RESOURCES. TRAINING. SUPPORT.

◄ ◄ ◄ ◄ Look inside for access to new assessment tools and multimedia resources!

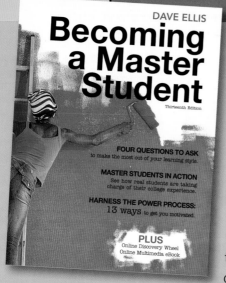

DAVE ELLIS

Becoming a Master Student

Thirteenth Edition

FOUR QUESTIONS TO ASK
to make the most out of your learning style.

MASTER STUDENTS IN ACTION
See how real students are taking charge of their college experience.

HARNESS THE POWER PROCESS:
13 ways to get you motivated.

PLUS
Online Discovery Wheel
Online Multimedia eBook

A message from *Becoming a Master Student* author Dave Ellis…

Becoming a Master Student is a book I wrote to help you help students be more successful in school and in life. The book presents lots of strategies, hints, tools, and techniques for students to pick from. It's a smorgasbord of suggestions so that students can pick what will work for them to be more successful by their definition of success.

When I first created *Becoming a Master Student*, I wanted a book that was more like a magazine with bite-sized articles divided into even smaller sections that could be read independently. Also, like in a magazine I wanted many of the pages to be an advertisement—not for a product, but for an idea about student success. The articles would advertise to students to read actively, to take notes frequently, to practice self-responsibility, to handle conflict, to manage distress, and much more.

The book is now in the thirteenth edition, and each time we revise it, it's because students and teachers let us know what works and what doesn't. As the population of students changes, and as the ideas about education change and develop, we add new elements to each chapter. The book evolves by our listening to you and to students.

For me one of the greatest joys of writing this book and of teaching this course is in my own development. As teachers, what works best is when we practice what we teach. And each time I practice the skills of *Becoming a Master Student*, I grow professionally and personally.

It really is a joy to put into practice stress management techniques and then live a more calm and relaxed life. It's a joy to practice what we teach about health and then experience the benefits of vibrant health. What I hear from teachers all the time is that when they implement these ideas, their lives change. I know that I have learned way more than students about becoming a master student—because when we teach it, we really learn it. That is the challenge and the joy of this book—not only developing the master students out there, but also developing the master student in you.

Dave

Hear more from author Dave Ellis, explore the philosophy behind *Becoming a Master Student*, and discover the full range of teaching and learning resources available with this edition at www.cengage.com/community/bams.

TEAMUP
THE USABILITY PEOPLE

TeamUP Faculty Programs

Our TeamUP program provides a range of services to help you implement new ideas and learning tools into your courses. Choose the level of support that works best for you, including:

- **Consultants** who understand your challenges and create a customized solution to meet your unique needs.

- **Trainers** who work with you and your students to fully utilize the power of your technology solutions.

- **Experts** in education who offer opportunities to explore new educational tools and ideas through peer-to-peer and professional insight.

To connect with your TeamUP Faculty Programs Consultant, call 1-800-528-8323 or visit www.cengage.com/teamup.

Free College Success eSeminars to Reinvigorate Your Teaching

Convenient, cutting-edge, and practical, the Wadsworth College Success eSeminar Series offers opportunities for professional development right at your desk. Our experts present relevant topics ranging from learning styles and active learning strategies to motivation and raising expectations.

Take advantage of this no-cost faculty development opportunity:
visit www.cengage.com/tlc/collegesuccess to access updated
eSeminar schedules and archival presentations.

Custom Solutions: Your Course, Your Way

Let Cengage Learning Custom Solutions help create the perfect learning solution for your course. Add key information about your campus and resources, a campus photo, planner pages, or other content from our College Success programs into your student's copy of **Becoming a Master Student**. Visit custom.cengage.com for more information.

Annotated Instructor's Edition

Becoming a
MASTER STUDENT

Thirteenth Edition

Doug Toft
Contributing Editor

Dean Mancina
Golden West College, CA
Faculty Advisor

WADSWORTH
CENGAGE Learning™

AUSTRALIA • BRAZIL • JAPAN • KOREA • MEXICO • SPAIN • UNITED KINGDOM • UNITED STATES

Becoming a Master Student
Thirteenth Edition
Ellis

Senior Publisher: Lyn Uhl

Director of College Success: Annie Todd

Senior Sponsoring Editor: Shani Fisher

Senior Development Editor: Julia Giannotti

Assistant Editor: Daisuke Yasutake

Editorial Assistant: Cat Salerno

Senior Marketing Manager: Kirsten Stoller

Marketing Coordinator: Ryan Ahern

Marketing Communications Manager: Martha Pfeiffer

Content Project Manager: Jessica Rasile

Art Director: Linda Jurras

Text Designer: Susan Gilday

Print Buyer: Julio Esperas

Permissions Editor: Tim Sisler

Project Management: Orr Book Services

Photo Manager: Leitha Etheridge-Sims

Photo Researcher: Walter Kopec

Cover Designer: Yvo Riezebos

Cover Image: Ted Humble-Smith/RF/Getty

Compositor: S4Carlisle Publishing Services

For product information and technology assistance, contact us at
Cengage Learning Customer & Sales Support, 1-800-354-9706

For permission to use material from this text or product,
submit all requests online at **cengage.com/permissions**
Further permissions questions can be emailed to
permissionrequest@cengage.com

Library of Congress Control Number: 209941954

Student Edition:

ISBN-13: 978-1-4390-8174-7

ISBN-10: 1-4390-8174-3

Annotated Instructor's Edition:

ISBN-13: 978-1-4390-8176-1

ISBN-10: 1-4390-8176-X

Wadsworth
20 Channel Center Street
Boston, MA 02210
USA

Cengage Learning is a leading provider of customized learning solutions with office locations around the globe, including Singapore, the United Kingdom, Australia, Mexico, Brazil and Japan. Locate your local office at **international.cengage.com/region**

Cengage Learning products are represented in Canada by Nelson Education, Ltd.

For your course and learning solutions, visit **www.cengage.com**.

Purchase any of our products at your local college store or at our preferred online store **www.ichapters.com**.

Printed in the United States of America
2 3 4 5 6 7 14 13 12 11 10

Contents

Chapter annotations

Please note: Chapter annotations can be found on an insert that appears before the beginning of each of the main text chapters, starting with the introduction.

Using the Annotated Instructor's Edition

Get familiar with the Annotated Instructor's Edition

The Annotated Instructor's Edition of *Becoming a Master Student,* Thirteenth Edition, will help guide you as you use this textbook. Whether you are a first-time user of *Becoming a Master Student* or a long-time fan, there is something here for you. In this Annotated Edition, strategies to aid your teaching are available at the front of the main text, and content-specific ideas appear prior to each chapter. All of these pages have a separate numbering system (AIE Chapter One, AIE Chapter Two, and so on) so that the textbook pages are numbered the same as the student edition of the text. This allows you to stay on the same page as your students when assigning readings and exercises.

Do a textbook reconnaissance

Flip through the pages of this textbook right now to get the big picture of the thirteenth edition. Look for fresh ideas you can use to support your course objectives. Explore new features, such as the new Skills Snapshot activity at the end of each chapter and the revised Put It to Work case study articles that help students see how the skills learned in each chapter can be applied in the workplace. Note how the annotated instructor information is organized and stands out visually from the student content for your handy reference.

Get to know your TeamUP College Survival consultant

For more than 20 years, TeamUP College Survival has provided consultation and training for the design and implementation of student success and first-year courses. All members of the team of consultants have extensive experience in teaching and administering the first-year course and in facilitating training sessions and conferences. Get to know your consultant today by calling 1-800-856-5727. Or visit the team online at **www .cengage.com/teamup.** Be sure to ask a consultant how you can attend a conference or workshop—for free!

Listen to your peers

Throughout the Annotated Instructor's Edition, you will find tips from the Faculty Advisor for *Becoming a Master Student,* Thirteenth Edition, Dean Mancina of Golden West Community College. Also look for suggestions from the Advisory Board and TeamUP consultants. As you dig into the following chapters, think about what you would say if you could add your voice to theirs. Send an e-mail to csweb.CollegeSurvival@ cengage.com to share your comments.

Use the transition guide to find your way

If you have used previous editions of *Becoming a Master Student,* you may need some help finding your favorite articles and exercises. The transition guide on the Instructor Web site will help you navigate the changes made to the thirteenth edition. A brief version of this guide is available on page AIE-17.

Make this book your own

The length of student success courses varies, so there may be more content here than you can share during your course. If some sections of the book don't apply to your course at all, skip them. Later, see if you can help your students gain value from these sections anyway. When you are committed to getting the most out of this book, your students will take note. Use the extra space in the annotated instructor pages to write ideas for lesson plans, activities, quiz questions, guest speakers, and homework assignments. Change the exercises in the book to fit your needs. Create a new technique by combining several others. Create a technique out of thin air! End your course by suggesting that students explore any unread sections of the book as one of the "ways to continue. . ." their journey of student success. See Chapter 12 for more about this.

Model the concepts

Action makes this book work. You are your students' best role model. Completing the exercises along with your students will enable you to stay involved and speak from experience when you discuss each chapter in class. The exercises and readings will help you write, touch, feel, move, see, search, ponder, speak, listen, recall, choose, commit, and create. In this way you join your students on their road to success.

Integrate learning styles into your teaching with the Master Student Map

On the opening page of each chapter, the Master Student Map (**M**etacognitive **A**pplication **P**rocess) guides students toward maximum learning by asking the four basic questions—*Why? What? How?* and *What if?*—that correlate to the Learning Style Inventory as explained in Chapter 1. By becoming aware of their preferred learning style and by using the Master Student Map, students will be better able to understand and practice new styles. Read more about the Master Student Map and how it works on page AIE-19. For additional reinforcement, use the Master Student Map in class as a structure for reviewing the previous chapter and previewing the upcoming one.

Note the style and design elements of each chapter

A toolbar at the top of each page signals when the chapter is coming to an end, with its Put It to Work feature, Quiz, Skills Snapshot, and Master Student Profile. Flip to the back of one of the chapters now. *Becoming a Master Student* provides the building blocks with which a creative and active mind can succeed.

Use the materials before each chapter to help you create lesson plans

There are four instructor pages before each chapter. These sections provide content-related ideas for guest speakers, lectures, activities, homework assignments, and previews/reviews to help bring the classroom alive for your students. The organization of these pages is based on the seven-part lesson plan structure described on page AIE-10. Flip to one of the chapters and review the instructor pages now.

Link to the Web

Throughout this book, students are reminded to visit the Web site for *Becoming a Master Student:* www .cengage.com/success/bams13e. There they'll find articles, videos, online exercises, and links to other useful Web sites. Part of the support for you when using this textbook is a password-protected instructor resource Web site that contains dozens of lesson plan and lecture ideas, activities, handouts, test questions, and more. These tools were submitted by faculty around the country who wanted to share effective strategies they have used in their classrooms. Register now (It's free!) so that you can explore additional resources to use with your students.

Power Processes

The Power Processes at the end of each chapter are a long-standing popular feature of *Becoming a Master Student*. These articles describe approaches to student success that are more philosophical in nature than most of the tools in the text. Review the pre-chapter instructor resources in the book or on the instructor resource Web site for strategies to help your students make full value of these special tools.

Help students take this book to work

Though the focus of this textbook is success in college, students can apply nearly all of the techniques in this book to any career. Students with less experience in the workplace, however, may not see how these tools apply at work. The Put It to Work articles at the end of each chapter use case studies to suggest key strategies that will help students make a seamless transition from success in school to success on the job. Skim one of them now.

Master Student Profiles

Becoming a Master Student has always concluded each chapter with a brief article about a real person who encompasses qualities of a master student. In each new edition of the textbook, several of the stories are replaced with new ones. Read the article "The Master Student" on page 45 and then check out the table of contents now to discover the 12 people on the special roster of master students for the thirteenth edition!

Master Teachers in Action

Instructors share their experiences with using *Becoming a Master Student!*

Overall

My retired husband was scanning the text on a plane one day while we were traveling and marveled at the content and scope of the issues covered. After his review, he then said to me, "Can I get a copy?" A former student liked the text so much that she planned to share it with her high school daughter and her daughter's friends because she thought it would help them improve their academic performance.

—JOYCE NORWOOD, SANTA ANA COLLEGE
Photo courtesy of Joyce Norwood

I have used BAMS since its first edition—then because it was the one selected by the course leader and one of the few available. After my first BAMS workshop I began to better understand the philosophy behind the text—a philosophy that I believe in and practice. But, more importantly, it is student and instructor friendly—filled with ideas and opportunities to practice what we teach (or should I say preach).

—FRANK BAKER, GOLDEN WEST COLLEGE
Photo courtesy of Frank Baker

Features

Discovery Wheel

The Discovery Wheel is brilliant because it allows the students to quickly identify where they may be weak and directs them to the chapter that can assist them.

—CHRIS DOUSE, INDIANA UNIVERSITY–PURDUE UNIVERSITY FORT WAYNE
Photo courtesy of Chris Douse

I really like the Discovery Wheel. I think it's so important for students to get a handle on where they are when they begin the semester, *and* where they are when they finish. I'm surprised how much growth there is! Sometimes it's not shown in "increased" scores on the

Discovery Wheel; sometimes the scores go down... that's a good thing. It shows that they are really examining their skills and abilities.

—TERRY CARLES, VALENCIA COMMUNITY COLLEGE
Photo courtesy of Terry Carles

Power Process

One of the assignments in my class is a group presentation on a Power Process. Early in the term, students pick a Power Process to work on. Small groups are formed with students interested in the same one. At midterm time, presentations are given. It is one of the highlights of the term.

—JOE RINE, MINNEAPOLIS COMMUNITY & TECHNICAL COLLEGE
Photo courtesy of Joe Rine

The Power Processes are my favorite feature in BAMS. They can be applied to all life situations. They're great for "teachable moments" during the semester as well. I've heard students tell their classmates to "Be Here Now" when they were engaged in side conversations or to apply "I Create It All" when they made excuses for not completing a homework assignment.

—DEBBIE WARFIELD, SEMINOLE COMMUNITY COLLEGE
Photo courtesy of Debbie Warfield

The Power Processes are my favorite feature. They are applicable and very timely. They give students an opportunity to consciously explore problem situations. Sometimes we have a problem, and until we bring it to consciousness, it persists. By presenting typical scenarios, my students are able to relate and begin to think outside the box.

—DAWN SHAFFER, CENTRAL PIEDMONT COMMUNITY COLLEGE
Photo courtesy of Dawn Shaffer

Journal Entries and Exercises

The Journal Entries information and exercises provide a format that invites students to become active participants in the learning process resulting in the acquisition of skills leading to behavior changes important to personal and academic success.

—LD LOVETT, TRUCKEE MEADOWS COMMUNITY COLLEGE
Photo courtesy of LD Lovett

Using the Annotated Instructor's Edition

Inevitably I end up having a class where what I've been doing just isn't working or, I'm just looking to try something different. I always find exciting ideas to take into class by reviewing these pages.

—TERRY CARLES, VALENCIA COMMUNITY COLLEGE
Photo courtesy of Terry Carles

As a new faculty member (former administrator) I was struggling with the concept of developing an engaging class. I am the product of traditional, lecture style classes, as my bachelor's degree is in finance. I knew that I wanted/needed to engage the students, I just didn't know how, as I had never personally experienced an engaging class! The article, "Creating an Engaging Classroom," was an excellent starting point for me. The course model gave me a great guideline to start with and try to follow. It also helped to keep me on task as the semester went along and I found myself lecturing too much, as that is what I experienced as a student.

—LEIGH SMITH, LAMAR INSTITUTE OF TECHNOLOGY
Photo courtesy of Leigh Smith

Content

Money

I find that many of our students have no experience with budgeting. They get money from their parents when they overspend, or work extra hours when they get in serious debt. Many will not buy textbooks because money is tight. This is a big, big problem on our large urban campus. Students get into debt and then work 30 or more hours per week to pay it down or for general living expenses. Because of

this extra workload their grades suffer and they lose financial aid and the cycle starts all over again... I like that the exercise makes students realize where (and on what) they're spending money each month. They often complain that they have no money for books or school-related expenses, not realizing that they've spent money on designer clothing and accessories, electronic gadgets, eating out, trips, etc.

—LETITIA THOMAS, UNIVERSITY AT BUFFALO
Photo courtesy of Letitia Thomas

Diversity

Diversity is such an important topic in today's world. In order to become a *master student,* students need to understand and appreciate diversity in order to hopefully, eventually *put it to work!* However, many instructors (myself included) feel very uncomfortable addressing this delicate subject in the classroom. The inclusion of Chapter 9 in the text has made the task much less daunting. The content focuses on facts, rather than emotions while the Journal Entry (especially number 26) gives the students a chance to think independently and objectively about their own feelings. The Mastering Technology section is also very helpful, as it gives students the opportunity to find additional information about different groups and cultures from reliable sources.

—LEIGH SMITH, LAMAR INSTITUTE OF TECHNOLOGY
Photo courtesy of Leigh Smith

Classroom Civility

I cover classroom civility in my classes. I have found that we can't assume that students know what is expected of them in terms of what are appropriate college classroom behaviors. For many they are the first in their family to attend college. There is a misconception among students that because they pay for classes any behavior is acceptable in the classroom. (The customer is always right!) Many of the students are also under a great deal of stress right now due to the state of the economy. This also influences their behaviors. During the first week of class, we have a discussion on classroom civility and I have them sign the student agreement.

—DEBBIE WARFIELD, SEMINOLE COMMUNITY COLLEGE
Photo courtesy of Debbie Warfield

Dean Mancina
. . . is a Master Student

Teaching student success classes has given me the humbling honor of facilitating the transformation of students' lives. It makes the hours of prep work and grading worthwhile when a student tells me that this is the best class she's taken in college, or that it has changed her life.

In 1985, I attended a workshop presented by Dave Ellis, hoping to learn new ways to help the students at my community college succeed. By the end of that workshop, I felt that Dave had the answer I was looking for. I returned to Southern California and, with Dave's and TeamUP College Survival's help, I developed a course for Golden West College that has become one of my institution's most popular classes.

Many students come to my college and to my class with low self-expectations. They aren't sure if they are "college material." Some think they might be too old or not smart enough. Some wonder if they have the motivation to do the work or the means to attend college. Most students leave my class with renewed enthusiasm about themselves and their dream of completing an educational program. Many of them get involved in student government and receive scholarships and awards. Two of my former students who became college educators have developed similar courses on their campuses for the students they now teach.

By modeling this book's concepts both in and outside the classroom, I've enjoyed the added side benefit of being happier in my personal life.

I've changed my habits, attitudes, and approaches to problem solving. I've gained confidence as a teacher and member of my campus community. By creating and implementing a course that has been popular and successful, I've earned respect from my colleagues. Over the last 20 years, I've had the wonderful opportunity to help other college and university faculty design and update their courses. And for the last 10 years, I've helped shape the updated editions of this book so that it continues to be current and relevant.

By learning more about learning style theory as presented in Chapter 1, I have become a better teacher. Like many instructors, I prefer to teach the way that I prefer to learn. I just wasn't aware that I was teaching this way and that there are equally effective ways of perceiving and processing information that work better for many of my students. Using the Learning Style Inventory and exercises in my classroom not only has helped my students develop understanding, tolerance, and the skills to adjust to different teaching styles, but it has also helped me understand and reach out to students who prefer to learn differently than I do.

I see myself as a facilitator in the classroom. This book is so well written by Dave Ellis that I just need to follow it, support it, and provide an environment in my classroom that is safe and inviting so that students are encouraged to reach for their dreams.

My suggestions throughout this Annotated Instructor's Edition are just that—suggestions. As you find your own voice in this material, you will develop your own way of teaching it to your students. Please change, adapt, alter, and re-create my ideas so they work for you and your students. I'd love to hear what you come up with. Write to me at csweb.CollegeSurvival@cengage.com.

Finding the master instructor in you

Teaching a student success course for the first time may seem intimidating. Most of us teach classes in our primary field of expertise, so teaching a course outside our knowledge base can be challenging on many levels. Here are a few suggestions to help you get started.

Model the behavior you want to see in your students

If you want your students to be organized, be organized in your class. If you want your students to show up on time, always be punctual yourself.

The textbook is for you, too

You can apply the strategies in this textbook to your professional and personal life. Use the same student success tools to sharpen your memory, manage your time, and improve relationships with colleagues, friends, and loved ones. Use the table of contents and the index to look for strategies to help you start, stop, or change habits in your life.

In a teacher training workshop, a dedicated instructor once asked, "How can I model and teach promptness if I'm always late to class?" This was an opportunity for personal and professional growth! For us, as for our students, however, change is a choice we choose to make.

Be inquisitive

There are many resources for you to use in the process of developing lesson plans for your student success course. In addition to this Annotated Instructor's Edition, with its suggestions here and on the pages preceding each chapter, explore these additional resources to help you create and improve lesson plans and organize all aspects of your course:

- **Instructor Web site**—provides specific tools to use while teaching your course, including video clips, PowerPoint slides, sample syllabi, chapter-by-chapter lecture outlines, teaching tips, exercises, quizzes, Web links, suggestions for service-learning activities, and more. You can edit most of the downloadable files to tailor them for your course.

- **DVDs/videos**—perfect for supplementing your lecture, videos can be used as "guest speakers" in your course. For a complete listing of available videos, and for information about new Power Process videos, flip to the "Master instructor resources" article on page AIE-22.

- **TeamUP consultants**—available by toll-free phone (1-800-856-5727) and e-mail (serviceandtraining@ cengage.com), a consultant can assist you with planning, class activities, research, and implementing a course on your campus. Ask about a customized on-campus training session or how you can attend a TeamUP conference for free.

- **Faculty members on your campus**—invite a respected colleague to lunch to find out how he solves grading, attendance, logistic, and classroom management issues.

Take it one step at a time

Creating the perfect course isn't likely to happen overnight. This textbook explains tools and techniques so clearly that you don't need to try to cover all of them in class. Start by identifying one or two topics in each chapter that you have personally found valuable. Look for activities or lecture ideas at the Instructor Web site or in this Annotated Instructor's Edition, and build your lesson plans around the topics that you want to emphasize. Use videos and guest speakers from your campus to augment your class meetings. Reinforce concepts by conducting review sessions and giving weekly quizzes. For additional lesson planning strategies, see the article "Creating engaging classes" on page AIE-10. ✳

Creating engaging classes
Using the seven-part course model in your classroom

USING THE FOLLOWING lesson planning model as a framework can provide more opportunities to engage students as active participants and partners in their learning process. The objective is to use varying modes of instruction to facilitate a course that accesses and maximizes each student's method of learning. Try using this seven-part course model as a weekly guideline when developing your lesson plans:

Lectures	20 percent
Exercises	20 percent
Sharing	20 percent
Guest speakers	20 percent
Evaluation Preview/review Assignments	} 20 percent

It will not always be possible to include all parts each week and that's OK. Ideally, over the entire term, the recommendation is to spend 20 percent of class time for lectures; 20 percent for exercises; 20 percent for conversations and sharing; 20 percent for guest speakers; and the remaining 20 percent for previewing/reviewing, quizzes and evaluations, and giving assignments. A complete overview of this course model is available on the Instructor Web site. The revised Annotated Instructor's Edition models this structure for every chapter. Flip to the four pages before one of the chapter to see this model put into action.

From Dean Mancina:

Using this seven-part course model can be challenging at first and may seem like more work than lecturing. Although the initial investment to create or redesign your lesson plans may be significant, I discovered that as a result of using this method to design my lesson plans, during class I get to have fun along with my students. Students tell me they enjoy the variety and that the class goes by much faster than many of their other classes.

Here is a sample lesson plan for my 170-minute, once-a-week student success course. If your course meets twice a week, you could do half of these things at each of the two weekly meetings.

CHAPTER 3: Memory
Collect homework (:03)
Preview the class agenda (:07)
Tutorial learning center—guest speakers (:15)
Review Chapter 3 (:30)
Lecture—mnemonic devices (:20)
Activity—loci system (:20)
Sharing successful memory experiences in
    groups (:20)
Activity—"Be here now" (:30)
Quiz on Chapter 3 (:20)
Assignment—read/do pages XX–XX
    (Chapter 4) (:05)

Collect homework

I collect homework at the beginning of the class to encourage students to arrive on time. If they are late, they don't get any points for their homework. The collected homework is a randomly selected Journal Entry or other writing assignment from within the text. Additional suggestions regarding collecting and grading homework assignments are available on the Instructor Web site.

Preview

I project a PowerPoint slide with the day's agenda before class. I encourage students to copy the agenda into their notes. The agenda can be used as a framework for note taking and helps explain to students the organization of the work we will do in class.

I randomly assign students to groups of four to conduct a review of the material they have read prior to coming to class. I provide poster paper and colored pens, and show them how to make a mind map. The students write their first names at the top of each poster and tape the posters to the walls using removable tape. Staying in their groups, they walk around to view the other mind maps, confirming what they have created and noticing what other groups included that they did not. Because they will be taking a quiz at the end of class, students stay motivated and focused for this activity.

Guest Speaker

Each week I invite guest speakers from support programs to make brief presentations on their services. This helps students learn what kinds of assistance are available at our college. If a guest speaker isn't available for a certain topic, consider showing one of the many videos that accompany this book in class.

Lecture

Lecturing on only one or two topics of the text encourages students to learn from the textbook and frees up class time for the many other activities planned for each class meeting. It's challenging to decide what topics to choose for my lecture. When I first started teaching, I selected topics I was most familiar with and felt I could add to beyond what the text said. As I became more confident about the content of the book, I began to focus on topics that students had difficulty fully understanding.

Activity

Though activities take time, they are often more effective than other methods for teaching skills that students retain. Additionally, groups promote more active involvement from students while they learn. The Instructor Web site has many activities provided by advisors, consultants, and instructors. Skim them, pick a few that fit your teaching style and time constraints, and try them with your class.

Sharing

Most of the time my students are in groups during class. Over the course of the semester, they get to know each other, and most form a few close friendships. Studies have shown that making friends on campus significantly reduces the likelihood that students will drop out of college. Participating in a sharing period allows students to talk candidly with their peers about their concerns, questions, and frustrations, both at college and at home. I give them a topic for discussion and sometimes, depending on the topic, will ask for group sharing at the end of this segment.

Evaluation

Each week I give a short quiz to my students at the end of the class. Doing so ensures that they read the textbook material, remain focused during class, and stay until the end of the session because they lose points if they miss the quiz.

Assignments

Each week I assign specific pages as a reading assignment, even if I want students to read the entire chapter. I call it "read/do" and list the specific page numbers because I require students to complete all Journal Entries, Discovery/Intention Statements, and Practicing Critical Thinking exercises within the assigned pages.

This seven-part course model is a proven strategy for organizing, planning, and revitalizing lesson plans. Whether you're a novice or a veteran teacher of student success courses, I encourage you to try it. ✻

Setting up your syllabus

BOTH THE STUDENTS and the purpose and focus of the course will be different at each school. *Becoming a Master Student* is designed to give students and instructors a variety of topics and ideas. By using this Annotated Instructor's Edition and the Instructor Web site, you can select material that is most appropriate both for your students and for your course purpose. Specific resources for "Writing your course purpose" and "Creating a course philosophy" are available on the Instructor Web site.

There are dozens of approaches to creating your student success course's syllabus. It may be as brief as one page, providing only the most essential information for students, or it may be several pages long, with detailed assignments, due dates, and other information about the course. Here are some ideas to consider:

Choose what to include. In addition to the course name, class time and room, instructor name, office hours, and instructor contact information, here are some common elements that may be included in your syllabus:

- Required and optional textbook information
- Other materials you will require students to have
- Class support Web site URL
- Assignments, with or without instructions and due dates
- Important dates, for midterm, final, and the like
- Official course outline
- Agendas for each class meeting
- Learning outcomes
- Grading method
- Additional recommended readings and/or resources
- Class rules

If you're creating a syllabus for your course for the first time, a more general syllabus may be a better choice. As you progress through the course material, you may discover that some topics take more or less time than you anticipated.

Organize and sequence the course topics. The official course outline of record and the total student contact hours for your course will provide you with parameters for organizing the material you will cover during the term. Based on the length of your course, decide how much time you will spend on each topic/chapter. Consider the order in which you will present the topics. Although the text chapters are organized in a logical sequence, once you complete the Introduction and First Steps chapters, each chapter has independent content, so you can teach the chapters in whatever order you prefer. Some teachers let the students prioritize the chapters by voting on each of the chapter topic names.

Identify key dates. After you have organized and sequenced the course topics/chapters, identify key dates for you and your students. Decide when the midterm will be given, when major projects will be due, and which guest speakers you want to invite and when during the term you want them to come.

Choose a grading method. Decide how you will weight quizzes, tests, homework, and other assignments. How many quizzes will you give? Will students be allowed to drop their lowest quiz score? Will there be an option for extra credit? Develop an objective system for grading that is applied consistently to each student.

Choose class rules. Class rules include written clarification of the boundaries you set for behavior in the classroom, instructions on the way assignments should be presented for grading, and parameters for how your students should interact with each other. Topics you may want to address include:

- Attendance
- Assignments turned in with no name
- Late assignments
- Word-processed (versus handwritten) assignments
- Side conversations
- Cell phone and laptop computer use in class
- Academic honesty
- Formatting requirements for electronically transmitted assignments (.pdf, .doc, etc.)
- Logging-in frequency for online courses

Evaluate and refine. Each semester, make notes about what works and what doesn't work in your syllabus so that you can modify it for the next term. Consider asking your students at the end of the term to provide feedback as to how the syllabus could have been more helpful to them. ✳

Sample Syllabus

College 100 - Becoming A Successful Student
Syllabus

Professor: Dean Mancina
Email: dmancina@aol.com
Office: Library 109
Hours: By appointment Tuesdays, and via email
Phone: 714.892.7711 x 51216
Classroom: Library 223 • Tuesdays 2:45-5:55 pm
Textbook: <u>Becoming A Master Student, 13th Edition</u>

The grading system in this course is points-based. Here is a list of graded activities in the course and the maximum points possible.

REGULAR POINTS:	Maximum
Text Exercises and other HW (14 @15 pts. each)	+210
Quizzes (12 @ 15 pts. each)	+180
Choose Your Grade	+15
Discovery Wheel #1	+15
Eureka Majors/Career Exploration	+15
Time Monitor	+30
Library Assignments (3 @15 pts each)	+45
Interview w/Campus Personnel	+30
Report on Campus Event	+30
Meeting with Course Instructor	+40
Oral Presentation	+100
Research Project	+100
Review Test #1	+50
Review Test #2	+50
Final Exam	+90
Total Points	**+1000**

MINUS POINTS:
1. missed class meeting, each	-30
2. missed appointment with /instructor *	-15
3. missed oral presentation *	-15
4. each final exam question skipped	-15

* Cancellations on #2 & 3 require 48 hours'
  notice to avoid minus points.

BONUS POINTS:	Maximum
1. Typing any assignment, each	+2
2. Others, to be assigned, each	+15
3. Individual/Group tutoring hour *(Maximum tutoring pts. = 90)*	+10
4. Assessment Portfolio Builder Exercise	+35

Maximum Total Bonus Per Student = 150

<u>**Grading Scale**</u>

900+ points =   A
800-899 =   B   685+ = CR
700-799 =   C   684- = NC *
600-699 =   D
500-599 =   F
below 500->   Subject to Withdrawal
*It is your responsibility to sign up for CR/NC
by the GWC Admissions Office deadline.

See also my Course Policies and Classroom Rules handout.

TeamUP College Survival: Committed to STUDENT SUCCESS

CENGAGE'S TEAMUP COLLEGE SURVIVAL GROUP is dedicated to providing educators with proven instructional strategies and tools that lead to student success. For the past 24 years, our team of consultants has provided guidance and training for the design and implementation of student success and first-year courses.

The College Survival consulting team is available to assist with any stage of student success program development, including:

- Developing student retention strategies
- Implementing student success courses
- Training faculty members
- Helping faculty engage students as active learners
- Transforming the learning environment
- Presenting conferences and workshops

Our team

Our team of consultants has extensive experience in teaching and administering the first-year course and in facilitating training at national education conferences throughout the year. We provide full-time support to help educators establish and maintain effective student success programs.

Web site

Visit our Web site at **www.cengage.com/teamup** for additional resources and more information about College Survival:

- Get the latest industry information
- Get updates on the latest technology available through Cengage Learning texts
- Get connected to our support services

Conferences/workshops

College Survival conferences and workshops offer highly interactive and informative sessions designed to equip you with ideas and activities that you can apply immediately in your classroom. All educators involved in enhancing instruction and improving students' motivation and performance are encouraged to attend.

About our national conferences. Our two- to three-day conferences provide informative, interactive sessions on a wide range of topics, such as adult learners, learning styles, student retention, motivation, technology, and much more. Presenters include nationally known authors, student success instructors, and College Survival consultants who offer invaluable instructional strategies based on their experience teaching the first-year course. This forum for learning and sharing with colleagues will furnish you with activities and ideas to implement immediately in your course.

About our on-campus workshops. Led by College Survival consultants, our on-campus workshops are customized to the needs of instructors on a particular campus. These workshops will equip you with ideas and activities to enliven the teaching and learning experience. The cost of a workshop is $1500 a day plus expenses, or free for schools ordering a minimum of $30,000 a year in College Success texts. Ask your Cengage Learning Representative to help you set up a training at your institution.

Who should attend? If you are an educator, new or experienced, who is dedicated to promoting student success in career schools, community colleges, or four-year colleges and universities, these events are for you! Those who will benefit from these workshops include:

- Academic and student affairs administrators
- Student success and freshman seminar coordinators
- Faculty members (full-time and adjunct instructors)
- Retention/enrollment management directors
- Counselors and orientation directors

How can your Cengage Learning Consultant help? Your Cengage Learning Consultant can help you with ideas for introducing a topic, creating community in the classroom, designing your syllabus, and figuring out what to do in class tomorrow. All you have to do is contact them. Check the TeamUP website to find your consultant: **www.cengage.com/teamup** ✳

Could your students use an extra $1,000?

CENGAGE STUDENT SUCCESS is proud to present three students each year with a $1,000 scholarship for tuition reimbursement. Students at postsecondary schools in the United States and Canada that offer a student success course are welcome to participate in this scholarship. To be considered, students must write an essay that answers the question "How do you define success?"

Here's one way to get your students to participate. Host a schoolwide competition for students enrolled in a first-year student success or study skills course. Consider having students participate by including the competition in your syllabus as a goal-setting or writing assignment. In your local contest, ask all of your students to write an essay on the topic "How do you define success?" The essay should not exceed 750 words.

Materials to advertise the scholarship competition are available on the Instructor Web site. Download flyers for posting on bulletin boards around campus, or for posting to online bulletin boards on your course Web site or in your course management system.

Students can send in their individual essays by filling out an entry form (available on the *Becoming a Master Student* Web site) to Cengage Learning. Multiple students from the same school may enter their essays. Entries are due each year on December 15. The winners are announced the following spring on the Web site. Invite your students to read the winning essays of previous entrants, also available on the Web site. ✳

Gaining support

Student success courses and first-year seminar programs help students learn to be more effective in school, thereby improving their academic performance and increasing their level of commitment.

Gaining approval and support from administrators is important to the success of your course and requires preparation and communication. This backing is necessary to sustain the course long enough to establish both its effectiveness and its value. These suggestions can help you establish that base of support:

Write a statement of purpose for your course. One possibility is "The purpose of our student success course is to improve students' academic performance and increase their level of commitment to our college."

Refer to your statement of purpose often. When negotiating any aspect of your course, be sure to avoid compromises that would sabotage its purpose from either the institution's or the students' perspective. For example, it would be a mistake to settle for too few course contact hours.

Seek grassroots support. The more people who have a vested interest in your proposal, the more likely it is to be accepted. Ask for assistance from the top of the administrative hierarchy. Draw a political road map encompassing crucial factors for gaining support and identifying key individuals. Include those who have behind-the-scenes influence. Enlist the support of colleagues who trust you. Spend time with key individuals who may not support your concept but are key curriculum decision makers.

Become a retention expert on your campus. Familiarize yourself with all the data, research, and institutional studies related to student performance and retention at your school. Explore options your institution might use to improve student performance and reduce attrition.

More suggestions for gaining support are available at the Instructor Web site: www.cengage.com/success/bams13e.

A guide for instructors who have used previous editions of this book

THE FOUNDATIONS AND THEMES for student success in *Becoming a Master Student* have been used by millions of students. Since the first edition, students and instructors have helped shape this book by providing strategies, insights, and suggestions. As a result of its continuous evaluation and refinement, students are inspired and motivated by this book to adopt, develop, and commit to using the skills needed for success in college and throughout life. These ideas are now a part of the thirteenth edition.

Every word in every article has been evaluated for its helpfulness to students. Statistics have been updated, recent research has been included, and articles have been shortened or lengthened as necessary to maximize clarity of concepts and strategies. Here are some of the major changes you will see in this edition. Please note that a detailed summary of all changes, including moved, deleted, and added articles, is located on the Instructor Web site to help you update your lesson plans.

Key textbook feature changes

- Each chapter starts on the same page as in the twelfth edition to make updating your assignments easier.

- Completely revised Put It to Work articles now feature case studies that will make it even easier for students to relate the themes and concepts to the workplace.

- The Power Process articles are more succinct and have been reduced to one page.

- A new chapter-end exercise "Skills Snapshot" helps students summarize what they learned in each chapter and connects back to their original responses in the Discovery Wheel. This new feature replaces the "Learning styles application exercise," which can now be found online.

- The Master Students in Action feature on the chapter openers help students connect to real students who have taken this course. Real students share their strategies for success or challenges that they have faced.

Key changes to specific chapters

Introduction: Making Transitions

- A new article "Classroom Civility—What's in It for You" on page 12 introduces the simple student behaviors that create a sense of safety, mutual respect, and community in any place where people gather—including a classroom, tutoring center, library, or instructor's office.

- A new article Power Process: "A User's Guide" on page 22 will help students get the most out of the Power Process articles.

Chapter 1: First Steps

Key revisions to the Learning Style Inventory include:

- Clearer directions on how to take the LSI.

- A new Journal Entry that prepares students for taking the Inventory.

- A new reflection activity, "Take a Snapshot of Your Learning Styles," that asks students to reflect on what they've learned. This activity is intended to be completed after students read all of the material about learning styles (including Multiple Intelligences and VAK).

- A learning styles across the curriculum chart that connects learning styles to specific strategies that students can use for their other courses.

- New material for students to connect their learning style to their courses, future career, and major.

Chapter 2: Time

- A new exercise "Seeing Where All the Time Goes" on page 69 that takes students beyond their time monitor and asks them to create a chart, diagram, or some other visual way to show the categories of activity that take up most of their time.

- New Master Student Profile: "Al Gore" on page 97.

Chapter 3: Memory

- New material on creating graphic organizers in the article "20 Memory Techniques" on page 102.

- New Master Student Profile: "Pablo Alvarado" on page 121.

Chapter 4: Reading

- A revised Mastering Technology feature "Find What You Want on the Internet" on page 131 will help students take their Internet searches to the next level.

- A new article "Staying Literate in the Digital Age" on page 137 gives tips to help students increase the time they spend on leisure reading.

- A new sidebar "Muscle Reading for ebooks" on page 137 links strategies for print books to online media.

- New Master Student Profile: "Chief Wilma Mankiller" on page 147.

Chapter 5: Notes

- A new sidebar article "Note This Information about Your Sources" on page 164 helps students avoid plagiarism and keep their source information organized.

- A new sidebar article "Taking Notes . . . despite PowerPoint" on page 165 suggests strategies to help students get the most out of PowerPoint presentations.

- A new Mastering Technology sidebar article "Your Mind, Online" on page 170 lists computer applications that can give students a variety of ways to store text and images, organize them, search them, and even share them with others when appropriate.

- New Master Student Profile: "Harvey Milk" on page 175.

Chapter 6: Tests

- A new section in the article "Cooperative Learning" on page 181 discusses the importance of understanding the learning styles of study group members.

- A new Mastering Technology sidebar article "Collaboration 2.0" on page 182 lists Web-based applications that allow students to create virtual study groups and collaborate online.

- Expanded coverage and more strategies in the article "Let Go of Test Anxiety" on page 188.

- A new exercise "Use Learning Styles for Math Success" on page 196.

- New Master Student Profile: "Bert and John Jacobs" on page 203.

Chapter 7: Thinking

- A new sidebar article "Four More Questions for Critical Thinking" on page 208 helps students think critically about what they read and hear.

- A new sidebar article "Creative Ways for Groups to get 'Unstuck'" on page 213 offers strategies to stimulate creative thinking in groups.

- The article "Don't Fool Yourself" on page 216 has been expanded and offers three additional common mistakes in logic:
  —Appealing to the people
  —Distracting from the real issue
  —Sliding a slippery slope.

- A new Mastering Technology article "Rethinking e-mail" on page 227 lists ways to use critical thinking to manage your inbox.

- New Master Student Profile: "Twyla Tharp" on page 233.

Chapter 8: Communicating

- A new article "Developing Emotional Intelligence" on page 243 helps students recognize feelings and respond to them in a skillful way.

- A new article "Collaborating for Success" on page 250 connects the Power Process articles in the book to strategies for working successfully with others.

- The revised/renamed article "Staying Smart in Cyberspace—Safe Social Networking" on page 251 has a new sidebar about text messaging etiquette.

- A new Mastering Technology sidebar article "Master Students—Get Networked" on page 251 shows ways to use the Internet to get connected to others.

- New Master Student Profile: "Mark Zuckerberg" on page 269.

Chapter 9: Diversity

- A major revision to the article "Building Relationships across Cultures" on page 274 includes a new section on the differences between individualist and collectivist cultures.

- A major revision to the article "Leadership in a Diverse World" on page 284 includes more concrete strategies for becoming an effective leader.

- A new Mastering Technology article "Making Technology Accessible" on page 288.

Chapter 10: Money

- A revision to the exercise "The Money Monitor/Money Plan" on page 296 simplifies the directions for creating and maintaining a budget.

- A major revision to the article "Spend Less Money" on page 304 offers more strategies that students can use now.

- A new article "Managing Money during Tough Times" on page 306 helps students form habits that will help them manage money both during tough times and when the economy rebounds.

- A new sidebar article "Common Credit Terms" on page 309 offers information to help students navigate the often confusing world of credit cards.

- A new article "Your Learning Styles and Your Money" on page 312 helps students understand how their learning style affects the way they manage money.

- New Master Student Profile: "Lisa Price" on page 319.

Chapter 11: Health

- A new chapter opener article "Wake Up to Health" on page 321 links healthy behavior to success in college.

- A major revision/renamed article "Choose Your Fuel" on page 323 replaces "Your Machine: Fuel It."

- A major revision/renamed article "Choose to Exercise" on page 324 replaces "Your Machine: Move It."

- A new article "Choose Mental Health" on page 325.

- A major revision/renamed article "Choose to Rest" on page 326 replaces "Your Machine: Rest It."

- A major revision/renamed article "Choose to Stay Safe" on page 327 replaces "Your Machine: Protect It."

- A renamed sidebar article "Observe Thyself" on page 328 replaces "Your Machine: Observe It."

- A major revision/renamed article "Choose Sexual Health: Prevent Infection" on page 329 replaces "Your Machine: Protect It."

- A new Mastering Technology sidebar article "Setting Limits on Screen Time" on page 334 helps students manage their time online.

- New Master Student Profile: "Randy Pausch" on page 351.

Chapter 12: What's Next?

- A new Mastering Technology sidebar article "Continue Your Education at Internet University" on page 355 offers online resources that can be applied for lifelong learning.

- A major revision/renamed sidebar "65 Transferable Skills" on page 362 replaces "25 Transferable Skills" and "Use the Scans Reports to Discover Your Skills."

- A new article "Surviving Your First Day on a New Job" on page 367 offers strategies for students entering the workforce.

- A new article "Becoming a Master Student Goes Green" on page 371.

- New Master Student Profile: "Lisa Ling" on page 385. ✳

Master Student Map

ONE OF THE MOST USEFUL FEATURES in *Becoming a Master Student* is the Master Student Map (**M**eta-cognitive **A**pplication **P**rocess) located on the opening page of each chapter. The Master Student Map is a reasoning model based on the Learning Style Inventory. Even the most inexperienced students can quickly begin to apply this simple, systematic process to monitor their thinking and learning. What makes this model so effective is that by utilizing the strengths of each learning style, students can implement the monitoring aspect of metacognition as soon as they achieve awareness.

Each category of the Master Student Map begins with a basic question designed to engage student interest and lead to the important ideas presented in the chapter. A closer look at the design and formatting of each question in the Master Student Map will reveal the logic behind this innovative approach to introducing chapter topics.

why this chapter matters . . .

The role of this question is to encourage personal interest and a need to know in the learner. Initiating the Master Student Map with this type of question leads Mode 1 learners toward a deeper metacognitive understanding of their thinking, allowing them to call on principles within their prior knowledge that help structure the ideas in the chapter.

what is included . . .

This question is followed by a list of specific, thought-provoking article titles from the chapter. This helps Mode 2 learners probe and analyze the factual and conceptual ideas presented in the chapter and become more aware of what will be expected of them.

how you can use this chapter . . .

Mode 3 students will experience the impact of acclaimed features of *Becoming a Master Student,* such as the Discovery and Intention Journal Entry system, Power Processes, and Master Student Profiles, which uplift and inspire students to make personal commitments and set goals to accomplish. By consciously choosing their attitude about a chapter topic before they begin to study, students gain confidence in their own ability to initiate action and synthesize solutions to pressing problems. In this stage, have students go through the list of articles and mark the ones they pre-

dict they will know something about. The articles they do not mark indicate topics they are least familiar with. Being aware of knowledge gaps will give students a better idea of what they need to study for tests.

as you read, ask yourself what if . . .

Taking advantage of the action-oriented strength of Mode 4 learners, *what if?* questions lead to more lateral thinking and thus better-quality decisions. Specific skills do not necessarily transfer from one mental schema to another. Asking provocative *what if?* questions triggers the students' imagination to transfer skills and create new schema for developing skills in their other classes. Students are intrigued by inquiry rather than pat answers. *What if?* questions stimulate discussion and

Using the Master Student Map

Begin to use the Master Student Map now by reviewing the Instructor Web site www.cengage.com/success/bams13e through the framework of the Master Student Map.

Why the Instructor Web site matters. Being prepared and organized for teaching your course will help you to teach first-year students the importance of becoming master students.

What is included. The Instructor Web site includes information on how to write your course outline, establish course objectives or student learning outcomes, determine instructional choices, integrate technology, use educational PowerPoint slides that illustrate key articles in the textbook, explore lectures and exercises for each chapter in the book, access DVD segments on the Power Processes to show your students during class, assess assignments and exercises, identify evaluation criteria, and create and maintain a supportive classroom atmosphere for your students.

How you can use this Web site. Ask yourself how you could adapt information, ideas, and exercises here to fit the needs of the students at your campus taking your course.

As you read, ask yourself: What if I could use the materials in this course and apply it to the other disciplines I teach?

further the transfer of skills in situations outside the classroom as well.

Based on the latest theories of brain-active learning, the Master Student Map feature helps students activate relevant memories with regard to the subject matter in the chapter. Since all learning depends on prior knowledge, beginning each chapter with this reasoning model helps students in several ways. First, distractions can be reduced or eliminated because the model allows students to study the most interesting or important topics first. Next, it helps increase the speed of students' learning by organizing the ideas in the beginning pages. Finally, it links all of the ideas in the entire textbook to the learning style of each student in a simple but powerful way.

Another important benefit of the Master Student Map is that it provides the instructor with a clear outline of what is going to be investigated in each chapter and a framework for guiding the discussion. In a pilot study using this model, instructors at Utah Valley University found these questions to be very helpful as teaching tools primarily because the questions gave them a place to begin instruction and a final destination.

The four basic questions not only help instructors better understand what the students need to know but also serve as a catalyst for both pre- and post-assessment in the students' minds. Instructors who were more adept at viewing the curriculum in a holistic fashion were able to use this feature of overarching guiding questions to help them convey to students the big picture of the chapter in an efficient and meaningful way. Those instructors who were more linear in their thinking leaned toward the *what?* category of guiding questions and allowed their students to discover how the other questions fit in during the course of the discussion. This flexibility instilled confidence in the instructors to teach the magazine format of *Becoming a Master Student* in their own preferred style and enabled them to be more comfortable with the teaching process. Consequently, students reported high satisfaction with both the course instructor and the material. ✳

Using the Instructor Web site

As you review the Instructor Web site, ask yourself

what if . . .

I need help teaching a certain skill or concept to my students?

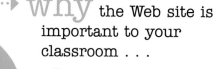

why the Web site is important to your classroom . . .

- Resources to support your instruction have been collected from educators whose previous experiences in the classroom have been met with success.

- Access to instructional materials, provided in electronic format, allows you to easily customize and then print, e-mail, or post materials to a Web site or course-management system.

how

you can use this resource . . .

- Evaluate resources chapter by chapter while planning your course to determine in-class activities and exercises you will use throughout the semester.

- View PowerPoint slides that are downloadable and customizable to fit your needs.

- Review sample syllabi instructors have generously shared for your inspiration.

- Read the guide and handouts created to accompany the Power-Up! Video/DVD series.

- Review lecture ideas you may adapt and adopt to clarify key concepts in the textbook.

- Invite guest speakers to your course at the start of the term.

- Practice using technology resources.

what is included . . .

- Pre- and post-test retention study materials
- Teaching tips
- Lecture ideas
- Warm-up exercises
- Guest speaker ideas
- Relationship building exercises
- Applying skills activities
- Closure exercises
- Prompts for conversation and sharing exercises
- Technology integration suggestions
- Video discussion questions
- Chapter tests
- Answer keys
- Final exam suggestions
- PowerPoint slide shows
- Video clips
- Bibliography
- Information on College Survival consulting services
- Resources for gaining support for your first-year experience course
- Information on supplementary resources

Master instructor resources

THE AIE RESOURCE PAGES in this Annotated Instructor's Edition of *Becoming a Master Student* highlight many chapter-specific resource materials that are available to you through Cengage Learning. Take advantage of these valuable tools to assist you in your course. Remember to call your TeamUp consultant if you have any questions about acquiring materials or integrating them into your course, or if you have a suggestion you would like to see implemented in the future.

Instructor Web site. This new one-stop resource provides all of the support materials users of previous editions of *Becoming a Master Student* have found in the paper Course Manual and the ClassPrep CD-ROM, plus new content. Material on the Web site includes icebreakers, lecture ideas, classroom activities, handouts, video excerpts you can use in your classroom, PowerPoint slides to integrate into classroom presentations, and additional ideas submitted by instructors who have shared tools they have developed for use with college students.

Powerlecture CD. This Powerlecture CD-ROM contains the *Becoming a Master Student* test bank in the ExamView test-generating software, enhanced instructor PowerPoints, and a PDF of the Course Manual.

Becoming a Master Student Premium Web site. The *Becoming a Master Student* Web site www.cengage .com/success/bams13e is easily accessible for students and instructors alike. The site includes new activities and resources for students, including the Discovery Wheel interactive exercise, Skillbuilders, Concept Maps, and a Master Student Hall of Fame featuring Master Student Profiles and biographical information about past and present master students.

WebTutor. The WebTutor on Blackboard offers a number of instructor resources to complement the main text including discussion questions and gradebook content. For students, Power Process media, Video Skillbuilders, and additional resources will enhance their understanding of the text's main points.

Multimedia eBook. The Multimedia eBook allows users to experience the textbook in a whole new way by instantly connecting students to resources including videos and Web site activities that will bring the content in the text to life.

Video Skillbuilders. This online tool combines video clips featuring discussions with students, instructors, and experts, with articles and activities designed to give students a fully engaging learning experience. Topics include:

· Keeping your mind and body in shape
· Taking notes to improve your grade
· Test-taking
· Time Management
· Exploring Majors
· Persuasive Communication
· Motivation and Goal Setting
· Textbook Note Taking
· Learning Styles
· Healthy Living: Making the right choices
· Career Planning
· Critical Thinking
· Diversity
· Memory Strategies
· Managing your finances

Master Students in Action. The new Maser Students and Teachers in Action video provides you with an inside look at how *Becoming a Master Student* is used by professors, including information on their favorite parts, and how specific articles and activities from the text prepare students for achieving success. Students will hear first-hand from other students where their challenges are and their strategies for success.

Power-Up! Power Process DVD. Show your students how to put the *power* into Power Processes with *Power-Up!* a new DVD that contains 8- to 9-minute segments on each of the thirteen Power Processes in *Becoming a Master Student*. These video segments will enhance your lecture by bringing to life the concepts and metaphors in the text while speaking to the auditory and visual learners in your class. This closed-captioned Power Process DVD is free to adopters. These videos are also found on the Student Web site.

Additional videos. A 30-minute video, *The Interviewing Process: Strategies for Making the Right Impression,* takes students through the interviewing process from start to finish, providing them with strategies for successful interviews. The video covers preparation for the interview with instruction on what to wear, questions and answers to think about, and research on the company. Real-life interviewing scenarios on the video provide students with examples of the actual interview process. Also covered is what to do after the interview, including evaluating how it went, seeing what you can learn, and following up.

A financial management video, *Money and Finances,* discusses strategies to help students gain control of their finances and overcome the money problems they may currently be experiencing. Students will hear advice from financial advisor Ann Egan on income and expenses, examine the general principles of budgeting and cash flow, and hear a discussion on financial aid. Through real-world money challenges, including the pitfalls of credit card spending, presented by real students, this video will teach your students to develop the skills of good money management.

Each of the above videos is accompanied by a program overview to guide instructors through its contents, as well as suggestions for classroom activities. These additional aids can be found at the Instructor Web site.

PowerPoint slides. PowerPoint slides for selected topics in *Becoming a Master Student* can be downloaded from the Instructor Web site. These slides can be edited to fit your teaching style and preferences.

CL Assessment and Portfolio Builder. The CL Assessment and Portfolio Builder tool is available for packaging, with *Becoming a Master Student,* as a passkey to a password-protected Web page. This is a personal assessment tool to help students learn more about themselves and prepare for success in college and career. Students will build their portfolios by responding to questions in the modules *Personal, Interpersonal, Career,* and *Community,* and by reflecting on their skills, attitudes, values, and behaviors. The *Accomplishments*

Report summarizes the results of students' responses in a format that is perfect for creating a résumé or preparing for interviews. More information about this resource begins on page AIE-27.

3x5 cards. Provided at no charge to instructors who purchase *Becoming a Master Student,* 3x5 cards facilitate classroom participation. The text suggests a variety of uses for 3x5 cards. Instructors and students often report becoming obsessed with them. They find them lurking in closets, hiding under their beds, stuck on their mirrors, pinned to bulletin boards, tucked into pockets, slipped into their notes, marking their places in books, resting next to their telephones, even replacing their address and recipe books. Some instructors ask students to carry 3x5 cards with them for a few days and jot down how they use their time. By doing so, students can monitor what they are doing and the amount of time they spend doing it.

Another way to use 3x5 cards is for attendance. Have students write their names and a question on a 3x5 card. Then have students bring their cards to class each day to hand in as their admission tickets to class. Their questions can then be used to stimulate classroom discussions.

Two-part exercise sheets. Two-part exercise sheets (up to five per book ordered) provide a way to encourage students to participate in class. The final step in any classroom exercise can be for students to write Journal Entries on two-part sheets. If you collect the original, letting students keep a copy for their own use, you can read some of the student discoveries and insights anonymously to the rest of the class. Students are interested in what their peers think. Collecting two-part sheets can also be a convenient way to take attendance. ✳

Selling this class to students on Day 1

IF YOUR STUDENT SUCCESS course is required, you are likely to have a number of student resisters in your class. In colleges and universities where taking such a course is an option, some students enroll because they think it looks like an "easy A" in the catalog. In either case, you, as the course instructor, can positively influence students on the first day of class so that they'll be more likely to stay and discover for themselves the value of this course. Here are seven suggestions to help build interest and commitment on Day 1:

1. Student testimonial letters. At the end of each semester, ask students to write a letter of advice to a future student in your course. Encourage them to include the information they would have liked to have known on the first day of class. Consider making this assignment part of the final or another assignment for which credit is granted. Distribute copies of these letters to your students during the first class meeting. Since these letters consist of opinions and not always facts, it may be useful to have the students exchange letters or share key information in the letters in groups or with the class as a whole. Students believe the content in these letters from unknown peers, and many will be inspired by what they read. Faculty Advisor Dean Mancina puts these letters in envelopes before handing them out—the sealed envelopes add to the impact!

2. Student guest speakers. This idea can be used as an alternative or in conjunction with the testimonial letters above. At the end of the semester, invite students to return as guest speakers on the first day of your class the following semester. Get their e-mail address and/or phone number so that you can send them a reminder a week or two before the next term begins. Having two or three students tell their peers how valuable the course is raises the commitment level of students who are still "shopping" for classes during the first week of the term.

3. Show your enthusiasm. If you've taught this course before, you know the profound impact it can have on your students. Share that in a dramatic and enthusiastic way. Let your students know how much impact this course can have on their lives. Share some stories of the success your prior students have achieved, but don't mention names to protect your students' privacy.

4. Ask "What do you want?" During the first class, ask students to write down three skills that would be so beneficial that if they could learn them, staying in this course would be "worth it." Brainstorm several such skills first to prompt their thinking. Use two-part paper. Have the students pass a copy forward. Read their responses aloud, anonymously, and announce whether each skill is part of the content of this course. This activity helps personalize the course and demonstrates that the content includes material that students want to learn. It also helps to clarify what this class is *not* about, as it's doubtful your course will cover everything the students want.

5. Talk about the text. *Becoming a Master Student* is one of the most used college textbooks on any subject in North America. This is a proven product that works. Hold the book up and turn to key pages such as the Discovery Wheel. Tell the students this is a book they will not want to burn or sell at the end of the semester, but will keep as a reference tool for the rest of their college years . . . and beyond!

6. Group discussion and anonymous questions. Divide students into groups of four and ask them to brainstorm questions about this course that they don't know the answers to. Have the students submit their questions anonymously on 3x5 cards. Read the questions aloud and answer them. Addressing concerns students may not wish to state openly can help quell anxiety and fears that could result in students dropping the course.

7. Tell the truth. Be honest about both the "good news" and the "bad news." "This course is *not* an easy A! But it's also about more than you thought it was when you enrolled." On the first day, Faculty Advisor Dean Mancina shares this thought with his students: "I don't know why you enrolled in this class, but today I get to convince you to commit to it and stay!" ✳

The Discovery Wheel

The Discovery Wheel is an opportunity for students to think about the kind of student they are and the kind of student that they want to become. Its twelve sections correspond to the twelve chapters in the text. This exercise is assigned at the outset of the course to help students assess their current strengths and weaknesses in different areas of student success. Students answer a series of questions and then plot their scores on their Discovery Wheel—a graphic illustration of their skill levels. This exercise is also available for students to complete on the *Becoming a Master Student* Web site (www.cengage .com/success/bams13e).

At the end of Chapter 12 is an identical Discovery Wheel. By repeating the exercise at the completion of the course, students can trace their progress in acquiring skills and techniques that can ensure their success in school and later in life.

The purpose of this exercise is to give students the opportunity to change their behavior. Completing the Discovery Wheel a second time allows students to see what behaviors they have changed on their journey to becoming a master student.

Having your students complete the Journal Entry that follows the second Discovery Wheel provides them with another opportunity to state how they intend to change. Encourage them to reconsider tools that they did not

think they could use the first time they encountered them in the text.

Note: Student scores may be lower on the second Discovery Wheel. That's OK. Lower scores might result from increased self-awareness and honesty, valuable assets in themselves.

Tips for teaching student success online

MANY OF THE STRATEGIES in the Instructor's Edition and on the Instructor Resources Web site can be adapted for use in your online student success course. For example, the icebreaker activity "Vote with your feet" (Page AIE-28) can be used online by having the students read a controversial article. Then at the Discussion Board, each student posts in the Subject Line— Strongly Agree, Agree, Disagree, or Strongly Disagree, with justification for their position in the body of the post. Further require that students respond to at least two other student posts in this thread.

One of the most important roles of the online instructor is to ensure a high degree of interactivity and participation by managing the discussion forum. In a classroom, the instructor builds motivation in front of the students by her on-stage demeanor. Online that role is portrayed in the projects, instructions, and guidance the instructor gives, which together promote a dynamic, interactive environment for online students. For example, when assigning text exercises such as the Discovery Wheel or Create a Lifeline, instead of having students turn in the reflective responses to the exercise, have them post a Discovery and/or Intention Statement to the Discussion Board and respond to at least two classmates' posts. If you use the eBook with your online students, assign students to complete the pre-chapter assessment that appears as a link icon at the beginning of each chapter and post an intention statement about the results on the Discussion Board.

Here are some suggestions to help you manage your online Discussion Board:

- Stagger due dates for postings and replies each week to keep the conversation moving.

- Require discussion participation and make it part of the student's grade in the course.

- Provide post expectations to receive full credit.

- Teach students to create succinct, accurate titles for the subject line of their posts.

- Don't let students use abbreviated writing, teach netiquette.

> After students read the article "Connect to resources" (Page 15) I have my students participate in an online scavenger hunt to discover what support programs are available to them while attending this community college. Many students do not attend classes on campus so I have them search the school website and then post on the Discussion Board what they discover. My assignment includes several different questions regarding student resources. Each student must respond to a different question.
>
> **—Connie Marten, Online Instructor, Golden West College**

Consider the following examples of online activities:

1. Don't fool yourself: 15 common mistakes in logic (Page 216). After students read the article, instruct them to pick one common mistake in logic and post a personal example to the Discussion Board. The second part of the assignment includes responding to classmates' posts.

2. Weekly Journal. The weekly journal is an avenue for students and the instructor to relate one-to-one. Solicit feedback from your students. Ask them how they are doing in class. Often an online class may be more difficult or time-consuming than they anticipated. In the journals, students often share frustrations with other classes, work, or not having enough time with family and friends. Direct them to a specific article in the textbook that may help, or quote something from the book in your reply.

3. Building Relationships across Cultures (Page 274). This activity is specifically for the eBook. After students have read the article, have them click on the *Activity* icon. Instruct the students to read the activity article "The face of diversity, remembering cultural differences." Then ask each student to complete an Internet search on the phrase "cultural generalization" from the article. Finally, ask students to post their discovery statements about cultural generalization to the Discussion Board, backing up their discoveries with links to the Web sites they researched. As noted above, each student should also respond to two of these posts to keep the discussion moving. ✳

CL Assessment and Portfolio Builder and Career Resource Center

THE CL ASSESSMENT AND PORTFOLIO BUILDER is a personal development tool that engages students in *self-assessment, critical thinking,* and *goal-setting* activities to prepare them for college and the workplace.

Students build a portfolio by responding to questions about their skills, attitudes, values, and behaviors in four key life areas: *Personal, Interpersonal, Career,* and *Community.* The *Accomplishments Report* summarizes the results of their responses and asks students to provide supporting evidence for responses in which they rate themselves as highly proficient. This provides great practice for honing critical thinking skills as well as for creating a résumé or preparing for interviews.

The Accomplishments Report module also provides access to additional resources, such as Cengage Learning's Web-based Career Resource Center, which offers tips, exercises, articles, and ideas to help students succeed on their journey from college to career. *The Bridge from College to Career* lets students practice new skills acquired in college that can be applied as they enter the job market. *Finding the Perfect Job* helps students fine-tune their résumé writing and interviewing skills. And *Skills for Your Future* provides strategies for problem solving and decision making to help students learn to work with others and communicate on the job.

Contact your sales representative or your TeamUp consultant about shrink-wrapping this tool as a passkey to a protected Web site with *Becoming a Master Student.*

A walk-through of the features

Demo this product via our Web site. Visit each of the areas described and try it yourself.

Each module (*Personal, Interpersonal, Career,* and *Community*) has a series of statements. Students assess their response to each statement by selecting from four choices. Feedback is provided for each response to help guide students in making the most appropriate selection. You can participate in the CL Assessment and Portfolio Builder by selecting the suitable response to each of the statements in the four sections. Those items that you mark as "usually and consistently" will be carried over to the *Accomplishments Report,* the fifth module.

Once the assessment portion has been completed, you are ready to enter evidence into your *Accomplishments Report.* In this section, you will provide supporting evidence for statements that were rated as "usually and consistently" most like your skills, attitudes, values, and behaviors.

The evidence is saved, and a portfolio of accomplishments is generated from these entries. Students can view and update their portfolios throughout the semester, and they can print a hard copy to bring to class or use as a reference during an interview.

After an *Accomplishments Report* is generated, students will see which areas still need documentation. They can explore information and resources for gaining experiences in college using the Career Resource Center. Students can access tips, exercises, articles, and additional Internet links to help them succeed in college and in the workplace. Suggestions for using the CL Assessment and Portfolio Builder to create a résumé and prepare for interviews are also available in the Career Resource Center. ✳

Icebreakers: Some ideas for first-day-of-class activities

CREATING A SENSE of community in your classroom starts during your first class meeting. Icebreakers can help both you and your students create a comfortable environment that supports self-discovery and honest reflection—two processes that will help your students achieve success. Here are several possible first-day icebreakers to get you started. Refer to the Instructor Web site for more activities related to specific chapters that can be used at any time throughout your course.

Becoming a Master Student has many unique messages in the beginning of the text. These messages are helpful for instructors to remember and highlight when starting the course.

"This book is worthless."

Have you ever seen a book start with this statement? All books are worthless unless read, so this book is useless unless students strive to adapt and adopt methods to attain personal and academic success. Students often complain about the cost of their textbooks. Yet the cost is even higher when they pay for a text but do not actively read it and implement its strategies to promote their success. Ask your students what specific steps they will take to ensure they get the most out of their investment in this textbook. Point out the following exercises as specific tasks to help them get started on this journey: "Textbook Reconnaissance," "The Discovery Wheel," and "Learning Style Inventory."

What is a master student?

Student success courses are offered at colleges and universities nationwide. Students often exhibit less resistance to taking this course when they realize that their school is not the only one requiring it. The qualities of a successful student are also the qualities of successful employees. This course can help students define the characteristics that promote excellence in their studies and relationships and in preparation for the world of work. Have your students review the article "The Master Student" in Chapter 1. Divide them into groups of four and ask them to list the qualities of people they admire (family members, celebrities, or friends). When each group has named ten characteristics, create a combined list of twenty for the entire class. Ask students to rank in order the qualities that might contribute to success in school, work, and life.

Ask your students to consider these qualities of success and then write an essay entitled "How do I define success?" Submit the best essay to the Cengage Learning Student Success scholarship competition (see complete details on page AIE-15).

Master Students in Action quotes

Each edition of *Becoming a Master Student* has been revised by considering the valuable insights and ideas of students and educators. Instructors over the years have used the Master Students in Action feature as part of the final examination for their course. Let your students know right from the outset that you will ask them to complete the Master Students in Action form on the *Becoming a Master Student* Web site www.cengage .com/success/bams13e or e-mail the forms to csweb .CollegeSurvival@cengage.com. Here they can share information about any article or exercise that they have found to be especially valuable to their growth during the course—and why. Ask them to suggest ways in which *Becoming a Master Student* could be valuable to next year's first-year students.

"What do you want?"

Research indicates that more than 60 percent of first-year college and university students are not yet sure of their career choice, even if they have declared a major. A student might choose a major because of parental pressure or the institution's policy rather than because of a passionate commitment to that field of study or career. This lack of clarity about her destination could negatively affect a student's level of dedication and involvement. She might experience a lack of desire or frustration when she encounters difficulties because she does not sense that current distresses might result in long-term benefits.

When they are asked "What do you want?" students can begin to find answers to what they hope to accomplish in the course, in the term, and in the academic year. Consider having your students share their answers in class, in small groups.

Create a college survival kit

Divide students into groups and ask them to brainstorm what this kit would have in it. Ask each group to report out to the class four items that have not been shared by another group.

Scavenger hunt

Create a scavenger hunt list about the services at the college. This encourages students to meet their peers, become familiar with the campus layout, and learn which services are available. The winner of the scavenger hunt might be rewarded by being taken to lunch by the college president.

Student success alumni

Invite former students to speak about their experiences taking the student success course and to describe specific successes they've had in college subsequent to completing this course.

Class as a worksite

Tell the class that you are the supervisor and they are the employees. Ask them the implications for being late, absent, attentive, and productive. Create a list of expected behaviors in the "workplace."

Naming names

Have each student introduce himself with a unique name that describes him. These aliases could be used throughout the term.

Choose your final grade

Many students wonder on the first day about the grade they'll get at the end of the term. Provide a list of each assignment, quiz, and test in the course and the maximum points possible. Ask students to set a goal score for each item. Then tell them to total their scores and see their final (goal) grade. This activity generates good first-day questions about course assignments throughout the term. It also demonstrates course goal setting.

Excuses brainstorm

Faculty Advisor Dean Mancina asks his students to commit to attend every class meeting. He asks students to brainstorm a list of reasons why a student might miss class. As reasons are suggested, he asks students to categorize them as "good," "poor," or "questionable." Students typically disagree about categorizing them, and most excuses end up in the "questionable" category. This activity helps students see how having to decide what exactly is a "good" excuse puts the faculty in an awkward position. It also sets the stage for Dean explaining his absence policy.

Group syllabus questions

Divide students into groups and ask each group to come up with three questions about the syllabus. Respond to the entire class about each of the groups' questions. Students are generally more attentive to responses to their inquiries than to your "lecture" about the syllabus.

Voting with your feet

Eldon McMurray from Utah Valley State College makes four signs: Agree, Disagree, Strongly Agree, and Strongly Disagree and posts them on the walls of the classroom. At the beginning of the activity, he has the students push the chairs aside and form a group in the middle. Next he reads a controversial statement like, "Being energy independent is more important than global warming."

Then he asks the students to vote with their feet. They simply move to stand by the sign that reflects how they feel about the issue at argument. He picks two or three students and has them defend their "stand." He also teaches them what it means to make a stand. He shows a video clip from the Tiananmen Square uprising in China. ✳

Encourage students to participate

Your student success course will benefit from class participation that motivates students to contribute and share. As you create a sense of community in your classroom, use these suggestions for increasing overall participation.

Facilitate students getting to know each other. Having students do projects in groups with non-threatening group assignments (such as "Plan participation activities" below) helps them to get to know each other. It's less intimidating to participate around people you've met than with strangers. Randomly assign students to different groups for a brief activity each week.

Plan participation activities. Divide your students into small groups (three to four students is ideal) to review articles from the textbook or assignments that may have been completed outside class. Provide some guidelines and post them (on a whiteboard, PowerPoint slide, etc.) so that all students can see them. Suggest the number of minutes that students should talk about each question you have assigned. For example, you may ask your students to do the following: "Identify the time-management strategy that was most interesting to you and describe how you plan to use it in the upcoming week (2 minutes per person)."

After your students have discussed this with their group, bring the discussion back to the classroom as a whole. Create a tally to show which strategy was the most popular. Consider discussing why some of the less popular strategies are beneficial, and challenge your students to try the one they selected and then one of the less popular strategies. As the instructor, also commit to planning to practice these new strategies and collectively report back on results during the next class period. Sharing enthusiasm with students is a master instructor quality that will help to increase positive feedback and results in your course.

Call on students rather than waiting for them to volunteer. Allow all of your students to think about questions that you are asking, permitting time for reflection and contemplation. Suggest that your students who frequently get called on first write down their answers while everyone in the class has time to think. Break the ice by selecting one of your eager students. Then select students who have not had a chance to share. Remind students that participating in class is a great way to connect with the instructor and that a student success class is a perfect classroom for practicing their public speaking skills. Challenge your students to participate in their other courses as much as they participate in this class—it's engaging!

Acknowledging uncomfortableness. Trying new techniques, changing habits, and practicing new behaviors can be uncomfortable at first. Nevertheless, these activities make up much of what a student success course is about. When describing the benefits of the course, it is wise to be honest about the challenges that students face while expressing confidence in their ability to succeed. Ask students to write their names with their nondominant hands, to introduce themselves to one another by shaking their left hands, or to cross their arms in reverse of the way they normally do. Everyone can relate when they all feel the awkwardness of these movements. But with practice, these movements will begin to feel natural. So will participating in class.

Reinforce speaking up. Surprise a student who speaks up with "bonus points" or a coupon for a beverage in the school food service. Dean Mancina's student success course has a required "materials fee" of about $3 per student. This small account funds the purchase of inexpensive educational supplies that are given to students through the term.

Teaching learning styles in your classroom

BECOMING A MASTER STUDENT includes three approaches to learning styles: the Learning Style Inventory, multiple intelligences, and the VAK (**v**isual, **a**uditory, and **k**inesthetic) system. That's a lot of information to absorb. It is important to recognize that each approach presents a valid option and is not the final word on learning styles. Encourage your students to look for ideas from any of these methods that they can put to immediate use. When they write Intention Statements, have your students keep these questions in mind: How can I use this idea to *be* more successful in school? What will I *do* differently as a result of reading about learning styles? If I develop new learning styles, what skill will I *have* that I don't have now?

The Learning Style Inventory (LSI). People are fascinated by why they do what they do—and students are no exception. Taking the Learning Style Inventory (LSI) in Chapter 1 gives students a chance to increase their self-awareness as learners. The LSI helps students make sense of what they're experiencing in college.

Developed by Dr. David Kolb at Case Western Reserve University in Cleveland, Ohio, the LSI measures a learner's preferences for *perceiving* information (taking it in) and *processing* information (making sense of what she takes in). When these preferences are plotted on two continuums, four unique modes of learning are formed. Students find that although every individual is capable of employing all four modes, each person has a preferred way of learning.

The Master Student Map on the first page of each chapter highlights these four modes to help students become more effective learners through an understanding of their own learning style preferences. More important, the Master Student Map can help increase students' effectiveness by encouraging them to use those modes that they have previously underutilized.

Detailed information about administering and helping your students interpret the Learning Style Inventory appears on the next page. Support materials are also available at the Instructor Web site.

Multiple intelligences. Howard Gardner of Harvard University believes that no single measure of intelligence can tell us how smart we are. Instead, Gardner identifies many types of intelligence, described in *Becoming a Master Student* on page 39. By applying Gardner's concepts, students can explore additional methods for achieving success in school, work, and relationships. *Becoming a Master Student* is designed to help students develop these different intelligences. Charts accompany the definitions of Gardner's multiple intelligences in the text, highlighting the characteristics of each intelligence, the learning strategies that are preferred by people with this type of intelligence, and the careers that might interest them. Have your students apply this information to their core courses. For example, a student with musical/rhythmic intelligence could write songs using lyrics based on class notes and could experiment with various kinds of background music while studying.

When students begin to acknowledge and trust all of their intelligences, they can understand and appreciate themselves more.

The VAK system. The VAK system is a simple and powerful technique that focuses on perception through three sense channels: seeing, or *visual* learning; hearing, or *auditory* learning; and movement, or *kinesthetic* learning. Invite your students to discover their VAK preferences by taking the informal inventory included in the text.

Strategies in the text highlight ways students can build on their current learning preferences and develop new options by utilizing their other sense channels. It is important that you teach students to take in information efficiently through their preferred learning style, but it is equally important that you teach them to study and learn information efficiently through a variety of other learning styles. As their instructor, you can set an example by using a mix of strategies to teach them ways to learn the largest amount of material in the least amount of time. Additional ideas for implementing variety in your teaching strategies can be found at the Instructor Web site. ✳

Applying the learning styles for critical thinking

Have students use the following scale to rate their confidence in their ability to utilize the four questions **Why? What? How?** and **What if?** to effectively accomplish the tasks listed below.

- 0 **Never confident**
- 1 **Rarely confident**
- 2 **Occasionally confident**
- 3 **Sometimes confident**
- 4 **Often confident**
- 5 **Almost always confident**

___ 1. You are a learner, and your biology professor only shows you *how* to do an experiment. Rate your confidence in your ability to answer any questions (*Why? What?* and/or *What if?*) you still have.

___ 2. After your professor repeats the instructions for an assignment, they are still not clear to you. How confident are you that you can gain the clarity you need to successfully complete the assignment by asking yourself the four questions?

___ 3. As you plan your schedule for the next semester, you find there are a number of English classes to choose from. How confident are you in your ability to discover which class would be best for you to take?

___ 4. You are preparing for a test, but you have little, if any, prior background knowledge about the subject.

___ 5. You have a problem, and you are trying to understand all the factors that have contributed to the problem so that you can solve it.

___ 6. You are reviewing your class notes for a test, and you do not remember why a certain entry was so important for you to remember.

___ 7. You need to choose your career and declare a major, but you are not sure what steps to take first.

___ 8. Your car breaks down, and you are the one responsible for fixing it.

___ 9. You are planning a party, and you have been elected to be in charge of buying the food and arranging for the entertainment.

___10. You are sending out Christmas cards, and you discover that you have more friends and family on your list than you have cards to send.

Administering and interpreting the Learning Style Inventory

THE LEARNING STYLE INVENTORY (LSI) is an important tool to help your students discover their preferred mode of learning. Some instructors have found their students feel overwhelmed when they are left on their own to take the LSI, score it, and interpret the results. Consider the following suggestions.

Begin by introducing the LSI to your students. The article "Learning Styles: Discovering How You Learn" will help you set the stage. Page 34 highlights the step-by-step directions for completing the LSI, which begins on page LSI-1. Review the directions with your students. If you are assigning the LSI as homework, consider walking students through the scoring process in class first. Or ask them to hold off scoring the inventory until they're in class with you. Guide them in using the interpretive material—help your students connect it with their own experience. Doing so will pay big dividends. Not only will your students begin to understand why they make the choices they do, but they'll be better partners in the learning process.

Be sure to review the cycle of learning with your students. The examples will be easily identifiable to your students and will encourage them to put the information they have discovered about themselves into practice right away. Begin your discussion by asking students about their preferred way to learn historical information or new technology. Once you have your students in the proper mindset to think about their learning style, they will be better prepared to read the Master Student Map at the beginning of each chapter and will understand the value of completing the Learning Styles Application on the Web site.

Beginning on page 35, the article "Using Your Learning Style Profile to Succeed" will have your students participating in a Mode 4 activity. In the Put It to Work feature at the end of Chapter 1, your students will be invited to think specifically about learning styles and their application in the workplace.

Students can use their understanding of learning styles to make choices that support their academic progress. Ask them to apply *what? why? how?* and *what if?* questions to the LSI:

- "**Why** should I involve myself in this learning situation?"

Self-awareness control is the ability to consciously monitor and intentionally control thinking and establish purposeful reasons for action. Asking the question *why?* helps students regulate their thinking by establishing purposeful reasons for their actions.

- "**What** will I need to do to understand the concept?"

Critical analysis is the ability to identify key ideas, gather necessary information, and recognize the importance of essential ideas. Asking *what?* questions helps students recognize the knowledge level of essential ideas by their order of importance.

- "**How** is this learning meaningful to me?"

Reasoned synthesis is the ability to combine essential ideas to create meaningful applications of knowledge. Asking *how?* questions helps students utilize essential ideas and create meaningful applications of their knowledge

- "**What if** I apply this strategy to my other courses or to my life?"

Creative transfer application is the ability to adapt applications for different concepts and choose the most effective strategies for specific situations. Asking *what if?* questions helps students imagine alternative applications and choose the most effective strategy for the situation.

Integrating knowledge of learning styles into the curriculum can help instructors design a course that promotes success for all students. As you choose your teaching methods to address various preferences at different points in the course, you meet different students' needs. Students in your classes typically represent all four modes of learning, so some students will sometimes find a good fit with what you are doing, while at other times they'll need to stretch beyond their preferences. Acknowledging different learning styles allows instructors to shift their energy from lecturing to facilitating. Rather than just focusing on the transfer of knowledge, you can use feedback about your students' learning to inform your teaching. Students come to realize that their interactions shape what happens in the classroom, and they become active participants in constructing their learning experience. Working together, instructors and students create an environment that promotes success.

More suggestions for creating lesson plans that support all four modes of learning are available at the Instructor Web site. In addition, video clips from the *Learning Style Inventory* video—an overview of the LSI and its application—are available at the Instructor Web site. ✳

Using learning styles to improve learning and problem-solving skills

Students can improve their ability to learn and solve problems in three ways:

1. Develop learning and work relationships with people whose learning strengths and weaknesses are different from theirs.

2. Improve the fit between their learning style strengths and the kinds of learning and problem-solving experiences they face.

3. Practice and develop learning skills in their areas of weakness.

First strategy: Develop supportive relationships. This is the easiest way to improve learning skills. It is important for students to recognize their own learning style strengths and build on them. At the same time, it is important to understand and value other people's different learning styles. Also, students should not assume that they have to solve problems alone. Learning power is increased by working with others. Although students might be drawn to people who have similar learning skills, they'll learn more and experience the learning cycle more fully with friends and coworkers who have different learning skills.

How? If someone has an abstract learning style, such as Mode 3, he can learn to communicate ideas more effectively by associating with those who are more concrete and people oriented, such as learners who prefer Mode 1. A person with a more reflective style can benefit from observing the risk taking and experimentation of people who are more active, such as learners who prefer Mode 4.

Second strategy: Improve the match or fit between students' learning styles and their life situation. This is a more difficult way to achieve better learning performance and life satisfaction.

How? There are a number of ways to do this. For some people, this might mean a change of career to a field where they feel more comfortable with the values and skills required of them. Most people, however, can improve the match between their learning style and their tasks by reorganizing their priorities and activities. They can concentrate on those tasks and activities that lie in their areas of learning strength and rely on other people's help in areas of learning weakness.

Third strategy: Become a flexible learner. Students can do this by strengthening the learning skills in which they are weak. This strategy is the most challenging but also the most rewarding. By becoming flexible, students will be able to cope with problems of all kinds, and they will be more adaptable in changing situations. Because this strategy is more difficult, it requires more time and tolerance for mistakes and failures.

How? First, students should develop a long-term plan. Look for improvements and payoffs over months and years, rather than right now. Next, look for safe opportunities to practice new skills. Students should find situations that can test new skills and will not punish them for failure. Lastly, students should reward themselves! Becoming a flexible learner is hard work.

Embracing diversity

RESEARCH INDICATES THAT although successful students benefit from having a relationship with a caring and competent adult, they are most likely to excel if they receive positive support from a peer group. The information below will help you foster that sense of belonging and assist students of all backgrounds in sharing with each other their discoveries and insights about higher education.

Research also shows that when students interact with diverse student groups, they experience many benefits including these:

- Improved cultural understanding and tolerance
- Decreased cultural prejudice and discrimination
- Stronger connection to the campus community
- Preparation for challenges of global society
- Development of creativity and critical thinking skills

These benefits can be realized only if students extend themselves beyond both real and imagined barriers that exist.

Anthony Antonio, a professor at Stanford University, claims, "The most influential experiences with diversity likely involve the development of interracial [and cross-cultural] friendships."* Learning tolerance and respect for the diversity that makes each student unique will be one of the most important skills students learn in college. By willingly stretching themselves to increase their sensitivity and feel empathy toward others, they will develop personal attributes that will benefit them throughout their lives.

Instructors and students are currently using *Becoming a Master Student* in the United States, Canada, and many other countries. In all probability, a variety of cultural and life experiences will be represented by the students in your class. They will have come from many places and have had varied experiences.

Additional activities in the Diversity chapter on the Instructor Web site offer ways to encourage communication among students of different races, ethnicity, ages, countries of origin, and levels of familiarity with the American language and American customs.

The video *Embracing Diversity* highlights a group of students representing diverse cultures, ages, races, and religious and ethnic backgrounds. They share their

*Antonio, A.L. (2004). When does race matter in college friendships? Exploring men's diverse and homogeneous friendship groups. *The Review of Higher Education.* 27(4), 553-575.

personal experiences and illustrate by example effective means of communicating across cultures. Attitudes, stereotypes, and biases are examined.

One of the major goals of diversity awareness is to understand how each person fits into the lives and worlds of others. For some of your students, college may be their first experience with someone different from themselves. As you prepare for your course, keep in mind that some kinds of diversity can be less obvious, though just as profound, as others. To the student from rural America, a classmate from New York or Chicago might seem nearly as strange as one from Finland or Zimbabwe, and vice versa.

International students will have additional adjustment issues beyond those of the other students in your class. They are far from home in an unfamiliar culture. Keep in mind that some statements, activities, or attitudes that seem perfectly natural in our society may seem curious or even offensive to students from other countries. Familiarize yourself with cultural differences and issues that could baffle or frustrate these students and work to overcome them before they become obstacles to learning.

Finding common ground can be an important learning experience in the classroom. Routinely pairing students from different backgrounds and circumstances when assigning group projects and activities can provide students with the opportunity to encounter ideas, attitudes, and experiences different from their own. Throughout the semester, schedule a variety of activities involving students in individual, partner, small-group, and whole-class settings that exercise and accentuate the similarities among your students, and also celebrate the wealth of their differences.

School strategies

Promote participation. Involving students in school activities challenges them and stimulates their interest. Promote the benefits of participating by placing ads in school newsletters and posting notes on bulletin boards. Design and display posters. Ask other teachers to announce school activities in their classrooms. Brainstorm ways to get more students involved. Don't overlook asking students for their ideas!

Provide tutors. Encourage students to take advantage of tutors. Maintaining or improving one's performance level and gaining confidence in academic ability help ensure student success.

Structure opportunities for friendships. Having friends is widely accepted as a critical component of making a healthy adjustment to college life and achieving academic success. Friendships can be expanded beyond immediate peer groups to include faculty members, administrative staff, counselors, role models, peers from home environments, community members, or graduate students. Organize icebreakers and get-acquainted exercises during orientation and at other school events. Encourage the use of name tags at these events. Sponsor social activities that include faculty and staff as well as students. Encourage broad participation in all social, academic, cultural, and extracurricular events.

Examine policies and procedures. Review policies and procedures, looking for any subtle (or blatant) messages of racism or other forms of discrimination. If there is no clear disciplinary procedure for infractions of any policy, implement one.

Promote resources. New students who are unfamiliar with the resources at your school cannot use them. Asking the administrators and staff who are responsible for these resources to describe their services during student orientation is only the beginning of what's possible.

Ask administrators and directors of service programs to speak in your class. Suggest that clubs and organizations offering services to diverse students sponsor programs to familiarize students with the resources at your school. Write articles about resources for the school newsletter. An open house at which refreshments are served will encourage students to get to know the facilities and the services that are available. Ask students who have benefited from the resources to give testimonials. Create contests and games that require students to visit various offices, facilities, and services personnel.

Promote the resources at your school so that they attract and serve students. Have tutors and counselors introduce themselves and make short presentations in class. Ask the student advisory board for help.

Make school inviting. Students who feel comfortable are more likely to experience success in school. Do the residence halls offer quiet places to study? Are exercise facilities available at convenient times? Are the needs for student transportation and day care facilities met? Are computers and software programs up-to-date? How long do students have to wait for assistance in the financial aid and other student services offices? What is the quality of the food service? How can registration procedures be made more efficient? Do instructors post office hours and keep them? What do admissions representatives say would attract more students?

Hire from different backgrounds. Whenever possible, hiring both men and women from a variety of backgrounds will provide role models for students. Whether they are faculty, staff, or administrators, they should be knowledgeable about diversity issues and committed to being involved with students on campus.

Evaluate faculty. Conduct regular student and peer evaluations of all instructors. Include the criteria of being sensitive to the needs of students and being responsive to the learning styles of all students.

Encourage leadership. Students from diverse backgrounds who are in leadership positions help promote acceptance and inclusion of all students in all areas of school life. Sponsor leadership training programs. Encourage students with leadership potential to consider running for student offices.

Sponsor panel discussions. Invite students from a variety of populations to participate in panel discussions on a wide range of topics. Each panel member can introduce himself (including a description of what it's like to be a member of his particular population on your campus, if appropriate) and then state his point of view about the topic. The discussion can then be opened for questions and answers.

Conduct workshops. Invite faculty and staff to attend workshops on the diverse backgrounds, circumstances, and cultures of students at your institution.

Classroom strategies

Help ensure success. You can individualize your instruction and structure your course so that students experience success. Total success in school is achieved by taking a series of small, successful steps. Set high but realistic expectations. If your course is too easy, students will lose interest. If it is too difficult, students may become discouraged. By continually evaluating students, monitoring their progress, and getting feedback from them, you can plan your classes in ways that help ensure student success.

Provide opportunities to talk. Invite students to speak about their perspectives. Suggest that students talk to others to share their concerns, celebrations, compliments, and complaints. Use small-group discussions and exercises. If you teach online or have a supplemental Web site for your class, use the Discussion Board for this purpose. Promote the idea of visiting with counselors and forming peer support groups. The suggestions for conversations and sharing at the Instructor Web site include many ideas for stimulating discussions.

Acknowledge and appreciate cultural differences. We can learn from each other and from exploring values that are different from our own. When we exchange ideas, we can expand our perceptions and examine our values. Use conversations, publications, and special events to recognize and celebrate diversity.

Communicate the advantages of being bicultural. Learning new ways of speaking and behaving does not mean denying or letting go of our traditional languages or customs. Adding alternatives does not eliminate anything. Expanding our options increases our ability to operate effectively in a variety of situations and improves our chances of success.

Discuss how the school environment is similar to, and different from, students' home environments. Then discuss ways to make effective transitions back and forth from one to the other. Explore how the expectations of one environment can be assets or liabilities in another. Recognize that a strength in one culture might be a disadvantage in another. Tennis rackets are great on a tennis court, but they don't work very well in a golf game. How can a student adapt so that she is successful in both environments?

Recognize different beliefs regarding time, competitiveness, and respect for authority. In some cultures, punctuality is a plus. In others, time is not measured in hours, minutes, and seconds; instead, it is measured by the movement of the sun, the changing of the seasons, and an intuitive sense of community readiness. In some cultures, competitiveness is a common incentive toward achievement. In others, it is considered antisocial and insulting. Eye contact during conversations is considered respectful in some cultures and disrespectful in others.

You can acknowledge a wide range of beliefs and, at the same time, communicate the expectations of your institution. An advantage to being bicultural is the ability to adopt behaviors that promote success in a specific environment.

Encourage exposure to different backgrounds. Encourage students to break out of old patterns and habits by associating with people from different backgrounds as well as with those whose backgrounds are similar to their own. They could choose new lab partners, form groups with people they don't know for in-class exercises, sit in new areas in the student union, or attend events that are likely to draw crowds different from those with whom they are comfortable. Invite your class to brainstorm ways to gain exposure to people with different backgrounds.

Survey student needs. Evaluate frequently. When you become aware that a student is struggling in a certain area, make an appointment with that student to formulate an action plan.

Individualize feedback. Students appreciate getting specific feedback about their individual performance. Students may initially share cultural concerns or issues in their writing rather than speaking up in class or even individually to you. Write sensitive, relevant comments on papers you return. Send messages and comments to students through the school e-mail. Thank a student who has actively participated as he leaves the classroom.

Set clear expectations. Communicate expectations clearly. State them several times in several different ways. Use examples to illustrate both what is acceptable and what isn't. Invite students to ask questions in class or to contact you during your office hours or via e-mail if they have any questions or concerns.

Be a mediator. As an instructor of a student success course, you can facilitate communication between students and administrators. Pass students' complaints and compliments on to the people who are most directly involved. Ask for responses from those people and report back to the students. Follow up on all communications until the matter is resolved.

Include other cultural experiences. Use speakers, textbooks, classroom materials, activities, and media presentations that incorporate diverse cultural experiences. Ask students, colleagues, administrators, and community members for recommendations.

Use a critical thinking approach. Ask students to decide what they think about relevant issues and why they think it. Then ask them to seek other views and gather evidence to support the various viewpoints. Discuss which view or views are the most reasonable. When discussing issues, you can apply the strategies outlined in the articles on critical thinking in the text to recognize any errors in thinking.

Encourage proaction. When students face uncomfortable, unfamiliar, and difficult situations, they sometimes choose avoidance. They may feel powerless or resentful and choose to withdraw rather than risk embarrassment. Help students consider the long-term costs of giving up. Help them see the benefits of a positive, healthy, and proactive approach. Suggest a variety of alternatives for dealing with the problems they face. Rather than giving up, students can garner support and find or create forums to discuss and resolve their issues.

Allow personal expression. Invite students to translate material into their own words. Ask them how certain techniques, or variations of those techniques, might be applied in their own culture. For example, a gay, lesbian, or transgender student may want to "come out" to the class while sharing in groups or with the whole class. Be ready to provide leadership and support in the event that another student's lack of sensitivity and understanding threatens to create an oppressive rather than supportive environment in your class.

Acknowledge student expertise. Ask students to communicate course content from their unique cultural perspective. Experiencing a concept from a different cultural perspective reinforces it. Give an assignment requiring students to combine a student success strategy with some cultural event, personality, tradition, or value. For example, they could create original music and lyrics or describe the role that a particular success strategy may have played in how a cultural hero changed history.

Use guest speakers. Invite guest speakers to your class who represent successful role models. Ask them to share struggles they have experienced and successes they have achieved. Be sure to include time for a question-and-answer period.

Personal strategies

Avoid generalizations. All generalizations are suspect—even this one. Avoid tendencies to lump together all people of one race or culture. Consider speaking up when you hear generalizations being made.

Examine your own prejudices. If you have painful memories that contribute to your prejudices, judgments, and generalizations, examine them. Tell the truth about the costs and benefits of holding on to them. Look at how your history encouraged you to be prejudiced in certain ways. Talk about your prejudices and formulate a plan to heal and grow.

Examine your assumptions about students. Where do you think your students go during their vacations? How would you expect them to spend extra money? What type of music do they enjoy? Who are their heroes? Which holidays do they celebrate? Consider how often your assumptions direct your teaching and your conversations with students. How would your teaching and your conversations be different if you assumed nothing about your students?

Find a translator. Taking a First Step by admitting that you are unfamiliar or uncomfortable with students from other cultures helps bridge the gap. Ask around to find someone who can act as a translator. In this sense, a translator is someone from the students' ethnic or cultural background who has successfully adapted to the mainstream environment. Ask students if they are willing to have this person present when you discuss various issues.

Increase your sensitivity to society's exclusions and inclusions. When you become aware of what to look for, you can see many examples of how one cultural or ethnic group excludes or includes others. Watch advertising and television shows. Listen to speeches. Examine the policies and notice the membership demographics of schools, business organizations, neighborhoods, religious institutions, athletic clubs, and social groups. Look for subtle or hidden messages of exclusion and inclusion as well as blatant, formal structures.

Reach out to students. Be sure students know your office hours. Send written invitations to each student in your class to come visit you during those hours. Talk in class about what students might gain if they schedule an appointment to see you or if they just drop in. Write your reactions to what students have written on papers before you return them. Maintain accurate records about attendance and call students when they miss a class. Use whatever appropriate methods you can think of to let individual students know that you are personally interested in their success. Be a person with whom students can form a supportive, interpersonal relationship.

Give specific feedback. Feedback promotes student success. Be especially sensitive to the unspoken expectations of the environment at your school and in your community. When feedback is given with a sincere desire to promote success, it is likely to be appreciated. ✳

Critical thinking:
It's all over this book

THINKING SKILLS ARE necessary from the first day of the semester, and tools throughout the text are designed to prepare students for the more in-depth coverage provided in Chapter 7: Thinking.

A first-year experience course can help students develop higher-level thinking and learning skills through self-awareness, self-regulation, and self-instruction. *Becoming a Master Student* offers many opportunities for critical thinking through the introduction of self-awareness tools; strategies for successful studying; and opportunities for connection with other students, faculty, and campus resources.

Self-discovery is encouraged in Chapter 1 through the Discovery Wheel, the Learning Style Inventory, and other learning styles models. The self-awareness that students gain through using these tools provides them with a foundation for honestly assessing their experiences for the rest of their lives. By completing the Discovery Wheel again at the end of the text, students can evaluate the work they have accomplished over the semester.

Time management is a crucial skill for students to develop. The exercises in Chapter 2 help students take a First Step in learning how to manage their time and set short-, medium-, and long-term goals.

As students develop effective thinking and study skills, mastering memory, reading, note taking, and test taking, encourage them to begin to transfer these concepts to their core courses. The application of these skills requires a higher level of thinking and promotes their overall success in college.

Once students reach the Thinking chapter, they have experienced the rigors of higher education and are ready to engage in *thorough thinking*. Master students use thorough thinking to select a major, choose courses for the second semester, and plan for their future. They have also actively employed decision-making skills and are ready to transition to the next step of solving problems more creatively and confidently. They exhibit a certain attitude toward success that is highlighted in the way they ask questions, make decisions, and solve problems.

The development of more advanced thinking skills helps students transition to later chapters. There they broaden their scope to consider the impact of decisions and experiences in higher education on such areas as diversity, communication, money, health, their careers, and life beyond.

Throughout the text, students are encouraged to participate actively in developing and implementing concepts. The ideas in the text are not a list of instructions; they are tools that students can try and then decide what works best for them.

The Master Student Map on the first page of each chapter encourages students to ask questions related to the four modes of learning identified in the Learning Style Inventory in Chapter 1. These questions promote curiosity and invite students to explore and investigate new materials.

Discovery and Intention Journal Entries, which appear throughout the text, promote a form of decision making that requires students to make declarations that lead to focused action.

Exercises and Practicing Critical Thinking activities promote the application of strategies and allow students to practice problem solving. Students develop thinking techniques and chart their own course.

Put It to Work articles provide students with the chance to begin making connections to their future and to think critically about the application of the skills they learn in college to the workplace. Endorse this type of thinking by asking students to create their own scenarios that apply the skills they are learning in this course to the careers they are considering.

The tools provided in *Becoming a Master Student* are a foundation for this success, and as the instructor, you have the ability to foster the attitudes of a critical thinker in your classroom. Ask your students *how* they will apply these skills. Advertise how these strategies work by suggesting that students ask *what if* questions: "*What if* I apply these test-taking strategies to prepare for exams in my biology course? And *what if* I do not?" ✳

Classroom management strategies

STUDENTS CAN ACHIEVE maximum success in an environment that fosters creativity, critical thinking, focus, and commitment. Developing your classroom management skills can help you create that environment. There are as many approaches to effective classroom management as there are instructors. To be effective, a strategy has to fit your style. For example, if you like a structured, linear environment, set up your class to fit that style. Brainstorm a list of answers to the following question: What is the optimum teaching environment for you and your students? The answers to this question may provide you with guidance in formulating strategies that will provide an environment conducive to learning. Consider asking tenured colleagues what works and what doesn't work for them. They know the culture of the students attending your institution.

After you decide what you want, make sure that you clearly communicate to your students how you conduct your class. Have a conversation with your students about this topic during the first week of class. Follow up with key aspects about your class in writing to enhance clarity. This information might be part of your syllabus or a separate handout.

Finally, implement consistently. Public institutions must be able to defend that students are not being discriminated against. No instructor wants to be accused of treating students with favoritism at any institution, public or private.

Class rules to consider

- *Respect—for peers, for the instructor, and for guest speakers.* What are the minimum standards you want to set?

- *Side conversations.* Some side conversations in class are related to the class topic being discussed, but others may be unrelated to the topic. Seating students in groups promotes more active learning, but may also facilitate more side conversations. Side conversations may distract you from your lecture. Further, when two students engage in a side conversation, not only do they miss what's actually happening in class, but the students around them may be distracted as well.

- *Absences.* What is your policy regarding missed class meetings? How will students get the assignments, handouts, information, and class experiences they missed? Flexibility here is helpful for students, but if you're teaching many courses or are a part-time instructor, providing copies of all of your previous handouts and class summaries and taking the time

to go over missed classes with students may not be realistic.

- *Arriving late to class.* Some instructors and students are distracted when students arrive late to class. How can late-arriving students minimize the disruption they cause? Will you still accept their homework?

- *Cell phones/laptops/other technologies.* Many students have come to believe that they need to stay in touch with their family and friends even during class. If you don't want students constantly stepping out of the classroom to answer their phones, checking their e-mail, surfing the Web, or texting instead of being engaged in what's happening in class, you'll need to set parameters for the use of such devices.

- *Turning in assignments late.* Will you accept assignments after they are due? If so, what are the limits to that policy, if any?

- *Makeups for missed quizzes and tests.* Can your students arrange to make up a quiz or test they miss?

- *Cheating.* What is your policy regarding cheating?

- *Progressive discipline.* How will you handle violations of your class rules?

Some instructors provide a written list of class rules and review them during class. Other instructors create such a list with the students at the beginning of the course. Such documents can even take the form of a class contract that the instructor and students must sign.

As for discipline, first find out your college's policies and procedures regarding student discipline for cheating and disruptive classroom behavior. Your dean or another administrator may be responsible for student discipline and can give you guidance and direction that is consistent with the institution's policies. Decide ahead of time what your progressive discipline plan will be if a student violates or refuses to follow your rules. Your behavior in that situation will set an example and inform other students of the consequences of not following your rules. Depending on the specific infraction, you might start by approaching the student individually and reminding him of the rule he has broken. If he repeats the violation, you might call him out in front of the class, remind him that you have already talked to him about this, and say that the next time you will tell him to leave the class. Then follow through with his removal if he violates the rule a third time.

See the example of Dean Mancina's class rules on the next page. ✳

Dean Mancina's Course Policies & Class Rules

1. The H1N1 flu virus is very contagious. If you're ill, stay home, or go to the GWC Health Center or to your private doctor. You'll lose some points, but just do bonus assignments to make up the points, and check the class website for assignments and handouts. Email me for a summary of the topics discussed in class that you missed.

2. Attendance at each class meeting and completing the Choose Your Grade assignment are required. Be in class on time. **No late assignments are accepted for point credit.**

3. Assignments, quizzes, etc turned in without your name on the front page get zero points.

4. Side Conversations are not permitted.

5. Turn cell phones to Off or Silent and keep them out of sight during class unless I authorize you to use them in class (e.g., to use the calculator).

6. Laptop computers may be used in class, but must focus at all times on College 100 content.

7. Read and follow the GWC Academic Honesty Policy as it is enforced in my class.

8. **Your grade will be based solely on the total points achieved on the activities you complete.** You must keep track of your own grade by using the Grade Monitor handout.

9. You must purchase a 3-ring binder for your text, handouts, notes, and other materials.

10. My course requires online access. Do not use an email address shared with others. Email attachments must be sent in WORD or PDF format. No other formats will be accepted. NOTE: The Blackboard Vista email system is not 100% reliable. To ensure that your emails reach me in a timely manner, I recommend you email me directly at dmancina@aol.com.

11. After 4 weeks, if your total points drop below 50% possible, you may be withdrawn from the course.

12. If you drop this course at any time during the semester, it is your responsibility to officially process the withdrawal paperwork.

13. My class and website are hate-free zones. **Inappropriate, disrespectful, or disruptive behavior will not be tolerated.**

14. Achievement of Student Learning Outcomes is based on the premise that you attend all class meetings, participate actively, and complete all outside of class activities. Generally, students should expect to spend an average of 2 hours outside of class for every hour spent in class in most transferable college courses, including this one.

15. Students with disabilities who believe they may need accommodations should contact the Accessibility Center for Education (ACE) as soon as possible in order to ensure that if ACE finds them qualified, such accommodations are made in a timely and confidential fashion. 714.895.8721 or 714.895.8350 TDD.

Helping your students become
master students

The new **chapter opener design** includes a Master Student Map to help students preview chapter concepts and chart their course to success. By using this map at the start of each chapter, your students can begin to address each of the four modes of learning described in Chapter 1.

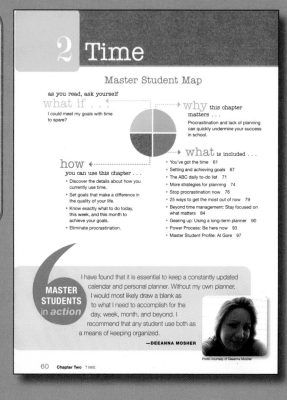

New to the chapter opener is the **Master Students in Action** feature. Students can read and relate to real stories of success and struggles in college from their peers.

The **Journal Entries** help students interact with the chapter content, declare their goals, and commit to taking action.

Action makes this book work. Student **exercises** encourage active learning and help develop critical thinking.

The **Discovery Wheel** has 12 spokes that represents the 12 themes (and chapters) in the book. The self-awareness that students gain through using this tool provides them with a foundation for honestly assessing their experiences for the rest of their lives. By completing the Discovery Wheel again at the end of the text, students can evaluate the work they have accomplished.

The Learning Style Inventory (LSI). People are fascinated by why they do what they do—and students are no exception. Students can take the Kolb Learning Style Inventory (LSI) in Chapter 1 to increase their self-awareness as learners. The LSI, which is printed on carbonless paper for easy scoring, helps students make sense of what they're experiencing in college. Key updates to the LSI for this edition include:

- Clearer directions on how to take the LSI.

- A new Journal Entry that prepares students for taking the Inventory.

- A new reflection activity, "Take a snapshot of your learning styles, " that asks students to reflect on what they've learned. This activity is intended to be completed after students read all of the material about learning styles (including multiple intelligences and VAK).

- A learning styles across the curriculum chart that connects learning styles to specific strategies that students can use for their other courses.

- New material to help students connect their learning style to their courses, future career, and major.

Sidebars highlight key information and concepts.

The **Mastering Technology** feature connects chapter content and themes to technology, providing concrete tips on how to effectively use technology to succeed.

Practicing Critical Thinking exercises reinforce concepts learned in each chapter through problem solving, creative thinking, and decision making.

Each chapter, including the Introduction, has a **Power Process,** a unique motivational article that empowers success through the application of strategies that relate to a wide variety of circumstances, issues, and problems. Revised for the 13th edition, the Power Process message is now more succinct.

Put it to Work reinforces the transferability of skills by encouraging students to think critically about applying what they learn to the workplace. Completely revised for the 13th edition, the articles now feature case studies that help students relate the chapter's themes and concepts to the workplace.

Quiz

Date ___ / ___ / ___

Name _____

1. Describe a strategy for managing interruptions when you study.

2. Rewrite the statement "I want to study harder" so that it becomes a specific goal.

3. The text suggests that you set long-term goals. Write one example of a long-term goal.

4. Write a mid-term and short-term goal that can help you achieve the long-term goal that you listed for Question 3.

5. What are at least five of the twenty-five ways to get the most out of now?

6. In time management terms, what is meant by "This ain't no piano"?

7. Define C *fever* as it applies to the ABC priority method.

8. Scheduling marathon study sessions once in a while is generally an effective strategy. True or False? Explain your answer.

9. According to the text, overcoming procrastination is a complex process that can take months or even years. True or False? Explain your answer.

10. The Power Process: "Be Here Now" rules out planning. True or False? Explain your answer.

BECOMING A MASTER STUDENT   95

The updated end-of-chapter **quiz** allows students to assess their comprehension of the materials covered in each chapter.

New to the 13th edition, the **Skills Snapshot** exercise helps students summarize what they have learned in each chapter and connects back to their original responses in the Discovery Wheel.

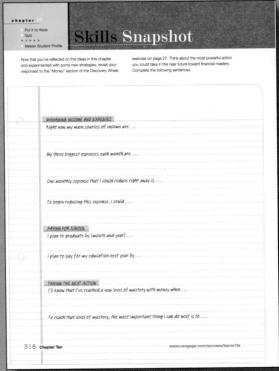

Skills Snapshot

Now that you've reflected on the ideas in this chapter and experimented with some new strategies, revisit your responses to the "Money" section of the Discovery Wheel exercise on page 27. Think about the most powerful action you could take in the near future toward financial mastery. Complete the following sentences.

MANAGING INCOME AND EXPENSES
Right now my main sources of income are . . .

My three biggest expenses each month are . . .

One monthly expense that I could reduce right away is . . .

To begin reducing this expense, I could . . .

PAYING FOR SCHOOL
I plan to graduate by (month and year) . . .

I plan to pay for my education next year by . . .

TAKING THE NEXT ACTION
I'll know that I've reached a new level of mastery with money when . . .

To reach that level of mastery, the most important thing I can do next is to . . .

318   Chapter Ten   www.cengage.com/success/bams13e

Master Student PROFILE

Lalita Booth
. . . is willing to work

Sitting in front of a classroom of LEAD Scholars, Lalita Booth looks like any other junior. The brown-eyed, freckle-faced student blends in with her peers in the University of Central Florida (UCF) leadership development program in every way.

That is, until she opens her mouth.

"You're looking at the face of a child abuse survivor, a perpetual runaway, a high school dropout," she says, as idle chitchat turns to complete silence.

"I was a teenage mother, a homeless parent, a former welfare recipient."

Lalita's parents divorced when she was young; by age 12 she was a runaway pro—asking for permission to go somewhere and then simply not returning for a few days or a few weeks.

. . . She became proficient in "couch surfing" at friends' homes. When there was no couch to crash on, the teen would take her nightly refuge behind the closest dumpster and rest in the park during the day.

Furthering her quest to be a grownup, at 17 she married her long-time buddy and fellow high school dropout, Quinn. Three months later, she found out she was pregnant with a son, Kieren. What normally would be a joyful time was instead a stressful one while the new couple struggled in a prison of deep poverty. The miserable situation began to take its toll, and after just two and a half years of marriage, Quinn was ready to call it quits.

With her new boyfriend, Carl, and her most precious cargo, Kieren, in tow, Lalita fled to Boulder, Colorado. Kieren lived with his paternal grandparents for 7 months while Lalita and Carl attempted to get back on their feet.

Being in Colorado proved to be fruitful for the 21-year-old Lalita. It started with an interesting job opportunity as an enrolled agent—an expert in U.S. taxation who can represent taxpayers before the Internal Revenue Service. Lalita could acquire the license without further schooling. Better yet, it would boost her income to $32,000. She buckled down and read all 4,000 pages of the study guide, and thanks to her nearly photographic memory, she aced the test.

But once again, she was in the wrong place at the wrong time. Carl's brother in Orlando was very ill, and he needed to move to Florida.

The only way to insure her independence was to do something that frightened her to the very core—go back to school. . . . And soon after, she enrolled at Seminole Community College.

. . . In May 2005, Lalita was selected to attend the Salzburg Global Seminar, where she brainstormed ways to solve global problems with a group of international students. The thought-provoking trip led to her mission: to help others escape the choke hold of poverty.

Back in the states, Lalita's world became even more dreamlike when she won the Jack Kent Cooke Foundation Scholarship. . . .

. . . Lalita strongly believes, and for good reason, that "things that are worth achieving are absolutely unreasonable." She advises, "Set unreasonable goals, and chase them unreasonably."

Jacque Brund/UCF News and Information

Once homeless, now a student at the University of Central Florida, and accepted to Harvard University Business School.

Find more biographical information about Lalita Booth at the Master Student Hall of Fame.

Adapted from Sarah Sekula, "Escape Artist," *Pegasus*, July/August 2008, UCF Alumni Life, 20–26. Reprinted with permission.

BECOMING A MASTER STUDENT   59

Each **Master Student Profile** highlights a person who embodies the qualities of a master student. This edition features 11 new profiles: Lalita Booth (Chapter 1), Al Gore (Chapter 2), Pablo Alvarado (Chapter 3), Chief Wilma Mankiller (Chapter 4), Harvey Milk (Chapter 5), Bert and John Jacobs (Chapter 6), Twyla Tharp (Chapter 7), Mark Zuckerberg (Chapter 8), Lisa Price (Chapter 10), Randy Pausch (Chapter 11), and Lisa Ling (Chapter 12).

Interactive learning opportunities for your students

With the Premium Web site for *Becoming a Master Student,* students have access to a variety of multimedia to strengthen their skills including:

The Online Multimedia eBook. This interactive text provides students with direct access to videos, audio, concept maps, and the opportunity to complete their homework online.

Video Skillbuilders. This online tool combines video clips featuring discussions with students, instructors, and experts, with articles and activities designed to give students a fully engaging learning experience. Topics include:

- Test-Taking
- Time Management
- Managing Your Finances
- Keeping Your Mind and Body in Shape
- Career Planning

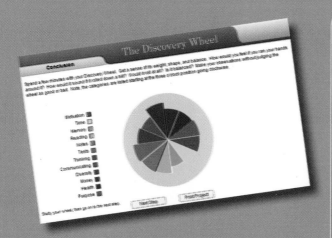

Power Process activities. See how the Power Process articles from the textbook can come to life and apply to different learning styles. Students can watch the video, read or listen to an audio version of the Power Process article, read the Case Study, and then answer the questions in the Power Process reflective journal.

Interactive exercises including a digital version of the **Discovery Wheel** and **Time and Money Management** charts.

Additional resources. These include practice quizzes, the Master Student Hall of Fame, and concept maps highlighting important chapter themes.

If you want your students to receive access to the premium Web site, you must request that the Printed Access Code be bundled with their text (ISBN: 1111083088). Contact your sales rep with any questions. www.cengage.com/findrep2.html

How much of a difference does your college success course make in your students' academic success?

The College Success Factors Index (CSFI) 2.0 *(Developed by Edmond Hallberg, Kaylene Hallberg, and Loren Sauer)* is an online survey that will give you the answers you're looking for. The CSFI assesses student's patterns of behavior and attitudes in areas that have been proven by research to affect student outcomes for success in higher education.

Accessed online, the CSFI is a perfect assessment tool for demonstrating the difference your college success course makes in your students' academic success. At the start of the course, the CSFI helps assess incoming students and allows you to tailor your course topics to meet their needs. As a post-test, it provides an opportunity for you and your students to measure their progress. And, CSFI 2.0 will provide specific page referenced remediation directly to *Becoming a Master Student,* Thirteenth Edition.

The **CSFI** includes 100 statements on ten areas that have been proven to correlate with college success:

Responsibility/Control	College Involvement
Competition/Collaboration	Time Management
Task Planning	Wellness
Expectations	Precision
Family Involvement	Persistence

An Early Alert indicator flags students who are the most at-risk in achieving college success. This information enables instructors to intervene at the beginning of the semester to increase their students' likelihood of success—and improve retention rates.

- Two new factors: Precision and Persistence.
- Book-specific remediation guides students who are struggling with specific factors.
- Increased reporting functionality provides instructors with access to more information and data about their students.
- Updated design makes the website easy to navigate.

Visit www.csfi-wadsworth.com for a product tour.

Printed Access Cards can be packaged with your book! Contact your Cengage Learning sales representative for more information on accessing the CSFI. www.cengage.com/findrep2.html

TeamUP Faculty Programs
College Success Staff Development
Get Trained. Get Connected. Get Support.

The TeamUP College Survival consulting team provides training in developing college success programs, revising existing programs, and integrating our products into your teaching. Whether we work with you online, on the phone, or on campus, we strive to deliver high-quality services through our Faculty Programs, Training, and Media Integration.

For more than a decade, our College Survival consultants have led the way in providing college success course expertise through on-campus consulting, training, and national workshops and conferences.

Look to TeamUP College Survival for:

- One- and two-day regional or on-campus training sessions presenting effective pedagogical strategies that can be applied to all disciplines and have proved effective in a variety of college success course curricula.

- Assistance from our College Survival consultants, each of whom has extensive experience in teaching the first-year course.

- Regional and nationwide conferences that provide two to three days of informative, interactive sessions covering a range of topics presented by authors, student success instructors, and College Survival consultants.

- Ideas and best practices on how to customize all elements of our technology.

- eSeminars facilitated by experts in the field that allow for professional development from the convenience of your desk.

To connect with your TeamUP Faculty Program Consultant, call 800-528-8323 or visit www.cengage.com/teamup.

Becoming a
MASTER STUDENT

Thirteenth Edition

Doug Toft
Contributing Editor

Dean Mancina
Golden West College, CA
Faculty Advisor

WADSWORTH
CENGAGE Learning™

AUSTRALIA • BRAZIL • JAPAN • KOREA • MEXICO • SPAIN • UNITED KINGDOM • UNITED STATES

Becoming a Master Student
Thirteenth Edition
Ellis

Senior Publisher: Lyn Uhl

Director of College Success: Annie Todd

Senior Sponsoring Editor: Shani Fisher

Senior Development Editor: Julia Giannotti

Assistant Editor: Daisuke Yasutake

Editorial Assistant: Cat Salerno

Senior Marketing Manager: Kirsten Stoller

Marketing Coordinator: Ryan Ahern

Marketing Communications Manager:
Martha Pfeiffer

Content Project Manager: Jessica Rasile

Art Director: Linda Jurras

Text Designer: Susan Gilday

Print Buyer: Julio Esperas

Permissions Editor: Tim Sisler

Project Management: Orr Book Services

Photo Manager: Leitha Etheridge-Sims

Photo Researcher: Walter Kopec

Cover Designer: Yvo Riezebos

Cover Image: Ted Humble-Smith/RF/Getty

Compositor: S4Carlisle Publishing Services

For product information and technology assistance, contact us at
Cengage Learning Customer & Sales Support, 1-800-354-9706

For permission to use material from this text or product,
submit all requests online at **cengage.com/permissions**
Further permissions questions can be emailed to
permissionrequest@cengage.com

Library of Congress Control Number: 2009941954

Student Edition:

ISBN-13: 978-1-4390-8174-7

ISBN-10: 1-4390-8174-3

Annotated Instructor's Edition:

ISBN-13: 978-1-4390-8176-1

ISBN-10: 1-4390-8176-X

Wadsworth
20 Channel Center Street
Boston, MA 02210
USA

Cengage Learning is a leading provider of customized learning solutions with office locations around the globe, including Singapore, the United Kingdom, Australia, Mexico, Brazil and Japan. Locate your local office at **international.cengage.com/region**

Cengage Learning products are represented in Canada by Nelson Education, Ltd.

For your course and learning solutions, visit **www.cengage.com**.

Purchase any of our products at your local college store or at our preferred online store **www.ichapters.com**.

Printed in the United States of America
1 2 3 4 5 6 7 14 13 12 11 10

Advisory Board

Marni Sanft
Utah Valley University

Sarah Schutt
J. Sargeant Reynolds Community College, VA

Dawn Shaffer
Central Piedmont Community College, NC

Jane Shearer
Suffolk County Community College, NY

Patricia Sheriff-Taylor
Jackson State University, MS

Samuel D. Sink
Wilkes Community College, NC

Leigh Smith
Lamar Institute of Technology, TX

Kim Smokowski
Bergen Community College, NJ

Al Soprano
Community College of Southern Nevada

Jane Speer
Alpena Community College, MI

John Sperry
Utah Valley University

Sharon M. Snyders
Ivy Tech Community College, IN

Letitia Thomas
University at Buffalo, NY

James Thomas
University of Albany, NY

Patricia Twaddle
Moberly Area Community College, MO

Karen N. Valencia
Volunteer State Community College, TN

Steve Walsh
California State University, Bakersfield

Peggy Walton
Howard Community College, MD

Deborah Warfield
Seminole Community College, FL

Paula Gaither Wimbish
Hinds Community College, MS

Eleanor F. Yapundich
American River College, CA

Student Advisory Board

Wylonda Bernstein
East-West University

William Couch
University of Maryland College Park

Jesse Decker
Ocean County College

Kanisha Jackson
Ohio University

Theresa Francis
Southwestern Illinois College

Steven Kelley
Drexel University

Jess Maggi
Le Moyne College

Ashley Molton
Central Texas College

Lindsay M. Ordone
Delgado Community College

Christopher Sampson
University of Houston-Downtown

Jason Shah
University of New Orleans

Lisa Shelley
University of Texas at Arlington

Katherine Wood
Washington and Lee University

Joyce King
Broward College

Melody Reese
Kent State

Vanessa Silva
Pace University

Bradford Johnson
Tallahassee Community College

Alecia Jackson
Phillips Community College of the University of Arizona

Christian Penaherrera
University at Buffalo

Valerie Cordes
Alpena Community College

Sally LaFleure
Alpena Community College

Kevin Kunz Jr
Mesa Community College

Jamila Williams
SUNY - University at Buffalo

Ivory D. Wiggins
Mesa College

Jose Ledesma II
San Diego Mesa College

Brief Table of Contents

© Graham Bell/Corbis

© image100/Corbis

© Masterfile Royalty Free

zimmytws/Shutterstock

Table of Contents

what if · · · · → why

how · · · · → what

2 Time 60

© Deborah Jaffe/The Image Bank/Getty

3 Memory 98

Angelo Cavalli/Digital Vision/ RF/Getty Images

Table of Contents

Goodshoot/RF/Jupiter Images

6 Tests

Yuri Arcurs/Shutterstock

7 Thinking

Rich Reed/National Geographic/Getty

Table of Contents

Pakhnyushcha/Shutterstock

Jeff Hunter/Getty

10 Money 294

Ted Humble-Smith/RF/Getty

11 Health
320

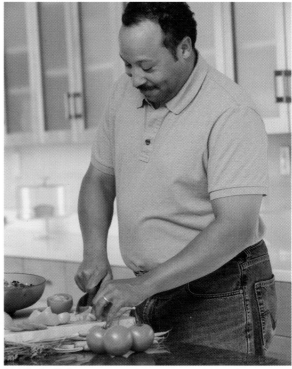

Ariel Skelley/Getty

12 What's Next?

Terry Vine/Blend Images/RF/Getty

Making Transitions

Instructor Tools & Tips

> Change and growth take place when a person has risked himself and dares to become involved with experimenting with his own life.
>
> **—Herbert Otto**

> The human ability to learn and remember is virtually limitless.
>
> **—Sheila Ostrander and Lynn Schroeder**

Each chapter in the Annotated Instructor Edition is preceded by pages with suggestions for instructors. These suggestions are organized using the 7-part course model on page AIE-10. You can quickly find ideas to use in your classroom for preview, guest speakers, lectures, class activities, sharing, homework, and evaluation.

Preview

The introductory chapter, "Making Transitions," is an important gateway to *Becoming a Master Student* because it sets the stage for entering the culture of higher education and connecting to new surroundings. It also explains how students should write the important Discovery and Intention Journal Entries throughout the book. Encourage your students to read "Making Transitions" the first week of class.

Guest Speaker

Two or three students from your class in the previous term can make great guest speakers for the first week of class. Students respond well to hearing from their peers. You might provide some guidance about the types of experiences the speakers should share. Ask them to briefly discuss why they enrolled in this course and the three most useful tools they learned in the class. Then invite students to ask the guests questions about the course. Consider taping the presentation in case no former students are available to speak.

Here is a guest speaker's comment on how she conducts her first week of class:

> During the first class, I ask my students to preview the text, paying particular attention to the table of contents. I then give students my course syllabus, which lists a suggested schedule of topics for the semester. The students' first assignment is to look at the table of contents and rearrange the schedule of topics in a way that fits their needs. (Another way to do this is to use students' completed Discovery Wheels—see Chapter 1.) During the second class meeting, we list the topics on a flip chart and vote on the order of the chapters. Then we rearrange the syllabus according to the preferences of the students. This method helps me design the course to meet students' immediate needs. Since the course is mandatory, some of the students have negative feelings when they come to class. Allowing them input on the order of the topics sparks interest and gives them ownership of the course.
>
> **—Dr. Jennifer Hurd, TeamUP Consultant**

Lecture

1. Master Student Map (page xiv) Teach students how to use the Master Student Map right from the start of *Becoming a Master Student*. If you have ever had trouble convincing your students to read the Introduction, this simply formatted framework will help them grasp the value of this book right away. Use the Master Student Map (**M**etacognitive **A**pplication **P**rocess) as a jumping-off point for sparking classroom discussion. Then teach your students how they can use this model to preview chapter content in this textbook. Take it a step further and show your students how creating a similar schema for textbooks in other courses can help activate background knowledge and provide a "hook" to get them ready for the material within the chapter. Start now by asking your students the following questions. Consider writing them on your whiteboard, posting them to your discussion board in an online course, or creating a PowerPoint presentation with them.

Why? Why is it important to read the Introduction?

What? What kind of information does an Introduction provide for the reader? What information does the Introduction to *Becoming a Master Student* provide?

How? Rate your level of effectiveness with the information presented in the Introduction now. (How much do you already know about the topics presented? How will this book help you become a better student?) Ask yourself, "How can I get more value from my textbook by reading the Introduction?"

What if? What if you skipped the Introduction? Ask yourself, "What if I could use this Introduction right now to become a better student?"

2. Discovery and Intention Statements (page 5) The Discovery and Intention Journal Entry system allows students to begin the reflective critical thinking process they will need to grasp the concepts and develop the skills studied in this student success course and to transfer those skills to their other classes. This simple yet powerful system is one of the foundations of the textbook. As students read the book, they are often asked to write Discovery Statements about what they are learning and Intention Statements about what they plan to do, based on the new information they are assimilating.

In addition to assigning the many Discovery and Intention Statements in the book, ask students to write statements in class after activities such as guest speakers, videos, or lectures. Here is one formula for writing Discovery Statements: "When I [what you experienced], I discovered that [specifically what you became aware of]." A formula for Intention Statements is: "I intend to [specifically what action you plan to take] by [time frame or date]. My reward will be [the tangible reward you'll give yourself if you complete your intended goal]."

3. Organize for success The inside front cover of *Becoming a Master Student* has a tool for master students: a place to organize key information to have "at their fingertips" throughout their college experience. Have your students fill in their information while they wait for you to begin class, or leave a few minutes at the end of your first meeting.

Illustrate how students can immediately apply this new strategy to their other courses. Although not every

textbook has a place to record information on the inside cover, students can use the inside front and back covers as quick references—for personal information, key facts such as formulas or Web site addresses, and any other information they will need to refer to frequently.

Encourage your students to identify a student in each class who seems responsible and dependable. Have them exchange e-mail addresses and phone numbers and record them. Suggest to students that if they know they won't be in class, they should contact this student ahead of time to ask her to pick up extra copies of handouts and request to copy her notes.

Take this opportunity to invite your students to visit you during office hours. Provide your e-mail address, phone number, and office location.

Exercises/Activities

1. Commitment exercise (page 4) After students have read the Introduction and completed this exercise, at the following class meeting ask them to open their books to this exercise so that they can review what they wrote. This simple exercise, which takes less than 5 minutes to complete, helps students confirm their commitment to this course and, indirectly, to their entire college experience. To reinforce this exercise and remind students of it throughout the semester, have them write in large letters on a sheet of paper the words of the level of commitment they chose and then sign their name at the bottom. Have them put this paper at the very front of their three-ring binder for this course so that every time they open their binder, they'll be reminded of their commitment to this textbook—and to their student success.

2. Making the transition to higher education (page 9) Have your students choose partners and review the list of expectations in this article. Ask them to predict the two transition areas in the list from the article that would cause students the most trouble and to discuss why. Then they should discuss some possible solutions for students who might be facing these problems. To help students connect to the article on a personal level, ask them which of the items listed in the article present a challenge for them.

3. Ways to change a habit (page 19) Challenge your students in class to brainstorm habits they would like to start, stop, or change. Then ask them to pick a habit that they would like to commit to change successfully within the next 16 weeks. Using the two-part note paper from TeamUP, have them write down their habit and separate the paper. Tell the students to put one part in a self-addressed envelope and to keep the copy for themselves as a reference and reminder of their habit change plan. Collect the self-addressed envelopes and mail them to the students in four months (after the course is over) as an incentive for them to keep working on their habit change.

4. Power Process: Discover What You Want (page 23)
Begin using the idea presented by the Master Student Map to think critically about the Power Process in the Introduction. Explain the purpose of each Power Process to your students: The Power Process will change the way they think, or change their consciousness, because it is their consciousness that determines their behavior. Ask students to consider and discuss in groups: (1) *Why* this Power Process might matter to them (or to their children, family, coworkers, and the like), (2) *What* this Power Process means with regard to the transition to college, (3) *How* they will make this transition work for them, and (4) *What* they risk by not making this transition now.

5. First day activity On the first day of class, ask your students, "What do you want?" Give them 10 minutes to write a list of ten skills they might learn in this class that would be useful for them in college and in their lives. Challenge them to think about things that are worth working hard for. Then have the students form groups of four to share what they wrote. Have them complete this list on two-part paper so that they can keep their list and you can have a copy. This will help you get to know your students right away.

Conversation/Sharing

1. This book is worthless (page 1) This article helps you "sell" this course to resistant students, whether your course is required or not. Consider going over the seven pitches on the first day of class, even though the students haven't read this article yet.

2. If you share with your class an experience that you had as a student in college, your students may feel that you are more of a partner with them in their educational explorations. Students particularly enjoy hearing stories of the mistakes you made while in college! Here's a success story Faculty Advisor Dean Mancina shares

with his students when discussing the value of connecting to campus resources:

> "When I applied for my first teaching position coordinating a Tutoring Program at Golden West College, I didn't know that 167 others had also applied! A few months after I was selected for the position, I asked my Dean why I had been selected over so many other applicants, many of whom might have had more experience. He shared with me that I was the only finalist who was able to answer the interview question about organizing, planning, publicizing, and evaluating college programs. I had spoken about my experiences working in student activities when I was a student in college. I had fun meeting other students and working with student government, but it wasn't until that point that I became aware of the other potential benefits of connecting to campus resources. Little did I know that I'd still be at Golden West College 34 years later!

Homework

Even though many students won't have purchased the textbook on the first day of class, hold up your copy of the book and show them the Textbook Reconnaissance exercise on page 2. When you assign textbook reading each week, tell students that they must read the articles *and* do all of the chapter exercises, Practicing Critical Thinking exercises, and Discovery/Intention Journal Entries within the assigned pages. The thinking/writing assignments in the book help students personalize what they are reading.

Evaluation

Frequent quizzes ensure that students focus attention during class and keep up with the text reading assignments. Quizzes also provide students with opportunities for written reflection regarding new discoveries and intentions. In addition, evaluations help you identify topics and concepts that students have not yet mastered. Questions may be based on the textbook reading assignment, guest speakers, class activities, and/or the lecture. Possible answers are provided for the end-of-chapter quizzes in the Annotated Instructor's Edition.

On your request, Cengage Learning will provide packages of three-part NCR quiz paper to facilitate quick quizzes in class. First make up your quiz question(s). These may be multiple-choice, true or false, short answer, or essay questions. Students answer the quiz question(s) on the white (top) sheet, simultaneously making two copies on the yellow and pink paper.

When the quiz time is up, direct students to tear off the white copy and pass it forward. They can no longer change their answers because you have the original white sheet. Then direct them to look up the correct answers in their book and grade their own quiz. Finally, have them pass the yellow copy forward for your review and to record their scores. Students keep the pink copy.

Additional Digital Resources

Course Manual

INTRO

The online *Course Manual* serves as an invaluable reference for those developing and teaching a College Success course with *Becoming a Master Student*. The *Course Manual* provides advice on general teaching issues such as preparing for classes, classroom management, grading, and communicating with students of various backgrounds, as well as specific strategies on getting the most out of various features in *Becoming a Master Student* such as the Discovery Wheel, Learning Styles Inventory, and book-specific Web sites. Do a *Course Manual* reconnaissance to find ideas that you can use in your course right now.

Instructor Web Site

The updated Instructor Web site provides resources to help you plan and customize your course. Content specific to the Introduction includes:

▶ Lecture Ideas
  • Selling the Course
  • What Are the Skills of Successful Students?
▶ In-Class Exercises
  • Advisor Role-Play Exercise
  • Icebreaker with Commitment
  • Student Agreement Contract
▶ Writing Assignments
  • Working with Academic Advisors
▶ In-Text Quiz Answers
▶ Learning Styles Application
▶ Discussion Topics
▶ PowerPoint Slides
▶ Reflection Questions
▶ Assessment Questions
▶ Experiment with chapter strategies

The Instructor Web site also contains the following book-specific content:

▶ ExamView Test Bank
▶ Online Course Manual

www.cengage.com/success/bams13e

▶ Articles from previous editions
▶ Master Student Profiles from previous editions
▶ Sample Syllabi
Detailed Transition Guide

Student Web Site

To help your students gain a better understanding of the topics discussed in *Becoming a Master Student*, encourage your students to visit the Student Web site, which provides the following resources specific to the Introduction:

▶ Online version of the Discovery Wheel.
▶ Connect to Text content expands on specific topics marked with an icon within the Introduction.
▶ Practice Tests allow students to see how well they understand the themes of *Becoming a Master Student*.
▶ Interactive Concept Maps promote critical thinking by highlighting related ideas to show relationships between concepts.
▶ Remembering Cultural Differences presents readers with brief articles that touch on aspects of diversity in our rapidly changing world. For the Introduction, the following article will prompt your students to look at contemporary issues in a new way:
  • What and How Cultures Teach
▶ Power Process Media contains video, PowerPoints, and audio files to take what your students have learned from the Power Processes in their book to the next level. For the Introduction, students will find additional media on:
  • Discover what you want

Along with the chapter-specific content, a General Resources folder is available that contains Toolboxes geared toward specific student types (Community College, Adult Learner, Student Athlete), the Plagiarism Prevention Zone, and the Career Resource Center.

Making Transitions

Master Student Map

as you read, ask yourself

what if . . .

I could use the ideas in this Introduction to master any transition in my life?

why the Introduction matters . . .

You can ease your transition to higher education and set up a lifelong pattern of success by following the strategies described here.

what is included . . .

how you can use this Introduction . . .

- Discover a way to interact with the book that multiplies its value.
- Use a journal to translate personal discoveries into powerful new behaviors.
- Connect with people and organizations that support your success.

MASTER STUDENTS in *action*

Use all of the resources on campus. Get to know your instructors and professors, attend every class, accept all new challenges, get a support group, have outside hobbies and passions, believe in yourself.

—TIMOTHY ALLEN

Photo courtesy of Timothy Allen/ American River College

This book is worthless— if you just read it

THE FIRST EDITION of this book began with the sentence *This book is worthless.* Many students thought beginning this way was a trick to get their attention. It wasn't. Others thought it was reverse psychology. It wasn't that, either. Still others thought it meant that the book was worthless if they didn't read it. It meant more than that.

This book is worthless *even if you read it*—if reading it is all you do. What was true of that first edition is true of this one as well. Until you take action and use the ideas in it, *Becoming a Master Student* really is worthless.

The purpose of this book is to help you make a successful transition to higher education by setting up a pattern of success that will last the rest of your life. You probably won't take action and use the ideas in this book until you are convinced that you have something to gain. That's the reason for this introduction—to persuade you to use this book actively.

Before you stiffen up and resist this sales pitch, remember that you have already bought the book. Now you can get something for your money by committing yourself to take action—in other words, by committing yourself to becoming a master student. Here is what's in it for you.

Pitch #1: You can save money now and make more money later. Start with money. Your college education is one of the most expensive things you will ever buy. You might find yourself paying $30 to $100 an hour to sit in class. (See Exercise 30: "Education by the hour" on page 308 to come up with a specific figure that applies to your own education.)

As a master student, you control the value you get out of your education, and that value can be considerable. The joy of learning aside, college graduates make more money during their lifetimes than do their nondegreed peers.[1] The income advantage you might gain through higher education could total over half a million dollars. It pays to be a master student.

Pitch #2: You can rediscover the natural learner in you. Joy is important, too. As you become a master student, you will learn to gain knowledge in the most effective way possible by discovering the joyful, natural learner within you.

Children are great natural students. They quickly master complex skills, such as language, and they have

fun doing it. For young children, learning is a high-energy process involving experimentation, discovery, and sometimes broken dishes. Then comes school. For some students, drill and drudgery replace discovery and dish breaking. Learning can become a drag. You can use this book to reverse that process and rediscover what you knew as a child—that laughter and learning go hand in hand.

Sometimes—and especially in college—learning does take effort. As you become a master student, you will learn many ways to get the most out of that effort.

Pitch #3: You can choose from hundreds of techniques. *Becoming a Master Student* is packed with hundreds of practical, nuts-and-bolts techniques. And you can begin using them immediately. For example, during the textbook reconnaissance on page 2, you might find three powerful learning techniques in one 15-minute exercise. Even if you doze in lectures, drift off during tests, or dawdle on term papers, you'll find ideas in this book that you can use to become a more effective student.

Not all of these ideas will work for you. That's why there are so many of them in *Becoming a Master Student.* You can experiment with the techniques. As you discover what works, you will develop a unique style of learning that you can use for the rest of your life.

Pitch #4: You get the best suggestions from thousands of students. The concepts and techniques in this book are here not just because learning theorists, educators, and psychologists say they work. They are here because tens of thousands of students from all kinds of backgrounds have tried them and agree that they work. These people are students who dreaded giving speeches, couldn't read their own notes, and fell behind in their course work. Then they figured out how to solve those problems. Now you can use their ideas.

Pitch #5: You can learn about yourself. The process of self-discovery is an important theme in *Becoming a Master Student.* Throughout the book, you can use Discovery Statements and Intention Statements for everything from organizing your desk to choosing long-term goals. Studying for an organic chemistry quiz is a lot easier with a clean desk and a clear idea of the course's importance to you.

Pitch #6: You can use a proven product.
The first twelve editions of this book have proved successful for hundreds of thousands of students. Feedback from students has been positive. In particular, students with successful histories have praised the techniques in this book.

Pitch #7: You can learn the secret of student success. If this sales pitch still hasn't persuaded you to use this book actively, maybe it's time to reveal the secret of student success. (Provide your own drumroll here.) The secret is . . . there are no secrets. Perhaps the ultimate formula is to give up formulas and keep inventing.

The strategies and tactics that successful students use are well known. You have hundreds of them at your fingertips right now, in this book. Use them. Modify them. Invent new ones. You're the authority on what works for you.

However, what makes any technique work is commitment—and action. Without them, the pages of *Becoming a Master Student* are just 2.1 pounds of expensive mulch. Add your participation to the mulch, and these pages become priceless.

This book is worth $1,000

Cengage Learning is proud to present three students each year with a $1,000 scholarship for tuition reimbursement. Any student in a post-secondary school in the United States and Canada is eligible for the scholarship. To be considered, students must write an essay that answers the question, How do you define success?

(www) For more details, visit the Web site.

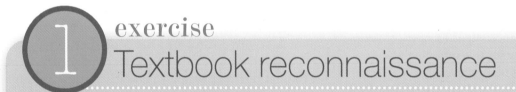

①exercise
Textbook reconnaissance

Start becoming a master student this moment by doing a 15-minute "textbook reconnaissance." Here's how.

First, read this book's Table of Contents. Do it in 3 minutes or less. Next, look at every page in the book. Move quickly. Scan headlines. Look at pictures. Notice forms, charts, and diagrams. Don't forget the last few pages in back, which include extra copies of planning forms that you might find useful.

A textbook reconnaissance shows you where a course is going. It gives you the big picture. That's useful because brains work best when going from the general to the specific. Getting the big picture before you start makes it easier to recall and understand details later on.

Your textbook reconnaissance will work even better if, as you scan, you look for ideas you can use. When you find one, write the page number and a short description of the idea in the space at the right. If you run out of room, just continue your list on a separate sheet of paper. You also can use Post-it Notes to flag pages that look useful. You might even use notes of different colors to signal priority, such as green for ideas to use right away and yellow for suggestions to apply later. The idea behind this technique is simple: It's easier to learn when you're excited, and it's easier to get

excited about a course if you know it's going to be useful, interesting, or fun.

Remember, look at every page, and do it quickly. And here's another useful tip for the master student: Do it now.

Page number	Description

(www) Complete this exercise online.

Get the most out of this book

1. Rip 'em out. The pages of *Becoming a Master Student* are perforated because some of the information here is too important to leave in the book . For example, Journal Entry #3 asks you to list some important things you want to get from your education. To keep yourself focused on these goals, rip that page out and post it on your bathroom mirror or some other place where you'll see it several times a day.

You can reinsert the pages later by sticking them into the spine of the book. A piece of tape will hold them in place.

2. Skip around. You can use this book in several different ways. You might read it straight through. Or pick it up, turn to any page, and find an idea you can use. Look for ideas you can use right now. For example, if you are about to choose a major or are considering changing schools, skip directly to the articles on these topics on pages 222 and 367, respectively.

You might note that this book presents similar ideas in more than one place. This repetition is intentional. Repetition reinforces key points. Also, a technique that works in one area of your life might work in others as well. Look especially to the Power Processes in this text for ideas that you can apply in many ways.

3. If it works, use it. If it doesn't, lose it. If some sections of this book don't apply to you at all, skip them—unless, of course, they are assigned. In that case, see if you can gain value from those sections anyway. When you are committed to getting value from this book, even an idea that seems irrelevant or ineffective at first can turn out to be a powerful tool.

4. Put yourself into the book. As you read about techniques in this book, create your own scenarios, and cast yourself in the lead roles. For example, when reading through Exercise #1: "Textbook Reconnaissance," picture yourself using this technique on your world history textbook.

5. Listen to your peers. At the beginning of each chapter you will find Master Students in Action. These short features contain quotations from students who used this text. As you dig into the following chapters, think about what you would say if you could add your voice to theirs.

6. Own this book. Right now, put your name, address, and related information on the inside cover of this book. Don't stop there, though. Determine what you want to get out of school, and create a record of how you intend to get it by reading the Power Process and completing the Journal Entries in this Introduction. Every time your pen touches a page, you move closer to mastery of learning.

7. Do the exercises. Action makes this book work. To get the most out of an exercise, read the instructions carefully before you begin. To get the most out of this book, do most of the exercises. The exercises invite you to write, touch, feel, move, see, search, ponder, speak, listen, recall, choose, commit, and create. You might even sing and dance. Learning often works best when it involves action. And by the way, it's never too late to go back and do the ones you skipped.

8. Practice critical thinking. Practicing Critical Thinking activities appear throughout this book. Their purpose is to encourage contemplation and problem solving. Use these activities to explore new ways of thinking about chapter topics. Note that other elements of this text, including Chapter 7: Thinking, the exercises, and Journal Entries, also promote critical thinking.

9. Learn about learning styles. Check out the Learning Style Inventory and related articles in Chapter 1. This material can help you discover your preferred learning styles and allow you to explore new styles. Then, throughout the rest of this book, you'll find suggestions for applying your knowledge of learning styles. The modes of learning can be accessed by asking four basic questions: *Why? What? How?* and *What if?*

10. Navigate through learning experiences with the Master Student Map. You can orient yourself for maximum learning every time you open this book by asking those same four questions: *Why? What? How?* and *What if?* That's the idea behind the Master Student Map included on the first page of each chapter, which includes sample answers to those questions. Remember that you can use the four-part structure of this map to cycle through several learning styles and effectively learn anything.

11. Link to the Web. Throughout this book, you'll notice reminders to visit the Web site for *Becoming a Master Student*. When you see these notices, go to the Web site for articles, online exercises, and links to other useful Web sites.

12. Read the sidebars. Look for sidebars—short bursts of words and pictures placed between longer articles—throughout this book. These short pieces might offer insights that transform your experience of higher education.

13. Practice using technology. Read and use the Mastering Technology features as you make your way through the book. These short boxes help you apply the techniques in the book to get the most out of online learning.

14. Take this book to work. With a little tweaking, you can apply nearly all of the techniques in this book to your career. For more details, see the Put It to Work articles in each chapter. Use these ideas to make a seamless transition from success in school to success on the job.

15. Get used to a new look and tone. This book looks different from traditional textbooks. *Becoming a Master Student* presents major ideas in magazine-style articles. You will discover lots of lists, blurbs, one-liners, pictures, charts, graphs, illustrations, and even a joke or two.

Even though this book is loaded with special features, you'll find some core elements. For example, the two pages that open each chapter include a "lead article" and an introductory Journal Entry. At the end of each chapter, you'll find Power Process, Put It to Work, a chapter quiz, Skills Snapshot, and Master Student Profile all noted in a toolbar at the top of the page.

Note: As a strategy for avoiding sexist language, this book alternates the use of feminine and masculine pronouns. ✳

② exercise Commitment

This book is worthless unless you actively participate in its activities and exercises. One powerful way to begin taking action is to make a commitment. Conversely, if you don't make a commitment, sustained action is unlikely—and the result is again a worthless book. Therefore, in the interest of saving your valuable time and energy, this exercise gives you a chance to declare your level of involvement up front. From the following options, choose the sentence that best reflects your commitment to using this book. Write the number in the space provided at the end of the list.

1. "Well, I'm reading this book right now, aren't I?"

2. "I will skim the book and read the interesting parts."

3. "I will read the book, think about it, and do the exercises that look interesting."

4. "I will read the book, do some exercises, and complete some of the Journal Entries."

5. "I will read the book, do some exercises and Journal Entries, and use some of the techniques."

6. "I will read the book, do most of the exercises and Journal Entries, and use some of the techniques."

7. "I will study this book, do most of the exercises and Journal Entries, and use some of the techniques."

8. "I will study this book, do most of the exercises and Journal Entries, and experiment with many of the techniques to discover what works best for me."

9. "I promise myself that I will create value from this course by studying this book, doing all the exercises and Journal Entries, and experimenting with most of the techniques."

10. "I will use this book as if the quality of my education depends on it—doing all the exercises and Journal Entries, experimenting with most of the techniques, inventing techniques of my own, and planning to reread this book in the future."

Enter your commitment level and today's date here:

Commitment level _____ Date _____

If you selected commitment level 1 or 2, you might consider passing this book on to a friend. If your commitment level is 9 or 10, you are on your way to terrific success in school. If your level is somewhere in between, experiment with the techniques and learning strategies in this book. If you find that they work, consider returning to this exercise and raising your level of commitment.

 Complete this exercise online.

The Discovery and Intention Journal Entry system

One way to become a better student is to grit your teeth and try harder. There is a better way, though. The Discovery and Intention Journal Entry system uses familiar tools and easily learned processes to help increase your effectiveness by showing you how to focus your energy.

USING THE DISCOVERY and Intention Journal Entry system is a little like flying a plane. An airplane is seldom exactly on course. Human and automatic pilots are always checking an airplane's position and making corrections. The resulting flight path looks like a zigzag. The plane is almost always flying in the wrong direction, but because of constant observation and course correction, it arrives at the right destination.

As a student, you can use a similar approach. Journal Entries throughout this book are labeled as Discovery Statements, Intention Statements, or Discovery/Intention Statements. Each Journal Entry contains a short set of suggestions that involve writing.

Through Discovery Statements, you gain **awareness** of "where you are." These statements are a record of what you are learning about yourself as a student—both your strengths and your weaknesses. Discovery Statements can also be declarations of your goals, descriptions of your attitudes, statements of your feelings, transcripts of your thoughts, and chronicles of your behavior.

Sometimes Discovery Statements chronicle an "aha!" moment—a flash of insight that results when you connect a new idea with your prior experiences, preferred styles of learning, or both. Perhaps a solution to a long-standing problem suddenly occurs to you. Or a life-changing insight wells up from the deepest recesses of your mind. Don't let such moments disappear. Capture them in Discovery Statements.

Intention Statements can be used to alter your course. These statements reflect your **commitment** to take action based on increased awareness. An intention arises out of your choice to direct your energy toward a specific task and to aim at a particular goal. The processes of discovery and intention reinforce each other.

Even simple changes in behavior can produce results. If you feel like procrastinating, then tackle just one small, specific task related to your intention. Find something you can complete in 5 minutes or less, and do it *now*. For example, access just one Web site related to the topic of your next assigned paper. Spend just 3 minutes previewing a reading assignment. Taking baby steps like these can move you into action with grace and ease.

That's the system in a nutshell. Discovery leads to awareness. Intention leads to commitment. And intention leads naturally to focused action.

The purpose of this system is not to get you pumped to go out there and try harder. In fact, Discovery and Intention Statements are intended to help you work smarter rather than harder.

The process of discovery, intention, and action creates a dynamic and efficient cycle. First, you write Discovery Statements about where you are now. Next, you write Intention Statements about where you want to be, and the specific steps you will take to get there. Finally, you follow up with action—the sooner, the better.

Then you start the cycle again. Write Discovery Statements about whether or how you act on your Intention Statements—and what you learn in the process. Follow up with more Intention Statements about what you will do differently in the future. Then move into action and describe what happens next.

This process never ends. Each time you repeat the cycle, you get new results. It's all about getting what you want and becoming more effective in everything you do. This is the path of mastery—a path that you can travel for the rest of your life.

Sometimes a Discovery or Intention Statement will be long and detailed. Usually it will be short—maybe just a line or two. With practice, the cycle will become automatic.

Don't panic when you fail to complete an intended task. Straying off course is normal. Simply make the necessary corrections. Consider the first word in the title of this book—*becoming*. This word implies that mastery is not an end state or final goal. Rather, mastery is a process that never ends—a path that you can travel for the rest of your life. The process of becoming more effective continues as long as you breathe. Miraculous progress might not come immediately. Do not be concerned. Stay with the cycle. Give it time. Use Discovery Statements to get a clear view of your world. Then use Intention Statements to direct your actions. Whenever you notice progress, record it.

The following statement might strike you as improbable, but it is true: It can take the same amount of energy to get what you *don't* want in school as it takes to get what you *do* want. In fact, sometimes getting what you don't want takes even more effort. An airplane burns the same amount of fuel flying away from its destination as it does flying toward it. It pays to stay on course.

You can use the Discovery and Intention Journal Entry system to stay on your own course and get what you want out of school. Start with the Journal Entries included in the text. Then go beyond them. Write Discovery and Intention Statements of your own at any time, for any purpose. Create new strategies whenever you need them, based on your current situation. Once you get the hang of it, you might discover you can fly. ✳

Hello Author I Agree ☺

Rewrite this book

Some books should be preserved in pristine condition. This book isn't one of them.

Something happens when you interact with a book by writing in it. *Becoming a Master Student* is about learning, and learning is an active pursuit, not a passive one. When you make notes in the margin, you can hear yourself talking with the author. When you doodle and underline, you can see the author's ideas taking shape. You can even argue with the author and come up with your own theories and explanations. In all of these ways, you can become a coauthor of this book. You can rewrite it to make it yours.

While you're at it, you can create symbols or codes that will help you review the text later on. You might insert a "Q" where you have a question or put exclamation points next to important ideas. You could also circle words to look up in a dictionary.

Remember, if any idea in this book doesn't work for you, you can rewrite it. Change the exercises to fit your needs. Create a new technique by combining several others. Even create a technique out of thin air!

Find something you agree or disagree with on this page, and write a short note in the margin about it. Or draw a diagram. Better yet, do both. Let creativity be your guide. Have fun.

Begin rewriting now.

Discovery and Intention Statement guidelines

Discovery Statements

1 Record the specifics about your thoughts, feelings, and behavior.
Thoughts include inner voices. We talk to ourselves constantly in our heads. When internal chatter gets in your way, write down what you are telling yourself. If this seems difficult at first, just start writing. The act of writing can trigger a flood of thoughts.

Thoughts also include mental pictures. These images are especially powerful. Picturing yourself flunking a test is like a rehearsal to do just that. One way to take away the power of negative images in your mind is to describe them in detail.

Also notice how you feel when you function well. Use Discovery Statements to pinpoint exactly where and when you learn most effectively.

In addition, observe your actions and record them accurately. If you spent 90 minutes chatting online with a favorite cousin instead of reading your anatomy text, write about it and include the details, such as when you did it, where you did it, and how it felt. Record your observations quickly, as soon as you make them.

2 Use discomfort as a signal. When you approach a daunting task, such as a difficult chemistry problem, notice your physical sensations—a churning stomach, perhaps, or shallow breathing or yawning. Feeling uncomfortable, bored, or tired might be a signal that you're about to do valuable work. Stick with it. Tell yourself you can handle the discomfort just a little bit longer. You will be rewarded.

You can experience those rewards at any time. Just think of the problem that poses the biggest potential barrier to your success in school. Choose a problem that you face right now, today. (Hint: It might be the thing that's distracting you from reading this article.) If you have a lot of emotion tied up in this problem, that's even better. Write a Discovery Statement about it.

3 Suspend judgment. When you are discovering yourself, be gentle. Suspend self-judgment. If you continually judge your behaviors as "bad" or "stupid" or "galactically imbecilic," sooner or later your mind will revolt. Rather than put up with the abuse, it will quit making discoveries. For your own benefit, be kind to yourself.

4 Tell the truth. Suspending judgment helps you tell the truth about yourself. "The truth will set you free" is a saying that endures for a reason. The closer you get to the truth, the more powerful your Discovery Statements will be. And if you notice that you are avoiding the truth, don't blame yourself. Just tell the truth about it.

Intention Statements

1 Make intentions positive. The purpose of writing Intention Statements is to focus on what you want rather than what you don't want. Instead of writing "I will not fall asleep while studying chemistry," write, "I intend to stay awake when studying chemistry." Also avoid the word *try*. Trying is not doing. When we hedge our bets with *try*, we can always tell ourselves, "Well, I *tried* to stay awake." We end up fooling ourselves into thinking we succeeded.

2 Make intentions observable. Experiment with an idea from educational trainer Robert Mager, who suggests that goals be defined through behaviors that can be observed and measured.[2] Rather than writing "I intend to work harder on my history assignments," write, "I intend to review my class notes, and I intend to make summary sheets of my reading." Then, when you review your progress, you can determine more precisely whether you have accomplished what you intended.

3 Make intentions small and achievable. Give yourself opportunities to succeed by setting goals you can meet. Break large goals into small, specific tasks that can be accomplished quickly. Small and simple changes in behavior—when practiced consistently over time—can have large and lasting effects. If you want to get an A in chemistry, ask yourself, "What can I do today?" You might choose to study chemistry for an extra hour. Make that your intention.

When setting your goals, anticipate self-sabotage. Be aware of what you might do, consciously or unconsciously, to undermine your best intentions. If you intend to study differential equations at 9 p.m., notice what you're doing when you sit down to watch a 2-hour movie that starts at 8 p.m.

Also, avoid intentions that depend on other people. If you write that you intend for your study group to complete an assignment by Monday, then your success depends on the other students in the group.

4 Set time lines that include rewards. Time lines can focus your attention. For example, if you are assigned a paper to write, break the assignment into small tasks and set a precise due date for each one. You might write, "I intend to select a topic for my paper by 9 a.m. Wednesday."

Time lines are especially useful when your intention is to experiment with a technique suggested in this book. The sooner you act on a new idea, the better. Consider practicing a new behavior within 4 hours after you first learn about it.

Remember that you create time lines to help yourself, not to set yourself up to feel guilty. Also remember that you can always change a time line.

When you meet your goal on time, reward yourself. Rewards that are an integral part of a goal are powerful. For example, your reward for earning a degree might be the career you've always dreamed of. External rewards, such as a movie or an afternoon in the park, are also valuable. These rewards work best when you're willing to withhold them. If you plan to take a nap on Sunday afternoon whether or not you've finished your chemistry assignment, the nap is not an effective reward.

Another way to reward yourself is to sit quietly after you have finished your task and savor the feeling. One reason why success breeds success is that it feels good. ✳

journal entry **1**

Discovery Statement

Recalling excellence

Welcome to the first Journal Entry in this book. You'll find Journal Entries in every chapter, all with a similar design that allows space for you to write.

In the space below, write a description of a time in your life when you learned or did something well. This experience does not need to be related to school. Describe the details of the situation, including the place, time, and people involved. Describe how you felt about the event, how it looked to you, and how it sounded. In other words, describe the physical sensations and emotions you associate with the event.

I discovered that . . .

_____

_____

_____

_____

_____

_____

_____

_____

You share one thing in common with other students at your vocational school, college, or university: Entering higher education represents a major change in your life. You've joined a new culture with its own set of rules, both spoken and unspoken.

© Andresr/Shutterstock

Making the transition to higher education

WHETHER YOU JUST graduated from high school or have been out of the classroom for decades, as a student new to higher education you'll readily discover many differences between secondary and post-secondary education. The sooner you understand such differences, the sooner you can deal with them. Some examples of what you might face include the following:

■ *New academic standards.* Once you enter higher education, you'll probably find yourself working harder in school than ever before. Instructors will often present more material at a faster pace. There probably will be fewer tests in higher education than in high school, and the grading might be tougher. Compared with high school, you'll have more to read, more to write, more problems to solve, and more to remember.

■ *A new level of independence.* College instructors typically give less guidance about how or when to study. You may not get reminders about when assignments are due or when quizzes and tests will take place. You probably won't get study sheets the night before a test. And anything that's said in class or included in assigned readings might appear on an exam. Overall, you might receive less consistent feedback about how well you are doing in each of

your courses. Don't let this tempt you into putting off work until the last minute. You will still be held accountable for all course work.

■ *Differences in teaching styles.* Instructors at colleges, universities, and vocational schools are often steeped in their subject matter. Many have never taken courses on how to teach and might not be as interesting as some of your high school teachers. And some professors might seem more focused on research than on teaching.

■ *A larger playing field.* The institution you've just joined might seem immense, impersonal, and even frightening. The sheer size of the campus, the variety of courses offered, the large number of departments—all of these opportunities can add up to a confusing array of options.

■ *More students and more diversity.* The school you're attending right now might enroll hundreds or thousands more students than your high school. And the range of diversity among these students might surprise you.

In summary, you are now responsible for structuring your time and creating new relationships. Perhaps more than ever before, you'll find that your life is your own creation. You are free to set different goals, explore alternative ways of thinking, change habits, and expand your circle of friends. All this can add up to a new identity—a new way of being in the world.

At first, this world of choices might seem overwhelming or even frightening. You might feel that you're just going through the motions of being a student or playing a role that you've never rehearsed.

That feeling is understandable. Use it to your advantage. Consider that you *are* assuming a new role in life—that of being a student in higher education. And just as actors enter the minds of the characters that they portray, you can take on the character of a master student.

When you're willing to assume responsibility for the quality of your education, you can create the future of your dreams. Keep the following strategies in mind.

Decrease the unknowns. To reduce surprise, anticipate changes. Before classes begin, get a map of the school property and walk through your first day's schedule, perhaps with a classmate or friend. Visit your instructors in their offices and introduce yourself. Anything you can do to get familiar with the new routine will help.

Admit your feelings—whatever they are. School can be an intimidating experience for new students. People of diverse cultures, adult learners, commuters, and people with disabilities may feel excluded. Anyone can feel anxious, isolated, homesick, or worried about doing well academically.

Those emotions are common among new students, and there's nothing wrong with them. Simply admitting the truth about how you feel—to yourself and to someone else—can help you cope. And you can almost always do something constructive in the present moment, no matter how you feel.

If your feelings about this transition make it hard for you to carry out the activities of daily life—going to class, working, studying, and relating to people—then get professional help. Start with a counselor at the student health service on your campus. The mere act of seeking help can make a difference.

Allow time for transition. You don't have to master the transition to higher education right away. Give it some time. Also, plan your academic schedule with your needs for transition in mind. Balance time-intensive courses with others that don't make as many demands.

Access resources. A supercharger increases the air supply to an internal combustion engine. The resulting difference in power can be dramatic. You can make just as powerful a difference in your education by using all of the resources available to students. In this case,

your "air supply" includes people, campus clubs and organizations, and school and community services.

Of all resources, people are the most important. You can isolate yourself, study hard, and get a good education. However, doing so is not the most powerful use of your tuition money. When you establish relationships with teachers, staff members, fellow students, and employers, you can get a *great* education. Build a network of people who will personally support your success in school.

Accessing resources is especially important if you are the first person in your family to enter higher education. As a first-generation student, you are having experiences that people in your family may not understand. Talk to your family about your activities at school. If they ask how they can help you, give specific answers. Also,

---

journal entry 2

Intention Statement

Plan for transition

As a way to ease your transition to higher education, consider setting a goal to meet at least one new person each week for the next month. You could introduce yourself to someone in each of your classes, for example. You could also see your teachers during office hours and meet with your academic advisor.

List your ideas for ways to meet people in the space below.

_____

_____

_____

_____

_____

I intend to . . .

_____

_____

_____

_____

_____

ask your advisor about programs for first-generation students on your campus.

Meet with your academic advisor. One person in particular—your academic advisor—can help you access resources and make the transition to higher education. Meet with this person regularly. Advisors generally see the big picture when it comes to course requirements, options for declaring majors, and the resources available at your school. Peer advisory programs might also be available.

When you work with an advisor, remember that you're a paying customer and have a right to be satisfied with the service you get. Don't be afraid to change advisors if that seems appropriate.

Learn the language of higher education. Terms such as *grade point average (GPA), prerequisite, accreditation, matriculation, tenure,* and *syllabus* might be new to you. Ease your transition to higher education by checking your school catalog or school Web site for definitions of these words and others that you don't understand. Also ask your academic advisor for clarification.

Attend class. In higher education, teachers generally don't take attendance. Yet you'll find that attending class is essential to your success. The amount that you pay in tuition and fees makes a powerful argument for going to classes regularly and getting your money's worth. In large part, the material that you're tested on comes from events that take place in class.

Showing up for class occurs on two levels. The most visible level is being physically present in the classroom. Even more important, though, is showing up mentally. This kind of attendance includes taking detailed notes, asking questions, and contributing to class discussions.

Research on college freshmen indicates a link between regular class attendance and academic success.[3] Succeeding in school can help you get almost anything you want, including the career, income, and relationships you desire. Showing up for class is an investment in yourself.

Manage out-of-class time. Time management takes on a new meaning for students in higher education. What you do *outside* class matters as much—or even more than—what you do in class. Instructors give you the raw materials for understanding a subject while a class meets. You then take those materials, combine them, and *teach yourself* outside of class.

To allow for this process, schedule 2 hours of study time for each hour that you spend in class. Also, get a calendar that covers the entire academic year. With the syllabus for each of your courses in hand, note key events for the entire term—dates for tests, papers, and other projects. Getting a big picture of your course load makes it easier to get assignments done on time and erases the need for all-night study sessions.

Don't assume that you already know how to study. You can cope with increased workloads and higher academic expectations by putting all of your study habits on the table and evaluating them. Don't assume that the learning strategies you used in the past—in high school or the workplace—will automatically transfer to your new role in higher education. Keep the habits that serve you, drop those that hold you back, and adopt new ones to promote your success. On every page of this book, you'll find helpful suggestions.

Take the initiative in meeting new people. Introduce yourself to classmates and instructors. Just before or after class is a good time. Realize that most of the people in this new world of higher education are waiting to be welcomed. You can help them and help yourself at the same time.

You might have envisioned higher education as a hotbed of social activity—and now find yourself feeling lonely and disconnected from campus during your first weeks of school. Your feelings are common. Remember that plugging into the social networks at any school takes time. And it's worth the effort. Connecting to school socially as well as academically promotes your success and your enjoyment.

Become a self-regulated learner. Reflect on your transition to higher education. Think about what's working well, what you'd like to change, and how you can make those changes. Psychologists use the term *self-regulation* to describe this kind of thinking.[4] Self-regulated learners set goals, monitor their progress toward those goals, and change their behavior based on the results they get.

Becoming a Master Student promotes self-regulation through the ongoing cycle of discovery, intention, and action. Write Discovery Statements to monitor your behavior and evaluate the results you're currently creating in any area of your life. Write about your level of commitment to school, your satisfaction with your classes and grades, your social life, and your family's support for your education.

Based on your discoveries, write Intention Statements about your goals for this term, this year, next year, and the rest of your college career. Describe exactly what you will do to create new results in each of these time frames. In this way, you can take charge of your transition to higher education, starting now. ✳

 Find more strategies for mastering the art of transition online.

The topic of this article might seem like a lesson in common sense, yet some students apparently lack this characteristic. They forget the simple behaviors that create a sense of safety, mutual respect, and community in any place where people gather—including a classroom, tutoring center, library, or instructor's office.

Classroom civility— what's in it for you

CONSIDER AN EXAMPLE: A student arrives 15 minutes late to a lecture and lets the door slam behind her. She pulls a fast-food burger out of a paper bag (hear the sound of that crackling paper). Then her cell phone rings at full volume—and she answers it. Behaviors like these send a message to everyone in the room: "I'm ignoring you."

Without civility, you lose. Even a modest lack of classroom civility creates problems for everyone. Learning gets interrupted. Trust breaks down. Your tuition dollars go down the drain. You invest hundreds of hours and thousands of dollars in getting a degree. You deserve to enter classrooms that are free of discipline problems and bullies.

Many schools have formal policies about classroom civility. Find out what policies apply to you. The consequences for violating them can be serious and may include dismissal or legal action.

With civility, you win. When you treat instructors with respect, you're more likely to be treated that way in return. A respectful relationship with an instructor could turn into a favorable reference letter, a mentorship, a job referral, or a friendship that lasts for years after you graduate. Politeness pays.

Classroom civility does not mean that you have to be passive or insincere. You can present your opinions with passion and even disagree with an instructor. Just make sure you do so in a way that leaves everyone enriched rather than threatened.

The basics of classroom civility are summarized in the following suggestions. They reflect simple common sense, and they make an uncommon difference.

Attend classes regularly. Show up for classes on time. If you know that you're going to miss a class or be late, let your instructor know. Take the initiative to ask your instructor or another student about what you missed.

If you arrive late, do not disrupt class. Close the door quietly and take a seat. When you know that you will have to leave class early, tell your instructor before class begins, and sit near an exit. If you leave class to use the restroom or handle an emergency, do so quietly.

During class, participate fully. Take notes and join in discussions. Turn off your cell phone or any other electronic device that you don't need for class. Remember that sleeping, texting, or doing work for another class is a waste of your time and money.

Instructors often give assignments or make a key point at the end of a class period. Be there when it happens. Wait until class has been dismissed to pack up your notebooks and other materials.

Communicate respect. When you speak in class, begin by addressing your instructor as *Ms., Mrs., Mr., Professor,* or whatever the teacher prefers.

Discussions gain value when everyone gets a chance to contribute. Show respect for others by not monopolizing class discussions. Refrain from side conversations and profanity. When presenting viewpoints that conflict with those of classmates or your instructor, combine the passion for your opinion with respect for the opinions of others.

Respect gets communicated in the smallest details, such as maintaining good hygiene. Avoid making distracting noises, and cover your mouth if you yawn or cough. Also avoid wearing inappropriate clothing. And even if you meet your future spouse in class, refrain from public displays of affection.

If you disagree with a class requirement or grade you received, talk to your instructor about it after class in a respectful way. In a private setting, your ideas will get more attention.

See civility as a contribution. Every class you enter has the potential to become a community of people who talk openly, listen fully, share laughter, and arrive at life-changing insights. Anything you do to make that vision a reality makes everyone a winner. ✳

Succeeding in higher education— at any age

David Buffington/Blend Images/Getty

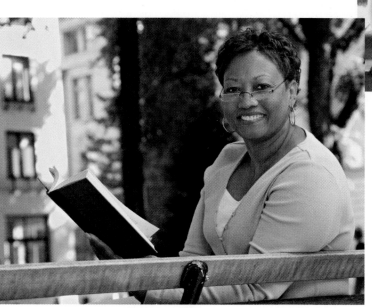

David Buffington/Blend Images/Getty

BEING AN ADULT learner puts you on a strong footing. Having a rich store of life experiences equips you to ask meaningful questions and make connections between course work and daily life.

Any abilities that you've developed to work on teams, manage projects, meet deadlines, and solve problems are assets. Many instructors will enjoy working with you.

Following are some suggestions for adult learners who want to ease their transition to higher education. If you're a younger student, commuting student, or community college student, look for useful ideas here as well.

Acknowledge your concerns. Adult learners might express any of the following fears:

- *I'll be the oldest person in all my classes.*
- *I've been out of the classroom too long.*
- *I'm concerned about my math, reading, and writing skills.*
- *I'm worried about making tuition payments.*
- *How will I ever make the time to study, on top of everything else I'm doing?*

Those concerns are understandable. Now consider some facts:

- College classrooms are more diverse than ever before. According to the U.S. Census Bureau, 37 percent of students in the nation's colleges are age 25 and older. The majority of these older students attend school part-time.[5]
- Adult learners can take advantage of evening classes, weekend classes, summer classes, distance learning, and online courses. Some classes may be held in off-campus locations, closer to where you work or live.
- Colleges offer financial aid—including scholarships, grants, and low-interest loans—for students of all ages.
- Orientation programs are designed for students to meet one another and make new friends. Look for programs targeted to adult learners.
- You are now enrolled in a course that can help boost your skills in math, reading, writing, note taking, and time management.

Ease into it. If you're new to higher education, consider easing into it. You can choose to attend school part-time before making a full-time commitment. If you've taken college-level classes in the past, find out if any of those credits will transfer into your current program.

Plan ahead. By planning a week or month at a time, you get a bigger picture of your multiple roles as a student, employee, and family member. With that awareness, you can make conscious adjustments in the number of hours you devote to each domain of activity in your life. Consider these examples:

- If your responsibilities at work or home will be heavy in the near future, then register for fewer classes next term.
- Choose recreational activities carefully, focusing on ones that relax you and recharge you the most.
- Don't load your schedule with classes that require unusually heavy amounts of reading or writing.

For related suggestions, see Chapter 2: Time.

Delegate tasks. If you have children, delegate some of the household chores to them. Or start a meal co-op in your neighborhood. Cook dinner for yourself and someone else one night each week. In return, ask that person to furnish you with a meal on another night. A similar strategy can apply to child care and other household tasks.

Get to know other returning students. Introduce yourself to other adult learners. Being in the same classroom gives you an immediate bond. You can exchange work, home, or cell phone numbers and build a network of mutual support. Some students adopt a buddy system, pairing up with another student in each class to complete assignments and prepare for tests.

Find common ground with traditional students. Traditional and nontraditional students have many things in common. They seek to gain knowledge and skills for their chosen careers. They desire financial stability and personal fulfillment. And many younger students, like their older peers, are concerned about whether they have the skills to succeed in higher education.

Consider pooling resources with younger students. Share notes, edit one another's papers, and form study groups. Look for ways to build on one another's strengths. If you want help with using a computer for assignments, you might find a younger student to guide you. In group projects and case studies, you can expand the discussion by sharing insights from your experiences.

Enlist your employer's support. Let your employer in on your educational plans. Point out how the skills you gain in the classroom will help you meet work objectives. Offer informal seminars at work to share what you're learning in school. You might find that your company reimburses its employees for some tuition costs or even grants time off to attend classes.

Get extra mileage out of your current tasks. Look for ways to relate your schoolwork to your job. For example, when you're assigned a research paper, choose a topic that relates to your current job tasks. Some schools even offer academic credit for work and life experience.

Review your subjects before you start classes. Say that you're registered for trigonometry and you haven't taken a math class since high school. Consider brushing up on the subject before classes begin. Also, talk with future instructors about ways to prepare for their classes.

"Publish" your schedule. After you plan your study and class sessions for the week, write up your schedule and post it in a place where others who live with you will see it. If you use an online calendar, print out copies to put in your school binder or on your refrigerator door, bathroom mirror, or kitchen cupboard.

Enroll family and friends in your success. School can cut into your social life. Prepare friends and family members by discussing this issue ahead of time. See Chapter 8: Communicating for ways to prevent and resolve conflict.

You can also involve your spouse, partner, children, or close friends in your schooling. Offer to give them a tour of the campus, introduce them to your instructors and classmates, and encourage them to attend social events at school with you.

Take this process a step further, and ask the key people in your life for help. Share your reason for getting a degree, and talk about what your whole family has to gain from this change in your life. Ask them to think of ways that they can support your success in school and to commit to those actions. Make your own education a joint mission that benefits everyone. ✱

 Find more strategies for adult learners online.

Connect to resources

AS A STUDENT in higher education, you can access a world of student services and community resources. Any of them can help you succeed in school. Many of them are free.

Name a problem that you're facing right now or that you anticipate facing in the future: finding money to pay for classes, resolving conflicts with a teacher, lining up a job after graduation. Chances are that a school or community resource can help you. The ability to access resources is a skill that will serve you long after you stop being a student.

Resources often go unused. Following are examples of what you can find. Check your school and city Web sites for more options.

Academic advisors can help you select courses, choose a major, plan your career, and adjust in general to the culture of higher education.

Arts organizations connect you to local museums, concert venues, clubs, and stadiums.

Athletic centers often open weight rooms, swimming pools, indoor tracks, basketball courts, and racquetball and tennis courts to all students.

© Losevsky Pavel, Shutterstock

Child care is sometimes made available to students at a reasonable cost through the early childhood education department on campus or community agencies.

Churches, synagogues, mosques, and temples have members who are happy to welcome fellow worshippers who are away from home.

Computer labs on campus are places where students can go to work on projects and access the Internet. Computer access is often available off campus as well. Check public libraries for this service. Some students get permission to use computers at their workplace after hours.

Consumer credit counseling can help even if you've really blown your budget. And it's usually free. Do your research, and choose a reputable and not-for-profit consumer credit counselor.

Counseling centers in the community can assist you with a problem when you can't get help at school. Look for career-planning services, rehabilitation offices, veterans' outreach programs, and mental health clinics.

The **financial aid office** assists students with loans, scholarships, work-study, and grants.

Governments (city, county, state, and federal) often have programs for students. Check the government listings in your local telephone directory.

Hotlines offer a way to get emergency care, personal counseling, and other kinds of help with just a phone call. Do an Internet search on *phone hotlines* in your area that assist with the specific kind of help you're looking for. Check your school catalog for more resources.

Job placement offices can help you find part-time employment while you are in school and a full-time job after you graduate.

Legal aid services provide free or inexpensive assistance to low-income people.

Libraries are a treasure on campus and in any community. They employ people who are happy to help you locate information.

Newspapers published on campus and in the local community list events and services that are free or inexpensive.

The **school catalog** lists course descriptions, tuition fees, requirements for graduation, and information on everything from the school's history to its grading practices.

School security agencies can tell you what's safe and what's not. They can also provide information about parking, bicycle regulations, and traffic rules.

Special needs/disability services assist college students who have learning disabilities or other disabilities.

Student health clinics often provide free or inexpensive counseling and other medical treatment.

Student organizations present opportunities for extracurricular activities. Explore student government, fraternities, sororities, service clubs, veterans' organizations, religious groups, sports clubs, and political groups. Find women's centers; multicultural student centers; and organizations for international students, students with disabilities, and gay and lesbian students.

Support groups exist for people with almost any problem, from drug addiction to cancer. You can find people who meet every week to share suggestions, information, and concerns about problems they share.

Tutoring is usually free and is available through academic departments or counseling centers. ✶

Extracurricular activities:
Reap the benefits

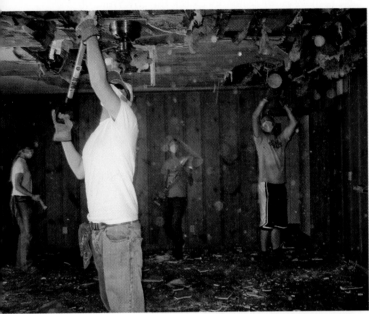

© 2006 Ben Loehrke, Youth Advocating Leadership and Learning.
www.yallrelief.org

AS YOU ENTER higher education, you may find that you are busier than you've ever been before. Often that's due to the variety of extracurricular activities available: athletics, fraternities, sororities, student newspapers, debate teams, study groups, service learning projects, internships, student government, and political action groups, to name just a few. Your school might also offer conferences, films, concerts, museums, art galleries, and speakers—all for free or reduced prices. Student organizations help to make these activities possible, and you can join any of them.

With this kind of involvement come potential benefits. People who participate in extracurricular activities are often excellent students. Such activities help them bridge the worlds inside and outside the classroom. Through student organizations, they develop new skills, explore possible careers, build contacts for jobs, and build a lifelong habit of giving back to their communities. They make new friends among both students and faculty, work with people from other cultures, and sharpen their skills in conflict resolution.

Getting involved in such organizations also comes with some risks. When students don't balance extracurricular activities with class work, their success in school can suffer. They can also compromise their health by losing sleep, neglecting exercise, skipping meals, or relying on fast food. These costs are easier to avoid if you keep a few suggestions in mind:

- *Make conscious choices* about how to divide your time between schoolwork and extracurricular activities. Decide up front how many hours each week or month you can devote to a student organization. Leave room in your schedule for relaxing and for unplanned events. For more ideas, see Chapter 2: Time.

- *Look to the future* when making commitments. Write down three or four of the most important goals you'd like to achieve in your lifetime. Then choose extracurricular activities that directly support those goals.

- *Create a career plan* that includes a list of skills needed for your next job. Then choose extracurricular activities to develop those skills. If you're unsure of your career choice, then get involved in campus organizations to explore your options.

- *Whenever possible, develop leadership experience* by holding an office in an organization. If that's too much of a commitment, then volunteer to lead a committee or plan a special event.

- *Get involved* in a variety of extracurricular activities. Varying your activities demonstrates to future employers that you can work with a variety of people in a range of settings.

- *Recognize reluctance* to follow through on a commitment. You might agree to attend meetings but find yourself forgetting them or consistently showing up late. If that happens, write a Discovery Statement about the way you're using time. Follow that with an Intention Statement about ways to keep your agreements—or consider renegotiating those agreements.

- *Say no* to activities that fail to create value for you. Avoid joining groups only because you feel guilty or obligated to do so.

- *Check out the rules* before joining any student organization. Ask about dues and attendance requirements. ✴

Link to the world of work

ONE THEORY OF education separates life into two distinct domains: work and school. One domain is the "real" world. The other is the place where you attend classes to prepare for the real world. Consider another point of view: Success in higher education promotes success on the job.

When you graduate from school, you don't leave your capacity for mastery locked inside a classroom. Excellence in one setting paves the way for excellence in other settings. For example, the student who knows how to show up for class on time is ready to show up for work on time. The student who knows how to focus attention during a lecture is ready to focus attention during a training session at work. And the student who's worked cooperatively in a study group brings skills to the table when joining a project team at work.

Staying current in the job market means continually expanding your knowledge and skills. You might change careers several times during your working life—a possibility that calls for continuous learning. As a master student, you can gain favor with employers by getting up to speed quickly on new jobs and new projects.

Starting now, read this book with a mental filter in place. Ask yourself, "How can I use this idea to meet my career goals? How can I apply this technique to my current job or the next job I see for myself?" The answers can help you thrive in any job, whether you work full-time or part-time.

To stimulate your thinking, look for the Put It to Work articles in each chapter. In addition, invent techniques of your own based on what you read, and test them at work. There's no limit to the possibilities.

For example, use the Discovery and Intention Journal Entry system while you're in the workforce. Write Discovery Statements to note your current job skills, as well as areas for improvement. Also use Discovery Statements to describe what you want from your career.

Follow up with Intention Statements that detail specifically what you want to be doing 1 year, 5 years, and 10 years or more from today. Write additional Intention Statements about specific actions you can take to meet those career goals.

Below is a textbook reconnaissance that lists articles in this book with workplace applications. These are just a few examples. As you read, look for more.

The techniques presented in *Setting and achieving goals* (page 67) can help you plan and complete projects on time. Supplement these ideas with suggestions from *The ABC daily to-do list* (page 71), *More strategies for planning* (page 74), and *Stop procrastination now* (page 76). The article *Twenty-five ways to get the most out of now* (page 79) is packed with ideas you can transfer to the workplace. For example, tackle difficult tasks first thing in the day, or at any other time when your energy peaks. Also find 5-minute tasks that you can complete while waiting for a meeting to start. The article *Twenty memory techniques* (page 102) will come in handy as you learn the policies and procedures for a new job.

Techniques presented in *Remembering names* (page 111) can help as you meet people during your job search and as you are being introduced to new coworkers.

Use *How muscle reading works* (page 124) to keep up with journals and books in your field. This set of techniques can also help you scan Web sites for the information you want, keep up with ever-increasing volumes of e-mail, and reduce mountains of interoffice memos to manageable proportions.

The article *Record* (page 153) explains different formats for taking notes—mind maps, concept maps, the Cornell format, and more. You can use these tools to document what happens at work-related meetings.

Adapt the ideas mentioned in *Cooperative learning— studying in groups* (page 181) in order to cooperate more effectively with members of a project team.

Let go of test anxiety (page 188) is full of strategies that can help you manage stress in any situation. Use them when you're under deadline pressure or dealing with a difficult customer. Use the thinking skills presented in *Gaining skill at decision making* (page 220) when it comes time to choose a career, weigh job offers, or make work-related decisions.

Robert Reich, former U.S. secretary of labor, said that jobs of the future will call for the abilities to "define problems, quickly assimilate relevant data, conceptualize and reorganize the information, make deductive and inductive leaps with it, ask hard questions about it, discuss findings with colleagues, work collaboratively to find solutions and then convince others."[6] See *Ways to create ideas* (page 212), *Becoming a critical thinker* (page 207), and *Four ways to solve problems* (page 221) for strategies related to each skill that Reich describes.

According to a survey of managers in government and business settings, workers who lack writing skills will struggle to advance in their careers.[7] Your own career path may require you to produce e-mails, reports, memos, articles, abstracts, proposals, job descriptions, and other business documents. *Three phases of effective writing* (page 253) offers a core process for completing all these assignments.

The U.S. Department of Labor issued an influential report on key skills needed by members of the workforce in the twenty-first century.[8] That report described the need for people with public speaking skills, including making group presentations, targeting messages to specific audiences, and responding to listener feedback. Take the next step in developing these skills with *Mastering public speaking* (page 260). Ideas from *Managing conflict* (page 244) can help you defuse tensions among coworkers.

The suggestions in *Building relationships across cultures* (page 274) can assist you in adapting to the culture of a new job. Each company, large or small, develops its own culture—a set of shared values and basic assumptions. Even if you are self-employed, you can benefit by discovering and adapting to a client's corporate culture.

Return to *Create your career now* (page 356) at any time in the future when you're redefining the kind of work that you want to do. Then hone your job-hunting skills with *Use résumés and interviews to "hire" an employer* (page 364).

The only job security available today is the ability to transfer skills from one position to another. *Now that you're done—begin* (page 353) opens up pathways to lifelong learning. Use these suggestions to continually update your job skills and explore new areas for personal development. ✳

You don't need this course— but you might want it

Some students don't believe they need a student success course. They might be right. These students may tell you that many schools don't even offer such a class. That's true.

Consider the benefits of taking this course anyway.

Start with a single question: What's one new thing that you could do on a regular basis to make a significant, positive difference in your life? This question might be the most important thing you ask yourself this term. The answer does not have to involve a huge behavior change. Over weeks and months, even a small shift in the way you take notes, read a textbook, or interact with instructors can make a major difference in how well you do in school.

Students who open up to this idea experience benefits. These comments from a recent student success course evaluation are typical:

I didn't expect to get anything out of this course except an easy A. Boy, was I ever wrong. This course has changed my life!

I entered college with no confidence. Now that I have taken this class, I feel like I can succeed in any class.

This course has truly showed that I have the power to change any situation for the better.

I am now ready for the rest of my college years.

A student success course gives you dozens of strategies for creating the life of your dreams. It's possible that you might arrive at these strategies on your own, given enough time. Why wait, though? Approach this book and your course as if the quality of your education depends on them. Then wait for the benefits to unfold.

Ways to change a habit

© Photodisc

©Photodisc

© Photodisc

CONSIDER A NEW way to think about the word *habit*. Imagine for a moment that many of our most troublesome problems and even our most basic traits are just habits.

That expanding waistline that your friend is blaming on her spouse's cooking—maybe that's just a habit called overeating.

That fit of rage that a student blames on a teacher—maybe that's just the student's habit of closing the door to new ideas.

Procrastination, stress, and money shortages might just be names that we give to collections of habits—scores of simple, small, repeated behaviors that combine to create a huge result. The same goes for health, wealth, love, and many of the other things that we want from life.

One way of thinking about success or failure is to focus on habits. Behaviors such as failing to complete reading assignments or skipping class might be habits leading to an outcome that "couldn't" be avoided—dropping out of school. In the same way, behaviors such as completing assignments and attending class might lead to the outcome of getting an "A."

When you confront a behavior that undermines your goals or creates a circumstance that you don't want, consider a new attitude: That behavior is just a habit. And it can be changed.

Thinking about ourselves as creatures of habit actually gives us power. Then we are not faced with the monumental task of changing our very nature. Rather, we can take on the doable job of changing our habits. One change in behavior that seems insignificant at first can have effects that ripple throughout your life. For example, you might get find you can accomplish more simply by waking up 30 minutes earlier each day.

After interviewing hundreds of people, psychologists James Prochaska, John Norcross, and Carlo DiClemente identified stages that people typically go through when adopting a new behavior.[9] These stages take people from *contemplating* a change and making a clear *determination* to change, to taking *action* and *maintaining* the new behavior. Following are ways to help yourself move successfully through each stage as you attempt to change a habit.

Tell the truth

Telling the truth about any habit—from chewing our fingernails to cheating on tests—frees us. Without taking this step, our efforts to change might be as ineffective as rearranging the deck chairs on the *Titanic*. Telling the truth allows us to see what's actually sinking the ship.

When we admit what's really going on in our lives, our defenses are down. We're open to accepting help from others. The support we need to change a habit has the opportunity to make an impact.

Choose and commit to a new behavior

It often helps to choose a new habit to replace an old one. First, make a commitment to practice the new habit. Tell key people in your life about your decision to change. Set up a plan for when and how. Answer questions such as these: When will I apply the new habit? Where will I be? Who will be with me? What will I be seeing, hearing, touching, saying, or doing? Exactly how will I think, speak, or act differently?

Take the student who always snacks when he studies. Each time he sits down to read, he positions a bag of potato chips within easy reach. For him, opening a book is a cue to start chewing. Snacking is especially easy given the place he chooses to study: the kitchen. He decides to change this habit by studying at a desk in his bedroom instead of at the kitchen table. And every time he feels the urge to bite into a potato chip, he drinks from a glass of water instead.

Richard Malott, a psychologist who specializes in helping people overcome procrastination, lists three key steps in committing to a new behavior.[10] First, *specify* your goal in numerical terms whenever possible. For example, commit to reading thirty pages per day, Monday through Friday. Next, *observe* your behavior and record the results—in this case, the number of pages that you actually read every day. Finally, set up a small *consequence* for failing to keep your commitment. For instance, pay a friend one quarter for each day that you read less than thirty pages.

Affirm your intention

You can pave the way for a new behavior by clearing a mental path for it. Before you apply the new behavior, rehearse it in your mind. Mentally picture what actions you will take and in what order.

Say that you plan to improve your handwriting when taking notes. Imagine yourself in class with a blank notebook poised before you. See yourself taking up a finely crafted pen. Notice how comfortable it feels in your hand. See yourself writing clearly and legibly. You can even picture how you will make individual letters: the *e*'s, *i*'s, and *r*'s. Then, when class is over, see yourself reviewing your notes and taking pleasure in how easy they are to read.

Start with a small change

You can sometimes rearrange a whole pattern of behaviors by changing one small habit. If you have a habit of always being late for classes, and if you want to change that habit, then be on time for one class. As soon as you change the old pattern by getting ready and going on time to one class, you'll likely find yourself arriving at all of your classes on time. You might even start arriving everywhere else on time, too.

The joy of this process is watching one small change of habit ripple through your whole life.

Get feedback and support

Getting feedback and support is a crucial step in adopting a new behavior. It is also the point at which many plans for change break down. It's easy to practice your new behavior with great enthusiasm for a few days. After the initial rush of excitement, though, things can get a little tougher. You begin to find excuses for slipping back into old habits: "One more cigarette won't hurt." "I can get back to my diet tomorrow." "It's been a tough day. I deserve this beer."

You may not see, or want to see, what you're doing. Feedback can help. One way to get feedback is to bring other people into the picture. Ask others to remind you that you are changing your habit if they see you backsliding. If you want to stop an old behavior, such as cramming for tests, it often works to tell everyone about your goal. When you want to start a new behavior, though, consider telling only a few people—those who truly support your efforts. Starting new habits might call for the more focused, long-lasting support that close friends or family members can give. Support from others can be as simple as a quick phone call: "Hi. Have you started that outline for your research paper yet?" Or it can be as formal as a support group that meets once a week to review everyone's goals and action plans.

Chances are, though, that the most effective source for your support and feedback is yourself. You know yourself better than anyone else does and can design a system to monitor your behavior. Create your own charts to track your behavior, or write about your progress in your journal. Figure out a way to monitor your progress.

Practice, practice, practice— without self-judgment

Psychologist B. F. Skinner defines learning as a stable change in behavior that comes as a result of practice.[11] This widely accepted idea is key to changing habits. Act on your intention. If you fail or forget, let go of any self-judgment. Just keep practicing the new habit, and allow whatever time it takes to make a change.

Accept the feelings of discomfort that might come with a new habit. Keep practicing the new behavior, even if it feels unnatural. Trust the process. You will grow into the new behavior. However, if this new habit doesn't work, simply note what happened (without guilt or blame), select a new behavior, and begin this cycle of steps over again.

Making mistakes as you practice doesn't mean that you've failed. Even when you don't get the results you want from a new behavior, you learn something valuable in the process. Once you understand ways to change one habit, you understand ways to change almost any habit. ✳

 Find more strategies for changing a habit online.

© Photodisc

© Photodisc

© Photodisc

Discovery Statement

Choosing your purpose

Success is a choice—your choice. To *get* what you want, it helps to *know* what you want. That is the purpose of this two-part Journal Entry.

You can begin choosing success right now by setting a date, time, and place to complete this Journal Entry. Write your choices here, and then block out the time on your calendar.

Date: _____

Time: _____

Place: _____

Part 1

Select a time and place when you know you will not be disturbed for at least 20 minutes. (The library is a good place to do this exercise.) Relax for 2 or 3 minutes, clearing your mind. Next, complete the following sentences—and then keep writing.

When you run out of things to write, stick with it just a bit longer. Be willing to experience a little discomfort. Keep writing. What you discover might be well worth the extra effort.

What I want from my education is . . .

_____

_____

_____

When I complete my education, I want to be able to . . .

_____

_____

_____

_____

I also want . . .

_____

_____

_____

_____

_____

_____

Part 2

After completing Part 1, take a short break. Reward yourself by doing something that you enjoy. Then come back to this Journal Entry.

Now, review the list you just created of things that you want from your education. See if you can summarize them in a one-sentence, polished statement. It will become a statement of your purpose for taking part in higher education.

Allow yourself to write many drafts of this mission statement, and review it periodically as you continue your education. With each draft, see if you can capture the essence of what you want from higher education and from your life. State it in a vivid way—in a short sentence that you can easily memorize, one that sparks your enthusiasm and makes you want to get up in the morning.

You might find it difficult to express your purpose statement in one sentence. If so, write a paragraph or more. Then look for the sentence that seems most charged with energy for you.

Following are some sample purpose statements:

- My purpose for learning is to gain skills that I can use to contribute to others.
- My purpose for acquiring an education is to live an abundant life that is filled with happiness, health, love, and wealth.
- My purpose for being in school is to enjoy myself by making lasting friendships and following my interests.

Write at least one draft of your purpose statement below:

_____

_____

_____

_____

_____

_____

_____

_____

_____

_____

A User's Guide

A POWER PROCESS is a suggestion to shift your perspective and try on a new habit or way of seeing the world. This book includes a baker's dozen of them. Reviewers of *Becoming a Master Student* consistently refer to the power of the Power Processes. Many students point to these short, offbeat, and occasionally outrageous articles as their favorite part of the book.

Why use the Power Processes?

People operate like holograms. But just what does that mean? Holograms are three-dimensional pictures made by using lasers and a special kind of film. You can cut holographic film into tiny pieces and reproduce the entire image from any piece. Each piece contains the whole.

Scientists have observed the same principle at work in biology, physics, sociology, politics, and management. Biologists know that the chromosomes in each cell are the blueprints for that whole organism. Careful study of any one cell can show a plan for the entire body.

The hologram-like nature of human behavior can be summed up in the word *process*. We have a natural tendency to live in patterns—to act out of habit. You can harness this idea for practical benefit. Altering a single attitude or basic behavior is like changing the blueprint for your life. One small change can open the door to many other changes, with a cascading series of positive effects. That's the reason why the word *power* goes with the term *process*.

The Power Processes in this book offer many more examples of this approach. Becoming a master student means setting up patterns of success that will last the rest of your life.

How do I use the Power Processes?

Approach each Power Process with an open mind. Then experiment with it right away. See if it works for you.

Psychologists have written thousands of pages on the subject of personal change. You can find countless theories of personality, techniques for reinforcing behaviors, and other complex schemes.

As an alternative, consider that personal change is simple. Just do something differently. Now. Then see what happens.

People often make personal change more complicated. They spend years trying to enhance their self-discipline, unearth their childhood memories, search for their hidden sources of motivation, discover their higher self, and on and on.

Another option is to just change, starting today. That's the idea behind the Power Processes. You'll find thirteen of them in this book:

To start unleashing the power, turn the page now. ✳

Discover What You Want

Imagine a person who walks up to a counter at the airport to buy a plane ticket for his next vacation. "Just give me a ticket," he says to the reservation agent. "Anywhere will do."

The agent stares back at him in disbelief. "I'm sorry, sir," she replies. "I'll need some more details. Just minor things—such as the name of your destination city and your arrival and departure dates."

"Oh, I'm not fussy," says the would-be vacationer. "I just want to get away. You choose for me."

Compare this scene with that of another traveler who walks up to the counter and says, "I'd like a ticket to Ixtapa, Mexico, departing on Saturday, March 23, and returning Sunday, April 7. Please give me a window seat, first class, with vegetarian meals."

Now, ask yourself which traveler is more likely to end up with an enjoyable vacation.

The same principle applies in any area of life. Knowing where we want to go increases the probability that we will arrive at our destination. Discovering what we want makes it more likely that we'll attain it. Once our goals are defined precisely, our brains reorient our thinking and behavior to align with those goals—and we're well on the way there.

The example about the traveler with no destination seems far-fetched. Before you dismiss it, though, do an informal experiment: Ask three other students what they want to get out of their education. Be prepared for hemming and hawing, vague generalities, and maybe even a helping of pie-in-the-sky à la mode.

What you hear will be amazing, considering the stakes involved. Our hypothetical vacationer is about to invest a couple weeks of his time and hundreds of dollars—all with no destination in mind. Students routinely invest years of their lives and thousands of dollars with an equally hazy idea of their destination in life.

Now suppose that you ask someone what she wants from her education and get this answer: "I plan to get a degree in journalism with double minors in earth science and Portuguese so that I can work as a reporter covering the environment in Brazil." Chances are you've found a master student. The details of a person's vision offer a clue to mastery.

Discovering what you want greatly enhances your odds of succeeding in higher education. Many students quit school simply because they are unsure about what they want from it. With well-defined goals in mind, you can look for connections between what you want and what you study. The more connections you discover, the more likely you'll stay in school—and the more likely you'll get what you want in every area of life.[12]

> "You either change things or you don't. Excuses rob you of power and induce apathy.
>
> **—Agnes Whistling Elk**
>
> In oneself lies the whole world, and if you know how to look and learn, then the door is there and the key is in your hand. Nobody on earth can give you either that key or the door to open, except yourself.
>
> **—J. Krishnamurti**

Preview

Many students taking a student success course start out the semester with a high level of enthusiasm and energy, and that's good because there's a lot of meaty and important foundation material in the Introduction and in Chapters 1 and 2. If students learn the important concepts presented in these chapters, they are well on the way to achieving their educational goals. Remind your students that this chapter is about First Steps—and this includes exercises in self-discovery, making transitions, and motivation. Use the Master Student Map on the chapter opener page to inspire your students, stimulate class discussion, and preview the chapter topics.

Guest Speaker

Consider inviting the elected President of Student Government to speak to your students as a follow-up to the "Extracurricular activities: Reap the benefits" article in the Introduction: Making Transitions. Prompt the President to discuss why he became involved in student activities and what he's gotten out of the experience.

If a speaker isn't available, consider using the Master Student Profile articles as guest speakers. Each chapter of this text includes a profile of a person who embodies several qualities of a master student. Invite your students to look for timeless qualities in the people they read about. Growing up with difficult situations, Lalita Booth observed the world around her and chose a different type of life for herself. She discovered that going back to school was the key to the life she wanted to create. Use this story to start a conversation about the external challenges students face while pursuing a post-secondary education.

Lecture

Learning Style Inventory (pages LSI-1–LSI-8) Being aware of learning styles is an important strategy for success because it helps students understand differences in the ways people like to perceive and process new information. Your students will learn about their own preferred style of learning and how this tool can help them observe and ascertain the preferred teaching styles of their professors.

The Learning Style Inventory (LSI) is a unifying theme woven throughout *Becoming a Master Student.* Activities are crafted to engage students not only in the strengths of their own learning preference but in the strengths of other styles as well. The Master Student Map at the beginning of each chapter can help students internalize the strategies taught in each chapter. Study skills do not transfer from a student success class to other courses accidentally. It takes a talented and prepared instructor to help students build other schema and develop the confidence that is necessary to transfer new strategies to different learning settings. Teaching this might seem intimidating for first-time instructors. Remember, when you teach with *Becoming a Master Student,* you are not alone. Your support materials include a talented team of TeamUP consultants. Call (1-800-528-8323) or visit **www.cengage.com/teamup** today!

Additional resources to help guide you in administering the LSI and applying the Master Student Map and Learning Styles Application are on the Instructor Web site. A video for instructors is also available online.

Claim your multiple intelligences (page 39) Howard Gardner's theory of several types of intelligence complements this chapter's discussion of different learning styles: both recognize that there are alternative ways for people to learn and assimilate knowledge. This article provides students with concepts for exploring additional methods to achieve success in school, work, and relationships. A chart on pages 40–41 presents an overview of the characteristics of each type of intelligence, suggests possible learning strategies for each, and links the different types with possible careers. Have your students further explore these career choices as they consider different majors or areas of focused study.

Exercises/Activities

1. **Learning by seeing, hearing, and moving: The VAK system (page 42)** Learning by seeing (visual learning), hearing (auditory learning), and moving (kinesthetic learning) allows students to perceive information through their senses. Engage your students by asking them to take the informal inventory and to continue to take First Steps of self-discovery. Have your students submit Discovery Statements to highlight the new strategies they have discovered and Intention Statements to describe the new options for learning that they intend to implement.

2. **The Master Student (pages 45–47)** After students read this article outside class, reinforce the concept of mastery with the following team-building activity in class. Randomly assign students to groups of four and ask each group to select five of the most important master student qualities. The group members must agree on the five qualities they pick and be able to justify their decision to choose them. Have each group report to the whole class on their choices.

3. **Attitudes, affirmations, and visualizations (pages 52–53)** Self-awareness is the key to self-regulation and eventually self-mastery. This article encourages students to begin positive self-talk early in the course. Affirmations are employed to help students sustain a positive self-image and develop attitudes that lead to success. To help students grasp the power of visualization, try the classroom exercise "Creating their place." Begin this exercise by providing students with names for this place such as power place, caring place, peaceful place, or happy place. Students select the name that feels best to them. This allows all students, introverts and extroverts, to be positive about their choice. Instruct students to close their eyes and create this place in their mind. Follow a script (which is available on the Instructor Web site) to help them discover the effectiveness of guided visualization. Once they have created this "mind place" in class two or three times, it can help reduce stress and test anxiety, and it can serve as a strategic memory tool.

4. **Power Process: Ideas Are Tools (page 55)** Each Power Process can be illustrated by a simple yet meaningful object lesson. For example, to illustrate this Power Process, bring a drinking straw, a spoon, a hammer, and a piece of chalk or whiteboard marker to class. Ask for volunteers to help write an assignment on the board. Hand out the various "ideas/tools" for them to use to write on the board. In seconds, all of the students will realize the power of this process. Although each of these ideas is an excellent tool for the job it was designed to do, only the student with the right tool is successful at the current task.

Conversation/Sharing

The article on Motivation (pages 50–51) provides students with tools that enable them to take responsibility for their own motivation in college. Motivation is often high at the beginning of the semester but may drop as the term progresses. Have students form groups of four and share which of the tools each student intends to use to keep motivation high for the entire term. Ask each group to report out a summary to the whole class.

Homework

The Discovery Wheel (pages 27–30) is an opportunity for students to take a First Step in telling the truth about the kind of student they are and the kind of student they want to become. This is not a test but an opportunity for change. Students complete the Discovery Wheel in Chapter 1 and then again in Chapter 12. This enables them to measure their progress. Results from the Discovery Wheel exercises can be used in your course in a variety of ways. Consider the following suggestions:

- Ask students to list their intentions or commitments for improving particular skills during the term. At the end of the term, they can assess their progress in those areas by using the Discovery Wheel in Chapter 12.

- As an alternative to the textbook version of the Discovery Wheel, have your students fill out the online interactive Discovery Wheel found on the Student Web site. Note that this online version does not include number ratings, so the results will be formatted differently from the results of the Discovery Wheel in the text.
- Create an assignment requiring students to contact people on campus or in the community who can assist them in enhancing particular skills. For example, the reading center can provide specific strategies for improving comprehension, word attack skills, and concentration.
- Allow the Discovery Wheel exercises to help shape course content. You can use the results to plan future lessons or to determine what students want to learn or accomplish during the course as a result of their self-assessments.
- Ask students to form small groups and coach each other. Coaching could include how to capitalize on and share talents and how to strengthen areas for growth. If you choose to do this activity, let students know your reasons for forming small groups. For many, self-assessment is personal, and sharing the results might seem risky. Ask students to coach themselves. They can imagine that the self-assessment is for someone special whose success in school and life is important to them. Ask students to take their best suggestions and implement them.
- Create a resource network. Take the titles of the sections of the Discovery Wheel (Attitude, Time, Memory, and so on) and list each title on a piece of paper. Ask students to sign their names to a particular piece of paper if they are willing to assist others in enhancing their skills in this area. Then distribute the lists to the class or post them on your course Web site.

Evaluation

Quiz Ideas for Chapter 1

- Ask about the role of truth in the mastery of student success.
- Ask about discoveries from completing the Discovery Wheel.
- Ask about their preferred Learning Style and the characteristics of students who like to learn using this style.
- What are challenges in college for someone with their Learning Style?
- Name and give examples of two multiple intelligences.
- Describe key points in the article "The value of higher education."
- Ask students to explain three of the master student qualities they desire to possess.

Here is a quiz idea from an Advisory Board Member:

> To save class time for instruction and discussion, I tell my students that I am going to select only one 10-point question for the quiz. It will be one of the questions in the book quiz. I present the question and ask students to respond using the three-part quiz forms (available through your sales rep). When they are through answering the question, I remind students to write their name on the quiz before tearing off the white sheet and handing it in. Then they compare answers with the person next to them to seek insights from each other. If they did not have the answer, I tell them that if they return the pink sheet with the answers to all ten questions, I will give them 7 out of 10 points.
>
> **—Eldon McMurray, Utah Valley State College**

Additional Digital Resources

Course Manual

The online *Course Manual* serves as an invaluable reference for those developing and teaching a College Success course with *Becoming a Master Student*. The *Course Manual* provides advice on general teaching issues such as preparing for classes, classroom management, grading, and communicating with students of various backgrounds, as well as specific strategies on getting the most out of various features in *Becoming a Master Student* such as the Discovery Wheel, Learning Styles Inventory, and book-specific Web sites.

Instructor Web Site

The updated Instructor Web site provides resources to help you plan and customize your course. Content specific to Chapter 1 includes:

▶ Lecture Ideas
  • Corkscrews Are Tools
  • Connecting VAK Self-Awareness, Brain Science, and Learning Styles in Your Mind
▶ In-Class Exercises
  • Co-creating a Syllabus
  • The Importance of Intention
  • Master Student Qualities
▶ Writing Assignments
  • Application Portfolio for Becoming a Master Student
▶ In-Text Quiz Answers
▶ Learning Styles Application
▶ Discussion Topics
▶ PowerPoint Slides
▶ Reflection Questions
▶ Assessment Questions
▶ Experiment with chapter strategies

The Instructor Web site also contains the following book-specific content:

▶ ExamView Test Bank
▶ Online Course Manual
▶ Articles from previous editions
▶ Master Student Profiles from previous editions
▶ Sample Syllabi

Student Web Site

To help your students gain a better understanding of the topics discussed in *Becoming a Master Student,* encourage your students to visit the Student Web site, which provides the following resources specific to Chapter 1:

www.cengage.com/success/bams13e

▶ Connect to Text content expands on specific topics marked with an icon within Chapter 1.
▶ Learning Style Applications invite students to cycle through the four styles of learning. In answering the four questions about Transitions posted in this chapter's Learning Styles Application, students explore the different modes and apply their new knowledge.
▶ Practice Tests allow students to see how well they understand the themes of *Becoming a Master Student.*
▶ Interactive Concept Maps promote critical thinking by highlighting related ideas to show relationships between concepts.
▶ Video Skillbuilders bring to life techniques that will help you to excel in college and beyond. The following videos should give your students more information regarding topics covered in Chapter 1:
  • Motivation and Goal Setting: Staying Motivated and Making a Contribution
  • Motivation and Goal Setting: Staying Motivated as an Adult Learner
  • Learning Styles: The VAK
  • Learning Styles: The Kolb Learning Style Inventory
▶ Remembering Cultural Differences presents readers with brief articles that touch on aspects of diversity in our rapidly changing world. For Chapter 1, the following article will prompt your students to look at contemporary issues in a new way:
  • Culture in the Classroom
▶ Master Student Profiles provide additional information on the people covered in this book feature. For Chapter 1, students will find expanded coverage and links about:
  • Lalita Booth
▶ Power Process Media contains video, PowerPoints, and audio files to take what your students have learned from the Power Processes in their book to the next level. For Chapter 1, students will find additional media on:
  • Ideas are tools

Along with the chapter-specific content, a General Resources folder is available that contains Toolboxes geared toward specific student types (Community College, Adult Learner, Student Athlete), the Plagiarism Prevention Zone, and the Career Resource Center.

1 First Steps

Master Student Map

as you read, ask yourself

what if . . .

I could create new outcomes in my life by accepting the way I am right now?

why this chapter matters . . .

Success starts with telling the truth about what *is* working—and what *isn't*—in our lives right now.

what is included . . .

how you can use this chapter . . .

- Experience the power of telling the truth about your current skills.
- Discover your preferred learning styles and develop new ones.
- Choose attitudes that promote your success.

MASTER STUDENTS in *action*

At the beginning of the term, I would have said that I learned best by doing (hands-on). But now that I have grown and expanded the boundaries of my mind's learning capabilities, I learn best with a mixture of all three (watching, listening, and doing). This is because I have come to realize that all three types of learning are connected through a balance; leading one to discover the "perfect" method of learning.

—DEONDRÉ LUCAS

Photo courtesy of Deondré Lucas

First Step:
Truth is a key to mastery

THE FIRST STEP technique is simple: Tell the truth about who you are and what you want. End of discussion. Now proceed to Chapter 2.

Well, it's not *quite* that simple.

The First Step is one of the most valuable tools in this book. It magnifies the power of all the other techniques. It is a key to becoming a master student.

Urging you to tell the truth sounds like moralizing, but there is nothing moralizing about a First Step. It is a practical, down-to-earth way to change behavior. No technique in this book has been field-tested more often or more successfully—or under tougher circumstances.

The principle of telling the truth is applied universally by people who want to turn their lives around. For members of Alcoholics Anonymous, the First Step is acknowledging that they are powerless over alcohol. For people who join Weight Watchers, the First Step is admitting how much they weigh.

It's not easy to tell the truth about our weaknesses. And for some of us, it's even harder to recognize our strengths. Maybe we don't want to brag. Maybe we're attached to a poor self-image. Yet using the First Step technique in *Becoming a Master Student* means telling the truth about our positive qualities, too.

It might help to remember that areas for improvement are often strengths taken to an extreme. The student who carefully revises her writing can make significant improvements in a term paper. If she revises too much and hands in the paper late, though, her grade might suffer. Any success strategy carried too far can backfire.

Whether written or verbal, the ways that we express our First Steps are more powerful when they are specific. For example, if you want to improve your note-taking skills, you might write, "I am an awful note taker." It would be more effective to write, "I can't read 80 percent of the notes I took in Introduction to Psychology last week, and I have no idea what was important in that class." Be just as specific about what you plan to achieve. You might declare, "I want to take legible notes that help me predict what questions will be on the final exam."

Completing the exercises in this chapter can help you tap resources you never knew you had. They're all First Steps. It's just that simple. The truth has power. ✳

journal entry 4

Discovery/Intention Statement

Create value from this chapter

Take 5 minutes to skim the Discovery Wheel exercise starting on page 27. Find one statement that describes a skill you already possess—a personal strength that will promote your success in school. Write that statement here:

_____

_____

_____

_____

The Discovery Wheel might also prompt some thoughts about skills you want to acquire. Describe one of those skills by completing the following sentence.

I discovered that . . .

_____

_____

_____

_____

Now, skim the appropriate chapter in this book for at least three articles that could help you develop this skill. For example, if you want to take more effective notes, turn to Chapter 5. List the names of your chosen articles here.

I intend to read . . .

_____

_____

_____

_____

③ exercise
Taking the First Step

The purpose of this exercise is to give you a chance to discover and acknowledge your own strengths, as well as areas for improvement. For many students, this exercise is the most difficult one in the book. To make the exercise worthwhile, do it with courage.

Some people suggest that looking at areas for improvement means focusing on personal weaknesses. They view it as a negative approach that runs counter to positive thinking. Well, perhaps. Positive thinking is a great technique. So is telling the truth, though, especially when we see the whole picture—the negative aspects as well as the positive ones.

If you admit that you can't add or subtract and that's the truth, then you have taken a strong, positive First Step toward learning basic math. In contrast, if you say that you are a terrible math student and that's not the truth, then you are programming yourself to accept unnecessary failure.

The point is to tell the truth. This exercise is similar to the Discovery Statements that appear in every chapter. The difference is that in this case, for reasons of confidentiality, you won't write down your discoveries in the book.

Be brave. If you approach this exercise with courage, you are likely to disclose some things about yourself that you wouldn't want others to read. You might even write down some truths that could get you into trouble. Do this exercise on separate sheets of paper; then hide them. Protect your privacy.

To make this exercise work, follow these suggestions.

Be specific. It is not effective to write, "I can improve my communication skills." Of course you can. Instead, write down precisely what you can *do* to improve your communication skills—for example, "I can spend more time really listening while the other person is talking, instead of thinking about what I'm going to say next."

Look beyond the classroom. What goes on outside school often has the greatest impact on your ability to be an effective student. Consider your strengths and weaknesses that you may think have nothing to do with school.

Be courageous. This exercise is a waste of time if it is done half-heartedly. Be willing to take risks. You might open a door that reveals a part of yourself that you didn't want to admit was there. The power of this technique is that once you know what is there, you can do something about it.

Part 1
Time yourself, and for 10 minutes write as fast as you can, completing each of the following sentences at least 10 times with anything that comes to mind. If you get stuck, don't stop. Just write something—even if it seems crazy.

I never succeed when I . . .

I'm not very good at . . .

Something I'd like to change about myself is . . .

Part 2
When you have completed the first part of the exercise, review what you have written, crossing off things that don't make any sense. The sentences that remain suggest possible goals for becoming a master student.

Part 3
Here's the tough part. Time yourself, and for 10 minutes write as fast as you can, completing the following sentences with anything that comes to mind. As in Part 1, complete each sentence at least 10 times. Just keep writing, even if it sounds silly.

I always succeed when I . . .

I am very good at . . .

Something I like about myself is . . .

Part 4
Review what you have written, and circle the things that you can fully celebrate. This list is a good thing to keep for those times when you question your own value and worth.

 Complete this exercise online.

4 The Discovery Wheel

The Discovery Wheel is another opportunity to tell the truth about the kind of student you are and the kind of student you want to become.

This is not a test. There are no trick questions, and the answers will have meaning only for you.

Here are two suggestions to make this exercise more effective. First, think of it as the beginning of an opportunity to change. There is another Discovery Wheel at the end of this book. You will have a chance to measure your progress there, so be honest about where you are now. Second, lighten up. A little laughter can make self-evaluations a lot more effective.

Here's how the Discovery Wheel works. By the end of this exercise, you will have filled in a circle similar to the one on this page. The Discovery Wheel circle is a picture of how you see yourself as a student. The closer the shading comes to the outer edge of the circle, the higher the evaluation of a specific skill. In the example to the right, the student has rated her reading skills low and her note-taking skills high.

The terms *high* and *low* are not meant to reflect a judgment. The Discovery Wheel is not a permanent picture of who you are. It is a picture of how you view your strengths and weaknesses as a student today. To begin this exercise, read the following statements and award yourself points for each one, using the point system described below. Then add up your point total for each section, and shade the Discovery Wheel on page 30 to the appropriate level.

> **5 points:** This statement is always or almost always true of me.
>
> **4 points:** This statement is often true of me.
>
> **3 points:** This statement is true of me about half the time.
>
> **2 points:** This statement is seldom true of me.
>
> **1 point:** This statement is never or almost never true of me.

 Complete this exercise online.

1. _____ I enjoy learning.

2. _____ I understand and apply the concept of multiple intelligences.

3. _____ I connect my courses to my purpose for being in school.

4. _____ I make a habit of assessing my personal strengths and areas for improvement.

5. _____ I am satisfied with how I am progressing toward achieving my goals.

6. _____ I use my knowledge of learning styles to support my success in school.

7. _____ I am willing to consider any idea that can help me succeed in school—even if I initially disagree with that idea.

8. _____ I regularly remind myself of the benefits I intend to get from my education.

> _____ **Total score (1) Attitude**

1. _____ I set long-term goals and periodically review them.

2. _____ I set short-term goals to support my long-term goals.

3. _____ I write a plan for each day and each week.

4. _____ I assign priorities to what I choose to do each day.

5. _____ I plan review time so I don't have to cram before tests.

6. _____ I plan regular recreation time.

7. _____ I adjust my study time to meet the demands of individual courses.

8. _____ I have adequate time each day to accomplish what I plan.

_____ **Total score (2) Time**

1. _____ I am confident of my ability to remember.

2. _____ I can remember people's names.

3. _____ At the end of a lecture, I can summarize what was presented.

4. _____ I apply techniques that enhance my memory skills.

5. _____ I can recall information when I'm under pressure.

6. _____ I remember important information clearly and easily.

7. _____ I can jog my memory when I have difficulty recalling.

8. _____ I can relate new information to what I've already learned.

_____ **Total score (3) Memory**

1. _____ I preview and review reading assignments.

2. _____ When reading, I ask myself questions about the material.

3. _____ I underline or highlight important passages when reading.

4. _____ When I read textbooks, I am alert and awake.

5. _____ I relate what I read to my life.

6. _____ I select a reading strategy to fit the type of material I'm reading.

7. _____ I take effective notes when I read.

8. _____ When I don't understand what I'm reading, I note my questions and find answers.

_____ **Total score (4) Reading**

1. _____ When I am in class, I focus my attention.

2. _____ I take notes in class.

3. _____ I am aware of various methods for taking notes and choose those that work best for me.

4. _____ I distinguish important material and note key phrases in a lecture.

5. _____ I copy down material that the instructor writes on the chalkboard or overhead display.

6. _____ I can put important concepts into my own words.

7. _____ My notes are valuable for review.

8. _____ I review class notes within 24 hours.

_____ **Total score (5) Notes**

1. _____ I use techniques to manage stress related to exams.

2. _____ I manage my time during exams and am able to complete them.

3. _____ I am able to predict test questions.

4. _____ I adapt my test-taking strategy to the kind of test I'm taking.

5. _____ I understand what essay questions ask and can answer them completely and accurately.

6. _____ I start reviewing for tests at the beginning of the term.

7. _____ I continue reviewing for tests throughout the term.

8. _____ My sense of personal worth is independent of my test scores.

_____ **Total score (6) Tests**

1. _____ I have flashes of insight and think of solutions to problems at unusual times.

2. _____ I use brainstorming to generate solutions to a variety of problems.

3. _____ When I get stuck on a creative project, I use specific methods to get unstuck.

4. _____ I see problems and tough choices as opportunities for learning and personal growth.

5. _____ I am willing to consider different points of view and alternate solutions.

6. _____ I can detect common errors in logic.

7. _____ I construct viewpoints by drawing on information and ideas from many sources.

8. _____ As I share my viewpoints with others, I am open to their feedback.

_____ **Total score (7) Thinking**

1. _____ I am candid with others about who I am, what I feel, and what I want.

2. _____ Other people tell me that I am a good listener.

3. _____ I can communicate my upset and anger without blaming others.

4. _____ I can make friends and create valuable relationships in a new setting.

5. _____ I am open to being with people I don't especially like in order to learn from them.

6. _____ I can effectively plan and research a large writing assignment.

7. _____ I create first drafts without criticizing my writing, then edit later for clarity, accuracy, and coherence.

8. _____ I know ways to prepare and deliver effective speeches.

_____ **Total score (8) Communicating**

1. _____ I build rewarding relationships with people from backgrounds different from my own.

2. _____ I use critical thinking to overcome stereotypes.

3. _____ I point out examples of discrimination and sexual harassment and effectively respond to them.

4. _____ I am constantly learning ways to thrive with diversity in school and/or the workplace— attitudes and behaviors that will support my success.

5. _____ I can effectively resolve conflict with people from other cultures.

6. _____ My writing and speaking are free of sexist expressions.

7. _____ I take diversity into account when assuming a leadership role.

8. _____ I respond effectively to changing demographics in my country and community.

_____ **Total score (9) Diversity**

1. _____ I am in control of my personal finances.

2. _____ I can access a variety of resources to finance my education.

3. _____ I am confident that I will have enough money to complete my education.

4. _____ I take on debts carefully and repay them on time.

5. _____ I have long-range financial goals and a plan to meet them.

6. _____ I make regular deposits to a savings account.

7. _____ I pay off the balance on credit card accounts each month.

8. _____ I can have fun without spending money.

_____ **Total score (10) Money**

1. _____ I have enough energy to study and work—and still enjoy other areas of my life.

2. _____ If the situation calls for it, I have enough reserve energy to put in a long day.

3. _____ The way I eat supports my long-term health.

4. _____ The way I eat is independent of my feelings of self-worth.

5. _____ I exercise regularly to maintain a healthy weight.

6. _____ My emotional health supports my ability to learn.

7. _____ I notice changes in my physical condition and respond effectively.

8. _____ I am in control of any alcohol or other drugs I put into my body.

_____ **Total score (11) Health**

1. _____ I see learning as a lifelong process.

2. _____ I relate school to what I plan to do for the rest of my life.

3. _____ I learn by contributing to others in need.

4. _____ I have a written career plan and update it regularly.

5. _____ I am gaining skills to support my success in the workplace.

6. _____ I take responsibility for the quality of my education—and my life.

7. _____ I live by a set of values that translates into daily actions.

8. _____ I am willing to accept challenges even when I'm not sure how to meet them.

_____ **Total score (12) Purpose**

Filling in your Discovery Wheel

Using the total score from each category, shade in each section of the Discovery Wheel. Use different colors, if you want. For example, you could use green to denote areas you want to work on. When you have finished, complete the Journal Entry on the next page.

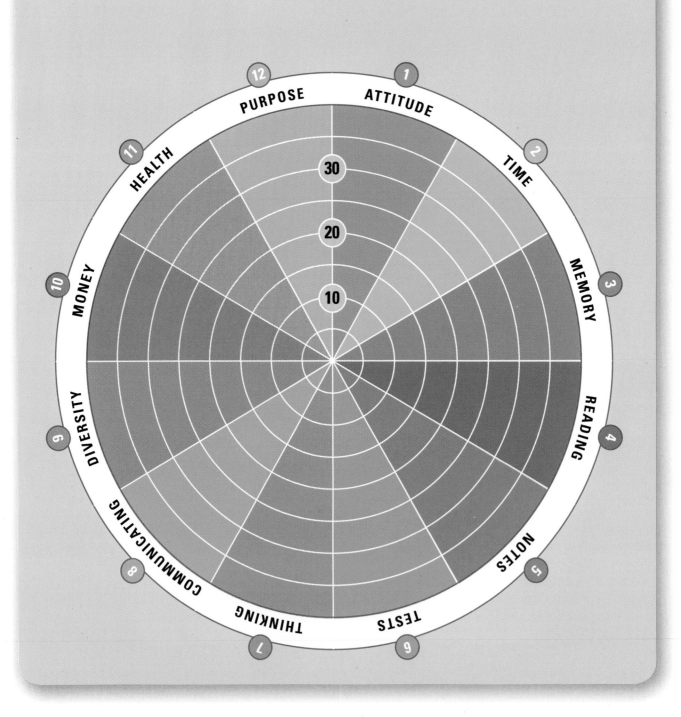

Discovery/Intention Statement

Roll your Discovery Wheel

Now that you have completed your Discovery Wheel, it's time to get a sense of its weight, shape, and balance. Can you imagine running your hands around it? If you could lift it, would it feel light or heavy? How would it sound if it rolled down a hill? Would it roll very far? Would it wobble? Make your observations without judging the wheel as good or bad. Simply be with the picture you have created.

After you have spent a few minutes studying your Discovery Wheel, complete the following sentences in the spaces below. Don't worry about what to write. Just put down whatever comes to mind. Remember, this is not a test.

This wheel is an accurate picture of my ability as a student because . . .

_____

_____

My self-evaluation surprises me because . . .

_____

_____

The two areas in which I am strongest are . . .

_____

_____

The areas in which I want to improve are . . .

_____

_____

I want to concentrate on improving these areas because . . .

_____

_____

Now, select one of your discoveries, and describe how you intend to benefit from it. Complete the statement below.

To gain some practical value from this Discovery, I will . . .

_____

_____

mastering technology

SUPPLEMENT YOUR TEXT WITH COMPUTER RESOURCES

Purchasing a textbook often gives you access to a suite of related resources, including companion Web sites that are regularly updated and other digital media. One way to get your money's worth from a text is to fully use these resources, even if they are not assigned:

• To begin, check out the Student Web site for *Becoming a Master Student*. There you'll discover ways to take your involvement with this book to a deeper level. For example, access the Web site to do an online version of the Discovery Wheel exercise. Then look for videos, additional exercises, articles, PowerPoint slides, practice tests, and forms.

• Look for Web sites created by your instructors for specific courses. Ask them for the URLs. Check your course syllabus for more details. When your course does have a Web site, explore its features in detail.

• Using key words related to your course, search the Internet for related sites. Look for content that expands on topics presented in class.

• Find out if your instructors offer "virtual office hours"— times when they are willing to answer questions via e-mail or other electronic messaging.

• Search for online homework help in specific subjects. Many schools and public libraries post such sites.

• Visit your school's Web site. Look for lists of campus organizations, extracurricular activities, and student services.

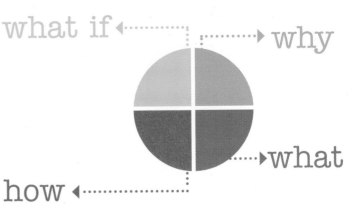

Learning styles: Discovering how you learn

RIGHT NOW, you are investing substantial amounts of time, money, and energy in your education. What you get in return for this investment depends on how well you understand the process of learning and use it to your advantage.

If you don't understand learning, you might feel bored or confused in class. After getting a low grade, you might have no idea how to respond. Over time, frustration can mount to the point where you question the value of being in school.

Some students answer that question by dropping out of school. These students lose a chance to create the life they want. Society loses the contributions of educated workers.

You can prevent that outcome. Gain strategies for going beyond boredom and confusion. Discover new options for achieving goals, solving problems, listening more fully, speaking more persuasively, and resolving conflicts between people. Start by understanding the different ways that people create meaning from their experience and change their behavior. In other words, learn about *how* we learn.

We learn by perceiving and processing

When we learn well, says psychologist David Kolb, two things happen.[1] First, we *perceive*— that is, we notice events and take in new experiences. Second, we *process,* or deal with, experiences in a way that helps us make sense of them.

Some people especially enjoy perceiving through *concrete experience.* They like to absorb information through their five senses. They learn by getting directly involved in new experiences. When solving problems, they rely on intuition as much as intellect. These people typically function well in unstructured classes that allow them to take initiative.

Other people favor perceiving by *abstract conceptualization.* They take in information best when they can think about it as a subject separate from themselves. They analyze, intellectualize, and create

theories. Often these people take a scientific approach to problem solving and excel in traditional classrooms.

People also process experiences differently. Some people favor processing information by *reflective observation.* They prefer to stand back, watch what is going on, and think about it. They consider several points of view as they attempt to make sense of things and generate many ideas about how something happens. They value patience, good judgment, and a thorough approach to learning.

Other people like to process experience by *active experimentation.* They prefer to jump in and start doing things immediately. These people do not mind taking risks as they attempt to make sense of things; risk taking helps them learn. They are results oriented and look for practical ways to apply what they have learned.

Perceiving and processing—an example

Suppose that you get a new cell phone. It has more features than any phone you've used before. You have many options for learning how to use it. For example, you could do any of the following:

- Just get your hands on the phone right away, press some buttons, and see if you can dial a number or send a text message.

- Read the instruction manual and view help screens on the phone before you try to make a call.

- Recall experiences you've had with phones in the past and what you've learned by watching other people use their cell phones.

- Ask a friend who owns the same type of phone to coach you as you experiment with making calls and sending messages.

These actions illustrate the different ways of perceiving and processing:

- Getting your hands on the phone right away and seeing if you can make it work is an example of learning through concrete experience.

- Reading the manual and help screens before you use the phone is an example of learning through abstract conceptualization.
- Recalling what you've experienced in the past is an example of learning through reflective observation.
- Asking a friend to coach you through a hands-on activity with the phone is an example of learning through active experimentation.

Four modes of learning and four questions

Your learning style is the unique way in which you blend the possible ways of perceiving and processing experience. Learning styles can be described in many ways. To keep things simple, just think in terms of four *modes* of learning.

Mode 1 learners are concrete and reflective. They seek a purpose for new information and a personal connection with the content. They want to know that a course matters, and how it challenges or fits in with what they already know. These learners embrace new ideas that relate directly to their current interests and career plans. In summary, Mode 1 learners ask, *Why* learn this?

Mode 2 learners are abstract and reflective. They crave information. When learning something, they want to know the main facts, ideas, and procedures. They seek a theory to explain events and are interested in what experts have to say. Often these learners like ideas that are presented in a logical, organized way. They break a subject down into its key elements or steps and master each one in a systematic way. Mode 2 learners ask, *What* is the content?

Mode 3 learners are abstract and active. They hunger for an opportunity to try out what they're studying. They want to take theories and test them by putting them into practice. These learners thrive when they have well-defined tasks, guided practice, and frequent feedback. Mode 3 learners ask, *How* does this work?

Mode 4 learners are concrete and active. They get excited about going beyond classroom assignments. They apply what they're learning in various situations and use theories to solve real problems. Mode 4 learners ask, *What if* I tried this in a different setting?

The four modes—an example

Becoming a Master Student is specifically designed to move you through all four modes of learning.

At the beginning of each chapter, you complete a Journal Entry designed to connect the chapter content to your current life experience. The aim is to help you see the chapter's possible benefits and discover a purpose for reading further. You answer the Mode 1 question—*Why* learn this?

Next, you read articles that are filled with ideas and suggestions for succeeding in school and the workplace. All these readings are answers to the Mode 2 question— *What* is the content?

You also use exercises to practice new skills and facilitate feedback from your instructor and other students. These exercises are answers to the Mode 3 question—*How* does this work?

Finally, at the end of each chapter, a Put It to Work article and Skills Snapshot exercise help you apply the chapter content to different situations and choose your next step toward mastery. You discover answers to the Mode 4 question—*What if* I tried this in a different setting?

Also notice the Master Student Map at the beginning of each chapter. It presents the chapter content as answers to these four questions. For example, the Master Student Map for this chapter (page 24) suggests *why* this chapter matters: "Success starts with telling the truth about what *is* working—and what *isn't*—in our lives right now." There's a list of *what* topics are included and suggestions for *how* you can use this chapter. Finally, you're encouraged to ask, "*What if* I could create new outcomes in my life by accepting the way I am right now?"

Becoming a flexible learner

Kolb believes that effective learners are flexible. They can learn using all four modes. They consistently ask *Why? What? How?* and *What if?*—and use a full range of activities to find the answers.

Becoming a flexible learner promotes your success in school and in the workplace. By developing all four modes of learning, you can excel in many types of courses. You can learn from instructors with many different styles of teaching. You can expand your options for declaring a major and choosing a career. You can experiment with a variety of strategies and create new options for learning *anything*.

Above all, you can recover your natural gift for learning. Rediscover a world where the boundaries between learning and fun, between work and play, all disappear. While immersing yourself in new experiences, blend the sophistication of an adult with the wonder of a child. This path is one that you can travel for the rest of your life.

The following elements of this chapter are designed to help you take the next steps toward becoming a flexible learner:

- To discover how you currently prefer to learn, take the Learning Style Inventory that follows.

- Read the article "Using your Learning Style Profile to Succeed" to learn ways to expand on your preferences.

- For additional perspectives on learning styles, see the articles "Claim your Multiple Intelligences" and "Learning by Seeing, Hearing, and Moving—The VAK System."

Directions for completing the Learning Style Inventory

To help you become more aware of learning styles, Kolb developed the Learning Style Inventory (LSI). This inventory is included on the next several pages. Responding to the items in the LSI can help you discover a lot about ways you learn.

The LSI is not a test. There are no right or wrong answers. Your goal is simply to develop a profile of your current learning style. So, take the LSI quickly. You might find it useful to recall a recent time when you learned something new at school, at home, or at work. However, do not agonize over your responses.

Note that the LSI consists of twelve sentences, each with four different endings. You will read each sentence, and then write a "4" next to the ending that best describes the way you currently learn. Then you will continue ranking the other endings with a "3," "2," or "1," representing the ending that least describes you. You must rank each ending. *Do not leave any endings blank.* Use each number only once for each question.

Following are more specific directions:

1. Read the instructions at the top of page LSI-1. When you understand example A, you are ready to begin.

2. Before you write on page LSI-1, remove the sheet of paper following page LSI-2.

3. While writing on page LSI-1, press firmly so that your answers will show up on page LSI-3.

4. After you complete the twelve items on page LSI-1, go to page LSI-3. ✻

 Find more information and examples related to learning styles online.

journal entry 6

Discovery Statement

Prepare for the Learning Style Inventory

As a warm-up for the LSI and articles that follow, spend a minute or two thinking about times in the past when you felt successful at learning. Underline or highlight any of the following statements that describe those situations:

I was in a highly structured setting, with a lot of directions about what to do and feedback on how well I did at each step.

I was free to learn at my own pace and in my own way.

I learned as part of a small group.

I learned mainly by working alone in a quiet place.

I learned in a place where there was a lot of activity going on.

I learned by forming pictures in my mind.

I learned by *doing* something—moving around, touching something, or trying out a process for myself.

I learned by talking to myself or explaining ideas to other people.

I got the "big picture" before I tried to understand the details.

I listened to a lecture and then thought about it after class.

I read a book or article and then thought about it afterward.

I used a variety of media—such as a video, audio recording, or computer—to assist my learning.

I went beyond taking notes and wrote in a personal journal.

I was considering where to attend school and knew I had to actually set foot on each campus before choosing.

I was shopping for a car and paid more attention to how I felt about test driving each one than to the sticker prices or mileage estimates.

I was thinking about going to a movie and carefully read the reviews before choosing one.

Review the list for any patterns in the way you prefer to learn. If you see any patterns, briefly describe them here.

_____

_____

_____

_____

Learning Style Inventory

Before completing the items, remove the sheet of paper following this page. While writing, press firmly.

1. When I learn: _____ I like to deal with my feelings. _____ I like to think about ideas. _____ I like to be doing things. _____ I like to watch and listen.

2. I learn best when: _____ I listen and watch carefully. _____ I rely on logical thinking. _____ I trust my hunches and feelings. _____ I work hard to get things done.

3. When I am learning: _____ I tend to reason things out. _____ I am responsible about things. _____ I am quiet and reserved. _____ I have strong feelings and reactions.

4. I learn by: _____ feeling. _____ doing. _____ watching. _____ thinking.

5. When I learn: _____ I am open to new experiences. _____ I look at all sides of issues. _____ I like to analyze things, breaking them down into their parts. _____ I like to try things out.

6. When I am learning: _____ I am an observing person. _____ I am an active person. _____ I am an intuitive person _____ I am a logical person.

7. I learn best from: _____ observation. _____ personal relationships. _____ rational theories. _____ a chance to try out and practice.

8. When I learn: _____ I like to see results from my work. _____ I like ideas and theories. _____ I take my time before acting. _____ I feel personally involved in things.

9. I learn best when: _____ I rely on my observations. _____ I rely on my feelings. _____ I can try things out for myself. _____ I rely on my ideas.

10. When I am learning: _____ I am a reserved person. _____ I am an accepting person. _____ I am a responsible person. _____ I am a rational person.

11. When I learn: _____ I get involved. _____ I like to observe. _____ I evaluate things. _____ I like to be active.

12. I learn best when: _____ I analyze ideas. _____ I am receptive and open-minded. _____ I am careful. _____ I am practical.

Take a snapshot of your learning styles

This page is intended to be completed as a culminating exercise. Before you work on this exercise, complete the Learning Styles Inventory and read the following articles:

Learning styles: Discovering how you learn, page 32

Using your learning style profile to succeed, page 35

Claim your multiple intelligences, page 39

Learning by seeing, hearing, and moving—the VAK system, page 42

An inventory of your learning styles is just a snapshot that gives a picture of who you are today. Your answers are not right or wrong. Your score does not dictate who you can become in the future. The key questions are simply "How do I currently learn?" and "How can I become a more successful learner?"

Take a few minutes right now to complete the following sentences describing your latest insights into the way you learn. When you finish, plan to follow up on those insights.

If someone asked me, "What do you mean by learning styles, and can you give me an example?" I'd say . . .

I would describe my current learning style(s) as . . .

If someone asked me to define intelligence, I'd say . . .

When learning well, I tend to use the following senses . . .

I apply my knowledge of learning styles and multiple intelligences by using certain strategies, such as . . .

When I study or work with people whose learning styles differ from mine, I will respond by . . .

To explore new learning styles, I will . . .

Remove this sheet before completing the Learning Style Inventory.

This page is inserted to ensure that the other writing you do in this book doesn't show through on page LSI-3.

Remove this sheet before completing the Learning Style Inventory.

This page is inserted to ensure that the other writing you do in this book doesn't show through on page LSI-3.

Scoring your Inventory

Now that you have taken the Learning Style Inventory, it's time to fill out the Learning Style Graph (page LSI-5) and interpret your results. To do this, please follow the next five steps.

1 First, add up all of the numbers you gave to the items marked with brown **F** letters. Then write down that total to the right in the blank next to "**Brown F**." Next, add up all of the numbers for "**Teal W**,"

"**Purple T**," and "**Orange D**," and also write down those totals in the blanks to the right.

2 Add the four totals to arrive at a GRAND TOTAL and write down that figure in the blank to the right. (Note: The grand total should equal 120. If you have a different amount, go back and re-add the colored letters; it was probably just an addition error.) Now remove this page and continue with Step 3 on page LSI-5.

F	T	D	W
W	T	F	D
T	D	W	F
F	D	W	T
F	W	T	D
W	D	F	T
W	F	T	D
D	T	W	F
W	F	D	T
W	F	D	T
F	W	T	D
T	F	W	D

Remove this page after you have
completed Steps 1 and 2 on page LSI-3.
Then continue with Step 3 on page LSI-5.

Learning Style Graph

3 Remove the sheet of paper that follows this page. Then transfer your totals from Step 1 on page LSI-3 to the lines on the Learning Style Graph below. On the brown (F) line, find the number that corresponds to your "**Brown F**" total from page LSI-3. Then write an X on this number. Do the same for your "**Teal W**," "**Purple T**," and "**Orange D**" totals. The graph on this page is yours to keep and to refer to and the graph on page LSI-7 is for you to turn into your professor if he or she requires it.

4 Now, pressing firmly, draw four straight lines to connect the four X's and shade in the area to form a kite. (For an example, see the illustration to the right.) This is your learning style profile. Each X that you placed on these lines indicates your preference for a different aspect of learning:

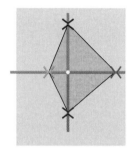

Concrete experience ("feeling"). The number where you put your X on this line indicates your preference for learning things that have personal meaning and have connections to experiences in your life. The higher your score on this line, the more you like to learn things that you feel are important and relevant to yourself.

Reflective observation ("watching"). Your number on this line indicates how important it is for you to reflect on the things you are learning. If your score is high on this line, you probably find it important to watch others as they learn about an assignment and then report on it to the class. You probably like to plan things out and take the time to make sure that you fully understand a topic.

Abstract conceptualization ("thinking"). Your number on this line indicates your preference for learning ideas, facts, and figures. If your score is high on this line, you probably like to absorb many concepts and gather lots of information on a new topic.

Active experimentation ("doing"). Your number on this line indicates your preference for applying ideas, using trial and error, and practicing what you learn. If your score is high on this line, you probably enjoy hands-on activities that allow you to test out ideas to see what works.

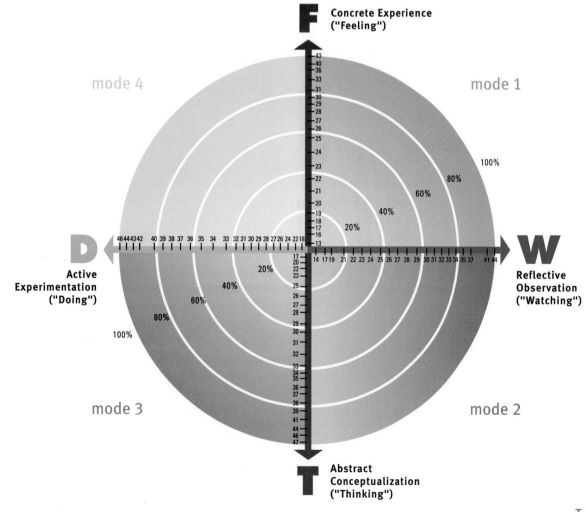

Learning styles across the curriculum

You can get another perspective on learning styles by thinking about ways to succeed in the various subjects that you study. For example, a math course will draw on different ways of perceiving and processing information than a course in African American literature or modern dance. When you feel stuck in a particular subject, see if you can get unstuck by applying a strategy based on your knowledge of learning styles. The following chart offers some examples. Start with them, and create more on your own.

Subject Area	Possible Strategies for Mastery
Humanities: English, literature, public speaking, history, religion, philosophy, fine arts	• Deepen your reading skills by previewing and reviewing each assignment (see Chapter 4: Reading). • Keep a dictionary handy and create an updated list of new words and their definitions. • Experiment with several different formats for taking notes (see Chapter 5: Notes). • Keep a personal journal to practice writing and make connections between the authors and ideas that you're studying. • Take part in class discussions and welcome chances to speak in front of groups.
Math and natural sciences: algebra, geometry, calculus, chemistry, biology, physics	• Before registering for a course, make sure that you are adequately prepared through prior course work. • In your notes, highlight basic principles—definitions, assumptions, axioms. • Learn concepts in the sequence presented by your instructor. • If you feel confused, ask a question immediately. • Attend all classes, practice solving problems every day, and check your work carefully. • Translate word problems into images or symbols; translate images and symbols into words. • Balance abstract ideas with concrete experiences, including laboratory sessions and study groups. • Take math courses back to back so you can apply what you learn in one level of a math course immediately to the next level.
Social sciences: sociology, psychology, economics, political science, anthropology, geography	• Pay special attention to theories—key terms and statements that are used to explain relationships between observations and predict events. • Expect complex and contradictory theories, and ask your instructor about ways to resolve disagreements among experts in the field. • Ask your instructor to explain the scientific method and how it is used to arrive at theories in each social science. • Ask about the current state of evidence for each theory. • Ask for examples of a theory and look for them in your daily life.
Foreign languages: learning to speak, read, and write any language that is new to you	• Pay special attention to the "rules"—principles of grammar, noun forms, and verb tense. For each principle, list correct and incorrect examples. • Spend some time reading, writing, or speaking the language every day. • Welcome the opportunity to practice speaking in class, where you can get immediate feedback. • Start or join a study group in each of your language classes. • Spend time with people who are already skilled in speaking the language. • Travel to a country where the language is widely spoken. • Similar to math courses, take your language courses back to back to ensure fluency.

Remove this sheet before completing the Learning Style Graph

This page is inserted to ensure that the other writing you do in this book doesn't show through on page LSI-7.

Remove this sheet before completing the Learning Style Graph

This page is inserted to ensure that the other writing you do in this book doesn't show through on page LSI-7.

Returning to the big picture about learning styles

This chapter introduces many ideas about how people learn—four modes, multiple intelligences, and the VAK system. That's a lot of information! And these are just a few of the available theories. You may have heard about inventories other than the Learning Style Inventory, such as the Myers-Briggs Type Indicator® (MBTI®) Instrument.* Do an Internet search on *learning styles,* and you'll find many more.

To prevent confusion, remember that there is one big idea behind these theories about learning styles. They all promote *metacognition* (pronounced "metta-cog-NI-shun"). *Meta* means "beyond" or "above." *Cognition* refers to everything that goes on inside your brain—perceiving, thinking, and feeling. So, metacognition refers to your ability to view your attitudes and behaviors from beyond—that is, understand more fully the way you learn. From that perspective, you can choose to think and act in new ways. *Metacognition is one of the main benefits of higher education.*

In addition, theories about learning styles share the following insights:

- People differ in important ways.
- We can see differences as strengths—not deficits.
- Relationships improve when we take differences into account.
- Learning is continuous—it is a *process,* as well as a series of outcomes.
- We *create* knowledge rather than simply absorbing it.
- We have our own preferences for learning.
- We can often succeed by matching our activities with our preferences.
- Our preferences can expand as we experiment with new learning strategies.
- The deepest learning takes place when we embrace a variety of styles and strategies.

Remember that teachers in your life will come and go. Some will be more skilled than others. None of them will be perfect. With a working knowledge of learning styles, you can view any course as one step along a path to learning what you want, using the ways that *you* choose to learn. Along this path toward mastery, you become your own best teacher.

*MBTI and Myer-Briggs Type Indicator are registered trademarks of Consulting Psychologists Press, Inc.

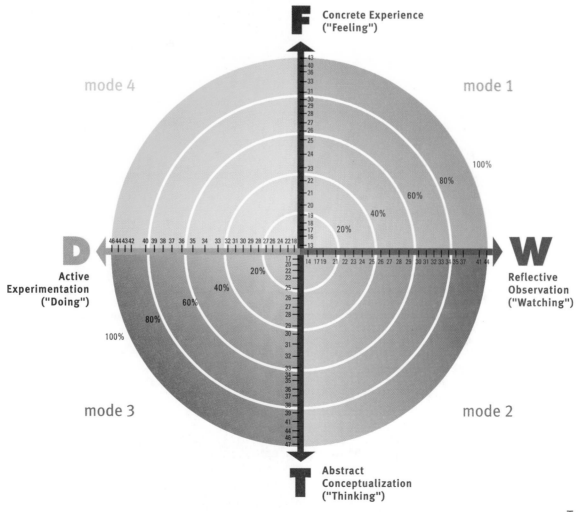

Balancing your preferences

The chart below identifies some of the natural talents as well as challenges for people who have a strong preference for any one mode of learning. For example, if most of your kite is in Mode 2 of the Learning Style Graph, then look at the lower right-hand corner of the following chart to see if this is an accurate description of yourself.

After reviewing the description of your preferred learning mode, read all of the sections for the other modes that start with the words "People with other preferred modes." These sections explain what actions you can take to become a more balanced learner.

Concrete Experience

mode 4

Strengths:
• Getting things done
• Leadership
• Risk taking

Too much of this mode can lead to:
• Trivial improvements
• Meaningless activity

Too little of this mode can lead to:
• Work not completed on time
• Impractical plans
• Lack of motivation to achieve goals

People with other preferred modes can develop Mode 4 by:
• Making a commitment to objectives
• Seeking new opportunities
• Influencing and leading others
• Being personally involved
• Dealing with people

mode 1

Strengths:
• Imaginative ability
• Understanding people
• Recognizing problems
• Brainstorming

Too much of this mode can lead to:
• Feeling paralyzed by alternatives
• Inability to make decisions

Too little of this mode can lead to:
• Lack of ideas
• Not recognizing problems and opportunities

People with other preferred modes can develop Mode 1 by:
• Being aware of other people's feelings
• Being sensitive to values
• Listening with an open mind
• Gathering information
• Imagining the implications of ambiguous situations

Active Experimentation ← → **Reflective Observation**

Strengths:
• Problem solving
• Decision making
• Deductive reasoning
• Defining problems

Too much of this mode can lead to:
• Solving the wrong problem
• Hasty decision making

Too little of this mode can lead to:
• Lack of focus
• Reluctance to consider alternatives
• Scattered thoughts

People with other preferred modes can develop Mode 3 by:
• Creating new ways of thinking and doing
• Experimenting with fresh ideas
• Choosing the best solution
• Setting goals
• Making decisions

Strengths:
• Planning
• Creating models
• Defining problems
• Developing theories

Too much of this mode can lead to:
• Vague ideals ("castles in the air")
• Lack of practical application

Too little of this mode can lead to:
• Inability to learn from mistakes
• No sound basis for work
• No systematic approach

People with other preferred modes can develop Mode 2 by:
• Organizing information
• Building conceptual models
• Testing theories and ideas
• Designing experiments
• Analyzing quantitative data

mode 3

mode 2

Abstract Conceptualization

Using your learning style profile to succeed

Develop all four modes of learning

Each mode of learning highlighted in the Learning Style Inventory represents a unique blend of concrete experience, reflective observation, abstract conceptualization, and active experimentation. You can explore new learning styles simply by adopting new habits related to each of these activities. Consider the following suggestions as places to start. Also remember that any idea about learning styles will make a difference in your life only when it leads to changes in your behavior.

To gain concrete experiences:

- See a live demonstration or performance related to your course content.

- Engage your emotions by reading a novel or seeing a video related to your course.

- Interview an expert in the subject you're learning or a master practitioner of a skill you want to gain.

- Conduct role-plays, exercises, or games based on your courses.

- Conduct an informational interview with someone in your chosen career or shadow that person for a day on the job.

- Look for a part-time job, internship, or volunteer experience that complements what you do in class.

- Deepen your understanding of another culture and extend your foreign language skills by studying abroad.

To become more reflective:

- Keep a personal journal, and write about connections among your courses.

- Form a study group to discuss and debate topics related to your courses.

- Set up a Web site, computer bulletin board, e-mail listserv, or online chat room related to your major.

- Create analogies to make sense of concepts; for instance, see if you can find similarities between career planning and putting together a puzzle.

- Visit your course instructor during office hours to ask questions.

- During social events with friends and relatives, briefly explain what your courses are about.

To develop abstract thinking:

- Take notes on your reading in outline form; consider using word-processing software with an outlining feature.

- Supplement assigned texts with other books, magazine and newspaper articles, and related Web sites.

- Attend lectures given by your current instructors and others who teach the same subjects.

- Take ideas presented in text or lectures and translate them into visual form—tables, charts, diagrams, and maps (see Chapter 5: Notes).

- Make hand-drawn visuals and use computer software to re-create them with more complex graphics and animation.

To become more active:

- Conduct laboratory experiments or field observations.

- Go to settings where theories are being applied or tested.

- Make predictions based on theories you learn, and then see if events in your daily life confirm your predictions.

- Try out a new behavior described in a lecture or reading, and observe its consequences in your life.

Use the modes while choosing courses

Remember your learning style profile when you're thinking about which classes to take and how to study for each class. Look for a fit between your preferred mode of learning and your course work.

If you prefer Mode 1, for example, look for courses that sound interesting and seem worthwhile to you. If you prefer Mode 2, consider classes that center on lectures, reading, and discussion. If you prefer Mode 3, choose courses that include demonstrations, lab sessions, role-playing, and others ways to take action. And if you enjoy Mode 4, look for courses that could apply to many situations in your life—at work, at home, and in your relationships.

You won't always be able to match your courses to your learning styles. View those situations as opportunities to practice becoming a flexible learner. By developing your skills in all four modes, you can excel in many types of courses. Also, see the sidebar "Use the modes to learn from *any* instructor" for specific strategies to make the most out of all your classes, regardless of your learning style.

Use the modes to explore your major

If you enjoy learning in Mode 1, you probably value creativity and human relationships. When choosing a major, consider the arts, English, psychology, or political science.

If Mode 2 is your preference, then you enjoy gathering information and building theories. A major related to math or science might be ideal for you.

If Mode 3 is your favorite, then you like to diagnose problems, arrive at solutions, and use technology. A major related to health care, engineering, or economics is a logical choice for you.

And if your preference is Mode 4, you probably enjoy taking the initiative, implementing decisions, teaching, managing projects, and moving quickly from planning into action. Consider a major in business or education.

As you prepare to declare a major, remain flexible. Use your knowledge of learning styles to open up possibilities rather than restrict them. Remember that regardless of your mode, you can excel at any job or major; it just may mean developing new skills in other modes.

Use the modes to explore your career

Knowing about learning styles becomes especially useful when planning your career.

People who excel at Mode 1 are often skilled at tuning in to the feelings of clients and coworkers. These people can listen with an open mind, tolerate confusion, be sensitive to people's feelings, open up to problems that are difficult to define, and brainstorm a variety of solutions. If you like Mode 1, you may be drawn to a career in counseling, social services, the ministry, or another field that centers on human relationships. You might also enjoy a career in the performing arts.

People who prefer Mode 2 like to do research and work with ideas. They are skilled at gathering data, interpreting information, and summarizing—arriving at the big picture. They may excel at careers that center on science, math, technical communications, or planning. Mode 2 learners may also work as college teachers, lawyers, technical writers, or journalists.

People who like Mode 3 are drawn to solving problems, making decisions, and checking on progress toward goals. Careers in medicine, engineering, information technology, or another applied science are often ideal for them.

People who enjoy Mode 4 like to influence and lead others. These people are often described as "doers" and "risk takers." They like to take action and complete projects. Mode 4 learners often excel at managing, negotiating, selling, training, and teaching. They might also work for a government agency.

Keep in mind that there is no strict match between certain learning styles and certain careers. Learning is essential to success in all careers. Also, any career can attract people with a variety of learning styles. For instance, the health care field is large enough to include people who prefer Mode 3 and become family physicians, *and* people who prefer Mode 2 and become medical researchers.

Expect to encounter different styles

As higher education and the workplace become more diverse and technology creates a global marketplace, you'll meet people who differ from you in profound ways. Your fellow students and coworkers will behave in ways that express a variety of preferences for perceiving information, processing ideas, and acting on what they learn. Consider these examples:

- A roommate who's continually moving while studying—reciting facts out loud, pacing, and gesturing—probably prefers concrete experience and learning by taking action.

- A coworker who talks continually on the phone about a project may prefer to learn by listening, talking, and forging key relationships.

- A supervisor who excels at abstract conceptualization may want to see detailed project plans and budgets submitted in writing, well before a project swings into high gear.

- A study group member who always takes the initiative, manages the discussion, delegates any work involved, and follows up with everyone probably prefers active experimentation.

Differences in learning style can be a stumbling block—or an opportunity. When differences intersect, there is the potential for conflict, as well as for creativity. Succeeding with peers often means seeing the classroom and workplace as a laboratory for learning from experience. Resolving conflict and learning from mistakes are all part of the learning cycle.

Look for specific clues to another person's style

You can learn a lot about other people's styles of learning simply by observing them during the workday. Look for clues such these:

Approaches to a task that requires learning. Some people process new information and ideas by sitting quietly and reading or writing. When learning to use a piece of equipment, such as a new computer, they'll read the instruction manual first. Others will skip the manual, unpack all the boxes, and start setting up equipment. And others might ask a more experienced colleague to guide them in person, step by step.

Word choice. Some people like to process information visually. You might hear them say, "I'll look into that" or "Give me the big picture first." Others like to solve problems verbally: "Let's talk though this problem" or "I hear you!" In contrast, some people focus on body sensations ("This product feels great") or action ("Let's run with this idea and see what happens").

Body language. Notice how often coworkers or classmates make eye contact with you and how close they sit or stand next to you. Observe their gestures, as well as the volume and tone of their voice.

Content preferences. Notice what subjects coworkers or classmates openly discuss and which topics they avoid. Some people talk freely about their feelings, their families, and even their personal finances. Others choose to remain silent on such topics and stick to work-related matters.

Process preferences. Look for patterns in the way your coworkers and classmates meet goals. When attending meetings, for example, some of them might stick closely to the agenda and keep an eye on the clock. Other people might prefer to go with the flow, even if it means working an extra hour or scrapping the agenda.

Accommodate differing styles

Once you've discovered differences in styles, look for ways to accommodate them. As you collaborate on projects with other students or coworkers, keep the following suggestions in mind:

Remember that some people want to reflect on the big picture first. When introducing a project plan, you might say, "This process has four major steps." Before explaining the plan in detail, talk about the purpose of the project and the benefits of completing each step.

Allow time for active experimentation and concrete experience. Offer people a chance to try out a new product or process for themselves—to literally get the feel of it.

Allow for abstract conceptualization. When leading a study group or conducting a training session, provide handouts that include plenty of visuals and step-by-step instructions. Visual learners and people who like to think abstractly will appreciate these handouts. Also schedule periods for questions and answers.

When planning a project, encourage people to answer key questions. Remember the four essential questions that guide learning. Answering *Why?* means defining the purpose and desired outcomes of the project. Answering *What?* means assigning major tasks, setting due dates for each task, and generating commitment to action. Answering *How?* means carrying out assigned tasks and meeting regularly to discuss things that are working well and ways to improve the project. And answering *What if?* means discussing what the team has learned from the project and ways to apply that learning to the whole class or larger organization.

When working on teams, look for ways the members can complement one another's strengths. If you're skilled at planning, find someone who excels at doing. Also seek people who can reflect on and interpret the team's experience. Pooling different styles allows you to draw on everyone's strengths.

Resolve conflict with respect for styles

When people's styles clash in educational or work settings, you have several options. One is to throw up your hands and resign yourself to personality conflicts. Another option is to recognize differences, accept them, and respect them as complementary ways to meet common goals. Taking that perspective allows you to act constructively. You might do one of the following:

Resolve conflict within yourself. In your mental pictures of classrooms and workplaces, are people all "supposed" to have the same style? Notice if you have such ideas, and gently let them go. If you *expect* to find differences in styles, you can more easily respect those differences.

Introduce a conversation about learning styles. Attend a workshop on learning styles. Then bring such training directly to your classroom or office.

Let people take on tasks that fit their learning styles. People gravitate toward the kinds of tasks they've succeeded at in the past, and that's fine. Remember, though, that learning styles are both stable and dynamic. People can broaden their styles by tackling new tasks to reinforce different modes of learning.

Rephrase complaints as requests. "This class is a waste of my time" can be recast as "Please tell me what I'll gain if I participate actively in class." "The instructor talks too fast" can become "What strategies can I use for taking notes when the instructor covers the material rapidly?"

Accept change—and occasional discomfort

Seek out chances to develop new modes of learning. If your instructor asks you to form a group to complete an assignment, avoid joining a group where everyone shares your learning style. Work on project teams with people who learn differently than you. Get together with people who both complement and challenge you.

Also look for situations where you can safely practice new skills. If you enjoy reading, for example, look for ways to express what you learn by speaking, such as leading a study group on a textbook chapter.

Discomfort is a natural part of the learning process. Allow yourself to notice any struggle with a task or lack of interest in completing it. Remember that such feelings are temporary and that you are balancing your learning preferences. By choosing to move through discomfort, you consciously expand your ability to learn in new ways. ✳

Use the modes to learn from any instructor

Students who experience difficulty in school might say, "My teacher doesn't get me" or "The tests are too hard for me" or "In class, we never have time for questions" or "The instructor doesn't teach to my learning style."

Such statements can become mental crutches—a set of beliefs that prevent you from taking responsibility for your education. To stay in charge of your learning, consider adopting attitudes such as the following:

I will look for the potential value in learning this information.

I can learn something useful in any situation, even if I don't like it at first.

I will experiment with this suggestion to see if it works.

No matter who's teaching a course, I am responsible for what I learn.

I will master this subject by using several modes of learning.

Remember that you can take action on such statements even if you don't fully agree with them yet. One way to change your attitudes is to adopt new behaviors, see how they work, and watch for new results in your life. This approach can be adapted to each mode:

- *To develop Mode 1,* ask questions that help you understand *why* it is important for you to learn about a specific topic. You might also want to form a study group.

- *To develop Mode 2,* ask questions that help you gather enough information to understand the main points and key facts. Also, learn a new subject in stages. For example, divide a large reading assignment into sections and then read each section carefully before moving on to the next one.

- *To develop Mode 3,* ask questions about how a theory relates to daily life. Also, allow time to practice what you learn. You can do experiments, conduct interviews, create presentations, find a relevant work or internship experience, or even write a song that summarizes key concepts. Learn through hands-on practice.

- *To develop Mode 4,* ask questions about ways to apply what you have just learned to several situations. Also, seek opportunities to demonstrate your understanding. You could coach a classmate about what you have learned, present findings from your research, explain how your project works, or perform a song that someone else created.

Even when teachers don't promote all four modes of learning, you can take charge of the way you learn. In the process, you consciously direct your growth and create new options.

Claim your multiple intelligences

PEOPLE OFTEN THINK that being smart means the same thing as having a high IQ, and that having a high IQ automatically leads to success. However, psychologists are finding that IQ scores do not always foretell which students will do well in academic settings—or after they graduate.[2]

Howard Gardner of Harvard University believes that no single measure of intelligence can tell us how smart we are. Instead, Gardner defines intelligence in a flexible way as "the ability to solve problems, or to create products, that are valued within one or more cultural settings." He also identifies several types of intelligence, as described below.[3]

People using **verbal/linguistic intelligence** are adept at language skills and learn best by speaking, writing, reading, and listening. They are likely to enjoy activities such as telling stories and doing crossword puzzles.

Individuals who use **mathematical/logical intelligence** are good with numbers, logic, problem solving, patterns, relationships, and categories. They are generally precise and are likely to enjoy science.

When people learn visually and by organizing things spatially, they display **visual/spatial intelligence.** They think in images and pictures, and understand best by seeing the subject. They enjoy charts, graphs, maps, mazes, tables, illustrations, art, and models.

People using **bodily/kinesthetic intelligence** prefer physical activity. They enjoy activities such as building things, woodworking, dancing, skiing, sewing, and crafts. They generally are coordinated and athletic, and they would rather participate in games than just watch.

Individuals using **musical/rhythmic intelligence** enjoy musical expression through songs, rhythms, and musical instruments. They are responsive to various kinds of sounds; remember melodies easily; and might enjoy drumming, humming, and whistling.

People using **intrapersonal intelligence** are exceptionally aware of their own feelings and values. They are generally reserved, self-motivated, and intuitive.

Outgoing people show evidence of **interpersonal intelligence.** They do well with cooperative learning and are sensitive to the feelings, intentions, and motivations of others. They often make good leaders.

People using **naturalist intelligence** love the outdoors and recognize details in plants, animals, rocks, clouds, and other natural formations. These people excel in observing fine distinctions among similar items.

Each of us has all of these intelligences to some degree. And each of us can learn to enhance them. Experiment with learning in ways that draw on a variety of intelligences—including those that might be less familiar. When we acknowledge all of our intelligences, we can constantly explore new ways of being smart. ✳

5 exercise
Develop your multiple intelligences

Gardner's theory of multiple intelligences complements the discussion of different learning styles in this chapter. The main point is that there are many ways to gain knowledge and acquire new behaviors. You can use Gardner's concepts to explore a range of options for achieving success in school, work, and relationships.

The Chart on the next page summarizes the content of "Claim your Multiple Intelligences" and suggests ways to apply the main ideas. Instead of merely glancing through this chart, get active. Place a check mark next to any of the "Possible Characteristics" that describe you. Also check off the "Possible Learning Strategies" that you intend to use. Finally, underline or highlight any of the "Possible Careers" that spark your interest.

Remember that the chart is *not* an exhaustive list or a formal inventory. Take what you find merely as points of departure. You can invent strategies of your own to cultivate different intelligences.

Type of intelligence	Possible characteristics	Possible learning strategies	Possible careers
Verbal/linguistic	❑ You enjoy writing letters, stories, and papers. ❑ You prefer to write directions rather than draw maps. ❑ You take excellent notes from textbooks and lectures. ❑ You enjoy reading, telling stories, and listening to them.	❑ Highlight, underline, and write notes in your textbooks. ❑ Recite new ideas in your own words. ❑ Rewrite and edit your class notes. ❑ Talk to other people often about what you're studying.	Librarian, lawyer, editor, journalist, English teacher, radio or television announcer
Mathematical/logical	❑ You enjoy solving puzzles. ❑ You prefer math or science class over English class. ❑ You want to know how and why things work. ❑ You make careful, step-by-step plans.	❑ Analyze tasks so you can order them in a sequence of steps. ❑ Group concepts into categories, and look for underlying patterns. ❑ Convert text into tables, charts, and graphs. ❑ Look for ways to quantify ideas—to express them in numerical terms.	Accountant, auditor, tax preparer, mathematician, computer programmer, actuary, economist, math or science teacher
Visual/spatial	❑ You draw pictures to give an example or clarify an explanation. ❑ You understand maps and illustrations more readily than text. ❑ You assemble things from illustrated instructions. ❑ You especially enjoy books that have a lot of illustrations.	❑ When taking notes, create concept maps, mind maps, and other visuals (see Chapter 5: Notes). ❑ Code your notes by using different colors to highlight main topics, major points, and key details. ❑ When your attention wanders, focus it by sketching or drawing. ❑ Before you try a new task, visualize yourself doing it well.	Architect, commercial artist, fine artist, graphic designer, photographer, interior decorator, engineer, cartographer
Bodily/kinesthetic	❑ You enjoy physical exercise. ❑ You tend not to sit still for long periods of time. ❑ You enjoy working with your hands. ❑ You use a lot of gestures when talking.	❑ Be active in ways that support concentration; for example, pace as you recite, read while standing up, and create flash cards. ❑ Carry materials with you, and practice studying in several different locations. ❑ Create hands-on activities related to key concepts; for example, create a game based on course content. ❑ Notice the sensations involved with learning something well.	Physical education teacher, athlete, athletic coach, physical therapist, chiropractor, massage therapist, yoga teacher, dancer, choreographer, actor

Type of intelligence	Possible characteristics	Possible learning strategies	Possible careers
Musical/rhythmic	❏ You often sing in the car or shower. ❏ You easily tap your foot to the beat of a song. ❏ You play a musical instrument. ❏ You feel most engaged and productive when music is playing.	❏ During a study break, play music or dance to restore energy. ❏ Put on background music that enhances your concentration while studying. ❏ Relate key concepts to songs you know. ❏ Write your own songs based on course content.	Professional musician, music teacher, music therapist, choral director, musical instrument sales representative, musical instrument maker, piano tuner
Intrapersonal	❏ You enjoy writing in a journal and being alone with your thoughts. ❏ You think a lot about what you want in the future. ❏ You prefer to work on individual projects over group projects. ❏ You take time to think things through before talking or taking action.	❏ Connect course content to your personal values and goals. ❏ Study a topic alone before attending a study group. ❏ Connect readings and lectures to a strong feeling or significant past experience. ❏ Keep a journal that relates your course work to events in your daily life.	Minister, priest, rabbi, professor of philosophy or religion, counseling psychologist, creator of a home-based or small business
Interpersonal	❏ You enjoy group work over working alone. ❏ You have plenty of friends and regularly spend time with them. ❏ You prefer talking and listening over reading or writing. ❏ You thrive in positions of leadership.	❏ Form and conduct study groups early in the term. ❏ Create flash cards, and use them to quiz study partners. ❏ Volunteer to give a speech or lead group presentations on course topics. ❏ Teach the topic you're studying to someone else.	Manager, school administrator, salesperson, teacher, counseling psychologist, arbitrator, police officer, nurse, travel agent, public relations specialist, creator of a midsize to large business
Naturalist	❏ As a child, you enjoyed collecting insects, leaves, or other natural objects. ❏ You enjoy being outdoors. ❏ You find that important insights occur during times you spend in nature. ❏ You read books and magazines on nature-related topics.	❏ During study breaks, take walks outside. ❏ Post pictures of outdoor scenes where you study, and play recordings of outdoor sounds while you read. ❏ Invite classmates to discuss course work while taking a hike or going on a camping trip. ❏ Focus on careers that hold the potential for working outdoors.	Environmental activist, park ranger, recreation supervisor, historian, museum curator, biologist, criminologist, mechanic, woodworker, construction worker, construction contractor or estimator

Learning by seeing, hearing, and moving: The VAK system

FIRST STEPS

YOU CAN APPROACH the topic of learning styles with a simple and powerful system—one that focuses on just three ways of perceiving through your senses:

- Seeing, or *visual learning*.
- Hearing, or *auditory learning*.
- Movement, or *kinesthetic learning*.

To recall this system, remember the letters *VAK*, which stand for **v**isual, **a**uditory, and **k**inesthetic. The theory is that each of us prefers to learn through one of these sense channels. And we can enrich our learning with activities that draw on the other channels.

To reflect on your VAK preferences, answer the following questions. Each question has three possible answers. Circle the answer that best describes how you would respond in the stated situation. This is not a formal inventory—just a way to prompt some self-discovery.

When you have problems spelling a word, you prefer to:

1. Look it up in the dictionary.
2. Say the word out loud several times before you write it down.
3. Write out the word with several different spellings and then choose one.

You enjoy courses the most when you get to:

1. View slides, overhead displays, videos, and readings with plenty of charts, tables, and illustrations.
2. Ask questions, engage in small-group discussions, and listen to guest speakers.
3. Take field trips, participate in lab sessions, or apply the course content while working as a volunteer or intern.

When giving someone directions on how to drive to a destination, you prefer to:

1. Pull out a piece of paper and sketch a map.
2. Give verbal instructions.
3. Say, "I'm driving to a place near there, so just follow me."

When planning an extended vacation to a new destination, you prefer to:

1. Read colorful, illustrated brochures or articles about that place.
2. Talk directly to someone who's been there.
3. Spend a day or two at that destination on a work-related trip before taking a vacation there.

You've made a commitment to learn to play the guitar. The first thing you do is:

1. Go to a library or music store and find an instruction book with plenty of diagrams and chord charts.
2. Put on your favorite songs, listen closely to the guitar solos, and see if you can sing along with them.
3. Buy or borrow a guitar, pluck the strings, and ask someone to show you how to play a few chords.

You've saved up enough money to lease a car. When choosing from among several new models, the most important factor in your decision is:

1. The cars' appearance.
2. The information you get by talking to people who own the cars you're considering.
3. The overall impression you get by taking each car on a test drive.

You've just bought a new computer system—monitor, central processing unit, keyboard, DVD drive, sound and video cards, and external speakers. When setting up the system, the first thing you do is:

1. Skim through the printed instructions that come with the equipment.
2. Call up someone with a similar system and ask her for directions.

3. Assemble the components as best as you can, see if everything works, and consult the instructions only as a last resort.

You get a scholarship to study abroad next semester, which starts in just 3 months. You will travel to a country where French is the most widely spoken language. To learn as much French as you can before you depart, you:

1. Buy a video-based language course that's recorded on a DVD.
2. Set up tutoring sessions with a friend who's fluent in French.
3. Sign up for a short immersion course in an environment in which you speak only French, starting with the first class.

Now take a few minutes to reflect on the meaning of your responses. All of the answers numbered "1" are examples of visual learning. The "2s" refer to auditory learning, and the "3s" illustrate kinesthetic learning. Finding a consistent pattern in your answers indicates that you prefer learning through one sense channel more than the others. Or you might find that your preferences are fairly balanced.

Listed below are suggestions for learning through each sense channel. Experiment with these examples, and create more techniques of your own. Use the suggestions to build on your current preferences and develop new options for learning.

To enhance visual learning:

■ Preview reading assignments by looking for elements that are highlighted visually—bold headlines, charts, graphs, illustrations, and photographs.

■ When taking notes in class, leave plenty of room to add your own charts, diagrams, tables, and other visuals later.

■ Whenever an instructor writes information on a blackboard or overhead display, copy it exactly in your notes.

■ Transfer your handwritten notes to your computer. Use word-processing software that allows you to format your notes in lists, add headings in different fonts, and create visuals in color.

■ Before you begin an exam, quickly sketch a diagram on scratch paper. Use this diagram to summarize the key formulas or facts you want to remember.

■ During tests, see if you can visualize pages from your handwritten notes or images from your computer-based notes.

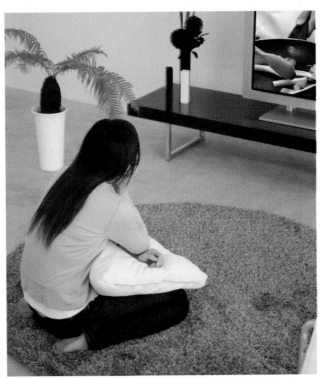

Diego Cervo/Shutterstock, collage by Walter Kopec

- Join study groups, and create short presentations about course topics.
- Visit your instructors during office hours to ask questions.

To enhance kinesthetic learning:

- Look for ways to translate course content into three-dimensional models that you can build. While studying biology, for example, create a model of a human cell using different colors of clay.
- Supplement lectures with trips to museums, field observations, lab sessions, tutorials, and other hands-on activities.
- Recite key concepts from your courses while you walk or exercise.
- Intentionally set up situations in which you can learn by trial and error.
- Create a practice test, and write out the answers in the room where you will actually take the exam.

To enhance auditory learning:

- Reinforce memory of your notes and readings by talking about them. When studying, stop often to recite key points and examples in your own words.
- After reciting several versions of key points and examples, record your favorite or write it out.
- Read difficult passages in your textbooks slowly and out loud.

DAJ/Getty Images

One variation of the VAK system has been called VARK.[4] The *R* describes a preference for learning by reading and writing. People with this preference might benefit from translating charts and diagrams into statements, taking notes in lists, and converting those lists into possible items on a multiple-choice test. *

Reminder: Go back to page LSI-2 to complete the "Take a Snapshot of Your Learning Styles" exercise.

In 1482, Leonardo da Vinci wrote a letter to a wealthy baron, applying for work. Here is an excerpt from the letter: "I can contrive various and endless means of offense and defense. . . . I have all sorts of extremely light and strong bridges adapted to be most easily carried. . . . I have methods for destroying every turret or fortress. . . . I will make covered chariots, safe and unassailable. . . . In case of need I will make big guns, mortars, and light ordnance of fine and useful forms out of the common type." And then he added, almost as an afterthought, "In times of peace I believe I can give perfect satisfaction and to the equal of any other in architecture . . . can carry out sculpture . . . and also I can do in painting whatever may be done." The *Mona Lisa*, for example.

The Master Student

THIS BOOK is about something that cannot be taught. It's about becoming a master student.

Mastery means attaining a level of skill that goes beyond technique. For a master, methods and procedures are automatic responses to the needs of the task. Work is effortless; struggle evaporates. The master carpenter is so familiar with her tools that they are part of her. To a master chef, utensils are old friends. Because these masters don't have to think about the details of the process, they bring more of themselves to their work.

Mastery can lead to flashy results—an incredible painting, for example, or a gem of a short story. In basketball, mastery might result in an unbelievable shot at the buzzer. For a musician, it might be the performance of a lifetime—the moment when everything comes together.

Often the result of mastery is a sense of profound satisfaction, well-being, and timelessness. Work seems self-propelled. The master is in control by being out of control. He lets go and allows the creative process to take over. That's why after a spectacular performance by an athlete or performer, observers often say, "He played full out—and made it look like he wasn't even trying."

Likewise, the master student is one who plays full out and makes learning look easy. She works hard without seeming to make any effort. She's relaxed and alert, disciplined and spontaneous, focused and fun loving.

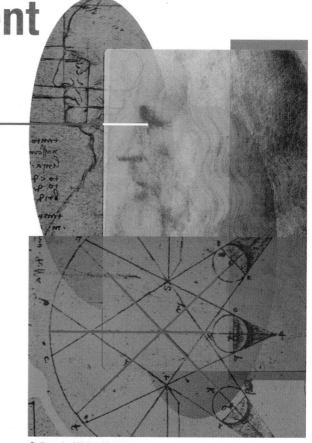

Collage by Walter Kopec

Of course, those statements seem contradictory—maybe even nonsensical. Mastery, in fact, doesn't make sense. It cannot be captured with words. It defies analysis. Mastery cannot be taught. It can only be learned and experienced.

Examine the following list of characteristics of master students in light of your own experience. The list is not complete. It merely points in a direction. Look in that direction, and you'll begin to see the endless diversity of master students. These people are old and young, male and female. They exist in every period of history. And they come from every culture, race, and ethnic group.

Also remember to look to yourself. No one can teach us to be master students; we already are master students. We are natural learners by design. As students, we can discover that every day.

Following are some traits shared by master students.

Inquisitive. The master student is curious about everything. By posing questions, she can generate interest in the most mundane, humdrum situations. When she is bored during a biology lecture, she thinks to herself, "I always get bored when I listen to this instructor. Why is that? Maybe it's because he reminds me of my boring Uncle Ralph, who always tells those endless fishing stories. He even looks like Uncle Ralph. Amazing! Boredom is certainly interesting." Then she asks herself, "What can I do to get value out of this lecture, even though it seems boring?" And she finds an answer.

Able to focus attention. Watch a 2-year-old at play. Pay attention to his eyes. The wide-eyed look reveals an energy and a capacity for amazement that keep his attention absolutely focused in the here and now. The master student's focused attention has a childlike quality. The world, to a child, is always new. Because the master student can focus attention, to him the world is always new, too.

Willing to change. The unknown does not frighten the master student. In fact, she welcomes it—even the unknown in herself. We all have pictures of who we think we are, and these pictures can be useful. But they also can prevent learning and growth. The master student is open to changes in her environment and in herself.

Able to organize and sort. The master student can take a large body of information and sift through it to discover relationships. He can play with information, organizing data by size, color, function, timeliness, and hundreds of other categories.

Determined. Mastery of skills is important to the master student. When she learns mathematical formulas, she studies them until they become second nature. She practices until she knows them cold, then puts in a few extra minutes. She also is able to apply what she learns to new and different situations.

Joyful. More often than not, the master student is seen with a smile on his face—sometimes a smile at nothing in particular other than amazement at the world and his experience of it.

Able to suspend judgment. The master student has opinions and positions, and she is able to let go of them when appropriate. She realizes she is more than her thoughts. She can quiet her internal dialogue and listen to an opposing viewpoint. She doesn't let judgment get in the way of learning. Rather than approaching discussions with a "Prove it to me and then I'll believe it" attitude, she asks herself, "What if this is true?" and explores possibilities.

Energetic. Notice the student with a spring in his step—the one who is enthusiastic and involved in class. When he reads, he often sits on the very edge of his chair, and he plays with the same intensity. He is a master student.

Well. Health is important to the master student, though not necessarily in the sense of being free of illness. Rather, she values her body and treats it with respect. She tends to her emotional and spiritual health, as well as her physical health.

Self-aware. The master student is willing to evaluate himself and his behavior. He regularly tells the truth about his strengths and those aspects that could be improved.

Responsible. There is a difference between responsibility and blame, and the master student knows it well. She is willing to take responsibility for everything in her life—even for events that most people would blame on others.

Willing to take risks. The master student often takes on projects with no guarantee of success. He participates in class dialogues at the risk of looking foolish. He tackles difficult subjects in term papers. He welcomes the risk of a challenging course.

Willing to participate. Don't look for the master student on the sidelines. She's in the game. She is a player who can be counted on. She is willing to make a commitment and to follow through on it.

A generalist. The master student is interested in everything around him. He has a broad base of knowledge in many fields and can apply it to his specialties.

Willing to accept paradox. The word *paradox* comes from two Greek words, *para* (beyond) and *doxen* (opinion). A paradox is something that is beyond opinion or, more accurately, something that might seem contradictory or absurd yet might actually have meaning.

For example, the master student can be committed to managing money and reaching her financial goals. At the same time, she can be totally detached from money, knowing that her real worth is independent of how much money she has. The master student recognizes the limitations of the mind and is at home with paradox. She can accept ambiguity.

Courageous. The master student admits his fear and fully experiences it. For example, he will approach a tough exam as an opportunity to explore feelings of anxiety and tension related to the pressure to perform. He does not deny fear; he embraces it.

Self-directed. Rewards or punishments provided by others do not motivate the master student. Her motivation to learn comes from within.

Spontaneous. The master student is truly in the here and now. He is able to respond to the moment in fresh, surprising, and unplanned ways.

Relaxed about grades. Grades make the master student neither depressed nor euphoric. She recognizes that sometimes grades are important, but grades are not the only reason she studies. She does not measure her worth as a human being by the grades she receives.

Intuitive. The master student has an inner sense that cannot be explained by logic. He has learned to trust his feelings, and he works to develop this intuitive sense.

Creative. Where others see dull details and trivia, the master student sees opportunities to create. She can gather pieces of knowledge from a wide range of subjects and put them together in new ways. The master student is creative in every aspect of her life.

Willing to be uncomfortable. The master student does not place comfort first. When discomfort is necessary to reach a goal, he is willing to experience it. He can endure personal hardships and can look at unpleasant things with detachment.

Optimistic. The master student sees setbacks as temporary and isolated, knowing that he can choose his response to any circumstance.

Willing to laugh. The master student might laugh at any moment, and his sense of humor includes the ability to laugh at himself.

Going to school is a big investment. The stakes are high. It's OK to be serious about that, but you don't have to go to school on the deferred-fun program. A master student celebrates learning, and one of the best ways to do that is to have a laugh now and then.

Hungry. Human beings begin life with a natural appetite for knowledge. In some people it soon gets dulled. The master student has tapped that hunger, and it gives her a desire to learn for the sake of learning.

Willing to work. Once inspired, the master student is willing to follow through with sweat. He knows that genius and creativity are the result of persistence and work. When in high gear, the master student works with the intensity of a child at play.

Caring. A master student cares about knowledge and has a passion for ideas. She also cares about people and appreciates learning from others. She flourishes in a community that values win-win outcomes, cooperation, and love.

Positive. The master student doesn't give in to negative thoughts or feelings. He is able to cope and deal with problems of daily life.

A leader. The master student looks for opportunities to make a difference. She is inspired and enables others to act.

The master student in you. The master student is in all of us. By design, human beings are learning machines. We have an innate ability to learn, and all of us have room to grow and improve.

It is important to understand the difference between learning and being taught. Human beings can resist being taught anything. Psychologist Carl Rogers goes so far as to say that anything that can be taught to a human being is either inconsequential or just plain harmful.[5] What is important in education, Rogers asserts, is learning. And everyone has the ability to learn.

Unfortunately, people also learn to hide that ability. As they experience the pain that sometimes accompanies learning, they shut down. If a child experiences embarrassment in front of a group of people, he may learn to avoid similar situations. In doing so, he restricts his possibilities.

Some children "learn" that they are slow learners. If they learn it well enough, their behavior comes to match that label.

As people grow older, they sometimes accumulate a growing list of ideas to defend—a catalog of familiar experiences that discourages them from learning anything new.

Still, the master student within survives. To tap that resource, you don't need to acquire anything. You already have everything you need. Every day you can rediscover the natural learner within you. ✳

The value of higher education

When you're waist-deep in reading assignments, writing papers, and studying for tests, you might well ask yourself, "Is all this effort going to pay off someday?"

THAT'S A FAIR QUESTION. And it addresses a core issue—the value of getting an education beyond high school.

Be reassured. The potential benefits of higher education are enormous. To begin with, there are economic benefits. Over their lifetimes, college graduates on average earn much more than high school graduates.

That's just one potential payoff. Consider the others explained below.

Gain a broad vision

It's been said that a large corporation is a collection of departments connected only by a plumbing system. This quip makes a point: As workers in different fields become more specialized, they run the risk of forgetting how to talk to one another.

Higher education can change that. One benefit of studying the liberal arts is the chance to gain a broad vision. People with a liberal arts background are aware of the various kinds of problems tackled in psychology and theology, philosophy and physics, literature and mathematics. They understand how people in all of these fields arrive at conclusions and how these fields relate to one another.

Master the liberal arts

According to one traditional model of education, people must master two essential tasks: the use of language and the use of numbers. To acquire these skills, students once immersed themselves in seven subjects: grammar, rhetoric, logic, arithmetic, geometry, music, and astronomy. These subjects were called the liberal arts. They complemented the fine arts, such as poetry, and the practical arts, such as farming.

nurse: © Masterfile Royalty Free, *statue:* © Ron Dahlquist/Getty, *nest:* © Judith Collins/Alamy; *money:* © Don Farrall/Getty, collage by Walter Kopec

This model of liberal arts education still has something to offer. Today we master the use of language through the basic processes of communication: reading, writing, speaking, and listening. In addition, courses in mathematics and science help us understand the world in quantitative terms. The abilities to communicate and calculate are essential to almost every profession. Excellence at these skills has long been considered an essential characteristic of an educated person.

The word *liberal* comes from the Latin verb *libero,* which means "to free." Liberal arts promote critical thinking. Studying them can free us from irrational ideas, half-truths, racism, and prejudice. The liberal arts grant us freedom to explore alternatives and create a system of personal values. These benefits are priceless—the very basis of personal fulfillment and political freedom.

Discover your values

We do not spend all of our waking hours at our jobs. That fact leaves us with a decision that affects the quality of our lives: how to spend leisure time. By cultivating our interest in the arts and community affairs, the liberal arts provide us with many options for activities outside work. Our studies add a dimension to life that goes beyond having a job and paying the bills.

We all have to focus on time and money to some extent. And managing time and money effectively calls for a clear sense of values. Our values define what we commit our time and money to. Higher education offers the opportunity to question and refine our values.

Discover new interests

Taking a broad range of courses has the potential to change your direction in life. A student previously committed to a career in science might try out a drawing class and eventually switch to a degree in studio art. Or a person who swears that she has no aptitude for technical subjects might change her major to computer science after taking an introductory computer course.

To make effective choices about your long-term goals, base those choices on a variety of academic and personal experiences. Even if you don't change majors or switch career directions, you might discover an important avocation or gain a complementary skill. For example, science majors who will eventually write for professional journals can benefit from taking English courses.

Hang out with the greats

Today we enjoy a huge legacy from our ancestors. The creative minds of our species have given us great works of art, systems of science, and technological advances that defy the imagination. Through higher education we can gain firsthand knowledge of humanity's greatest creations. The poet Ezra Pound defined literature as "news that stays news."[6] Most of the writing in newspapers and magazines becomes dated quickly. In contrast, many of the books you read in higher education have passed the hardest test of all—time. Such works have created value for people for decades, sometimes for centuries. These creations are inexhaustible. We can return to them time after time and gain new insights. These are the works we can justifiably deem great. Hanging out with them transforms us. Getting to know them exercises our minds, just as running exercises our bodies.

By studying the greatest works in many fields, we raise our standards. We learn ways to distinguish what is superficial and fleeting from what is lasting and profound.

The criteria for a great novel, poem, painting, or piece of music or dance might vary among individuals. Differences in taste reflect the differences in our backgrounds. The point is to discover those works that have enduring value—and enjoy them for a lifetime.

Learn skills that apply across careers

Jobs that involve responsibility, prestige, and higher incomes depend on self-management skills. These skills include knowing ways to manage time, resolve conflicts, set goals, learn new skills, and relate to people of diverse cultures. Higher education is a place to learn and practice such skills.

Judging by recent trends, most of us will have multiple careers in our lifetimes. In this environment of constant change, it makes sense to learn skills that apply across careers.

Join the conversation

Long ago, before the advent of printing presses, televisions, and computers, people educated themselves by conversing with one another. Students in ancient Athens were often called *peripatetic* (a word that means "walking around") because they were frequently seen strolling around the city, engaged in heated philosophical debate.

Since then, the debate has deepened and broadened. The world's finest scientists and artists have joined voices in a conversation that spans centuries and crosses cultures. This conversation is about the nature of truth and beauty, knowledge and compassion, good and evil—ideas that form the very basis of human society.

Robert Hutchins, former president of the University of Chicago, called this exchange the "great conversation."[7] By studying this conversation, we take on the most basic human challenges: coping with death and suffering, helping create a just global society, living with meaning and purpose.

Our greatest thinkers have left behind tangible records. You'll find them in libraries, concert halls, museums, and scientific laboratories across the world. Through higher education, you gain a front-row seat for the great conversation—and an opportunity to add your own voice. ✳

Olly/Shutterstock

Motivation—
I'm just not in the mood

IN LARGE PART, this chapter is about your motivation to succeed in school. There are at least two ways to think about motivation.

In one view of motivation, the terms *self-discipline, willpower,* and *motivation* describe something missing in ourselves. We use these words to explain another person's success—or our own shortcomings: "If I were more motivated, I'd get more involved in school." "Of course she got an A. She has self-discipline." "If I had more willpower, I'd lose weight." It seems that certain people are born with lots of motivation, while others miss out on it.

A second approach to thinking about motivation is to stop assuming that motivation is mysterious, determined at birth, or hard to come by. Perhaps there's nothing missing in you. What we call motivation could be something that you already possess—the ability to do a task even when you don't feel like it. Motivation is a habit that you can develop with practice. The following suggestions offer ways to do that.

Promise it. Motivation can come simply from being clear about your goals and acting on them. Say that you want to start a study group. You can commit yourself to inviting people and setting a time and place to meet. Promise your classmates that you'll do this, and ask them to hold you accountable. Self-discipline, willpower, motivation—none of these mysterious characteristics needs to get in your way. Just make a promise and keep your word.

Befriend your discomfort. Sometimes keeping your word means doing a task you'd rather put off. The mere thought of doing laundry, reading a chapter in a statistics book, or proofreading a term paper can lead to discomfort. In the face of such discomfort, you can

procrastinate. Or you can use this barrier as a means to getting the job done.

Begin by investigating the discomfort. Notice the thoughts running through your head, and speak them out loud: "I'd rather walk on a bed of coals than do this." "This is the last thing I want to do right now."

Also observe what's happening with your body. For example, are you breathing faster or slower than usual? Is your breathing shallow or deep? Are your shoulders tight? Do you feel any tension in your stomach?

Once you're in contact with your mind and body, stay with the discomfort a few minutes longer. Don't judge it as good or bad. Accepting the thoughts and body sensations robs them of power. They might still be there, but in time they can stop being a barrier for you.

Discomfort can be a gift—an opportunity to do valuable work on yourself. On the other side of discomfort lies mastery.

Change your mind—and your body. You can also get past discomfort by planting new thoughts in your mind or changing your physical stance. For example, instead of slumping in a chair, sit up straight or stand up. You can also get physically active by taking a short walk. Notice what happens to your discomfort.

Work with your thoughts, also. Replace "I can't stand this" with "I'll feel great when this is done" or "Doing this will help me get something I want."

Sweeten the task. Sometimes it's just one aspect of a task that holds you back. You can stop procrastinating merely by changing that aspect. If distaste for your physical environment keeps you from studying, you can change that environment. Reading about social psychology might seem like a yawner when you're alone in a dark corner of the house. Moving to a cheery, well-lit library can sweeten the task.

Galina Barskaya/Shutterstock

Talk about how bad it is. One way to get past negative attitudes is to take them to an extreme. When faced with an unpleasant task, launch into a no-holds-barred gripe session. Pull out all the stops: "There's no way I can start my income taxes now. This is terrible beyond words—an absolute disaster. This is a catastrophe of global proportions!" Griping taken this far can restore perspective. It shows how self-talk can turn inconveniences into crises.

Turn up the pressure. Sometimes motivation is a luxury. Pretend that the due date for your project has been moved up 1 month, 1 week, or 1 day. Raising the stress level slightly can spur you into action. Then the issue of motivation seems beside the point, and meeting the due date moves to the forefront.

Turn down the pressure. The mere thought of starting a huge task can induce anxiety. To get past this feeling, turn down the pressure by taking baby steps. Divide a large project into small tasks. In 30 minutes or less, you could preview a book, create a rough outline for a paper, or solve two or three math problems. Careful planning can help you discover many such steps to make a big job doable.

Ask for support. Other people can become your allies in overcoming procrastination. For example, form a support group and declare what you intend to accomplish before each meeting. Then ask members to hold you accountable. If you want to begin exercising regularly, ask another person to walk with you three times weekly. People in support groups ranging from Alcoholics Anonymous to Weight Watchers know the power of this strategy.

Adopt a model. One strategy for succeeding at any task is to hang around the masters. Find someone you consider successful, and spend time with her. Observe this person and use her as a model for your own behavior. You can try on this person's actions and attitudes. Look for tools that feel right for you. This person can become a mentor for you.

Compare the payoffs to the costs. All behaviors have payoffs and costs. Even unwanted behaviors such as cramming for exams or neglecting exercise have payoffs. Cramming might give you more time that's free of commitments. Neglecting exercise can give you more time to sleep.

One way to let go of such unwanted behaviors is first to celebrate them—even embrace them. Openly acknowledge the payoffs.

Celebration can be especially powerful when you follow it up with the next step—determining the costs. For example, skipping a reading assignment can give you time to go to the movies. However, you might be unprepared for class and have twice as much to read the following week.

Maybe there is another way to get the payoff (going to the movies) without paying the cost (skipping the reading assignment). With some thoughtful weekly planning, you might choose to give up a few hours of television and end up with enough time to read the assignment *and* go to the movies.

Comparing the costs and benefits of any behavior can fuel our motivation. We can choose new behaviors because they align with what we want most.

Do it later. At times, it's effective to save a task for later. For example, writing a résumé can wait until you've taken the time to analyze your job skills and map out your career goals. Putting it off does not show a lack of motivation—it shows planning.

When you do choose to do a task later, turn this decision into a promise. Estimate how long the task will take, and schedule a specific date and time for it on your calendar.

Heed the message. Sometimes lack of motivation carries a message that's worth heeding. An example is the student who majors in accounting but seizes every chance to be with children. His chronic reluctance to read accounting textbooks might not be a problem. Instead, it might reveal his desire to major in elementary education. His original career choice might have come from the belief that "real men don't teach kindergarten." In such cases, an apparent lack of motivation signals a deeper wisdom trying to get through. ✳

Attitudes, affirmations, and visualizations

"I HAVE A BAD ATTITUDE." Some of us say this as if we were talking about having the flu. An attitude is certainly as strong as the flu, but it isn't something we have to succumb to or accept.

Attitudes are powerful. They mold behavior. If your attitude is that you're not interesting at a party, then your behavior will probably match your attitude. If your attitude is that you are fun at a party, then your behavior is more likely to be playful.

Visible measures of success—such as top grades and résumés filled with accomplishments—start with invisible assets called attitudes. Some attitudes will help you benefit from all the money and time you invest in higher education. Other attitudes will render your investment worthless.

You can change your attitudes through regular practice with affirmations and visualizations.

Affirm it. An affirmation is a statement describing what you want. The most effective affirmations are personal, positive, and written in the present tense.

To use affirmations, first determine what you want; then describe yourself as if you already have it. To get what you want from your education, you could write, "I, Malika Jones, am a master student. I take full responsibility for my education. I learn with joy, and I use my experiences in each course to create the life that I want."

If you decide that you want a wonderful job, you might write, "I, Peter Webster, have a wonderful job. I respect and love my colleagues, and they feel the same way about me. I look forward to going to work each day."

Effective affirmations include detail. Use brand names, people's names, and your own name. Involve all of your senses—sight, sound, smell, taste, touch. Take a positive approach. Instead of saying, "I am not fat," say, "I am slender."

Once you have written an affirmation, repeat it. Practice saying it out loud several times a day. Do this at a regular time, such as just before you go to sleep or just after you wake up. Sit in a chair in a relaxed position. Take a few deep and relaxing breaths, and then repeat your affirmation with emotion. It's also effective to look in a mirror while saying the affirmation. Keep looking and repeating until you are saying your affirmation with conviction.

Visualize it. You can improve your golf swing, tennis serve, or batting average while lying in bed. You can become a better driver, speaker, or cook while sitting silently in a chair. In line at the grocery store, you

Attitude replacements

You can use affirmations to replace a negative attitude with a positive one. There are no limitations other than your imagination and your willingness to practice. Here are some sample affirmations. Modify them to suit your individual hopes and dreams, and then practice them.

I, _____, have abundant energy and vitality throughout the day.

I, _____, exercise regularly.

I, _____, work effectively with many different kinds of people.

I, _____, eat wisely.

I, _____, plan my days and use time wisely.

I, _____, have a powerful memory.

I, _____, take tests calmly and confidently.

I, _____, fall asleep quickly and sleep soundly.

I, _____, have relationships that are mutually satisfying.

I, _____, contribute to other people through my job.

I, _____, know ways to play and have fun.

I, _____, focus my attention easily.

I, _____, like myself.

I, _____, have an income that far exceeds my expenses.

I, _____, live my life in positive ways for the highest good of all people.

www Find an online version of these affirmations.

can improve your ability to type or to take tests. These goals are all possible through visualization—the technique of seeing yourself being successful.

Here's one way to begin. Choose what you want to improve. Then describe in writing what it would look like, sound like, and feel like to have that improvement in your life. If you are learning to play the piano, write down briefly what you would see, hear, and feel if you were playing skillfully. If you want to improve your relationships with your children, write down what you would see, hear, and feel if you were communicating with them successfully.

Once you have a sketch of what it would be like to be successful, practice it in your imagination. Whenever you toss the basketball, it swishes through the net. Every time you invite someone out on a date, the person says yes. Each test the teacher hands back to you is graded an A. Practice at least once a day. Then wait for the results to unfold in your life.

You can also use visualizations to replay errors. When you make a mistake, replay it in your imagination. After a bad golf shot, stop and imagine yourself making that same shot again, this time very successfully. If you just had a discussion with your roommate that turned into a fight, replay it successfully.

Visualizations and affirmations can restructure your attitudes and behaviors. Be clear about what you want—and then practice it. ✳

I am a Loving Parent!

6 exercise
Reprogram your attitude

You can employ affirmations and visualizations to successfully reprogram your attitudes and behaviors. Use this exercise to change your approach to any situation in your life.

Step 1
Pick something in your life that you would like to change. It can be related to anything—relationships, work, money, or personal skills. Below, write a brief description of what you choose to change.

_____

_____

_____

Step 2
Add more details about the change you described in Step 1. Write down how you would like the change to come about. Be outlandish. Imagine that you are about to ask your fairy godmother for a wish that you know she will grant. Be detailed in your description of your wish.

_____

_____

_____

_____

Step 3
Here comes the fairy godmother. Use affirmations and visualizations to start yourself on the path to creating exactly

what you wrote about in Step 2. Below, write at least two affirmations that describe your dream wish. Also, briefly outline a visualization that you can use to picture your wish. Be specific, detailed, and positive.

_____

_____

_____

_____

Step 4
Put your new attitudes to work. Set up a schedule to practice them. Let the first time you practice be right now. Then set up at least five other times and places where you intend to practice your affirmations and visualizations.

I intend to relax and practice my affirmations and visualizations for at least 5 minutes on the following dates and at the time(s) and location(s) given.

	Date	Time	Location
1.			
2.			
3.			
4.			
5.			

www Complete this exercise online.

Master Student Profiles

Each chapter of this text has an example of a person who embodies on or more qualities of a master student. As you read about these people and others like them, ask yourself, "How can I apply this?" Look for the timeless qualities in the people you read about. Many of the strategies used by master students from another time or place are tools that you can use today.

The master students in this book were chosen because they demonstrate unusual and effective ways to learn. Remember that these are just twelve examples of master students (one for each chapter). You can read more about them in the Master Student Hall of Fame on the Web site.

As you read the Master Student Profiles, ask questions based on each mode of learning: Why is this person considered a master student? What attitudes or behaviors helped to create her mastery? How can I develop those qualities? What if I could use his example to create positive new results in my own life?

Also reflect on other master students you've read about or know personally. Focus on people who excel at learning. The master student is not a vague or remote ideal. Rather, master students move freely among us.

In fact, there's one living inside your skin.

practicing critical thinking

Review the article "The Master Student" in this chapter. Then skim the Master Student Profiles throughout this book. Finally, choose one of the people profiled, and describe in the space below how this person embodies qualities of a master student.

 Complete this exercise online.

The Practicing Critical Thinking exercises that appear throughout this book incorporate ideas from Peter Facione, dean of the College of Arts and Sciences, Santa Clara University, and creator of the California Critical Thinking Disposition Inventory. Facione provided substantial suggestions for these exercises and edited them. More information on critical thinking assessment is available at www.insightassessment.com/.

Adapted with permission from *Critical Thinking: What It Is and Why It Counts* by Peter Facione, Millbrae, CA: The California Academic Press, 1996.

Ideas Are Tools

There are many ideas in this book. When you first encounter them, don't believe any of them. Instead, think of the ideas as tools.

For example, you use a hammer for a purpose—to drive a nail. You don't try to figure out whether the hammer is "right." You just use it. If it works, you use it again. If it doesn't work, you get a different hammer.

People have plenty of room in their lives for different kinds of hammers, but they tend to limit their openness to different kinds of ideas. A new idea, at some level, is a threat to their very being—unlike a new hammer, which is simply a new hammer.

Most of us have a built-in desire to be right. Our ideas, we often think, represent ourselves.

Some ideas are worth dying for. But please note: This book does not contain any of those ideas. The ideas on these pages are strictly "hammers."

Imagine someone defending a hammer. Picture this person holding up a hammer and declaring, "I hold this hammer to be self-evident. Give me this hammer or give me death. Those other hammers are flawed. There are only two kinds of people in this world: people who believe in this hammer and people who don't."

That ridiculous picture makes a point. This book is not a manifesto. It's a toolbox, and tools are meant to be used.

If you read about a tool in this book that doesn't sound "right" or one that sounds a little goofy, remember that the ideas here are for using, not necessarily for believing. Suspend your judgment. Test the idea for yourself. If it works, use it. If it doesn't, don't use it.

Any tool—whether it's a hammer, a computer program, or a study technique—is designed to do a specific job. A master mechanic carries a variety of tools, because no single tool works for all jobs. If you throw a tool away because it doesn't work in one situation, you won't be able to pull it out later when it's just what you need. So if an idea doesn't work for you and you are satisfied that you gave it a fair chance, don't throw it away. File it away instead. The idea might come in handy soon.

And remember, this book is not about figuring out the "right" way. Even the ideas-are-tools approach is not "right."

It's a hammer . . . or maybe a saw.

 Complete this exercise online.

Edmond Van Hoorick/Digital Vision/Getty Images

Put it to Work

Shortly after graduating with an associate in arts degree in business administration, Sylvia Lopez joined a market research firm as a staff accountant. After a week, she wanted to quit. She didn't think she would ever learn to deal with her coworkers. Their personalities just seemed too different.

For example, there was project manager Ed Washington. He spent hours a day on the phone calling prospective customers who had responded to the corporate Web site. Since Ed's office door was always open and he had a loud voice, people inevitably overheard his calls. It seemed to Sylvia that Ed spent a lot of time socializing with clients—asking about their hobbies and family lives. Even though Ed was regarded as a skilled salesperson, Sylvia wondered when he actually got any work done.

Sylvia also felt uncomfortable with Linda Martinez, the firm's accounting analyst and her direct supervisor. Linda kept her office door closed most of the time. In contrast to Ed, Linda hardly ever stopped to chat informally. Instead of taking lunch breaks, she typically packed a bag lunch and ate it while checking e-mail or updating the company databases. Linda had a reputation as a top-notch employee. Yet the only time people saw her was at scheduled staff meetings. Linda led those meetings and distributed a detailed agenda in advance. And while Ed was on a first-name basis with everyone in the office, Linda made it clear that she wished to be addressed as "Ms. Martinez."

After thinking for several days about how to survive in the same office with such different coworkers, Sylvia chose to simply accept those differences. In her journal, she reflected on her experiences with Ed and Linda, noting her observations and listing specific ways to improve her working relationships with both of them.

Sylvia made it her intention to stop by Ed's office several times each week, always allowing some time for small talk before asking a work-related question.

She sent an e-mail to Linda with this request: "I value working with you, and I'd like to make sure my performance is up to par. Is there any way I can get regular feedback from you about how I'm doing?"

Sylvia applied several strategies from this chapter:

- She observed her coworkers and looked for clues to their styles.
- She accepted the differences in her coworkers and looked for ways to build on each person's strengths.

Andrew Taylor/Shutterstock

- She used her journal as a tool for reflective observation.
- She used other modes of learning by planning new responses to Ed and Linda—and taking action on her plans.

List more strategies that would be useful to Sylvia in this situation.

_____

_____

_____

_____

_____

Once you've discovered differences in people's styles, look for ways to accommodate them. As you collaborate on projects with coworkers, for example, encourage them to answer the four learning style questions:

Ask *Why?* to define the purpose and desired outcomes of a project. Help participants answer the questions, what's in this for our organization? And what's in this for me?

Ask *What?* to set goals, assign major tasks, and set due dates for each task.

Ask *How?* as you complete your tasks. In project meetings, discuss what's working well, and brainstorm ways to improve performance.

Ask *What if?* to discuss what the team is learning from the project and ways to apply that learning to the larger organization.

Quiz

chapter 1

■ Put it to Work
◄ ◄ ◄ ◄ ◄
■ Skills Snapshot
■ Master Student Profile

Name_____   Date____/____/____

1. Write an example of an effective affirmation and an example of an ineffective affirmation.

   Effective: I am a confident student who is responsible for her own education. Ineffective: I want to be a confident student who is responsible for his own education. (Answers may vary.) (*Attitudes, affirmations, visualizations,* p. 52)

2. Define the term *mastery* as it is used in this chapter.

   Mastery implies a level of skill that goes beyond technique; it is something that cannot be taught. Often the result of mastery is a sense of profound satisfaction, well-being, and timelessness. A master allows the creative process to take over. With this in mind, it is hard to concretely define what mastery is as it is an individual experience. Most master students do have certain qualities in common including inquisitiveness, responsibility, willingness to change, and willingness to take risks. Considering how these qualities are reflected in your own experience will give you direction toward mastery. (Answers may vary.) (*The master student,* p. 45)

3. The First Step technique refers only to telling the truth about your areas for improvement. True or false? Explain your answer.

   False. While the First Step is all about telling the truth, telling the truth about your areas for improvement is just one part. Taking the First Step involves telling the truth about what is working as well as what isn't, who you are, and what you want. (Answers may vary.) (*First Step: Truth is a key to mastery,* p. 25)

4. The four modes of learning are associated with certain questions. Give the appropriate question for each mode.

   Mode 1: Why? Mode 2: What? Mode 3: How? Mode 4: What if? (*Learning styles: Discovering how you learn,* p. 32)

5. Give a brief example of learning, and relate it to one of the four questions you listed above.

   Learning about history. For me, it's important to know how I can use information. So, if I'm going to be motivated to learn about history, I have to figure out how I can use this knowledge—to be happier, more successful, etc.   (Answers may vary.) (*Using your learning style profile to succeed,* p. 35)

6. Describe the difference between liberal education and vocational education as defined in the text.

   Liberal education is about discovering what is worth doing. (Answers may vary.) (*The value of higher education,* p. 48)

7. List several types of intelligence defined by Howard Gardner. Then describe one learning strategy related to each type of intelligence that you listed.

   Verbal/linguistic: Practice learning by reciting new ideas in your own words. Mathematical/logical: Practice learning by looking for ways to quantify ideas. Visual/spatial: Find pictures and graphs in a book and practice analyzing them without reading the accompanying text. Musical/rhythmic: Try studying with different kinds of music in the background and analyze which, if any, seem to aid in your learning. Interpersonal: Form a study group with classmates to discuss homework, text, and class discussions. (Answers may vary.) (*Claim your multiple intelligences,* p. 39)

8. According to the Power Process, ideas are tools; if you want the ideas in this book to work, you must believe in them. True or false? Explain your answer.

   False. On the contrary, it is probably best when encountering one of the many new ideas in this book to not believe it all. Each idea presented can be used as a tool to help you on your way to becoming a master student. Not every idea will fit you—the challenge is to discover why an idea is not right for you and to ask yourself the questions that will expand your toolbox with more ideas. (Answers may vary). (*Power Process: Ideas Are Tools,* p. 55)

9. Define the word *metacognition,* and give an example of it.

   Metacognition refers to your ability to view your attitudes and behaviors from beyond—that is, to understand more fully the way you learn. An example is studying for an hour, then stepping back and reviewing your learning process—how you paced yourself, how you approached the material, the learning strategies you used, the challenges you encountered—and then making a decision to continue with the same study method or to modify it to become more effective during study. (*Learning Styles Inventory,* p. LSI-11)

10. This chapter presents two views of the nature of motivation. Briefly explain the difference between them.

    According to the article, one view of motivation is that it is a quality or personality trait that people either have or don't have. The other view is that motivation is a habit or inherent quality we already possess. In the first view, we are powerless to change our motivation. In the second view, we can improve on the ability to motivate ourselves to accomplish the goals we want to achieve. (*Motivation,* p. 50)

Skills Snapshot

The Discovery Wheel in this chapter includes a section labeled *Attitude*. For the next 10 to 15 minutes, go beyond your initial responses to that exercise. Take a snapshot of your skills as they exist today, after reading and doing this chapter.

Begin by reflecting on some recent experiences. Then take another step toward mastery by choosing to follow up on your reflections with a specific action.

SELF-AWARENESS

Three things I do well as a student are . . .

Three areas in which I'd like to improve as a student are . . .

STYLES

If asked to describe my learning style in one sentence, I would say that I am . . .

To become a more flexible learner, I could . . .

FLEXIBILITY

When I disagree with what someone else says, my first response is usually to . . .

In these situations, I could be more effective by . . .

NEXT ACTION

I'll know that I've adopted new attitudes to support my success when I'm able to say . . .

To reach that level of mastery, the most important thing I can do next is to . . .

chapter 1
....

■ Put it to Work
■ Quiz
■ Skills Snapshot

◄ ◄ ◄ ◄ ◄

Master Student PROFILE

Lalita Booth
. . . is willing to work

Jacque Brund/UCF News
and Information

Sitting in front of a classroom of LEAD Scholars, Lalita Booth looks like any other junior. The brown-eyed, freckle-faced student blends in with her peers in the University of Central Florida (UCF) leadership development program in every way.

That is, until she opens her mouth.

"You're looking at the face of a child abuse survivor, a perpetual runaway, a high school dropout," she says, as idle chitchat turns to complete silence.

"I was a teenage mother, a homeless parent, and a former welfare recipient."

Lalita's parents divorced when she was young; by age 12 she was a runaway pro—asking for permission to go somewhere and then simply not returning for a few days or a few weeks.

. . . She became proficient in "couch surfing" at friends' homes. When there was no couch to crash on, the teen would take her nightly refuge behind the closest dumpster and rest in the park during the day.

Furthering her quest to be a grownup, at 17 she married her long-time buddy and fellow high school dropout, Quinn. Three months later, she found out she was pregnant with a son, Kieren. What normally would be a joyful time was instead a stressful one while the new couple struggled in a prison of deep poverty. The miserable situation began to take its toll, and after just two and a half years of marriage, Quinn was ready to call it quits.

With her new boyfriend, Carl, and her most precious cargo, Kieren, in tow, Lalita fled to Boulder, Colorado. Kieren lived with his paternal grandparents for 7 months while Lalita and Carl attempted to get back on their feet.

Being in Colorado proved to be fruitful for the 21-year-old Lalita. It started with an interesting job opportunity as an enrolled agent—an expert in U.S. taxation who can represent taxpayers before the Internal Revenue Service. Lalita could acquire the license without further schooling. Better yet, it would boost her income to $32,000. She buckled down and read all 4,000 pages of the study guide, and thanks to her nearly photographic memory, she aced the test.

But once again, she was in the wrong place at the wrong time. Carl's brother in Orlando was very ill, and he needed to move to Florida.

The only way to insure her independence was to do something that frightened her to the very core—go back to school. . . .

. . . And soon after, she enrolled at Seminole Community College.

. . . In May 2005, Lalita was selected to attend the Salzburg Global Seminar, where she brainstormed ways to solve global problems with a group of international students. The thought-provoking trip led to her mission: to help others escape the choke hold of poverty.

Back in the states, Lalita's world became even more dreamlike when she won the Jack Kent Cooke Foundation Scholarship. . . .

. . . Lalita strongly believes, and for good reason, that "things that are worth achieving are absolutely unreasonable." She advises, "Set unreasonable goals, and chase them unreasonably."

Adapted from Sarah Sekula, "Escape Artist," *Pegasus,* July/August 2008, *UCF Alumni Life,* 20–26. Reprinted with permission.

Once homeless, now a student at the University of Central Florida, and accepted to Harvard University Business School.

Find more biographical information about Lalita Booth at the Master Student Hall of Fame.

2 Time

Instructor Tools & Tips

> Even if you are on the right track, you'll get run over if you just sit there.
>
> **—Will Rogers**

> Dost thou love life, then do not squander time, for that's the stuff life is made of.
>
> **—Benjamin Franklin**

> An hour of effective, precise, hard, disciplined and integrated thinking can be worth a month of hard work.
>
> **—David Kekich**

> I think the Time Monitor exercise is one of the most valuable in the book. Until students track their time, most have no idea how they use/waste their time. They just know that they don't have enough of it. This visual really brings home the reality of time. Because time management is so very important, have students do the same exercise of tracking their time toward the end of the semester. Comparing the two should reflect changes the students have made with regard to their time management. There should be a direct correlation between their time management and the success they are having in school, work, and life.
>
> **—Jo Ella Fields, Oklahoma State University**

Preview

Chapter 2 addresses one of the great challenges for students—managing their time. Whether they are traditional students attending college right out of high school or returning students attending college for the first time after an absence from formal education, your students each have only 168 hours per week to allocate to their many priorities. Time is an equal opportunity resource: All people, regardless of race, gender, creed, or national origin, have exactly the same number of hours per week. As you help your students choose how to allocate their 168 hours per week, set goals, and overcome procrastination, remind them that planning increases their options. Planning offers them the freedom to act in response to their intentions rather than to their moods. And planning vastly increases the odds of getting what they want.

Guest Speaker

Consider inviting experts from your college or from off-campus who work in fields that emphasize planning, goal setting, or organization. A representative from the Counseling Department may provide some planning tips and also share information about advisement, scheduling, and personal counseling services. Here is a guest speaker for you:

Lecture

Suggested lecture topics for this chapter include:

- Planning strategies
- Structure and freedom
- Organizing your space
- Committing to attend class
- Completing projects
- Power Process: Be here now

For specific lecture ideas and key lecture points on text articles, visit the lecture ideas area of the chapter-by-chapter instructor materials at the Online Instructor Resources Web site.

Exercises/Activities

1. Why? What? How? and What if? Consider writing these questions on the chalkboard or whiteboard. Post them to your online course discussion board. Tap into all the different learning styles of your students by asking these questions in class:

Why? Why does *Becoming a Master Student* cover the topic of planning?

What? What is planning? Read through the list of articles in this chapter and pick three that look interesting. What about these three articles interests you?

How? How would you rate your level of success with the ideas covered in this chapter? (How much do you already know about prioritizing your time, setting goals, or avoiding procrastination?)

What if? What if you start to apply these strategies to your life right now? And what if you don't?

2. The ABC daily to-do list (pages 71–72) Some students have had prior experience with to-do lists. Their testimonials in class can help convince students who have not yet tried to-do lists to experiment with them. The ABC priority aspect is usually a new concept for all students. Learning this technique helps them make better decisions about *what* to do and *when* to do it. Practicing this skill in groups during class helps students get started with to-do lists.

3. Stop procrastination NOW (pages 76–77) Many students report that procrastination is their number one obstacle to success in school, work, and their personal lives. After they have read the antiprocrastination article and sidebar, divide them into groups of four and ask them to list situations in which they often procrastinate. Then discuss as a group which of the antiprocrastination strategies might be most appropriate for each situation. Making this an active-learning exercise puts the strategies in motion. Have the students create summary charts on poster paper and then present a brief report to the rest of the class.

4. 25 ways to get the most out of now (pages 79–83) After students have read this article, divide them into groups of four and ask them to discuss which of the 25 tools they have had success with in the past. Then ask them to discuss five tools that they are interested in trying and to make a verbal commitment to each of their group members. At the beginning of the next class, ask students to report back to their groups to discuss which strategies worked and which did not.

5. Big Rock Planning (submitted by Eldon McMurray) This activity helps students build on the ideas they learned in the Time Monitor/Time Plan exercise. Order a text bundle that includes the Master Student Planner. (Ask your TeamUP consultant or sales representative about how to order this special package.) Start the process with a week at a glance by asking students to identify their A's—their most time-sensitive activities,

such as relationships, class and study time, work commitments, or exercise. Remind students to start their daily plan with a look at the week before it starts. One way to do this is to take seven 3x5 cards (also available for your students through Cengage Learning) and write the date and day of the week at the top of each card. After students first list their most time-sensitive activities for the week, adding B's and C's as their second- and third-level priorities, respectively, becomes a less daunting task.

An in-class strategy to illustrate planning and prioritizing is to bring three stones to class: Stone A is roughly the size of a softball, stone B is the size of a golf ball, and stone C is the size of a hazelnut or a small marble. Begin by asking for three volunteers. Hand each of the students a stone and ask them to hold the stones at arm's length above their heads for a minute. Ask the student holding the smallest stone (stone C) to let it go so that it hits the student on the head. Then ask, "Did you feel that? Was it painful?" After the student responds, the suspense will build as you turn to the student holding stone B. Explain that the three stones are analogous to planning and prioritizing; if you don't accomplish your plan by prioritizing and completing, it can be *painful*. Then ask the students holding stones A and B how they are feeling about dropping their stones. After they respond, have them put their rocks down without dropping them on their heads. Pause for a moment to let the students get back to their seats. Ask the student who held stone B how it felt to be able to put it down. After the student answers, ask the same question of the student who held stone A. "Even better than B" is a typical response. Summarize by making the point that priority equals *pleasure* (finishing on time) or *pain* (missing class, late assignments or failing tests). Figuratively, suggest that their education is a Big Rock. The more important the goal, the bigger the rock that they should imagine is suspended above their head.

6. Power Process: Be Here Now (page 93) This Power Process teaches the skill of focusing attention—a skill essential for taking effective notes in class, maximizing comprehension when reading textbooks, and memorizing content. After students read the article and you review it with them in class, have them stand up and find a partner for this brief "hand mirror" exercise.

Facing their partner, students put their hands up, palms facing toward their partner, without touching. In this position, students appear as a mirror image of their partner. Without speaking, for 1 minute, one student is in charge of moving her hands slowly in different directions—up, down, left, right, forward, backward. Her partner focuses his attention and mirrors the movement of her hands with his hands, even when they do not move symmetrically. After 1 minute, they reverse roles for another minute. Afterwards, discuss the paradox that it feels both easy and difficult to focus attention for just 60 seconds. It may be beneficial to bring a student forward and demonstrate the activity with him first.

Conversation/Sharing

The Master Student Profile about Al Gore describes ways to approach and solve problems. In groups of four, ask students to select either a world or a local problem toward which they would like to contribute their time and energy. Then brainstorm creative solutions to the problem. As a whole class, share ideas and discuss master student qualities that students can develop while attending college. More information about Al Gore and other master students is available on the *Becoming a Master Student* Web site, in a special Master Student Hall of Fame. Biographical information about Al Gore is also available, along with links to outside resources that can help you and your students explore his master student qualities further.

Homework

The Time Monitor/Time Plan Process (pages 62–66)
Assign the monitoring step of this exercise the week before you get to this chapter because the exercise asks students to monitor their activities first so that they will have a detailed picture of how they spend their time. When students complete this exercise *before* they read the chapter, they are motivated to learn strategies to make the most of their 168 hours per week. It is not easy to keep track of oneself for 24 hours a day for a week, so talk about the importance of this exercise ahead of time. To show students that you know how challenging this exercise really is, share with them that you did it yourself.

Create a lifeline (page 69) Have students tape two sheets of paper side by side to allow for a long lifeline,

drawn diagonally from the bottom left-hand corner to the upper right-hand corner. Have them spread the next 10 years across the left-hand page and then 50 years of highlights across the right-hand page. An alternative to doing this on paper is using the "Create a lifeline" online exercise on the Student Web site.

Master monthly calendar (page 87) The words *planning* and *time management* strike terror into many students' hearts. Yet this is the number one skill research tells us that students need. Tell students that they cannot control time, but they *can* control the way they respond to it. They cannot control the past, but they *can* have an impact on their future by planning the semester. The master monthly calendar is an opportunity for you to work with your students to plan an entire semester. Using the blank monthly calendar in the textbook (with additional sheets at the back of the text or available on the Student Web site), have students create their master plan based on the course syllabi from all of their classes. Have them transfer key dates for tests and papers and ask them to plug in interim deadlines, such as "Write draft of English paper." Some students have success with developing master plans if, during this exercise, they also create a timeline for each of the bigger projects. An example of such a timeline is available on the Instructor Web site.

Evaluation

Frequent quizzes ensure that students focus attention during class and keep up with the text reading assignments. In addition, quizzes provide students with opportunities for written reflection regarding new discoveries and intentions. Evaluation instruments also help you identify topics and concepts that students have not yet mastered. In addition to the questions listed here, find more test questions on the Instructor Web site.

Quiz ideas for Chapter 2:

- Discovery statement regarding time monitoring/planning.
- Intention statement regarding goal setting.
- Name antiprocrastination tools.
- Describe strategies for getting the most out of now.
- Discovery statement regarding the Power Process: Be here now.

Additional Digital Resources

Course Manual

The online *Course Manual* serves as an invaluable reference for those developing and teaching a College Success course with *Becoming a Master Student*. The *Course Manual* provides advice on general teaching issues such as preparing for classes, classroom management, grading, and communicating with students of various backgrounds, as well as specific strategies on getting the most out of various features in *Becoming a Master Student* such as the Discovery Wheel, Learning Styles Inventory, and book-specific Web sites.

Instructor Web Site

The updated Instructor Web site provides resources to help you plan and customize your course. Content specific to Chapter 2 includes:

► Lecture Ideas
  • Committing to Coming to Class
  • Planning Sets You Free
  • Structured Time and Freedom
► In-Class Exercises
  • 3x5 Goal Setting
  • How Do I Manage My Time?
  • When Is a Notebook a Portfolio?
► Writing Assignments
  • Goal-Setting Paper
► In-Text Quiz Answers
► Learning Styles Application
► Discussion Topics
► PowerPoint Slides
► Reflection Questions
► Assessment Questions
► Experiment with chapter strategies

The Instructor Web site also contains the following book-specific content:

► ExamView Test Bank
► Online Course Manual
► Articles from previous editions
► Master Student Profiles from previous editions
► Sample Syllabi

Student Web Site

To help your students gain a better understanding of the topics discussed in *Becoming a Master Student,* encour-

 www.cengage.com/success/bams13e

age your students to visit the Student Web site, which provides the following resources specific to Chapter 2:

► Connect to Text content expands on specific topics marked with an icon within Chapter 2.

► Learning Style Applications invite students to cycle through the four styles of learning. In answering the four questions about freeing up for extra hours per week posted in this chapter's Learning Styles Application, students explore the different modes and apply their new knowledge.

► Practice Tests allow students to see how well they understand the themes of *Becoming a Master Student.*

► Interactive Concept Maps promote critical thinking by highlighting related ideas to show relationships between concepts.

► Video Skillbuilders bring to life techniques that will help you to excel in college and beyond. The following video should give your students more information regarding topics covered in Chapter 2:
  • Time Management

► Remembering Cultural Differences presents readers with brief articles that touch on aspects of diversity in our rapidly changing world. For Chapter 2, the following article will prompt your students to look at contemporary issues in a new way:
  • The Concept of Time

► Master Student Profiles provide additional information on the people covered in this book feature. For Chapter 2, students will find expanded coverage and links about:
  • Al Gore

► Power Process Media contains video, PowerPoints, and audio files to take what your students have learned from the Power Processes in their book to the next level. For Chapter 2, students will find additional media on:
  • Be here now

Along with the chapter-specific content, a General Resources folder is available that contains Toolboxes geared toward specific student types (Community College, Adult Learner, Student Athlete), the Plagiarism Prevention Zone, and the Career Resource Center.

2 Time

Master Student Map

as you read, ask yourself

what if . . .

I could meet my goals with time to spare?

why this chapter matters . . .

Procrastination and lack of planning can quickly undermine your success in school.

what is included . . .

how you can use this chapter . . .

- Discover the details about how you currently use time.
- Set goals that make a difference in the quality of your life.
- Know exactly what to do today, this week, and this month to achieve your goals.
- Eliminate procrastination.

MASTER STUDENTS in *action*

I have found that it is essential to keep a constantly updated calendar and personal planner. Without my own planner, I would most likely draw a blank as to what I need to accomplish for the day, week, month, and beyond. I recommend that any student use both as a means of keeping organized.

—DEEANNA MOSHER

Photo courtesy of Deeanna Mosher

You've got the time

THE WORDS *time management* may call forth images of restriction and control. You might visualize a prune-faced Scrooge hunched over your shoulder, stopwatch in hand, telling you what to do every minute. Bad news.

Good news: You do have enough time for the things you want to do. All it takes is thinking about the possibilities and making conscious choices.

Time is an equal opportunity resource. All of us, regardless of gender, race, creed, or national origin, have exactly the same number of hours in a week. No matter how famous we are, no matter how rich or poor, we get 168 hours to spend each week—no more, no less.

Time is also an unusual commodity. It cannot be saved. You can't stockpile time like wood for the stove or food for the winter. It can't be seen, heard, touched, tasted, or smelled. You can't sense time directly. Even scientists and philosophers find it hard to describe. Because time is so elusive, it is easy to ignore. That doesn't bother time at all. Time is perfectly content to remain hidden until you are nearly out of it. And when you are out of it, you are out of it.

Time is a nonrenewable resource. If you're out of wood, you can chop some more. If you're out of money, you can earn a little extra. If you're out of love, there is still hope. If you're out of health, it can often be restored. But when you're out of time, that's it. When this minute is gone, it's gone.

Time seems to pass at varying speeds. Sometimes it crawls, and sometimes it's faster than a speeding bullet. On Friday afternoons, classroom clocks can creep. After you've worked a 10-hour day, reading the last few pages of an economics assignment can turn minutes into hours. A year in school can stretch out to an eternity.

At the other end of the spectrum, time flies. There are moments when you are so absorbed in what you're doing that hours disappear like magic.

Approach time as if you are in control. Sometimes it seems that your friends control your time, that your boss controls your time, that your teachers or your parents or your kids or somebody else controls your time. Maybe that is not true, though. When you say you don't have enough time, you might really be saying that you are not spending the time you *do* have in the way that you want.

Everything written about time management boils down to two topics. One is knowing exactly *what* you want. The other is knowing *how* to get what you want. State your wants as written goals. Then choose activities that will help you meet those goals.

Spend your most valuable resource in the way you choose. Start by observing how you use time. On the following pages, Exercise 7: The Time Monitor/Time Plan Process gives you this opportunity. ✳

journal entry 7

Discovery/Intention

Create value from this chapter

Think back to a time during the past year when you rushed to finish a project or when you did not find time for an activity that was important to you. List one thing you might have done to create this outcome.

I discovered that I . . .

_____

_____

_____

_____

_____

Now take a few minutes to skim this chapter. Find eight techniques that you intend to use. List them below, along with their associated page numbers.

Strategy	Page number

exercise

The Time Monitor/ Time Plan Process

The purpose of this exercise is to transform time into a knowable and predictable resource. Complete this exercise over a 2-week period:

- During the first week, you *monitor* your activities to get detailed information about how you actually spend your time.

- After you analyze your first week in Journal Entry 8, you *plan* the second week.

- During the second week, you *monitor* your activity again and compare it with your plan.

- Based on everything you've learned, you *plan* again.

For this exercise, monitor your time in 15-minute intervals, 24 hours a day, for 7 days. Record how much time you spend sleeping, eating, studying, attending lectures, traveling to and from class, working, watching television, listening to music, taking care of the kids, running errands—everything.

If this sounds crazy, hang on for a minute. This exercise is not about keeping track of the rest of your life in 15-minute intervals. It is an opportunity to become conscious of how you spend your time—your life. Use the Time Monitor/Time Plan process only for as long as it helps you do that.

When you know exactly how you spend your time, you can make choices with open eyes. You can spend more time on the things that are most important to you and less time on the unimportant. Monitoring your time puts you in control of your life.

Here's an eye opener for many students. If you think you already have a good idea of how you manage time, predict how many hours you will spend in a week on each category of activity listed in the form on page 64. (Four categories are already provided; you can add more at any time.) Make your predictions before your first week of monitoring. Write them in the margin to the left of each category. After monitoring your time for 1 week, see how accurate your predictions were.

Following are charts for monitoring and planning, along with instructions for using them. Some students choose other materials, such as 3x5 cards, calendars, campus planners, or time management software. You might even develop your own way to monitor your time.

 Do this exercise online.

1. **Get to know the Time Monitor/Time Plan.** Look at the sample Time Monitor/Time Plan on page 63. Note that each day has two columns—one labeled "Monitor" and the other labeled "Plan." During the first week, you will use only the "Monitor" column, just like this student did.

On Monday, the student in this example got up at 6:45 a.m., showered, and got dressed. He finished this activity and began breakfast at 7:15. He put this new activity in at the time he began and drew a line just above it. He ate from 7:15 to 7:45. It took him 15 minutes to walk to class (7:45 to 8:00), and he attended classes from 8:00 to 11:00.

When you begin an activity, write it down next to the time you begin. Round off to the nearest 15 minutes. If, for example, you begin eating at 8:06, enter your starting time as 8:00. Over time, it will probably even out. In any case, you will be close enough to realize the benefits of this exercise.

Keep your Time Monitor/Time Plan with you every minute you are awake for 1 week. Take a few moments every 2 or 3 hours to record what you've done. Or enter a note each time you change activities.

2. **Remember to use your Time Monitor/Time Plan.** It might be easy to forget to fill out your Time Monitor/ Time Plan. One way to remember is to create a visual reminder for yourself. You can use this technique for any activity you want to remember.

Relax for a moment, close your eyes, and imagine that you see your Time Monitor/Time Plan. Imagine that it has arms and legs and is as big as a person. Picture the form sitting at your desk at home, in your car, in one of your classrooms, or in your favorite chair. Visualize it sitting wherever you're likely to sit. When you sit down, the Time Monitor/Time Plan will get squashed unless you pick it up and use it.

You can make this image more effective by adding sound effects. The Time Monitor/Time Plan might scream, "Get off me!" Or since time can be related to money, you might associate the Time Monitor/Time Plan with the sound of an old-fashioned cash register. Imagine that every time you sit down, a cash register rings to remind you it's there.

MONDAY 9 / 12	
Monitor	**Plan**
Get up	
Shower	
7:00 ————	7:00
7:15 Breakfast	
7:30 ⊥	
7:45 Walk to class	
8:00 Econ 1	8:00
8:15	
8:30	
8:45	
9:00	9:00
9:15	
9:30	
9:45	
10:00 Bio 1	10:00
10:15	
10:30	
10:45	
11:00	11:00
11:15 Study	
11:30	
11:45	
12:00	12:00
12:15 Lunch	
12:30	
12:45	
1:00	1:00
1:15 Eng. Lit	
1:30	
1:45	
2:00	2:00
2:15 Coffeehouse	
2:30	
2:45	
3:00	3:00
3:15	
3:30	
3:45	
4:00	4:00
4:15 Study	
4:30	
4:45	
5:00	5:00
5:15 Dinner	
5:30	
5:45	
6:00	6:00
6:15	
6:30 Babysit	
6:45	
7:00	7:00

TUESDAY 9 / 13	
Monitor	**Plan**
Sleep	
7:00	7:00
7:15	
7:30	
7:45 Shower	
8:00 Dress	8:00
8:15 Eat	
8:30	
8:45	
9:00 Art	9:00
9:15 Apprec.	
9:30 Project	
9:45	
10:00	10:00
10:15	
10:30	
10:45	
11:00 Data	11:00
11:15 process	
11:30	
11:45	
12:00	12:00
12:15	
12:30	
12:45	
1:00	1:00
1:15 Lunch	
1:30	
1:45	
2:00 Work	2:00
2:15 on book	
2:30 report	
2:45	
3:00 Art	3:00
3:15 Apprec.	
3:30	
3:45	
4:00	4:00
4:15	
4:30	
4:45	
5:00 Dinner	5:00
5:15	
5:30	
5:45	
6:00 Letter to	6:00
6:15 Uncle Jim	
6:30	
6:45	
7:00	7:00

3. **Evaluate the Time Monitor/Time Plan.** After you've monitored your time for 1 week, group your activities together by categories. The form on page 64 lists the categories "sleep," "class," "study," and "meals." Think of other categories you could add. "Grooming" might include showering, putting on makeup, brushing teeth, and getting dressed. "Travel" could include walking, driving, taking the bus, and riding your bike. Other categories might be "exercise," "entertainment," "work," "television," "domestic," and "children."

Write in the categories that work for you, and then do the following:

• Guess how many hours you *think* you spent on each category of activity. List these hours in the "Estimated" column.

- List the *actual* number of hours you spent on each activity, adding up the figures from your daily time monitoring. List these hours in the "Monitored" column. Make sure that the grand total of all categories is 168 hours.

- Now take a minute, and let these numbers sink in. Compare the totals in the "Estimated" and "Monitored" columns.

Notice your reactions. You might be surprised. You might feel disappointed or even angry about where your time goes.

Use those feelings as motivation to plan your time differently. Go to the "Planned" column, and choose how much time you *want* to spend on various categories during the coming week. As you do this, allow yourself to have fun. Approach planning in the spirit of adventure. Think of yourself as an artist who's creating a new life.

In several months you might want to take another detailed look at how you spend your life. Fill in the "Monitor" and "Plan" columns on pages 65–66 simultaneously. Use a continuous cycle of monitoring and planning to get the full benefits of this exercise for the rest of your life. Let time management become more than a technique. Transform it into a habit—a constant awareness of how you spend your lifetime.

WEEK OF ___ / ___ / ___ /			
Category	**Estimated**	**Monitored**	**Planned**
Sleep			
Class			
Study			
Meals			

MONDAY ___ / ___ / ___ /	
Monitor	**Plan**
7:00	7:00
7:15	
7:30	
7:45	
8:00	8:00
8:15	
8:30	
8:45	
9:00	9:00
9:15	
9:30	
9:45	
10:00	10:00
10:15	
10:30	
10:45	
11:00	11:00
11:15	
11:30	
11:45	
12:00	12:00
12:15	
12:30	
12:45	
1:00	1:00
1:15	
1:30	
1:45	
2:00	2:00
2:15	
2:30	
2:45	
3:00	3:00
3:15	
3:30	
3:45	
4:00	4:00
4:15	
4:30	
4:45	
5:00	5:00
5:15	
5:30	
5:45	
6:00	6:00
6:15	
6:30	
6:45	
7:00	7:00
7:15	
7:30	
7:45	
8:00	8:00
8:15	
8:30	
8:45	
9:00	9:00
9:15	
9:30	
9:45	
10:00	10:00
10:15	
10:30	
10:45	
11:00	11:00
11:15	
11:30	
11:45	
12:00	12:00

TUESDAY ___ / ___ / ___ /	
Monitor	**Plan**
7:00	7:00
7:15	
7:30	
7:45	
8:00	8:00
8:15	
8:30	
8:45	
9:00	9:00
9:15	
9:30	
9:45	
10:00	10:00
10:15	
10:30	
10:45	
11:00	11:00
11:15	
11:30	
11:45	
12:00	12:00
12:15	
12:30	
12:45	
1:00	1:00
1:15	
1:30	
1:45	
2:00	2:00
2:15	
2:30	
2:45	
3:00	3:00
3:15	
3:30	
3:45	
4:00	4:00
4:15	
4:30	
4:45	
5:00	5:00
5:15	
5:30	
5:45	
6:00	6:00
6:15	
6:30	
6:45	
7:00	7:00
7:15	
7:30	
7:45	
8:00	8:00
8:15	
8:30	
8:45	
9:00	9:00
9:15	
9:30	
9:45	
10:00	10:00
10:15	
10:30	
10:45	
11:00	11:00
11:15	
11:30	
11:45	
12:00	12:00

WEDNESDAY ___ / ___ / ___ /	
Monitor	**Plan**
7:00	7:00
7:15	
7:30	
7:45	
8:00	8:00
8:15	
8:30	
8:45	
9:00	9:00
9:15	
9:30	
9:45	
10:00	10:00
10:15	
10:30	
10:45	
11:00	11:00
11:15	
11:30	
11:45	
12:00	12:00
12:15	
12:30	
12:45	
1:00	1:00
1:15	
1:30	
1:45	
2:00	2:00
2:15	
2:30	
2:45	
3:00	3:00
3:15	
3:30	
3:45	
4:00	4:00
4:15	
4:30	
4:45	
5:00	5:00
5:15	
5:30	
5:45	
6:00	6:00
6:15	
6:30	
6:45	
7:00	7:00
7:15	
7:30	
7:45	
8:00	8:00
8:15	
8:30	
8:45	
9:00	9:00
9:15	
9:30	
9:45	
10:00	10:00
10:15	
10:30	
10:45	
11:00	11:00
11:15	
11:30	
11:45	
12:00	12:00

THURSDAY ___ / ___ / ___ /		FRIDAY ___ / ___ / ___ /		SATURDAY ___ / ___ / ___ /	
Monitor	**Plan**	**Monitor**	**Plan**	**Monitor**	**Plan**
7:00	7:00	7:00	7:00		
7:15		7:15			
7:30		7:30			
7:45		7:45			
8:00	8:00	8:00	8:00		
8:15		8:15			
8:30		8:30			
8:45		8:45			
9:00	9:00	9:00	9:00		
9:15		9:15			
9:30		9:30			
9:45		9:45			
10:00	10:00	10:00	10:00		
10:15		10:15			
10:30		10:30			
10:45		10:45			
11:00	11:00	11:00	11:00		
11:15		11:15			
11:30		11:30			
11:45		11:45			
12:00	12:00	12:00	12:00		
12:15		12:15			
12:30		12:30			
12:45		12:45			
1:00	1:00	1:00	1:00		
1:15		1:15			
1:30		1:30			
1:45		1:45			
2:00	2:00	2:00	2:00		
2:15		2:15			
2:30		2:30			
2:45		2:45			
3:00	3:00	3:00	3:00		
3:15		3:15			
3:30		3:30			
3:45		3:45			
4:00	4:00	4:00	4:00		
4:15		4:15			
4:30		4:30			
4:45		4:45			
5:00	5:00	5:00	5:00		
5:15		5:15			
5:30		5:30			
5:45		5:45			
6:00	6:00	6:00	6:00		

SUNDAY ___ / ___ / ___ /	
Monitor	**Plan**

THURSDAY		FRIDAY	
6:15		6:15	
6:30		6:30	
6:45		6:45	
7:00	7:00	7:00	7:00
7:15		7:15	
7:30		7:30	
7:45		7:45	
8:00	8:00	8:00	8:00
8:15		8:15	
8:30		8:30	
8:45		8:45	
9:00	9:00	9:00	9:00
9:15		9:15	
9:30		9:30	
9:45		9:45	
10:00	10:00	10:00	10:00
10:15		10:15	
10:30		10:30	
10:45		10:45	
11:00	11:00	11:00	11:00
11:15		11:15	
11:30		11:30	
11:45		11:45	
12:00	12:00	12:00	12:00

Many of us have vague, idealized notions of what we want out of life. These notions float among the clouds in our heads. They are wonderful, fuzzy, safe thoughts such as "I want to be a good person," "I want to be financially secure," or "I want to be happy."

Setting and achieving goals

SUCH OUTCOMES ARE great possible goals. When we keep these goals in a generalized form, however, we may become confused about ways to actually achieve them. If you really want to meet a goal, translate it into specific, concrete behaviors. Find out what that goal looks like. Listen to what it sounds like. Pick it up and feel how heavy that goal is. Inspect the switches, valves, joints, cogs, and fastenings of the goal. Make your goal as real as a chain saw.

There is nothing vague or fuzzy about chain saws. You can see them, feel them, and hear them. They have a clear function. Goals can be every bit as real and useful.

Writing down your goals exponentially increases your chances of meeting them. Writing exposes undefined terms, unrealistic time frames, and other symptoms of fuzzy thinking. If you've been completing Intention Statements as explained in the Introduction to this book, then you've already had experience writing goals. Both goals and Intention Statements address changes you want to make in your behavior, your values, your circumstances—or all of these. To keep track of your goals, write each one on a separate 3x5 card, or key them all into a word-processing file on your computer.

There are many useful methods for setting goals. You're about to learn one of them. This method is based on writing specific goals that relate to several time frames and areas of your life. Experiment with this method, and modify it as you see fit. Also, reflect regularly on your goals. The key words to remember are *specific, time, areas,* and *reflect.* Combine the first letter of each word, and you get *STAR.* Use this acronym to remember the suggestions that follow.

Write specific goals. In writing, state your goals as observable actions or measurable results. Think in detail about how things will be different once your goals are attained. List the changes in what you'd see, feel, touch, taste, hear, be, do, or have.

Suppose that one of your goals is to become a better student by studying harder. You're headed in a powerful direction; now translate that goal into a concrete action, such as "I will study 2 hours for every hour I'm in class." Specific goals make clear what actions are needed or what results are expected. Consider these examples:

Vague goal	Specific goal
Get a good education.	Graduate with B.S. degree in engineering, with honors, by 2012.
Enhance my spiritual life.	Meditate for 15 minutes daily.
Improve my appearance.	Lose 6 pounds during the next 6 months.

When stated specifically, a goal might look different to you. If you examine it closely, a goal you once thought you wanted might not be something you want after all. Or you might discover that you want to choose a new path to achieve a goal that you are sure you want.

Write goals in several time frames. To get a comprehensive vision of your future, write down the following:

- *Long-term goals.* Long-term goals represent major targets in your life. These goals can take 5 to 20 years to achieve. In some cases, they will take a lifetime. They can include goals in education, careers, personal relationships, travel, financial security—whatever is important to you. Consider the answers to the following questions as you create your long-term goals: What do you want to accomplish in your life? Do you want your life to make a statement? If so, what is that statement?

- *Mid-term goals.* Mid-term goals are objectives you can accomplish in 1 to 5 years. They include goals such as completing a course of education, paying off a car loan, or achieving a specific career level. These goals usually support your long-term goals.

Short-term goals. Short-term goals are the ones you can accomplish in a year or less. These goals are specific achievements, such as completing a particular course or group of courses, hiking down the Appalachian Trail, or organizing a family reunion. A short-term financial goal would probably include an exact dollar amount. Whatever your short-term goals are, they will require action now or in the near future.

Write goals in several areas of life. People who set goals in only one area of life—such as their career—may find that their personal growth becomes one-sided. They might experience success at work while neglecting their health or relationships with family members and friends.

To avoid this outcome, set goals in a variety of categories. Consider what you want to experience in your:

- education
- career
- financial life
- family life
- social life
- spiritual life
- level of health

Add goals in other areas as they occur to you.

Reflect on your goals. Each week, take a few minutes to think about your goals. You can perform the following spot checks:

- *Check in with your feelings.* Think about how the process of setting your goals felt. Consider the satisfaction you'll gain in attaining your objectives. If you don't feel a significant emotional connection with a written goal, consider letting it go or filing it away to review later.

- *Check for alignment.* Look for connections among your goals. Do your short-term goals align with your mid-term goals? Will your mid-term goals help you achieve your long-term goals? Look for a fit between all of your goals and your purpose for taking part in higher education, as well as your overall purpose in life.

- *Check for obstacles.* All kinds of things can come between you and your goals, such as constraints on time and money. Anticipate obstacles, and start looking now for workable solutions.

- *Check for immediate steps.* Here's a way to link goal setting to time management. Decide on a list of small, achievable steps you can take right away to accomplish each of your short-term goals. Write these small steps down on a daily to-do list. If you want to accomplish some of these steps by a certain date, enter them in a calendar that you consult daily. Then, over the coming weeks, review your to-do list and calendar. Take note of your progress, and celebrate your successes. ✳

journal entry 8

Discovery Statement

Assess your use of time

Now that you have monitored one week, reflect on how you spend the time of your life:

After 1 week of monitoring my time, I discovered that . . .

_____

_____

_____

I want to spend more time on . . .

_____

_____

_____

I want to spend less time on . . .

_____

_____

_____

I was surprised that I spent so much time on . . .

_____

_____

_____

I was surprised that I spent so little time on . . .

_____

_____

_____

⑧ exercise
Seeing where all the time goes

You've probably heard people say, "I just don't know where my time goes." Well, this chapter offers ways to find out.

First, discover the details about how you spend your lifetime by doing the Time Monitor/Time Plan process on page 62.

Next, get a big picture of those results—literally. Create a chart, diagram, or some other visual way to show the categories of activity that take up most of your time. Consider creating a pie chart like the example shown below.

Using a pie chart to display your activities is useful for at least two reasons. First, a circle is a fixed shape. It reinforces the idea that you have only a fixed amount of time to work with—24 hours per day, 168 hours per week. Second, seeing your life represented on the chart can help you adjust the size of each slice in the pie—that is, each category of activity.

After looking at the example, fill in the first blank circle with your totals from the "Monitored" column on page 64. Label this pie chart "Monitored." Then fill in the second blank circle with the totals from your "Planned" column on that page. Label this pie chart "Planned."

 Create your pie chart online.

- Class (15 hours)
- Sleep (49 hours)
- Study/Reading for Classes (45 hours)
- Personal Maintenance (7 hours)
- Work (10 hours)
- Call Family (2 hours)
- Laundry (2 hours)
- Clean Apartment (3 hours)
- Exercise (4 hours)
- Free Time (10 hours)
- Meals (including cooking) (21 hours)

⑨ exercise
Create a lifeline

On a large sheet of paper, draw a horizontal line. This line will represent your lifetime. Now add key events in your life to this line in chronological order. Examples are birth, first day at school, graduation from high school, and enrollment in higher education.

Now extend the lifeline into the future. Write down key events you would like to see occur 1 year, 5 years, and 10 or more years from now. Choose events that align with your core values. Work quickly in the spirit of a brainstorm, bearing in mind that this plan is not a final one.

Afterward, take a few minutes to review your lifeline. Select one key event for the future, and list any actions you could take in the next month to bring yourself closer to that goal. Do the same with the other key events on your lifeline. You now have the rudiments of a comprehensive plan for your life.

Finally, extend your lifeline another 50 years beyond the year when you would reach age 100. Describe in detail what changes in the world you'd like to see as a result of the goals you attained in your lifetime.

exercise
10 Get real with your goals

One way to make goals effective is to examine them up close. That's what this exercise is about. Using a process of brainstorming and evaluation, you can break a long-term goal into smaller segments until you have taken it completely apart. When you analyze a goal to this level of detail, you're well on the way to meeting it. For this exercise, you will use a pen, extra paper, and a watch with a second hand. (A digital watch with a built-in stopwatch feature is even better.) Timing is an important part of the brainstorming process, so follow the stated time limits. This entire exercise takes about an hour.

Part one: Long-term goals

Brainstorm.   Begin with an 8-minute brainstorm. Use a separate sheet of paper for this part of the exercise. For 8 minutes, write down everything you think you want in your life. Write as fast as you can, and write whatever comes into your head. Leave no thought out. Don't worry about accuracy. The object of a brainstorm is to generate as many ideas as possible.

Evaluate.   After you have finished brainstorming, spend the next 6 minutes looking over your list. Analyze what you wrote. Read the list out loud. If something is missing, add it. Look for common themes or relationships among your goals. Then select three long-term goals that are important to you—goals that will take many years to achieve. Write these goals below in the space provided.

_____

_____

_____

Before you continue, take a minute to reflect on the process you've used so far. What criteria did you use to select your top three goals? On a separate sheet of paper, write about your criteria for selecting these three goals.

Part two: Mid-term goals

Brainstorm.   Read out loud the three long-term goals you selected in Part One. Choose one of them. Then brainstorm a list of goals you might achieve in the next 1 to 5 years that would lead to the accomplishment of that one long-term goal. These are mid-term goals. Spend 8 minutes on this brainstorm. Go for quantity.

Evaluate.   Analyze your brainstorm of mid-term goals. Then select three that you determine to be important in meeting the long-term goal you picked. Allow yourself 6 minutes for this part of the exercise. Write your selections below in the space provided.

_____

_____

_____

Again, pause for reflection before going on to the next part of this exercise. Why do you see these three goals as more important than the other mid-term goals you generated? On a separate sheet of paper, write about your reasons for selecting these three goals.

Part three: Short-term goals

Brainstorm.   Review your list of mid-term goals, and select one. In another 8-minute brainstorm, generate a list of short-term goals—those you can accomplish in a year or less that will lead to the attainment of that mid-term goal. Write down everything that comes to mind. Do not evaluate or judge these ideas yet. For now, the more ideas you write down, the better.

Evaluate.   Analyze your list of short-term goals. The most effective brainstorms are conducted by suspending judgment, so you might find some bizarre ideas on your list. That's fine. Now is the time to cross them out. Next, evaluate your remaining short-term goals, and select three that you are willing and able to accomplish. Allow yourself 6 minutes for this part of the exercise. Then write your selections below in the space provided.

_____

_____

_____

The more you practice, the more effective you can be at choosing goals that have meaning for you. You can repeat this exercise, employing the other long-term goals you generated or creating new ones.

 Complete this exercise online.

One of the most effective ways to stay on track and actually get things done is to use a daily to-do list. While the Time Monitor/Time Plan gives you a general picture of the week, your daily to-do list itemizes specific tasks you want to complete within the next 24 hours.

© Deborah Jaffe/The Image Bank/Getty

The ABC daily to-do list

ONE ADVANTAGE OF keeping a daily to-do list is that you don't have to remember what to do next. It's on the list. A typical day in the life of a student is full of separate, often unrelated tasks—reading, attending lectures, reviewing notes, working at a job, writing papers, researching special projects, running errands. It's easy to forget an important task on a busy day. When that task is written down, you don't have to rely on your memory.

The following steps present one method for creating and using to-do lists. This method involves ranking each item on your list according to three levels of importance—A, B, and C. Experiment with these steps, modify them as you see fit, and invent new techniques that work for you.

Step 1 Brainstorm tasks

To get started, list all of the tasks you want to get done tomorrow. Each task will become an item on a to-do list. Don't worry about putting the entries in order or scheduling them yet. Just list everything you want to accomplish on a sheet of paper or planning calendar, or in a special notebook. You can also use 3x5 cards, writing one task on each card. Cards work well because you can slip them into your pocket or rearrange them, and you never have to copy to-do items from one list to another.

Step 2 Estimate time

For each task you wrote down in Step 1, estimate how long it will take you to complete it. This can be tricky. If

you allow too little time, you end up feeling rushed. If you allow too much time, you become less productive. For now, give it your best guess. If you are unsure, overestimate rather than underestimate how long it will take for each task. Overestimating has two benefits: (1) it avoids a schedule that is too tight, missed deadlines, and the resulting feelings of frustration and failure; and (2) it allows time for the unexpected things that come up every day—the spontaneous to-dos. Now pull out your calendar or Time Monitor/Time Plan. You've probably scheduled some hours for activities such as classes or work. This leaves the unscheduled hours for tackling your to-do lists.

Add up the time needed to complete all your to-do items. Also add up the number of unscheduled hours in your day. Then compare the two totals. The power of this step is that you can spot overload in advance. If you have 8 hours' worth of to-do items but only 4 unscheduled hours, that's a potential problem. To solve it, proceed to Step 3.

Step 3 Rate each task by priority

To prevent overscheduling, decide which to-do items are the most important, given the time you have available. One suggestion for making this decision comes from the book *How to Get Control of Your Time and Your Life*, by Alan Lakein: Simply label each task A, B, or C.[1]

The A's on your list are those things that are the most critical. They include assignments that are coming due or jobs that need to be done immediately. Also included are activities that lead directly to your short-term goals.

Step 1: Brainstorm tasks

Step 2: Estimate time

Step 3: Rate each task by priority

Step 4: Cross off tasks

Step 5: Evaluate

The B's on your list are important, but less so than the A's. B's might someday become A's. For the present, these tasks are not as urgent as A's. They can be postponed, if necessary, for another day.

The C's do not require immediate attention. C priorities include activities such as "shop for a new blender" and "research genealogy on the Internet." C's are often small, easy jobs with no set time line. They, too, can be postponed.

Once you've labeled the items on your to-do list, schedule time for all of the A's. The B's and C's can be done randomly during the day when you are in between tasks and are not yet ready to start the next A.

Step 4 Cross off tasks

Keep your to-do list with you at all times. Cross off activities when you finish them, and add new ones when you think of them. If you're using 3x5 cards, you can toss away or recycle the cards with completed items. Crossing off tasks and releasing cards can be fun—a visible reward for your diligence. This step fosters a sense of accomplishment.

When using the ABC priority method, you might experience an ailment common to students: C fever. Symptoms include the uncontrollable urge to drop that A task and begin crossing C's off your to-do list. If your history paper is due tomorrow, you might feel compelled to vacuum the rug, call your third cousin in Tulsa, and make a trip to the store for shoelaces. The reason C fever is so common is that A tasks are usually more difficult or time-consuming to achieve, with a higher risk of failure.

If you notice symptoms of C fever, ask yourself, "Does this job really need to be done now? Do I really need to alphabetize my CD collection, or might I better use this time to study for tomorrow's data-processing exam?" Use your to-do list to keep yourself on task, working on your A's. But don't panic or berate yourself when you realize that in the last 6 hours, you have completed eleven C's and not a single A. Just calmly return to the A's.

Step 5 Evaluate

At the end of the day, evaluate your performance. Look for A priorities you didn't complete. Look for items that repeatedly turn up as B's or C's on your list and never seem to get done. Consider changing them to A's or dropping them altogether. Similarly, you might consider changing an A that didn't get done to a B or C priority. When you're done evaluating, start on tomorrow's to-do list. Be willing to admit mistakes. You might at first rank some items as A's only to realize later that they are actually C's. And some of the C's that lurk at the bottom of your list day after day might really be A's. When you keep a daily to-do list, you can adjust these priorities *before* they become problems.

The ABC system is not the only way to rank items on your to-do list. Some people prefer the 80-20 system. This method is based on the idea that 80 percent of the value of any to-do list comes from only 20 percent of the tasks on that list. So on a to-do list of ten items, find the two that will contribute most to your life, and complete those tasks without fail.

Another option is to rank items as "yes," "no," or "maybe." Do all of the tasks marked "yes." Ignore those marked "no." And put all of the "maybes" on the shelf for later. You can come back to the "maybes" at a future point and rank them as "yes" or "no."

Or you can develop your own style for to-do lists. You might find that grouping items by categories such as "errands" or "reading assignments" works best. Be creative.

Keep in mind the power of planning a whole week or even 2 weeks in advance. Planning in this way can make it easier to put activities in context and see how your daily goals relate to your long-term goals. Weekly planning can also free you from feeling that you have to polish off your whole to-do list in 1 day. Instead, you can spread tasks out over the whole week.

In any case, make starting your own to-do list an A priority. ✳

 Find more strategies for daily planning.

USE WEB-BASED TOOLS TO SAVE TIME

Time management tools generally fall into three major categories, no matter which system or set of techniques you use:

- **Lists** of goals and planned actions for meeting those goals (to-do items).
- **Calendars** for scheduling appointments and keeping track of due dates.
- **Contact managers**—sometimes called *personal relationship managers*—for keeping track of other people's addresses, phone numbers, e-mail addresses, and other contact information, along with notes from meetings with clients, customers, or coworkers.

Today you can choose from dozens of free online applications that fill these functions. Online applications can save you time because they're available from *any* computer that you can access, in any location—as long as it's connected to the Web. Cell phone applications are also available to help you organize your time. If you use online or cell phone applications, you don't have to keep track of information scrawled on pieces of paper or transfer files from computer to computer. All the data you've entered from any computer are at your fingertips, at any time.

Many Web-based applications are aimed directly at students. A few of the options are described below. To find more, do an Internet search using the key words *web, tools,* and *students.*

Purpose	Application	Uses
Calendar	Google Calendar (www.google.com/calendar)	Keep track of scheduled events and share them with other people; coordinate your data with other Google online applications.
Calendar	30 Boxes (30boxes.com)	Keep track of scheduled events, and share them with other people.
Goal setting	43Things (www.43things.com)	List goals, and track your progress toward them as part of an online community.
Goal setting	myGoals.com (www.mygoals.com)	List goals, get automatic action reminders, and choose from a library of "GoalPlans" based on expert-recommended content.
Lists	Gubb (www.gubb.net)	Create and edit lists (including to-do lists), check off completed items, assign due dates to items, and send lists via e-mail or text messaging.
Lists	Remember the Milk (www.rememberthemilk.com)	Create and manage tasks online and offline, and send yourself reminders.
Multipurpose	Google Docs (docs.google.com)	Create and share documents, spreadsheets, presentations, and forms.
Multipurpose	Zoho (www.zoho.com)	Create and share documents, spreadsheets, presentations, and forms; create a wiki (a Web site that anyone can edit); send and receive e-mail; manage to-do lists; create a calendar; chat online; and clip content (audio, video, text, and images) from the Web.
Multipurpose	Yahoo (www.yahoo.com)	Send and receive e-mail, manage contact information, take notes, and create a calendar.
Multipurpose	OpenOffice (www.openoffice.org)	Create documents, spreadsheets, presentations, graphics, and databases.

 Find an updated list of Web-based applications online.

More strategies for planning

PLANNING SETS YOU FREE. When you set goals and manage time, your life does not just happen by chance. You are on equal terms with the greatest sculptor, painter, or playwright. More than creating a work of art, you are designing a life.

Without planning, we fall prey to simply digging in—engaging in frantic activity with uncertain results. Planning replaces this behavior with clearly defined outcomes and action steps.

An effective plan is flexible, not carved in stone. You can change your plans frequently and still preserve the advantages of planning—choosing your overall direction and taking charge of your life. And even when other people set the goal, you can choose how to achieve it.

Planning is a self-creative venture that lasts for a lifetime. Following are nine ways to get the most from this process. The first four are suggestions about goal setting. The rest cover the details of scheduling activities based on your goals.

Back up to a bigger picture. When choosing activities for the day or week, take some time to lift your eyes to the horizon. Step back for a few minutes and consider your longer-range goals—what you want to accomplish in the next 6 months, the next year, the next 5 years, and beyond.

Ask whether the activities you're about to schedule actually contribute to those goals. If they do, great. If not, ask whether you can delete some items from your calendar or to-do list to make room for goal-related activities. See if you can free up at least 1 hour each day for doing something you love instead of putting it off to a more "reasonable" or "convenient" time.

You can back up to a bigger picture even when your goals are not precisely defined. You might suddenly sense that now is the time in your life to start a new relationship, take a long trip, or move to a new apartment or house. Pay attention to these intuitions. Allow space in your daily and weekly schedule to explore and act on your dreams.

Look boldly for things to change. It's fascinating to note the areas that are off limits when people set goals. Goals that involve money, sex, career, marriage, and other topics can easily fall into the category "I'll just have to live with this."

When creating your future, expand your thinking about what aspects of your life can be changed and what cannot. Be willing to put every facet of your life on the table. Staying open-minded can lead to a future you never dreamed was possible.

Look for what's missing—and what to maintain. Goals often arise from a sense of what's missing in our lives. Goal setting is fueled by problems that are not resolved, projects that are incomplete, relationships we want to develop, and careers we still want to pursue.

However, not all planning has to spring from a sense of need. You can set goals to maintain things that you already have, or to keep doing the effective things that you already do. If you exercise vigorously three times each week, you can set a goal to keep exercising. If you already have a loving relationship with your spouse, you can set a goal to nurture that relationship for the rest of your life.

Think even further into the future. To have fun and unleash your creativity, set goals as far in the future as you can. The specific length of time doesn't matter. For some people, long-range planning might mean 10, 20, or even 50 years from now. For others, imagining 3 years feels right. Do whatever works for you.

Once you've stated your longest-range goals, work backward until you can define a next step to take. Suppose your 30-year goal is to retire and maintain your present standard of living. Ask yourself, "To do that, what financial goals do I need to achieve in 20 years? In 10 years? In 1 year? In 1 month? In 1 week?" Put the answers to these questions in writing.

Schedule fixed blocks of time first. When planning your week, start with class time and work time. These time periods are usually determined in advance, so other activities must be scheduled around them. Then schedule essential daily activities such as sleeping and eating. In addition, schedule some time each week for actions that lead directly to one of your written goals.

Set clear starting and stopping times. Tasks often expand to fill the time we allot to them. "It always takes me an hour just to settle into a reading assignment" might become a self-fulfilling prophecy.

Try scheduling a certain amount of time for a reading assignment—set a timer, and stick to it. Students often find that they can decrease study time by forcing themselves to read faster. They can usually do so without sacrificing comprehension.

A variation of this technique is called *time boxing*. Set aside a specific number of minutes or hours to spend on a certain task. Instead of working on that task until it's done, commit to work on it just for that specific amount of time. Then set a timer, and get to work. In effect, you're placing the task inside a definite "box"—a specific space on your daily calendar.

Time boxing is one way to overcome resistance to a task, focus your attention, and make a meaningful dent in large projects. The amount of time you choose can be relatively small—such as 10 minutes. Start with short periods, and gradually increase them.

Scheduling a fixed time can apply to other tasks. Some people find they can get up 15 minutes earlier in the morning and still feel alert throughout the day. Plan 45 minutes for a trip to the grocery store instead of an hour. Over the course of a year, those extra minutes can add up to hours.

Feeling rushed or sacrificing quality is not the goal here. The point is to push yourself a little and discover what your time requirements really are.

Schedule for flexibility and fun. Recognize that unexpected things will happen, and allow for them. Leave some holes in your schedule. Build in blocks of unplanned time. Consider setting aside time each week marked "flex time" or "open time." Use these hours for emergencies, spontaneous activities, catching up, or seizing new opportunities.

Include time for errands. The time we spend buying toothpaste, paying bills, and doing laundry is easy to overlook. These little errands can destroy a tight schedule and make us feel rushed and harried all week. Plan for them, and remember to allow for travel time between locations.

Also make room for fun. Fun is important. Brains that are constantly stimulated by new ideas and new challenges need time off to digest them. Take time to browse aimlessly through the library, stroll with no destination, ride a bike, or do other things you enjoy. It's important to "waste" time once in a while.

To maintain flexibility and fun, be realistic. Don't set yourself up for failure by telling yourself you can do a 4-hour job in 2 hours. There are only 168 hours in a week. If you schedule 169 hours, you're sunk.

Plan for changes in your workload. You might find yourself with a lighter load of assignments to complete during the first few days or weeks of any course. This typically happens when instructors give an overview of the subject or take time to review material that you already know from another course.

Faced with this situation, some students are tempted to let early homework slide. They figure that they'll have plenty of time to catch up later. These students often get a rude surprise when the course shifts into warp speed. After reviewing the basics, instructors may cover new and more difficult material at a faster pace, piling on extra readings, writing assignments, and quizzes.

To stay on top of your workload over the entire term, plan for such a change of pace. Stay on top of your assignments right from the start. Whenever possible, work ahead. This tactic gives you an edge when the load for a course gets heavier, or when big assignments for several courses are due during the same week.

Involve others when appropriate. Sometimes the activities you schedule depend on gaining information, assistance, or direct participation from other people. If you neglect to inform others of your plans or forget to ask for their cooperation at the outset—surprise! Your schedule can crash.

Statements such as these often follow the communications breakdown: "I just assumed you were going to pick up the kids from school on Tuesday." "I'm working overtime this week and hoped that you'd take over the cooking for a while."

When you schedule a task that depends on another person's involvement, let that person know—the sooner, the better. ✳

Poleze/Shutterstock

Stop procrastination NOW

CONSIDER A BOLD IDEA: The way to begin to stop procrastinating is to choose to stop procrastinating. Giving up procrastination is actually a simple choice; people make it complicated.

Test this idea for yourself. Think of something that you've been putting off. Choose a small, specific task—one that you can complete in 5 minutes or less. Then do that task today.

Tomorrow, choose another task and do it. Repeat this strategy each day for 1 week. Notice what happens to your habit of procrastination.

If the above suggestion just doesn't work for you, then experiment with any strategy from the list on page 77. (Just don't put it off.)

Discover the costs. Find out if procrastination keeps you from getting what you want. Clearly seeing the side effects of procrastination can help you kick the habit.

Discover your procrastination style. Psychologist Linda Sapadin identifies different styles of procrastination.[2] For example, *dreamers* have big goals that they seldom translate into specific plans. *Worriers* focus on the worst-case scenario and are likely to talk more about problems than about solutions. *Defiers* resist new tasks or promise to do them and then don't follow through. *Overdoers* create extra work for themselves by refusing to delegate tasks and neglecting to set priorities. And *perfectionists* put off tasks for fear of making a mistake.

Awareness of your procrastination style is a key to changing your behavior. If you exhibit the characteristics of an overdoer, for example, then say no to new projects. Also ask for help in completing your current projects.

To discover your procrastination style, observe your behavior. Avoid judgments. Just be a scientist: Record the facts. Write Discovery Statements about specific ways you procrastinate. Follow up with Intention Statements about what to do differently.

Trick yourself into getting started. If you have a 50-page chapter to read, then grab the book and say to yourself, "I'm not really going to read this chapter right now. I'm just going to flip through the pages and scan the headings for 10 minutes." Tricks like these can get you started on a task you've been dreading.

Let feelings follow action. If you put off exercising until you feel energetic, you might wait for months. Instead, get moving now. Then watch your feelings change. After 5 minutes of brisk walking, you might be in the mood for a 20-minute run. This principle—action generates motivation—can apply to any task that you've put on the back burner.

Choose to work under pressure. Sometimes people thrive under pressure. As one writer puts it, "I don't do my *best* work under deadline. I do my *only* work under deadline." Used selectively, this strategy might also work for you.

Put yourself in control. If you choose to work with a due date staring you right in the face, then schedule a big block of time during the preceding week. Until then, enjoy!

Think ahead. Use the monthly calendar on page 88 or the long-term planner on page 91 to list due dates for assignments in all your courses. Using these tools, you can anticipate heavy demands on your time and take action to prevent last-minute crunches. Make *Becoming a Master Student* your home base—the first place to turn in taking control of your schedule.

Give up "someday." Procrastination rests on this vague notion: *I'll do it someday.* Other people reinforce this notion by telling you that your life will *really* start when you . . . . (Fill in the blank with phrases like *graduate from college, get married, have kids, get promoted,* or *retire.*) Using this logic, you could wait your whole life to start living. Avoid this fate. Take action today.

Create goals that draw you forward. A goal that grabs you by the heartstrings is an inspiration to act now. If you're procrastinating, then set some goals that excite you. Then you might wake up one day and discover that procrastination is part of your past. ✳

 Find more strategies for ending procrastination.

The 7-day antiprocrastination plan

Listed here are seven strategies you can use to reduce or eliminate many sources of procrastination. The suggestions are tied to the days of the week to help you remember them. Use this list to remind yourself that each day of your life presents an opportunity to stop the cycle of procrastination.

MONDAY Make it Meaningful What is important about the task you've been putting off? List all the benefits of completing that task. Look at it in relation to your short-, mid-, or long-term goals. Be specific about the rewards for getting it done, including how you will feel when the task is completed. To remember this strategy, keep in mind that it starts with the letter *M,* as in the word *Monday.*

TUESDAY Take it Apart Break big jobs into a series of small ones you can do in 15 minutes or less. If a long reading assignment intimidates you, divide it into two- or three-page sections. Make a list of the sections, and cross them off as you complete them so you can see your progress. Even the biggest projects can be broken down into a series of small tasks. This strategy starts with the letter *T,* so mentally tie it to *Tuesday.*

WEDNESDAY Write an Intention Statement If you can't get started on a term paper, you might write, "I intend to write a list of at least ten possible topics by 9 p.m. I will reward myself with an hour of guilt-free recreational reading." Write your intention on a 3x5 card. Carry it with you or post it in your study area, where you can see it often. In your memory, file the first word in this strategy—*write*—with *Wednesday.*

THURSDAY Tell Everyone Publicly announce your intention to get a task done. Tell a friend that you intend to learn ten irregular French verbs by Saturday. Tell your spouse, roommate, parents, and children. Include anyone who will ask whether you've completed the assignment or who will suggest ways to get it done. Make the world your support group. Associate *tell* with *Thursday.*

FRIDAY Find a Reward Construct rewards to yourself carefully. Be willing to withhold them if you do not complete the task. Don't pick a movie as a reward for studying biology if you plan to go to the movie anyway. And when you legitimately reap your reward, notice how it feels. Remember that *Friday* is a fine day to *find* a reward. (Of course, you can find a reward on any day of the week. Rhyming *Friday* with *fine* day is just a memory trick.)

SATURDAY Settle it Now Do it now. The minute you notice yourself procrastinating, plunge into the task. Imagine yourself at a cold mountain lake, poised to dive. Gradual immersion would be slow torture. It's often less painful to leap. Then be sure to savor the feeling of having the task behind you. Link *settle* with *Saturday.*

SUNDAY Say No When you keep pushing a task into a low-priority category, reexamine your purpose for doing that task at all. If you realize that you really don't intend to do something, quit telling yourself that you will. That's procrastinating. Just say no. Then you're not procrastinating. You don't have to carry around the baggage of an undone task. *Sunday*—the last day of this 7-day plan—is a great day to finally let go and just *say* no.

practicing critical thinking

1. List five areas of your life in which you procrastinate, and describe them briefly in the first column below.

2. Look back at the articles you just read about procrastination, and pick a procrastination tool that you think might work to help you overcome each of your five procrastination areas. Write that tool in the second column.

3. In the third column, describe specifically how you will implement the procrastination tool.

Example:

Procrastination Area

1. Not starting my research project.

Potential Tool

Take it Apart

Specific Plan

Break down the project as follows:

1. Topic/thesis statement (week 1).
2. Preliminary research (week 2).
3. In-depth research (week 3).
4. First draft (week 4).
5. Revision for final version (week 5).

(www) Complete this exercise online.

25 ways to get the most out of now

The following techniques are about getting the most from study time. They're listed in four categories:

- When to study.
- Where to study.
- Ways to handle the rest of the world.
- Things to ask yourself if you get stuck.

Don't feel pressured to use all of the techniques or to tackle them in order. As you read, note the suggestions you think will be helpful. Pick one technique to use now. When it becomes a habit, come back to this article and select another one. Repeat this cycle, and enjoy the results as they unfold in your life.

Ferenc Szelepcsenyi/Shutterstock

When to study

Study difficult (or boring) subjects first. If your chemistry problems put you to sleep, get to them first, while you are fresh. We tend to give top priority to what we enjoy studying, yet the courses that we find most difficult often require the most creative energy. Save your favorite subjects for later. If you find yourself avoiding a particular subject, get up an hour earlier to study it before breakfast. With that chore out of the way, the rest of the day can be a breeze.

Continually being late with course assignments indicates a trouble area. Further action is required. Clarify your intentions about the course by writing down your feelings in a journal, talking with an instructor, or asking for help from a friend or counselor. Consistently avoiding study tasks can also be a signal to reexamine your major or course program.

Be aware of your best time of day. Many people learn best in daylight hours. If this is true for you, schedule study time for your most difficult subjects before nightfall.

Unless you grew up on a farm, the idea of being conscious at 5 a.m. might seem ridiculous. Yet many successful businesspeople begin the day at 5 a.m. or earlier. Athletes and yoga practitioners use the early morning, too. Some writers complete their best work before 9 a.m.

Others experience the same benefits by staying up late. They flourish after midnight. If you aren't convinced, then experiment. When you're in a time crunch, get up early or stay up late. You might even see a sunrise.

Use waiting time. Five minutes waiting for a subway, 20 minutes waiting for the dentist, 10 minutes in between classes—waiting time adds up fast. Have short study tasks ready to do during these periods. For example, you can carry 3x5 cards with facts, formulas, or definitions and pull them out anywhere.

A CD or mp3 player can help you use commuting time to your advantage. Use your computer to make a recording of yourself reading your notes. Then transfer that recording onto a CD or mp3 player. Play it as you drive, or listen through headphones as you ride on the bus or subway.

Study 2 hours for every hour you're in class. Students in higher education are regularly advised to allow 2 hours of study time for every hour spent in class. If you are taking 15 credit hours, then plan to spend 30 hours a week studying. The benefits of following this advice will be apparent at exam time.

This guideline is just that—a guideline, not an absolute rule. Consider what's best for you. If you do the Time Monitor/Time Plan exercise in this chapter, note how many hours you actually spend studying for each hour of class. Then ask how your schedule is working. You might want to allow more study time for some subjects.

Keep in mind that the "2 hours for 1" rule doesn't distinguish between focused time and unfocused time. In one 4-hour block of study time, it's possible to use up two of those hours with phone calls, breaks, daydreaming, and doodling. With study time, quality counts as much as quantity.

Avoid marathon study sessions. When possible, study in shorter sessions. Three 3-hour sessions are usually more productive than one 9-hour session. If you must study in a large block of time, work on several subjects, and avoid studying similar topics one after the other.

Where to study

Use a regular study area. Your body and your mind know where you are. Using the same place to study, day after day, helps train your responses. When you arrive at that particular place, you can focus your attention more quickly.

Study where you'll be alert. In bed, your body gets a signal. For most students, that signal is more likely to be "Time to sleep!" than "Time to study!" Just as you train

your body to be alert at your desk, you also train it to slow down near your bed. For that reason, don't study where you sleep.

Easy chairs and sofas are also dangerous places to study. Learning requires energy. Give your body a message that energy is needed. Put yourself in a situation that supports this message. For example, some schools offer empty classrooms as places to study. Many students report that they find themselves studying effectively in a classroom setting.

Use a library. Libraries are designed for learning. The lighting is perfect. The noise level is low. A wealth of material is available. Entering a library is a signal to focus the mind and get to work. Many students can get more done in a shorter time frame at the library than anywhere else. Experiment for yourself.

Ways to handle the rest of the world

Pay attention to your attention. Breaks in concentration are often caused by internal interruptions. Your own thoughts jump in to divert you from your studies. When this happens, notice these thoughts, and let them go. Perhaps the thought of getting something else done is distracting you. One option is to handle that other task now and study later. Or you can write yourself a note about it, or schedule a specific time to do it.

Agree with living mates about study time. This agreement includes roommates, spouses, and children. Make the rules about study time clear, and be sure to follow them yourself. Explicit agreements—even written contracts—work well. One student always wears a colorful hat when he wants to study. When his wife and children see the hat, they respect his wish to be left alone.

Get off the phone. The phone is the ultimate interrupter. People who wouldn't think of distracting you in person might call or text you at the worst times because they can't see that you are studying. You don't have to be a victim of your cell phone. If a simple "I can't talk; I'm studying" doesn't work, use dead silence. It's a conversation killer. Or short-circuit the whole problem: Turn off your phone or silence it.

Learn to say no. Saying no is a time-saver and a valuable life skill for everyone. Some people feel it is rude to refuse a request. But you can say no effectively and courteously. Others want you to succeed as a student. When you tell them that you can't do what they ask because you are busy educating yourself, most people will understand.

Hang a "do not disturb" sign on your door. Many hotels will give you a free sign, for the advertising. Or you can create a sign yourself. They work. Using signs can relieve you of making a decision about cutting off each interruption—a time-saver in itself.

Get ready the night before. Completing a few simple tasks just before you go to bed can help you get in gear the next day. If you need to make some phone calls first thing in the morning, look up those numbers, write them on 3x5 cards, and set them near the phone. If you need to drive to a new location, make a note of the address and check the directions online, then put them next to your car keys. If you plan to spend the next afternoon writing a paper, get your materials together: dictionary, notes, outline, paper, pencil, flash drive, laptop—whatever you need. Pack your lunch or put gas in the car. Organize the baby's diaper bag and your briefcase or backpack.

Call ahead. We often think of talking on the telephone as a prime time-waster. Used wisely, though, the telephone can actually help manage time. Before you go shopping, call the store to see if it carries the items you're looking for. If you're driving, call for directions to your destination (or look them up online). A few seconds on the phone or computer can save hours in wasted trips and wrong turns.

Avoid noise distractions. To promote concentration, avoid studying in front of the television, and turn off the radio. Many students insist that they study better with background noise, and it might be true. Some students report good results with carefully selected and controlled music. For many others, silence is the best form of music to study by.

At times noise levels might be out of your control. A neighbor or roommate might decide to find out how far she can turn up her music before the walls crumble. Meanwhile, your ability to concentrate on the principles of sociology goes down the drain. To avoid this scenario, schedule study sessions during periods when your living environment is usually quiet. If you live in a residence hall, ask if study rooms are available. Or go somewhere else where it's quiet, such as the library. Some students have even found refuge in quiet coffee shops, self-service laundries, and places of worship.

Manage interruptions. Notice how others misuse your time. Be aware of repeat offenders. Ask yourself if there are certain friends or relatives who consistently interrupt your study time.

If avoiding the interrupter is impractical, send a clear message. Sometimes others don't realize that they are breaking your concentration. You can give them a gentle, yet firm, reminder: "What you're saying is important. Can we schedule a time to talk about it when I can give you my full attention?" If this strategy doesn't work, there are other ways to make your message more effective. For more ideas, see Chapter 8: Communicating.

See if you can "firewall" yourself for selected study periods each week. Find a place where you can count on being alone and working without interruption.

Sometimes interruptions still happen, though. Create a system for dealing with them. One option is to take an index card and write a quick note about what you're doing the moment an interruption occurs. As soon as possible, return to the card and pick up the task where you left off.

Things to ask yourself if you get stuck

Ask: "What is one task I can accomplish toward achieving my goal?" This technique is helpful when you face a big, imposing job. Pick out one small accomplishment, preferably one you can complete in about 5 minutes; then do it. The satisfaction of getting one thing done can spur you on to get one more thing done. Meanwhile, the job gets smaller.

Ask: "Am I being too hard on myself?" If you are feeling frustrated with a reading assignment, if your attention wanders repeatedly, or if you've fallen behind on math problems that are due tomorrow, take a minute to listen to the messages you are giving yourself. Are you scolding yourself too harshly? Lighten up. Allow yourself to feel a little foolish, and then get on with

Keep on going?

Some people keep on going, even when they get stuck or fail again and again. To such people belongs the world. Consider the hapless politician who compiled this record:

- Failed in business, 1831.
- Defeated for legislature, 1832.
- Failed in business a second time, 1833.
- Suffered a nervous breakdown, 1836.
- Defeated for speaker of the house, 1838.
- Defeated for elector, 1840.
- Defeated for Congress, 1843.
- Defeated for Senate, 1855.
- Defeated for vice president, 1856.
- Defeated for Senate, 1858.
- Elected president, 1860.

Who was the fool who kept on going in spite of so many failures?

Answer: The fool was Abraham Lincoln.

the task at hand. Don't add to the problem by berating yourself.

Worrying about the future is another way people beat themselves up: "How will I ever get all this done?" "What if every paper I'm assigned turns out to be this hard?" "If I can't do the simple calculations now, how will I ever pass the final?" Instead of promoting learning, such questions fuel anxiety.

Labeling and generalizing weaknesses are other ways people are hard on themselves. Being objective and specific in the messages you send yourself will help eliminate this form of self-punishment and will likely generate new possibilities. An alternative to saying "I'm terrible in algebra" is to say "I don't understand factoring equations." This rewording suggests a plan to improve.

You might be able to lighten the load by discovering how your learning styles affect your behavior. For example, you may have a bias toward concrete experience rather than abstract thinking. If so, after setting a goal, you might want to move directly into action.

In large part, the ability to learn through concrete experience is a valuable trait. After all, action is necessary to achieve goals. At the same time, you might find it helpful to allow extra time to plan. Careful planning can help you avoid unnecessary activity. Instead of using a planner that shows a day at a time, experiment with a calendar that displays a week or month at a glance. The expanded format can help you

Remember cultural differences

There are as many different styles for managing time as there are people. These styles vary across cultures.

In the United States and England, for example, business meetings typically start on time. That's also true in Scandinavian countries such as Norway and Sweden. However, travelers to Panama might find that meetings start about a half-hour late. And people who complain about late meetings while doing business in Mexico might be considered rude.

When you study or work with people of different races and ethnic backgrounds, look for differences in their approach to time. A behavior that you might view as rude or careless—such as showing up late for appointments—could simply result from seeing the world in a different way.

 Find more information about cultural differences in time management online.

look farther into the future and stay on track as you set out to meet long-term goals.

Ask: "Is this a piano?" Carpenters who construct rough frames for buildings have a saying they use when they bend a nail or accidentally hack a chunk out of a two-by-four: "Well, this ain't no piano." It means that perfection is not necessary. Ask yourself if what you are doing needs to be perfect. Perhaps you don't have to apply the same standards of grammar to lecture notes that you would apply to a term paper. If you can complete a job 95 percent perfectly in 2 hours and 100 percent perfectly in 4 hours, ask yourself whether the additional 5 percent improvement is worth doubling the amount of time you spend.

Sometimes, though, it *is* a piano. A tiny miscalculation can ruin an entire lab experiment. A misstep in solving a complex math problem can negate hours of work. Computers are notorious for turning little errors into nightmares. Accept lower standards only when appropriate.

A related suggestion is to weed out low-priority tasks. The to-do list for a large project can include dozens of items, not all of which are equally important. Some can be done later, while others can be skipped altogether, if time is short.

Apply this idea when you study. In a long reading assignment, look for pages you can skim or skip. When it's appropriate, read chapter summaries or article abstracts. As you review your notes, look for material that might not be covered on a test, and decide whether you want to study it.

Ask: "Would I pay myself for what I'm doing right now?" If you were employed as a student, would you be earning your wages? Ask yourself this question when you notice that you've taken your third snack break in 30 minutes. Then remember that you are, in fact, employed as a student. You are investing in your own productivity and are paying a big price for the privilege of being a student. Doing a mediocre job now might result in fewer opportunities in the future.

Ask: "Can I do just one more thing?" Ask yourself this question at the end of a long day. Almost always you will have enough energy to do just one more short task. The overall increase in your productivity might surprise you.

Ask: "Am I making time for things that are important but not urgent?" If we spend most of our time putting out fires, we can feel drained and frustrated. According to Stephen R. Covey, this chain of events occurs when we forget to take time for things that are not urgent but are truly important.[3] Examples of truly important activities include exercising regularly, reading, praying or meditating, spending quality time alone or with family members and friends, traveling, and cooking nutritious meals. Each of these activities can contribute directly to a long-term goal or life mission. Yet when schedules get tight, we often forgo these things, waiting for that elusive day when we'll "finally have more time."

That day won't come until we choose to make time for what's truly important. Knowing this, we can use some of the suggestions in this chapter to free up more time.

Ask: "Can I delegate this?" Instead of slogging through complicated tasks alone, you can draw on the talents and energy of other people. Busy executives know the value of delegating tasks to coworkers. Without delegation, many projects would flounder or die.

You can apply the same principle in your life. Instead of doing all the housework or cooking by yourself, for example, you can assign some of the tasks to family members or roommates. Rather than making a trip to the library to look up a simple fact, you can call and ask a library assistant to research it for you. Instead of driving across town to deliver a package, you can hire a delivery service to do so. All of these tactics can free up extra hours for studying.

It's not practical to delegate certain study tasks, such as writing term papers or completing reading assignments. However, you can still draw on the ideas of others in completing such tasks. For instance, form a writing group to edit and critique papers, brainstorm topics or titles, and develop lists of sources.

If you're absent from a class, find a classmate to summarize the lecture, discussion, and any upcoming assignments. Presidents depend on briefings. You can use the same technique.

Ask: "How did I just waste time?" Notice when time passes and you haven't accomplished what you had planned to do. Take a minute to review your actions, and note the specific ways you wasted time. We tend to operate by habit, wasting time in the same ways over and over again. When you are aware of things you do that drain your time, you are more likely to catch yourself in the act next time. Observing one small quirk might save you hours. But keep this in mind: Asking

you to notice how you waste time is not intended to make you feel guilty. The point is to increase your skill by getting specific information about how you use time.

Ask: "Could I find the time if I really wanted to?" The way people speak often rules out the option of finding more time. An alternative is to speak about time with more possibility.

The next time you're tempted to say, "I just don't have time," pause for a minute. Question the truth of this statement. Could you find 4 more hours this week for studying? Suppose that someone offered to pay you $10,000 to find those 4 hours. Suppose, too, that you will get paid only if you don't lose sleep, call in sick for work, or sacrifice anything important to you. Could you find the time if vast sums of money were involved?

Remember that when it comes to school, vast sums of money *are* involved.

Ask: "Am I willing to promise it?" This time management idea might be the most powerful of all: If you want to find time for a task, promise yourself—and others—that you'll get it done.

To make this technique work, do more than say that you'll try or that you'll give it your best shot. Take an oath, as you would in court. Give it your word.

One way to accomplish big things in life is to make big promises. There's little reward in promising what's safe or predictable. No athlete promises to place seventh in the Olympic games. Chances are that if you're not making big promises, you're not stretching yourself.

The point of making a promise is not to chain yourself to a rigid schedule or impossible expectations. You can promise to reach goals without unbearable stress. You can keep schedules flexible and carry out your plans with ease, joy, and satisfaction.

At times, though, you might go too far. Some promises may be truly beyond you, and you might break them. However, failing to keep a promise is just that—failing to keep a promise. A broken promise is not the end of the world.

Promises can work magic. When your word is on the line, it's possible to discover reserves of time and energy you didn't know existed. Promises can push you to exceed your expectations. ✳

 Discover even more ways to get the most out of now.

Beyond time management:
Stay focused on what matters

Ask some people about managing time, and a dreaded image appears in their minds.

THEY SEE A PERSON with a 100-item to-do list clutching a calendar chock full of appointments. They imagine a robot who values cold efficiency, compulsively accounts for every minute, and has no time for people.

These stereotypes about time management hold a kernel of truth. Sometimes people fixate so much on time management that they fail to appreciate what they are doing. Time management becomes a burden, a chore, a process that prevents them from actually enjoying the task at hand.

At other times, people who pride themselves on efficiency are merely keeping busy. In their rush to check items off a to-do list, they might be fussing over activities that create little value in the first place.

It might help you to think beyond time management to the larger concept of *planning*. The point of planning is not to load your schedule with obligations. Instead, planning is about getting the important things done and still having time to be human. An effective planner is productive and relaxed at the same time.

Discover your style

Many time management techniques appeal to "left-brained" people—those who thrive on making lists, scheduling events, and handling details. Those suggestions might not work for people who like to see wholes and think visually.

Remember that there are many styles of planning. Some people prefer a written action plan that carefully details each step leading to a long-range goal. If you prefer a Mode 2 or Mode 3 learning style as explained

Woman: Hill Street Studios/Getty; *clock:* Falko Matte/Shutterstock; collage by Walter Kopec

in Chapter 1, written action plans might appeal to you. Other people just keep a list of current projects and periodically assess their progress. Both approaches can work.

Give time management strategies a fair chance. Strategies that don't seem to your taste at first might be suitable with a few modifications. Instead of writing a conventional to-do list, for instance, you can plot your day on a mind map. (Mind maps are explained in Chapter 5: Notes.) Doing so might feel especially comfortable if you're blessed with a natural visual intelligence, as explained in the discussion of Howard Gardner's theory of multiple intelligences in Chapter 1.

Another approach might be to write to-do items, one per 3x5 card, in any order in which tasks occur to you. Later you can edit, sort, and rank the cards, choosing which items to do. This method will probably appeal to you if you learn best through active experimentation and using your kinesthetic intelligence, which involves movement and the sense of touch.

Focus on values

View your activities from the perspective of an entire lifetime. Given the finite space between birth and death, determine what matters most to you.

As a way to define your values, write your own obituary. Describe the ways you want to be remembered. List the contributions you intend to make during your lifetime and the kind of person you wish to become. If this exercise is too spooky, then complete the lifeline exercise on page 69 instead. Or simply write your life purpose—a sentence or short paragraph that describes what's most important to you.

Next, return to the Time Monitor/Time Plan exercise on page 62. Look at your completed Time Monitor, and place a check mark next to the activities that are directly aligned with your values. Write a Discovery Statement about how "on purpose" you were for the week. Follow it with an Intention Statement about any resulting changes in your plan for next week.

Focus on outcomes

You might feel guilty when you occasionally stray from your schedule and spend 2 hours napping or watching soap operas. But if you're regularly meeting your goals, there's probably no harm done.

Managing time and getting organized are not ends in themselves. It's possible to be efficient, organized, and miserable. Larger outcomes such as personal satisfaction and effectiveness count more than the means used to achieve them.

Visualizing a desired outcome can be as important as having a detailed action plan. Here's an experiment: Write a list of goals you plan to accomplish over the next 6 months. Next, create a vivid mental picture of yourself attaining those goals and enjoying the resulting benefits. Visualize this image several times in the next few weeks. Then file the list away, making a note on your calendar to review it in 6 months. When 6 months have passed, look over the list, and note how many of your goals you have actually accomplished.

Do less

Planning is as much about dropping worthless activities as about adding new ones. See if you can reduce or eliminate activities that contribute little to your values. When you add a new item to your calendar or to-do list, consider dropping a current one.

Buy less

Before you purchase an item, estimate how much time it will take to locate, assemble, use, repair, and maintain it. You might be able to free up hours by doing without. If the product comes with a 400-page manual or 20 hours of training, beware. Before rushing to the store to add another possession to your life, see if you can reuse or adapt something you already own.

Woman: Hill Street Studios/Getty; *clock:* Janaka Dharmasena/Shutterstock; collage by Walter Kopec

Slow down

Sometimes it's useful to hurry, such as when you're late for a meeting or about to miss a plane. At other times, haste is a choice that serves no real purpose. If you're speeding through the day like a launched missile, consider what would happen if you got to your next destination a few minutes later than planned. Rushing might not be worth the added strain.

Handle it now

A long to-do list can result from postponing decisions and procrastinating. An alternative is to handle a task or decision immediately. Answer that letter now. Make that phone call as soon as it occurs to you. Then you don't have to add the task to your calendar or to-do list.

The same idea applies when someone asks you to volunteer for a project and you realize immediately that you don't want to do it. Save time by graciously telling the truth up front. Saying "I'll think about it and get back to you" just postpones the conversation until later, when it might take more time.

Remember people

Few people on their deathbeds ever say, "I wish I'd spent more time at the office." They're more likely to say, "I wish I'd spent more time with my family and friends." The pace of daily life can lead us to neglect the people we cherish.

Efficiency is a concept that applies to things—not people. When it comes to maintaining and nurturing relationships, we can often benefit from loosening up our schedules. We can allow extra time for conflict management, spontaneous visits, and free-ranging conversations.

Forget about time

Take time away from time. Schedule downtime—a space in your day where you ignore to-do lists, appointments, and accomplishments. This period is when you're accountable to no one else and have nothing to accomplish. Even a few minutes spent in this way can yield a sense of renewal. One way to manage time is periodically to forget about it.

Experiment with decreasing your overall awareness of time. Leave your watch off for a few hours each day.

Spend time in an area that's free of clocks. Notice how often you glance at your watch, and make a conscious effort to do so less often.

If you still want some sense of time, use alternatives to the almighty, unforgiving clock. Measure certain activities with a sundial, hourglass, or egg timer. Or synchronize your activities with the rhythms of nature—for example, by rising at dawn.

You can also plan activities to harmonize with the rhythms of your body. Schedule your most demanding tasks for times when you're normally most alert. Eat when you're hungry, not according to the clock. Toss out schedules when it's appropriate. Sometimes the best-laid plans are best laid to rest.

Strictly speaking, time cannot be managed. The minutes, hours, days, and years simply march ahead. What we can do is manage *ourselves* with respect to time. A few basic principles can help us do that as well as a truckload of cold-blooded techniques. ✳

Forget time management—just get things done

David Allen, author of *Getting Things Done: The Art of Stress-free Productivity*, says that a lack of time is not the real issue for the people he coaches in time management. Instead, the problem is "a lack of clarity and definition about what a project really is, and what the associated next-action steps required are."[4] Allen translates this idea into the following suggestions.

1. **Collect.** To begin, gather every unfinished project, incomplete task, misplaced object—or anything else that's nagging you—and dump it into a "bucket," or collection area. This area could be an actual bucket that's big enough to hold various objects, a file folder, a traditional in-basket, or all of these receptacles. If an item is too big to store in a bucket, write a reminder of it on a 3x5 card or a piece of paper—one item per card or sheet—so that it's easier to file later. Stick this reminder in one of your buckets.

2. **Process.** Now go to each of your buckets, one at a time. Take whatever item is at the top of the pile and ask, "Do I truly want to or need to do something about this?" If the answer is no, calmly dispose of the item. If the answer is yes, then choose immediately how to respond:

   - If you can take action on this item in 2 minutes or less, do so now.

   - If you're dealing with an item that can best be handled by someone else, delegate it to that person.

   - If you're dealing with an item that will take more than 2 minutes for you to do, write a reminder to do it later.

   Repeat the above procedure for each item in each of your buckets. The overall goal is to *empty* the buckets at least once each week.

3. **Organize.** Now group your reminders into appropriate lists by category. The categories are ultimately up to you, but Allen's recommendations include the following:

   - A calendar for listing actions to be completed on a specific date or at a specific time.

   - A list of current projects. A *project* is an outcome that requires two or more actions to produce.

   - A to-do list. Group the items on this list by the physical location where you will do them—for example, *at phone* or *at computer*.

4. **Review.** Every week, review your reminders and ask yourself, "What are all my current projects? And what is the *very next physical action* (such as a phone call or errand) that I can take to move each project forward?"

5. **Do.** Every day, review your calendar or lists. Based on this information and on your intuition, make moment-to-moment choices about how to spend your time.

Master monthly calendar

This exercise will give you an opportunity to step back from the details of your daily schedule and get a bigger picture of your life. The more difficult it is for you to plan beyond the current day or week, the greater the benefit of this exercise.

Your basic tool is a 1-month calendar. Use it to block out specific times for upcoming events such as study group meetings, due dates for assignments, review periods before tests, and other time-sensitive tasks.

To get started, you might want to copy the blank monthly calendar on pages 88–89 onto both sides of a sheet of paper. Or make several copies of these pages, and tape them together so that you can see several months at a glance.

Be creative. Experiment with a variety of uses for your monthly calendar. For instance, you can note day-to-day changes in your health or moods, list the places you visit while you are on vacation, or circle each day that you practice a new habit. For examples of filled-in monthly calendars, see below.

 Find printable copies of this monthly calendar online.

TIME

MONDAY	TUESDAY	WEDNESDAY	THURSDAY	FRIDAY	SATURDAY	SUNDAY

Month

Name

MONDAY	TUESDAY	WEDNESDAY	THURSDAY	FRIDAY	SATURDAY	SUNDAY

Name

Month

2

TIME

Gearing up:
Using a long-term planner

Planning a day, a week, or a month ahead is a powerful practice. Using a long-term planner—one that displays an entire quarter, semester, or year at a glance—can yield even more benefits.

WITH A LONG-TERM PLANNER you can eliminate a lot of unpleasant surprises. Long-term planning allows you to avoid scheduling conflicts—the kind that obligate you to be in two places at the same time 3 weeks from now. You can also anticipate busy periods, such as finals week, and start preparing for them now. Good-bye, all-night cram sessions. Hello, serenity.

Find a long-term planner, or make your own. Many office supply stores carry academic planners in paper form that cover an entire school year. Computer software for time management offers the same features. You can also be creative and make your own long-term planner. A big roll of newsprint pinned to a bulletin board or taped to a wall will do nicely.

Enter scheduled dates that extend into the future. Use your long-term planner to list commitments that extend beyond the current month. Enter test dates, lab sessions, days that classes will be canceled, and other events that will take place over this term and next term.

Create a master assignment list. Find the syllabus for each course you're currently taking. Then, in your long-term planner, enter the due dates for all of the assignments in all of your courses. This step can be a powerful reality check.

The purpose of this technique is to not to make you feel overwhelmed with all the things you have to do. Rather, its aim is to help you take a First Step toward recognizing the demands on your time. Armed with the truth about how you use your time, you can make more accurate plans.

Include nonacademic events. In addition to tracking academic commitments, you can use your long-term planner to mark significant events in your life outside school. Include birthdays, doctors' appointments, concert dates, credit card payment due dates, and car maintenance schedules.

Use your long-term planner to divide and conquer. Big assignments such as term papers or major presentations pose a special risk. When you have 3 months to do a project, you might say to yourself, "That looks like a lot of work, but I've got plenty of time. No problem." But 2 months, 3 weeks, and 6 days from now, it could suddenly be a huge problem.

For some people, academic life is a series of last-minute crises punctuated by periods of exhaustion. You can avoid that fate. The trick is to set due dates *before* the final due date.

When planning to write a term paper, for instance, enter the final due date in your long-term planner. Then set individual due dates for each milestone in the writing process—creating an outline, completing your research, finishing a first draft, editing the draft, and preparing the final copy. By meeting these interim due dates, you make steady progress on the assignment throughout the term. That sure beats trying to crank out all those pages at the last minute. ✱

 Find printable copies of this long-term planner online.

Week of	Monday	Tuesday	Wednesday	Thursday	Friday	Saturday	Sunday
9 / 5							
9 / 12		English quiz					
9 / 19			English paper due		Speech #1		
9 / 26	Chemistry test					Skiing at the lake	
10 / 3		English quiz			Speech #2		
10 / 10				Geography project due			

LONG-TERM PLANNER ___ / ___ / ___ to ___ / ___ / ___

Week of	Monday	Tuesday	Wednesday	Thursday	Friday	Saturday	Sunday
___ / ___							
___ / ___							
___ / ___							
___ / ___							
___ / ___							
___ / ___							
___ / ___							
___ / ___							
___ / ___							
___ / ___							
___ / ___							
___ / ___							
___ / ___							
___ / ___							
___ / ___							
___ / ___							
___ / ___							
___ / ___							
___ / ___							
___ / ___							
___ / ___							
___ / ___							
___ / ___							
___ / ___							
___ / ___							
___ / ___							
___ / ___							
___ / ___							
___ / ___							
___ / ___							
___ / ___							
___ / ___							
___ / ___							

TIME

LONG-TERM PLANNER ___ / ___ / ___ to ___ / ___ / ___

Week of	Monday	Tuesday	Wednesday	Thursday	Friday	Saturday	Sunday
___ / ___							
___ / ___							
___ / ___							
___ / ___							
___ / ___							
___ / ___							
___ / ___							
___ / ___							
___ / ___							
___ / ___							
___ / ___							
___ / ___							
___ / ___							
___ / ___							
___ / ___							
___ / ___							
___ / ___							
___ / ___							
___ / ___							
___ / ___							
___ / ___							
___ / ___							
___ / ___							
___ / ___							
___ / ___							
___ / ___							
___ / ___							
___ / ___							
___ / ___							
___ / ___							
___ / ___							
___ / ___							

TIME

Be Here Now

Being right here, right now is such a simple idea. It seems obvious. Where else can you be but where you are? When else can you be there but when you are there? The answer is that you can be somewhere else at any time—in your head. It's common for our thoughts to distract us from where we've chosen to be. When we let this happen, we lose the benefits of focusing our attention on what's important to us in the present moment.

To "be here now" means to do what you're doing when you're doing it. It means to be where you are when you're there. Students consistently report that focusing attention on the here and now is one of the most powerful tools in this book.

We all have a voice in our head that hardly ever shuts up. If you don't believe it, conduct this experiment: Close your eyes for 10 seconds, and pay attention to what is going on in your head. Please do this right now.

Notice something? Perhaps a voice in your head was saying, "Forget it. I'm in a hurry." Another might have said, "I wonder when 10 seconds is up." Another could have been saying, "What little voice? I don't hear any little voice."

That's the voice.

This voice can take you anywhere at any time—especially when you are studying. When the voice takes you away, you might appear to be studying, but your brain is at the beach.

All of us have experienced this voice, as well as the absence of it.

When our inner voices are silent, time no longer seems to exist. We forget worries, aches, pains, reasons, excuses, and justifications. We fully experience the here and now. Life is magic.

Do not expect to get rid of daydreams entirely. That is neither possible nor desirable. Inner voices serve a purpose. They enable us to analyze, predict, classify, and understand events out there in the "real" world. The trick is to consciously choose when to be with your inner voice and when to let it go.

Instead of trying to force a stray thought out of your head—a futile enterprise—simply notice it. Accept it. Tell yourself, "There's that thought again." Then gently return your attention to the task at hand. That thought, or another, will come back. Your mind will drift. Simply notice again where your thoughts take you, and gently bring yourself back to the here and now.

The idea behind this Power Process is simple. When you plan for the future, plan for the future. When you listen to a lecture, listen to a lecture. When you read this book, read this book. And when you choose to daydream, daydream. Do what you're doing when you're doing it.

Be where you are when you're there. Be here now . . . and now . . . and now.

 Learn more about this Power Process online.

© Luca Tettoni/Corbis

Put it to Work

You can use strategies you learn in *Becoming a Master Student* to succeed at work. Get started by reflecting on the following case study.

Steve Carlson is a technical writer. He works for DCS, a company that makes products for multimedia teleconferencing—both hardware and software. He joined DCS a year ago, after graduating with a B.A. in technical communications.

Steve works in a department that creates sales brochures, user manuals, and Web sites that relate to DCS products. His manager is Louise Chao.

One Friday afternoon, Louise knocks on the door of Steve's office. She wants Steve to do a rush project—a new product brochure to be researched, written, designed, and printed in 2 weeks. Louise is on the way to another meeting and only has 5 minutes to talk.

After Louise describes the project, Steve checks a large paper calendar hanging on a wall in his office. This calendar shows the status of Steve's active projects. On this calendar are due dates for researching, outlining, and writing about a dozen documents. Each due date is color coded—red for urgent projects, green for other active projects, and gray for planned projects that are not yet active. Steve uses the wall calendar to plan his work and visually represent his project load.

"I need at least 3 full days to research and write the brochure you're talking about," Steve says. "In addition, meetings with our designer and revisions would take up another 2 days. So, I'd want to free up at least 1 week of my time to get this brochure done."

Steve points to the projects shown in red on his wall calendar. It's clear that his schedule is full of urgent projects.

"Louise, I know this brochure is important to you," he says. "Can we schedule a time to meet about this? We could choose one project to delay for a week so that I could meet your request."

Steve applied several strategies from this chapter:

- Estimate time.
- Rate each task by priority.
- Create a master monthly calendar.
- Set clear starting and stopping times.
- Use a long-term planner to divide and conquer.

Asia Images Group/Getty

List more strategies that would be useful to Steve in this situation.

_____

_____

_____

_____

Consider the following ideas if you feel overwhelmed at work:

- Use the Time Monitor/Time Plan process to analyze the way you currently use your time at work.
- Look for low-value activities to delegate or eliminate.
- Before committing to a project, brainstorm a list of project-related tasks, and estimate the amount of time each task requires.
- Note your peak periods of energy during the workday, and schedule your most challenging tasks for those times.
- Schedule fixed blocks of time during the week when you will not be available for meetings; use this time to tackle your to-do list.
- Set aside 1 hour each week to review the status of each long-term project.
- When delegating tasks to members of a project team, set a clear due date for each task.
- Keep a "waiting for" list of things that coworkers have promised to send you or tasks that they've agreed to complete.

Find more strategies for managing time at work.

Quiz

Name _____   Date ____/____/____

1. Describe a strategy for managing interruptions when you study.
   Make a plan that addresses the types of interruptions I experience when I study. For example, make an agreement with living mates about my study time, turn off my cell phone, and practice saying no to my friends. (Answers will vary.) (*25 ways to get the most out of now,* p. 79)

2. Rewrite the statement "I want to study harder" so that it becomes a specfic goal.
   I will study one more hour each night, Monday through Friday, for the next 30 days. After that, I will reflect and evaluate on the impact it has had on my performance in college. (Answers will vary.) (*Setting and achieving goals,* p. 67)

3. The text suggests that you set long-term goals. Write one example of a long-term goal.
   Six years from now I want to be finished with my college degree and have an entry-level professional career position in my field. (Answers will vary.) (*Setting and achieving goals,* p. 67)

4. Write a mid-term and short-term goal that can help you achieve the long-term goal that you listed for Question 3.
   I will meet with my counselor each year to be sure I'm on track to finish my educational plan within the next 6 years. In 5 years, I will update my résumé, begin looking for career opportunities, and apply for at least twenty open positions. (Answers will vary.) (*Setting and achieving goals,* p. 67)

5. What are at least five of the twenty-five ways to get the most out of now?
   List at least five. Answers will vary. See page reference for full list. (*25 ways to get the most out of now,* p. 79)

6. In time management terms, what is meant by "This ain't no piano"?
   If a nail is bent or a chunk is accidentally hacked out of a two-by-four during the rough framing of a building, a carpenter might say, "This ain't no piano." It means perfection is not necessary. Consider if what you are doing needs to be perfect: Is it a piano or not? (*25 ways to get the most out of now,* p. 79)

7. Define *C fever* as it applies to the ABC priority method.
   The C items on your to-do list do not require immediate attention. C fever is the uncontrollable urge to drop that A task and begin crossing C's off of the list. A and B tasks are often more difficult and time-consuming. (*The ABC daily to-do list,* p. 71)

8. Scheduling marathon study sessions once in a while is generally an effective strategy. True or False? Explain your answer.
   False. When possible, study in shorter sessions; three 3-hour sessions are usually far more productive than one 9-hour session. If you do study for long periods of time, it is important take short breaks and work on a variety of subjects. (*25 ways to get the most out of now,* p. 79)

9. According to the text, overcoming procrastination is a complex process that can take months or even years. True or False? Explain your answer.
   False. Most of the strategies are easy and can be done immediately. The challenge is to replace the procrastination habits with nonprocrastination habits. (*Stop procrastination now,* p. 76)

10. The Power Process: "Be Here Now" rules out planning. True or False? Explain your answer.
    False. "Be here now" is about focusing your attention on whatever you are doing. It does not mean live for today and forget about the future. It means when you are planning, focus 100 percent on that task. (Explanation will vary.) (*Power Process: Be Here Now,* p. 93)

Skills Snapshot

The Discovery Wheel in Chapter 1, Exercise 4, includes a section labeled "Time." For the next 10 to 15 minutes, go beyond your initial responses to that exercise. Take a snapshot of your skills as they exist today, after reading and doing this chapter.

Begin by reflecting on some recent experiences. Then take the next step in your mastery of time by choosing the strategy you'd like to experiment with next.

GOALS

I would describe my ability to set specific goals as . . .

The most important goal for me to achieve during this school year is . . .

DAILY PLANNING

When setting priorities for what to do each day, the first thing I consider is . . .

I keep track of my daily to-do items by . . .

PROCRASTINATION

The kinds of tasks on which I tend to procrastinate include . . .

My strategies for overcoming procrastination currently include . . .

BALANCE

My ability to balance recreation with working and studying can be described as . . .

If I sense that I'm not making enough time for family and friends, I respond by . . .

NEXT ACTION

I'll know that I've reached a new level of mastery with planning when . . .

To reach that level of mastery, the most important thing I can do next is to . . .

Master Student PROFILE

Al Gore ... is optimistic

© Joseph Sohm/Visions of America/Corbis

One hundred and nineteen years ago, a wealthy inventor read his own obituary, mistakenly published years before his death. Wrongly believing the inventor had just died, a newspaper printed a harsh judgment of his life's work, unfairly labeling him "The Merchant of Death" because of his invention—dynamite. Shaken by this condemnation, the inventor made a fateful choice to serve the cause of peace.

Seven years later, Alfred Nobel created this prize and the others that bear his name.

Seven years ago tomorrow, I read my own political obituary in a judgment that seemed to me harsh and mistaken—if not premature. But that unwelcome verdict also brought a precious if painful gift: an opportunity to search for fresh new ways to serve my purpose.

Unexpectedly, that quest has brought me here. Even though I fear my words cannot match this moment, I pray what I am feeling in my heart will be communicated clearly enough that those who hear me will say, "We must act." . . .

In the last few months, it has been harder and harder to misinterpret the signs that our world is spinning out of kilter. Major cities in North and South America, Asia and Australia are nearly out of water due to massive droughts and melting glaciers. Desperate farmers are losing their livelihoods. Peoples in the frozen Arctic and on low-lying Pacific islands are planning evacuations of places they have long called home. Unprecedented wildfires have forced a half million people from their homes in one country and caused a national emergency that almost brought down the government in another. Climate refugees have migrated into areas already inhabited by people with different cultures, religions, and traditions, increasing the potential for conflict. Stronger storms in the Pacific and Atlantic have threatened whole cities. Millions have been displaced by massive flooding in South Asia, Mexico, and 18 countries in Africa. As temperature extremes have increased, tens of thousands have lost their lives. We are recklessly burning and clearing our forests and driving more and more species into extinction.

There is an African proverb that says, "If you want to go quickly, go alone. If you want to go far, go together." We need to go far, quickly. . . .

Fifteen years ago, I made that case at the "Earth Summit" in Rio de Janeiro. Ten years ago, I presented it in Kyoto. This week, I will urge the delegates in Bali to adopt a bold mandate for a treaty that establishes a universal global cap on emissions and uses the market in emissions trading to efficiently allocate resources to the most effective opportunities for speedy reductions.

This treaty should be ratified and brought into effect everywhere in the world by the beginning of 2010—two years sooner than presently contemplated. The pace of our response must be accelerated to match the accelerating pace of the crisis itself. . . .

Make no mistake, the next generation will ask us one of two questions. Either they will ask: "What were you thinking; why didn't you act?"

Or they will ask instead: "How did you find the moral courage to rise and successfully resolve a crisis that so many said was impossible to solve?"

Al Gore, "Nobel Lecture," December 10, 2007. Copyright © 2007 The Nobel Foundation, Stockholm, 2007. Reproduced by permission.

(1948–) Former vice president of the United States. Gore refocused his career on climate change, won a Nobel Peace Prize, and—in his film *An Inconvenient Truth*—invented a new type of documentary.

Learn more about Al Gore and other master students at the Master Student Hall of Fame.

3 Memory

Instructor Tools & Tips

> The art of true memory is the art of attention.
> —**Samuel Johnson**
>
> Memory is the mother of imagination, reason and skill....This is the companion, this is the tutor, the poet, the library with which you travel.
> —**Mark Van Doren**

> I have always loved the 20 memory techniques. . . . In my classes I stress the importance of making all techniques your own. Needless to say, the custom-made memory system is right on target! Throughout the list of techniques, I especially like that each technique has a clear-cut example for the student. It also gives each student choices. "Be aware of attitudes" and "Give your 'secret brain' a chance" also fit right in with the information I'm already teaching my students. This also helps to show the reader what is significant.
> —**Maria Parnell, Brevard Community College, Florida**

Preview

A primary objective of student success courses is to foster the fundamental skill of memorizing key information. Simplified memory is a biological brain change. In one of the most remarkable discoveries about memory and the human brain, neuroscientists at Washington University in St. Louis, using functional MRI technology, point to literal changes in the brain's activity as different learning processes take place. Educational psychologists recently discovered that all long-term memories are set by emotional markers.[1] New learning is accomplished when, within the brain's cognitive neural structure, the student's existing emotional markers match or connect the new information to be learned within the existing brain structure. Understanding the principles of brain-active learning presented in this chapter will help students learn more in less time. It is frustrating when we can't remember something we're certain that we know, especially in a high-stakes situation, such as during a test or at a job interview.

This chapter opens with new information about the brain—how it changes physically by growing more connections between neurons. Understanding that the limbic processor is the gateway to learning and to remembering what they learn can help students become more confident that their brain really is "college material." How your students feel about what they are learning has become more important than ever. Help your students improve their memory by learning to "wire" those neural networks into place.

Guest Speaker

Here is a guest speaker for you:

Consider inviting a Psychology or Anatomy colleague as your guest speaker to talk to your students about how the brain works. Your current or former students can also be used as guest speakers. Faculty Advisor Eldon McMurray from Utah State College invites student leaders (upperclassmen who help teach this course) to present the Master Student Profiles. Most students are more receptive to hearing about these profiles from their peers. Having a student presentation also helps to break up the amount of time I spend as the instructor in front of the classroom. For this chapter, I ask my student leaders to talk about *Why* Pablo Alvarado is an example of a master student; *What* qualities Alvarado has that they would like to emulate; *How* they could obtain and practice these qualities; and *What if*, like Pablo Alvarado, they fought for what they believed in.

Lecture

Consider lecturing about some of the 20 memory techniques you used when you were a student, clarifying how students can use these techniques to maximize their effectiveness in college classes.

Another approach is to invite students to ask you for additional information about articles in this chapter. Here's how Eldon McMurray explained Q-Cards (page 108) to a student. This explanation could be expanded as a lecture for all students about this useful tool.

> I had a frustrated student tell me that, although she had studied and studied, she had failed her exam in biology. We reviewed her study methods: She had created flash cards by putting a question on one side and the answer on the other. Her review questions did not align well with the instructor's test questions, so she was unable to retrieve answers from her memory during the exam. Q-Cards have a question on both sides. Here's the trick: The question on each side of the card contains the answer to the question on the other side. This portable studying device helps students break information into manageable pieces and forces them to use a higher level of thinking. You can promote even further connection with materials by asking students to draw pictures to help them remember concepts. Reviewing these materials consistently before an exam will aid students' recall.
>
> **—Eldon McMurray**

For additional lecture ideas, visit the Chapter 3 Lecture Ideas on the Instructor Web site.

Exercises/Activities

1. The memory jungle (page 100) Students enjoy the book's analogy of the memory as a jungle. For the visual learner, it is helpful to use the interactive version on the *Becoming a Master Student* Web site to illustrate the concept in a step-by-step manner. You can project it onto a screen in class as a means for review, or you can have students visit the site outside class.

2. Remembering names (page 111) This exercise can be used as an opportunity for building relationships. Start students off in groups of four. Have them use tools described in the article to help remember the names of the people in each small group. Then the groups combine to make groups of 8, then 16, then 32, and so on, until everyone in the class can say the first name of every classmate. Then talk about how it feels when someone remembers your name.

3. Mnemonic devices (page 112) Get your students involved in creating mnemonic devices in class, and they will discover how easy it is to apply these devices outside class. Have your students memorize the Bill of Rights using the peg system that is explained on page 113. To enhance recall, use Q-Cards. To reinforce neural connections, draw pictures.

4. The loci system (page 112) Humor can be an effective memory motivator. Demonstrate in class how making up a funny story can help with memorizing word lists. Start by asking for a show of hands from students who think they can memorize 12 words in 12 minutes. Some students will raise their hands. Then ask how many students think they can remember the words in order—that is, if asked for word number 7, number 3, or number 5, can they recall that word after 12 minutes? Usually, only one or two students will raise their hands. Then have the students create a list of 12 nouns. For example, they might create the following list, which you write on the board for reference:

1. Alligator
2. Clown
3. Kitten
4. Hummer (car)
5. Shopping mall
6. Shoes
7. Hamburger
8. Hot air balloon
9. Television
10. Criminal
11. Pillow
12. Monkey

Now, make a note of the time on the clock, and the goal completion time 12 minutes later. As a class, make up a funny story using the numbers and words. If you don't want to make up a story on the spot, use the list above so that you can have the following story ready to go:

Once upon a time, 1 alligator came across 2 clowns with 3 kittens. The alligator was initially surprised when they gave him one of the kittens, but was shocked when he watched 4 of them get into a Hummer and drive off! At 5 p.m. that afternoon, the alligator went to the local shopping mall because he wanted to buy 6 new shoes. After all that shopping, he was very hungry so he ate 7 hamburgers. On his way home, he saw 8 hot air balloons on the horizon. He returned home, and at 9 p.m. that evening he turned on his television to watch his favorite reality show about 10 criminals. In this particular episode, they were fighting over 11 pillows. When 12 monkeys were released into their cell, chaos broke out!

The students usually find the story foolishly humorous, which helps them remember it. Repeat the story again, reminding them to focus completely on the story you're telling ("Be here now"). Repeat it a third time, and ask them to join you and talk through the story in unison. The next step is to erase or cover up the words on the board and recite the story again in unison. Next, go up and down the rows telling the story, but have each student in turn give the word that goes with that number. If a student can't recall the word, ask him to say the story aloud from the beginning. By the time the student gets to the word, he usually can recall it. This usually takes a total of about 9 to 10 minutes. Next, say a number, and ask students to raise their hands if they know the word that goes with that number. Select one student to confirm the word. Continue until it is clear that everyone knows all the words and the numbers associated with them.

In conclusion, point out that if students can memorize 12 random words in 12 minutes, in order, then they can also memorize important terms for tests fairly quickly if they focus their attention and create a system for memorization. This chapter contains many memorization tools. Most students initially think they can't memorize 12 words in order in 12 minutes, so this exercise boosts confidence in their memory, too.

5. **Power Process: Love Your Problems (And Experience Your Barriers) (page 117)** One of many problem-solving tools in *Becoming a Master Student*, this Power Process helps students explore an alternative to avoiding problems that they encounter in college. By embracing a problem, you can diffuse its energy and find a solution. To illustrate this process with an in-class activity, bring a word puzzle or mind game to class. Students who hate these types of puzzles get frustrated. Competitive students become anxious because each wants to be the first to solve it. Allow time for your students to try to solve the problem by loving it. Tell them to relax; enjoy the process; notice their frustration level, competitiveness, and anxiety; and just love the problem. Many students are able to solve the puzzle, individually or in groups. The Instructor Web site has a sample puzzle that you can hand out to your students as part of this exercise.

Conversation/Sharing

Divide students into small groups to discuss the topic of memorization in college. Students should share their frustration with memorization as well as a successful experience they've had remembering something important.

You can also facilitate a conversation using the Master Student Map. After your students begin to read about memory and learn to activate the connections between neurons, you will have empowered them to connect memory to their Learning Styles.

Why? Why do master students need to have confidence in their ability to remember what they study?

What? What is memory? Read through the list of articles in this chapter and pick three that look interesting. What about these three articles interests you?

How? How can knowing more about how your memory works improve your memory skills? How will this help you in college and in life?

What if? What if you start to apply these memory techniques to your other classes? And what if you don't?

Homework

Remembering your car keys—or anything else (page 110) This exercise helps students practice Learning Styles Mode 3 "How can I use this?" Students are asked to apply the strategies they are learning to a specific, personal memorization situation. An alternative to this assignment would be to ask students to bring in a memorization task from one of their current classes for discussion and analysis in class in groups.

Get creative (page 113) Students enjoy this creative opportunity to invent their own mnemonic device.

Move from problems to solutions (page 116) Here students discover that they can solve their own problems, and that such solutions are usually the most effective.

Evaluation

Ask students to describe four memory techniques from the chapter that work for them and to explain how they have used them. Ask students to describe the tool of setting a trap for your memory. Ask students to explain three ways to keep their brain fit for life. Ask students to explain what "love your problems" means. Ask students why Pablo Alvarado is considered a master student.

Additional Digital Resources

CHAPTER 3

Course Manual
The online *Course Manual* serves as an invaluable reference for those developing and teaching a College Success course with *Becoming a Master Student*. The *Course Manual* provides advice on general teaching issues such as preparing for classes, classroom management, grading, and communicating with students of various backgrounds, as well as specific strategies on getting the most out of various features in *Becoming a Master Student* such as the Discovery Wheel, Learning Styles Inventory, and book-specific Web sites.

Instructor Web Site
The updated Instructor Web site provides resources to help you plan and customize your course. Content specific to Chapter 3 includes:

- ▶ Lecture Ideas
  - • Four Ways to Forget
- ▶ In-Class Exercises
  - • Your Memory Is Better Than You May Think!
  - • The Memory Story
  - • Mental Stretch Breaks
- ▶ In-Text Quiz Answers
- ▶ Learning Styles Application
- ▶ Discussion Topics
- ▶ PowerPoint Slides
- ▶ Reflection Questions
- ▶ Assessment Questions
- ▶ Experiment with chapter strategies

The Instructor Web site also contains the following book-specific content:

- ▶ ExamView Test Bank
- ▶ Online Course Manual
- ▶ Articles from previous editions
- ▶ Master Student Profiles from previous editions
- ▶ Sample Syllabi

Student Web Site
To help your students gain a better understanding of the topics discussed in *Becoming a Master Student,* encourage your students to visit the Student Web site that provides the following resources specific to Chapter 3:

- ▶ Connect to Text content expands on specific topics marked with an icon within Chapter 3.
- ▶ Learning Style Applications invite students to cycle through the four styles of learning. In answering the

www.cengage.com/success/bams13e

four questions about memory skills posted in this chapter's Learning Styles Application, students explore the different modes and apply their new knowledge.

- ▶ Practice Tests allow students to see how well they understand the themes of *Becoming a Master Student*.
- ▶ Interactive Concept Maps promote critical thinking by highlighting related ideas to show relationships between concepts.
- ▶ Video Skillbuilders bring to life techniques that will help you to excel in college and beyond. The following video should give your students more information regarding topics covered in Chapter 3:
  - • Memory Strategies
- ▶ Remembering Cultural Differences presents readers with brief articles that touch on aspects of diversity in our rapidly changing world. For Chapter 3, the following article will prompt your students to look at contemporary issues in a new way:
  - • The Value of Oral Tradition
- ▶ Master Student Profiles provide additional information on the people covered in this book feature. For Chapter 3, students will find expanded coverage and links about:
  - • Pablo Alvarado
- ▶ Power Process Media contains video, PowerPoints, and audio files to take what your students have learned from the Power Processes in their book to the next level. For Chapter 3, students will find additional media on:
  - • Love your problems

Along with the chapter-specific content, a General Resources folder is available that contains Toolboxes geared toward specific student types (Community College, Adult Learner, Student Athlete), the Plagiarism Prevention Zone, and the Career Resource Center.

[1] J. G. Ojemann, R. L. Buckner, E. Akbudak, A. Z. Snyder, J. M. Ollinger, R. C. Mckinstry, B. R. Rosen, S. E. Petersen, M. E. Raichle, and T. E. Conturo, "Functional MRI Studies of Word-Stem Completion: Reliability across Laboratories and Comparison to Blood Flow Imaging with PET," *Human Brain Mapping* 6, no. 4 (1998): 203–215; M. I. Posner and M. E. Raichle, "The Neuroimaging of Human Brain Function," *Proceedings of the National Academy of Sciences of the United States of America* 95, no. 3 (1998): 763–764.

3 Memory

Master Student Map

as you read, ask yourself

what if . . .

I could use my memory to its full potential?

why this chapter matters . . .

Learning memory techniques can boost your skills at test taking, reading, note taking, and many other tasks.

what is included . . .

how you can use this chapter . . .

- Focus your attention.
- Make conscious choices about what to remember.
- Recall facts and ideas with more ease.

MASTER STUDENTS in *action*

Before I read the Memory chapter, I had trouble remembering what I had studied when taking a test or quiz. Visualization is by far the most useful technique I have come across in this book. While I'm taking the test, I visualize the book or paper that I had studied from. It also helps with names. I visualize something funny to go along with someone's name.

—TAUNI ALDINGER

Photo courtesy of Tauni Aldinger

Take your memory out of the closet

ONCE UPON A TIME, people talked about human memory as if it were a closet. You stored individual memories there as you would old shirts and stray socks. Remembering something was a matter of rummaging through all that stuff. If you were lucky, you found what you wanted.

This view of memory creates some problems. For one thing, closets can get crowded. Things too easily disappear. Even with the biggest closet, you eventually run out of space. If you want to pack some new memories in there—well, too bad. There's no room.

Brain researchers have shattered this image to bits. Memory is not a closet. It's not a place or a thing. Instead, memory is a *process*.

On a conscious level, memories appear as distinct and unconnected mental events: words, sensations, images. They can include details from the distant past—the smell of cookies baking in your grandmother's kitchen or the feel of sunlight warming your face through the window of your first-grade classroom.

On a biological level, each of those memories involves millions of nerve cells, or neurons, firing chemical messages to one another. If you could observe these exchanges in real time, you'd see regions of cells all over the brain glowing with electrical charges at speeds that would put a computer to shame.

When a series of cells connects several times in a similar pattern, the result is a memory. Psychologist Donald Hebb uses the aphorism to describe this principle: "Neurons which fire together, wire together."[1] It means that memories are not really stored. Instead, remembering is a process in which you *encode* information as links between active neurons that fire together. You also *decode,* or reactivate, neurons that wired together in the past.

Memory is the probability that certain patterns of brain activity will occur again in the future. In effect, you re-create a memory each time you recall it.

Whenever you learn something new, your brain changes physically by growing more connections between neurons. The more you learn, the greater the number of connections. For all practical purposes, there's no limit to how many memories your brain can encode.

There's a lot you can do to wire those neural networks into place. That's where the memory techniques described in this chapter come into play. Step out of your crowded mental closet into a world of infinite possibilities. ✳

journal entry 9

Discovery/Intention Statement

Create value from this chapter

Write a sentence or two describing the way you feel when you want to remember something but have trouble doing so. Think of a specific incident in which you experienced this problem, such as trying to remember someone's name or a fact you needed during a test.

I discovered that I . . .

_____

_____

_____

_____

_____

_____

Now spend 5 minutes skimming this chapter, and find three to five memory strategies you intend to use. List the strategies below, and note the page numbers where they are explained.

Strategy	Page number

The memory jungle

Think of your memory as a vast, overgrown jungle. This memory jungle is thick with wild plants, exotic shrubs, twisted trees, and creeping vines. It spreads over thousands of square miles— dense, tangled, forbidding.

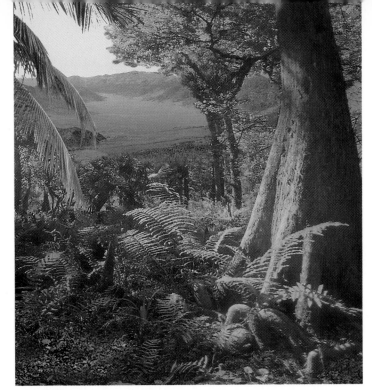

IMAGINE THAT THE jungle is encompassed on all sides by towering mountains. There is only one entrance to the jungle, a small meadow that is reached by a narrow pass through the mountains.

In the jungle there are animals, millions of them. The animals represent all of the information in your memory. Imagine that every thought, mental picture, or perception you ever had is represented by an animal in this jungle. Every single event ever perceived by any of your five senses—sight, touch, hearing, smell, or taste—is a thought animal that has also passed through the meadow and entered the jungle. Some of the thought animals, such as the color of your seventh-grade teacher's favorite sweater, are well hidden. Other thoughts, such as your cell phone number or the position of the reverse gear in your car, are easier to find.

The memory jungle has two rules: Each thought animal must pass through the meadow at the entrance to the jungle. And once an animal enters the jungle, it never leaves.

The meadow represents short-term memory. You use this kind of memory when you look up a telephone number and hold it in your memory long enough to make a call. Short-term memory appears to have a limited capacity (the meadow is small) and disappears fast (animals pass through the meadow quickly).

The jungle itself represents long-term memory. This kind of memory allows you to recall information from day to day, week to week, and year to year. Remember that thought animals never leave the long-term memory jungle. The following visualizations can help you recall useful concepts about memory.

Visualization #1: A well-worn path

Imagine what happens as a thought—in this case, we'll call it an elephant—bounds across short-term memory and into the jungle. The elephant leaves a trail of broken twigs and hoof prints that you can follow. Brain research suggests that thoughts can wear paths in the brain.[2] These paths are called *neural traces*. The more well-worn a neural trace, the easier it is to retrieve (find) the thought. In other words, the more often the elephant retraces the path, the clearer the path becomes. The more often you recall information, and the more often you put the same information into your memory, the easier it is to find. When you buy a new car, for example, the first few times you try to find reverse, you have to think for a moment. After you have found reverse gear every day for a week, the path is worn into your memory. After a year, the path is so well-worn that when you dream about driving your car backward, you even dream the correct motion for putting the gear in reverse.

Visualization #2: A herd of thoughts

© Photodisc

The second picture you can use to your advantage in recalling concepts about memory is the picture of many animals gathering at a clearing—like thoughts gathering at a central location in memory. It is easier to retrieve thoughts that are grouped together, just as it is easier to find a herd of animals than it is to find a single elephant.

Pieces of information are easier to recall if you can associate them with similar information. For example, you can more readily remember a particular player's batting average if you can associate it with other baseball statistics.

Visualization #3: Turning your back

© Photodisc

Imagine releasing the elephant into the jungle, turning your back, and counting to 10. When you turn around, the elephant is gone. This is exactly what happens to most of the information you receive.

Generally, we can recall only 50 percent of the material we have just read. Within 24 hours, most of us can recall only about 20 percent. This means that 80 percent of the material has not been encoded and is wandering around, lost in the memory jungle.[3]

The remedy is simple: Review quickly. Do not take your eyes off the thought animal as it crosses the short-term memory meadow. Look at it again (review it) soon after it enters the long-term memory jungle. Wear a path in your memory immediately.

Visualization #4: Directing the animal traffic

© Photodisc

The fourth picture is one you are in. You are standing at the entrance to the short-term memory meadow, directing herds of thought animals as they file through the pass, across the meadow, and into your long-term memory. You are taking an active role in the learning process. You are paying attention. You are doing more than sitting on a rock and watching the animals file past into your brain. You have become part of the process, and in doing so, you have taken control of your memory. ✳

 Find guided visualizations based on the memory jungle online.

20 memory techniques

Experiment with these techniques to develop a flexible, custom-made memory system that fits your style of learning.

THE 20 TECHNIQUES below are divided into four categories, each of which represents a general principle for improving memory:

Organize it. Organized information is easier to find.

Use your body. Learning is an active process; get all of your senses involved.

Use your brain. Work *with* your memory, not *against* it.

Recall it. Recite and apply key information.

As you read this article, mark the techniques you like best, and use them. Also look for ways to combine techniques.

Organize it

1 Be selective. During your stay in higher education, you will be exposed to thousands of facts and ideas. No one expects you to memorize all of them. To a large degree, the art of memory is the art of selecting what to remember in the first place.

As you dig into your textbooks and notes, make choices about what is most important to learn. Imagine that you are going to create a test on the material, and consider the questions you would ask.

When reading, look for chapter previews, summaries, and review questions. Pay attention to anything printed in bold type. Also notice visual elements—tables, charts, graphs, and illustrations. They are all clues pointing to what's important. During lectures, notice what the instructor emphasizes. Anything that's presented visually—on the board, in overheads, or with slides—is probably key.

2 Make it meaningful. You remember things better if they have meaning for you. One way to create meaning is to learn from the general to the specific. Before you begin your next reading assignment, skim the passage to locate the main idea. You can use the same techniques you learned in Exercise #1: "Textbook Reconnaissance" on page 2. If you're ever lost, step back and look at the big picture. The details then might make more sense.

You can organize any list of items—even random items—in a meaningful way to make them easier to remember. In his book *Information Anxiety*, Richard Saul Wurman proposes five principles for organizing any body of ideas, facts, or objects:[4]

Principle	Example
Organize by **time**	Events in history or in a novel flow in chronological order.
Organize by **location**	Addresses for a large company's regional offices are grouped by state and city.
Organize by **category**	Nonfiction library materials are organized by subject categories.
Organize by **continuum**	Products rated in most consumer guides or online stores are grouped from highest in price to lowest in price, or highest in quality to lowest in quality.
Organize by **alphabet**	Entries in a book index are listed in ABC order.

3 Create associations. The data already encoded in your neural networks are arranged according to a scheme that makes sense to you. When you introduce new data, you can remember them more effectively if you associate them with similar or related data.

Think about your favorite courses. They probably relate to subjects that you already know something about. If you are interested in politics over the last few years, you'll find it easier to remember the facts in a modern history course. Even when you're tackling a new subject, you can build a mental store of basic background information—the raw material for creating associations. Preview reading assignments, and complete those readings before you attend lectures. Before taking upper-level courses, master the prerequisites.

Use your body

4 **Learn actively.** Action is a great memory enhancer. Test this theory by studying your assignments with the same energy that you bring to the dance floor or the basketball court.

You can use simple, direct methods to infuse your learning with action. When you sit at your desk, sit up straight. Sit on the edge of your chair, as if you were about to spring out of it and sprint across the room.

Also experiment with standing up when you study. It's harder to fall asleep in this position. Some people insist that their brains work better when they stand. Pace back and forth and gesture as you recite material out loud. Use your hands. Get your body moving.

Don't forget to move your mouth. During a lecture, ask questions. With your textbooks, read key passages out loud. Use a louder voice for the main points.

Active learning also involves a variety of learning styles. In Chapter 1, the article "Learning Styles: Discovering How You Learn" explains four aspects of learning: concrete experience, abstract conceptualization, active experimentation, and reflective observation. Many courses in higher education lean heavily toward abstract conceptualization—lectures, papers, and reading. These courses might not offer chances to actively experiment with ideas or test them in concrete experience.

Create those opportunities yourself. For example, your introductory psychology book probably offers some theories about how people remember information. Choose one of those theories, and test it on yourself. See if you can discover a new memory technique.

To remember an idea, go beyond thinking about it. *Do* something with it.

5 **Relax.** When you're relaxed, you absorb new information quickly and recall it with greater ease and accuracy. Students who can't recall information under the stress of a final exam can often recite the same facts later when they are relaxed.

Relaxing might seem to contradict the idea of active learning as explained in technique #4, but it doesn't. Being relaxed is not the same as being drowsy, zoned out, or asleep. Relaxation is a state of alertness, free of tension, during which your mind can play with new information, roll it around, create associations with it, and apply many of the other memory techniques. You can be active *and* relaxed. See Exercise #16: "Relax" in Chapter 4 for some tips on how to relax.

6 **Create pictures.** Draw diagrams. Make cartoons. Use these images to connect facts and illustrate relationships. You can "see" and recall associations within and among abstract concepts more easily when you visualize both the concepts and the associations. The key is to use your imagination. Creating pictures reinforces visual and kinesthetic learning styles.

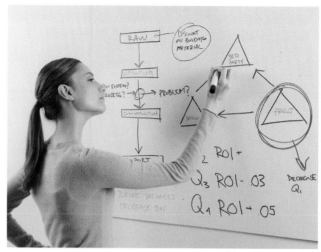

Influx Productions/Getty

For example, Boyle's law states that at a constant temperature, the volume of a confined ideal gas varies inversely with its pressure. Simply put, cutting the volume in half doubles the pressure. To remember this concept, you might picture someone "doubled over" using a bicycle pump. As she increases the pressure in the pump by decreasing the volume in the pump cylinder, she seems to be getting angrier. By the time she has doubled the pressure (and halved the volume), she is boiling ("Boyle-ing") mad.

Another reason to create pictures is that visual information is associated with a part of the brain that is different from the part that processes verbal information. When you create a picture of a concept, you are anchoring the information in a second part of your brain. Doing so increases your chances of recalling that information.

To visualize abstract relationships effectively, create an action-oriented image, such as the person using the pump. Make the picture vivid, too. The person's face could be bright red. And involve all of your senses. Imagine how the cold metal of the pump would feel, and how the person would grunt as she struggled with it.

You can also create pictures as you study by using *graphic organizers*. One example is a *topic-point-details* chart. At the top of this chart, write the main topic of a lecture or reading assignment. In the left column, list the main points you want to remember. And in the right column, list key details related to each point. See Example 1 for the beginning of a chart based on this article:

Example 1

20 MEMORY TECHNIQUES

Point	Details
1. Be selective	Choose what not to remember. Look for clues to important material.
2. Make it meaningful	Organize by time, location, category, continuum, or alphabet.
3. Create associations	Link new facts with facts you already know.
4. Learn actively	Sit straight. Stand while studying. Recite while walking.
5. Relax	Release tension. Remain alert.

You could use a similar chart to prompt critical thinking about an issue. Express that issue as a question, and write it at the top. In the left column, note the opinion about the issue. In the right column, list notable facts, expert opinions, reasons, and examples that support each opinion. Example 2 in the top right column is about tax cuts as a strategy for stimulating the economy.

Sometimes you'll want to remember the main actions in a story or historical event. Create a time line by drawing a straight line. Place points in order on that line to represent key events. Place earlier events toward the left end of the line and later events toward the right. At the bottom of this page, Example 3 shows the start of a time line of events relating to the beginning of the U.S. war with Iraq.

When you want to compare or contrast two things, play with a Venn diagram. Represent each thing as a circle. Draw the circles so that they overlap. In the overlapping area, list characteristics that the two things share. In the outer parts of each circle, list the unique characteristics of each thing. Example 4 on page 105 compares the two types of journal entries included in this book—Discovery Statements and Intention Statements.

Example 2

STIMULATE THE ECONOMY WITH TAX CUTS?

Opinion	Support
Yes	Savings from tax cuts allow businesses to invest money in new equipment. Tax cuts encourage businesses to expand and hire new employees.
No	Years of tax cuts under the Bush administration failed to prevent the mortgage credit crisis. Tax cuts create budget deficits.
Maybe	Tax cuts might work in some economic conditions. Budget deficits might be only temporary.

The graphic organizers described here are just a few of the many kinds available. To find more examples, do an Internet search. Have fun, and invent graphic organizers of your own.

7 Recite and repeat. When you repeat something out loud, you anchor the concept in two different senses. First, you get the physical sensation in your throat, tongue, and lips when voicing the concept. Second, you hear it. The combined result is synergistic, just as it is when you create pictures. That is, the effect of using two different senses is greater than the sum of their individual effects.

The "out loud" part is important. Reciting silently in your head can be useful—in the library, for example— but it is not as effective as making noise. Your mind can trick itself into thinking it knows something when it doesn't. Your ears are harder to fool.

Example 3

● 3/19/03 U.S. invades Iraq	● 3/30/03 Rumsfeld announces location of WMD	● 4/9/03 Soldiers topple statue of Saddam	● 5/1/03 Bush declares mission accomplished	● 5/29/03 Bush: We found WMD

www.cengage.com/success/bams13e

Example 4

Discovery Statements   Intention Statements

- Describe specific thoughts
- Describe specific feelings
- Describe current and past behaviors

- Are a type of journal entry
- Are based on telling the truth
- Can be written at any time on any topic
- Can lead to action

- Describe future behaviors
- Can include timelines
- Can include rewards

The repetition part is important, too. Repetition is a common memory device because it works. Repetition blazes a trail through the pathways of your brain, making the information easier to find. Repeat a concept out loud until you know it; then say it five more times.

Recitation works best when you recite concepts in your own words. For example, if you want to remember that the acceleration of a falling body due to gravity at sea level equals 32 feet per second per second, you might say, "Gravity makes an object accelerate 32 feet per second faster for each second that it's in the air at sea level." Putting a concept into your own words forces you to think about it.

Have some fun with this technique. Recite by writing a song about what you're learning. Sing it in the shower. Use any style you want. (Country, jazz, rock, or rap—when you sing out loud, learning's a snap!).

Or imitate someone. Imagine your textbook being read by Will Ferrell, Madonna, or Clint Eastwood ("Go ahead, punk. Make my density equal mass over volume").

8 Write it down. The technique of writing things down is obvious, yet easy to forget. Writing a note to yourself helps you remember an idea, even if you never look at the note again.

You can extend this technique by writing down an idea not just once, but many times. Let go of the old image of being forced to write "I will not throw paper wads" a hundred times on the chalkboard after school. When you choose to remember something, repetitive writing is a powerful tool.

Writing engages a different kind of memory than speaking. Writing prompts us to be more logical, coherent, and complete. Written reviews reveal gaps in knowledge that oral reviews miss, just as oral reviews reveal gaps that written reviews miss.

Another advantage of written reviews is that they more closely match the way you're asked to remember materials in school. During your academic career, you'll probably take far more written exams than oral exams. Writing can be an effective way to prepare for such tests.

Finally, writing is physical. Your arm, your hand, and your fingers join in. Remember, learning is an active process—you remember what you *do*.

Use your brain

9 Engage your emotions. One powerful way to enhance your memory is to make friends with your amygdala. This area of your brain lights up with extra neural activity each time you feel a strong emotion. When a topic excites love, laughter, or fear, the amygdala sends a flurry of chemical messages that say, in effect: *This information is important and useful. Don't forget it.*

You're more likely to remember course material when you relate it to a goal—whether academic, personal, or career—that you feel strongly about. This is one reason why it pays to be specific about what you want. The more goals you have and the more clearly they are defined, the more channels you create for incoming information.

You can use this strategy even when a subject seems boring at first. If you're not naturally interested in a topic, then create interest. Find a study partner in the class—if possible, someone you know and like—or form a study group. Also consider getting to know the instructor personally. When a course creates a bridge to human relationships, you engage the content in a more emotional way.

10 Overlearn. One way to fight mental fuzziness is to learn more than you need to know about a subject simply to pass a test. You can pick a subject apart, examine it, add to it, and go over it until it becomes second nature.

This technique is especially effective for problem solving. Do the assigned problems, and then do more problems. Find another textbook, and work similar problems. Then make up your own problems and solve them. When you pretest yourself in this way, the potential rewards are speed, accuracy, and greater confidence at exam time.

11 Escape the short-term memory trap.
Short-term memory is different from the kind of memory you'll need during exam week. For example, most of us can look at an unfamiliar seven-digit phone number once and remember it long enough to dial it. See if you can recall that number the next day.

Short-term memory can fade after a few minutes, and it rarely lasts more than several hours. A short review within minutes or hours of a study session can move material from short-term memory into long-term memory. That quick mini-review can save you hours of study time when exams roll around.

12 Use your times of peak energy.
Study your most difficult subjects during the times when your energy peaks. Some people can concentrate more effectively during daylight hours. The early morning hours can be especially productive, even for those who hate to get up with the sun. Observe the peaks and valleys in your energy flow during the day, and adjust study times accordingly. Perhaps you experience surges in memory power during the late afternoon or evening.

13 Distribute learning.
As an alternative to marathon study sessions, experiment with several shorter sessions spaced out over time. You might find that you can get far more done in three 2-hour sessions than in one 6-hour session.

For example, when you are preparing for your American history exam, study for an hour or two and then wash the dishes. While you are washing the dishes, part of your mind will be reviewing what you studied. Return to American history for a while, then call a friend. Even when you are deep in conversation, part of your mind will be reviewing history.

You can get more done if you take regular breaks. You can even use the breaks as mini-rewards. After a productive study session, give yourself permission to log on and check your e-mail, listen to a song, or play 10 minutes of hide-and-seek with your kids.

Distributing your learning is a brain-friendly activity. You cannot absorb new information and ideas during all of your waking hours. If you overload your brain, it will find a way to shut down for a rest—whether you plan for it or not. By taking periodic breaks while studying, you allow information to sink in. During these breaks, your brain is taking the time to rewire itself by growing new connections between cells. Psychologists call this process *consolidation*.[5]

The idea of allowing time for consolidation does have an exception. When you are so engrossed in a textbook that you cannot put it down, when you are consumed by an idea for a term paper and cannot think of anything else—keep going. The master student within you has taken over. Enjoy the ride.

14 Be aware of attitudes.
People who think history is boring tend to have trouble remembering dates and historical events. People who believe math is difficult often have a hard time recalling mathematical equations and formulas. All of us can forget information that contradicts our opinions.

If you think a subject is boring, remind yourself that everything is related to everything else. Look for connections that relate to your own interests.

For example, consider a person who is fanatical about cars. He can rebuild a motor in a weekend and has a good time doing so. From this apparently specialized interest, he can explore a wide realm of knowledge. He can relate the workings of an engine to principles of physics, math, and chemistry. Computerized parts in newer cars can lead him to the study of data processing. He can research how the automobile industry has changed our cities and helped create suburbs, a topic that relates to urban planning, sociology, business, economics, psychology, and history.

Being aware of your attitudes is not the same as fighting them or struggling to give them up. Just notice your attitudes and be willing to put them on hold.

15 Elaborate.
According to Harvard psychologist Daniel Schacter, all courses in memory improvement are based on a single technique—elaboration. *Elaboration* means consciously encoding new information. Repetition is one basic way to elaborate. However, current brain research indicates that other types of elaboration are more effective for long-term memory.[6]

One way to elaborate is to ask yourself questions about incoming information: "Does this remind me of something or someone I already know?" "Is this similar to a technique that I already use?" and "Where and when can I use this information?"

When you learned to recognize Italy on a world map, your teacher probably pointed out that the country is shaped like a boot. This is a simple form of elaboration.

The same idea applies to more complex material. When you meet someone new, for example, ask yourself, "Does she remind me of someone else?" Or when reading this book, preview the material using the Master Student Map that opens each chapter.

16 Intend to remember. To instantly enhance your memory, form the simple intention to *learn it now* rather than later. The intention to remember can be more powerful than any single memory technique.

You can build on your intention with simple tricks. During a lecture, for example, pretend that you'll be quizzed on the key points at the end of the period. Imagine that you'll get a $5 reward for every correct answer.

Also pay attention to your attention. Each time your mind wanders during class, make a tick mark in the margins of your notes. The act of writing reengages your attention.

If your mind keeps returning to an urgent or incomplete task, then write an Intention Statement about how you will handle it. With your intention safely recorded, return to what's important in the present moment.

Recall it

17 Remember something else. When you are stuck and can't remember something that you're sure you know, remember something else that is related to it.

If you can't remember your great-aunt's name, remember your great-uncle's name. During an economics exam, if you can't remember anything about the aggregate demand curve, recall what you do know about the aggregate supply curve. If you cannot recall specific facts, remember the example that the instructor used during her lecture. Any piece of information is encoded in the same area of the brain as a similar piece of information. You can unblock your recall by stimulating that area of your memory.

A brainstorm is a good memory jog. If you are stumped when taking a test, start writing down lots of answers to related questions, and—pop!—the answer you need is likely to appear.

18 Notice when you do remember. Everyone has a different memory style. Some people are best at recalling information they've read. Others have an easier time remembering what they've heard, seen, or done.

To develop your memory, notice when you recall information easily, and ask yourself what memory techniques you're using naturally. Also notice when you find it difficult to recall information. Be a reporter. Get the facts, and then adjust your learning techniques. And remember to congratulate yourself when you remember.

19 Use it before you lose it. Even information encoded in long-term memory becomes difficult to recall when we don't use it regularly. The pathways to the information become faint with disuse. For example, you can probably remember your current phone number. What was your phone number 10 years ago?

This example points to a powerful memory technique. To remember something, access it a lot. Read it, write it, speak it, listen to it, apply it—find some way to make contact with the material regularly. Each time you do so, you widen the neural pathway to the material and make it easier to recall the next time.

Another way to make contact with the material is to teach it. Teaching demands mastery. When you explain the function of the pancreas to a fellow student, you discover quickly whether you really understand it yourself.

Study groups are especially effective because they put you on stage. The friendly pressure of knowing that you'll teach the group helps focus your attention.

20 Adopt the attitude that you never forget. You might not believe that an idea or a thought never leaves your memory. That's OK. In fact, it doesn't matter whether you agree with the idea or not. It can work for you anyway.

Test the concept. Instead of saying, "I don't remember," you can say, "It will come to me." The latter statement implies that the information you want is encoded in your brain and that you can retrieve it—just not right now. You'll probably be surprised to find that the information was in there all along.

People who use the flip side of this technique often get the opposite results. "I never remember anything," they say over and over again. "I've always had a poor memory. I'm such a scatterbrain." That kind of negative talk is self-fulfilling.

Instead, use positive affirmations that support you in developing your memory: "I recall information easily and accurately." "At any time I choose, I will be able to recall key facts and ideas." "My memory serves me well."

Or even "I never forget!" ✱

 Find more memory strategies online.

Use Q-Cards to reinforce memory

One memory strategy you might find useful involves a special kind of flash card. It's called a *Question Card*, or *Q-Card* for short.

To create a standard flash card, you write a question on one side of a 3x5 card and its answer on the other side. Q-Cards have a question on *both* sides. Here's the trick: The question on one side of the card contains the answer to the question on the other side.

The questions you write on Q-Cards can draw on both lower- and higher-order thinking skills. Writing these questions forces you to encode material in different ways. You activate more areas of your brain and burn the concepts even deeper into your memory.

For example, say that you want to remember the subject of the Eighteenth Amendment to the U.S. Constitution—the one that prohibited the sale of alcohol. On one side of a 3x5 card, write *Which amendment prohibited the sale of alcohol?* Turn the card over, and write *What did the Eighteenth Amendment do?*

To get the most from Q-Cards:

- Add a picture to each side of the card. Doing so helps you learn concepts faster and develop a more visual learning style.

- Read the questions and recite the answers out loud. Two keys to memory are repetition and novelty, so use a different voice whenever you read and recite. Whisper the first time you go through your cards, then shout or sing the next time. Doing this develops an auditory learning style.

- Carry Q-Cards with you, and pull them out during waiting times. To develop a kinesthetic learning style, handle your cards often.

- Create a Q-Card for each new and important concept within 24 hours after attending a class or completing an assignment. This is your *active stack* of cards. Keep answering the questions on these cards until you learn each new concept.

- Review all of the cards for a certain subject on one day each week. For example, on Monday, review all cards from biology; on Tuesday, review all cards from history. These cards make up your *review stacks*.

Get started with Q-Cards right now. Use the blanks below. One blank represents the front of the card; the other blank represents the back. Start by creating a Q-Card about remembering how to use Q-Cards!

Shark and windmill: © Digital Vision/Getty; *illustration:* Walter Kopec

Set a trap for your memory

> When you want to remind yourself to do something, link this activity to another event you know will take place. The key is to "trap" your memory by picking events that are certain to occur.

Phone: © Index Stock/Alamy; door: © Ryan McVay/Photodisc Green/ Getty; illustration: Walter Kopec

SAY THAT YOU'RE walking to class and suddenly remember that your accounting assignment is due tomorrow. Switch your watch to the opposite wrist. Now you're "trapped." Every time you glance at your wrist and remember that you have switched your watch, it becomes a reminder that you were supposed to remember something else. (You can do the same with a ring.)

If you empty your pockets every night, put an unusual item in your pocket in the morning to remind yourself to do something before you go to bed. For example, to remember to call your younger sister on her birthday, pick an object that reminds you of her—a photograph, perhaps—and put it in your pocket. When you empty your pocket that evening and find the photo, you're more likely to make the call.

Everyday rituals that you seldom neglect, such as feeding a pet, listening to the weather report, and unlacing your shoes, provide opportunities for setting traps. For example, tie a triple knot in your shoelace as a reminder to set the alarm for your early morning study group meeting. You can even use imaginary traps. To remember to write a check for the phone bill, picture your phone hanging on the front door. In your mind, create the feeling of reaching for the doorknob and grabbing the phone instead. When you get home and reach to open the front door, the image is apt to return to you.

Link two activities together, and make the association unusual. ✳

journal entry 10

Discovery Statement

Revisit your memory skills

Take a minute to reflect on the memory techniques in this chapter. You probably use some of them already without being aware of it. In the space below, list at least three memory techniques you have used in the past, and describe how you have used them.

_____

_____

_____

_____

_____

_____

_____

_____

_____

_____

13 exercise
Remembering your car keys—
or anything else

Pick something you frequently forget. Some people chronically lose their car keys or forget to write down checks in their check register. Others let anniversaries and birthdays slip by.

Pick an item or a task you're prone to forget. Then design a strategy for remembering it. Use any of the techniques from this chapter, research others, or make up your own from scratch. Describe your technique and the results in the space provided.

In this exercise, as in most of the exercises in this book, a failure is also a success. Don't be concerned with whether your technique will work. Design it, and then find out if it works. If it doesn't work for you this time, use another method.

Keep your brain fit for life

Memories are encoded as physical changes in the brain. And your brain is an organ that needs regular care and exercise. Higher education gives you plenty of chances to exercise that organ. Don't let those benefits fade after you leave school. Starting now, adopt habits to keep your brain lean and fit for life. Consider these research-based suggestions from the Alzheimer's Association.[7]

Stay mentally active If you sit at a desk most of the workday, take a class. If you seldom travel, start reading maps of new locations and plan a cross-country trip. Seek out museums, theaters, concerts, and other cultural events. Even after you graduate, consider learning another language or taking up a musical instrument. Learning gives your brain a workout, much like sit-ups condition your abs.

Stay socially active Having a network of supportive friends can reduce stress levels. In turn, stress management helps to maintain connections between brain cells. Stay socially active by working, volunteering, and joining clubs.

Stay physically active Physical activity promotes blood flow to the brain. It also reduces the risk of diabetes, cardiovascular disease, and other diseases that can impair brain function.

Adopt a brain-healthy diet A diet rich in dark-skinned fruits and vegetables boosts your supply of antioxidants—natural chemicals that nourish your brain. Examples of these foods are raisins, blueberries, blackberries, strawberries, raspberries, kale, spinach, brussels sprouts, alfalfa sprouts, and broccoli. Avoid foods that are high in saturated fat and cholesterol, which may increase the risk of Alzheimer's disease.

Drink alcohol moderately, if at all A common definition of moderate consumption for people of legal drinking age is a limit of one drink per day for women and two drinks per day for men. Heavier drinking can affect memory. In fact, long-term alcoholics tend to develop conditions that impair memory. One such condition is Korsakoff's syndrome, a disorder that causes people to forget incidents immediately after they happen.

Protect your heart In general, what's good for your heart is good for your brain. Protect both organs by eating well, exercising regularly, managing your weight, staying tobacco-free, and getting plenty of sleep. These habits reduce your risk of heart attack, stroke, and other cardiovascular conditions that interfere with blood flow to the brain.

Remembering names

NEW FRIENDSHIPS, job contacts, and business relationships all start with remembering names. Here are some suggestions for remembering them.

Recite and repeat in conversation. When you hear a person's name, repeat it. Immediately say it to yourself several times without moving your lips. You can also repeat the name out loud in a way that does not sound forced or artificial: "I'm pleased to meet you, Maria."

Ask the other person to recite and repeat. You can let other people help you remember their names. After you've been introduced to someone, ask that person to spell his name and pronounce it correctly for you. Most people will be flattered by the effort you're making to learn their names.

While you're at it, verify what name people want to be called. "Bob" may actually prefer "Robert."

Visualize. After the conversation, construct a brief visual image of the person. For a memorable image, make it unusual. Imagine the name painted in hot pink fluorescent letters on the person's forehead.

Admit you don't know. Admitting that you can't remember someone's name can actually put people at ease. Most of them will sympathize if you say, "I'm working to remember names better. Yours is right on the tip of my tongue. What is it again?"

Introduce yourself again. Most of the time we assume introductions are one-shot affairs. If we miss a name the first time around, our hopes for remembering it are dashed. Instead of giving up, reintroduce yourself: "We met earlier. I'm Jesse. Please tell me your name again."

Use associations. Link each person you meet with one characteristic that you find interesting or unusual. For example, you could make a mental note: "Vicki Cheng—long, black hair" or "James Washington—horn-rimmed glasses." To reinforce your associations, write them on 3x5 cards as soon as you can.

Limit the number of new names you learn at one time. Occasionally, we find ourselves in situations where we're introduced to several people at the same time: "Dad, these are all the people in my Boy Scout troop." "Let's take a tour so you can meet all thirty-two people in this department."

When meeting a large group of people, concentrate on remembering just two or three names. Free yourself from feeling obligated to remember everyone. Few of the people in mass introductions expect you to remember their names. Another way to avoid memory overload is to limit yourself to learning just first names. Last names can come later.

Ask for photos. In some cases, you might be able to get photos of all the people you meet. For example, a small business where you work might have a brochure with pictures of all the employees. If you're having trouble remembering names the first week of work, ask for individual or group photos, and write in the names if they're not included. You can use these photos as flash cards to drill yourself on names.

Go early. Consider going early to conventions, parties, and classes. Sometimes just a few people show up on time for these occasions. That's fewer names for you to remember. And as more people arrive, you can overhear them being introduced to others—an automatic review for you.

Make it a game. In situations where many people are new to one another, consider pairing up with another person and staging a contest. Challenge each other to remember as many new names as possible. Then choose an award—such as a movie ticket or free meal—for the person who wins.

Use technology. After you meet new people, enter their names as contacts in your e-mail or add them to a database. If you get business cards, enter phone numbers, e-mail addresses, and other contact information as well.

Intend to remember. The simple act of focusing your attention at key moments can do wonders for your memory. Test this idea for yourself. The next time you're introduced to someone, direct 100 percent of your attention to hearing that person's name. Do this consistently, and see what happens to your ability to remember names. ✳

The peg system is a mneumonic device based on matching words that rhyme, such as *one* and *bun*.

Mnemonic devices

It's pronounced *ne-MON-ik*. The word refers to tricks that can increase your ability to recall everything from grocery lists to speeches.

SOME ENTERTAINERS use mnemonic devices to perform "impossible" feats of memory, such as recalling the names of everyone in a large audience after hearing them just once. Using mnemonic devices, speakers can go for hours without looking at their notes. The possibilities for students are endless.

There is a catch, though. Mnemonic devices have three serious limitations:

- They don't always help you understand or digest material. Mnemonics rely only on rote memorization.
- The mnemonic device itself is sometimes complicated to learn and time-consuming to develop.
- Mnemonic devices can be forgotten.

In spite of their limitations, mnemonic devices can be powerful. There are five general categories: new words, creative sentences, rhymes and songs, the loci system, and the peg system.

Make up new words. Acronyms are words created from the initial letters of a series of words. Examples include NASA (**N**ational **A**eronautics and **S**pace **A**dministration) and laser (**l**ight **a**mplification by **s**timulated **e**mission of **r**adiation).

You can make up your own acronyms to recall a series of facts. A common mnemonic acronym is Roy G. Biv, which has helped millions of students remember the colors of the visible spectrum (**r**ed, **o**range, **y**ellow, **g**reen, **b**lue, **i**ndigo, and **v**iolet). IPMAT helps biology students remember the stages of cell division

(**i**nterphase, **p**rophase, **m**etaphase, **a**naphase, and **t**elophase).

Use creative sentences. Acrostics are sentences that help you remember a series of letters that stand for something. For example, the first letters of the words in the sentence *Every good boy does fine* (E, G, B, D, and F) are the music notes of the lines of the treble clef staff.

Create rhymes and songs. Madison Avenue advertising executives spend billions of dollars a year on advertisements designed to burn their messages into your memory. The song "It's the Real Thing" was used to market Coca-Cola, despite the soda's artificial ingredients.

Rhymes have been used for centuries to teach basic facts. "*I before e, except after c*" has helped many a student on spelling tests.

Use the loci system. The word *loci* is the plural of *locus,* a synonym for *place* or *location*. Use the loci system to create visual associations with familiar locations. Unusual associations are the easiest to remember.

The loci system is an old one. Ancient Greek orators used it to remember long speeches, and politicians use it today. For example, if a politician's position was that road taxes must be raised to pay for school equipment, his loci visualizations before a speech might have looked like the following.

First, as he walks in the door of his house, he imagines a large *porpoise* jumping through a hoop.

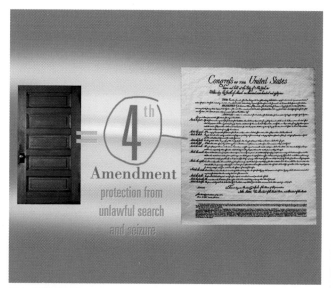

Door: © Photospin

You can use the peg system to remember the Bill of Rights (the first ten amendments to the U.S. Constitution). For example, amendment number *four* is about protection from unlawful search and seizure. Imagine people knocking at your *door* who are demanding to search your home. This amendment means that you do not have to open your door unless those people have a proper search warrant. ✳

This reminds him to begin by telling the audience the *purpose* of his speech.

Next, he visualizes his living room floor covered with paving stones, forming a road leading into the kitchen. In the kitchen, he pictures dozens of schoolchildren sitting on the floor because they have no desks.

Now it's the day of the big speech. The politician is nervous. He's perspiring so much that his clothes sticks to his body. He stands up to give his speech, and his mind goes blank. Then he starts thinking to himself:

> I can remember the rooms in my house. Let's see, I'm walking in the front door and—wow!—I see a porpoise. That reminds me to talk about the purpose of my speech. And then there's that road leading to the kitchen. Say, what are all those kids doing there on the floor? Oh, yeah, now I remember—they have no desks! We need to raise taxes on roads to pay for their desks and the other stuff they need in classrooms.

Try the peg system. The peg system is a technique that employs key words that are paired with numbers. Each word forms a "peg" on which you can "hang" mental associations. To use this system effectively, learn the following peg words and their associated numbers well:

bun goes with 1

shoe goes with 2

tree goes with 3

door goes with 4

hive goes with 5

sticks goes with 6

heaven goes with 7

gate goes with 8

wine goes with 9

hen goes with 10

14 exercise
Get creative

Construct your own mnemonic device for remembering some of the memory techniques in this chapter. Make up a poem, jingle, acronym, or acrostic. Or use another mnemonic system. Describe your mnemonic device in the space below.

MEMORY

3

mastering technology

USE YOUR COMPUTER TO ENHANCE MEMORY

The outlining feature of a word-processing program offers a powerful way to apply some of the memory techniques in this chapter. Use this feature to create summaries of textbooks and lecture notes:

- Divide a book chapter or set of handwritten notes into sections.

- Open up a new document in your word-processing program, and list the main points from each section.

- Shift to the outline view of your document, and turn each point into a level one heading.

- Enter key facts and other details as normal text under the appropriate heading.

- When reviewing for a test, shift your document into outline view so that only the headings are displayed. Scan them as you would scan the headlines in a newspaper.

- In the outline view, see if you can recall the details you included. Then open up the normal text underneath each headline to check the accuracy of your memory.

Outlining your notes allows you to organize information in a meaningful way. And stating key points in your own words helps you learn actively.

You can also use PowerPoint or other presentation software to create flash cards. Add illustrations, color, and other visual effects—a simple and fun way to draw on your visual intelligence.

A related option is to go online. Do an Internet search with the words *flash, card,* and *online.* You'll find a list of sites that allow you to select from a library of printable flash cards—or create and print your own cards.

Notable failures

As you experiment with memory techniques, you may try a few that fail at crucial moments—such as during a test. Just remember that many people before you have failed miserably before succeeding brilliantly. Consider a few examples.

In his first professional race, cyclist **Lance Armstrong** finished last.

The first time **Jerry Seinfeld** walked onstage at a comedy club as a professional comic, he looked out at the audience and froze.

When **Lucille Ball** began studying to be an actress in 1927, she was told by the head instructor of the John Murray Anderson Drama School, "Try any other profession."

In high school, actor and comic **Robin Williams** was voted "Least Likely to Succeed."

Walt Disney was fired by a newspaper editor because "he lacked imagination and had no good ideas."

R. H. Macy failed seven times before his store in New York City caught on.

Emily Dickinson had only seven poems published in her lifetime.

Decca Records turned down a recording contract with the **Beatles** with an unprophetic evaluation: "We don't like their sound. Groups of guitars are on their way out."

In 1954, Jimmy Denny, manager of the Grand Ole Opry, fired **Elvis Presley** after one performance.

Babe Ruth is famous for his past home run record, but for decades he also held the record for strikeouts. **Mark McGwire** broke that record.

After **Carl Lewis** won the gold medal for the long jump in the 1996 Olympic Games, he was asked to what he attributed his longevity, having competed for almost 20 years. He said, "Remembering that you have both wins and losses along the way. I don't take either one too seriously."

"I've missed more than 9,000 shots in my career," **Michael Jordan** said. "I've lost almost 300 games. Twenty-six times I've been trusted to take the game winning shot . . . and missed. I've failed over and over and over again in my life. That is why I succeed."

Adapted from "But They Did Not Give Up," http://www.des.emory.edu/mfp/OnFailingG.html (accessed February 20, 2009).

practicing critical thinking

3

Take 5 minutes to remember a time when you enjoyed learning something. In the space below, describe that experience in a sentence or two. Then make a brief list of the things you found enjoyable about that experience.

 Complete this exercise online.

_____

_____

_____

_____

_____

_____

_____

_____

Within the next 24 hours, compare your list with those of other classmates. Look for similarities and differences in the descriptions of your learning experiences.

Based on your comparison of lists, form a tentative explanation about what makes learning enjoyable for people. Summarize your explanation here:

_____

_____

_____

_____

_____

_____

_____

_____

_____

_____

_____

15 exercise
Move from problems to solutions

Many students find it easy to complain about school and to dwell on problems. This exercise gives you an opportunity to change that habit and respond creatively to any problem you're currently experiencing—whether it be with memorizing or some other aspect of school or life.

The key is to dwell more on solutions than on problems. Do that by inventing as many solutions as possible for any given problem. See if you can turn a problem into a *project* (a plan of action) or a *promise* to change some aspect of your life. Shifting the emphasis of your conversation from problems to solutions can raise your sense of possibility and unleash the master learner within you.

In the space below, describe at least three problems that could interfere with your success as a student. The problems can be related to courses, teachers, personal relationships, finances, or anything else that might get in the way of your success.

My problem is that . . .

My problem is that . . .

My problem is that . . .

Next, brainstorm at least five possible solutions to each of those problems. Ten solutions would be even better. (You can continue brainstorming on a separate piece of paper or on a computer.) You might find it hard to come up with that many ideas. That's OK. Stick with it. Stay in the inquiry, give yourself time, and ask other people for ideas.

I can solve my problem by . . .

I can solve my problem by . . .

I can solve my problem by . . .

MEMORY

3

Love Your Problems
(And Experience Your Barriers)

We all have problems and barriers that block our progress or prevent us from moving into new areas. Often, the way we respond to our problems places limitations on what we can be, do, and have.

Problems often work like barriers. When we bump up against one of our problems, we usually turn away and start walking along a different path. And all of a sudden—bump!—we've struck another barrier. And we turn away again.

As we continue to bump into problems and turn away from them, our lives stay inside the same old boundaries. Inside these boundaries, we are unlikely to have new adventures. We are unlikely to keep learning.

If we respond to problems by loving them instead of resisting them, we can expand the boundaries in which we live our lives.

The word *love* might sound like an overstatement. In this Power Process, the word means to unconditionally accept the fact that your problems exist. The more we deny or resist a problem, the stronger it seems to become. When we accept the fact that we have a problem, we can find effective ways to deal with it.

Suppose one of your barriers is being afraid of speaking in front of a group. You could get up in front of the group and pretend that you're not afraid. Or you could tell yourself, "I'm not going to be scared," and then try to keep your knees from knocking. Generally, these strategies don't work.

A more effective approach is to love your fear. Go to the front of the room, look out into the audience, and say to yourself, "I am scared. I notice that my knees are shaking and my mouth feels dry, and I'm having a rush of thoughts about what might happen if I say the wrong thing. Yup, I'm scared, and I'm not going to fight it. I'm going to give this speech anyway."

The beauty of this Power Process is that you continue to take action—giving your speech, for example—no matter what you feel. You walk right up to the barrier and then *through* it. You might even find that if you totally accept and experience a barrier, such as fear, it shrinks or disappears. Even if that does not happen right away, you still open up to new experiences and gain new chances to learn. Loving a problem does not need to stop us from solving it. In fact, fully accepting and admitting a problem usually helps us take effective action—which can free us of the problem once and for all.

 Discover more ways to love your problems online.

Put it to Work

You can use strategies in *Becoming a Master Student* to succeed at work. Get started by reflecting on the following case study.

Paula Chang is a nurse at a large urban hospital. Paula just joined the staff in the cardiology department, which includes forty nurses, doctors, and other health care workers. She was hired 2 months after graduating with a nursing degree from a nearby university.

Among Paula's goals for her new career was to learn the names of her colleagues by the end of the first week on the job. She succeeded.

One afternoon, the department head, Dr. Frank Rangel, invited Paula into his office for an informal chat. Frank had heard several colleagues talking about Paula's ability to remember names. He wanted to congratulate her—and learn a thing or two about memory techniques from his youngest team member.

"You're the first person on my staff who's ever managed to learn so many names so quickly," said Frank. "What's your secret?"

"No secrets, honest," Paula replied. "It's all about attitude, I guess. I simply made it a priority to remember names. I remember a teacher I had in college who had anywhere from fifty to a hundred students in his lecture classes. On the first day of class, he went around the room and asked each of us for our name. It took a lot of time, but then he called us by name for the rest of the semester. I remember feeling so touched by that. I promised I would do the same thing when I started my first job."

Frank smiled and said, "That's impressive. Memorizing so many names so quickly is a neat trick. But I'm just wondering: Does it really make a difference?"

"Yes, I think so," Paula said. "For one thing, I feel more confident right away about my surroundings. I feel more comfortable asking questions when I remember names."

Paula also shared an idea with Frank for future new employees. As a visual learner, she learns better by seeing photos of people and associating pictures with names. So Paula volunteered to take pictures of her colleagues to help everyone learn names.

Paula applied several strategies from this chapter:

* Create pictures.
* Engage your emotions.
* Intend to remember.

Stephen Coburn/Shutterstock

List more memory strategies that Paula could use:

_____

_____

_____

_____

Also consider the following suggestions when you want to sharpen your memory for names in the workplace. You can adapt these techniques to remembering any kind of detailed, factual information.

* Think of someone you already know who has the same first name as a new coworker. Visualize these two people standing side by side. Look for strong differences or similarities between them.
* Use rhymes or alliteration (the repetition of sounds). If Tim is slim or Sandra wears a scarf, you've got a natural "hook" for remembering their names.
* Use a new person's name every chance you get. In a meeting, for example, refer to "Jim's idea" or "Susan's question."
* Make small talk with people when you first meet them. Associate one key fact—such as a person's hometown or favorite hobby—with an image of the person's face.

www.cengage.com/success/bams13e

Quiz

Name _____   Date ____/____/____

1. In the article about the memory jungle, the meadow:
    (a) Is a place that every animal (thought or perception) must pass through.
    (b) Represents short-term memory.
    (c) Represents the idea that one type of memory has a limited capacity.
    (d) All of the above.
    (d) All of the above. (*The memory jungle,* p. 100)

2. Give a specific example of "setting a trap" for your memory.
    One example of setting a trap for your memory is tying a triple knot in your shoelace. (Answers will vary.) (*Set a trap for your memory,* p. 109)

3. Give two examples of ways in which you can organize a long list of items.
    One way of organizing a long list for memorization is by location. An example would be a biology student memorizing the leg muscles from the foot up to the hip. She could organize the muscles by location by grouping the muscles in the foot, those in the calf, those in the knee, and so on. Another way of organizing a list is by continuum. An example would be a student memorizing the types of business organization. He could organize them on a continuum, from the smallest and simplest type (a sole proprietorship) to the largest and most complex (a multinational corporation). (Answers will vary.) (*20 memory techniques,* p. 102)

4. Define *acronym,* and give an example of one.
    An acronym is a word created from the first letters in a series of words. Examples include NASA (**N**ational **A**eronautics and **S**pace **A**dministration), radar (**r**adio **d**etecting **a**nd **r**anging), scuba (**s**elf-**c**ontained **u**nderwater **b**reathing **a**pparatus), and laser (**l**ight **a**mplification by **s**timulated **e**mission of **r**adiation). (*Mnemonic devices,* p. 112)

5. Memorization on a deep level can take place if you:
    (a) Repeat the idea.
    (b) Repeat the idea.
    (c) Repeat the idea.
    (d) All of the above.
    (d) All of the above. (*20 memory techniques,* p. 102)

6. Mnemonic devices are the most efficient ways to memorize facts and ideas. True or False? Explain your answer.
    True. These memory tricks can help you learn information quickly. Therefore, they are efficient. However, they may not be effective for long-term memorization or for understanding. (*Mnemonic devices,* p. 112)

7. Briefly describe at least three memory techniques other than mnemonics.
    Briefly describe any three of the following:
    a. Any of the 20 memory techniques.
    b. Set a trap for your memory.
    c. Any of the 11 techniques for remembering names.
    (*20 memory techniques,* p. 102; *Set a trap for your memory,* p. 109; *Remembering names,* p. 111)

8. List three techniques that can be used to remember the names of three specific people you've recently met.
    The student should explain how to use one or more of the remembering names techniques, applying them to the three names chosen. Sample answer: Jerry—I will associate his name with the comedian Jerry Seinfeld. Darwish—I will recite and repeat his name several times to him and others in conversation. Maria—She seems to know all the answers in class, so I will write an intention to remember her name as a way to get to know her better. (*Remembering names,* p. 111)

9. Briefly define the word *love* as it is used in the Power Process: "Love Your Problems (and Experience Your Barriers)."
    Embrace your problems, instead of resisting or avoiding them. (*Power Process: Love your problems [and experience your barriers],* p. 117)

10. According to the text, "One powerful way to enhance your memory is to make friends with your amygdala." Briefly explain the meaning of this sentence.
    The amygdala is the area of your brain that activates when you feel a strong emotion. Because the amygdala tells the brain that the incoming information is important and should be remembered, you should be as aware of it as possible. (Answers will vary.) (*20 memory techniques,* p. 102)

Skills Snapshot

The Discovery Wheel in Chapter 1 includes a section labeled *Memory*. For the next 10 to 15 minutes, go beyond your initial responses to that exercise. Take a snapshot of your skills as they exist today, after reading and doing this chapter.

Begin by reflecting on some recent experiences. Then take the next step toward memory mastery by committing to a specific action in the near future.

Recalling key facts more quickly and accurately could help me be more effective in the following situations . . .

Memory techniques that I already use include . . .

I'll know that I've reached a new level of mastery with remembering ideas and information when . . .

To reach that level of mastery, the most important thing I can do next is to . . .

Master Student PROFILE

Pablo Alvarado
. . . is caring

Photo by Misha Erwitt

As an immigrant worker from El Salvador, Pablo Alvarado has a special connection to the Latin American immigrants who have traveled far from their homes in search of work to support their families. These are the people who wait on street corners, in parking lots, or in parks hoping for temporary employment—which is usually hard physical labor. Their average monthly earnings range from $350 to $1,000. They suffer discrimination, unsafe working conditions, and underpayment or nonpayment for their work, and many live in fear of deportation. Also, in many parts of the country, new civic ordinances prevent day laborers from soliciting work in public places, which makes finding work even more difficult. In addition, day laborers are frequent targets of violence and law enforcement hostility.

In El Salvador, Alvarado's family members were farmers who grew beans, corn, and coffee for their own use. Every day, his father hauled water from a nearby town to sell in their village. At harvest time, young Alvarado worked 10 hours a day at nearby coffee plantations to have money to buy his clothes and school supplies. Although Alvarado's mother never went to school and his father only attended as far as the third grade, his parents insisted that he and his siblings get an education.

In the midst of civil war, when he was 12 years old, Alvarado became a teaching assistant for a literacy class that served his neighbors, and he witnessed the power of education to bring social improvement and better living conditions. "On my way to and from school, I would walk over bodies, which were left on the side of the road. When I was in eighth grade, several teachers were killed and others fled because they were accused of being guerrilla sympathizers," Alvarado recalls.

At 16, Alvarado used his communications skills to serve as a lay preacher. His teachings contained elements of Liberation Theology, applying the Gospels to current socioeconomic and political struggles. He earned high school teaching credentials in 1989 from Universidad de El Salvador, but "just as many immigrants have done, I fled my country because of political and economic reasons."

Working as an undocumented immigrant in the United States, Alvarado toiled as a gardener, factory assembly line worker, driver, and painter, and he experienced the pain of isolation and discrimination. While working at a studio-equipment factory, he witnessed hostility between Salvadorans and Mexicans. "Drawing on my childhood experiences, I engaged other co-workers and organized a soccer team that greatly improved relations among workers." That was the beginning of Alvarado's leadership in the United States. "The soccer experience is now part of the national movement, as day laborers in Los Angeles and Washington D.C. have created their own soccer leagues," he says.

Some of his organizing techniques are unusual, but effective. Besides soccer teams, his organization also sponsors chess teams, marathon races, and popular theater. "On the street corners, workers start by relating to each other as competition (for jobs)," Alvarado explains. "When brought together on a soccer field, their dynamic changes to camaraderie, which then extends back to organizing on the street corners."

"Pablo Alvarado, National Day Laborer Organizing Network (NDLON)—Los Angeles, CA: 2004 Award Recipients," Institute for Sustainable Communities, Leadership for a Changing World, Institute for Sustainable Communities, 2009, http://www.leadershipforchange.org/awardees/awardee.php3?ID=201.

(1954–)
Executive director of the National Day Laborer Organizing Network who uses soccer, music, and coalition building to foster humane conditions for day laborers.

Find more biographical information about Pablo Alvarado at the Master Student Hall of Fame.

Instructor Tools & Tips

> "Reading furnishes our mind only with materials of knowledge; it is thinking that makes what we read ours.
>
> **—John Locke**

> There would seem to be almost no limit to what people can and will misunderstand when they are not doing their utmost to get at a writer's meaning.
>
> **—Ezra Pound**

Preview

Chapter 4 is the first chapter in the text's academic development section, which includes Chapters 4 through 6. This section of the book employs a time-sensitive critical thinking approach to organize academic learning by considering strategies to employ before, during and after learning. All three chapters (Chapter 4: Reading, Chapter 5: Notes, and Chapter 6: Tests) follow this approach, which makes Chapter 2: Time even more relevant to student success.

Although much of this chapter appears to be simply a review of what students should have learned in elementary or high school, the reality is that many students do not learn the critical reading skills they need to survive and thrive in the academic rigors of college. College reading is more than just the ability to read the words. Critical reading is a complex thinking process and thus is unlike any other "subject" they study in school. The academic literacy training that students receive in this chapter will prove invaluable throughout their academic careers. Our motivation, maturity, and life experiences all lead us to value the skills of reading comprehension and reading speed more than we might have as children.

Most importantly, you can help your students accelerate their ability to learn new material by helping them activate any prior knowledge to engage with the reading they must do to succeed. Encourage your students to use the information they have learned about the brain in the memory chapter to enhance their skill at reading. Also included in this chapter is an updated article about how to use the library. Consider the Master Student Map at the beginning of the chapter as a stepping-stone.

Guest Speaker

This is a good time to invite a librarian as your guest speaker to talk to students about how they can use the library to research topics for classes. See also a related assignment in the **"Homework"** section.

Another possibility is to invite instructors from a variety of disciplines to talk about reading strategies appropriate to their course content. Ask them to come prepared to answer the following questions for your students:

Why? Why is the reading material in your discipline area unique?

What? What strategies would work best for tackling the reading material in your discipline area? Suggest that your discipline expert bring a sample passage (as a handout) for students so that they can use this new strategy to read it.

How? How can students improve their reading comprehension in your discipline area using these strategies?

What if? What if the students are still having trouble with reading in this discipline? What resources do you suggest (on-campus labs, ancillary textbooks, Web sites, and the like)?

Here's a guest speaker for you:

Lecture

Students may ask, "Why use Muscle Reading? I have been reading since first grade!" Muscle Reading is designed as a balanced literacy approach. It incorporates the three aspects of a metacognitive learning system. This means that it presents specific strategies for students to use before, during, and after reading.

Students may also grumble that this approach to reading requires "too much." Lecture on Muscle Reading by walking them through the nine steps for the next chapter, "Notes." Tell them to *Preview* the chapter by turning the pages, looking at graphs, pictures, article titles, and anything else that stands out for them. Next, on a sheet of paper, create an *Outline* by listing the titles of the articles, double spacing between the article titles. Instruct the students to turn each title into a *Question*. Then *Read* the chapter, highlighting/*Underlining* the *Answers* they discover to their outline list of questions. *Recite, Review,* and periodically *Review Again* their outline questions and highlighted answers in the book. This lecture and demonstration will help your students see

how the nine-step process can be efficiently streamlined while retaining its effectiveness. For more information, review the sidebar article, "Muscle Reading—a leaner approach," on page 129.

Exercises/Activities

1. **Muscle Reading (page 123)** Divide your class into three groups: Before, During, and After. Have each group prepare a 10-minute presentation on the three steps within their given phase. Each group aims for a memorable lesson that provides examples of their strategies. In conclusion, the three groups come up with a sample test question to help determine how the rest of the class understood their presentation.

2. **Power Process: Notice Your Pictures and Let Them Go (page 143)** Present this Power Process as a problem-solving technique. When students feel frustrated because reality does not match their expectations, "Notice your pictures and let them go" helps them let go of those expectations and experience what their reality *does* have to offer. In class, have students individually brainstorm "pictures" that interfere with their success in college. Examples include "I'm not smart enough to get a college degree" or "I'll never graduate—I can't stick with anything for four years." Then ask students to select one picture to "let go." Have them write their picture on a piece of paper and fold it up. Take the entire class outside and have the students tear their papers (negative pictures) into shreds and throw them in the Dumpster—literally letting them go! Return to class and have students write briefly about a new, positive picture to replace the negative one they have let go. For some students, this will be a personal exercise, and they may not feel comfortable talking about it with others. Other students may be willing to share with the class their experience of letting their negative picture go.

3. **Master Student Profile: Wilma Mankiller** Divide students into groups and ask each group to come up with ways that they can be leaders on their college campus or in their local community. Have them write their ideas on large sheets of poster paper and tape them to the walls in your classroom. Have students stay in groups and walk around the room to read the other lists.

Conversation/Sharing

Now that your students have practiced using the Master Student Map in previous chapters, see if they can generate their own questions before you present yours to the class.

Why? Why does *Becoming a Master Student* include a chapter on reading?

What? Read through the list of articles and select three that you believe will enhance your reading skills.

How? How can you be more successful in college with these additional strategies for successful reading?

What if? What if you apply these reading strategies to your coursework for other classes?

Homework

The twenty-first century-researcher—using your library (page 135) After students have read this article and heard from a librarian (as a guest speaker), give them an assignment to go to the college library to (1) find a broad, current issue topic for a college research paper and (2) use the online catalog to discover narrow topics within the broad topic. For the first step, have them use *CQ Researcher,* a reference book most college libraries have, so they learn about a useful book in the library that can help them find current issue topics for future research paper assignments.

Developing critical thinking strategies throughout the semester will help your students master their college-level reading. Use this exercise to help students further develop their skills. This assignment works best as either an extra-credit assignment or as homework.

Practicing Critical Thinking #4 (page 142) One of the strategies suggested for understanding difficult reading material is to read another publication on the same subject. This is one example of critical thinking skills—explaining and assessing alternative views on an issue.

Apply this strategy now. Ask your students to find and read a newspaper or magazine article that's relevant to one of their current reading assignments. Have your students summarize and compare the viewpoints on the subject presented by both authors. Ask them to list the major questions addressed, along with the answers that are offered, and have them highlight points of disagreement and agreement. Finally, have your students consider the methods that the authors use to reach their conclusions and the evidence they present. Have students determine if one author's viewpoint is more reasonable, given all of the suitable evidence, and then write a paragraph that supports their conclusion.

If you assign this for extra credit or homework, be sure to clarify for your students exactly which materials they should submit. Consider asking them to submit their articles or a bibliography page. If you are trying to encourage students to become familiar with technology, ask them to forward the materials to you in an e-mail attachment or post the materials to your online course management system.

Evaluation

Frequent quizzes ensure that students face attention during class and keep up with the text reading assignments. In addition, quizzes provide students with opportunities for written reflection regarding new discoveries and intentions. Evaluation instruments also help you identify topics and concept that students have not yet mastered. In addition to the questions listed here, find more test questions on the Instructor Web site.

Quiz ideas for Chapter 4:

- Ask students to explain the nine steps of the Muscle Reading process.
- Ask students to describe tools to use when reading tough material.
- Ask students to list techniques for reading faster.
- Ask students to explain in writing to a student who is a single parent how to study with children underfoot.

Additional Digital Resources

Course Manual

The online *Course Manual* serves as an invaluable reference for those developing and teaching a College Success course with *Becoming a Master Student.* The *Course Manual* provides advice on general teaching issues such as preparing for classes, classroom management, grading, and communicating with students of various backgrounds, as well as specific strategies on getting the most out of various features in *Becoming a Master Student* such as the Discovery Wheel, Learning Styles Inventory, and book-specific Web sites.

Instructor Web Site

The updated Instructor Web site provides resources to help you plan and customize your course. Content specific to Chapter 4 includes:

► Lecture Ideas
  • Liking the Instructor—or Form versus Content
  • Appropriate Reading Rates
► In-Class Exercises
  • First Impressions
  • Critical Reading as a Process
  • Numbered Notes
► In-Text Quiz Answers
► Learning Styles Application
► Discussion Topics
► PowerPoint Slides
► Reflection Questions
► Assessment Questions
► Experiment with chapter strategies

The Instructor Web site also contains the following book-specific content:

► ExamView Test Bank
► Online Course Manual
► Articles from previous editions
► Master Student Profiles from previous editions
► Sample Syllabi

 www.cengage.com/success/bams13e

Student Web Site

To help your students gain a better understanding of the topics discussed in *Becoming a Master Student,* encourage your students to visit the Student Web site, which provides the following resources specific to Chapter 4:

► Connect to Text content expands on specific topics marked with an icon within Chapter 4.
► Learning Style Applications invite students to cycle through the four styles of learning. In answering the four questions about Muscle Reading posted in this chapter's Learning Styles Application, students explore the different modes and apply their new knowledge.
► Practice Tests allow students to see how well they understand the themes of *Becoming a Master Student.*
► Interactive Concept Maps promote critical thinking by highlighting related ideas to show relationships between concepts.
► Remembering Cultural Differences presents readers with brief articles that touch on aspects of diversity in our rapidly changing world. For Chapter 4, the following article will prompt your students to look at contemporary issues in a new way:
  • Where Have All the Readers Gone?
► Master Student Profiles provide additional information on the people covered in this book feature. For Chapter 4, students will find expanded coverage and links about:
  • Chief Wilma Mankiller
► Power Process Media contains video, PowerPoints, and audio files to take what your students have learned from the Power Processes in their book to the next level. For Chapter 4, students will find additional media on:
  • Notice your pictures and let them go

Along with the chapter-specific content, a General Resources folder is available that contains Toolboxes geared toward specific student types (Community College, Adult Learner, Student Athlete), the Plagiarism Prevention Zone, and the Career Resource Center.

4 Reading

Master Student Map

as you read, ask yourself

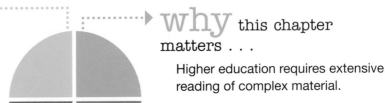

what if . . .

I could finish my reading with time to spare and easily recall the key points?

why this chapter matters . . .

Higher education requires extensive reading of complex material.

what is included . . .

how you can use this chapter . . .

- Analyze what effective readers do and experiment with new techniques.
- Increase your vocabulary and adjust your reading speed for different types of material.
- Comprehend difficult texts with more ease.

MASTER STUDENTS in *action*

One night when I was reading I had so much on my mind I reread the page probably 5 times. I finally just put the book down and cleared my mind.

I put on some of my favorite music, and I took a fantasy trip by thinking about all my upcoming exciting things that I would be doing. When I was done, I got back to my reading with no trouble at all.

—LINDSEY GIBLIN

Photo courtesy of Lindsey Giblin

Muscle Reading

PICTURE YOURSELF SITTING at a desk, a book in your hands. Your eyes are open, and it looks as if you're reading. Suddenly your head jerks up. You blink. You realize your eyes have been scanning the page for 10 minutes, and you can't remember a single thing you have read.

Or picture this: You've had a hard day. You were up at 6 a.m. to get the kids ready for school. A coworker called in sick, and you missed your lunch trying to do his job as well as your own. You picked up the kids, then had to shop for dinner. Dinner was late, of course, and the kids were grumpy.

Finally, you get to your books at 8 p.m. You begin a reading assignment on something called "the equity method of accounting for common stock investments." "I am preparing for the future," you tell yourself, as you plod through two paragraphs and begin the third. Suddenly, everything in the room looks different. Your head is resting on your elbow, which is resting on the equity method of accounting. The clock reads 11:00 p.m. Say good-bye to 3 hours.

Sometimes the only difference between a sleeping pill and a textbook is that the textbook doesn't have a warning on the label about operating heavy machinery.

Contrast this scenario with the image of an active reader. This person does the following:

■ Stays alert, poses questions about what she reads, and searches for the answers.

■ Recognizes levels of information within the text, separating the main points and general principles from supporting details.

■ Quizzes herself about the material, makes written notes, and lists unanswered questions.

■ Instantly spots key terms and takes the time to find the definitions of unfamiliar words.

■ Thinks critically about the ideas in the text and looks for ways to apply them.

That sounds like a lot to do. Yet skilled readers routinely accomplish all these things and more—while enjoying reading.[1]

One way to experience this kind of success is to approach reading with a system in mind. An example is Muscle Reading. You can use Muscle Reading to avoid mental minivacations and reduce the number of unscheduled naps during study time, even after a hard day.

Muscle Reading is a way to decrease difficulty and struggle by increasing energy and skill. Once you learn this system, you might actually spend less time on your reading and get more out of it.

This is not to say that Muscle Reading will make your education a breeze. Muscle Reading might even look like more work at first. Effective textbook reading is an active, energy-consuming, sit-on-the-edge-of-your-seat business. That's why this strategy is called Muscle Reading. ✳

journal entry 11

Discovery/Intention Statement

Discover what you want from this chapter

Recall a time when you encountered problems with reading, such as words you didn't understand or paragraphs you paused to reread more than once. Sum up the experience and how you felt about it by completing the following statement.

I discovered that I . . .

_____

_____

_____

_____

Now list three to five specific reading skills you want to gain from this chapter.

I intend to . . .

_____

_____

_____

_____

_____

_____

_____

How Muscle Reading works

Images: © Masterfile Royalty Free, collage by Walter Kopec

MUSCLE READING is a three-phase technique you can use to extract the ideas and information you want.

Phase 1 includes steps to take *before* you read.

Phase 2 includes steps to take *while* you read.

Phase 3 includes steps to take *after* you read.

Each phase has three steps.

PHASE ONE:
Before you read
Step 1: **Preview**
Step 2: **Outline**
Step 3: **Question**

PHASE TWO:
While you read
Step 4: **Read**
Step 5: **Underline**
Step 6: **Answer**

PHASE THREE:
After you read
Step 7: **Recite**
Step 8: **Review**
Step 9: **Review again**

To assist your recall of Muscle Reading strategies, memorize three short sentences:

Pry Out Questions.

Root Up Answers.

Recite, Review, and Review again.

These three sentences correspond to the three phases of the Muscle Reading technique. Each sentence is an acrostic. The first letter of each word stands for one of the nine steps listed above.

Take a moment to invent images for each of those sentences.

For *Phase 1,* visualize or feel yourself prying out questions from a text. These questions are ones you want answered based on a brief survey of the assignment. Make a mental picture of yourself scanning the material, spotting a question, and reaching into the text to pry it out. Hear yourself saying, "I've got it. Here's my question." Then for *Phase 2,* get your muscles involved. Feel the tips of your fingers digging into the text as you root up the answers to your questions.

Finally, you enter *Phase 3.* Hear your voice reciting what you have learned. Listen to yourself making a speech or singing a song about the material as you review it.

To jog your memory, write the first letters of the Muscle Reading acrostic in a margin or at the top of your notes. Then check off the steps you intend to follow. Or write the Muscle Reading steps on 3x5 cards and then use them for bookmarks.

Muscle Reading might take a little time to learn. At first you might feel it's slowing you down. That's natural when you're gaining a new skill. Mastery comes with time and practice.

PHASE 1

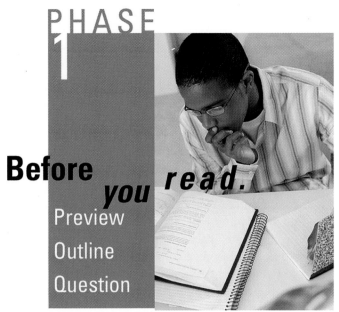

Before *you* **read.**

Preview

Outline

Question

Images: © Masterfile Royalty Free, collage by Walter Kopec

Step 1: Preview

Before you start reading, preview the entire assignment. You don't have to memorize what you preview to get value from this step. Previewing sets the stage for incoming information by warming up a space in your mental storage area.

If you are starting a new book, look over the table of contents, and flip through the text page by page. If you're going to read one chapter, flip through the pages of that chapter. Even if your assignment is merely a few pages in a book, you can benefit from a brief preview of the table of contents.

Keep the preview short. If the entire reading assignment will take less than an hour, your preview might take 5 minutes. Previewing is also a way to get yourself started when an assignment looks too big to handle. It is an easy way to step into the material.

Keep an eye out for summary statements. If the assignment is long or complex, read the summary first. Many textbooks have summaries in the introduction or at the end of each chapter.

Read all chapter headings and subheadings. Like the headlines in a newspaper, these are usually printed in large, bold type. Often headings are brief summaries in themselves.

When previewing, seek out familiar concepts, facts, or ideas. These items can help increase comprehension by linking new information to previously learned material. Look for ideas that spark your imagination or curiosity. Inspect drawings, diagrams, charts, tables, graphs, and photographs. Imagine what kinds of questions will show up on a test. Previewing helps to clarify your purpose for reading. Ask yourself what you will do with this material and how it can relate to your long-term goals. Will you be reading just to get the main

points? Key supporting details? Additional details? All of the above? Your answers will guide what you do with each step that follows.

Step 2: Outline

With complex material, take time to understand the structure of what you are about to read. Outlining actively organizes your thoughts about the assignment and can help make complex information easier to understand.

If your textbook provides chapter outlines, spend some time studying them. When an outline is not provided, sketch a brief one in the margin of your book or at the beginning of your notes on a separate sheet of paper. Later, as you read and take notes, you can add to your outline.

Headings in the text can serve as major and minor entries in your outline. For example, the heading for this article is "Phase 1: Before You Read," and the subheadings list the three steps in this phase. When you outline, feel free to rewrite headings so that they are more meaningful to you.

The amount of time you spend on this outlining step will vary. For some assignments, a 10-second mental outline is all you might need. For other assignments (fiction and poetry, for example), you can skip this step altogether.

Step 3: Question

Before you begin a careful reading, determine what you want from the assignment. Then write down a list of questions, including any questions that resulted from your preview of the materials.

Another useful technique is to turn chapter headings and subheadings into questions. For example, if a heading is "Transference and Suggestion," you can ask yourself, "What are *transference* and *suggestion*? How does *transference* relate to *suggestion*?" Make up a quiz as if you were teaching this subject to your classmates.

If there are no headings, look for key sentences and turn them into questions. These sentences usually show up at the beginnings or ends of paragraphs and sections.

Have fun with this technique. Make the questions playful or creative. You don't need to answer every question that you ask. The purpose of making up questions is to get your brain involved in the assignment. Take your unanswered questions to class, where they can be springboards for class discussion.

Demand your money's worth from your textbook. If you do not understand a concept, write specific questions about it. The more detailed your questions, the more powerful this technique becomes.

 Find examples of Phase 1 strategies online.

PHASE 2

While you read.

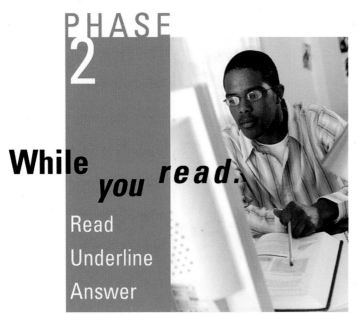

Read

Underline

Answer

Images: © Masterfile Royalty Free, collage by Walter Kopec

Step 4: Read

At last! You have previewed the reading assignment, organized it in your mind, and formulated questions. Now you are ready to begin reading.

Before you dive into the first paragraph, take a few moments to reflect on what you already know about this subject. Do so even if you think you know nothing. This technique prepares your brain to accept the information that follows.

As you read, be conscious of where you are and what you are doing. Use the Power Process: "Be Here Now" in Chapter 2. When you notice your attention wandering, gently bring it back to the present moment.

One way to stay focused is to avoid marathon reading sessions. Schedule breaks, and set a reasonable goal for the entire session. Then reward yourself with an enjoyable activity for 5 or 10 minutes every hour or two.

For difficult reading, set more limited goals. Read for a half-hour and then take a break. Most students find that shorter periods of reading distributed throughout the day and week can be more effective than long sessions. You can use the following four techniques to stay focused as you read.

First, visualize the material. Form mental pictures of the concepts as they are presented. If you read that a voucher system can help control cash disbursements, picture a voucher handing out dollar bills. Using visual imagery in this way can help deepen your understanding of the text while allowing information to be transferred into your long-term memory.

Second, read the material out loud, especially if it is complicated. Some of us remember better and understand more quickly when we hear an idea.

Third, get a "feel" for the subject. For example, let's say you are reading about a microorganism—a paramecium—in your biology text. Imagine what it would feel like to run your finger around the long, cigar-shaped body of the organism. Imagine feeling the large fold of its gullet on one side and the tickle of the hairy little cilia as they wiggle in your hand.

Fourth, remember that a goal of your reading is to answer the questions you listed during Phase 1. After you've identified the key questions, predict how the author will answer them. Then read to find out if your predictions were accurate.

A final note: It's easy to fool yourself about reading. Just having an open book in your hand and moving your eyes across a page doesn't mean you are reading effectively. Reading textbooks takes energy, even if you do it sitting down.

If you do an informal study of chief executive officers, you'll find some who wear out the front of their chairs first. Approach your reading assignment as a company president would. Sit up. Keep your spine straight. Use the edge of your chair. And avoid reading in bed—except for fun.

Step 5: Underline

Deface your books. Have fun writing in them. Indulge yourself as you never could with your grade school books. The purpose of making marks in a text is to call out important concepts or information that you will need to review later. Be aware, though, that underlining a text with a pen can make underlined sections—the important parts—harder to read. As an alternative, many students underline in pencil or use colored highlighters to flag key words and sentences. Using a highlighter to mark key information can save lots of time when you are studying for tests.

Underlining offers a secondary benefit. When you read with a highlighter, pen, or pencil in your hand, you involve your kinesthetic senses of touch and motion. Being physical with your books can help build strong neural pathways in your memory.

Avoid underlining too soon. Wait until you complete a chapter or section to make sure you know the key points. Then mark up the text. Sometimes, underlining after you read each paragraph works best.

Underline sparingly—usually less than 10 percent of the text. If you mark up too much on a page, you defeat the purpose—to flag the most important material for review.

In addition to underlining, you can mark up a text in the following ways:

- Place an asterisk (*) or an exclamation point (!) in the margin next to an especially important sentence or term.
- Circle key terms and words to look up later in a dictionary.
- Write short definitions of key terms in the margin.
- Write a Q in the margin to highlight possible test questions, passages you don't understand, and questions to ask in class.
- Write personal comments in the margin—points of agreement or disagreement with the author.
- Write mini-indexes in the margin—that is, the numbers of other pages in the book where the same topic is discussed.
- Write summaries by listing the main points or key events covered in a chapter.
- Rewrite chapter titles, headings, and subheadings so that they're more meaningful to you.

- Draw diagrams, pictures, tables, or maps that translate text into visual terms.
- Number each step in a list or series of related points.

Step 6: Answer

As you read, seek out the answers to your questions and write them down. Fill in your outline. Jot down new questions, and note when you don't find the answers you are looking for. Use these notes to ask questions in class, or see your instructor personally.

When you read, create an image of yourself as a person in search of the answers. You are a detective, watching for every clue, sitting erect in your straight-back chair, demanding that your textbook give you what you want—the answers.

 Find examples of Phase 2 strategies online.

Five smart ways to highlight a text

Step 5 in Muscle Reading presents a powerful tool: highlighting. It also presents a danger—the ever-present temptation to highlight too much text. Excessive highlighting leads to wasted time during reviews and can also spoil the appearance of your books. Get the most out of all that money you pay for books. Highlight in an efficient way that leaves texts readable for years to come.

Read carefully first   Read an entire chapter or section at least once before you begin highlighting. Don't be in a hurry to mark up your book. Get to know the text first. Make two or three passes through difficult sections before you highlight.

Make choices up front about what to highlight   Perhaps you can accomplish your purposes by highlighting only certain chapters or sections of a text. When you highlight, remember to look for passages that directly answer the questions you posed during Step 3 of Muscle Reading. Within these passages, highlight individual words, phrases, or sentences rather than whole paragraphs. The important thing is to choose an overall strategy before you put highlighter to paper.

Recite first   You might want to apply Step 7 of Muscle Reading before you highlight. Talking about what you read—to yourself or with other people—can help you grasp the essence of a text. Recite first; then go back and highlight. You'll probably highlight more selectively.

Underline, then highlight   Underline key passages lightly in pencil. Then close your text and come back to it later. Assess your underlining. Perhaps you can highlight less than you underlined and still capture the key points.

Use highlighting to monitor your comprehension   Critical thinking plays a role in underlining and highlighting. When highlighting, you're making moment-by-moment decisions about what you want to remember from a text. You're also making inferences about what material might be included on a test.

Take your critical thinking a step further by using highlighting to check your comprehension. Stop reading periodically, and look back over the sentences you've highlighted. See if you are making accurate distinctions between main points and supporting material. Highlighting too much—more than 10 percent of the text—can be a sign that you're not making this distinction and that you don't fully understand what you're reading. See the article "When Reading Is Tough" later in this chapter for suggestions that can help.

 Find an example of smart highlighting online.

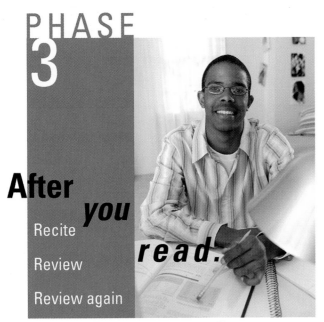

PHASE 3

After *you* *read.*

Recite

Review

Review again

Images: © Masterfile Royalty Free, collage by Walter Kopec

Step 7: Recite

Talk to yourself about what you've read. Or talk to someone else. When you finish a reading assignment, make a speech about it. A classic study suggests that you can profitably devote up to 80 percent of your study time to active reciting.[2] When you recite, you practice an important aspect of metacognition—synthesis, or combining individual ideas and facts into a meaningful whole.

One way to get yourself to recite is to look at each underlined point. Note what you marked; then put the book down and start talking out loud. Explain as much as you can about that particular point.

To make this technique more effective, do it in front of a mirror. It might seem silly, but the benefits can be enormous. Reap them at exam time.

Classmates are even better than mirrors. Form a group, and practice teaching one another what you have read. One of the best ways to learn anything is to teach it to someone else.

In addition, talk about your reading whenever you can. Tell friends and family members what you're learning from your textbooks.

Talking about your reading reinforces a valuable skill—the ability to summarize. To practice this skill, pick one chapter (or one section of one chapter) from any of your textbooks. State the main topic covered in this chapter. Then state the main points that the author makes about this topic.

For example, the main topic up to this point in this chapter is Muscle Reading. The main point about this topic is that Muscle Reading includes three phases—steps to take before you read, while you read, and after you read. For a more detailed summary, you could name each of the nine steps.

Note: This topic-point method does not work so well when you want to summarize short stories, novels, plays, and other works of fiction. Instead, focus on action. In most stories, the main character confronts a major problem and takes a series of actions to solve it. Describe that problem and talk about the character's key actions—the turning points in the story.

Step 8: Review

Plan to do your first complete review within 24 hours of reading the material. Sound the trumpets! This point is critical: A review within 24 hours moves information from your short-term memory to your long-term memory.

Review within 1 day. If you read it on Wednesday, review it on Thursday. During this review, look over your notes and clear up anything you don't understand. Recite some of the main points again.

This review can be short. You might spend as little as 15 minutes reviewing a difficult 2-hour reading assignment. Investing that time now can save you hours later when studying for exams.

Step 9: Review again

The final step in Muscle Reading is the weekly or monthly review. This step can be very short—perhaps only 4 or 5 minutes per assignment. Simply go over your notes. Read the highlighted parts of your text. Recite one or two of the more complicated points.

The purpose of these reviews is to keep the neural pathways to the information open and to make them more distinct. That way, the information can be easier to recall. You can accomplish these short reviews anytime, anywhere, if you are prepared.

Conduct a 5-minute review while you are waiting for a bus, for your socks to dry, or for the water to boil. Three-by-five cards are a handy review tool. Write ideas, formulas, concepts, and facts on cards, and carry them with you. These short review periods can be effortless and fun.

Sometimes longer review periods are appropriate. For example, if you found an assignment difficult, consider rereading it. Start over, as if you had never seen the material before. Sometimes a second reading will provide you with surprising insights.

Decades ago, psychologists identified the primacy-recency effect, which suggests that we most easily remember the first and last items in any presentation.[3] Previewing and reviewing your reading can put this theory to work for you. ✳

 Find examples of Phase 3 strategies online.

Muscle Reading—a leaner approach

Keep in mind that Muscle Reading is an overall approach, not a rigid, step-by-step procedure. Here's a shorter variation that students have found helpful. Practice it with any chapter in this book:

- **Preview and question.** Flip through the pages, looking at anything that catches your eye—headings, subheadings, illustrations, photographs. Turn the title of each article into a question. For example, "How Muscle Reading Works" can become "How does Muscle Reading work?" List your questions on a separate sheet of paper, or write each question on a 3×5 card.

- **Read to answer your questions.** Read each article. Then go back over the text and underline or highlight answers to the appropriate questions on your list.

- **Recite and review.** When you're done with the chapter, close the book. Recite by reading each question—and answering it—out loud. Review the chapter by looking up the answers to your questions. (It's easy—they're already highlighted.) Review again by quizzing yourself one more time with your list of questions.

journal entry 12

Discovery/Intention Statement

Experimenting with Muscle Reading

After reading the steps included in Muscle Reading, reflect on your reading skills. Are you a more effective reader than you thought you were? Less effective? Record your observations below.

_____

_____

_____

_____

_____

_____

_____

_____

_____

_____

_____

_____

_____

_____

Many students find that they only do the "read" step with their textbooks. You've just read about the advantages of eight additional steps you should perform. Depending on the text, reading assignment, your available time, and your commitment level to the material, you may discover through practice which additional steps work best for you. Right now, make a commitment to yourself to experiment with all or several of the additional Muscle Reading steps by completing the following Intention Statement.

I intend to use the following Muscle Reading steps for the next 2 weeks in my _____ class:

- ❑ Preview
- ❑ Outline
- ❑ Question
- ❑ Read
- ❑ Underline
- ❑ Answer
- ❑ Recite
- ❑ Review
- ❑ Review again

When reading is tough

Sometimes ordinary reading methods are not enough. It's easy to get bogged down in a murky reading assignment. The solution starts with a First Step: When you are confused, tell the truth about it. Successful readers monitor their understanding of reading material. They do not see confusion as a mistake or a personal shortcoming. Instead, they take it as a cue to change reading strategies and process ideas at a deeper level.

© Graham Bell/Corbis

Read it again. Somehow, students get the idea that reading means opening a book and dutifully slogging through the text—line by line, page by page—moving in a straight line from the first word until the last. Actually, this method can be an ineffective way to read much of the published material you'll encounter in college.

Feel free to shake up your routine. Make several passes through any reading material. During a preview, for example, just scan the text to look for key words and highlighted material. Next, skim the entire chapter or article again, spending a little more time and taking in more than you did during your preview. Finally, read in more depth, proceeding word by word through some or all of the text.

Difficult material—such as the technical writing in science texts—is often easier the second time around. Isolate difficult passages and read them again, slowly.

If you read an assignment and are completely lost, do not despair. Sleep on it. When you return to the assignment the next day, you'll see it with fresh eyes.[4]

Look for essential words. If you are stuck on a paragraph, mentally cross out all of the adjectives and adverbs, and then read the sentences without them. Find the important words—usually verbs and nouns.

Hold a mini-review. Pause briefly to summarize—either verbally or in writing—what you've read so far. Stop at the end of a paragraph and recite, in your own words, what you have just read. Jot down some notes, or create a short outline or summary.

Read it out loud. Make noise. Read a passage out loud several times, each time using a different inflection and emphasizing a different part of the sentence. Be creative. Imagine that you are the author talking.

Talk to your instructor. Admit when you are stuck, and make an appointment with your instructor. Most teachers welcome the opportunity to work individually with students. Be specific about your confusion. Point out the paragraph that you found toughest to understand.

Stand up. Changing positions periodically can combat fatigue. Experiment with standing as you read, especially if you get stuck on a tough passage and decide to read it out loud.

Skip around. Jump to the next section or to the end of a tough article or chapter. You might have lost the big picture. Simply seeing the next step, the next main point, or a summary might be all you need to put the details in context. Retrace the steps in a chain of ideas, and look for examples. Absorb facts and ideas in whatever order works for you—which may be different than the author's presentation.

Find a tutor. Many schools provide free tutoring services. If your school does not, other students who have completed the course can assist you.

Use another text. Find a similar text in the library. Sometimes a concept is easier to understand if it is expressed another way. Children's books—especially children's encyclopedias—can provide useful overviews of baffling subjects.

Pretend you understand, and then explain it. We often understand more than we think we do. Pretend that the material is clear as a bell and explain it to another person, or even to yourself. Write down your explanation. You might be amazed by what you know.

Ask, "What's going on here?" When you feel stuck, stop reading for a moment and diagnose what's happening. At these stop points, mark your place in the margin of the page with a penciled *S* for *Stuck*. A pattern to your marks over several pages might indicate a question you want to answer before going further. Or you might discover a reading habit you'd like to change.

Stop reading. When none of the above suggestions work, do not despair. Admit your confusion and then take a break. Catch a movie, go for a walk, study another subject, or sleep on it. The concepts you've already absorbed might come together at a subconscious level as you move on to other activities. Allow some time for that process. When you return to the reading material, see it with fresh eyes. ✳

FIND WHAT YOU WANT ON THE INTERNET

At one level, searching the Internet is simple. Just go online to a site such as Ask, Google, or Yahoo! Look for the search box, and enter a key word or two to describe what you want to find. Then hit the enter key.

You might find exactly what you're looking for in this way. If you don't, then take your Internet searches to the next level:

Use specific key words. Entering *firefox* or *safari* will give you more focused results than entering *web browser*. *Reading strategies* or *note-taking strategies* will get more specific results than *study strategies*.

Use unique key words. Whenever possible, use proper names. Enter *Beatles* or *Radiohead* rather than *British rock bands*. If you're looking for nearby restaurants, enter *restaurant* and your zip code rather than the name of your city.

Start with fewer key words rather than more. Instead of *ways to develop your career plan,* just enter *career plan*. The extra words might lead to irrelevant results or narrow your search too much.

If you're looking for certain words in a certain order, use quotation marks. *"Audacity of hope"* will return a list of pages with that exact phrase.

Search within a site. If you're looking only for articles about college tuition from the *New York Times,* then add *new york times* or *nytimes.com* to the search box.

When you're not sure of a key word, add a wild card character. In most search engines, that character is the asterisk (*). If you're looking for the title of a film directed by Clint Eastwood and just can't remember the name, enter *clint eastwood directed* *.

Look for more search options. The previous suggestions will keep you from drowning in a sea of useless search results. Many search engines also offer advanced search features and explain how to use them. Look for the word *advanced* or *more* on the site's home page, and click on the link.

Experiment with meta-search engines. Meta-search engines combine results from several search engines. Examples include Clusty, Dogpile, and SurfWax.

Create your own search engine. Google allows you to customize your search engine. Go online to www.google.com/coop/cse.

 Discover more search strategies.

Reading *fast*

One way to read faster is to read faster. This idea might sound like double-talk, but it is a serious suggestion. The fact is, you can probably read faster—without any loss in comprehension—simply by making a conscious effort to do so. Your comprehension might even improve.

EXPERIMENT WITH THE "just do it" method right now. Read the rest of this article as fast as you can. After you finish, come back and reread the same paragraphs at your usual rate. Note how much you remember from your first sprint through the text. You might be surprised to find out how well you comprehend material even at dramatically increased speeds. Build on that success by experimenting with the following guidelines.

Get your body ready. Gear up for reading faster. Get off the couch. Sit up straight at a desk or table, on the edge of your chair, with your feet flat on the floor. If you're feeling adventurous, read standing up.

Set a time limit. When you read, use a clock or a digital watch with a built-in stopwatch feature to time yourself. You are not aiming to set speed records, so be realistic. For example, set a goal to read two or three sections of a chapter in an hour, using all of the Muscle Reading steps. If that works, set a goal of 50 minutes for reading the same number of sections. Test your limits. The idea is to give yourself a gentle push, increasing your reading speed without sacrificing comprehension.

Relax. It's not only possible to read fast when you're relaxed; it's easier. Relaxation promotes concentration. And remember, relaxation is not the same as sleep. You can be relaxed *and* alert at the same time.

Move your eyes faster. When we read, our eyes leap across the page in short bursts called *saccades* (pronounced *sa-käds*). A saccade is also a sharp jerk on the reins of a horse—a violent pull to stop the animal quickly. Our eyes stop like that, too, in pauses called *fixations.*

Although we experience the illusion of continuously scanning each line, our eyes actually take in groups of words, usually about three at a time. For more than 90 percent of reading time, our eyes are at a dead stop, in those fixations.

One way to decrease saccades is to follow your finger as you read. The faster your finger moves, the faster

your eyes move. You can also use a pen, pencil, or 3x5 card as a guide.

Your eyes can move faster if they take in more words with each burst—for example, six instead of three. To practice taking in more words between fixations, find a newspaper with narrow columns. Then read down one column at a time, and fixate only once per line.

In addition to using the above techniques, simply make a conscious effort to fixate less. You might feel a little uncomfortable at first. That's normal. Just practice often, for short periods of time.

Notice and release ineffective habits. Our eyes make regressions; that is, they back up and reread words. You can reduce regressions by paying attention to them. Use the handy 3x5 card to cover words and lines that you have just read. You can then note how often you stop and move the card back to reread the text. Don't be discouraged if you stop often at first. Being aware of it helps you regress less frequently.

Also notice vocalizing. You are more likely to read faster if you don't read out loud or move your lips. You can also increase your speed if you don't subvocalize—that is, if you don't mentally "hear" the words as you read them. To stop doing it, just be aware of it.

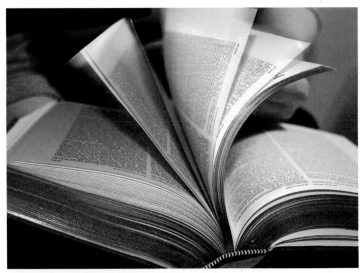
© Chris Pancewicz/Alamy

4

READING

Another habit to release is reading letter by letter. When we first learn to read, we do it one letter at a time. By now you have memorized many words by their shape, so you don't have to focus on the letters at all. Read this example: "Rasrhcers at Cbmrigae Uivnretisy funod taht eprxert raeedrs dno't eevn look at the lteters." You get the point. Skilled readers recognize many words and phrases in this way, taking them in at a single glance.

When you first attempt to release these habits, choose simpler reading material. That way, you can pay closer attention to your reading technique. Gradually work your way up to more complex material.

If you're pressed for time, skim. When you're in a hurry, experiment by skimming the assignment instead of reading the whole thing. Read the headings, subheadings, lists, charts, graphs, and summary paragraphs. Summaries are especially important. They are usually found at the beginning or end of a chapter or section.

Stay flexible. Remember that speed isn't everything. Skillful readers vary their reading rate according to their purpose and the nature of the material. An advanced text in analytic geometry usually calls for a different reading rate than the Sunday comics.

You also can use different reading rates on the same material. For example, you might first sprint through an assignment for the key words and ideas, and then return to the difficult parts for a slower and more thorough reading.

Explore more resources. You can find many books about speed-reading. Ask a librarian to help you find a few. Using them can be a lot of fun. For more possibilities, including courses and workshops, go to your favorite search engine on the Internet, and key in the word *speed-reading*.

In your research, you might discover people who offer to take you beyond speed-reading. According to some teachers, you can learn to flip through a book and "mentally photograph" each page—hundreds or even thousands of words at once. To prepare for this feat, you first do relaxation exercises to release tension while remaining alert. In this state, you can theoretically process vast quantities of information at a level other than your conscious mind.

You might find these ideas controversial. Approach them in the spirit of the Power Process in Chapter 1: "Ideas Are Tools." Also remember that you can use more conventional reading techniques at any time.

One word of caution: Courses and workshops in speed-reading range from free to expensive. Before you lay out any money, check the instructor's credentials and talk to people who've taken the course. Also find out whether the instructor offers free "sampler sessions" and whether you can cancel at some point in the course for a full refund.

Finally, remember the first rule of reading fast: Just do it! ✳

16 exercise
Relax

Eyestrain can be the result of continuous stress. Take a break from your reading and use this exercise to release tension.

1. Sit on a chair or lie down, and take a few moments to breathe deeply.

2. Close your eyes, place your palms over them, and visualize a perfect field of black.

3. Continue to be aware of the blackness for 2 or 3 minutes while you breathe deeply.

4. Now remove your hands from your eyes, and open your eyes slowly.

5. Relax for a minute more; then continue reading.

READING

4

Read with a laptop or dictionary in your lap

HAVING A LARGE vocabulary makes reading more enjoyable and increases the range of materials you can explore. In addition, building your vocabulary gives you more options for self-expression when speaking or writing.

Strengthen your vocabulary by taking delight in words. Look up unfamiliar terms. Pay special attention to words that arouse your curiosity.

Students regularly use two kinds of paper dictionaries: the desk dictionary and the unabridged dictionary. A desk dictionary is an easy-to-handle abridged dictionary that you can use many times in the course of a day. Keep this book within easy reach (maybe in your lap) so you can look up unfamiliar words while reading. You can find a large, unabridged dictionary in a library or bookstore. It provides more complete information about words and definitions not included in your desk dictionary, as well as synonyms, usage notes, and word histories. Or, you may prefer using one of several online dictionaries, such as Dictionary.com.

Construct a word stack. When you come across an unfamiliar word, write it down on a 3x5 card. Below the word, copy the sentence in which it was used, along with the page number. You can look up each word immediately, or you can accumulate a stack of these cards and look up the words later. Write the definition of each word on the back of the 3x5 card, adding the diacritics—marks that tell you how to pronounce it.

To expand your vocabulary and learn the history behind the words, take your stack of cards to an unabridged dictionary. As you find related words in the dictionary, add them to your stack. These cards become a portable study aid that you can review in your spare moments.

Learn—even when your dictionary is across town. When you are listening to a lecture and hear an unusual word, or when you are reading on the bus and encounter a word you don't know, you can still build your word stack. Pull out a 3x5 card and write down the word and its sentence. Later, you can look up the definition and write it on the back of the card.

Divide words into parts. Another suggestion for building your vocabulary is to divide an unfamiliar word into syllables and look for familiar parts. This strategy works well if you make it a point to learn

© Stockbyte

common prefixes (beginning syllables) and suffixes (ending syllables). For example, the suffix *-tude* usually refers to a condition or state of being. Knowing this makes it easier to conclude that *habitude* refers to a usual way of doing something and that *similitude* means being similar or having a quality of resemblance.

Infer the meaning of words from their context. You can often deduce the meaning of an unfamiliar word simply by paying attention to its context—the surrounding words, phrases, sentences, paragraphs, or images. Later, you can confirm your deduction by consulting a dictionary.

Practice looking for context clues such as these:

- *Definitions.* A key word might be defined right in the text. Look for phrases such as *defined as* or *in other words.*

- *Examples.* Authors often provide examples to clarify a word meaning. If the word is not explicitly defined, then study the examples. They're often preceded by the phrases *for example, for instance,* or *such as.*

- *Lists.* When a word is listed in a series, pay attention to the other items in the series. They might define the unfamiliar word through association.

- *Comparisons.* You might find a new word surrounded by synonyms—words with a similar meaning. Look for synonyms after words such as *like* and *as.*

- *Contrasts.* A writer might juxtapose a word with its antonym. Look for phrases such as *on the contrary* and *on the other hand.* ✳

The twenty-first-century researcher—using your library

© Masterfile Royalty Free

LIBRARIES HOUSE TREASURES. They include materials that will help you complete assignments, improve your writing, develop presentations, and plan your career. In addition to housing print and audiovisual publications, libraries give you access to online sources. With skills to mine all this wealth, you can acquire new knowledge for the rest of your life.

Remember that much published material is available only in print. The book—a form of information technology that's been with us for centuries—still has something to offer the twenty-first-century researcher.

Ask a librarian. They enjoy helping people. They chose this line of work because they enjoy helping people. They also understand that some people feel nervous about finding materials. Asking a librarian for help can save you hours.

Start with a reference librarian. If the library has the material that you want, this person will find it. If not, he will direct you to another source. This source might be a business, community agency, or government office.

If you have trouble finding something in your library, don't give up. Perhaps the book you want is on a cart waiting to be reshelved. A librarian can find out.

Take a tour. Libraries—from the smallest one in your hometown to the Smithsonian in Washington, D.C.—consist of just three basic elements:

- *Catalogs*—online databases that list all of the library's accessible sources.

- *Collections*—materials, such as periodicals (magazines and newspapers), books, pamphlets, audiovisual materials, and materials available from other collections via interlibrary loan.

- *Computer resources*—Internet access; connections to campuswide computer networks; and databases stored on CD-ROMs, on CDs, on DVDs, or online.

Before you start your next research project, take some time to investigate all three elements of your campus or community library. Start with a library orientation session or tour. Step into each room, and ask what's available there. Also find out whether the library houses any special collections. You might find one related to your major or another special interest.

Search the catalog. The library catalog is a database that lists all available materials. Some catalogs include listings for several libraries. To find materials, do a key word search—much like using a search engine on the Internet.

The catalog lists materials by subject, author, and title. Each listing includes a Library of Congress or Dewey decimal system number. These call numbers are used to shelve and locate materials. When you find a book by its call number, look at the materials around it on the shelf. There you will find sources of information on the same topic.

Some catalogs let you see if material is on the shelf or checked out. You may even be able to put a hold on materials that are currently in circulation. Ask a librarian if you can do these things from a computer at your home or workplace.

Inspect the collection. When inspecting a library's collections, look for materials such as the following:

- *Encyclopedias.* Use leading print and online encyclopedias, such as *Encyclopaedia Britannica*. Specialized encyclopedias cover many fields and include, for example, *Encyclopedia of Psychology, Encyclopedia of Asian History,* and *McGraw-Hill Encyclopedia of Science and Technology*.

- *Biographies.* Read accounts of people's lives in biographical works such as *Who's Who* and *Biography Index: A Cumulative Index to Biographical Material in Books and Magazines*.

- *Critical works.* Read what scholars have to say about works of art and literature in Oxford Companion volumes (such as *Oxford Companion to Art* and *Oxford Companion to African American Literature*).

- *Statistics and government documents.* Among the many useful sources are *Statistical Abstract of*

4

READING

the United States, *Handbook of Labor Statistics, Occupational Outlook Handbook,* and U.S. Census Bureau publications.

- *Almanacs, atlases, and gazetteers.* For population statistics and boundary changes, see the *World Almanac and Book of Facts,* the *New York Times Almanac,* or the *CIA World Factbook.*

- *Dictionaries.* Consult the *American Heritage Dictionary of the English Language, Oxford English Dictionary,* and other specialized dictionaries such as the *Penguin Dictionary of Literary Terms and Literary Theory* and the *Dictionary of the Social Sciences.*

- *Indexes and databases.* Databases contain publication information and an abstract, or sometimes the full text, of an article available for downloading or printing from your computer. Your library houses print and CD-ROM databases and subscribes to some online databases; others are accessible through online library catalogs or Web links.

- *Reference works in specific subject areas.* These references cover a vast range of material. Examples include the *Encyclopedia of the Biological Sciences* and the *Concise Oxford Companion to Classical Literature.* Ask a librarian for more information.

- *Periodical articles.* Find articles in periodicals (works issued periodically, such as scholarly journals, popular magazines, and newspapers) by using a periodical index. Use electronic indexes for recent works and print indexes for earlier works—especially for works written before 1980. Check to see which services your library subscribes to and the dates the indexes cover. Indexes might provide abstracts. Some indexes, such as Lexis-Nexis Academic Universe, InfoTrac, OCLC FirstSearch, and New York Times Ondisc, provide the full text of articles. You might be able to access such indexes from a computer in your dorm room or apartment.[5]

Access computer resources. Many libraries have access to special databases that are not available on the Internet. A reference librarian can tell you about them.

Also ask about e-books (electronic books). These free texts are delivered straight to your computer.

Inspect your finds. Once you find materials about a particular topic, inspect each one. Allow time for this step. Scan all the materials to find the most useful ones, and read them several times. Do this in a place where you can write notes—not while you're riding a stationary bike or watching TV.

With print sources, give special attention to the preface, publication data, table of contents, bibliography, glossary, endnotes, and index. (Nonprint materials, including online documents, often include similar types of information.) Also scan any headings, subheadings, and summaries. If you have time, read a chapter or section.

Then evaluate materials according to the following:

Relevance. Look for sources that deal directly with your research questions. If you're in doubt about the relevance of a particular source, ask yourself, "Will this material help me achieve the purpose of my research and support my thesis?

Currentness. Notice the publication date of your source material (usually found in the front matter on the copyright page). If your topic is time sensitive, set some guidelines about how current you want your sources to be.

Credibility. Scan the source for biographical information about the author. Look for education, training, and work experience that qualifies this person to publish on the topic. Also notice any possible sources of bias, such as political affiliations or funding sources.

You might also find that it helps to close your books, stop taking notes, and get away from your computer for a while. Digest your first impressions of the materials you've gathered. Take a walk—outdoors, if possible—and ask yourself the following questions:

- What are the main topics that these authors cover?

- What are the main problems that these authors want to solve?

- What are the authors' main areas of agreement and disagreement?

- If I could meet with these authors in person, what would I ask them?

- What personal experiences do I have with these topics?

- If I were limited to only one 3x5 card to express my thoughts on these topics, what would I write?

- If I were being interviewed about these topics on a talk show, what would I say?

The idea behind these questions is to use the work of others to get to the heart of an issue and stimulate your *own* thinking. It's amazing how many students go through higher education without doing this.

Discover the pleasures of solitary reflection, emerging insights, and sudden inspiration. A library furnished with plush chairs and wooden bookcases is a traditional setting for these experiences. Add computer technology and library skills to the mix, and you get an ideal environment for the twenty-first-century researcher. ✳

Staying literate in the digital age

READING BOOKS FOR pleasure is strongly linked to success in school and in the workplace. Skilled readers generally go on to higher-paying jobs and have more opportunities to advance in their careers.[6]

However, *To Read or Not To Read*, a 2007 report from the National Endowment for the Arts, states the following:[7]

- Nearly half of all Americans aged eighteen to twenty-four read no books for pleasure.

- Only about one-third of high school seniors read proficiently.

- Companies now rank reading and writing as skills lacking in new employees.

If you'd like to begin or increase your leisure reading, here are a few suggestions for how to get started.

Read for pleasure. Look for fun things to read—books that are not required for your classes or job and that reflect your personal interests. Scan the *New York Times* best seller lists. Look for book reviews in your local newspaper. Ask friends and instructors to recommend books. Sample a few of them.

Make time to read. Keep track of how much time you spend online or in front of the TV. Consider trading some of that time for pleasure reading.

Let books read to you. Comb your local library for audiobooks. Many are available on CD or as digital downloads.

Slow down and reflect. When you read for pleasure, forget about speed reading. Take in the words at your own pace.

In addition, look up from the page once in a while to think about what you've just read, or write a journal entry. In a Discovery Statement, list the main points or events that you want to remember. Also note what surprised you or led to a flash of insight. Whenever you disagree, argue with the author in writing.

In an Intention Statement, describe any follow-up action you want to take. Perhaps what you've read suggests a goal for you to achieve or an idea that you want to use. Describe it in more detail. List the next action you could take to get started.

Make reading a social event. Good readers tend to revel in conversation, so talk about what you're reading. Also consider joining a book group. ✳

Muscle Reading for ebooks

Today you can read ebooks on many platforms—computers, mobile phones, and dedicated devices such as the Amazon Kindle and Sony Reader. Muscle your way into this new medium by using features that are not available with printed books. Though ebook features vary, see if you can do the following.

Find navigation tools To flip electronic pages, look for *previous* and *next* buttons or arrows on the right and left borders of each page. Many ebooks also offer a "go to page" feature that allows you to key in a specific page number.

For a bigger picture of the text, look for a table of contents that lists chapter headings and subheadings. Note that charts, illustrations, photos, tables, diagrams, and other visuals might be listed separately.

Search Look for a search box that allows you to enter key words and find all the places in the text where those words are mentioned.

Customize page appearance For more readable text, adjust the font size or zoom in on a page.

Look for links to related information Many ebook readers will supply a definition of any word in the text. All you need to do is highlight a word and click on it. Also find out if your ebook reader will connect you to Web sites related to the topic of your ebook.

Mark it up Look for ways to electronically underline or highlight text. In addition, see if you can annotate the book by keying in your own notes tied to specific pages. You might be able to tag each note with a key word and then sort your notes into categories.

Print See if you can connect your ebook device to a printer. You might find it easier to study difficult passages on paper.

Sit back and listen Some ebook readers will convert highlighted text into speech.

Monitor battery life Recharge the battery for your ebook device or laptop computer so that it has enough power to last throughout your work or school day.

English as a Second Language

If you grew up reading and speaking a language other than English and are new to the English language, you might fall under the category of English as a Second Language (ESL) student, or English Language Learner (ELL). Experiment with the following suggestions to learn English with more success.

Build confidence

Many ESL/ELL students feel insecure about using English in social settings, including the classroom. Choosing not to speak, however, can delay your mastery of English and isolate you from other students.

As an alternative, make it your intention to speak up in class. List several questions beforehand, and plan to ask them. Also schedule a time to meet with your instructors during office hours to discuss any material that you find confusing. These strategies can help you build relationships while developing English skills.

In addition, start a conversation with at least one native speaker of English in each of your classes. For openers, ask about their favorite instructors or ideas for future courses to take.

English is a complex language. Whenever you extend your vocabulary and range of expression, the likelihood of making mistakes increases. The person who wants to master English yet seldom makes mistakes is probably being too careful. Do not look upon mistakes as a sign of weakness. Mistakes can be your best teachers—if you are willing to learn from them.

Remember that the terms *English as a Second Language* and *English Language Learner* describe a difference—not a deficiency. The fact that you've entered a new culture and are mastering another language gives you a broader perspective than people who speak only one language. And if you currently speak two or more languages, you've already demonstrated your ability to learn.

Errors	Corrections
Sun is bright.	The sun is bright.
He cheerful.	He is cheerful.
I enjoy to play chess.	I enjoy playing chess.
Good gifts received everyone.	Everyone received good gifts.
I knew what would present the teachers.	I knew what the teachers would present.
I like very much burritos.	I like burritos very much.
I want that you stay.	I want you to stay.
Is raining.	It is raining.
My mother she lives in Iowa.	My mother lives in Iowa.
I gave the paper to she.	I gave the paper to her.
They felt safety in the car.	They felt safe in the car.
He has three car.	He has three cars.
I have helpfuls family members.	I have helpful family members.
She don't know nothing.	She knows nothing.

Analyze errors in using English

To learn from your errors, make a list of those that are most common for you. Next to the error, write a corrected version. For examples, see the chart above.

Remember that native speakers of English also use this technique—for instance, by making lists of words they frequently misspell.

Learn by speaking and listening

You probably started your English studies by using textbooks. Writing and reading in English are important. Both can help you add to your English vocabulary and master grammar. To gain greater fluency and improve your pronunciation, also make it your goal to *hear* and *speak* English.

For example, listen to radio talk shows. Imitate the speaker's pronunciation by repeating phrases and sentences that you hear. During conversations, notice the facial expressions and gestures that accompany certain English words and phrases.

If you speak English with an accent, do not be concerned. Many people speak clear, accented English. Work on your accent only if you can't be easily understood.

Take advantage of opportunities to read and hear English at the same time. For instance, turn on English subtitles when watching a film on DVD. Also, check your library for books on tape or CD. Check out the printed book, and follow along as you listen.

Use computer resources

Some online dictionaries allow you to hear words pronounced. They include Answers.com (www.answers .com) and Merriam-Webster Online (www.m-w.com). Other resources include online book sites with a read-aloud feature. An example is Project Gutenberg (www .gutenberg.org; search on "Audio Books"). Speaks for Itself (www.speaksforitself.com) is a free download that allows you to hear text from Web sites read aloud.

Also, check general Web sites for ESL students. A popular one is Dave's ESL Café (www.eslcafe.com), which will lead you to others.

Gain skills in note taking and testing

When taking notes, remember that you don't have to capture everything that an instructor says. To a large extent, the art of note taking consists of choosing what *not* to record. Listen for key words, main points, and important examples. Remember that instructors will often repeat these things. You'll have more than one chance to pick up on the important material. When you're in doubt, ask for repetition or clarification. For additional suggestions, see Chapter 5: Notes.

Taking tests is a related challenge. You may find that certain kinds of test questions—such as multiple-choice items—are more common in the United States than in your native country. Chapter 6: Tests can help you master these and many other types of tests.

When in doubt, use expressions you understand

Native speakers of English use many informal expressions that are called *slang*. You are more likely to find slang in spoken conversation than in written English.

Native speakers also use *idioms*—colorful expressions with meanings that are not always obvious. Idioms can often be misunderstood. For instance, a "fork in the road" does not refer to an eating utensil discarded on a street but rather to a place where a part of the road branches off.

Learning how to use slang and idioms is part of gaining fluency in English. However, these elements of the language are tricky. If you mispronounce a key word or leave one out, you can create a misunderstanding. In important situations—such as applying for a job, writing an essay, or meeting with a teacher—use only those expressions you fully understand. Later, during informal conversations with friends, try out new expressions and ask for feedback about your use of them.

Create a community of English learners

Learning as part of a community can increase your mastery. For example, when completing a writing assignment in English, get together with other people who are learning the language. Read each other's papers and suggest revisions. Plan on revising your paper a number of times based on feedback from your peers.

You might feel awkward about sharing your writing with other people. Accept that feeling—and then remind yourself of everything you have to gain by learning from a group. In addition to learning English more quickly, you can raise your grades and make new friends.

Native speakers of English might be willing to assist your group. Ask your instructors to suggest someone. This person can benefit from the exchange of ideas and the chance to learn about other cultures.

Celebrate your gains

Every time you analyze and correct an error in English, you make a small gain. Celebrate those gains. Taken together over time, they add up to major progress in mastering English as a second language. ✳

Reading with children underfoot

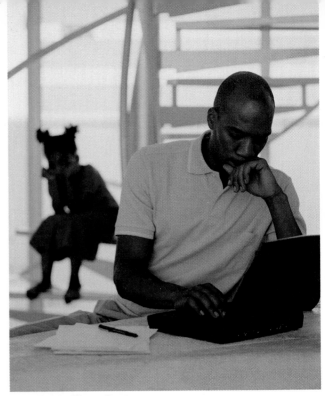
© Digital Vision/Picture Quest

IT IS POSSIBLE to have both effective study time and quality time with your children. The following suggestions come mostly from students who are also parents. The specific strategies you use will depend on your schedule and the ages of your children.

Attend to your children first. When you first come home from school, keep your books out of sight. Spend at least 10 minutes with your children before you settle in to study. Give them hugs, and ask about their day. Then explain that you have some work to do. Your children might reward you with 30 minutes of quiet time. A short time of full, focused attention from a parent can be more satisfying than longer periods of partial attention.

Of course, this suggestion won't work with the youngest children. If your children are infants or toddlers, schedule sessions of concentrated study for when they are asleep.

Use "pockets" of time. See if you can arrange study time at school before you come home. If you arrive at school 15 minutes earlier and stay 15 minutes later, you can squeeze in an extra half-hour of study time that day. Also look for opportunities to study between classes.

Before you shuttle children to soccer games or dance classes, throw a book in the car. While your children are warming up for the game or changing clothes, steal another 15 minutes to read.

Plan special activities for your child. Find a regular playmate for your child. Some children can pair off with close friends and safely retreat to their rooms for hours of private play. You can check on them occasionally and still get lots of reading done.

Another option is to take your children to a public playground. While they swing, slide, and dig in the sand, you can dig into your textbooks. Lots of physical activity will tire out your children in constructive ways. If they go to bed a little early, that's extra time for you to read.

After you set up appropriate activities for your children, don't attend to them every second, even if you're nearby as they play. Obviously, you want to break up fights, stop unsafe activity, and handle emergencies. Short of such incidents, though, you're free to read.

Create a special space for your child. Set aside one room or area of your home as a play space. Child-proof this space. The goal is to create a place where children can roam freely and play with minimal supervision. Consider allowing your child in this area *only* when you study. Your homework time then becomes your child's reward.

If you're cramped for space, just set aside some special toys for your child to play with during your study time. When you're sitting at your desk, your child might enjoy sitting at a small table and doing an "assignment." While she plays with stickers or flips through some children's books, you can review your notes.

Use television responsibly. Another option is to use television as a babysitter—when you can control the programming. Rent a videotape for your child to watch as you study. If you're concerned about your child becoming a couch potato, select educational programs that keep his mind active and engaged.

See if your child can use headphones while watching television. That way, the house stays quiet while you study.

Allow for interruptions. It's possible that you'll be interrupted even if you set up special activities for your child in advance. If so, schedule the kind of studying that can be interrupted. For instance, you could write out or review flash cards with key terms and definitions. Save the tasks that require sustained attention for other times.

Plan study breaks with children. Another option is to spend 10 minutes with your children for every 50 minutes that you study. View this time not as an interruption but as a study break.

Or schedule time to be with your children when you've finished studying. Let your children in on the plan: "I'll be done reading at 7:30. That gives us a whole hour to play before you go to bed."

Many children love visible reminders that "their time" is approaching. An oven timer works well for this purpose. Set it for 15 minutes of quiet time. Follow that with 5 minutes of show-and-tell, storybooks, or another activity with your child. Then set the timer for another 15 minutes of studying, another break, and so on.

Develop a routine. Many young children love routines. They often feel more comfortable and secure when they know what to expect. You can use this characteristic to your benefit. One option is to develop a regular time for studying and let your child know this schedule: "I have to do my homework between 4 p.m. and 5 p.m. every day." Then enforce it.

Bargain with children. Reward them for respecting your schedule. In return for quiet time, give your child an extra allowance or a special treat. Children might enjoy gaining "credits" for this purpose. Each time they give you an hour of quiet time for studying, make an entry on a chart, put a star on their bulletin board, or give them a coupon. After they've accumulated a certain number of entries, stars, or coupons, they can cash them in for a big reward—a movie or a trip to the zoo.

Ask other adults for help. This suggestion for studying with children is a message repeated throughout the book: Enlist other people to help support your success. Getting help can be as simple as asking your spouse, partner, neighbor, or fellow student to take care of the children while you study. Offer to trade child care with a neighbor: You will take his kids and yours for 2 hours on Thursday night if he'll take them for 2 hours on Saturday morning. Some parents start blockwide babysitting co-ops based on the same idea.

Find community activities and services. Ask if your school provides a day care service. In some cases, these services are available to students at a reduced cost.

Community agencies such as the YMCA might offer similar programs.

You can also find special events that appeal to children. Storytelling hour at the library is one example. While your child is being entertained and supervised, you can stay close by. Use the time in this quiet setting to read a chapter or review class notes.

Make it a game. Reading a chemistry textbook with a 3-year-old in the same room is not as preposterous as it sounds. The secret is to involve your child. For instance, use this time to recite. Make funny faces as you say the properties of the transition elements in the periodic table. Talk in a weird voice as you repeat Faraday's laws. Draw pictures and make up an exciting story about the process of titration.

Read out loud to your children, or use them as an audience for a speech. If you invent rhymes, poems, or songs to help you remember formulas or dates, teach them to your children. Be playful. Kids are attracted to energy and enthusiasm.

Whenever possible, involve family members in tasks related to reading. Older children can help you with research tasks—finding books at the library, looking up news articles, or even helping with typing.

When you can't read everything, just read something. Your objection to reading with children nearby may be this one: "I just can't concentrate. There's no way I can get it all done while children are around."

That's OK. Even if you can't absorb an entire chapter while the kids are running past your desk, you can skim the chapter. Or you can just read the introduction and summary. When you can't get it *all* done, just get *something* done.

Caution: If you always read this way, your education might be compromised. Supplement this strategy with others so that you can get all of your reading done. ✳

www Discover more ways to study with children underfoot.

practicing critical thinking

Read an editorial in a newspaper or magazine. Analyze that editorial by taking notes in the three-column format below. Use the first column for listing major points, the second for listing supporting points, and the third for writing key facts or statistics that support the major or supporting points.

For example:

Major point	**Supporting point**	**Key fact**
The "female" condom" has not yet been proved effective as a method of birth control.	Few studies on this method exist.	One of the few studies showed a 26 percent failure rate for the female condom.

Major point	**Supporting point**	**Key fact**

Ask another student to do this exercise with you. Read the same editorial. Then compare and discuss your notes. See if you identified the same main points.

Complete this exercise online.

Notice Your Pictures and Let Them Go

One of the brain's primary jobs is to manufacture images. We use mental pictures to make predictions about the world, and we base much of our behavior on those predictions.

Pictures can sometimes get in our way. Take the student who plans to attend a school he hasn't visited. He chose this school for its strong curriculum and good academic standing, but his brain didn't stop there. In his mind, the campus has historic buildings with ivy-covered walls and tree-lined avenues. The professors, he imagines, will be as articulate as Barack Obama and as entertaining as Conan O'Brien. The cafeteria will be a cozy nook serving everything from delicate quiche to strong coffee. He will gather there with fellow students for hours of stimulating, intellectual conversation. The library will have every book, while the computer lab will boast the newest technology.

The school turns out to be four gray buildings downtown next to the bus station. The first class he attends is taught by an overweight, balding professor wearing a purple and orange bird-of-paradise tie. The cafeteria is a nondescript hall with machine-dispensed food, and the student's apartment is barely large enough to accommodate his roommate's tuba. This hypothetical student gets depressed. He begins to think about dropping out of school.

The problem with pictures is that they can prevent us from seeing what is really there. That is what happened to the student in this story. His pictures prevented him from noticing that his school is in the heart of a culturally vital city—close to theaters, museums, government offices, clubs, and all kinds of stores. The professor with the weird tie is not only an expert in his field but also a superior teacher. The school cafeteria is skimpy because it can't compete with the variety of inexpensive restaurants in the area.

Our pictures often lead to us becoming angry or disappointed. We set up expectations of events before they occur. Sometimes we don't even realize that we have these expectations. The next time you discover you are angry, disappointed, or frustrated, look to see which of your pictures aren't being fulfilled.

When you notice that pictures are getting in your way, in the most gentle manner possible, let your pictures go. Let them drift away like wisps of smoke picked up by a gentle wind.

Sometimes when you let go of old pictures, it's helpful to replace them with new, positive pictures. These new images can help you take a fresh perspective. The new pictures might not feel as comfortable and genuine as your old ones, but it's important to let those old pictures go. No matter what picture is in your head, you can still be yourself.

 Learn more about this Power Process online.

Put it to Work

You can use strategies you learn in *Becoming a Master Student* to succeed at work. For examples, reflect on the following case study.

Sachin Aggarwal worked as a bank teller during the summers while he was in school. After he earned an associate of science degree in marketing, the bank promoted him and gave him a new job title: personal banker. When bank customers want to open a new account or take out a car loan, Sachin is the first person they see.

While working as a teller, Sachin gained a reputation as a quick study. When the bank installed a new computer system, he completed the online tutorials and stayed on top of the software updates. Within a few weeks, Sachin was training new tellers to use the system. In addition, he often fielded questions from some of the bank's older employees who described themselves as "computer challenged." Sachin's most recent performance review acknowledged his patience and ability to adapt his explanations to people with various levels of computer experience.

Right now, Sachin's biggest challenge is job-related reading. He never anticipated the number of documents—both in print and online—that would cross his desk after he got promoted. His supervisor has asked him to read technical manuals for each of the bank's services and account plans. He's also taking a customer service course with a 200-page textbook.

In addition, Sachin gets about sixty e-mail messages each day, some of them several screens long. He checks his in-box twice a day, scans each new message, and then files it in one of three folders:

- If a message requires some kind of response, Sachin sends it to a folder titled *action*. He checks this folder daily.
- If no response is required but Sachin might refer to the message again, he sends it to a folder named *archives*. He can search this folder any time he wants to retrieve a message.
- If the message requires no response and there's little chance that Sachin will refer to it again, he sends it straight to the trash folder.

Sachin applied several strategies from this chapter. For example, he previewed each message while keeping a couple

PhotosIndia.com/Getty

questions in mind: *Does this call for a response from me? Will I ever refer to this message again?*

List more strategies that Sachin could use to stay on top of his reading load:

_____

_____

_____

_____

In addition to online documents, workplace reading often includes technical manuals, sales manuals, policies and procedures, memos, newsletters, invoices, application forms, meeting minutes, brochures, annual reports, and job descriptions. Consider the following strategies for managing those piles of paper and still getting the rest of your work done:

- Determine your purpose in reading each document, and extract only what you need to produce that outcome.
- Look for executive summaries at the front of long documents. Everything you want to know might be there, all in a few pages.
- Create "read anytime" files. Most of the papers and online documents that cross your desk will probably consist of basic background material—items that are important to read but not urgent. Place these documents in a folder, and save them for a Friday afternoon or a plane trip.

chapter 4

Quiz

■ Put it to Work
◄ ◄ ◄ ◄ ◄
■ Skills Snapshot
■ Master Student Profile

Name _____ Date ____/____/____

1. Name the acrostic that can help you remember the steps of Muscle Reading.
   POQ, RUA, RRR = **P**ry **O**ut **Q**uestions, **R**oot **U**p **A**nswers, **R**ecite, **R**eview, and **R**eview again. (*How Muscle Reading works*, p. 124)

2. You must complete all nine steps of Muscle Reading to get the most out of any reading assignment. True or False? Explain your answer.
   False. The nine-step process is not an all-or-nothing package. Use it appropriately and choose what steps to apply as you read. (*Muscle Reading—a leaner approach*, p. 129)

3. Give three examples of what to look for when previewing a reading assignment.
   Describe at least three of the following: a. Look over the table of contents.   b. Survey the entire assignment by looking at each page.   c. Keep the preview short.   d. Look for summary statements.   e. Look for familiar concepts, facts, or ideas while previewing.   f. Read all chapter headings and subheadings.   g. Inspect drawings, diagrams, charts, tables, graphs, and photographs.   h. Ask yourself what you will do with this material and how it can relate to your long-term goals. (*Phase 1: Before you read*, p. 125)

4. Briefly explain how to use headings in a text to create an outline.
   The headings of the text can be used as the major points of an outline, and the subheadings could serve as the subcategories in the outline. (*Phase 1: Before you read*, p. 125)

5. In addition to underlining and highlighting, there are other ways to mark up a text. List three possibilities.
   List any three of the following: a. Use asterisks or exclamation points near important sentences.   b. Circle key terms.   c. Write short definitions of key terms in the margin.   d. Mark possible test questions with a Q in the margin.   e. Write personal comments in the margin.   f. Write related page number references in the margin.   g. Write summaries of main points.   h. Rewrite chapter titles, headings, and subheadings.   i. Draw diagrams, pictures, or maps.   j. Number steps in a list or series of related points.   (*Phase 2: While you read*, p. 127)

6. To get the most benefit from marking a book, underline at least 20 percent of the text. True or False? Explain your answer.
   False. Underlining is generally more effective when only the most important material is flagged. A small portion of underlined text, less than 10 percent, is usually sufficient for review. (*Phase 2: While you read*, p. 127)

7. Explain at least three techniques you can use when reading is tough.
   Explain at least three of the following: a. Read it again.   b. Look for essential words.   c. Hold a minireview.   d. Read it out loud.   e. Talk to your instructor.   f. Stand up.   g. Jump to the next section or the end of the article or chapter.   h. Find a tutor.   i. Use another text.   j. Pretend you understand and then explain it.   k. Ask, "What's going on here?"   l. Stop reading.   (*When reading is tough*, p. 130)

8. The Power Process in this chapter includes this sentence: "The next time you discover you are angry, disappointed, or frustrated, look to see which of your pictures aren't being fulfilled." Give an example from your own experience.
   Answers will vary. Example: On my first day of college, I thought everything was going to be fun and much easier than high school with all of its rules and regulations. But when I arrived, I couldn't find a parking spot, the line at the bookstore was around the building, and I couldn't find my classrooms. Had I not been persistent, the disconnect between my pictures of college and reality might have resulted in my dropping out of college on the first day of the term. (*Power Process: Notice Your Pictures and Let Them Go*, p. 143)

9. Define the topic-point method of summarizing, and give a brief example based on an article in this book.
   The topic-point method of summarization involves defining the main topic of a work or passage, then stating the main points made about this topic within the text. This should be followed by an example of using the topic-point method on any article in this chapter. (*Phase 3: After you read*, p. 128)

10. List at least three techniques for increasing your reading speed.
    Discuss at least three of the following: a. Experiment with intentionally reading as fast as possible.   b. Get your body ready: Sit up straight at a desk, sit on the edge of your chair, or read standing up.   c. Set a time limit: Use a clock or stopwatch while reading to time yourself—but be realistic.   d. Relax.   e. Move your eyes faster.   f. Take in more words with each fixation.   g. Follow your finger as you read, or use a 3×5 card as a guide.   h. Avoid vocalizing and subvocalizing.   i. Practice on easy material. (*Reading fast*, p. 132)

Skills Snapshot

Now that you've learned about Muscle Reading, review the *Reading* section of the Discovery Wheel on page 28. Think about whether that evaluation of your reading skills is still accurate. After studying this chapter, you might want to make some major changes in the way you read. Or, perhaps you are a more effective reader than you thought you were.

In either case, take a snapshot of your current reading skills by completing the following sentences.

BEFORE YOU READ

If someone asked me how well I keep up with my assigned reading, I would say that . . .

To get the most out of a long reading assignment, I start by . . .

WHILE YOU READ

To focus my attention while I read, I . . .

When I take notes on my reading, my usual method is to . . .

AFTER YOU READ

When it's important for me to remember what I read, I . . .

When I don't understand something that I've read, I overcome confusion by . . .

NEXT ACTION

I'll know that I've reached a new level of mastery with reading when . . .

To reach that level of mastery, the most important thing I can do next is to . . .

Master Student PROFILE

Chief Wilma Mankiller ... is a leader

© Peter Turnley/CORBIS

Wilma Mankiller came from a large family that spent many years on the family farm in Oklahoma. They were, of course, poor, but not desperately so. "As far back as I can remember there were always books around our house," she recalls in her autobiography, *Mankiller: A Chief and Her People.* "This love of reading came from the traditional Cherokee passion for telling and listening to stories. But it also came from my parents, particularly my father. . . ."

Unfortunately, a poor local economy made the Mankiller family an easy target for the Bureau of Indian Affairs relocation program of the 1950s. . . . In 1959 the family moved to San Francisco, where Wilma's father could get a job and where Wilma began her junior high school years. This was not a happy time for her. She missed the farm and she hated the school where white kids teased her about being Native American and about her name.

Mankiller decided to leave her parents and go to live with her maternal grandmother, Pearl Sitton, on a family ranch inland from San Francisco. The year she spent there restored her confidence and after returning to the Bay Area, she got increasingly involved with the world of the San Francisco Indian Center. . . .

When a group of Native Americans occupied Alcatraz Island in November 1969, in protest of U.S. Government policies, which had, for hundreds of years, deprived them of their lands, Mankiller participated in her first major political action.

"It changed me forever," she wrote. "It was on Alcatraz . . . where at long last some Native Americans, including me, truly began to regain our balance."

. . . She returned to Oklahoma in the 1970s where she worked at the Urban Indian Resource Center and volunteered in the community. In 1981 she founded and then became director of the Cherokee Community Development Department, where she orchestrated a community-based renovation of the water system and was instrumental in lifting an entire town, Bell, Oklahoma, out of squalor and despair. In 1983, she ran for Deputy Chief of the Cherokee Nation.

The campaign was not an easy one. There had never been a woman leader of a Native American tribe. She had many ideas to present and debate, but encountered discouraging opposition from men who refused to talk about anything but the fact that she was a woman. Her campaign days were troubled by death threats, and her tires were slashed. She sought the advice of friends for ways to approach the constant insults, finally settling on a philosophy summed up by the epithet, "Don't ever argue with a fool, because someone walking by and observing you can't tell which one is the fool." In the end, Mankiller had her day: she was elected as first woman Deputy Chief, and over time her wise, strong leadership vindicated her supporters and proved her detractors wrong.

In 1985, when Chief Ross Swimmer left for Washington, D.C., Mankiller was obligated to step into his position, becoming the first woman to serve as Principal Chief of the Cherokee Nation.

Susannah Abbey, "Community Hero: Chief Wilma Mankiller," My Hero, 11/17/2006, http://www.myhero .com/myhero/hero.asp?hero=w_mankiller. Copyright © 2006 the My Hero Project. All rights reserved. Reproduced by permission of The My Hero Project . http://myhero.com

(1945–) The first woman to become Principal Chief of the Cherokee Nation. Chief Wilma Mankiller also was awarded the Presidential Medal of Freedom, the nation's highest civilian honor.

Find more biographical information on Wilma Mankiller at the Master Student Hall of Fame.

Instructor Tools & Tips

> Rather than try to gauge your note-taking skill by quantity, think in this way: Am I simply doing clerk's work or am I assimilating new knowledge and putting down my own thoughts? To put down your own thoughts you must put down your own words. . . . If the note taken shows signs of having passed through a mind, it is a good test of its relevance and adequacy.
>
> **—Jacques Barzun and Henry Graff**

Preview

Linking Chapters 4, 5, and 6 together is very important because students sometimes tend to compartmentalize these chapters. Introducing note taking as a four-part process asks students to understand *Why* it is important to capture the context of *What* they are taking notes on. This chapter will help your students identify *What* note-taking strategies are effective: observing, recording, and reviewing. Each part of the process is essential and interdependent with the others. After your students learn new strategies for taking notes, ask them *How* they will apply these techniques to their other courses. Practice is an important element in adopting or adapting effective note-taking techniques. Encourage your students to test the new methods over time before they evaluate the effectiveness of a particular method. In class discussions, give students time to interpret the effectiveness of their note taking. Remember to suggest that learning styles have a significant impact on note-taking skill. Students can also apply *What if* by connecting Chapters 4, 5, and 6 together into a study-skills section for the course.

Guest Speaker

At this point in the term, students should be aware of how they are doing in their classes. It may be a good time to invite guest speakers from academic support services to talk to your students about how to get additional help they may need. Possibilities include the coordinators of the Writing Center, Tutoring Program, or Academic Success Center.

Here is a colleague from North Carolina discussing another note-taking tool:

> I share an additional tool for note-taking with my students: **Use the power of doodling.** If you find that you often have drawn circles around every hole on the paper and have added doodles in every open space in your notes, perhaps you need to use your "doodle power" to your advantage. Doodlers often find that they put more effort into their artistic efforts than they do into the content of their notes. Consider using this energy to create notes in the style of a comic strip with stick figures (for speed) and balloons for dialogue. As you invest your energy in depicting the information on paper, you will become more involved in the presentation instead of allowing the doodles to distract you.
>
> **—Sam Sink, Wilkes Community College, North Carolina**

Lecture

Eldon McMurray tells his students, "You are your own best instructor." As an in-class discussion, he asks the students to tell him about their favorite recording artist or sports figure. He asks questions such as "Where does she live?" and "How old is he?" Then he switches over to asking students about their professors. He almost always gets a blank stare when he asks, "What do you know about your math instructor?" Then he reviews the article in the text, challenging his students to brainstorm ideas on how they can learn more about their instructors and how this connectedness will help them in class. Some shy students particularly like the idea of conducting Internet research and reading about their instructors online.

Many new college students have no idea what they should do when they miss a class. They fail to contact either their instructor or their classmates to find out what handouts, information, and assignments they missed. As a follow-up to the article "What to do when you miss a class" (page 151), consider providing a brief lecture on this topic. It's also a good time to review classroom and campus attendance policies with your students.

Consider using the PowerUp DVD segment "I Create It All" as a lecture review of this important Power Process about self-responsibility.

Exercises/Activities

1. Target class exercise Ask your students to select three of their other courses in which they would like to put their advanced note-taking system into practice. By applying the note-taking concepts to their other courses, they start to realize the power of the ideas presented in *Becoming a Master Student*. To give them a head start and to help them understand how setting the stage can contribute to effective note taking, have them prepare for taking notes in class by outlining the textbook reading that the professor's lecture will cover that day.

2. Getting your money's worth, or "What am I paying for this ticket?" Set up this demonstration by having a student come up at the beginning of the class and pay you $20 for a front-row seat. If there is no front-row seat available, ask a student to move so that the paying student can sit there. Do this very seriously, and the irony of the object lesson will catch everyone's attention.

Ask students where they like to sit at a concert that costs $40 or more to attend. Then ask why tickets are so much more expensive for front-row center seats at a concert, or at the center court of a professional basketball game, or on the 50-yard line of a football game. All they have to do to get the best seat in class is be on time or come a little early.

3. "Be here now" in class Ask students to designate the upper right-hand corner of their class note page as their "Be here now" corner. When they catch their mind wandering, they can jot down a note and then bring their attention back to the speaker. Practicing this helps them stay focused.

4. Note-taking tools After students have read about the various note-taking strategies, discuss them in class. Divide the class into groups of four, and assign each group one of the new techniques to practice while you give a short lecture. Provide a safety net for this exercise by telling students that you will give them a detailed handout of the lecture at the end of class. This way, they don't have to worry about missing important information while they are trying out a new note-taking tool. After the lecture, the students discuss—with their group and then as a class—what they discovered about using the new strategy, including their initial perceptions of its strengths and weaknesses. This in-class practice encourages students to try a new note-taking tool in their other courses.

5. Power Process: I Create It All This in-class activity helps bring this process alive. After students have read this process and seen the "I Create It All" segment from the PowerUp DVD, ask them to recall a recent situation that went well for them at college, work, or home. Give them a few minutes to summarize the situation in their notes. Then ask them to list six ways that they created that successful situation. After they are done, ask for volunteers to share their success and how they created it. Then repeat the exercise, this time identifying a recent situation that did *not* work out well for them. For some students, this part may be much harder to do. Discuss this in class, with students volunteering to share their stories.

6. Put it to work This is a good time to start making connections to what students are learning to the workplace. An Advisory Board member remarks on the value of the Put it to work feature:

> I think that this feature, Put it to work, is excellent. I really like the way you take the various articles in the chapter and apply them to the work force. The students will definitely be receptive to this application of the articles in the chapter. I do stress work force applications…and this article will follow the concept that the skills that are being successfully learned in college can be applied successfully in the work force and in life. This is a wonderful feature.
>
> **—Paula Wimbish, Hinds Community College**

Conversation/Sharing

Ask students to discuss the characteristics that made Harvey Milk a master student, using the list of words and phrases provided in Chapter 1. Also ask them to identify *What* traits Milk had that they feel they do not personally possess. This is followed by further sharing on *How* students can gain these qualities.

This chapter is a good time to facilitate a conversation and sharing about online courses. Some students love them; some hate them. Ask students to share what they have liked and/or disliked about online courses so that those who haven't tried them will have more information before it's time to register for the next term.

Homework

Master Student Map (page 148) Students can begin practicing new note-taking techniques immediately after reading this chapter. As your students begin to transfer and apply what they learn in this course to their other courses, more aha! moments will begin to occur.

Why? Why learn about new methods of note taking?

What? What is the Cornell format? What is mind mapping?

How? How can reviewing your notes help you be more successful in school?

What if? What if you observe, record, and review your notes in a new way in all of your classes?

Review: The note-taking process flows (page 158) For many students, 24 hours is too long to wait before reviewing and processing their notes into long-term memory. For difficult classes or upper-division theory-based courses, ask your students to answer the questions using the strengths of each mode in the Master Student Map exercises. Students can summarize their notes during their review by answering these key questions: *Why*

is this idea important? *What* are the details I need to know? *How* will I remember and prepare to be tested on this material? *What if* the test is multiple choice? *What if* the test is an essay format?

Exercise #18: "Revisit your goals" (page 166) One powerful way to achieve any goal is to periodically assess your progress in meeting it. Exercise #18 provides your students an opportunity to reflect on the materials that have been covered to date. Students are asked to reflect on their goals set in Exercise #10 (on page 70) and make adjustments to their plan. While discussing this exercise, suggest that your students look back at their Discovery Wheel and review their progress to date. Students will be given a formal post-course Discovery Wheel in Chapter 12.

Evaluation

Frequent quizzes ensure that students face attention during class and keep up with the text reading assignments. In addition, quizzes provide students with opportunities for written reflection regarding new discoveries and intentions. Evaluation instruments also help you identify topics and concept that students have not yet mastered. In addition to the questions listed here, find more test questions on the Instructor Web site.

Quiz ideas for Chapter 5:

- Ask students to describe the Cornell note-taking system.
- Ask students to describe strategies for taking notes when instructors talk fast.
- Ask students what it takes to become an online learner.
- Ask students to explain how the Power Process: "I create it all" can help them be more successful in college.

Additional Digital Resources

Course Manual

The online *Course Manual* serves as an invaluable reference for those developing and teaching a College Success course with *Becoming a Master Student*. The *Course Manual* provides advice on general teaching issues such as preparing for classes, classroom management, grading, and communicating with students of various backgrounds, as well as specific strategies on getting the most out of various features in *Becoming a Master Student* such as the Discovery Wheel, Learning Styles Inventory, and book-specific Web sites.

Instructor Web Site

The updated Instructor Web site provides resources to help you plan and customize your course. Content specific to Chapter 5 includes:

- Lecture Ideas
  - Exploring Note-Taking Methods
- In-Class Exercises
  - Adapt Your Note-Taking Style
  - Mind Map Review
  - Recording Your Notes
  - Now, This Is Studying
  - What Level Are You On?
- In-Text Quiz Answers
- Learning Styles Application
- Discussion Topics
- PowerPoint Slides
- Reflection Questions
- Assessment Questions
- Experiment with chapter strategies

The Instructor Web site also contains the following book-specific content:

- ExamView Test Bank
- Online Course Manual
- Articles from previous editions
- Master Student Profiles from previous editions
- Sample Syllabi
- Detailed Transition Guide

Student Web Site

To help your students gain a better understanding of the topics discussed in *Becoming a Master Student,* encourage your students to visit the Student Web site, which provides the following resources specific to Chapter 5:

 www.cengage.com/success/bams13e

- Connect to Text content expands on specific topics marked with an icon within Chapter 5.
- Learning Style Applications invite students to cycle through the four styles of learning. In answering the four questions about note-taking techniques posted in this chapter's Learning Styles Application, students explore the different modes and apply their new knowledge.
- Practice Tests allow students to see how well they understand the themes of *Becoming a Master Student.*
- Interactive Concept Maps promote critical thinking by highlighting related ideas to show relationships between concepts.
- Video Skillbuilders bring to life techniques that will help you to excel in college and beyond. The following videos should give your students more information regarding topics covered in Chapter 5:
  - Taking Notes to Improve Your Grade
  - Textbook Note Taking: Student Methods
  - Textbook Note Taking: Traditional Methods
- Remembering Cultural Differences presents readers with brief articles that touch on aspects of diversity in our rapidly changing world. For Chapter 5, the following article will prompt your students to look at contemporary issues in a new way:
  - From Hieroglyphics to Handwriting in the Computer Age
- Master Student Profiles provide additional information on the people covered in this book feature. For Chapter 5, students will find expanded coverage and links about:
  - Harvey Milk
- Power Process Media contains video, PowerPoints, and audio files to take what your students have learned from the Power Processes in their book to the next level. For Chapter 5, students will find additional media on:
  - I create it all

Along with the chapter-specific content, a General Resources folder is available that contains Toolboxes geared toward specific student types (Community College, Adult Learner, Student Athlete), the Plagiarism Prevention Zone, and the Career Resource Center.

5 Notes

Master Student Map

as you read, ask yourself

what if . . .

I could take notes that remain informative and useful for weeks, months, or even years to come?

why this chapter matters . . .

Note taking helps you remember information and influences how well you do on tests.

how

you can use this chapter . . .

- Experiment with several formats for note taking.
- Create a note-taking format that works especially well for you.
- Take effective notes in special situations—such as while reading and when instructors talk fast.

what is included . . .

MASTER STUDENTS in *action*

Being responsible is what your career depends on—going to class, turning in assignments on time, studying for exams in advance, and, most importantly, knowing when to go out and when to stay home. Becoming a master student means setting and accomplishing goals—not to prove anything to anyone but to yourself.

—MAURICIO RUEDA

Photo courtesy of Mauricio Rueda

The note-taking process flows

ONE WAY TO understand note taking is to realize that taking notes is just one part of the process. Effective note taking consists of three parts: observing, recording, and reviewing. First, you observe an "event"—a statement by an instructor, a lab experiment, a slide show of an artist's works, or a chapter of required reading. Then you record your observations of that event; that is, you "take notes." Finally, you review what you have recorded.

Each part of the note-taking process is essential, and each depends on the others. Your observations determine what you record. What you record determines what you review. And the quality of your review can determine how effective your next observations will be. For example, if you review your notes on the Sino-Japanese War of 1894, the next day's lecture on the Boxer Rebellion of 1900 will make more sense.

Legible and speedy handwriting is also useful in taking notes. Knowledge about outlining is handy, too. A nifty pen, a new notebook, and a laptop computer are all great note-taking devices. And they're all worthless—unless you participate as an energetic observer *in* class and regularly review your notes *after* class. If you take those two steps, you can turn even the most disorganized chicken scratches into a powerful tool.

Sometimes note taking looks like a passive affair, especially in large lecture classes. One person at the front of the room does most of the talking. Everyone else is seated and silent, taking notes. The lecturer seems to be doing all of the work.

Don't be deceived. Observe more closely, and you'll see some students taking notes in a way that radiates energy. They're awake and alert, poised on the edge of their seats. They're writing—a physical activity that expresses mental engagement. These students listen for levels of ideas and information, make choices about what to record, and compile materials to review.

In higher education, you might spend hundreds of hours taking notes. Making them more effective is a direct investment in your success. Think of your notes as a textbook that *you* create—one that's more current and more in tune with your learning preferences than any textbook you could buy. ✷

journal entry 13

Discovery/Intention Statement

Get what you want from this chapter

Think about the possible benefits of improving your skills at note taking. Recall a recent incident in which you had difficulty taking notes. Perhaps you were listening to an instructor who talked fast, or you got confused and stopped taking notes altogether. Describe the incident in the space below.

_____

_____

_____

Now preview this chapter to find at least five strategies that you can use right away to help you take better notes. Sum up each of those strategies in a few words, and note page numbers where you can find out more about each suggestion.

Strategy	Page number

Reflect on your intention to experiment actively with this chapter. Describe a specific situation in which you promise to apply the strategies you listed above. If possible, choose a situation that will occur within the next 24 hours. I intend to . . .

_____

_____

_____

OBSERVE
The note-taking process flows

SHERLOCK HOLMES, a fictional master detective and student of the obvious, could track down a villain by observing the fold of his scarf and the mud on his shoes. In real life, a doctor can save a life by observing a mole—one a patient has always had—that undergoes a rapid change.

An accountant can save a client thousands of dollars by observing the details of a spreadsheet. A student can save hours of study time by observing that she gets twice as much done at a particular time of day.

Keen observers see facts and relationships. They know ways to focus their attention on the details and then tap their creative energy to discover patterns. To sharpen your classroom observation skills, experiment with the following techniques, and continue to use those that you find most valuable. Many of these strategies can be adapted to the notes you take while reading.

Set the stage

Complete outside assignments. Nothing is more discouraging (or boring) than sitting through a lecture about the relationship of Le Chatelier's principle to the principle of kinetics if you've never heard of Henri Louis Le Chatelier or kinetics. The more familiar you are with a subject, the more easily you can absorb important information during class lectures. Instructors usually assume that students complete assignments, and they construct their lectures accordingly.

Bring the right materials. A good pen does not make you a good observer, but the lack of a pen or notebook can be distracting enough to take the fine edge off your concentration. Make sure you have a pen, pencil, notebook, or any other materials you need. Bring your textbook to class, especially if the lectures relate closely to the text.

If you are consistently unprepared for a class, that might be a message about your intentions concerning the course. Find out if it is. The next time you're in a frantic scramble to borrow pen and paper 37 seconds before the class begins, notice the cost. Use the borrowed pen and paper to write a Discovery Statement about your lack of preparation. Consider whether you intend to be successful in the course.

Woman: Getty; *frames:* Shutterstock, collage by Walter Kopec

Sit front and center. Students who get as close as possible to the front and center of the classroom often do better on tests for several reasons. The closer you sit to the lecturer, the harder it is to fall asleep. The closer you sit to the front, the fewer interesting or distracting classmates are situated between you and the instructor. Material on the board is easier to read from up front. Also, the instructor can see you more easily when you have a question.

Instructors are usually not trained to perform. Some can project their energy to a large audience, but some cannot. A professor who sounds boring from the back of the room might sound more interesting up close.

Sitting up front enables you to become a constructive force in the classroom. By returning the positive energy that an engaged teacher gives out, you can reinforce the teacher's enthusiasm and enhance your experience of the class.

In addition, sound waves from the human voice begin to degrade at a distance of 8 to 12 feet. If you sit more than 15 feet from the speaker, your ability to hear and take effective notes might be compromised. Get close to the source of the sound. Get close to the energy.

Sitting close to the front is a way to commit yourself to getting what you want out of school. One reason students gravitate to the back of the classroom is that they think the instructor is less likely to call on them. Sitting in back can signal a lack of commitment. When you sit up front, you are declaring your willingness to take a risk and participate.

What to do when you miss a class

For most courses, you'll benefit by attending every class session. If you miss a class, catch up as quickly as possible.

Clarify policies on missed classes   On the first day of classes, find out about your instructors' policies on absences. See if you will be allowed to make up assignments, quizzes, and tests. Also inquire about doing extra-credit assignments.

Contact a classmate   Early in the semester, identify a student in each class who seems responsible and dependable. Exchange e-mail addresses and phone numbers. If you know you won't be in class, contact this student ahead of time. When you notice that your classmate is absent, pick up extra copies of handouts, make assignments lists, and offer copies of your notes.

Contact your instructor   If you miss a class, e-mail, phone, or fax your instructor, or put a note in his mailbox. Ask if he has another section of the same course that you can attend so you won't miss the lecture information. Also ask about getting handouts you might need before the next class meeting.

Consider technology   If there is a Web site for your class, check it for assignments and the availability of handouts you missed. Free online services such as NoteMesh allow students to share notes with one another. These services use wiki software, which allows you to create and edit Web pages using any browser. Before using such tools, however, check with instructors for their policies on note sharing.

Conduct a short preclass review.   Arrive early, and then put your brain in gear by reviewing your notes from the previous class. Scan your reading assignment. Look at the sections you have underlined or highlighted. Review assigned problems and exercises. Note questions you intend to ask.

Clarify your intentions.   Take a 3x5 card to class with you. On that card, write a short Intention Statement about what you plan to get from the class. Describe your intended level of participation or the quality of attention you will bring to the subject. Be specific. If you found your previous class notes to be inadequate, write down what you intend to do to make your notes from this class session more useful.

"Be here now" in class

Accept your wandering mind.   The techniques in Chapter 2's Power Process: "Be Here Now" can be especially useful when your head soars into the clouds. Don't fight daydreaming. When you notice your mind wandering during class, look at it as an opportunity to refocus your attention. If thermodynamics is losing out to beach parties, let go of the beach.

Notice your writing.   When you discover yourself slipping into a fantasyland, feel the weight of your pen in your hand. Notice how your notes look. Paying attention to the act of writing can bring you back to the here and now.

You also can use writing in a more direct way to clear your mind of distracting thoughts. Pause for a few seconds, and write those thoughts down. If you're distracted by thoughts of errands you need to run after class, list them on a 3x5 card, and stick it in your pocket. Or simply put a symbol, such as an arrow or asterisk, in your notes to mark the places where your mind started to wander. Once your distractions are out of your mind and safely stored on paper, you can gently return your attention to taking notes.

Be with the instructor.   In your mind, put yourself right up front with the instructor. Imagine that you and the instructor are the only ones in the room and that the lecture is a personal conversation between the two of you. Pay attention to the instructor's body language and facial expressions. Look the instructor in the eye.

Remember that the power of this suggestion is immediately reduced by digital distractions—Web surfing, e-mail checking, or text messaging. Taking notes is a way to stay focused. The physical act of taking notes signals your mind to stay in the same room as the instructor.

Notice your environment.   When you become aware of yourself daydreaming, bring yourself back to class by paying attention to the temperature in the room, the feel of your chair, or the quality of light coming through the window. Run your hand along the surface of your desk. Listen to the chalk on the blackboard or the sound of the teacher's voice. Be in that environment. Once your attention is back in the room, you can focus on what's happening in class.

Postpone debate.   When you hear something you disagree with, note your disagreement and let it go. Don't allow your internal dialogue to drown out subsequent material. If your disagreement is persistent and strong, make note of it and then move on. Internal debate can prevent you from absorbing new information. It is OK to absorb information you don't agree with. Just absorb it with the mental tag "My instructor says . . . , and I don't agree with it."

Let go of judgments about lecture styles. Human beings are judgment machines. We evaluate everything, especially other people. If another person's eyebrows are too close together (or too far apart), if she walks a certain way or speaks with an unusual accent, we instantly make up a story about her. We do this so quickly that the process is usually not a conscious one.

Don't let your attitude about an instructor's lecture style, habits, or appearance get in the way of your education. You can decrease the power of your judgments if you pay attention to them and let them go.

You can even let go of judgments about rambling, unorganized lectures. Turn them to your advantage. Take the initiative, and organize the material yourself. While taking notes, separate the key points from the examples and supporting evidence. Note the places where you got confused, and make a list of questions to ask.

Participate in class activities. Ask questions. Volunteer for demonstrations. Join in class discussions. Be willing to take a risk or look foolish, if that's what it takes for you to learn. Chances are, the question you think is dumb is also on the minds of several of your classmates.

Relate the class to your goals. If you have trouble staying awake in a particular class, write at the top of your notes how that class relates to a specific goal. Identify the reward or payoff for reaching that goal.

Think critically about what you hear. This suggestion might seem contrary to the previously mentioned technique "postpone debate." It's not. You might choose not to think critically about the instructor's ideas during the lecture. That's fine. Do it later, as you review and edit your notes. This is the time to list questions or write down your agreements and disagreements.

Watch for clues

Be alert to repetition. When an instructor repeats a phrase or an idea, make a note of it. Repetition is a signal that the instructor thinks the information is important.

Listen for introductory, concluding, and transition words and phrases. Introductory, concluding, and transition words and phrases include phrases such as *the following three factors, in conclusion, the most important consideration, in addition to,* and *on the other hand.* These phrases and others signal relationships, definitions, new subjects, conclusions, cause and effect, and examples. They reveal the structure of the lecture. You can use these phrases to organize your notes.

Watch the board or PowerPoint presentation. If an instructor takes the time to write something down on the board or show a PowerPoint presentation, consider the material to be important. Copy all diagrams and drawings, equations, names, places, dates, statistics, and definitions.

Watch the instructor's eyes. If an instructor glances at her notes and then makes a point, it is probably a signal that the information is especially important. Anything she reads from her notes is a potential test question.

Highlight the obvious clues. Instructors often hint strongly or tell students point-blank that certain information is likely to appear on an exam. Make stars or other special marks in your notes next to this information. Instructors are not trying to hide what's important.

Notice the instructor's interest level. If the instructor is excited about a topic, it is more likely to appear on an exam. Pay attention when she seems more animated than usual. ✳

WWW Find more strategies for observing online.

journal entry 14

Discovery/Intention Statement

Create more value from lectures

Think back on the last few lectures you have attended. How do you currently observe (listen to) lectures? What specific behaviors do you have as you sit and listen? Briefly describe your responses in the space below.

I discovered that I . . .

_____

_____

_____

_____

Now write an Intention Statement about any changes you want to make in the way you respond to lectures.

I intend to . . .

_____

_____

_____

_____

RECORD
The note-taking process flows

THE FORMAT AND STRUCTURE of your notes are more important than how fast you write or how elegant your handwriting is. The following techniques can improve the effectiveness of your notes.

General techniques for note taking

Use key words. An easy way to sort the extraneous material from the important points is to take notes using key words. Key words or phrases contain the essence of communication. They include

- Concepts, technical terms, names, and numbers.

- Linking words, including words that describe action, relationship, and degree (for example, *most, least,* and *faster*).

Key words evoke images and associations with other words and ideas. They trigger your memory. That characteristic makes them powerful review tools. One key word can initiate the recall of a whole cluster of ideas. A few key words can form a chain from which you can reconstruct an entire lecture.

To see how key words work, take yourself to an imaginary classroom. You are now in the middle of an anatomy lecture. Picture what the room looks like, what it feels like, how it smells. You hear the instructor say:

OK, what happens when we look directly over our heads and see a piano falling out of the sky? How do we take that signal and translate it into the action of getting out of the way? The first thing that happens is that a stimulus is generated in the neurons—receptor neurons—of the eye. Light reflected from the piano reaches our eyes. In other words, we see the piano.

The receptor neurons in the eye transmit that sensory signal—the sight of the piano—to the body's nervous system. That's all they can do—pass on information. So we've got a sensory signal coming into the nervous system. But the neurons that initiate movement in our legs are effector neurons. The information from the sensory neurons must be transmitted to effector neurons or we will get squashed by the piano. There must be some kind of interconnection between receptor and effector neurons. What happens between the two? What is the connection?

Key words you might note in this example include *stimulus, generated, receptor neurons, transmit, sensory*

signals, nervous system, effector neurons, and *connection.* You can reduce the instructor's 163 words to these 12 key words. With a few transitional words, your notes might look like this:

> Stimulus (piano) generated in receptor neurons (eye)
>
> Sensory signals transmitted by nervous system to effector neurons (legs)
>
> What connects receptor to effector?

Note the last key word of the lecture above: *connection.* This word is part of the instructor's question and leads to the next point in the lecture. Be on the lookout for questions like this. They can help you organize your notes and are often clues for test questions.

Use pictures and diagrams. Make relationships visual. Copy all diagrams from the board, and invent your own.

A drawing of a piano falling on someone who is looking up, for example, might be used to demonstrate the relationship of receptor neurons to effector neurons. Label the eyes "receptor" and the feet "effector." This picture implies that the sight of the piano must be translated into a motor response. By connecting the explanation of the process with the unusual picture of the piano falling, you can link the elements of the process together.

Write notes in paragraphs. When it is difficult to follow the organization of a lecture or put information into outline form, create a series of informal paragraphs. These paragraphs should contain few complete sentences. Reserve complete sentences for precise definitions, direct quotations, and important points that the instructor emphasizes by repetition or other signals—such as the phrase "This is an important point."

RECORD

Woman: Getty; *frame:* Shutterstock, collage by Walter Kopec

Copy material from the board and a PowerPoint presentation. Record all formulas, diagrams, and problems that the teacher presents on the board or in a PowerPoint presentation. Copy dates, numbers, names, places, and other facts. If it's presented visually in class, put it in your notes. You can even use your own signal or code to flag that material.

Use a three-ring binder. Three-ring binders have several advantages over other kinds of notebooks. First, pages can be removed and spread out when you review. This way, you can get the whole picture of a lecture. Second, the three-ring-binder format allows you to insert handouts right into your notes. Third, you can insert your own out-of-class notes in the correct order.

Use only one side of a piece of paper. When you use one side of a page, you can review and organize all your notes by spreading them out side by side. Most students find the benefit well worth the cost of the paper. Perhaps you're concerned about the environmental impact of consuming more paper. If so, you can use the blank side of old notes and use recycled paper.

Use 3×5 cards. As an alternative to using notebook paper, use 3×5 cards to take lecture notes. Copy each new concept onto a separate 3×5 card.

Keep your own thoughts separate. For the most part, avoid making editorial comments in your lecture notes. The danger is that when you return to your notes, you might mistake your own ideas for those of the instructor. If you want to make a comment, clearly label it as your own.

Use an "I'm lost" signal. No matter how attentive and alert you are, you might get lost and confused in a lecture. If it is inappropriate to ask a question, record

in your notes that you were lost. Invent your own signal—for example, a circled question mark. When you write down your code for "I'm lost," leave space for the explanation or clarification that you will get later. The space will also be a signal that you missed something. Later, you can speak to your instructor or ask to see a fellow student's notes.

Label, number, and date all notes. Develop the habit of labeling and dating your notes at the beginning of each class. Number the page, too. Sometimes the sequence of material in a lecture is important. Write your name and phone number in each notebook in case you lose it.

Use standard abbreviations. Be consistent with your abbreviations. If you make up your own abbreviations or symbols, write a key explaining them in your notes. Avoid vague abbreviations. When you use an abbreviation such as *comm.* for *committee,* you run the risk of not being able to remember whether you meant *committee, commission, common,* or *commit.* One way to abbreviate is to leave out vowels. For example, *talk* becomes *tlk, said* becomes *sd, American* becomes *Amrcn.*

Leave blank space. Notes tightly crammed into every corner of the page are hard to read and difficult to use for review. Give your eyes a break by leaving plenty of space.

Later, when you review, you can use the blank spaces in your notes to clarify points, write questions, or add other material.

Take notes in different colors. You can use colors as highly visible organizers. For example, you can signal important points with red. Or use one color of ink for notes about the text and another color for lecture notes.

Use graphic signals. The following ideas can be used with any note-taking format:

- Use brackets, parentheses, circles, and squares to group information that belongs together.
- Use stars, arrows, and underlining to indicate important points. Flag the most important points with double stars, double arrows, or double underlines.
- Use arrows and connecting lines to link related groups.
- Use equal signs and greater-than and less-than signs to indicate compared quantities.

To avoid creating confusion with graphic symbols, use them carefully and consistently. Write a "dictionary" of your symbols in the front of your notebooks; an example is shown on the next page.

[ ], ( ), ⬭, ▭ = info
   that belongs together

*, ↘, ═ = important

**, ↘↘, ≡, !!! = extra important

> = greater than   < = less than
═ = equal to

⟶ = leads to, becomes
   Ex: school → job → money

? = huh?, lost

?? = big trouble, clear up
      immediately

Use recorders effectively. Some students record lectures with audio or digital recorders, but there are persuasive arguments against doing so. When you record a lecture, there is a strong temptation to daydream. After all, you can always listen to the lecture again later on. Unfortunately, if you let the recorder do all of the work, you are skipping a valuable part of the learning process.

There are other potential problems as well. Listening to recorded lectures can take a lot of time—more time than reviewing written notes. Recorders can't answer the questions you didn't ask in class. Also, recording devices malfunction. In fact, the unscientific Hypothesis of Recording Glitches states that the tendency of recorders to malfunction is directly proportional to the importance of the material. With those warnings in mind, you can use a recorder effectively if you choose. For example, you can use recordings as backups to written notes. (Check with your instructor first. Some prefer not to be recorded.) Turn the recorder on; then take notes as if it weren't there. Recordings can be especially useful if an instructor speaks fast.

The Cornell method

A note-taking system that has worked for students around the world is the *Cornell method*.[1] Originally developed by Walter Pauk at Cornell University during the 1950s, this approach continues to be taught across the United States and in other countries as well.

The cornerstone of this method is what Pauk calls the *cue column*—a wide margin on the left-hand side of the paper. The cue column is the key to the Cornell method's many benefits. Here's how to use it.

Format your paper. On each sheet of your notepaper, draw a vertical line, top to bottom, about 2 inches from the left edge of the paper. This line creates the cue column—the space to the left of the line. You can also find Web sites that allow you to print out pages in this format. Just do an Internet search using the key words *cornell method pdf*.

Take notes, leaving the cue column blank. As you read an assignment or listen to a lecture, take notes on the right-hand side of the paper. Fill up this column with sentences, paragraphs, outlines, charts, or drawings. Do not write in the cue column. You'll use this space later, as you do the next steps.

Condense your notes in the cue column. Think of the notes you took on the right-hand side of the paper as a set of answers. In the cue column, list potential test questions that correspond to your notes. Write one question for each major term or point.

As an alternative to questions, you can list key words from your notes. Yet another option is to pretend that your notes are a series of articles on different topics. In the cue column, write a newspaper-style headline for each "article." In any case, be brief. If you cram the cue column full of words, you defeat its purpose—to reduce the number and length of your notes.

Write a summary. Pauk recommends that you reduce your notes even more by writing a brief summary at the bottom of each page. This step offers you another way to engage actively with the material.

5

NOTES

Cue column	Notes
What are the 3 phases of Muscle Reading?	Phase 1: Before you read Phase 2: While you read Phase 3: After you read
What are the steps in phase 1?	1. Preview 2. Outline 3. Question
What are the steps in phase 2?	4. Read 5. Underline 6. Answer
What are the steps in phase 3?	7. Recite 8. Review 9. Review again
What is an acronym for Muscle Reading?	Pry = preview Out = outline Questions = question Root = read Up = underline Answers = answer Recite Review Review again
Summary	
Muscle Reading includes 3 phases: before, during, and after reading. Each phase includes 3 steps. Use the acronym to recall all the steps.	

BECOMING A MASTER STUDENT 155

Use the cue column to recite. Cover the right-hand side of your notes with a blank sheet of paper. Leave only the cue column showing. Then look at each item you wrote in the cue column and talk about it. If you wrote questions, answer each question. If you wrote key words, define each word and talk about why it's important. If you wrote headlines in the cue column, explain what each one means and offer supporting details. After reciting, uncover your notes and look for any important points you missed.

Mind mapping

Mind mapping, a system developed by Tony Buzan,[2] can be used in conjunction with the Cornell method to take notes. In some circumstances, you might want to use mind maps exclusively.

To understand mind maps, first review the features of traditional note taking. Outlines (explained in the next section) divide major topics into minor topics, which, in turn, are subdivided further. They organize information in a sequential, linear way.

The traditional outline reflects only a limited range of brain function—a point that is often made in discussions about "left-brain" and "right-brain" activities. People often use the term *right brain* when referring to creative, pattern-making, visual, intuitive brain activity. They use the term *left brain* when talking about orderly, logical, step-by-step characteristics of thought. Writing teacher Gabrielle Rico uses another metaphor. She refers to the left-brain mode as our "sign mind" (concerned with words) and the right-brain mode as our "design mind" (concerned with visuals).[3] A mind map uses both kinds of brain functions. Mind maps can contain lists and sequences and show relationships. They can also provide a picture of a subject. They work on both verbal and nonverbal levels.

One benefit of mind maps is that they quickly, vividly, and accurately show the relationships between ideas. Also, mind mapping helps you think from general to specific. By choosing a main topic, you focus first on the big picture, then zero in on subordinate details. And by using only key words, you can condense a large subject into a small area on a mind map. You can review more quickly by looking at the key words on a mind map than by reading notes word for word.

Give yourself plenty of room. To create a mind map, use blank paper that measures at least 11 by 17 inches. If that's not available, turn regular notebook paper on its side so that you can take notes in a horizontal (instead of vertical) format. If you use a computer in class to take notes, consider software that allows you to create digital mind maps that can include graphics, photos, and URL links.

Determine the main concept of the lecture, article, or chapter. As you listen to a lecture or read, figure out the main concept. Write it in the center of the paper and circle it, underline it, or highlight it with color. You can also write the concept in large letters. Record concepts related to the main concept on lines that radiate outward from the center. An alternative is to circle or box in these concepts.

Use key words only. Whenever possible, reduce each concept to a single word per line or circle/box in your mind map. Although this reduction might seem awkward at first, it prompts you to summarize and to condense ideas to their essence. That means fewer words for you to write now and fewer to review when it's time to prepare for tests. (Using shorthand symbols and abbreviations can help.) Key words are usually nouns and verbs that communicate the bulk of the speaker's ideas. Choose words that are rich in associations and that can help you re-create the lecture.

Create links. A single mind map doesn't have to include all of the ideas in a lecture, book, or article. Instead, you can link mind maps. For example, draw a mind map that sums up the five key points in a chapter, and then make a separate, more detailed mind map for each of those key points. Within each mind map, include references to the other mind maps. This technique helps explain and reinforce the relationships among many ideas. Some students pin several mind maps next to one another on a bulletin board or tape them to a wall. This allows for a dramatic—and effective—look at the big picture.

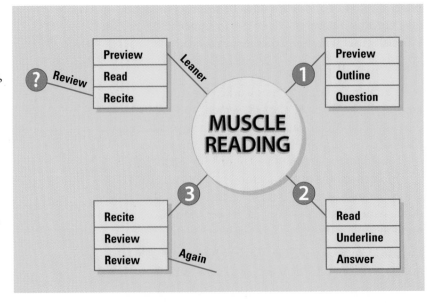

Outlining

A traditional outline shows the relationships among major points and supporting ideas. One benefit of taking notes in the outline format is that doing so can totally occupy your attention. You are recording ideas and also organizing them. This process can be an advantage if the material has been presented in a disorganized way. By playing with variations, you can discover the power of outlining to reveal relationships among ideas. Technically, each word, phrase, or sentence that appears in an outline is called a *heading*. Headings are arranged in different levels:

■ In the first, or top, level of headings, note the major topics presented in a lecture or reading assignment.

■ In the second level of headings, record the key points that relate to each topic in the first-level headings.

■ In the third level of headings, record specific facts and details that support or explain each of your second-level headings. Each additional level of subordinate heading supports the ideas in the previous level of heading.

Roman numerals offer one way to illustrate the difference between levels of headings. See the examples below and to the right.

Distinguish levels with indentations only:

Muscle Reading includes 3 phases
    Phase 1: Before you read
        Preview

Distinguish levels with bullets and dashes:

MUSCLE READING INCLUDES 3 PHASES
    • Phase 1: Before you read
        – Preview

Distinguish headings by size:

MUSCLE READING INCLUDES 3 PHASES

Phase 1: Before you read

Preview

First-level heading

Second-level heading

Third-level heading

I. Muscle Reading includes 3 phases.
    A. Phase 1: Before you read
        1. Preview
        2. Outline
        3. Question
    B. Phase 2: While you read
        4. Read
        5. Underline
        6. Answer
    C. Phase 3: After you read
        7. Recite
        8. Review
        9. Review again

Combining formats

Feel free to use different note-taking systems for different subjects and to combine formats. Do what works for you.

For example, combine mind maps along with the Cornell method. You can modify the Cornell format by dividing your notepaper in half. Reserve one half for mind maps and the other for linear information

such as lists, graphs, and outlines, as well as equations, long explanations, and word-for-word definitions. You can incorporate a mind map into your paragraph-style notes whenever you feel one is appropriate. Mind maps are also useful for summarizing notes taken in the Cornell format.

John Sperry, a teacher at Utah Valley State College, developed the following note-taking system that includes all of the formats discussed in this article:

■ Fill up a three-ring binder with fresh paper. Open your notebook so that you see two blank pages—one on the left and one on the right. Plan to take notes across this entire two-page spread.

■ During class or while reading, write your notes only on the left-hand page. Place a large dash next to each main topic or point. If your instructor skips a step or switches topics unexpectedly, just keep writing.

■ Later, use the right-hand page to review and elaborate on the notes that you took earlier. This page is for anything you want. For example, add visuals such as mind maps. Write review questions, headlines, possible test questions, summaries, outlines, mnemonics, or analogies that link new concepts to your current knowledge.

■ To keep ideas in sequence, place appropriate numbers on top of the dashes in your notes on the left-hand page. Even if concepts are presented out of order during class, they'll still be numbered correctly in your notes. ✳

 See more examples of notes in various formats online.

REVIEW
The note-taking process flows

Woman: Getty; *frame:* Shutterstock, collage by Walter Kopec

THINK OF REVIEWING as an integral part of note taking rather than an added task. To make new information useful, encode it in a way that connects it to your long-term memory. The key is reviewing.

Review within 24 hours. In Chapter 4, when you read the suggestion to review what you've read within 24 hours, you were asked to sound the trumpet. If you have one, get it out and sound it again. This note-taking technique might be the most powerful one you can use. It might save you hours of review time later in the term.

Many students are surprised that they can remember the content of a lecture in the minutes and hours after class. They are even more surprised by how well they can read the sloppiest of notes at that time. Unfortunately, short-term memory deteriorates quickly. The good news is that if you review your notes soon enough, you can move that information from short-term to long-term memory. And you can do it in just a few minutes—often 10 minutes or less.

The sooner you review your notes, the better, especially if the content is difficult. In fact, you can start reviewing during class. When your instructor pauses to set up the overhead display or erase the board, scan your notes. Dot the *i*'s, cross the *t*'s, and write out unclear abbreviations. Another way to use this technique is to get to your next class as quickly as you can. Then use the 4 or 5 minutes before the lecture begins to review the notes you just took in the previous class. If you do not get to your notes immediately after class, you can still benefit by reviewing them later in the day. A review right before you go to sleep can also be valuable.

Think of the day's unreviewed notes as leaky faucets, constantly dripping and losing precious information until you shut them off with a quick review. Remember, it's possible to forget most of the material within 24 hours—unless you review.

Edit your notes. During your first review, fix words that are illegible. Write out abbreviated words that might be unclear to you later. Make sure you can read everything. If you can't read something or don't understand something you *can* read, mark it, and make a note to ask your instructor or another student about it. Check to see that your notes are labeled with the date and class and that the pages are numbered.

Fill in key words in the left-hand column. This task is important if you are to get the full benefit of using the Cornell method. Using the key word principles described earlier in this chapter, go through your notes and write key words or phrases in the left-hand column.

These key words will speed up the review process later. As you read your notes, focus on extracting important concepts.

Use your key words as cues to recite. Cover your notes with a blank sheet of paper so that you can see only the key words in the left-hand margin. Take each key word in order, and recite as much as you can about the point. Then uncover your notes and look for any important points you missed.

Conduct short weekly review periods. Once a week, review all of your notes again. These review sessions don't need to take a lot of time. Even a 20-minute weekly review period is valuable. Some students find that a weekend review—say, on Sunday afternoon—helps them stay in continuous touch with the material. Scheduling regular review sessions on your calendar helps develop the habit.

As you review, step back to see the larger picture. In addition to reciting or repeating the material to yourself, ask questions about it: Does this relate to my goals? How does this compare to information I already know, in this field or another? Will I be tested on this material?

What will I do with this material? How can I associate it with something that deeply interests me?

Consider typing your notes. Some students type up their handwritten notes on the computer. The argument for doing so is threefold. First, typed notes are easier to read. Second, they take up less space. Third, the process of typing them forces you to review the material.

Another alternative is to bypass handwriting altogether and take notes in class on a laptop. This solution has a potential drawback, though: Computer errors can wipe out your notes files. If you like using this method of taking notes, save your files frequently, and back up your work onto a jump drive or other portable drive.

Create summaries. Mind mapping is an excellent way to summarize large sections of your course notes or reading assignments. Create one map that shows all the main topics you want to remember. Then create another map about each main topic. After drawing your maps, look at your original notes, and fill in anything you missed. This system is fun and quick.

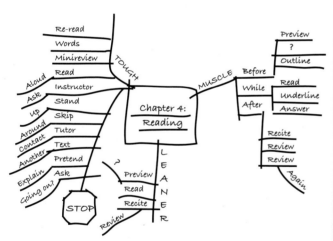

Another option is to create a "cheat sheet." There's only one guideline: Fit all your review notes on a single sheet of paper. Use any note-taking format that you want—mind map, outline, Cornell method, or a combination of all of them. The beauty of this technique is that it forces you to pick out main ideas and key details. There's not enough room for anything else!

If you're feeling adventurous, create your cheat sheet on a single index card. Start with the larger sizes (5×7 or 4×6) and then work down to a 3×5 card.

Some instructors might let you use a summary sheet during an exam. But even if you can't use it, you'll benefit from creating one while you study for the test. Summarizing is a powerful way to review. *

To study the process of memory and forgetting, Hermann Ebbinghaus devised a method for testing memory. The results, shown here in what has come to be known as the Ebbinghaus forgetting curve, demonstrate that forgetting occurs most rapidly shortly after learning and then gradually declines over time.

journal entry 15

Discovery Statement

Reflect on your review habits

Respond to the following statements by checking "Always," "Often," "Sometimes," "Seldom," or "Never" after each.

1. I review my notes immediately after class.

_____ Always _____ Often _____ Sometimes

_____ Seldom _____ Never

2. I conduct weekly reviews of my notes.

_____ Always _____ Often _____ Sometimes

_____ Seldom _____ Never

3. I make summary sheets of my notes.

_____ Always _____ Often _____ Sometimes

_____ Seldom _____ Never

4. I edit my notes within 24 hours.

_____ Always _____ Often _____ Sometimes

_____ Seldom _____ Never

5. Before class, I conduct a brief review of the notes I took in the previous class.

_____ Always _____ Often _____ Sometimes

_____ Seldom _____ Never

Enroll your instructor in your education

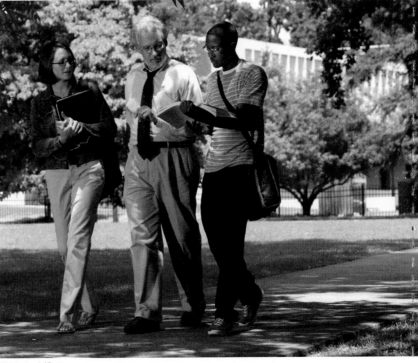

Thinkstock/Getty

FACED WITH AN instructor you don't like, you have two basic choices. One is to label the instructor a "dud" and let it go at that. When you make this choice, you get to endure class and complain to other students. This choice puts you at the mercy of circumstance. It gives your instructor sole responsibility for the quality of your education and the value of your tuition payments.

There is another option. Don't give away your power. Instead, take responsibility for your education.

The word *enroll* in this headline is a play on words. Usually, we think of students as the people who enroll in school. Turn this idea on its head. See if you can enlist instructors as partners in getting what you want from higher education.

Research the instructor. When deciding what classes to take, you can look for formal and informal sources of information about instructors. One source is the school catalog. Alumni magazines or newsletters or the school newspaper might run articles on teachers. At some schools, students post informal evaluations of instructors on Web sites. Also talk to students who have taken courses from the instructor you're researching.

Or introduce yourself to the instructor. Set up a visit during office hours, and ask about the course. This conversation can help you get the flavor of a class and clues to the instructor's teaching style.

Show interest in class. Students give teachers moment-by-moment feedback in class. That feedback comes through posture, eye contact, responses to questions, and participation in class discussions. If you find a class boring, re-create the instructor through a massive display of interest. Ask lots of questions. Sit up straight, make eye contact, take detailed notes. Your enthusiasm might enliven your instructor. If not, you are still creating a more enjoyable class for yourself.

Release judgments. Maybe your instructor reminds you of someone you don't like—your annoying Aunt Edna, a rude store clerk, or the fifth-grade teacher who kept you after school. Your attitudes are in your own head and beyond the instructor's control. Likewise, an instructor's beliefs about politics, religion, or feminism are not related to teaching ability. Being aware of such things can help you let go of negative judgments.

Instructors are a lot like you. They have opinions about politics, sports, and music. They worry about their health, finances, and career path. They're sometimes in a good mood and sometimes sad or angry. What distinguishes them is a lifelong passion for the subject that they teach.

Get to know the instructor. Meet with your instructor during office hours. Teachers who seem boring in class can be fascinating in person. Prepare to notice your pictures and let them go.

Students who do well in higher education often get to know at least one instructor outside of class. In some cases, these instructors become mentors and informal advisors.

Open up to diversity. Sometimes students can create their instructors by letting go of pictures about different races and ethnic groups. According to one picture, a Hispanic person cannot teach English literature. According to other pictures, a white teacher cannot have anything valid to say about African music, a teacher in a wheelchair cannot command the attention of a hundred people in a lecture hall, and a male instructor cannot speak credibly about feminism. All of those pictures can clash with reality. Releasing them can open up new opportunities for understanding and appreciation.

Separate liking from learning. You don't have to like an instructor to learn from them. See if you can focus on content instead of form. *Form* is the way something is organized or presented. If you are irritated at the sound of an instructor's voice, you're focusing on form. When you put aside your concern about her voice and turn your attention to the points she's making, you're focusing on *content*.

Form your own opinion about each instructor. You might hear conflicting reports about teachers from other students. The same instructor could be described by two different students as a riveting speaker and as completely lacking in charisma. Decide for yourself what descriptions are accurate.

Seek alternatives. You might feel more comfortable with another teacher's style or method of organizing course materials. Consider changing teachers, asking another teacher for help outside class, or attending an additional section taught by a different instructor. You can also learn from other students, courses, tutors, study groups, books, and DVDs. Be a master student, even when you have teachers you don't like. Your education is your own creation.

Avoid excuses. Instructors know them all. Most teachers can see a snow job coming before the first flake hits the ground. Accept responsibility for your own mistakes, and avoid thinking that you can fool the teacher.

Submit professional work. Prepare papers and projects as if you were submitting them to an employer. Imagine that your work will determine whether you get a promotion and raise. Instructors often grade hundreds of papers during a term. Your neat, orderly, well-organized paper can stand out and lift a teacher's spirits.

Accept criticism. Learn from your teachers' comments about your work. It is a teacher's job to give feedback. Don't take it personally.

Use course evaluations. In many classes you'll have an opportunity to evaluate the instructor. Respond honestly. Write about the aspects of the class that did not work well for you. Offer specific ideas for improvement. Also note what *did* work well.

Take further steps, if appropriate. Sometimes severe conflict develops between students and instructors. In such cases, you might decide to file a complaint or ask for help from an administrator.

Be prepared to document your case in writing. Describe specific actions that created problems. Stick to

the facts—events that other class members can verify. Your school might have a set of established grievance procedures to use in these cases. Use them. You are a consumer of education and have a right to fair treatment. ✳

 Discover more ways to create positive relationships with instructors online.

Meeting with your instructor

Meeting with an instructor outside class can save hours of study time and help your grade. To get the most from these meetings, consider doing the following:

- Schedule a meeting time during the instructor's office hours.

- If you need to cancel or reschedule, let your instructor know well in advance.

- During the meeting, relax. This activity is not graded.

- Come prepared with a list of questions and any materials you'll need. During the meeting, take notes on the instructor's suggestions.

- Show the instructor your class notes to see if you're capturing essential material.

- Get feedback on outlines that you've created for papers.

- Ask about ways to prepare for upcoming exams.

- If the course is in a subject area that interests you, ask about the possibilities of declaring a major in that area and the possible careers that are associated with that major.

- Avoid questions that might offend your instructor—for example, "I missed class on Monday. Did we do anything important?"

- Ask if your instructor is willing to answer occasional short questions via e-mail or a phone call.

- When the meeting is over, thank your instructor for making time for you.

Instead of trying to resolve a conflict with an instructor in the few minutes before or after class, schedule a time during office hours. During this meeting, state your concerns in a respectful way. Then focus on finding solutions.

When your instructor talks *fast*

Take more time to prepare for class. Familiarity with a subject increases your ability to pick up on key points. If an instructor lectures quickly or is difficult to understand, conduct a thorough preview of the material to be covered.

Be willing to make choices. When an instructor talks fast, focus your attention on key points. Instead of trying to write everything down, choose what you think is important. Occasionally, you will make a wrong choice and neglect an important point. Worse things could happen. Stay with the lecture, write down key words, and revise your notes immediately after class.

Exchange photocopies of notes with classmates. Your fellow students might write down something you missed. At the same time, your notes might help them. Exchanging photocopies can fill in the gaps.

Leave large empty spaces in your notes. Leave plenty of room for filling in information you missed. Use a symbol that signals you've missed something, so you can remember to come back to it.

See the instructor after class. Take your class notes with you, and show the instructor what you missed.

Use an audio recorder. Recording a lecture gives you a chance to hear it again whenever you choose. Some audio recording software allows you to vary the speed of the recording. With this feature, you can perform magic and actually slow down the instructor's speech.

Before class, take notes on your reading assignment. You can take detailed notes on the text before class. Leave plenty of blank space. Take these notes with you to class, and simply add your lecture notes to them.

Go to the lecture again. Many classes are taught in multiple sections. That gives you the chance to hear a lecture at least twice—once in your regular class and again in another section of the class.

Learn shorthand. Some note-taking systems, known as shorthand, are specifically designed for getting ideas down fast. Books and courses are available to help you learn these systems. You can also devise your own shorthand method by inventing one- or two-letter symbols for common words and phrases.

Ask questions—even if you're totally lost. Many instructors allow a question session. This is the time to ask about the points you missed.

At times you might feel so lost that you can't even formulate a question. That's OK. One option is to report this fact to the instructor. He can often guide you to a clear question. Another option is to ask a related question. Doing so might lead you to the question you really wanted to ask.

Ask the instructor to slow down. This solution is the most obvious. If asking the instructor to slow down doesn't work, ask her to repeat what you missed. ✳

17 exercise
Television note taking

You can use evening news broadcasts to practice listening for key words, writing quickly, focusing your attention, and reviewing. With note taking, as with other skills, the more you practice, the better you become.

The next time you watch the news, use pen and paper to jot down key words and information. During the commercials, review and revise your notes. At the end of the broadcast, spend 5 minutes reviewing all of your notes. Create a mind map of a few news stories; then sum up the news of the day for a friend.

This exercise will help you develop an ear for key words. Since you can't ask questions or request that the speaker slow down, you train yourself to stay totally in the moment. If you get behind, relax, leave a space, and return your attention to the broadcast.

Don't be discouraged if you miss a lot the first time around. Do this exercise several times, and observe how your mind works.

If you find it too difficult to take notes during a fast-paced television news show, check your local broadcast schedule for a news documentary. Documentaries are often slower paced. Another option is to record a program and then take notes. You can stop the recording at any point to review your notes. You can also ask a classmate to do the same exercise, and then compare notes the next day.

Taking notes while reading

TAKING NOTES WHILE reading requires the same skills that apply to taking class notes: observing, recording, and reviewing. Use these skills to take notes for review and for research.

Review notes

Take review notes when you want more detailed notes than writing in the margin of your text allows. You might want to single out a particularly difficult section of a text and make separate notes. Or make summaries of overlapping lecture and text material. You can't underline or make notes in library books, so these sources will require separate notes, too.

To take more effective review notes, follow these suggestions:

- *Use a variety of formats.* Translate text into Cornell notes, mind maps, or outlines. Combine these formats to create your own. Translate diagrams, charts, and other visual elements into words. Then reverse the process by translating straight text into visual elements.

- *However, don't let the creation of formats get in your way.* Even a simple list of key points and examples can become a powerful review tool.

- *Condense a passage to key quotes.* Authors embed their essential ideas in key sentences. As you read, continually ask yourself, "What's the point?" Then see if you can point to a specific sentence on the page to answer your question. Look especially at headings, subheadings, and topic sentences of paragraphs. Write these key sentences word for word in your notes, and put them within quotation marks. Copy as few sentences as you can and still retain the core meaning of the passage.

- *Condense by paraphrasing.* Pretend that you have to summarize a chapter, article, or book on a postcard. Limit yourself to a single paragraph—or a single sentence—and use your own words. This is a great way to test your understanding of the material.

- *Take a cue from the table of contents.* Look at the table of contents in your book. Write each major heading on a piece of paper, or key those headings into a word-processing file on your computer. Include page numbers. Next, see if you can improve on the table of contents. Substitute your own headings for those that appear in the book. Turn single words or phrases into complete sentences, and use words that are meaningful to you.

- *Note special concepts in math and science.* When you read mathematical, scientific, or other technical materials, copy important formulas or equations. Re-create important diagrams, and draw your own visual representations of concepts. Also write down data that might appear on an exam.

Research notes

Take research notes when preparing to write a paper or deliver a speech. One traditional method of research is to take notes on index cards. You write one idea, fact, or quotation per card. The advantage of limiting each card to one item of information is that you can easily arrange cards according to the sequence of your outline—and ongoing changes in your outline.

Taking notes on a computer offers the same flexibility as index cards. In addition, you can take advantage of software features that help you create tables of contents, indexes, graphics, and other elements you might want to use in your project later on.

No matter which method you use, your research notes will fall into two main categories.

The first category is information about your sources. For example, a source card for a book will show the author, title, date and place of publication, and publisher. You'll need such information later in the writing process as you create a formal list of your sources—especially sources of quotes or paraphrased material that is included in the body of your paper or presentation. By keeping track of your sources as you conduct research, you create a working bibliography. Ask your instructor about what source information to record (and also see the sidebar to this article). When recording your own ideas, simply note the source as "me."

The second category of research notes includes the actual ideas and facts that you will use to create the content of your paper or presentation. Again, if you're using index cards, write only *one* piece of information on each information card—a single quotation, fact, or concept. Doing so makes it easier for you to sort cards later.

Be sure to avoid plagiarism. When people take words or images from a source and present them as their own, they are committing plagiarism. Even when plagiarism is accidental, the consequences can be harsh. For essential information on this topic, see "Academic integrity: Avoid plagiarism" on page 259.

If you're taking notes on a computer and using Internet sources, be especially careful to avoid plagiarism. When you copy text or images from a Web site, separate those notes from your own ideas. Use a different font for copied material, or enclose it in quotation marks.

Schedule time to review all the information and ideas that your research has produced. By allowing time for rereading and reflecting on all the notes you've taken, you create the conditions for genuine understanding.

Start by summarizing major points of view on your topic. Note points of agreement and disagreement among your sources.

Also see if you can find direct answers to the questions that you had when you started researching. These answers could become headings in your paper.

Look for connections in your material, including ideas, facts, and examples that occur in several sources. Also look for connections between your research and your life—ideas that you can verify based on personal experience.

Adapt to special cases

The style of your notes can vary according to the nature of the reading material. For example, if you are assigned a short story or poem, read the entire work once without taking any notes. On your first reading, simply enjoy the piece. When you finish, write down your immediate impressions. Then go over the piece and make brief notes on characters, images, symbols, settings, plot, point of view, or other aspects of the work. ✳

 Find examples of effective research and review notes online.

Note this information about your sources

Following are checklists of the information to record about various types of sources. Whenever possible, print out or make photocopies of each source. For books, include a copy of the title page and copyright page, both of which are found in the front matter. For magazines and scholarly journals, copy the table of contents.

For each book you consult, record the following:

- ☐ Author
- ☐ Editor (if listed)
- ☐ Translator (if listed)
- ☐ Edition number (if listed)
- ☐ Full title, including the subtitle
- ☐ Name and location of the publisher
- ☐ Copyright date
- ☐ Page numbers for passages that you quote, summarize, or paraphrase

For each article you consult, record the following:

- ☐ Author
- ☐ Editor (if listed)
- ☐ Translator (if listed)
- ☐ Full title, including the subtitle
- ☐ Name of the periodical
- ☐ Volume number
- ☐ Issue number
- ☐ Issue date
- ☐ Page numbers for passages that you quote, summarize, or paraphrase

For each computer-based source you consult (CD-ROMs and Internet documents), record the following:

- ☐ Author
- ☐ Editor (if listed)
- ☐ Translator (if listed)
- ☐ Full title of the page or article, including the subtitle
- ☐ Name of the organization that posted the site or published the CD-ROM
- ☐ Dates when the page or other document was published and revised
- ☐ Date when you accessed the source
- ☐ URL for Web pages (the uniform resource locator, or Web site address, which often starts with http://)
- ☐ Version number (for CD-ROMs)
- ☐ Volume, issue number, and date for online journals

Note: Computer-based sources may not list all the above information. For Web pages, at a minimum, record the date you accessed the source and the URL.

For each interview you conduct, record the following:

- ☐ Name of the person you interviewed
- ☐ Professional title of the person you interviewed
- ☐ Contact information for the person you interviewed—mailing address, phone number, e-mail address
- ☐ Date of the interview

Taking notes . . . despite PowerPoint

PowerPoint presentations can be lethal for students who want to take effective notes (or simply stay awake). When they can access a presentation online or get a printout of the slides, some students are tempted to zone out during class: *Might as well take a mental break now. After all, I can look at the slides later.*

This choice can be hazardous to your academic health. If your attention drifts during a PowerPoint show, you might get confused about the material that's presented next. To get the most value from PowerPoint presentations, try the following:

Stay active. Keep observing, recording, and reviewing. See slides as a way to *supplement* and guide rather than to *replace* your own note taking.

Preview. If your instructor makes PowerPoint files available before a lecture, download them. Scan the slides, just as you would preview a reading assignment.

Annotate. Add notes directly to the slides. Print out the slides, bring them to class, and add your written comments. If you take notes on a laptop and can open up the PowerPoint file during class, consider taking notes in the window that appears at the bottom of the screen. After class, you can print out the slides in note view. You'll see the slides plus all your notes.

Add slide numbers. If the PowerPoint file is not available before class, take notes during the presentation. Capture the main points and key details as you normally would. Also add slide numbers to your notes. Numbering the slides can help you make more sense of your notes if you get a copy of the presentation later.

Use slides as a cue to recite. After taking notes on a printout of the slides, review them just as you would review notes taken in the Cornell format. Cover up your notes so that only the slides are visible. See if you can remember the main points you noted about each slide.

"Edit" the presentation. If you have the PowerPoint file on your computer, make another copy of it. Open up this copy, and see if you can condense the presentation. Cut slides that don't include anything you want to remember. Also rearrange slides so that the order makes more sense to you. Remember that you can open up the original file later if you want to see exactly what your instructor presented.

18 exercise
Revisit your goals

One powerful way to achieve any goal is to periodically assess your progress in meeting it. This step is especially important with long-term goals—those that can take years to achieve.

When you did Exercise # 10: "Get Real with Your Goals" on page 70, you focused on one long-term goal and planned a detailed way to achieve it. This process involved setting mid-term and short-term goals that will lead to achieving your long-term goal. Take a minute to review that exercise and revisit the goals you set. Then complete the following steps.

1. Take your long-term goal from Exercise #10, and rewrite it in the space below. If you can think of a more precise way to state it, feel free to change the wording.

2. Next, check in with yourself. How do you feel about this goal? Does it still excite your interest and enthusiasm? On a scale of 1 to 10, how committed are you to achieving this goal? Write down your level of commitment in the space below.

3. If your level of commitment is 5 or less, you might want to drop the goal and replace it with a new one. To set a new goal, just turn back to Exercise #10 and do it again. And release any self-judgment about dropping your original long-term goal. Letting go of one goal creates space in your life to set and achieve a new one.

4. If you're committed to the goal you listed in Step 1 of this exercise, consider whether you're still on track to achieve it. Have you met any of the short-term goals related to this long-term goal? If so, list your completed goals here.

Before going on to the next step, take a minute to congratulate yourself and celebrate your success.

5. Finally, consider any adjustments you'd like to make to your plan. For example, write additional short-term or mid-term goals that will take you closer to your long-term goal. Or cross out any goals that you no longer deem necessary. Make a copy of your current plan in the space below.

Long-term goal (to achieve within your lifetime):

Supporting mid-term goals (to achieve in 1 to 5 years):

Supporting short-term goals (to achieve within the coming year):

Get to the bones of your book with concept maps

CONCEPT MAPPING, pioneered by Joseph Novak and D. Bob Gowin, is a tool to make major ideas in a book leap off the page.[4] In creating a concept map, you reduce an author's message to its essence—its bare bones. Concept maps can also be used to display the organization of lectures and discussions.

Concepts and links are the building blocks of knowledge. A *concept* is a name for a group of related things or ideas. *Links* are words or phrases that describe the relationship between concepts. Consider the following paragraph:

> Muscle Reading consists of three phases. Phase 1 includes tasks to complete before reading. Phase 2 tasks take place during reading. Finally, Phase 3 includes tasks to complete after reading.

In this paragraph, examples of concepts are *Muscle Reading, reading, phases, tasks, Phase 1, Phase 2,* and *Phase 3.* Links include *consists of, includes, before, during,* and *after.*

To create a concept map, list concepts and then arrange them in a meaningful order from general to specific. Then fill in the links between concepts, forming meaningful statements.

Concept mapping promotes critical thinking. It alerts you to missing concepts or faulty links between concepts. In addition, concept mapping mirrors the way that your brain learns—that is, by linking new concepts to concepts that you already know.

To create a concept map, use the following steps:

1. **List the key concepts in the text.** Aim to express each concept in three words or less. Most concept words are nouns, including terms and proper names. At this point, you can list the concepts in any order.

2. **Rank the concepts so that they flow from general to specific.** On a large sheet of paper, write the main concept at the top of the page. Place the most specific concepts near the bottom. Arrange the rest of the concepts in appropriate positions throughout the middle of the page. Circle each concept.

3. **Draw lines that connect the concepts.** On these connecting lines, add words that describe the relationship between the concepts. Again, limit yourself to the fewest words needed to make an accurate link—three words or less. Linking words are often verbs, verb phrases, or prepositions.

4. **Finally, review your map.** Look for any concepts that are repeated in several places on the map. You can avoid these repetitions by adding more links between concepts. ✳

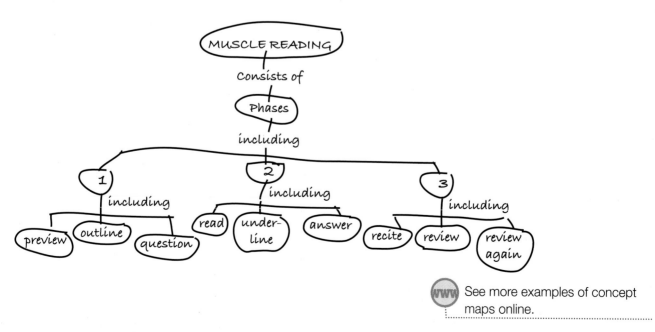

See more examples of concept maps online.

practicing critical thinking

Use a concept map as a tool to interpret and evaluate a piece of writing. First, list the key concepts from a chapter (or section of a chapter) in a textbook you're reading. Create a concept map in the space provided below. Connect the concepts from your text with linking words, using the format described in the article "Get to the bones of your book with concept maps." Then take a few minutes to assess the author's presentation as reflected in your concept map. Pay special attention to the links between concepts. Are they accurate? Do they reveal false assumptions or lack of evidence? Write your evaluation of your concept map below.

_____

_____

_____

_____

_____

_____

_____

_____

_____

_____

_____

_____

_____

Concept Map

NOTES

5

Online classes—taking notes and using other review tools

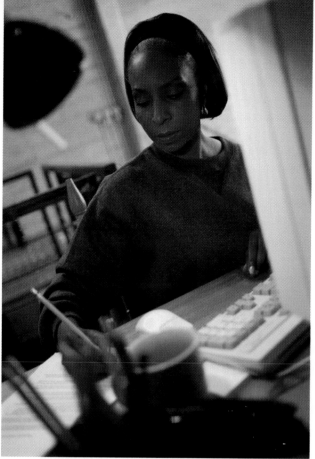

© JUPITERIMAGES/Brand X Pictures/Alamy

IF YOU ARE taking an online course or a course that is heavily supported by online materials, note taking could be a new challenge. You can print out anything that appears on a computer screen. This includes online course materials, articles, books, manuscripts, e-mail messages, chat room sessions, and more.

One potential problem is that you might skip the note-taking process altogether. ("I can just print out everything!") You would then miss the chance to internalize a new idea by restating it in your own words—a principal benefit of note taking.

Result: Material passes from computer to printer without ever intersecting with your brain.

To prevent this problem, find ways to engage actively with online materials. Take review notes in Cornell, mind map, concept map, or outline format. Write Discovery and Intention Statements to capture key insights from the materials and to state ways you intend to apply them. Also talk about what you're learning. Recite key points out loud, and discuss what you read online with other students.

Of course, it's fine to print out online material. If you do, treat your printouts like textbooks, and apply the steps of Muscle Reading explained in Chapter 4. In addition, consider the following ways to create the most value from course content that's delivered online.

Do a trial run with technology. Verify your access to course Web sites, including online tutorials, PowerPoint presentations, readings, quizzes, tests, assignments, bulletin boards, and chat rooms. Ask your instructors for Web site addresses, e-mail addresses, and passwords. Work out any bugs when you start the course and well before that first assignment is due.

If you're planning to use a computer lab on campus, find one that meets course requirements. Remember that on-campus computer labs may not allow you to install all the software needed to access Web sites for your courses or textbooks.

Develop a contingency plan. Murphy's Law of Computer Crashes states that technology tends to break down at the moment of greatest inconvenience. You

might not believe this piece of folklore, but it's still wise to prepare for it:

- Find a "technology buddy" in each of your classes—someone who can contact the instructor if you lose Internet access or experience other computer problems.
- Every day, make backup copies of files created for your courses.
- Keep extra printer supplies—paper and toner or ink cartridges—on hand at all times. Don't run out of necessary supplies on the day a paper is due.

Set up folders and files for easy reference. Create a separate folder for each class on your computer's hard drive. Give each folder a meaningful name, such as *biology–spring2009.* Place all files related to a course in the appropriate folder. Doing this can save you from one of the main technology-related time wasters: searching for lost files.

Also name individual files with care. Avoid changing extensions that identify different types of files, such as .ppt for PowerPoint presentations or .pdf for files in the Adobe Reader portable document format. Changing extensions might lead to problems when you're looking for files later or sharing them with other users.

Take responsibility. If you register for an online course with no class meetings, you might miss the motivating presence of an instructor and classmates.

Instead, manufacture your own motivation. Be clear about what you'll gain by doing well in the course. Relate course content to your major and career goals. Don't wait to be contacted by your classmates and instructor. Initiate that contact on your own.

If you feel confused about anything you're learning, ask for help right away. This is especially important when you don't see the instructor face to face in class. Some students simply drop online courses rather than seek help. E-mail or call the instructor before you make that choice. If the instructor is on campus, you might be able to arrange for a meeting during office hours.

Prevent procrastination. Courses that take place mostly or totally online can become invisible in your weekly academic schedule. This tendency reinforces the temptation to put off dealing with these courses until late in the term. You can avoid this fate:

- Early in the term, create a detailed schedule for online courses. In your calendar, list a due date for each assignment. Break big assignments into smaller steps, and schedule a due date for each step.

- Consider scheduling times in your daily or weekly calendar to complete online course work. Give these scheduled sessions the same priority as regular classroom meetings. At these times, check for online announcements relating to assignments, tests, and other course events.

- When you receive an online assignment, e-mail any questions immediately. If you want to meet with an instructor in person, request an appointment several days in advance.

- Download or print out online course materials as soon as they're posted on the class Web site. These materials might not be available later in the term.

- If possible, submit online assignments early. Staying ahead of the game will help you avoid an all-nighter at the computer during finals week.

Focus your attention. Some students are used to visiting Web sites while watching television, listening to loud music, or using instant messaging software. When applied to online learning, these habits can reduce your learning and imperil your grades. To succeed with technology, turn off the television, quit online chat sessions, and turn down the music. Whenever you go online, stay in charge of your attention.

Ask for feedback. To get the most from online learning, request feedback from your instructor via e-mail. When appropriate, also ask for conferences by phone or in person.

Sharing files offers another source of feedback. For example, Microsoft Word has a Track Changes feature that allows other people to insert comments into your documents and make suggested revisions. These edits are highlighted on the screen. Use such tools to get feedback on your writing from instructors and peers.

Note: Be sure to check with your instructors to see how they want students enrolled in their online courses to address and label their e-mails. Many teachers ask their online students to use a standard format for the subject area so they can quickly recognize e-mails from them.

Contact other students. Make personal contact with at least one other student in each of your classes—especially classes that involve lots of online course work. Create study groups to share notes, quiz each other, critique papers, and do other cooperative learning tasks. This kind of support can help you succeed as an online learner. ✳

mastering technology

YOUR MIND, ONLINE

Imagine how useful—and fun—it would be to download everything you've ever read or thought and then instantly locate what you know about a particular topic. Something like this *is* possible today. Computer applications give you a variety of ways to store text and images, organize them, search them, and even share them with others when appropriate. These applications fall into three categories.

Online Notebooks Google Notebook, Zoho Notebook, and similar applications allow you to "clip" images and text from various Web pages, categorize all this content, and add your own notes.

Personal Information Managers Examples of personal information managers include Evernote, Yojimbo, and DEVONThink. These applications share many features with online notebooks. However, some of them allow you to add "offline" content, such as digital photos of business cards and receipts. You can search through all this content by using tags and key words.

Browser Extensions Zotero is a Firefox extension that allows you to store Web pages, PDF files, and notes in rich-text format. This tool makes it easy to cite the sources of text and images and to convert your citations into a bibliography—a great way to avoid plagiarism.

I Create It All

This article describes a powerful tool for times of trouble. In a crisis, "I create it all" can lead the way to solutions. "I create it all" means treating experiences, events, and circumstances in your life as if you created them.

"I create it all" is one of the most unusual and bizarre suggestions in this book. It certainly is not a belief. Use it when it works. Don't when it doesn't.

Keeping that in mind, consider how powerful this Power Process can be. It is really about the difference between two distinct positions in life: being a victim or being responsible.

A victim of circumstances is controlled by outside forces. We've all felt like victims at one time or another. Sometimes we felt helpless.

In contrast, we can take responsibility. Responsibility is "response-ability"—the ability to choose a *response* to any event. You can choose your *response* to any event, even when the event itself is beyond your control.

Many students approach grades from the position of being victims. When the student who sees the world this way gets an F, she reacts something like this:

"Another F! That teacher couldn't teach her way out of a wet paper bag. She can't teach English for anything. And that textbook—what a bore!"

The problem with this viewpoint is that in looking for excuses, the student is robbing herself of the power to get any grade other than an F. She's giving all of her power to a bad teacher and a boring textbook.

There is another way, called *taking responsibility*. You can recognize that you choose your grades by choosing your actions. Then you are the source, rather than the result, of the grades you get. The student who got an F could react like this:

"Another F! Oh, shoot! Well, hmmm. . . . What did I do to create it?"

Now, that's power. By asking, "How did I contribute to this outcome?" you are no longer the victim. This student might continue by saying, "Well, let's see. I didn't review my notes after class. That might have done it." Or "I went out with my friends the night before the test. Well, that probably helped me fulfill some of the requirements for getting an F."

The point is this: When the F is the result of your friends, the book, or the teacher, you probably can't do anything about it. However, if you *chose* the F, you can choose a different grade next time. You are in charge.

Learn more about using this Power Process online.

Goodshoot/RF/Jupiter Images

Put it to Work

Developing the ability to take useful notes during meetings is one way to make yourself valued in the workplace. It might even help you get promoted. With this in mind, look for ways to apply suggestions from this chapter at work.

sozaijiten/Datacraft/Getty

Hanae Niigata is a part-time office manager for a large cardiovascular clinic. Her responsibilities include handling incoming calls, scheduling patient visits, maintaining medical records, and completing other tasks assigned by physicians and nurses.

Hanae's career focus is health care. She has worked as a home health aide and is currently enrolled in school. Her goal is to obtain a degree in nursing and work as a registered nurse.

Hanae has a reputation as a hard worker. Even in a noisy environment with frequent interruptions, she completes tasks that require attention to detail and sustained concentration. She catches errors on medical records that her coworkers tend to miss. In addition, Hanae is often the first person in the office to whom people turn when they have a problem to solve. Even in the most difficult circumstances, she can generate a list of options—including solutions that occur to no one else.

Recently, Hanae attended a 2-hour course on a new telephone system soon to be installed in her office. She was told to take detailed notes so she could teach the system to several receptionists. Hanae was shocked that the old system was being replaced. In her opinion, it was user-friendly.

As the training session began, Hanae diligently attempted to write down almst everything the instructor said. While doing so, she repeatedly found herself distracted by the thought that her manager was replacing a perfectly good phone system with some "sure-to-be-a-nightmare, high-tech garbage."

After completing the course, Hanae sat down with her manager to fill him in on the new system. As she thumbed through her notes, she realized they didn't make much sense to her, even though she had just finished writing them. She couldn't recall much of the course from memory, either, leaving her with little information to share with her manager.

Hanae routinely applies strategies from this book to many areas of her work. For example, she applies the Power Process: "Be Here Now" to help her pay attention amid distractions and catch errors on medical records. In addition, she is a creative thinker and problem solver, using several strategies you will learn in Chapter 7: Thinking. But when it came to the training session, she didn't apply any of the book's note-taking strategies. List strategies that Hanae could have used to take more effective notes on the training session that she attended:

_____

_____

_____

_____

When you are at work, consider using the three "A's" when you take notes during a meeting. Record key details about the following:

- *Attendance*. Notice who shows up. Your employer might expect meeting notes to include a list of attendees.
- *Agreements*. The purpose of most meetings is to reach an agreement about something—a policy, project, or plan. Note each agreement. If you're not sure whether an agreement was reached, ask for clarification.
- *Actions*. During meetings, people often commit to take some type of action in the future. Record each proposed follow-up action and who agreed to do it.

Skilled meeting planners often put an agenda in writing and distribute it in advance. You can use this agenda as a way to organize your notes. However, be prepared for times when people depart from the agenda and introduce new topics.

Quiz

chapter 5
....

■ Put it to Work
◄ ◄ ◄ ◄ ◄
■ Skills Snapshot
■ Master Student Profile

Name _____   Date ____/____/____

1. What are the three major steps of effective note taking as explained in this chapter? Summarize each step in one sentence.

   List each of the following and describe in a sentence (answers will vary):   a. Observe—notice spoken or written words.   b. Record—take notes.   c. Review— reread notes frequently.   (*The note-taking process flows*, p. 149)

2. According to the text, neat handwriting and a knowledge of outlining are the only requirements for effective notes. True or False? Explain your answer.

   False. Neat handwriting and knowing how to outline are useful, but not requirements. (*The note-taking process flows*, p. 149)

3. What are some advantages of sitting in the front and center of the classroom?

   Possible advantages to sitting front and center in a lecture include (answers will vary):   a. The closer you sit to the lecturer, the harder it is to fall asleep.   b. The closer you sit to the front, the fewer interesting or distracting classmates between you and instructor there are to watch.   c. Material on the board is easier to read from up front.   d. The instructor can see you more easily when you have a question.   e. A professor who sounds boring from the back of the room might sound more interesting if you're closer.   f. Sitting up front is a way to commit yourself to getting what you want out of your education.   g. When you sit in front, you are declaring your willingness to take a risk and participate.   (*Observe: The note-taking process flows*, p. 150)

4. Instructors sometimes give clues that the material they are presenting is important. List at least three of these clues.

   List at least three of the following: a. Be alert to repetition.   b. Listen for introductory, concluding, and transition words and phrases.   c. Watch the board or PowerPoint presentation.   d. Watch the instructor's eyes.   e. Highlight the obvious clues.   f. Notice the instructor's interest level.   (*Observe: The note-taking process flows*, p. 150)

5. Postponing judgment while taking notes means that you have to agree with everything that the instructor says. True or False? Explain your answer.

   False. The purpose of postponing debate is to prevent your internal dialogue about what is being presented from drowning out subsequent material. Thinking critically and postponing debate are not contradictory. Aim to understand the instructor's point before you criticize it. (*Observe: The note-taking process flows*, p. 150)

6. Graphic signals include which of the following?

   (a) Brackets and parentheses.
   (b) Stars and arrows.
   (c) Underlining and connecting lines.
   (d) Equal signs and greater-than and less-than signs.
   (e) All of the above.

   (e) All of the above.   (*Record: The note-taking process flows*, p. 153)

7. Describe the two types of key words. Then write down at least five key words from this chapter.

   The two types of key words are concepts, which are usually nouns, and linking words, which are usually verbs. Key words in this chapter include Cornell format, mind mapping, source cards, information cards, critical thinking, "I create it all," observe, record, review, front and center, preclass review, and postpone debate. (Answers will vary.) (*Record: The note-taking process flows*, p. 153; *Get to the bones of your book with concept maps*, p. 167)

8. Describe a way to apply the Power Process: "Be Here Now" to the job of taking notes in class.

   One can apply "Be here now" in note taking to help make decisions about what to write down in one's notes. (Answers will vary.) (*Observe: The note-taking process flows*, p. 150)

9. Describe at least three strategies for reviewing notes.

   Describe at least three of the following: a. Review within 24 hours.   b. Edit your notes.   c. Fill in key words in the left-hand column.   d. Use key words as recitation cues.   e. Conduct short weekly review periods.   f. Type up your notes.   g. Create summaries.   (*Review: The note-taking process flows*, p. 158)

10. Briefly define the word *responsibility* as it is used in the Power Process: "I Create It All."

    As used in this process, responsibility means taking ownership of your actions and responses to things that happen in your life. (Answers will vary.) (*Power Process: I create it all*, p. 171)

Skills Snapshot

The Discovery Wheel in Chapter 1 includes a section labeled *Notes*. For the next 10 to 15 minutes, go beyond your initial responses to that exercise. Take a snapshot of your skills as they exist today, after reading and doing this chapter.

Begin by reflecting on some of your recent experiences with note taking. These experiences can include classroom notes, as well as notes on your reading assignments. Then take the next step toward mastery by committing to a specific action in the near future.

OBSERVING

If my attention wanders while taking notes, I refocus by . . .

When I strongly disagree with the opinion of a speaker or author, I respond by . . .

RECORDING

The formats I usually use to take notes are . . .

A new note-taking format that I'd like to experiment with is . . .

REVIEWING

If asked to rate the overall quality of the notes that I've taken in the last week, I would say that . . .

In general, I find my notes to be most useful when they . . .

NEXT ACTION

I'll know that I've reached a new level of mastery with note taking when . . .

www.cengage.com/success/bams13e

Master Student PROFILE

Harvey Milk

. . . was courageous

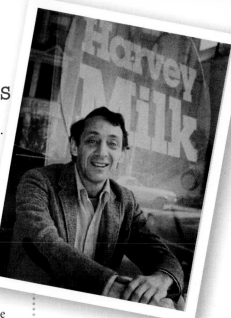

© Bettmann/CORBIS

People told Harvey Milk that no openly gay man could win political office. Fortunately, he ignored them.

There was a time when it was impossible for people—straight or gay—even to imagine a Harvey Milk. The funny thing about Milk is that he didn't seem to care that he lived in such a time. After he defied the governing class of San Francisco in 1977 to become a member of its board of supervisors, many people—straight and gay—had to adjust to a new reality he embodied: that a gay person could live an honest life and succeed. That laborious adjustment plods on—now forward, now backward—though with every gay character to emerge on TV and with every presidential speech to a gay group, its eventual outcome favoring equality seems clear.

The few gays who had scratched their way into the city's [San Francisco's] establishment blanched when Milk announced his first run for supervisor in 1973, but Milk had a powerful idea: he would reach downward, not upward, for support. He convinced the growing gay masses of "Sodom by the Sea" that they could have a role in city leadership, and they turned out to form "human billboards" for him along major thoroughfares. In doing so, they outed themselves in a way once unthinkable. It was invigorating.

While his first three tries for office failed, they lent Milk the credibility and positive media focus that probably no openly gay person ever had. Not everyone cheered, of course, and death threats multiplied. Milk spoke often of his ineluctable assassination, even recording a will naming acceptable successors to his seat and containing the famous line: "If a bullet should enter my brain, let that bullet destroy every closet door."

Two bullets actually entered his brain. It was Nov. 27, 1978, in city hall, and Mayor George Moscone was also killed. Fellow supervisor Daniel White, a troubled anti-gay conservative, had left the board, and he became unhinged when Moscone denied his request to return. White admitted the murders within hours. . . .

A jury gave him just five years with parole. Defense lawyers had barred anyone remotely pro-gay from the jury and brought a psychologist to testify that junk food had exacerbated White's depression. (The so-called Twinkie defense was later banned.) Milk's words had averted gay riots before, but after the verdict, the city erupted. More than 160 people ended up in the hospital.

Milk's killing probably awakened as many gay people as his election had. His death inspired many associates—most notably Cleve Jones, who later envisioned the greatest work of American folk art, the AIDS quilt. But while assassination offered Milk something then rare for openly gay men—mainstream empathy—it would have been thrilling to see how far he could have gone as a leader. He had sworn off gay bathhouses when he entered public life, and he may have eluded the virus that killed so many of his contemporaries. He could have guided gay America through the confused start of the AIDS horror. Instead, he remains frozen in time, a symbol of what gays can accomplish and the dangers they face in doing so.

John Cloud, "The Pioneer," *Time*, June 14, 1999, http://www.time.com/time/time100/heroes/profile/milk01/html.

(1930–1978) One of America's first openly gay men to win political office, Harvey Milk was assassinated by a former San Francisco city supervisor.

Learn more about Harvey Milk and other master students at the Master Student Hall of Fame.

Instructor Tools & Tips

> Learn from the mistakes of others—you can never live long enough to make them all yourself.
>
> **—John Luther**
>
> Keep in mind that neither success nor failure is ever final.
>
> **—ROGER BABSON**

Preview

Test taking is a high-priority issue for students. Discussing this topic together in class can help students prepare more successfully before tests while learning to manage anxiety during tests. This chapter reinforces how the strategies in *Becoming a Master Student* can help students reduce stress at school, at work, and at home. An article on math test strategies can help your students achieve higher test scores. Encourage your students to do a chapter reconnaissance to discover ways to predict test questions or to glean information from a test after it has been returned.

Guest Speaker

Consider inviting faculty members from different departments to talk to your class about their expectations regarding tests. Ask them to prepare a few suggestions for studying materials in their discipline. Prompt them to provide information on the importance of attending class, reading assigned textbook materials, and completing homework assignments. Have students prepare questions to ask these faculty members during a question-and-answer session.

Another guest speaker idea is to invite the administrator responsible for student discipline. In addition to explaining the office's broader role at the college, prompt the administrator to talk about the college's policies regarding cheating. When students cheat and get caught, they don't talk about it, so students have a misperception that no one's getting caught. The administrator's firsthand discussion of the topic may hit home with students who have considered cheating or have cheated in the past.

Another suggestion for a guest speaker is to invite a counselor or staff member from the Student Health Center to talk about test anxiety and relaxation techniques.

Lecture

What to do when you're stuck Lecture on what students should do when they are stuck on a test question. Here are some strategies. A copy of this material is available on the Instructor Web site.

- **Read it again.** Eliminate the simplest sources of confusion, such as misreading the question.

- **Skip the question for now.** This advice is simple—and it works. Tell students to let their subconscious mind work on the answer while they respond to other questions. The trick is to truly let go of the puzzling question—for the moment. Questions that nag at the back of your mind can undermine your concentration and interfere with your recall while you are answering other questions.

- **Look for answers in other test questions.** A term, name, date, or other fact that escapes you might appear in another question on the test itself. Use other questions to stimulate your memory.

- **Treat intuition with care.** In quick-answer questions (multiple choice, true/false), go with your first instinct about which answer is correct. If you think your first answer is wrong because you misread the question, though, do change your answer.

- **Visualize the answer's "location."** Think of the answer to any test question as being recorded someplace in your notes or assigned reading. Close your eyes, take a deep breath, and see if you can visualize that place—its location on a page in the materials you studied for the test.

- **Rewrite the question.** See if you can put a confusing question into your own words. Doing so might release the answer.

- **Free-write.** Just start writing anything at all. On scratch paper or in the margins of your test booklet, record any response to the test question that pops into your head. Instead of just sitting there, stumped, you're doing something—and that can reduce anxiety. Writing might also trigger a mental association that answers the question.

- **Write a close answer.** If you simply cannot think of a direct, accurate answer to the question, give it a shot anyway. Answer the question as best as you can, even if you don't think your answer is fully correct. This technique might help you get partial credit for short-answer questions, essay questions, and problems on math or science tests.

Celebrate mistakes (page 197) From Faculty Advisor Dean Mancina:

> "Sometimes I flub up a piece of my lecture or an in-class group activity. My students love to see that happen! I made a sign with the eight reasons to celebrate mistakes and had our graphics center blow it up into a poster that I have posted in my classroom. When I make a mistake, rather than trying to cover it up, I walk over to the poster, review the list, and pick one of the reasons to celebrate it, right then and there! The students see me model making a mistake without shame—a real application of the tool. Depending on how many mistakes I make during the semester, some of my students get a frequent review of this strategy!"

Exercises/Activities

1. Cooperative learning: Studying in groups (page 181) This article addresses the topic of working together in group study sessions. Use the Master Student Map to begin the discussion of tests and cooperative learning. Divide your class into four groups, assigning each group one of the learning styles. Next, with their books closed, ask students to write down as many answers to their question (*Why? What? How? What if?*) in relation to test taking as they can in 1 minute. After a minute, have each group pick their best answer and report about it to the class. Then have the students open their textbooks and compare their lists to the Master Student Map.

Why? Why does this chapter appear in *Becoming a Master Student*?

What? What is included in this chapter?

How? How can you use this chapter?

What if? What if you use the techniques in this chapter to be better prepared for tests?

2. What to do before the test (page 178) This article is important to students because so many of them cram at the last minute and therefore have never practiced these strategies. Mind maps are powerful visual review tools that can be an effective tool for students who don't know how to study effectively for tests. Have your students get into groups of four, pick a chapter from *Becoming a Master Student,* and create a mind map of the chapter's content on poster paper with colored markers. Tell them to sign their names at the top of the paper. This helps ensure that everyone is actively participating in the group. Hang the completed posters on the wall in the classroom, and then have the students walk around in their groups to review their classmates' work. Having had an opportunity to practice creating mind map summaries in class, they are likely to be more comfortable trying the technique on their own outside class. This activity also allows students to practice the important skill of working in groups.

3. Ways to predict test questions (page 180) Divide students into groups and have them practice predicting test questions for the weekly quizzes that you give in class. Their questions should be based on what they see as the key points you have presented in lectures, activities, and homework, and the key points in the articles in the text. They are often surprised at how easy and effective this tool is!

4. Power Process: DETACH (page 199) After you have lectured on how to develop and write good essay exam answers, and have emphasized the importance of thinking, planning, and clear writing, divide students into groups of four and have them answer the following question: "Fully explain the Power Process: 'Detach.'" This provides them with an opportunity to practice developing an essay answer in a cooperative learning environment. It's also valuable because some students don't fully understand this process without class discussion. After the groups write their group essay answers, have them pass their papers to another group who then "grade" the essay. Read the highest-scoring answer, and provide your analysis as to the essay's strengths and weaknesses. Here's a modification of this exercise from an instructor:

> One thing that I tell my students about essay tests is to write as if they were writing to someone who knows absolutely nothing about the subject. In that way they should include all the basic information that they might not otherwise think of. I also use LIBEC, which was in a College Survival newsletter several years ago. LIBEC stands for **l**egible, **i**ntroduction, **b**ody, **e**xample, and **c**onclusion. We talk about these steps and then my students (in groups) write answers to questions I make up from the reading in the chapter. With their group members they exchange answers and check to see if all the areas were covered. They enjoy working on an essay question with others and then evaluating what others have done.
>
> **—Barbara Fowler, Longview Community College, Missouri**

Conversation/Sharing

As the article "The test isn't over until…" (page 186) explains, it is vital for students to find out what questions they missed on a test and to understand why they missed them. Students can use the learning styles questions *(Why? What? How? What if?)* to review their tests. *Why* did I get this question wrong? *What* is the correct answer? *How* should I have studied this material? And they need to understand the consequences: *What if* I do not learn the correct answer for future tests? These four questions are a great foundational structure for this self-analysis. After a quiz or test, divide students into groups and have them share their analyses with each other so that they can all do better on the next evaluation. On a related note, here's a suggestion from an instructor:

> I have always tried to instruct my students to learn something from the tests that they take. This can be an area where the students can gain so much information and yet it is often overlooked. The information in the chart (page 186) is also helpful. This is a great way to say a lot in a small space.
>
> **—Ray Emett, Salt Lake Community College**

Homework

Journal Entry #17 Discovery/Intention Statement (page 192) Ask students to take a look at how they sabotage their opportunity to "create it all" by making excuses. This self-analysis will help them break the excuses habit by writing their discoveries and intentions about excuses.

Journal Entry #18 Discovery Statement (page 192) Having students complete and turn in this journal entry regarding how they feel about tests can be helpful to you in understanding the key problem areas for your students before, during, and after a test. Review students' responses to this exercise and tailor your lectures and activities to address the needs expressed.

Exercise #20: Use learning styles for math success (page 196) This exercise helps students see how they can use their preferred learning style to create tools to help them succeed in math.

Evaluation

Giving a quiz that includes multiple-choice, true/false, short-answer, and essay questions will give students an opportunity to practice new skills they've learned in this chapter and provide them with feedback about where they have achieved success in building new skills and where more practice is needed. For example, ask the following quiz question about Master Students Bert and John Jacobs: "Briefly describe their attitude about keeping a positive attitude. Then state whether you agree with it or not, and justify your position." Using the three-part quiz forms available from your Cengage sales representative facilitates students' self-evaluation of their quiz performance and provides them with immediate feedback about their test-taking skills.

Additional Digital Resources

Course Manual

The online *Course Manual* serves as an invaluable reference for those developing and teaching a College Success course with *Becoming a Master Student*. The *Course Manual* provides advice on general teaching issues such as preparing for classes, classroom management, grading, and communicating with students of various backgrounds, as well as specific strategies on getting the most out of various features in *Becoming a Master Student* such as the Discovery Wheel, Learning Styles Inventory, and book-specific Web sites.

Instructor Web Site

The updated Instructor Web site provides resources to help you plan and customize your course. Content specific to Chapter 6 includes:

► Lecture Ideas
  • Comparing Athletic Competitions to Tests
  • Using Bloom's Taxonomy to Prepare for Tests
  • Test Anxiety and Stress
► In-Class Exercises
  • The Fribbled What?
  • Mid-Term Project
  • The Power of Positive Peer Influence
► In-Text Quiz Answers
► Learning Styles Application
► Discussion Topics
► PowerPoint Slides
► Reflection Questions
► Assessment Questions
► Experiment with chapter strategies

The Instructor Web site also contains the following book-specific content:

► ExamView Test Bank
► Online Course Manual
► Articles from previous editions
► Master Student Profiles from previous editions
► Sample Syllabi
► Detailed Transition Guide

Student Web Site

To help your students gain a better understanding of the topics discussed in *Becoming a Master Student,* encour-

 www.cengage.com/success/bams13e

age your students to visit the Student Web site, which provides the following resources specific to Chapter 6:

► Connect to Text content expands on specific topics marked with an icon within Chapter 6.
► Learning Style Applications invite students to cycle through the four styles of learning. In answering the four questions about managing test anxiety posted in this chapter's Learning Styles Application, students explore the different modes and apply their new knowledge.
► Practice Tests allow students to see how well they understand the themes of *Becoming a Master Student*.
► Interactive Concept Maps promote critical thinking by highlighting related ideas to show relationships between concepts.
► Video Skillbuilders bring to life techniques that will help you to excel in college and beyond. The following videos should give your students more information regarding topics covered in Chapter 6:
  • Test Taking: Understanding Tests
  • Test Taking: Preparing for Tests
► Remembering Cultural Differences presents readers with brief articles that touch on aspects of diversity in our rapidly changing world. For Chapter 6, the following article will prompt your students to look at contemporary issues in a new way:
  • A Historical Look at Exams
► Master Student Profiles provide additional information on the people covered in this book feature. For Chapter 6, students will find expanded coverage and links about:
  • Bert and John Jacobs
► Power Process Media contains video, PowerPoints, and audio files to take what your students have learned from the Power Processes in their book to the next level. For Chapter 6, students will find additional media on:
  • Detach

Along with the chapter-specific content, a General Resources folder is available that contains Toolboxes geared toward specific student types (Community College, Adult Learner, Student Athlete), the Plagiarism Prevention Zone, and the Career Resource Center.

6 Tests

Master Student Map

as you read, ask yourself

what if . . .

I could let go of anxiety about tests—or anything else?

why this chapter matters . . .

Adopting a few simple techniques can make a major difference in how you feel about tests—and how you perform on them.

what is included . . .

how you can use this chapter . . .

- Predict test questions and use your study time more effectively.
- Harness the power of cooperative learning by studying with other people.
- Gain strategies for raising your scores on tests.
- Separate your self-image from your test scores.

MASTER STUDENTS in *action*

When studying for a test, the first thing I usually do is to read over my notes. Sometimes I re-read the chapter just to make sure I comprehend what the chapter is saying. I find it very helpful to go online to the publisher's website and do the practice exams. By doing the practice exams, I get a better perspective of what the critical points are in the chapters. I like to go through the chapter outline because sometimes the answers are in the outlines.   **—LEA DEAN**

Photo courtesy of Lea Dean

Disarm tests

ON THE SURFACE, tests don't look dangerous. Maybe that's why we sometimes treat them as if they were land mines. Suppose a stranger walked up to you on the street and asked, "Does a finite abelian P-group have a basis?" Would you break out in a cold sweat? Would your muscles tense up? Would your breathing become shallow?

Probably not. Even if you had never heard of a finite abelian P-group, you probably would remain coolly detached. However, if you find the same question on a test and you have never heard of a finite abelian P-group, your hands might get clammy.

Grades (A to F) are what we use to give power to tests. And there are lots of misconceptions about what grades are. Grades are not a measure of intelligence or creativity. They are not an indication of our ability to contribute to society. Grades are simply a measure of how well we do on tests.

Some people think that a test score measures what a student has accomplished in a course. This idea is false. A test score is a measure of what a student scored on a test. If you are anxious about a test and blank out, the grade cannot measure what you've learned. The reverse is also true: If you are good at taking tests and you are a lucky guesser, the score won't be an accurate reflection of what you know.

Grades are not a measure of self-worth. Yet we tend to give test scores the power to determine how we feel about ourselves. Common thoughts include "If I fail a test, I am a failure" or "If I do badly on a test, I am a bad person." The truth is that if you do badly on a test, you are a person who did badly on a test. That's all.

Carrying around misconceptions about tests and grades can put undue pressure on your performance. It's like balancing on a railroad track. Many people can walk along the rail and stay balanced for long periods. Yet the task seems entirely different if the rail is placed between two buildings, fifty-two stories up.

It is easier to do well on exams if you don't put too much pressure on yourself. Don't give the test some magical power over your own worth as a human being. Academic tests are not a matter of life and death. Scoring low on important tests—standardized tests for medical school, bar exams, CPA exams—usually means only a delay.

Whether the chance of doing poorly is real or exaggerated, worrying about it can become paralyzing. The way to deal with tests is to keep them in perspective. Keep the railroad track on the ground. ✱

journal entry 16

Discovery/Intention Statement

Use this chapter to transform your experience of tests

Mentally re-create a time when you had difficulty taking a test. Do anything that helps you reexperience this event. Briefly describe that experience in the space below. You could draw a picture of yourself in this situation, list some of the questions you had difficulty answering, or explain how you felt after finding out your score on the test.

I discovered that I . . .

_____

_____

_____

Now wipe your mental slate clean, and declare your intention to replace it with a new scenario. Describe how you want your experience of test taking to change. For example, you might write: "I intend to walk into every test I take feeling well rested and thoroughly prepared."

I intend to . . .

_____

_____

_____

Preview this chapter, looking for at least five strategies that can help you accomplish your goal. List those strategies below, and note the page numbers where you can find out more about them.

Strategy	Page number

What to do before the test

Do daily reviews. Daily reviews include short preclass and postclass reviews of lecture notes. Also conduct brief daily reviews with textbooks: Before reading a new assignment, scan your notes and the sections you underlined or highlighted in the previous assignment. In addition, use the time you spend waiting for the bus or doing the laundry to conduct short reviews.

Concentrate daily reviews on two kinds of material. One is material you have just learned, either in class or in your reading. Second is material that involves simple memorization—equations, formulas, dates, definitions.

Begin to review on the first day of class. Most instructors outline the whole course at that time. You can even start reviewing within seconds after learning. During a lull in class, go over the notes you just took. Immediately after class, review your notes again.

Do weekly reviews. Review each subject at least once a week, allowing about 1 hour per subject. Include reviews of assigned reading and lecture notes. Look over any mind map summaries or flash cards you have created. Also practice working on sample problems.

Do major reviews. Major reviews are usually most helpful when conducted the week before finals or other critical exams. They help you integrate concepts and deepen your understanding of material presented throughout the term. These are longer review periods—2 to 5 hours at a stretch, with sufficient breaks. Remember that the effectiveness of your review begins to drop after an hour or so unless you give yourself a short rest.

After a certain point, short breaks every hour might not be enough to refresh you. That's when it's time to quit. Learn your limits by being conscious of the quality of your concentration.

During long sessions, study the most difficult subjects when you are the most alert: at the beginning of the session.

Schedule reviews. Schedule specific times in your calendar for reviews. Start reviewing key topics at least 5 days before you'll be tested on them. This allows plenty of time to find the answers to questions and close any gaps in your understanding.

Create study checklists. You can use study checklists the way a pilot uses a preflight checklist.

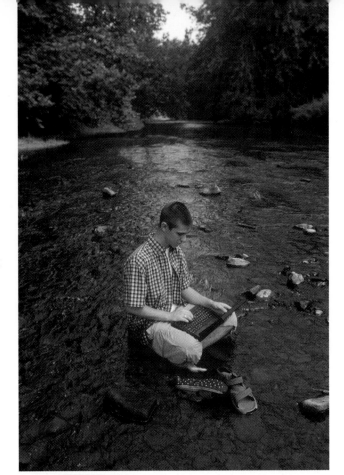

© Gaetano Images Inc./Alamy

Pilots go through a standard routine before they take off. They physically mark off each item: test flaps, check magnetos, check fuel tanks, adjust instruments, check rudder. A written list helps them to be sure they don't miss anything. Once they are in the air, it's too late. Taking an exam is like flying a plane. Once the test begins, it's too late to memorize that one equation you forgot to include in your review.

Make a checklist for each subject. List reading assignments by chapters or page numbers. List dates of lecture notes. Write down various types of problems you will need to solve. Write down other skills to master. Include major ideas, definitions, theories, formulas, and equations. For math and science tests, choose some problems and do them over again as a way to review for the test.

Remember that a study checklist is not a review sheet; it is a to-do list. Checklists contain the briefest possible description of each item to study.

Instead of a checklist, you may want to use a test prep plan. This written plan goes beyond a study checklist to include the following:

- The date and time of each test, along with the name of the course and instructor.
- The type of items—such as essay or multiple choice—that are likely to appear on each test.

- Specific dates and times that you intend to study for each test (which you then enter on your calendar).
- Specific strategies that you intend to use while studying for each test.

Create mind map summary sheets. There are several ways to make a mind map as you study for tests. Start by creating a map totally from memory. You might be surprised by how much you already know. After you have gone as far as you can using recall alone, go over your notes and text, and fill in the rest of the map. Another option is to go through your notes and write down key words as you pick them out. Then, without looking at your notes, create a mind map of everything you can recall about each key word. Finally, go back to your notes, and fill in material you left out.

Create flash cards. Flash cards are like portable test questions. On one side of some 3×5 cards, write questions. On the other side, write the answers. It's that simple. Always carry a pack of flash cards with you, and review them whenever you have a minute to spare. Use flash cards for formulas, definitions, theories, key words from your notes, axioms, dates, foreign language phrases, hypotheses, and sample problems. Create flash cards regularly as the term progresses. Buy an inexpensive card file to keep your flash cards arranged by subject.

Monitor your reviews. Each day that you prepare for a test, assess what you have learned and what you still want to learn. See how many items you've covered from your study checklist. Look at the tables of contents in your textbooks, and write an X next to the sections that you've summarized. This helps you gauge the thoroughness of your reviews and alerts you to areas that still need attention.

Take a practice test. Write up your own questions, and take this practice test several times before the actual exam. You might type this "test" so that it looks like the real thing. If possible, take your practice test in the same room where you will take the actual test.

Also meet with your instructor to go over your practice test. Ask whether your questions focus on appropriate topics and represent the kind of items you can expect to see. The instructor might decline to give you any of this information. More often, though, instructors will answer some or all of your questions about an upcoming test.

Get copies of old exams. Copies of previous exams for the class might be available from the instructor, the instructor's department, the library, or the counseling office. Old tests can help you plan a review strategy. One caution: If you rely on old tests exclusively, you might gloss over material the instructor has added since the last test. Also, check your school's policy about making past tests available to students. Some schools might not allow it. ✳

 See examples of mind map summary sheets and other review tools online.

How to cram (even though you "shouldn't")

Know the limitations of cramming, and be aware of its costs. Cramming won't work if you've neglected all of the reading assignments, or if you've skipped most of the lectures and daydreamed through the rest. The more courses you have to cram for, the less effective cramming will be. Also, cramming is not the same as learning: You won't remember what you cram.

If you *are* going to cram, however, then avoid telling yourself that you *should* have studied earlier, you *should* have read the assignments, or you *should* have been more conscientious. All those shoulds get you nowhere. Instead, write an Intention Statement about how you will change your study habits. Give yourself permission to be the fallible human being you are. Then make the best of the situation.

Make choices Pick out a *few* of the most important elements of the course and learn them backward, forward, and upside down. For example, devote most of your attention to the topic sentences, tables, and charts in a long reading assignment.

Make a plan After you've chosen what elements you want to study, determine how much time to spend on each one.

Recite and recite again The key to cramming is repetition. Go over your material again and again.

Ways to predict test questions

PREDICTING TEST questions can do more than get you a better grade. It can also keep you focused on the purpose of a course and help you design your learning strategies. Making predictions can be fun, too—especially when they turn out to be accurate.

Ask about the nature of the test. Eliminate as much guesswork as possible. Ask your instructor to describe upcoming tests. Do this early in the term so you can be alert for possible test questions throughout the course. Some questions to ask are:

- What course material will the test cover—readings, lectures, lab sessions, or a combination?
- Will the test be cumulative, or will it cover just the most recent material you've studied?
- Will the test focus on facts and details or major themes and relationships?
- Will the test call on you to solve problems or apply concepts?
- Will you have choices about which questions to answer?
- What types of questions will be on the test—true/false, multiple choice, short answer, essay?

Note: In order to study appropriately for essay tests, find out how much detail the instructor wants in your answers. Ask how much time you'll be allowed for the test and about the length of essay answers (number of pages, blue books, or word limit). Having that information before you begin studying will help you gauge your depth for learning the material.

Put yourself in your instructor's shoes. If you were teaching the course, what kinds of questions would you put on an exam? You can also brainstorm test questions with other students—a great activity for study groups.

Look for possible test questions in your notes and readings. Have a separate section in your notebook labeled "Test questions." Add several questions to this section after every lecture and assignment. You can also create your own code or graphic signal—such as a *T!* in a circle—to flag possible test questions in your notes. Use the same symbol to flag review questions and problems in your textbooks that could appear on a test.

Look for clues to possible questions during class. During lectures, you can predict test questions by observing what an instructor says and how he says it. Instructors often give clues. They might repeat important points several times, write them on the board, or return to them in later classes.

Gestures can indicate critical points. For example, your instructor might pause, look at notes, or read passages word for word.

Notice whether your teacher has any strong points of view on certain issues. Questions on those issues are likely to appear on a test. Also pay attention to questions the instructor poses to students, and note questions that other students ask.

When material from reading assignments is covered extensively in class, it is likely to be on a test. For science courses and other courses involving problem solving, work on sample problems using different variables.

Save all quizzes, papers, lab sheets, and graded materials of any kind. Quiz questions have a way of reappearing, in slightly altered form, on final exams. If copies of previous exams and other graded materials are available, use them to predict test questions.

Apply your predictions. To get the most value from your predictions, use them to guide your review sessions.

Remember the obvious. Be on the lookout for these words: *This material will be on the test.*[1] ✳

 Find more ways to predict a variety of test questions online.

Cooperative learning: Studying in groups

Yuri Arcurs/Shutterstock

STUDY GROUPS CAN lift your mood on days when you just don't feel like working. If you skip a solo study session, no one else will know. If you declare your intention to study with others who are depending on you, your intention gains strength.

Study groups are especially important if going to school has thrown you into a new culture. Joining a study group with people you already know can help ease the transition. To multiply the benefits of working with study groups, seek out people of other backgrounds, cultures, races, and ethnic groups. You can get a whole new perspective on the world, along with some valued new friends. And you can experience what it's like to be part of a diverse team—an important asset in today's job market.

Form a study group

Choose a focus for your group. Many students assume that the purpose of a study group is to help its members prepare for a test. That's one valid purpose—and there are others.

Through his research on cooperative learning, psychologist Joe Cuseo has identified several kinds of study groups.[2] For instance, members of *test review* groups compare answers and help one another discover sources of errors. *Note-taking* groups focus on comparing and editing notes, often meeting directly after the day's class. Members of *research* groups meet to help one another find, evaluate, and take notes on background materials for papers and presentations. *Reading* groups can be useful for courses in which test questions are based largely on textbooks. Meet with classmates to compare the passages you underlined or highlighted and the notes you made in the margins of your books.

Look for dedicated students. Find people you are comfortable with and who share your academic goals. Look for students who pay attention, participate in class, and actively take notes. Invite them to join your group.

Of course, you can recruit members in other ways. One way is to make an announcement during class. Another option is to post signs asking interested students to contact you. Or pass around a sign-up sheet before class. These methods can reach many people, but they do take more time to achieve results. And you have less control over who applies to join the group.

Limit groups to four people. Research on cooperative learning indicates that four people is an ideal group size.[3] Larger ones can be unwieldy.

Studying with friends is fine, but if your common interests are pizza and jokes, you might find it hard to focus.

Hold a planning session. Ask two or three people to get together for a snack and talk about group goals, meeting times and locations, and other logistics. You don't have to make an immediate commitment.

As you brainstorm about places to meet, aim for a quiet meeting room with plenty of room to spread out materials.

Do a trial run. Test the group first by planning a one-time session. If that session works, plan another. After a few successful sessions, you can schedule regular meetings.

Conduct your group

Ask your instructor for guidelines on study group activity. Many instructors welcome and encourage study groups. However, they have different ideas about what kinds of collaboration are acceptable. Some activities—such as sharing test items or writing papers from a shared outline—are considered cheating and can have serious consequences. Let your instructor know that you're forming a group, and ask for clear guidelines.

Set an agenda for each meeting. At the beginning of each meeting, reach agreement on what you intend to do. Set a time limit for each agenda item, and determine a quitting time. End each meeting with assignments for all members to complete before the next meeting.

Assign roles. To make the most of your time, ask one member to lead each group meeting. The leader's role is to keep the discussion focused on the agenda and ask for contributions from all members. Assign another person to act as recorder. This person will take notes on the meeting, recording possible test questions, answers, and main points from group discussions. Rotate both of these roles so that every group member takes a turn.

Cycle through learning styles. As you assign roles, think about the learning styles present in your group. Some people excel at raising questions and creating lots of ideas. Others prefer to gather information and think critically. Some like to answer questions and make decisions, while others excel at taking action. All of these distinct modes of learning are explained in "Learning Styles: Discovering How You Learn" on page 32. To create an effective group, match people with their preferred activities. Also change roles periodically. This gives group members a chance to explore new learning styles.

Teach each other. Teaching is a great way to learn something. Turn the material you're studying into a list of topics and assign a specific topic to each person, who will then teach it to the group. When you're done presenting your topic, ask for questions or comments. Prompt each other to explain ideas more clearly, find gaps in understanding, consider other points of view, and apply concepts to settings outside the classroom.

Test one another. During your meeting, take a practice test created from questions contributed by group members. When you're finished, compare answers. Or turn testing into a game by pretending you're on a television game show. Use sample test questions to quiz one another.

Compare notes. Make sure that all the group's members heard the same thing in class and that you all recorded the important information. Ask others to help explain material in your notes that is confusing to you.

Create wall-size mind maps or concept maps to summarize a textbook or series of lectures. Work on large sheets of butcher paper, or tape together pieces of construction paper. When creating a mind map, assign one branch to each member of the study group. Use a different colored pen or marker for each branch of the mind map. (For more information on concept maps and mind maps, see Chapter 5: Notes.)

Monitor effectiveness. On your meeting agenda, include an occasional discussion about your group's effectiveness. Are you meeting consistently? Is the group helping members succeed in class?

Use this time to address any issues that are affecting the group as a whole. If certain members are routinely unprepared for study sessions, brainstorm ways to get them involved. If one person tends to dominate meetings, reel her in by reminding her that everyone's voice needs to be heard.

To resolve conflict among group members, keep the conversation constructive. Focus on solutions. Move from vague complaints ("You're never prepared") to specific requests ("Will you commit to bringing ten sample test questions next time?"). Asking a "problem" member to lead the next meeting might make an immediate difference. ✳

mastering technology

COLLABORATION 2.0

Web-based applications allow you to create virtual study groups and collaborate online. For example, create and revise documents with sites such as Google Docs (www.docs.google.com) and Zoho Writer (www.writer.zoho.com).

Create and share PowerPoint and keynote presentations with tools such as SlideShare (www.slideshare.net).

Use Basecamp (www.basecamphq.com), Joint Contact (www.jointcontact.com), or 5pm (www.5pmweb.com) to manage projects. You can share files, create a group calendar, assign tasks, chat online, post messages, and track progress toward milestones (key due dates).

Create group mind maps with MindMeister (www.mindmeister.com) and Mindomo (www.mindomo.com).

For more options, do an Internet search with the key words *collaborate online*.

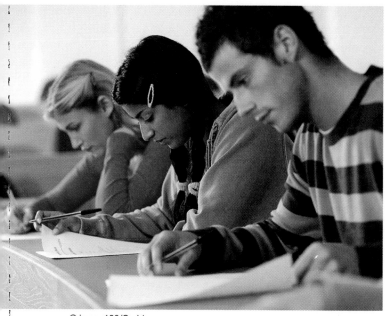
© image100/Corbis

What to do during the test

PREPARE YOURSELF FOR the test by arriving early. Being early often leaves time to do a relaxation exercise. While you're waiting for the test to begin and talking with classmates, avoid asking the question, "How much did you study for the test?" This question might fuel anxious thoughts that you didn't study enough.

As you begin

Ask the teacher or test administrator if you can use scratch paper during the test. (If you use a separate sheet of paper without permission, you might appear to be cheating.) If you *do* get permission, use this paper to jot down memory aids, formulas, equations, definitions, facts, or other material you know you'll need and might forget. An alternative is to make quick notes in the margins of the test sheet.

Pay attention to verbal directions given as a test is distributed. Then scan the whole test immediately. Evaluate the importance of each section. Notice how many points each part of the test is worth; then estimate how much time you'll need for each section, using its point value as your guide. For example, don't budget 20 percent of your time for a section that is worth only 10 percent of the points.

Read the directions slowly. Then reread them. It can be agonizing to discover that you lost points on a test merely because you failed to follow the directions. When the directions are confusing, ask to have them clarified.

Now you are ready to begin the test. If necessary, allow yourself a minute or two of "panic" time. Notice any tension you feel, and apply one of the techniques explained in the article "Let Go of Test Anxiety" later in this chapter.

Answer the easiest, shortest questions first. This gives you the experience of success. It also stimulates associations and prepares you for more difficult questions. Pace yourself, and watch the time. If you can't think of an answer, move on. Follow your time plan.

If you are unable to determine the answer to a test question, keep an eye out throughout the test for context clues that may remind you of the correct answer or provide you with evidence to eliminate wrong answers.

Multiple-choice questions

- *Answer each question in your head first.* Do this step before you look at the possible answers. If you come up with an answer that you're confident is right, look for that answer in the list of choices.

- *Read all possible answers before selecting one.* Sometimes two answers will be similar and only one will be correct.

- *Test each possible answer.* Remember that multiple-choice questions consist of two parts: the stem (an incomplete statement or question at the beginning) and a list of possible answers. Each answer, when combined with the stem, makes a complete statement or question-and-answer pair that is either true or false. When you combine the stem with each possible answer, you are turning each multiple-choice question into a small series of true/false questions. Choose the answer that makes a true statement.

- *Eliminate incorrect answers.* Cross off the answers that are clearly not correct. The answer you cannot eliminate is probably the best choice.

True/false questions

- *Read the entire question.* Separate the statement into its grammatical parts—individual clauses and phrases—and then test each part. If any part is false, the entire statement is false.

- *Look for qualifiers.* Qualifiers include words such as *all, most, sometimes,* or *rarely.* Absolute qualifiers such as *always* or *never* generally indicate a false statement.

- *Find the devil in the details.* Double-check each number, fact, and date in a true/false statement. Look for numbers that have been transposed or facts that have been slightly altered. These are signals of a false statement.

- *Watch for negatives.* Look for words such as *not* and *cannot.* Read the sentence without these words and see if you come up with a true or false statement. Then reinsert the negative words and see if the statement makes more sense. Watch especially for sentences with two negative words. As in math operations, two negatives cancel each other out: *We cannot say that Chekhov never succeeded at short story writing* means the same as *Chekhov succeeded at short story writing.*

Computer-graded tests

- Make sure that the answer you mark corresponds to the question you are answering.

- Check the test booklet against the answer sheet whenever you switch sections and whenever you come to the top of a column.

- Watch for stray marks on the answer sheet; they can look like answers.

- If you change an answer, be sure to erase the wrong answer thoroughly, removing all pencil marks completely.

Open-book tests

- Carefully organize your notes, readings, and any other materials you plan to consult when writing answers.

- Write down any formulas you will need on a separate sheet of paper.

- Bookmark the table of contents and index in each of your textbooks. Place sticky notes and stick-on tabs or paper clips on other important pages of books (pages with tables, for instance).

- Create an informal table of contents or index for the notes you took in class.

- Predict which material will be covered on the test, and highlight relevant sections in your readings and notes.

Short-answer/fill-in-the-blank tests

- Concentrate on key words and facts. Be brief.

- Overlearning material can really pay off. When you know a subject backward and forward, you can answer this type of question almost as fast as you can write.

Matching tests

- Begin by reading through each column, starting with the one with fewer items. Check the number of items in each column to see if they're equal. If they're not, look for an item in one column that you can match with two or more items in the other column.

- Look for any items with similar wording, and make special note of the differences between these items.

- Match words that are similar grammatically. For example, match verbs with verbs and nouns with nouns.

- When matching individual words with phrases, first read a phrase. Then look for the word that logically completes the phrase.

- Cross out items in each column when you are through with them.

Essay questions

Managing your time is crucial in answering essay questions. Note how many questions you have to answer, and monitor your progress during the test period. Writing shorter answers and completing all of the questions on an essay test will probably yield a better score than leaving some questions blank.

Find out what an essay question is asking—precisely. If a question asks you to *compare* the ideas of Sigmund Freud and Karl Marx, no matter how eloquently you *explain* them, you are on a one-way trip to No Credit City.

Before you write, make a quick outline. An outline can help speed up the writing of your detailed answer; you're less likely to leave out important facts; and if you don't have time to finish your answer, your outline could win you some points. To use test time efficiently, keep your outline brief. Focus on key words to use in your answer.

Introduce your answer by getting to the point. General statements such as "There are many interesting facets to this difficult question" can cause acute irritation to teachers grading dozens of tests.

One way to get to the point is to begin your answer with part of the question. Suppose the question is, "Discuss how increasing the city police budget might or might not contribute to a decrease in street crime." Your first sentence might be this: "An increase in police expenditures will not have a significant effect on street crime for the following reasons." Your position is clear. You are on your way to an answer.

Then expand your answer with supporting ideas and facts. Start out with the most solid points. Be brief and avoid filler sentences.

Write legibly. Grading essay questions is in large part a subjective process. Sloppy, difficult-to-read handwriting might actually lower your grade.

Write on one side of the paper only. If you write on both sides of the paper, writing may show through and obscure the words on the other side. If necessary, use the blank side to add points you missed. Leave a generous left-hand margin and plenty of space between your answers, in case you want to add points that you missed later on.

Finally, if you have time, review your answers for grammar and spelling errors, clarity, and legibility. ✳

F is for feedback, not failure

When some students get an F on an assignment, they interpret that letter as a message: "You are a failure." That interpretation is not accurate. Getting an F means only that you failed a test—not that you failed your life.

From now on, imagine that the letter *F* when used as a grade represents another word: *feedback.* An F is an indication that you didn't understand the material well enough. It's a message to do something differently before the next test or assignment.

If you interpret F as *failure,* you don't get to change anything. But if you interpret F as *feedback,* you can change your thinking and behavior in ways that promote your success.

Words to watch for in essay questions

The following words are commonly found in essay test questions. They give you precise directions about what to include in your answer. Get to know these words well. When you see them on a test, underline them. Also look for them in your notes. Locating such key words can help you predict test questions.

> *Analyze:* Break into separate parts and discuss, examine, or interpret each part. Then give your opinion.
>
> *Compare:* Examine two or more items. Identify similarities and differences.
>
> *Contrast:* Show differences. Set in opposition.
>
> *Criticize:* Make judgments. Evaluate comparative worth. Criticism often involves analysis.
>
> *Define:* Explain the exact meaning—usually, a meaning specific to the course or subject. Definitions are usually short.
>
> *Describe:* Give a detailed account. Make a picture with words. List characteristics, qualities, and parts.
>
> *Discuss:* Consider and debate or argue the pros and cons of an issue. Write about any conflict. Compare and contrast.

> *Explain:* Make an idea clear. Show logically how a concept is developed. Give the reasons for an event.
>
> *Prove:* Support with facts (especially facts presented in class or in the text).
>
> *Relate:* Show the connections between ideas or events. Provide a larger context for seeing the big picture.
>
> *State:* Explain precisely.
>
> *Summarize:* Give a brief, condensed account. Include conclusions. Avoid unnecessary details.
>
> *Trace:* Show the order of events or the progress of a subject or event.

Notice how these words differ. For example, *compare* asks you to do something different than *contrast.* Likewise, *criticize* and *explain* call for different responses. If any of these terms are still unclear to you, look them up in an unabridged dictionary.

 Review these key words and other helpful vocabulary terms by using the flash cards online.

The test isn't over until . . .

MANY STUDENTS believe that a test is over as soon as they turn in the test. Consider another point of view: You're not done with a test until you know the answer to any question that you missed.

This point of view offers major benefits. Tests in many courses are cumulative. The content included on the first test is assumed to be working knowledge for future tests. When you discover what questions you missed and understand the reasons for lost points, you learn something—and you increase your odds of achieving better scores later.

Take control of what you do at two critical points: the time immediately following the test and the time when the test is returned to you.

Immediately following the test. After finishing a test, your first thought might be to nap, snack, or go out with friends to celebrate. Restrain those impulses for a short while so that you can reflect on the test.

To begin with, sit down in a quiet place. Take a few minutes to write some Discovery Statements related to your experience of taking the test. Describe how you felt about taking the test, how effective your review strategies were, and whether you accurately predicted the questions that appeared on the test.

Follow up with an Intention Statement or two. State what, if anything, you will do differently to prepare for the next test. The more specific you are, the better.

When the test is returned. View a returned test as a treasure trove of intellectual gold.

First, make sure that the point totals add up correctly, and double-check for any other errors in grading. Even the best teachers make an occasional mistake.

Next, ask these questions:

- On what material did the teacher base test questions—readings, lectures, discussions, or other class activities?
- What types of questions appeared in the test—objective, short answer, or essay?
- What types of questions did you miss?
- Can you learn anything from the instructor's comments that will help you on the next test?
- How can you prepare differently for your next test?

Also see if you can correct any answers that lost points. Carefully analyze the source of your errors, and find a solution. Consult the chart below for help. ✳

Source of test error	Possible solutions
Study errors—studying material that was not included on the test, or spending too little time on material that *did* appear on the test	• Ask your teacher about specific topics that will be included on a test. • Practice predicting test questions. • Form a study group with class members to create mock tests.
Careless errors, such as skipping or misreading directions	• Read directions more carefully—especially when tests are divided into several sections. • Set aside time during the next test to proofread your answers.
Concept errors—mistakes made when you do not understand the underlying principles needed to answer a question or solve a problem	• Look for patterns in the questions you missed. • Make sure that you complete all assigned readings, attend all lectures, and show up for laboratory sessions. • Ask your teacher for help with specific questions.
Application errors—mistakes made when you understand underlying principles but fail to apply them correctly	• Rewrite your answers correctly. • Spend more time solving sample problems. • Predict application questions that will appear in future tests, and practice answering them.
Test mechanics errors—missing more questions in certain parts of the test than others, changing correct answers to incorrect ones at the last minute, leaving items blank, miscopying answers from scratch paper to the answer sheet	• Set time limits for taking each section of a test. • Proofread your test answers carefully. • Look for patterns in the kind of answers you change at the last minute. • Change answers only if you can state a clear and compelling reason to do so.

The high costs of cheating

Cheating on tests can be a tempting strategy. It offers the chance to get a good grade without having to study.

INSTEAD OF STUDYING, we could spend more time watching TV, partying, sleeping, or doing anything that seems like more fun. Another benefit of cheating is that we could avoid the risk of doing poorly on a test—which could happen even if we *do* study.

Remember that cheating carries costs. Here are some consequences to consider.

We risk failing the course or getting expelled from college. The consequences for cheating are serious. Cheating can result in failing the assignment, failing the entire course, getting suspended, or getting expelled from college entirely. Documentation of cheating may also prevent you from being accepted to other colleges.

We learn less. While we might think that some courses offer little or no value, we can create value from any course. If we look deeply enough, we can discover some idea or acquire some skill to prepare us for future courses or a career after graduation.

We lose time and money. Getting an education costs a lot of money. It also calls for years of sustained effort. Cheating sabotages our purchase. We pay full tuition and invest our energy without getting full value for it.

Fear of getting caught promotes stress. When we're fully aware of our emotions about cheating, we might discover intense stress. Even if we're not fully aware of our emotions, we're likely to feel some level of discomfort about getting caught.

Violating our values promotes stress. Even if we don't get caught cheating, we can feel stress about violating our own ethical standards. Stress can compromise our physical health and overall quality of life.

Cheating on tests can make it easier to violate our integrity again. Human beings become comfortable with behaviors that they repeat. Cheating is no exception.

Think about the first time you drove a car. You might have felt excited—even a little frightened. Now driving is probably second nature, and you don't give it much thought. Repeated experience with driving creates familiarity, which lessens the intense feelings you had during your first time at the wheel.

We can experience the same process with almost any behavior. Cheating once will make it easier to cheat again. And if we become comfortable with compromising our integrity in one area of life, we might find it easier to compromise in other areas.

Cheating lowers our self-concept. Whether or not we are fully aware of it, cheating sends us the message that we are not smart enough or responsible enough to make it on our own. We deny ourselves the celebration and satisfaction of authentic success.

An alternative to cheating is to become a master student. Ways to do this are described on every page of this book. *

Perils of high-tech cheating

Digital technology offers many blessings, but it also expands the options for cheating during a test. For example, one student loaded class notes into a Sidekick (a hand-held device) and tried to read them. Another student dictated his class notes into files stored on his iPod and tried to listen to them. At one school, students used cell phones to take photos of test questions. They sent the photos to classmates outside the testing room, who responded by text-messaging the answers.[4]

All of these students were caught. Schools are becoming sophisticated about detecting high-tech cheating. Some install cameras in exam rooms. Others use software that monitors the programs running on students' computers during tests. And some schools simply ban all digital devices during tests.

There's no need to learn the hard way—through painful consequences—about the high costs of high-tech cheating. Using the suggestions in this chapter can help you succeed on tests *and* preserve your academic integrity.

Let go of test anxiety

If you freeze during tests and flub questions when you know the answers, you might be dealing with test anxiety.

© Masterfile Royalty Free

A LITTLE TENSION before a test is fine. That tingly, butterflies-in-the-stomach feeling you get from extra adrenaline can sharpen your awareness and keep you alert. You can enjoy the benefits of a little tension while you stay confident and relaxed.

Sometimes, however, tension is persistent and extreme. If it interferes with your daily life and consistently prevents you from doing your best in school, it might be test anxiety.

Symptoms of anxiety include the following:[5]

- Inability to concentrate.
- Insomnia.
- Sweating.
- Shortness of breath.
- Fatigue.
- Irritability.
- Stomachache.
- Diarrhea.
- Headache.

Anxiety has three elements: mental, physical, and emotional. The mental element includes your thoughts, including predictions of failure. The physical component includes physical sensations such as shallow breathing and muscle tension. The emotional element occurs when thoughts and physical sensations combine. The following techniques can help you deal with these elements of stress in *any* situation, from test anxiety to stage fright.

Dealing with thoughts

Yell "Stop!" When you notice that your mind is consumed with worries and fears—that your thoughts are spinning out of control—mentally yell "Stop!" If you're in a situation that allows it, yell it out loud. This action can allow you to redirect your thoughts. Once you've broken the cycle of worry or panic, you can use any of the following techniques.

Dispute your thoughts. Certain thoughts tend to increase test anxiety. They often boil down to this statement: *Getting a low grade on a test is a disaster.* Do the math, however: A 4-year degree often involves taking about 32 courses (8 courses per year over 4 years for a full-time student). This means that your final grade on any one course amounts to about only 3 percent of your total grade point average.

Also consider that your final grade in any one course is usually based on more than one test. This means that a single test score is not going to make or break your college career.

This argument is not meant to convince you to stop preparing for tests. It *is* an argument to keep each test in perspective—and to dispute thoughts that only serve to create anxiety.

Praise yourself. Talk to yourself in a positive way. Many of us take the first opportunity to belittle ourselves: "Way to go, dummy! You don't even know the answer to the first question on the test." We wouldn't dream of treating a friend this way, yet we do it to ourselves. An alternative is to give yourself some encouragement. Treat yourself as if you were your own best friend. Consider telling yourself, "I am prepared. I can do a great job on this test."

Consider the worst. Rather than trying to put a stop to your worrying, consider the very worst thing that could happen. Take your fear to the limit of absurdity.

Imagine the catastrophic problems that might occur if you were to fail the test. You might say to yourself, "Well, if I fail this test, I might fail the course, lose my financial aid, and get kicked out of school. Then I won't be able to get a job, so the bank will repossess my car, and I'll start drinking." Keep going until you see the absurdity of your predictions. After you stop chuckling, you can backtrack to discover a reasonable level of concern. Your worry about failing the entire course if you fail the test might be justified. At that point, ask yourself, "Can I live with that?" Unless you are taking a test in parachute packing and the final question involves jumping out of a plane, the answer will almost always be yes. (If the answer is no, use another technique. In fact, use several other techniques.)

Dealing with physical sensations

Breathe. You can calm physical sensations within your body by focusing your attention on your breathing. Concentrate on the air going in and out of your lungs. Experience it as it passes through your nose and mouth. Do this exercise for 2 to 5 minutes. If you notice that you are taking short, shallow breaths, begin to take longer and deeper breaths. Imagine your lungs to be a pair of bagpipes. Expand your chest to bring in as much air as possible. Then listen to the plaintive chords as you slowly release the air.

Describe sensations. In your mind, describe your anxiety to yourself in detail; don't resist it. When you completely experience a physical sensation, it will often disappear. People suffering from chronic pain have used this technique successfully.[6]

Scan your body. Simple awareness is an effective response to unpleasant physical sensations. Discover this for yourself by bringing awareness to each area of your body.

To begin, sit comfortably and close your eyes. Focus your attention on the muscles in your feet, and notice if they are relaxed. Tell the muscles in your feet that they can relax.

Move up to your ankles, and repeat the procedure. Next, go to your calves and thighs and buttocks, telling each group of muscles to relax.

Do the same for your lower back, diaphragm, chest, upper arms, lower arms, fingers, upper back, shoulders, neck, jaw, face, and scalp.

Use guided imagery. Relax completely, and take a quick fantasy trip. Close your eyes, free your body of tension, and imagine yourself in a beautiful, peaceful, natural setting. Create as much of the scene as you can. Be specific. Use all of your senses.

For example, you might imagine yourself at a beach. Hear the surf rolling in and the seagulls calling to each other. Feel the sun on your face and the hot sand between your toes. Smell the sea breeze. Taste the salty mist from the surf. Notice the ships on the horizon and the rolling sand dunes. Use all of your senses to create a vivid imaginary trip.

Find a place that works for you, and practice getting there. When you become proficient, you can return to it quickly for trips that might last only a few seconds.

With practice, you can use this technique even while you are taking a test.

Exercise aerobically. Performing aerobic exercise is one technique that won't work in the classroom or while you're taking a test. Yet it is an excellent way to reduce body tension. Exercise regularly during the days you review for a test. See what effect it has on your ability to focus and relax during the test.

Do some kind of exercise that will get your heart beating at twice your normal rate and keep it beating at that rate for 15 or 20 minutes. Aerobic exercise includes rapid walking, jogging, swimming, bicycling, basketball, and anything else that elevates your heart rate and keeps it elevated.

Find alternatives to chemicals. When faced with stress, some people turn to relief in the form of a pill, a drink, or a drug in some other form. Chemicals such as caffeine and alcohol *can* change the way you feel. They also come with costs that go beyond money. For example, drinking alcohol can relax you *and* interfere with your attention and memory. Caffeine or energy drinks might make you feel more confident in the short term. Watch what happens, though, when you start to come down from a caffeine-induced high. You might feel even more irritable than you did *before* drinking that double espresso.

All moral lectures aside, chemicals that you take without a prescription are ineffective ways to manage anxiety. Use other techniques instead.

Dealing with emotions

Accept emotions—whatever they are. Consider our typical response to problems. If a car has a flat tire, that's a problem. The solution is to repair or replace the tire. If a bathroom faucet drips, that's a problem. The solution is to repair or replace part of the faucet.

This problem-solution approach often works well when applied to events outside us. It does not work so well, however, when applied to events *inside* us. When we define anger, sadness, fear, or any emotion as a problem, we tend to search for a solution. However, emotions respond differently than flat tires and drippy faucets.

Typical attempts to "solve" unpleasant emotions include eating, drinking, watching TV, or surfing the Internet. These are actually attempts to resist the emotions and try to make them go away. For a short time, this strategy might work. Over the long term, however, our efforts to repair or replace emotions often have the opposite effect: The emotions persist or even get stronger. Our solutions actually become part of the problem.

An alternative to problem solving is *acceptance*. We can stop seeing emotions as problems. This attitude frees us from having to search for solutions (which often fail anyway).

Acceptance means just letting our emotions be. It means releasing any resistance to emotions. This approach is a wise one, since what we *resist* usually *persists*. Our emotions are just bundles of thoughts and physical sensations. Even the most unpleasant ones fade sooner or later.

The next time you are feeling anxious before a test, simply let that feeling arise and then pass away.

Practice detachment. To *detach* means to step back from something and see it as separate from ourselves. When we detach from an emotion, we no longer identify with it. We no longer say, "*I am afraid*" or "*I am sad.*" We say something like "There's fear again" or "I feel sadness right now." Using language such as this offers us a way to step back from our internal experiences and keep them in perspective.

Before a test, you might find it especially useful to detach from your thoughts. Borrow some ideas from acceptance and commitment therapy, which is used by a growing number of therapists.[7] Take an anxiety-producing thought—such as *I always screw up on tests*—and do any of the following:

- Repeat the thought over and over again out loud until it becomes just a meaningless series of sounds.
- Repeat the thought while using the voice of a cartoon character such as Mickey Mouse or Homer Simpson.
- Rephrase the thought so that you can sing it to the tune of a nursery rhyme or the song "Happy Birthday."
- Preface the thought with "I'm having the thought that . . ." (*I'm having the thought that I always screw up on tests.*)
- Talk back to your mind by saying, "That's an interesting thought, mind; thanks a lot for sharing." Or simply say, "Thanks, mind."

Make contact with the present moment. If you feel anxious, see if you can focus your attention on a specific sight, sound, or other sensation that's happening in the present moment. Examine the details of a painting. Study the branches on a tree. Observe the face of your watch right down to the tiny scratches in the glass. During an exam, take a few seconds to listen to the sounds of squeaking chairs, the scratching of pencils, the muted coughs. Touch the surface of your desk and notice the texture. Focus all of your attention on one point—anything other than the flow of thoughts through your head. Focusing in this manner is one way to use the Power Process: "Be Here Now."

Get help

If you use any of the above techniques for a couple of weeks and they fail to work, then turn to other people. Sometimes help with a specific situation—such as a lack of money—can relieve a source of stress that affects your test performance. Turn to the appropriate campus resource, such as the financial aid office.

If you become withdrawn, have thoughts about death or suicide, feel depressed for more than a few days, or have prolonged feelings of hopelessness, then see your doctor or a counselor at your student health center. No matter what the source of anxiety, help is always available. ✳

Have some FUN!

Contrary to popular belief, finals week does not have to be a drag.

In fact, if you have used techniques in this chapter, exam week can be fun. You will have done most of your studying long before finals arrive.

When you are well prepared for tests, you can even use fun as a technique to enhance your performance. The day before a final, go for a run or play a game of basketball. Take in a movie or a concert. A relaxed brain is a more effective brain. If you have studied for a test, your mind will continue to prepare itself even while you're at the movies.

Get plenty of rest, too. There's no need to cram until 3 a.m. when you have reviewed material throughout the term.

On the first day of finals, you can wake up refreshed, have a good breakfast, and walk into the exam room with a smile on your face. You can also leave with a smile on your face, knowing that you are going to have a fun week. It's your reward for studying regularly throughout the term.

exercise
20 things I like to do

One way to relieve tension is to mentally yell "Stop!" and substitute a pleasant daydream for the stressful thoughts and emotions you are experiencing.

To create a supply of pleasant images to recall during times of stress, conduct an 8-minute brainstorm about things you like to do. Your goal is to generate at least twenty ideas. Time yourself, and write as fast as you can in the space below.

When you have completed your list, study it. Pick out two activities that seem especially pleasant, and elaborate on them by creating a mind map in the space below. Write down all of the memories you have about that activity.

You can use these images to calm yourself in stressful situations.

TESTS

6

Discovery/Intention Statement

Notice your excuses and let them go

Do a timed, 4-minute brainstorm of all the reasons, rationalizations, justifications, and excuses you have used to avoid studying. Be creative. List your thoughts in the space below:

_____

_____

_____

_____

Now write a Discovery Statement about the list you just created.

I discovered that I . . .

_____

_____

_____

_____

_____

_____

_____

_____

Next, review your list, pick the excuse that you use the most, and circle it. In the space below, write an Intention Statement about what you will do to begin eliminating your favorite excuse. Make this Intention Statement one that you can keep, with a time line and a reward.

I intend to . . .

_____

_____

_____

_____

_____

Discovery Statement

Explore your feelings about tests

Complete the following sentences.

As exam time gets closer, one thing I notice that I do is . . .

_____

_____

When it comes to taking tests, I have trouble . . .

_____

_____

The night before a test, I usually feel . . .

_____

_____

The morning of a test, I usually feel . . .

_____

_____

During a test, I usually feel . . .

_____

_____

After a test, I usually feel . . .

_____

_____

When I learn a test score, I usually feel . . .

_____

_____

 An online version of this exercise is available.

6

TESTS

Getting ready for math tests

© Bloomimage/Corbis

MANY STUDENTS who could succeed in math shy away from the subject. Some had negative experiences in past courses. Others believe that math is only for gifted students.

At some level, however, math is open to all students. There's more to this subject than memorizing formulas and manipulating numbers. Imagination, creativity, and problem-solving skills are important, too.

Consider a three-part program for math success. Begin with strategies for overcoming math anxiety. Next, boost your study skills. Finally, let your knowledge shine during tests.

Overcome math anxiety

Many schools offer courses in overcoming math anxiety. Ask your advisor about resources on your campus. Also experiment with the following suggestions.

Connect math to life. Think of the benefits of mastering math courses. You'll have more options for choosing a major and a career. Math skills can also put you at ease in everyday situations—calculating the tip for a waiter, balancing your checkbook, working with a spreadsheet on a computer. If you follow baseball statistics, cook, do construction work, or snap pictures with a camera, you'll use math. And speaking the language of math can help you feel at home in a world driven by technology.

Pause occasionally to get an overview of the branch of math that you're studying. What's it all about? What basic problems is it designed to solve? How do people apply this knowledge in daily life? For example, many architects, engineers, and space scientists use calculus daily.

Take a first step. Math is cumulative. Concepts build upon each other in a certain order. If you struggled with algebra, you may have trouble with trigonometry or calculus.

To ensure that you have an adequate base of knowledge, tell the truth about your current level of knowledge and skill. Before you register for a math course, locate assigned texts for the prerequisite courses. If the material in those books seems new or difficult for you, see the instructor. Ask for suggestions on ways to prepare for the course.

Remember that it's OK to continue your study of math from your current level of ability, whatever that level might be.

Notice your pictures about math. Sometimes what keeps people from succeeding at math is their mental picture of mathematicians. They see a man dressed in a baggy plaid shirt and brown wingtip shoes. He's got a calculator on his belt and six pencils jammed in his shirt pocket.

These pictures are far from realistic. Succeeding in math won't turn you into a nerd. Actually, you'll be able to enjoy school more, and your friends will still like you.

Mental pictures about math can be funny, but they can have serious effects. If math is seen as a field for white males, then women and people of color are likely to get excluded. Promoting math success for all students helps to overcome racism and sexism.

Change your conversation about math. When students fear math, they often say negative things to themselves about their abilities in this subject. Many times this self-talk includes statements such as *I'll never be fast enough at solving math problems* or *I'm good with words, so I can't be good with numbers.*

Get such statements out in the open, and apply some emergency critical thinking. You'll find two self-defeating assumptions lurking there: *Everybody else is better at math and science than I am* and *Since I don't understand a math concept right now, I'll never understand it.* Both of these statements are illogical.

Replace negative beliefs with logical, realistic statements that affirm your ability to succeed in math: *Any confusion I feel now can be resolved. I learn math without comparing myself to others.* And *I ask whatever questions are needed to aid my understanding.*

Choose your response to stress. Math anxiety is seldom just "in your head." It can also register as sweaty palms, shallow breathing, tightness in the chest, or a mild headache. Instead of trying to ignore these sensations, just notice them without judgment. Over time, simple awareness decreases their power.

In addition, use stress management techniques. "Let Go of Test Anxiety" on page 188 offers a bundle of them.

No matter what you do, remember to breathe. You can relax in any moment just by making your breath slower and deeper. Practice doing this while you study math. It will come in handy at test time.

Boost study skills for math

Choose teachers with care. Whenever possible, find a math teacher whose approach to math matches your learning style. Talk with several teachers until you find one you enjoy.

Another option is to ask around. Maybe your academic advisor can recommend math teachers. Also ask classmates to name their favorite math teachers—and to explain the reasons for their choices.

In some cases, only one teacher will be offering the math course you need. The suggestions that follow can be used to learn from a teacher regardless of her teaching style.

Take math courses back to back. Approach math in the same way that you learn a foreign language. If you take a year off in between Spanish I and Spanish II, you won't gain much fluency. To master a language, you take courses back to back. It works the same way with math, which is a language in itself.

Form a study group. During the first week of each math course, organize a study group. Ask each member to bring five problems to group meetings, along with solutions. Also exchange contact information so that you can stay in touch via e-mail, phone, and text messaging.

Avoid short courses. Courses that you take during summer school or another shortened term are condensed. You might find yourself doing far more reading and homework each week than you do in longer courses. If you enjoy math, the extra intensity can provide a stimulus to learn. But if math is not your favorite subject, give yourself extra time. Enroll in courses spread out over more calendar days.

Participate in class. Success in math depends on your active involvement. Attend class regularly. Complete homework assignments *when they're due*—

not just before the test. If you're confused, get help right away from an instructor, tutor, or study group. Instructors' office hours, free on-campus tutoring, and classmates are just a few of the resources available to you. Also support class participation with time for homework. Make daily contact with math.

Prepare for lab sessions. Laboratory work is crucial to many science classes. To get the most out of these sessions, be prepared. Complete required reading before you enter the lab. Also gather the materials you'll need ahead of time.

Prepare for several types of tests. Math tests often involve lists of problems to solve. Ask your instructor about what type of tests to expect. Then prepare for the tests using strategies from this chapter.

Ask questions fearlessly. It's a cliché, and it's true: In math, there are no dumb questions. Ask whatever questions will aid your understanding. Keep a running list of them, and bring the list to class.

Make your text top priority. Math courses are often text driven. Class activities closely follow the book. This fact underscores the importance of completing your reading assignments. Master one concept before going on to the next, and stay current with your reading. Be willing to read slowly and reread sections as needed.

Read actively. To get the most out of your math texts, read with paper and pencil in hand. Work out examples. Copy diagrams, formulas, and equations. Use chapter summaries and introductory outlines to organize your learning.

From time to time, stop, close your book, and mentally reconstruct the steps in solving a problem. Before you memorize a formula, understand the basic concepts behind it.

Practice solving problems. To get ready for math tests, work *lots* of problems. Find out if practice problems or previous tests are on file in the library, in the math department, or with your math teacher.

Isolate the types of problems that you find the most difficult. Practice them more often. Be sure to get help with these kinds of problems *before* exhaustion or frustration sets in.

To prepare for tests, practice working problems fast. Time yourself. This activity is a great one for math study groups.

Approach problem solving with a three-step process, as shown in the chart on the following page. During each step, apply an appropriate strategy.

1: Prepare

- Read each problem two or three times, slowly and out loud whenever possible.
- Consider creating a chart with three columns labeled *What I already know, What I want to find out,* and *What connects the two.* The third column is the place to record a formula that can help you solve the problem.
- Determine which arithmetic operations (addition, subtraction, multiplication, division) or formulas you will use to solve the problem.
- See if you can estimate the answer before you compute it.

2: Compute

- Reduce the number of unknowns as much as you can. Consider creating a separate equation to solve each unknown.
- When solving equations, carry out the algebra as far as you can before plugging in the actual numbers.
- Cancel and combine. For example, if the same term appears in both dividend and divisor, they will cancel each other out.
- Remember that it's OK to make several attempts at solving the problem before you find an answer.

3: Check

- Plug your answer back into the original equation or problem and see if it works out correctly.
- Ask yourself if your answer seems likely when compared with your estimate. For example, if you're asked to apply a discount to an item, that item should cost less in your solution.
- Perform opposite operations. If a problem involves multiplication, check your work by division; add, then subtract; factor, then multiply; find the square root, then the square; differentiate, then integrate.
- Keep units of measurement clear. Say that you're calculating the velocity of an object. If you're measuring distance in meters and time in seconds, the final velocity should be in meters per second.

Use tests to show what you know

Practice test taking. Part of preparing for any math test is rehearsal. Instead of passively reading through your text or scanning class notes, do a practice test:

- Print out a set of practice problems, and set a timer for the same length of time as your testing period.
- Whenever possible, work practice problems in the same room where you will take the actual test.
- Use only the kinds of supporting materials—such as scratch paper or lists of formulas—that will be allowed during the test.
- As you work problems, use deep breathing or another technique to enter a more relaxed state.

Ask appropriate questions. If you don't understand a test item, ask for clarification. The worst that can happen is that an instructor or proctor will politely decline to answer your question.

Write legibly. Put yourself in the instructor's place. Imagine the prospect of grading stacks of illegible answer sheets. Make your answers easy to read. If you show your work, underline key sections and circle your answer.

Do your best. There are no secrets involved in getting ready for math tests. Master some stress management techniques, do your homework, get answers to your questions, and work sample problems. If you've done those things, you're ready for the test and deserve to do well. If you haven't done all those things, just do the best you can.

Remember that your personal best can vary from test to test, and even from day to day. Even if you don't answer all test questions correctly, you can demonstrate what you *do* know right now.

During the test, notice when solutions come easily. Savor the times when you feel relaxed and confident. If you ever feel math anxiety in the future, these are the times to remember.[8] ✳

Succeeding in science courses

Many of the strategies that help you prepare for math tests can also help you succeed in science courses. For example, forming small study groups can be a fun way to learn these subjects.

Relating science to your career interests and daily life is also important. People in many professions—from dentists to gardeners—rely on science to do their job. And even if you don't choose a science-driven career, you will live in a world that's driven by technology. Understanding how scientists observe, collect data, and arrive at conclusions can help you feel more at home in this world.

In addition, use some strategies that are unique to succeeding in science courses.

Prepare for Variety   Remember that the word *science* refers to a vast range of subjects—astronomy, biology, chemistry, physics, physiology, geology, ecology, geography, and more. Most of these subjects include math as one of their tools. Beyond that, however, are key differences.

You can take advantage of this variety. Choose courses in a science that matches your personal interests and comfort level for technical subjects.

Prepare forLab Sessions   Laboratory work is crucial to many science classes. To get the most out of these sessions, be prepared. Complete required reading before you enter the lab. Also gather the materials you'll need ahead of time.

 Find more strategies for succeeding in science online.

20 exercise
Use learning styles for math success

Review the articles about learning styles in Chapter 1: First Steps. Look for strategies that could promote your success in math. Modify any of the suggested strategies so that they work for you, or invent new techniques of your own.

If you're a visual learner, for example, you might color code your notes by writing key terms and formulas in red ink. If you like to learn by speaking and listening, consider reading key passages in your textbooks out loud. And if you're a kinesthetic learner, use "manipulatives"—such as magnetic boards with letters and numbers—when you study math.

Whatever you choose, commit to using at least one new strategy. In the space below, describe what you will do.

Celebrate mistakes

Most of us are haunted by the fear of failure. We dread the thought of making mistakes or being held responsible for a major breakdown. We shudder at the missteps that could cost us grades, careers, money, or even relationships.

IT'S POSSIBLE to take an entirely different attitude toward mistakes. Rather than fearing them, we could actually celebrate them. We could revel in our redundancies, frolic in our failures, and glory in our goof-ups. We could marvel at our mistakes and bark with loud laughter when we blow it.

A creative environment is one in which failure is not fatal. Businesses striving to be on the cutting edge of competition desperately seek innovative changes. They know that innovation requires risk taking, despite the chance of failure.

This is not idle talk. There are people who actually celebrate mistakes:[9]

- The Coca-Cola Company launched a number of beverages that bombed—including Choglit, OK Soda, Surge, and New Coke. But at the company's annual meeting in 2006, chair and chief executive officer E. Neville Isdell told investors to accept failures as a way to regenerate the company.

- Scott Anthony, director of a consulting firm named Innosight, coaches companies to fumble to success by failing early and cheaply as they develop new products.

- Thomas D. Kuczmarski, a Chicago-based consultant, suggests that companies hold "failure parties" to reward mistakes that lead to better products.

Note: Nothing in this article amounts to an argument in favor of *making* mistakes in the first place. Rather, the goal is to shine a light on mistakes so that we can examine them and fix them. Mistakes that are hidden cannot be corrected.

Eight solid reasons to celebrate mistakes

1 Celebration allows us to notice the mistake. Celebrating mistakes gets them out into the open. This activity is the opposite of covering up mistakes or blaming others for them. Hiding mistakes takes a lot of energy—energy that could be channeled into correcting errors.

PKruger/Shutterstock

2 Mistakes are valuable feedback. There's an old story about the manager of a major corporation who made a mistake that cost his company $100,000. He predicted that he would be fired. Instead, his boss said, "Fire you? I can't afford to do that. I just spent $100,000 training you." This story may be fictional, but it makes a point: Mistakes are part of the learning process. In fact, mistakes are often more interesting and more instructive than are successes.

3 Mistakes demonstrate that we're taking risks. People who play it safe make few mistakes. Making mistakes can be evidence that we're stretching to the limit of our abilities—growing, risking, and learning. Fear of making mistakes can paralyze us into inaction. Celebrating mistakes helps us move into gear and get things done.

4 Celebrating mistakes reminds us that it's OK to make them. When we celebrate a mistake, we remind ourselves that the person who made the mistake is not bad—just human. This is not a recommendation that you purposely set out to make mistakes. Mistakes are not an end in themselves. Rather, their value lies in what we learn from them. When we make a mistake, we can admit it and correct it.

5 Celebrating mistakes includes everyone. Celebrating mistakes reminds us that the exclusive club named the Perfect Performance Society has no members. All of us make mistakes. When we notice them, we can work together. Blaming others or the system prevents the cooperative efforts that can improve our circumstances.

6 Mistakes occur only when we aim at a clear goal. We can express concern about missing a target only if the target is there in the first place. If there's no target or purpose, there's no concern about missing it. Making a mistake affirms something of great value—that we have a plan.

7 Mistakes happen only when we're committed to making things work. Systems work when people are willing to be held accountable. Openly admitting mistakes promotes accountability. Imagine a school where there's no concern about quality and effectiveness. Teachers usually come to class late.

Residence halls are never cleaned, and scholarship checks are always late. The administration is in chronic debt, students seldom pay tuition on time, and no one cares. In this school, the word *mistake* would have little meaning. Mistakes become apparent only when people are committed to improvement. Mistakes go hand in hand with a commitment to quality.

8 Celebrating mistakes cuts the problem down to size. On top of the mistake itself, there is often a layer of regret, worry, and desperation about having made the mistake in the first place. Not only do people have a problem with the consequences of their mistake; they also have a problem with themselves for making a mistake in the first place. When we celebrate mistakes, we eliminate that layer of concern. When our anxiety about making a mistake is behind us, we can get down to the business of correcting the mistake. ✳

practicing critical thinking

Create a short multiple-choice test on a topic in a course you're taking right now. Ask several people from the class to take this exam.

Then, as a group, discuss the answer you chose for each question. Also talk about **why** and **how** you chose each answer. The purpose is to identify the strategies that different people use when answering a multiple-choice question—especially when they are unsure of the correct answer.

You might discover some test-taking strategies that you would use in the future. List those strategies in the space below.

Repeat this exercise by creating and discussing tests in other formats: short answer, true/false, and essay.

DETACH

This Power Process helps you release the powerful, natural student within you. It is especially useful whenever negative emotions are getting in your way.

Attachments are addictions. When we are attached to something, we think we cannot live without it, just as a drug addict feels he cannot live without drugs. We believe our well-being depends on maintaining our attachments.

We can be attached to just about anything: beliefs, emotions, people, roles, objects. The list is endless.

One person, for example, might be so attached to his car that he takes an accident as a personal attack. Pity the poor unfortunate who backs into this person's car. He might as well have backed into the owner himself.

Another person might be attached to her job. Her identity and sense of well-being depend on it. She could become suicidally depressed if she got fired.

When we are attached and things don't go our way, we can feel angry, sad, afraid, or confused.

Suppose you are attached to getting an A on your physics test. You feel as though your success in life depends on getting that A. As the clock ticks away, you work harder on the test, getting more stuck. That voice in your head gets louder: "I must get an A. I MUST get an A. I MUST GET AN A!"

Now is a time to detach. Practice observer consciousness. See if you can just *observe* what's going on, letting go of all your judgments. When you just observe, you reach a quiet state above and beyond your usual thoughts. This is a place where you can be aware of being aware. It's a tranquil spot, apart from your emotions. From here, you can observe yourself objectively, as if you were someone else. Pay attention to your thoughts and physical sensations. If you are confused and feeling stuck, tell yourself, "Here I am, confused and stuck." If your palms are sweaty and your stomach is one big knot, admit it. Practice perspective by putting current circumstances into a broader perspective. View your personal issues within the larger context of your community, nation, or even planet.

Practice breathing. Calm your mind and body with relaxation techniques.

Practice detaching before the big test. The key is to let go of automatic emotional reactions when you don't get what you want.

Caution: Giving up an *attachment* to being an A student does not mean giving up *being* an A student. Giving up an attachment to a job doesn't mean giving up the job. When you detach, you get to keep your values and goals. However, you know that you will be OK even if you fail to achieve a goal. You are more than your goals. You are more than your thoughts and feelings. These things come and go. Meanwhile, the part of you that can *just observe* is always there and always safe, no matter what happens.

Behind your attachments is a master student. Release that mastery. Detach.

 Learn more about using this Power Process online.

Katsuo Yamagishi/SPORT/Jupiter Images

Put it to Work

You can use strategies you learn in *Becoming a Master Student* to succeed at work. To discover how your test-taking skills can transfer to your career, reflect on the following case study.

During his senior year of high school, Chang Lee read about the favorable job market for medical assistants. He set a goal to enroll in a local community college, earn his associate of arts (A.A.) degree in medical assisting, work for a few years, and then return to school for a nursing degree.

This career plan was a logical one for Chang. His mother worked as a psychiatric nurse, and he'd always been interested in health care. He figured that his degree would equip him with marketable skills and a way to contribute to society.

Chang's choice was a good one for him. He excelled in classes. With his career goal in mind, he often asked himself, "How could I use this information to become a better medical assistant?"

During his second year of college, Chang landed an internship with a large medical clinic near campus. The clinic offered him a job after he graduated, and he accepted.

Chang enjoyed the day-to-day tasks of medical assisting. He helped doctors run medical tests and perform physical exams. In addition, he ordered lab work and updated medical records.

After 3 months on the job, Chang was on a first-name basis with many of the clinic's regular patients. No matter how busy the clinic's schedule, Chang made time for people. When they finished describing their symptoms, he frequently asked, "Is there anything else that's on your mind?" Then he listened without interrupting. Chang's ability to put people at ease made him popular with patients, who often asked specifically to see him.

The only part of his job that Chang dreaded was performance reviews, which took place twice during each year of employment. Even though he was respected by coworkers, Chang felt nervous whenever the topic of evaluating work performance came up. "It just reminds me too much of final exams during school," he said. "I like my job, and I try to do it well every day. Having a performance review just raises my anxiety level and doesn't really benefit me."

Red Chopsticks/Getty

Chang could apply several strategies recommended in this book. He demonstrated a knowledge of learning styles by tying the content of his courses to concrete experience ("How can I *use* this information?").

Describe some strategies that Chang could use to deal with anxiety related to performance reviews:

_____

_____

_____

_____

You can apply other techniques from this chapter to the workplace. Remember that you might face licensing exams, certification exams, and other tests in your career field. Also, joining study groups while you are in school can help you expand your learning styles and succeed in project teams. In doing so, you can use higher education to develop teamwork skills.

Quiz

chapter 6

- Put it to Work
- ◄ ◄ ◄ ◄ ◄
- Skills Snapshot
- Master Student Profile

Name _____   Date ____/____/____

1. According to the text, test scores measure your accomplishments in a course. True or False? Explain your answer.

   False. Test scores are a measure of how well we do on tests. (*Disarm tests*, p. 177)

2. When answering multiple-choice questions, it is better to read all of the possible answers before answering the question in your head. True or False? Explain your answer.

   False. Answer the question in your head before you look at any of the options. If you come up with an answer you are confident is right, then look for that answer in the list of choices. (*What to do during the test*, p. 183)

3. The presence of absolute qualifiers, such as *always* or *never*, generally indicates a false statement. True or False? Explain your answer.

   True. Qualifiers include words such as *all, most, sometimes,* or *rarely*. Absolute qualifiers are words like *always* or *never*—such extremes generally indicate a false statement. (*What to do during the test*, p. 183)

4. Briefly explain the differences between a daily review and a major review.

   Daily reviews include short preclass and postclass reviews of lecture notes and brief text reviews. Major reviews are usually done about a week before an exam and are much longer study periods, such as 2 to 5 hours per session. (*What to do before the test*, p. 178)

5. Define the term *study checklist*, and give three examples of what to include on such checklists.

   Study checklists are lists of everything one needs to review for a given test. They are similar to a to-do list or a study plan. List at least three of the following examples of what to include: a. Reading assignments listed by page or chapter number.   b. Dates of lecture notes.   c. Types of problems to be solved.   d. Other skills to master.   e. A brief description of each item to study.   (Answers will vary.)   (*What to do before the test*, p. 178)

6. Describe how using the Power Process: "Detach" differs from giving up.

   "Giving up" means to stop taking action toward a goal you have. In contrast, detachment involves accepting emotions and understanding the details of those emotions. Once you accept and fully experience your emotions, you can more easily move beyond them. Yet, the more you deny them, the more they persist. When we are detached, we perform better. (*Power Process: Detach*, p. 199)

7. Study groups can focus on which of the following?

   (a) Comparing and editing class notes.

   (b) Doing research to prepare for papers and presentations.

   (c) Finding and understanding key passages in assigned readings.

   (d) Creating and taking practice tests.

   (e) All of the above.

   (e) All of the above.   (*Cooperative learning: Studying in groups*, p. 181)

8. The text offers a three-step process for solving math problems. Name these steps, and list a strategy related to each one.

   First, Prepare.   a. Read each problem.   b. Create a three-column chart: What I know, what I want to find out, and what connects the two.   c. Determine which arithmetic operations or formulas you will use.   d. Estimate the answer before computing it.   Second, Compute.   a. Reduce the number of unknowns.   b. Carry out algebraic equations before using actual numbers.   c. Cancel and combine.   d. Remember that it's OK to make several attempts.   Third, Check.   a. Plug your answer in to see if it works out correctly.   b. Compare your answer to your estimate.   c. Perform opposite operations.   d. Keep units of measurement clear.   (Answers will vary.)   (*Getting ready for math tests*, p. 193)

9. Describe at least three techniques for dealing with the thoughts connected to test anxiety.

   Describe at least three of the following: a. Yell "Stop!"   b. Dispute your thoughts.   c. Praise yourself.   d. Consider the worst.   (*Let go of test anxiety*, p. 188)

10. Describe at least three techniques for dealing with the physical sensations or emotions connected to test anxiety.

   Describe at least three of the following: a. Breathe.   b. Describe sensations.   c. Scan your body.   d. Use guided imagery.   e. Exercise aerobically.   f. Find alternatives to chemicals.   g. Accept your emotions.   h. Practice detachment.   i. Make contact with the present moment.   (*Let go of test anxiety*, p. 188)

Skills Snapshot

Now that you've had some concrete experience with the strategies presented in this chapter, take a minute to reflect on your responses to the "Tests" section of the Discovery Wheel on page 27. Expand on those responses by completing the following sentences.

PREPARING FOR TESTS

When studying for a test, the first thing I usually do is to . . .

In addition, I . . .

TAKING TESTS

One strategy that helps me with objective tests (true/false and multiple choice) is . . .

One strategy that helps me with short-answer and essay tests is . . .

MANAGING TEST ANXIETY

On the day of a test, my level of confidence is generally . . .

If I feel stressed about a test, I respond by . . .

NEXT ACTION

I'll know that I've reached a new level of mastery with tests when . . .

To reach that level of mastery, the most important thing I can do next is to . . .

Master Student PROFILE

chapter 6

- Put it to Work
- Quiz
- Skills Snapshot

◄ ◄ ◄ ◄ ◄

Bert and John Jacobs

. . . are positive

© John Rich Photography

"Life is good" says the T-shirt, the hoodie, the baseball cap, and the onesie, to which one might reasonably respond in these days of doom and gloom: Really?

When Bert and John Jacobs launched their self-described optimistic apparel company out of a Boston apartment 15 years ago, we were smack in the middle of the go-go '90s and those three little words—part lifestyle, part mantra, part last-ditch effort by a pair of struggling T-shirt entrepreneurs to make rent money—seemed to mirror the national mood.

Today, not so much. Which oddly enough might make this something of a golden moment for the Life is good company.

"It is generally people who face the greatest adversity who embrace this message the most," says Bert Jacobs, whose company website features a section of "inspiring letters that fuel us all to keep spreading good vibes." The letters include testimonials from survivors of a grizzly bear attack, a young amputee, and a soldier stationed in Iraq. "People have a higher sense and appreciation of the simple things when they've been through something difficult. It's our job to see the glass half full."

Life is good doesn't have a demographic, the brothers like to say, but rather a psychographic: the optimists. And while one might imagine that their numbers are dwindling at roughly the same rate as their retirement accounts, some observers suggest otherwise. . . .

That's not to say Life is good is immune to the downturn, but in this company's case it's all relative. . . .

Until last year the company, whose annual sales top $100 million, had never had a year with less than 30 percent growth. In 2008 it grew only 10 percent, a slowdown that Jacobs notes (in apropos parlance) is "not exactly something you bum out about." Especially since the company hasn't spent a dime on advertising. . . .

Life is good was tested once before, not by the company's customers but its employees. In the days following 9/11 a number of managers approached Bert Jacobs and said that they weren't feeling right about spreading the company's signature tidings. Some had lost friends in the attacks. The news was all about anthrax and terrorism and tips on turning your basement into a bunker. Maybe life wasn't so good, and maybe this was not the message the American people wanted to hear.

But the company forged ahead, launching its first (wildly successful) nationwide fund-raiser. Jacobs calls its the pivotal moment in his business life.

"Our company has this fantastic positive energy and our brand is capable of bringing people together," he says. "We know there's trauma and violence and hardship. Life is good isn't the land of Willy Wonka. We're not throwing Frisbees all day. We live in the real world. But you can look around you and find good things any time."

Joan Anderson, "A Positive Outlook? Apparel company says bad times make its message more vital," *The Boston Globe,* March 17, 2009, http://www.boston.com/lifestyle/fashion/articles/2009/03/17/a_positive_outlook/?page=1.

Bert Jacobs (1965–) and John Jacobs (1968–), whose job titles are "chief executive optimist" and "chief creative optimist," started their business by selling T-shirts out of the back of a van

Learn more about Bert and John Jacobs at the Master Student Hall of Fame.

7 Thinking

Instructor Tools & Tips

Preview

Critical thinking is an essential skill for success in the classroom and in the workplace. Although critical thinking has already been introduced through the Master Student Map, Learning Styles Applications, chapter exercises, Journal Entries, and Practicing Critical Thinking exercises, Chapter 7 takes a more in-depth look at how students can practice the strategies presented in Chapters 1 through 6 using higher levels of thinking. At this point, your students will have taken their first tests in their other courses and will have become familiar with the learning strategies presented in the earlier chapters of *Becoming a Master Student*. Now you can help them take the next step toward thinking critically in higher education. The skills they learn in this chapter can be applied immediately to one decision that most of your students must make—choosing a major.

A primary objective of the student success course is to nurture the fundamental skill of critical thinking. From the beginning of this text, your students have been using the Master Student Map as a means of thinking critically.

When they ask *Why* they need this chapter, have them complete a chapter reconnaissance of *What* new materials are in this chapter. Together you can discuss *How* these new ideas will help them become better students. Remind your students that, with these techniques, they can open the door of possibility (*What if?*) to solve problems more creatively and make decisions with confidence.

Guest Speaker

Critical thinking is a priority for many workplace scenarios. A police officer, attorney, or law school professor would be a great guest speaker for this chapter. These guests can provide students with a dramatic reality check that will help you reinforce the importance of critical thinking in the real world. Ask your guests to prepare to talk for approximately 10 minutes on the importance of critical thinking in their jobs.

Another guest speaker idea is to invite a colleague from the department that offers critical and/or creative thinking courses, or logic courses, to talk about classes that students can take to expand on the concepts they learn in this chapter.

Lecture

Use the following excerpt from Vincent Ryan Ruggiero's *Instructor's Resource Manual to Accompany Becoming a Critical Thinker,* Fifth Edition, copyright 2006 (reprinted by permission) to help you prepare lectures for this chapter:

As a result of the historic neglect of thinking, many people harbor misconceptions about thinking instruction. The following misconceptions are the most damaging:

That thinking can't be taught. A related misconception is that thinking can be taught only to "gifted" people. The basis of both misconceptions is the pessimistic view that intelligence is fixed and therefore cannot be increased. Formal research and the experience of innumerable thinking-skills instructors disprove this notion.

That thinking is taught automatically in certain courses. Some people reason that English courses teach thinking automatically because they deal with the expression of ideas and because expression is intimately connected to thought. Others make similar claims for science because it deals with scientific method, history because it deals with the record of human thought and action, or psychology because it deals with behavior. Research has long made clear that no course content, by itself, can teach thinking; in other words, thinking skills are developed only when students receive direct instruction in them and have frequent opportunities for guided practice.

That thinking skills are necessarily subject-specific. According to this view, economists use one set of thinking skills, biologists another, and anthropologists yet another; no generic thinking skills exist. Yet close examination of what thinkers do in everyday situations reveals great similarity in their patterns of thought. Moreover, the patterns of error are also remarkably similar. That is why the list of logical fallacies has remained essentially the same since the time of the ancient Greeks. Though different academic disciplines may employ certain patterns of thinking more often and in slightly different ways than others, the fundamental fact is that the human mind created the academic disciplines and is neither defined nor limited by them.

That students learn to think by being exhorted or inspired. Exhortation and inspiration can surely motivate students to learn, but these approaches have little if any teaching force, particularly where skills are involved. No one ever learned to master driving a car or playing the piccolo or dribbling a basketball by hearing a lecture. Similarly, intellectual skills are learned by doing and by receiving guidance and encouragement from knowledgeable people.

Exercises/Activities

1. Have students practice problem solving and noticing assumptions by completing an in-class case study. Have them do this in groups of four. Individually, they read the short case study in class. Then they discuss it in their group. Facilitate a full-class discussion so that students can hear what other groups came up with. For examples and more information about using case studies in your classroom, go to the Instructor Web site.

2. Here's a suggestion from TeamUp Consultant Michelle Martin:

> As a warm-up exercise or icebreaker for this chapter, I put my students into groups and give each group an ordinary household object (such as a napkin, candle, coaster, cup). Then I have the groups brainstorm ways to use the objects in a different fashion than the most obviously intended purpose. This helps students embrace different ways of thinking, and stretches their minds to see things in new ways.

3. Select a current controversial topic and bring in background information from newspapers and magazines about the topic. Divide students into groups and have them work through the issue using the four-step process in the article "Becoming a critical thinker" (page 207). Have each group make a 90-second summary report to the class about their position on the issue and their justification for that position.

Conversation/Sharing

Begin with a discussion about the media's influence on our lives, using the think-pair-share discussion pattern. Ask the students to think critically about the topic and then have them free-write for a minute about their thoughts on the matter and about the learning style questions. They need to feel that they can jot down their own ideas without worrying about what you might expect or want them to say. Then have students work in pairs to share their ideas. Cycle through the learning style questions and then discuss the topic as a class. More detailed information about this exercise is available on the Instructor Web site.

Homework

Examining different points of view This is an in-class and homework alternative to the Conversation/Sharing activity above. Have students read a newspaper article about a current, controversial issue and then answer the first two learning style questions (*Why?* and *What?*) based on the information in the article. Then have them form groups of four to discuss their ideas. Eventually, someone will say that there is not enough information in the article to explore all of the various views on the topic. This provides an opportunity to ask students to continue this project outside the classroom, using campus resources (such as the library and the Internet) to fully answer the second and third (*What?* and *How?*) learning style questions. They should also work on the fourth question (*What if?*) at home. At the next class meeting, have the students discuss their findings and draw conclusions.

Selecting classes Too often, the hectic process of registering for classes results in a schedule based on convenience rather than critical decision making. Ask students to follow the systematic procedure described in the article "Gaining skill at decision making" (page 220) to decide which classes to take next semester—before the schedule of classes has been published.

Choosing a major Invite the director of your Career Center to be the guest speaker during a class period to talk about the center's services. Then have the students do a follow-up assignment that involves visiting the Career Center and exploring possible majors. Ask them to write a brief report on what they learned at the center about themselves and about potential careers and/or majors. Have students work through Exercise #22 and Journal Entry #20 to further explore their thoughts on selecting a major.

Here is a suggestion from an instructor:

> "Choosing your major is a major topic in my course. My background is in career counseling, and statistics back up the assumption that students make better grades and are less likely to drop out if they have selected a major and have a good handle on a future career. In my class (and at our school) students are required to complete an exploration paper. In my class we set academic and career goals (even if it's to select a major and career) [and] generate career ideas using a variety of methods (including interest/skills/personality inventories). Students select one career and major to research, complete an informational interview, and finally write a paper reviewing what they have done/researched and any conclusions they have drawn.
>
> **—Terry Carles, Valencia Community College**

Power Process: Find a Bigger Problem (page 229) Some students feel trapped by their personal situation or by learning problems to the point that their ability to succeed in school is seriously impaired. This article can help students recognize that there are other ways to view their problems. Students can look for a way to get involved in activities that take them outside their own circumstances. Each term organize a community service project with a local agency as a way to demonstrate that "finding a bigger problem" helps bring their own problems into perspective.

Evaluation

With the skills students have learned about essay test answers in Chapter 6, they are prepared to answer an essay question that requires critical thinking. Ask them to justify their answers to open-ended questions about common mistakes in logic, learning through inquiry, or thinking critically about information on the Internet.

Additional Digital Resources

Course Manual

The online *Course Manual* serves as an invaluable reference for those developing and teaching a College Success course with *Becoming a Master Student.* The *Course Manual* provides advice on general teaching issues such as preparing for classes, classroom management, grading, and communicating with students of various backgrounds, as well as specific strategies on getting the most out of various features in *Becoming a Master Student* such as the Discovery Wheel, Learning Styles Inventory, and book-specific Web sites.

Instructor Web Site

The updated Instructor Web site provides resources to help you plan and customize your course. Content specific to Chapter 7 includes:

▶ Lecture Ideas
  • Thriving in the Age of Information
▶ In-Class Exercises
  • Increasing Awareness
  • Circle Brainstorming
  • Speech Creativity Exercise
  • Who Says So? A Critical Thinking Lesson
▶ In-Text Quiz Answers
▶ Learning Styles Application
▶ Discussion Topics
▶ PowerPoint Slides
▶ Reflection Questions
▶ Assessment Questions
▶ Experiment with chapter strategies

The Instructor Web site also contains the following book-specific content:

▶ ExamView Test Bank
▶ Online Course Manual
▶ Articles from previous editions
▶ Master Student Profiles from previous editions
▶ Sample Syllabi

Student Web Site

To help your students gain a better understanding of the topics discussed in *Becoming a Master Student,* encourage your students to visit the Student Web site, which provides the following resources specific to Chapter 7:

www.cengage.com/success/bams13e

▶ Connect to Text content expands on specific topics marked with an icon within Chapter 7.

▶ Learning Style Applications invite students to cycle through the four styles of learning. In answering the four questions about decision making posted in this chapter's Learning Styles Application, students explore the different modes and apply their new knowledge.

▶ Practice Tests allow students to see how well they understand the themes of *Becoming a Master Student.*

▶ Interactive Concept Maps promote critical thinking by highlighting related ideas to show relationships between concepts.

▶ Video Skillbuilders bring to life techniques that will help you to excel in college and beyond. The following videos should give your students more information regarding topics covered in Chapter 7:
  • Critical Thinking: What Is Critical Thinking?
  • Critical Thinking in Action: Career Planning
  • Exploring Majors

▶ Remembering Cultural Differences presents readers with brief articles that touch on aspects of diversity in our rapidly changing world. For Chapter 7, the following article will prompt your students to look at contemporary issues in a new way:
  • Perceptions of Engagement

▶ Master Student Profiles provide additional information on the people covered in this book feature. For Chapter 7, students will find expanded coverage and links about:
  • Twyla Tharp

▶ Power Process Media contains video, PowerPoints, and audio files to take what your students have learned from the Power Processes in their book to the next level. For Chapter 7, students will find additional media on:
  • Find a bigger problem

Along with the chapter-specific content, a General Resources folder is available that contains Toolboxes geared toward specific student types (Community College, Adult Learner, Student Athlete), the Plagiarism Prevention Zone, and the Career Resource Center.

7 Thinking

Master Student Map

as you read, ask yourself

what if . . .

I could solve problems more creatively and make decisions in every area of life with more confidence?

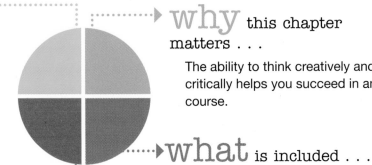

why this chapter matters . . .

The ability to think creatively and critically helps you succeed in any course.

how

you can use this chapter . . .

- Read, write, speak, and listen more effectively.
- Learn strategies to enhance your success in problem solving.
- Apply thinking skills to practical decisions, such as choosing a major.

what is included . . .

MASTER STUDENTS in *action*

I think critical thinking is when you're presented with a problem or a scenario and you don't just go with your gut reaction. You have to look at the problem from many different angles and weigh different options before you decide what is the right answer.

—LAUREN SWIDLER

Photo courtesy of Lauren Swidler

Critical thinking:
A survival skill

SOCIETY DEPENDS ON persuasion. Advertisers want us to spend money on their products. Political candidates want us to "buy" their stands on the issues. Teachers want us to agree that their classes are vital to our success. Parents want us to accept their values. Authors want us to read their books. Broadcasters want us to spend our time in front of the radio or television, consuming their programs and not those of the competition. The business of persuasion has an impact on all of us.

A typical American sees thousands of television commercials each year—and TV is just one medium of communication. Add to that the writers and speakers who enter our lives through radio shows, magazines, books, billboards, brochures, Internet sites, and fundraising appeals—all with a product, service, cause, or opinion for us to embrace.

This flood of appeals leaves us with hundreds of choices about what to buy, where to go, and who to be. It's easy to lose our heads in the crosscurrent of competing ideas—unless we develop skills in critical thinking. When we think critically, we can make choices with open eyes.

Uses of critical thinking. *Critical thinking informs reading, writing, speaking, and listening.* These elements are the basis of communication—a process that occupies most of our waking hours.

Critical thinking promotes social change. The institutions in any society—courts, governments, schools, businesses, nonprofit groups—are the products of cultural customs and trends. All social movements—from the American Revolution to the Civil Rights movement—came about through the work of engaged individuals who actively participated in their communities and questioned what was going on around them. As critical thinkers, we strive to understand and influence the institutions in our society.

Critical thinking uncovers bias and prejudice. Working through our preconceived notions is a first step toward communicating with people of other races, ethnic backgrounds, and cultures.

Critical thinking reveals long-term consequences. Crises occur when our thinking fails to keep pace with reality. An example is the world's ecological crisis, which arose when people polluted the earth,

journal entry 19

Discovery/Intention Statement

Choose to Create Value from This Chapter

Think back to a time when you felt unable to choose among several different solutions to a problem or several stands on a key issue in your life. In the space below, describe this experience.

I discovered that . . .

_____

_____

Now scan this chapter to find useful suggestions for decision making, problem solving, and critical thinking. Note below at least four techniques that look especially promising to you.

Strategy	Page number

Finally, declare your intention to explore these techniques in detail and apply them to a situation coming up during this term.

I intend to use critical thinking strategies to . . .

_____

_____

_____

_____

_____

7

THINKING

air, and water without considering the long-term consequences. Imagine how different our world would be if our leaders had thought like the first female chief of the Cherokees. Asked about the best advice her elders had given her, she replied, "Look forward. Turn what has been done into a better path. If you are a leader, think about the impact of your decision on seven generations into the future."

Critical thinking reveals nonsense. Novelist Ernest Hemingway once said that anyone who wants to be a great writer must have a built-in, shockproof "crap" detector.[1] That inelegant comment points to a basic truth: As critical thinkers, we are constantly on the lookout for thinking that's inaccurate, sloppy, or misleading.

Critical thinking is a skill that will never go out of style. At various times in human history, nonsense has been taken for the truth. For example, people have believed the following:

- Use of blood-sucking leeches is the only recommended treatment for disease.

- Illness results from an imbalance in the four vital fluids: blood, phlegm, water, and bile.

- Caucasians are inherently more intelligent than people of other races.

- Racial intermarriage will lead to genetically inferior children.

- Racial integration of the armed forces will lead to destruction of soldiers' morale.

- Women are incapable of voting intelligently.

- We will never invent anything smaller than a transistor. (That was before the computer chip.)

- Computer technology will usher in the age of the paperless office.

The critical thinkers of history arose to challenge short-sighted ideas such as those above. These courageous men and women pointed out that—metaphorically speaking—the emperor had no clothes.

Even in mathematics and the hard sciences, the greatest advances take place when people reexamine age-old beliefs. Scientists continually uncover things that contradict everyday certainties. For example, physics presents us with a world where solid objects are made of atoms spinning around in empty space—where matter and energy are two forms of the same substance. At a moment's notice, the world can deviate from the "laws of nature." That is because those "laws" exist in our heads—not in the world.

Critical thinking is a path to freedom from half-truths and deception. You have the right to question everything that you see, hear, and read. Acquiring this ability is a major goal of a liberal education.

Critical thinking as thorough thinking. For some people, the term *critical thinking* has negative connotations. If you prefer, use *thorough thinking* instead. Both terms point to the same activities: sorting out conflicting claims, weighing the evidence, letting go of personal biases, and arriving at reasonable conclusions. These activities add up to an ongoing conversation—a constant process, not a final product.

We live in a culture that values quick answers and certainty. These concepts are often at odds with effective thinking. Thorough thinking is the ability to examine and reexamine ideas that might seem obvious. This kind of thinking takes time and the willingness to say three subversive words: *I don't know.*

Thorough thinking is also the willingness to change our opinions as we continue to examine a problem. This calls for courage and detachment. Just ask anyone who has given up a cherished point of view in light of new evidence.

Thorough thinking is the basis for much of what you do in school—reading, writing, speaking, listening, note taking, test taking, problem solving, and other forms of decision making. Skilled students have strategies for accomplishing all these tasks. They distinguish between opinion and fact. They ask probing questions and make detailed observations. They uncover assumptions and define their terms. They make assertions carefully, basing them on sound logic and solid evidence. Almost everything that we call *knowledge* is a result of these activities. This means that critical thinking and learning are intimately linked.

One kind of thorough thinking—planning—has the power to lift the quality of our lives almost immediately. When you plan, you are the equal of the greatest sculptor, painter, or playwright. More than creating a work of art, you are designing your life. *Becoming a Master Student* invites you to participate in this form of thinking by choosing your major, planning your career, and setting long-term goals.

It's been said that human beings are rational creatures. Yet no one is born a thorough thinker. Critical thinking is a learned skill. Use the suggestions in this chapter to claim the thinking powers that are your birthright. The critical thinker is one aspect of the master student who lives inside you. ✳

Becoming a critical thinker

Critical thinking is a path to intellectual adventure. Although there are dozens of possible approaches, the process boils down to asking and answering questions.

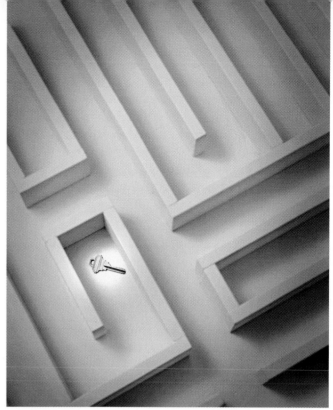
© Steve Cole/Getty

According to "Learning Styles: Discovering How You Learn" (p.32), there are four modes of learning based on four questions: *Why? What? How?* and *What if?* These questions are also powerful guides to critical thinking. Following are a variety of tools for answering those questions. For more handy implements, see *Becoming a Critical Thinker* by Vincent Ryan Ruggiero.

1 Why am I considering this issue? Critical thinking and personal passion go together. Begin critical thinking with a question that matters to you. Seek a rationale for your learning. Understand why it is important for you to think about a specific topic. You might want to arrive at a new conclusion, make a prediction, or solve a problem. By finding a personal connection with an issue, your interest in acquiring and retaining new information increases.

2 What are various points of view on this issue? Imagine Karl Marx, Cesar Chavez, and Warren Buffett assembled in one room to choose the most desirable economic system. Picture Mahatma Gandhi, Nelson Mandela, and General George Patton lecturing at a United Nations conference on conflict resolution. Visualize Al Gore, Bill Gates, and Kofi Annan in a discussion about distributing the world's resources equitably. When seeking out alternative points of view, let such scenarios unfold in your mind.

Dozens of viewpoints exist on every important issue—reducing crime, ending world hunger, preventing war, educating our children, and countless other concerns. In fact, few problems have any single, permanent solution. Each generation produces its own answers to critical questions, based on current conditions. Our search for answers is a conversation that spans centuries. On each question, many voices are waiting to be heard.

You can take advantage of this diversity by seeking out alternative views with an open mind. When talking to another person, be willing to walk away with a new point of view—even if it's the one you brought to the table, supported with new evidence.

Examining different points of view is an exercise in analysis, which you can do with the suggestions that follow.

Define terms. Imagine two people arguing about whether an employer should limit health care benefits to members of a family. To one person, the word *family* means a mother, father, and children; to the other person, the word *family* applies to any individuals who live together in a long-term, supportive relationship. Chances are, the debate will go nowhere until these two people realize that they're defining the same word in different ways.

Conflicts of opinion can often be resolved—or at least clarified—when we define our key terms up front. This is especially true with abstract, emotion-laden terms such as *freedom, peace, progress,* or *justice.* Blood has been shed over the meaning of those words. Define them with care.

Look for assertions. Speakers and writers present their key terms in a larger context called an *assertion.* An assertion is a complete sentence that directly answers a key question. For example, consider this sentence from the article "The Master Student" in Chapter 1: "Mastery means attaining a level of skill that goes beyond technique." This sentence is an assertion that answers an important question: How do we recognize mastery?

Look for at least three viewpoints. When asking questions, let go of the temptation to settle for just a single answer. Once you have come up with an answer, say to yourself, "Yes, that is one answer. Now what's another?" Using this approach can sustain honest inquiry, fuel creativity, and lead to conceptual breakthroughs. Be prepared: The world is complicated, and critical thinking is a complex business. Some of your answers might contradict others. Resist the temptation to have all of your ideas in a neat, orderly bundle.

Practice tolerance. One path to critical thinking is tolerance for a wide range of opinions. Taking a position on important issues is natural. When we stop having an opinion on things, we've probably stopped breathing.

Problems occur when we become so attached to our current viewpoints that we refuse to consider alternatives. Many ideas that are widely accepted in Western cultures—for example, civil liberties for people of color and the right of women to vote—were once considered dangerous. Viewpoints that seem outlandish today might become widely accepted a century, a decade, or even a year from now. Remembering this idea can help us practice tolerance for differing beliefs and, in doing so, make room for new ideas that might alter our lives.

3 How well is each point of view supported? Uncritical thinkers shield themselves from new information and ideas. As an alternative, you can follow the example of scientists, who constantly search for evidence that contradicts their theories. The following suggestions can help you do so.

Look for logic and evidence. The aim of using logic is to make statements that are clear, consistent, and coherent. As you examine a speaker's or writer's assertions, you might find errors in logic—assertions that contradict each other or assumptions that are unfounded.

Also assess the evidence used to support points of view. Evidence comes in several forms, including facts, expert testimony, and examples. To think critically about evidence, ask questions such as the following:

- Are all or most of the relevant facts presented?
- Are the facts consistent with one another?
- Are facts presented accurately—or in a misleading way?
- Are enough examples included to make a solid case for the viewpoint?
- Do the examples truly support the viewpoint?

Four more questions for critical thinking

The four main questions presented in "Becoming a Critical Thinker" offer one approach to this skill. In their classic *How to Read a Book*, Mortimer Adler and Charles Van Doren offer another approach. They list four different questions to sum up the whole task of thinking critically about a body of ideas:[2]

What is the writing or speech about as a whole? To answer this question, state the main topic in one sentence. Then list the related subtopics.

What is being said in detail, and how? List the main terms, assertions, and arguments. Also state what problems the writer or speaker is trying to solve.

Is it true? Examine the logic and evidence behind the ideas. Look for missing information, faulty information, and errors in reasoning. Also determine which problems were solved and which remain unsolved.

What of it? After answering the first three questions, prepare to change your thinking or behavior as a result of encountering new ideas.

- Are the examples typical? That is, could the author or speaker support the assertion with other examples that are similar?
- Is the expert credible—truly knowledgeable about the topic?

Consider the source. Look again at that article on the problems of manufacturing cars powered by natural gas. It might have been written by an executive from an oil company. Check out the expert who disputes the connection between smoking and lung cancer. That "expert" might be the president of a tobacco company.

This is not to say that we should dismiss the ideas of people who have a vested interest in stating their opinions. Rather, we should take their self-interest into account as we consider their ideas.

Understand before criticizing. Polished debaters are good at summing up their opponents' viewpoints—often better than the people who support those viewpoints themselves. Likewise, critical thinkers take the time to understand a statement of opinion before agreeing or disagreeing with it.

Effective understanding calls for listening without judgment. Enter another person's world by expressing her viewpoint in your own words. If you're conversing with that person, keep revising your summary until she agrees that you've stated her position accurately. If you're reading an article, write a short summary of it. Then scan the article again, checking to see if your synopsis is on target.

Watch for hot spots. Many people have mental "hot spots"—topics that provoke strong opinions and feelings. Examples are abortion, homosexuality, gun control, and the death penalty.

To become more skilled at examining various points of view, notice your own particular hot spots. Make a clear intention to accept your feelings about these topics and to continue using critical thinking techniques in relation to them.

One way to cool down our hot spots is to remember that we can change or even give up our current opinions without giving up ourselves. That's a key message behind the Power Processes: "Ideas Are Tools" and "Detach." These articles remind us that human beings are much more than the sum of their current opinions.

Be willing to be uncertain. Some of the most profound thinkers have practiced the art of thinking by using a magic sentence: "I'm not sure yet."

Those are words that many people do not like to hear. Our society rewards quick answers and quotable sound bites. We're under considerable pressure to utter the truth in 10 seconds or less.

In such a society, it is courageous and unusual to take the time to pause, to look, to examine, to be thoughtful, to consider many points of view—and to be unsure. When a society adopts half-truths in a blind rush for certainty, a willingness to embrace uncertainty can move us forward.

4 **What if I could combine various points of view or create a new one?** The search for truth is like painting a barn door by tossing an open can of paint at it. Few people who throw at the door miss it entirely. Yet no one can cover the whole door in a single toss.

People who express a viewpoint are seeking the truth. And no reasonable person claims to cover the whole barn door—to understand the whole truth about anything. Instead, each viewpoint can be seen as one approach among many possible alternatives. If you don't think that any one opinion is complete, combine different perspectives on the issue. Experiment with the following strategies.

Create a critical thinking "spreadsheet." When you consult authorities with different stands on an issue, you might feel confused about how to sort, evaluate, and combine their points of view. To overcome confusion, create a critical thinking "spreadsheet." List the authorities (and yourself) across the top of a page and key questions down the left side. Then indicate each authority's answer to each question, along with your own answers.

For example, the spreadsheet below clarifies different points of view on the issue of whether to outlaw boxing.

You could state your own viewpoint by combining your answers to the questions in the spreadsheet: "I favor legalized boxing. Although boxing poses dangers, so do other sports. And like other sports, the risk of injury can be reduced when boxers get proper training."

Write about it. Thoughts can move at blinding speed. Writing slows down that process. Gaps in logic that slip by us in thought or speech are often exposed when we commit the same ideas to paper. Writing down our thoughts allows us to compare, contrast, and combine points of view more clearly—and therefore to think more thoroughly.

Accept your changing perspectives. Researcher William Perry found that students in higher education move through stages of intellectual development.[3] In earlier stages, students tend to think there is only one correct viewpoint on each issue, and they look to their instructors to reveal that truth. Later, students acknowledge a variety of opinions on issues and construct their own viewpoints.

	Medical doctor	**Former boxer**	**Sports journalist**	**Me**
Is boxing a sport?	No	Yes	Yes	Yes
Is boxing dangerous?	Yes	Yes	Yes	Yes
Is boxing more dangerous than other sports?	Yes	No	Yes	No
Can the risk of injury be overcome by proper training?	No	No	No	Yes

Source: Vincent Ryan Ruggiero, *Becoming a Critical Thinker*, Sixth Edition. Copyright © 2009 by Cengage Learning. Reprinted with permission.

Monitor changes in your thinking processes as you combine viewpoints. Distinguish between opinions that you accept from authorities and opinions that are based on your own use of logic and your search for evidence. Also look for opinions that result from objective procedures (such as using the *Why? What? How?* and *What if?* questions in this article) and personal sources (using intuition or "gut feelings").

Remember that the process of becoming a critical thinker will take you through a variety of stages. Give yourself time, and celebrate your growing mastery. ✳

 Find more strategies for becoming a critical thinker online.

Attitudes of a critical thinker

The American Philosophical Association invited a panel of forty-six scholars from the United States and Canada to come up with answers to the following two questions: "What is college-level critical thinking?" and "What leads us to conclude that a person is an effective critical thinker?"[4] After 2 years of work, this panel concluded that critical thinkers share the attitudes summarized in the following chart.

Attitude	Sample statement
Truth seeking	"Let's follow this idea and see where it leads, even if we feel uncomfortable with what we find out."
Open minded	"I have a point of view on this subject, and I'm anxious to hear yours as well."
Analytical	"Taking a stand on the issue commits me to take some new action."
Systematic	"The speaker made several interesting points, and I'd like to hear some more evidence to support each one."
Self-confident	"After reading the book for the first time, I was confused. I'll be able to understand it after studying the book some more."
Inquisitive	"When I first saw that painting, I wanted to know what was going on in the artist's life when she painted it."
Mature	"I'll wait until I gather some more facts before reaching a conclusion on this issue."

Finding "aha!"— creativity fuels critical thinking

THIS CHAPTER OFFERS you a chance to practice two types of critical thinking: convergent thinking and divergent thinking.

Convergent thinking involves a narrowing-down process. Out of all the possible viewpoints on an issue or alternative solutions to a problem, you choose the one that is the most reasonable or that provides the most logical basis for action.

Some people see convergent thinking and critical thinking as the same thing. However, convergent thinking is just one part of critical thinking. Before you choose among viewpoints, generate as many of them as possible. Open up alternatives, and consider all of your options. Define problems in different ways. Keep asking questions and looking for answers. This opening-up process is called *divergent thinking* or *creative thinking*.

Creative thinking provides the basis for convergent thinking. One path toward having good ideas is to have *lots* of ideas. Then you can pick and choose from among them, combining and refining them as you see fit.

Choose when to think creatively. The key is to make conscious choices about what kind of thinking to do in any given moment. Generally speaking, creative thinking is more appropriate in the early stages of planning and problem solving. Feel free to dwell in this domain for a while. If you narrow down your options too soon, you run the risk of missing an exciting solution or of neglecting a novel viewpoint.

Creative thinking and convergent thinking take place in a continuous cycle. After you've used convergent thinking to narrow down your options, you can return to creative thinking at any time to generate new ones.

Cultivate "aha!" Central to creative thinking is something called the "aha!" experience. Nineteenth-century poet Emily Dickinson described aha! this way: "If I feel physically as if the top of my head were taken off, I know that is poetry." Aha! is the burst of creative energy heralded by the arrival of a new, original idea. It is the sudden emergence of an unfamiliar pattern, a previously undetected relationship, or an unusual combination of familiar elements.

Aha! It can be inspired by anything from playing a new riff on a guitar to figuring out why your car's fuel pump doesn't work. A nurse might notice a patient's symptom that everyone else missed. That's an aha! An accountant might discover a tax break for a client. That's an aha! A teacher might devise a way to reach a difficult student. Aha!

Follow through. The flip side of aha! is following through. Thinking is both fun and work. It is both effortless and uncomfortable. It's the result of luck and persistence. It involves planning and action, convergent and creative thinking.

The necessary skills for finding aha! include the ability to spot assumptions, weigh evidence, separate fact from opinion, organize thoughts, and avoid errors in logic. All these skills involve demanding work. Just as often, they can be energizing and fun. ✳

Tangram

A tangram is an ancient Chinese puzzle game that stimulates the play instinct so critical to creative thinking. The cat figure here was created by rearranging seven sections of a square. Hundreds of images can be devised in this manner. Playing with tangrams allows us to see relationships we didn't notice before.

The rules of the game are simple: Use these seven pieces to create something that wasn't there before. Be sure to use all seven. You might start by mixing up the pieces and seeing whether you can put them back together to form a square. Make your own tangram by cutting pieces like these out of poster board. When you come up with a pattern you like, trace around the outside edges of it, and see if a friend can discover how you did it.

Ways to create ideas

ANYONE CAN THINK creatively. Use the following techniques to generate ideas about anything—whether you're studying math problems, remodeling a house, or writing a best seller.

Conduct a brainstorm

Brainstorming is a technique for creating plans, finding solutions, and discovering new ideas. When you are stuck on a problem, brainstorming can break the logjam. For example, if you run out of money 2 days before payday every week, you can brainstorm ways to make your money last longer. You can brainstorm ways to pay for your education. You can brainstorm ways to find a job.

The overall purpose of brainstorming is to generate as many solutions as possible. Sometimes the craziest, most outlandish ideas, while unworkable in themselves, can lead to new ways to solve problems. Use the following steps to try out the brainstorming process:

- *Focus on a single problem or issue.* State your focus as a question. Open-ended questions that start with the words *what, how, who, where*, and *when* often make effective focusing questions.

- *Relax.* Creativity is enhanced by a state of relaxed alertness. If you are tense or anxious, use relaxation techniques such as those described in "Let Go of Test Anxiety" in Chapter 6.

- *Set a quota or goal for the number of solutions you want to generate.* Goals give your subconscious mind something to aim for.

- *Set a time limit.* Use a clock to time it to the minute. Digital sports watches with built-in stopwatches work well. Experiment with various lengths of time. Both short and long brainstorms can be powerful.

- *Allow all answers.* Brainstorming is based on attitudes of permissiveness and patience. Accept every idea. If

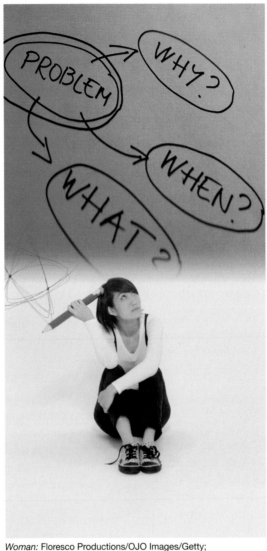

Woman: Floresco Productions/OJO Images/Getty; *words:* Shutterstock; collage by Walter Kopec

it pops into your head, put it down on paper. Quantity, not quality, is the goal. Avoid making judgments and evaluations during the brainstorming session. If you get stuck, think of an outlandish idea, and write it down. One crazy idea can unleash a flood of other, more workable solutions.

- *Brainstorm with others.* Group brainstorming is a powerful technique. Group brainstorms take on lives of their own. Assign one member of the group to write down solutions. Feed off the ideas of others, and remember to avoid evaluating or judging anyone's ideas during the brainstorm.

After your brainstorming session, evaluate the results. Toss out any truly nutty ideas, but not before you give them a chance.

Focus and let go

Focusing and letting go are alternating parts of the same process. Intense focus taps the resources of your conscious mind. Letting go gives your subconscious mind time to work. When you focus for intense periods and then let go for a while, the conscious and subconscious parts of your brain work in harmony.

Focusing attention means being in the here and now. To focus your attention on a project, notice when you pay attention and when your mind starts to wander. And involve all of your senses. For example, if you are having difficulty writing a paper at a computer, practice focusing by listening to the sounds as you type. Notice the feel of the keys as you strike them. When you know the sights, sounds, and sensations you associate with being truly in focus, you'll be able to repeat the experience and return to your paper more easily.

Be willing to recognize conflict, tension, and discomfort in yourself. Notice them and fully accept

7

THINKING

them rather than fight against them. Look for the specific thoughts and body sensations that make up the discomfort. Allow them to come fully into your awareness, and then let them pass.

You might not be focused all of the time. Periods of inspiration might last only seconds. Be gentle with yourself when you notice that your concentration has lapsed. In fact, that might be a time to let go. *Letting go* means not forcing yourself to be creative. Practice focusing for short periods at first, and then give yourself a break. Take a nap when you are tired. Thomas Edison took frequent naps. Then the lightbulb clicked on.

Cultivate creative serendipity

The word *serendipity* was coined by the English author Horace Walpole from the title of an ancient Persian fairy tale, "The Three Princes of Serendip." The princes had a knack for making lucky discoveries. Serendipity is that knack, and it involves more than luck. It is the ability to see something valuable that you weren't looking for.

History is full of people who make serendipitous discoveries. Country doctor Edward Jenner noticed "by accident" that milkmaids seldom got smallpox. The result was his discovery that mild cases of cowpox immunized them. Penicillin was also discovered "by accident." Scottish scientist Alexander Fleming was growing bacteria in a laboratory petri dish. A spore of *Penicillium notatum,* a kind of mold, blew in the window and landed in the dish, killing the bacteria. Fleming isolated the active ingredient. A few years later, during World War II, it saved thousands of lives. Had Fleming not been alert to the possibility, the discovery might never have been made.

You can train yourself in the art of serendipity. Keep your eyes open. You might find a solution to an accounting problem in a Saturday morning cartoon. You might discover a topic for your term paper at the corner convenience store. Multiply your contacts with the world. Resolve to meet new people. Join a study or discussion group. Read. Go to plays, concerts, art shows, lectures, and movies. Watch television programs you normally wouldn't watch.

Also expect discoveries. One secret for success is being prepared to recognize "luck" when you see it.

Keep idea files

We all have ideas. People who treat their ideas with care are often labeled "creative." They not only recognize ideas but also record them and follow up on them.

One way to keep track of ideas is to write them down on 3×5 cards. Invent your own categories, and number the cards so you can cross-reference them. For example, if you have an idea about making a

Creative ways for groups to get "unstuck"

Sometimes creative thinking dies in committee. People are afraid to disagree with a forceful leader and instead keep their mouths shut. Or a longstanding group ignores new members with new ideas. The result can be "group think," where no one questions the prevailing opinion. To stimulate creative thinking in groups, try these strategies:

Put your opinion on hold. If you're leading a meeting, ask other people to speak up first. Then look for the potential value in *any* idea. Avoid nonverbal language that signals a negative reaction, such as frowning or rolling your eyes.

Rotate group leadership. Ask group members to take turns. This strategy can work well in groups where people have a wide range of opinions.

Divide larger groups into several teams. People might be more willing to share their ideas in a smaller group.

Assign a devil's advocate. Give one person free permission to poke holes in any proposal.

Invite a guest expert. A fresh perspective from someone outside the group can spark an aha!

Set up a suggestion box. Let people submit ideas anonymously, in writing.

new kind of bookshelf, you might file a card under "Remodeling." A second card might also be filed under "Marketable Ideas." On the first card, you can write down your ideas, and on the second, you can write "See card #321—Remodeling."

Include in your files powerful quotations, random insights, notes on your reading, and useful ideas that you encounter in class. Collect jokes, too.

Keep a journal. Journals don't have to be exclusively about your own thoughts and feelings. You can record observations about the world around you, conversations with friends, important or offbeat ideas—anything.

To fuel your creativity, read voraciously, including newspapers and magazines. Keep a clip file of interesting articles. Explore beyond mainstream journalism. Hundreds of low-circulation specialty magazines and online news journals cover almost any subject you can imagine. Keep letter-size file folders of important correspondence, magazine and news articles, and other material. You can also create idea files on a computer using word-processing, outlining, or database software.

Safeguard your ideas, even if you're pressed for time. Jotting down four or five words is enough to capture the essence of an idea. You can write down one quotation in a minute or two. And if you carry 3x5 cards in a pocket or purse, you can record ideas while standing in line or sitting in a waiting room.

Review your files regularly. Some amusing thought that came to you in November might be the perfect solution to a problem in March.

Collect and play with data

Look from all sides at the data you collect. Switch your attention from one aspect to another. Examine each fact, and avoid getting stuck on one particular part of a problem. Turn a problem upside down by picking a solution first and then working backward. Ask other people to look at the data. Solicit opinions.

Living with the problem invites a solution. Write down data, possible solutions, or a formulation of the problem on 3×5 cards, and carry them with you. Look at them before you go to bed at night. Review them when you are waiting for the bus. Make them part of your life, and think about them frequently.

Look for the obvious solutions or the obvious "truths" about the problem—then toss them out. Ask yourself, "Well, I know X is true, but if X were *not* true, what would happen?" Or ask the reverse: "If that *were* true, what would follow next?"

Put unrelated facts next to each other and invent a relationship between them, even if it seems absurd at first. In *The Act of Creation,* novelist Arthur Koestler says that finding a context in which to combine opposites is the essence of creativity.

Make imaginary pictures with the data. Condense it. Categorize it. Put it in chronological order. Put it in alphabetical order. Put it in random order. Order it from most to least complex. Reverse all of those orders. Look for opposites.[5]

It has been said that there are no new ideas—only new ways to combine old ideas. Creativity is the ability to discover those new combinations.

Create while you sleep

A part of our mind works as we sleep. You've experienced this fact directly if you've ever fallen asleep with a problem on your mind and awakened the next morning with a solution. For some of us, the solution appears in a dream or just before we fall asleep or wake up.

You can experiment with this process. Ask yourself a question as you fall asleep. Keep pencil and paper or a recorder near your bed. The moment you wake up, begin writing or speaking, and see if an answer to your question emerges.

Many of us have awakened from a dream with a great idea, only to fall asleep again and lose it forever. To capture your ideas, keep a notebook by your bed at all times. Put the notebook where you can find it easily.

There is a story about how Benjamin Franklin used this suggestion. Late in the evenings, as he was becoming drowsy, he would sit in his rocking chair with a rock in his right hand and a metal bucket on the floor beneath the rock. The moment he fell asleep, the rock would fall from his grip into the bottom of the bucket, making a loud noise that awakened him. Having placed a pen and paper nearby, he immediately wrote down what he was thinking. Experience taught him that his thoughts at these moments were often insightful and creative.

Refine ideas and follow through

Many of us ignore the part of the creative process that involves refining ideas and following through. How many great moneymaking schemes have we had that we never pursued? How many good ideas have we had for short stories that we never wrote? How many times have we said to ourselves, "You know, what they ought to do is attach two handles to one of those things, paint it orange, and sell it to police departments. They'd make a fortune." And we never realize that we are "they."

Genius resides in the follow-through—the application of perspiration to inspiration. One powerful tool you can use to follow through is the Discovery and Intention Journal Entry system. First write down your idea in a Discovery Statement, and then write what you intend to do about it in an Intention Statement. You also can explore the writing techniques discussed in Chapter 8: Communicating as a guide for refining your ideas.

Another way to refine an idea is to simplify it. And if that doesn't work, mess it up. Make it more complex.

Finally, keep a separate file in your ideas folder for your own inspirations. Return to it regularly to see if there is anything you can use. Today's defunct term paper idea could be next year's A in speech class.

Create success strategies

Use creative thinking techniques to go beyond the pages of this book and create your own ways to succeed in school. Read other books on success. Interview successful people. Reflect on any of your current behaviors that help you do well in school. Change any habits that fail to serve you.

If you have created a study group with people from one of your classes, set aside time to talk about the ways to succeed in any class. Challenge each other to practice your powers of intervention. Test any new strategies you create and report to the group on how well they're working for you.

Trust the process

Learn to trust the creative process—even when no answers are in sight. We are often reluctant to look at problems if no immediate solution is at hand. Trust that a solution will show up. Frustration and a feeling of being stuck are often signals that a solution is imminent.

Sometimes solutions break through in a giant AHA! More often they come in a series of little aha!s. Be aware of what your aha!s look, feel, and sound like. This understanding sets the stage for even more flights of creative thinking. ✳

Create on your feet

A popular trend in executive offices is the stand-up desk—a raised working surface at which you stand rather than sit.

Standing has advantages over sitting for long periods. You can stay more alert and creative when you're on your feet. One theory is that our problem-solving ability improves when we stand, due to increased heart rate and blood flow to the brain.

Standing can ease lower-back pain, too. Sitting for too long aggravates the spine and its supporting muscles.

Standing while working is a technique with tradition. If you search the Web for stand-up desks, you'll find models based on desks used by Thomas Jefferson, Winston Churchill, and writer Virginia Woolf. Consider setting your desk up on blocks or putting a box on top of your desk so that you can stand while writing, preparing speeches, or studying. Discover how long you can stand comfortably while working, and whether this approach works for you.

Photo courtesy of David Ellis

21 exercise
Explore emotional reactions

Each of us has certain "hot spots"—issues that trigger strong emotional reactions. These topics may include abortion, gay and lesbian rights, capital punishment, and funding for welfare programs. There are many other examples, varying from person to person. Examine your own hot spots on a separate sheet of paper by writing a word or short phrase summarizing each issue about which you feel very strongly. Then describe what you typically say or do when each issue comes up in conversation.

After you have completed your list, think about what you can do to become a more effective thinker when you encounter one of these issues. For example, you could breathe deeply and count to five before you offer your own point of view. Or you might preface your opinion with an objective statement such as "There are many valid points of view on this issue. Here's the way I see it, and I'm open to your ideas."

THINKING

7

Don't fool yourself: Fifteen common mistakes in logic

LOGIC IS A branch of philosophy that seeks to distinguish between effective and ineffective reasoning. Students of logic look for valid steps in an *argument,* or a series of statements. The opening statements of the argument are the premises, and the final statement is the conclusion.

Effective reasoning is not just an idle pastime for unemployed philosophers. Learning to think logically offers many benefits: When you think logically, you take your reading, writing, speaking, and listening skills to a higher level. You avoid costly mistakes in decision making. You can join discussions and debates with more confidence, cast your election votes with a clear head, and become a better-informed citizen. People have even improved their mental health by learning to dispute illogical beliefs.[6]

Over the last 2,500 years, specialists have listed some classic land mines in the field of logic—common mistakes in thinking that are called *fallacies.* The study of fallacies could fill a year-long course. Following are fifteen examples to get you started. Knowing about them before you string together a bunch of assertions can help you avoid getting fooled.

1 Jumping to conclusions. Jumping to conclusions is the only exercise that some lazy thinkers get. This fallacy involves drawing conclusions without sufficient evidence. Take the bank officer who hears about a student's failing to pay back an education loan. After that, the officer turns down all loan applications from students. This person has formed a rigid opinion on the basis of hearsay. Jumping to conclusions—also called *hasty generalization*—is at work here.

Rich Reed/National Geographic/Getty

Following are more examples of this fallacy:

- When I went to Mexico for spring break, I felt sick the whole time. Mexican food makes people sick.

- Google's mission is to "organize the world's information." Their employees must be on a real power trip.

- During a recession, more people go to the movies. People just want to sit in the dark and forget about their money problems.

Each item in the above list includes two statements, and the second statement does not necessarily follow from the first. More evidence is needed to make any possible connection.

2 Attacking the person. The mistake of attacking the person is common at election time. An example is the candidate who claims that her opponent has failed to attend church regularly during the campaign. People who indulge in personal attacks are attempting an intellectual sleight of hand to divert our attention away from the truly relevant issues.

3 Appealing to authority. A professional athlete endorses a brand of breakfast cereal. A famous musician features a soft drink company's product in a rock video. The promotional brochure for an advertising agency lists all of the large companies that have used its services.

In each case, the people involved are trying to win your confidence—and your dollars—by citing authorities. The underlying assumption is usually this: *Famous people and organizations buy our product. Therefore, you should buy it too.* Or: *You should accept this idea merely because someone who's well known says it's true.*

THINKING

7

Appealing to authority is usually a substitute for producing real evidence. It invites sloppy thinking. When our only evidence for a viewpoint is an appeal to authority, it's time to think more thoroughly.

4 Pointing to a false cause. The fact that one event follows another does not necessarily mean that the two events have a cause-and-effect relationship. All we can actually say is that the events might be correlated. For example, as children's vocabularies improve, they can get more cavities. This does not mean that cavities are the result of an improved vocabulary. Instead, the increase in cavities is due to other factors, such as physical maturation and changes in diet or personal care.

5 Thinking in all-or-nothing terms. Consider these statements: *Doctors are greedy. You can't trust politicians. Students these days are in school just to get high-paying jobs; they lack idealism. Homeless people don't want to work.*

These opinions imply the word *all*. They gloss over individual differences, claiming that all members of a group are exactly alike. They also ignore key facts—for instance, that some doctors volunteer their time at free medical clinics and that many homeless people are children who are too young to work. All-or-nothing thinking is one of the most common errors in logic.

6 Basing arguments on emotion. The politician who ends every campaign speech with flag waving and slides of his mother eating apple pie is staking his future on appeals to emotion. So is the candidate who paints a grim scenario of the disaster and ruination that will transpire unless she is elected. Get past the fluff and histrionics to see if you can uncover any worthwhile ideas.

7 Using a faulty analogy. An *analogy* states a similarity between two things or events. Some arguments rest on analogies that hide significant differences. On June 25, 1987, the Associated Press reported an example: U.S. representative Tom DeLay opposed a bill to ban chlordane, a pesticide that causes cancer in laboratory animals. Supporting this bill, he argued, would be like banning cars because they kill people. DeLay's analogy was faulty. Banning automobiles would have a far greater impact on society than banning a single pesticide, especially if safer pesticides are available.

8 Creating a straw man. The name of this fallacy comes from the scarecrows traditionally placed in gardens to ward off birds. A scarecrow works because it looks like a man. Likewise, a person can attack ideas that *sound like* his opponent's ideas but

are actually absurd. For example, some legislators attacked the Equal Rights Amendment by describing it as a measure to abolish separate bathrooms for men and women. In fact, supporters of this amendment proposed no such thing.

9 Begging the question. Speakers and writers beg the question when their colorful language glosses over an idea that is unclear or unproven. Consider this statement: *Support the American tradition of individual liberty and oppose mandatory seat belt laws!* Anyone who makes such a statement "begs" (fails to answer) a key question: Are laws that require drivers to use seat belts actually a violation of individual liberty?

10 Confusing fact and opinion. Facts are statements verified by direct observation or compelling evidence that creates widespread agreement. In recent years, some politicians argued for tax cuts on the grounds that the American economy needed to create more jobs. However, it's not a fact that tax cuts automatically create more jobs. This statement is almost impossible to verify by direct observation, and there's actually evidence against it.

11 Creating a red herring. When hunters want to throw a dog off a trail, they can drag a smoked red herring (or some other food with a strong odor) over the ground in the opposite direction. This distracts the dog, who is fooled into following a false trail. Likewise, people can send our thinking on false trails by raising irrelevant issues. Case in point: In 2008, some people who opposed the presidential campaign by U.S. senator Barack Obama emphasized his middle name: Hussein. This was an irrelevant attempt to link the senator to Saddam Hussein, the dictator and former ruler of Iraq.

12 Appealing to tradition. Arguments based on an appeal to tradition take a classic form: *Our current beliefs and behaviors have a long history; therefore, they are correct.* This argument has been used to justify the divine right of kings, feudalism, witch burnings, slavery, child labor, and a host of other traditions that are now rejected in most parts of the world. Appeals to tradition ignore the fact that unsound ideas can survive for centuries before human beings realize that they are being fooled.

13 Appealing to "the people." Consider this statement: *Millions of people use Wikipedia as their main source of factual information. Wikipedia must be the best reference work in the world.* This is a perfect example of the *ad populum* fallacy. (In Latin, that phrase means "to the people.") The essential error is assuming that popularity, quality, and accuracy are the same.

Appealing to "the people" taps into our universal desire to be liked and to associate with a group of people who agree with us. No wonder this fallacy is also called "jumping on the bandwagon." Following are more examples:

- *Internet Explorer is the most widely used Web browser. It must be the best one.*

- *Dan Brown's books, including* The Da Vinci Code, *did not sell as well as the Harry Potter books by J. K. Rowling. I guess we know who's the better writer.*

- *Same-sex marriages must be immoral. Most Americans think so.*

You can refute such statements by offering a single example: Many Americans once believed that slavery was moral and that people of color should not be allowed to vote. That did not make either belief right.

14 Distracting from the real issue. The fallacy of distracting from the real issue occurs when a speaker or writer makes an irrelevant statement and then draws a conclusion based on that statement. For example: *The most recent recession was caused by people who borrowed too much money and bankers who loaned too much money. Therefore, you should never borrow money to go to school.* This argument ignores the fact that a primary source of the recession was loans to finance housing—not loans to finance education. Two separate topics are mentioned, and statements about one do not necessarily apply to the other.

15 Sliding a slippery slope. The fallacy of sliding a slippery slope implies that if one undesired event occurs, then other, far more serious events will follow: *If we restrict our right to own guns,* *then all of our rights will soon be taken away. If people keep downloading music for free, pretty soon they'll demand to get everything online for free. I notice that more independent bookstores are closing; it's just a matter of time before people stop reading.* When people slide a slippery slope, they assume that different types of events have a single cause. They also assume that a particular cause will operate indefinitely. In reality, the world is far more complex. Grand predictions about the future often prove to be wrong.

Finding fallacies before they become a fatal flaw (bonus suggestions). Human beings have a long history of fooling themselves. This article presents just a partial list of logical fallacies. You can prevent them and many more by following a few suggestions:

- When outlining a paper or speech, create a two-column chart. In one column, make a list of your main points. In the other column, summarize the evidence for each point. If you have no evidence for a point, a logical fallacy may be lurking in the wings.

- Go back to some of your recent writing—assigned papers, essay tests, journal entries, and anything else you can find. Look for examples of logical fallacies. Note any patterns, such as repetition of one particular fallacy. Write an Intention Statement about avoiding this fallacy.

- Be careful when making claims about people who disagree with you. One attitude of a critical thinker is treating everyone with fairness and respect. ✳

 Practice hunting for fallacies.

THINKING

7

Uncovering assumptions

Consider the following argument:

- Orcas (killer whales) mate for life.
- Orcas travel in family groups.
- Science has revealed that orcas are intelligent.
- Therefore, orcas should be saved from extinction.

One idea—or assumption—underlies this line of thought: *Any animal that displays significant human characteristics deserves special protection.* Whether or not you agree with this argument, consider for a moment the process of making assumptions. Assumptions are assertions that guide our thinking and behavior.

Assumptions are invisible and powerful

Often assumptions are unconscious. People can remain unaware of their most basic and far-reaching assumptions—the very ideas that shape their lives.

Spotting assumptions can be tricky because they are usually unstated and offered without evidence. And scores of assumptions can be held at the same time. Those assumptions might even contradict each other, resulting in muddled thinking and confused behavior. This makes uncovering assumptions a feat worthy of the greatest detective.

Assumptions drive our attitudes and actions

Letting assumptions remain in our subconscious can erect barriers to our success. Take the person who says, "I don't worry about saving money for the future. I think life is meant to be enjoyed today—not later." This statement rests on at least two assumptions: *saving money is not enjoyable* and *we can enjoy ourselves only when we're spending money.*

It would be no surprise to find out that this person runs out of money near the end of each month and depends on cash advances from high-interest credit cards. He is shielding himself from some ideas that could erase his debt: Saving money can be a source of satisfaction, and many enjoyable activities cost nothing.

The stakes in uncovering assumptions are high. Prejudice thrives on the beliefs that certain people are inferior or dangerous due to their skin color, ethnic background, or sexual orientation. Those beliefs have led to flawed assumptions such as *mixing the blood of the races will lead to genetically inferior offspring* and *racial integration of the armed forces will lead to the destruction of morale.*

When we remain ignorant of our assumptions, we also make it easier for people with hidden agendas to do our thinking for us. Demagogues and unethical advertisers know that unchallenged assumptions are potent tools for influencing our attitudes and behavior.

Assumptions can create conflict

Heated conflict and hard feelings often result when people argue on the level of opinions—forgetting that the real conflict lies at the level of their assumptions.

An example is the question about whether the government should fund public works programs that create jobs during a recession. People who advocate such programs might assume that creating such jobs is an appropriate task for the federal government. In contrast, people who argue against such programs might assume that the government has no business interfering with the free workings of the economy. There's little hope of resolving this conflict of opinion unless we deal with something more basic: our assumptions about the proper role of government.

Look for assumptions

You can follow a three-step method for testing the validity of any viewpoint. First, look for the assumptions—the assertions implied by that viewpoint. Second, write down these assumptions. Third, see if you can find any exceptions to the assumptions. This technique helps detect many errors in logic. ✳

THINKING

7

Gaining skill at decision making

WE MAKE DECISIONS all the time, whether we realize it or not. Even avoiding decisions is a form of decision making. The student who puts off studying for a test until the last minute might really be saying, "I've decided this course is not important" or "I've decided not to give this course much time." In order to escape such a fate, decide right now to experiment with the following suggestions.

Recognize decisions. Decisions are more than wishes or desires. There's a world of difference between "I wish I could be a better student" and "I will take more powerful notes, read with greater retention, and review my class notes daily." Decisions are specific and lead to focused action. When we decide, we narrow down. We give up actions that are inconsistent with our decision. Deciding to eat fruit for dessert instead of ice cream rules out the next trip to the ice cream store.

Establish priorities. Some decisions are trivial. No matter what the outcome, your life is not affected much. Other decisions can shape your circumstances for years. Devote more time and energy to the decisions with big outcomes.

Base your decisions on a life plan. The benefit of having long-term goals for our lives is that they provide a basis for many of our daily decisions. Being certain about what we want to accomplish this year and this month makes today's choices more clear.

Balance learning styles when making decisions. To make decisions more effectively, use all four modes of learning explained in Chapter 1: First Steps. The key is to balance reflection with action, and thinking with experience. First, take the time to think creatively, and generate many options. Then think critically about the possible consequences of each option before choosing one. Remember, however, that thinking is no substitute for experience. Act on your chosen option, and notice what happens. If you're not getting the results that you want, then quickly return to creative thinking to invent new options.

Choose an overall strategy. Every time you make a decision, you choose a strategy—even when you're not aware of it. Effective decision makers can articulate and choose from among several strategies. For example:

- *Find all of the available options, and choose one deliberately.* Save this strategy for times when you have a relatively small number of options, each of which leads to noticeably different results.

- *Find all of the available options, and choose one randomly.* This strategy can be risky. Save it for times when your options are basically similar and fairness is the main issue.

- *Limit the options, and then choose.* When deciding which search engine to use on the World Wide Web, visit many sites and then narrow the list down to two or three that you choose.

Use time as an ally. Sometimes we face dilemmas—situations in which any course of action leads to undesirable consequences. In such cases, consider putting a decision on hold. Wait it out. Do nothing until the circumstances change, making one alternative clearly preferable to another.

Use intuition. Some decisions seem to make themselves. A solution pops into our mind, and we gain newfound clarity. Using intuition is not the same as forgetting about the decision or refusing to make it. Intuitive decisions usually arrive after we've gathered the relevant facts and faced a problem for some time.

Evaluate your decision. Hindsight is a source of insight. After you act on a decision, observe the consequences over time. Reflect on how well your decision worked and what you might have done differently.

Think *choices*. This final suggestion involves some creative thinking. Consider that the word *decide* derives from the same root as *suicide* and *homicide*. In the spirit of those words, a decision forever "kills" all other options. That's kind of heavy. Instead, use the word *choice,* and see if it frees up your thinking. When you *choose,* you express a preference for one option over others. However, those options remain live possibilities for the future. Choose for today, knowing that as you gain more wisdom and experience, you can choose again. ✳

THINKING

7

Four ways to solve problems

THINK OF PROBLEM solving as a process with four Ps: Define the *problem,* generate *possibilities,* create a *plan,* and *perform* your plan.

1 Define the problem. To define a problem effectively, understand what a problem is: a mismatch between what you want and what you have. Problem solving is all about reducing the gap between these two factors.

Start with what you have. Tell the truth about what's present in your life right now, without shame or blame. For example: "I often get sleepy while reading my physics assignments, and after closing the book I cannot remember what I just read."

Next, describe in detail what you want. Go for specifics: "I want to remain alert as I read about physics. I also want to accurately summarize each chapter I read."

Remember that when we define a problem in limiting ways, our solutions merely generate new problems. As Albert Einstein said, "The world we have made is a result of the level of thinking we have done thus far. We cannot solve problems at the same level at which we created them."[7]

This idea has many applications for success in school. An example is the student who struggles with note taking. The problem, she thinks, is that her notes are too sketchy. The logical solution, she decides, is to take more notes, and her new goal is to write down almost everything her instructors say. No matter how fast and furiously she writes, she cannot capture all of the instructors' comments.

Consider what happens when this student defines the problem in a new way. After more thought, she decides that her dilemma is not the *quantity* of her notes but their *quality.* She adopts a new format for taking notes, dividing her notepaper into two columns. In the right-hand column, she writes down only the main points of each lecture. And in the left-hand column, she notes two or three supporting details for each point.

Over time, this student makes the joyous discovery that there are usually just three or four core ideas to remember from each lecture. She originally thought the solution was to take more notes. What really worked was taking notes in a new way.

2 Generate possibilities. Now put on your creative thinking hat. Open up. Brainstorm as many possible solutions to the problem as you can. At this stage, quantity counts. As you generate possibilities, gather relevant facts. For example, when you're faced with a dilemma about what courses to take next term, get information on class times, locations, and instructors. If you haven't decided which summer job offer to accept, gather information on salary, benefits, and working conditions.

3 Create a plan. After rereading your problem definition and list of possible solutions, choose the solution that seems most workable. Think about specific actions that will reduce the gap between what you have and what you want. Visualize the steps you will take to make this solution a reality, and arrange them in chronological order. To make your plan even more powerful, put it in writing.

4 Perform your plan. This step gets you off your chair and out into the world. Now you actually *do* what you have planned. Ultimately, your skill in solving problems lies in how well you perform your plan. Through the quality of your actions, you become the architect of your own success.

Note that the four Ps of this problem-solving process closely parallel the four key questions listed in the article "Becoming a Critical Thinker":

Define the **problem**	**What** is the problem?
Generate **possibilities**	**What if** there are several possible solutions?
Create a **plan**	**How** would this possible solution work?
Perform your plan	**Why** is one solution more workable than another?

When facing problems, experiment with these four Ps, and remember that the order of steps is not absolute. Also remember that any solution has the potential to create new problems. If that happens, cycle through the four Ps of problem solving again. ✻

 Find more strategies for problem solving online.

Choosing your major

Man: © Masterfile Royalty Free; *boy with remote:* © Ron Chapple/Corbis; *plane:* © Corbis; collage by Walter Kopec

ONE DECISION that troubles many students in higher education is the choice of an academic major. Here is an opportunity to apply your skills at critical thinking, decision making, and problem solving. The following four suggestions can guide you through the process.

1 Discover options

Follow the fun. Perhaps you look forward to attending one of your classes and even like completing the assignments. This is a clue to your choice of major.

See if you can find lasting patterns in the subjects and extracurricular activities that you've enjoyed over the years. Look for a major that allows you to continue and expand on these experiences.

Also sit down with a stack of 3×5 cards and brainstorm answers to the following questions:

- What do you enjoy doing most with your unscheduled time?
- Imagine that you're at a party and having a fascinating conversation. What is this conversation about?
- What Web sites do you frequently visit or have bookmarked in a Web browser?
- What kind of problems do you enjoy solving—those that involve people? Products? Ideas?
- What interests are revealed by your choices of reading material, television shows, and other entertainment?
- What would an ideal day look like to you? Describe where you'd be, who would be with you, and what activities you'd do. Do any of these visions suggest a possible major?

Questions like these are not frivolous. They can uncover a "fun factor" that energizes you to finish the work of completing a major.

Consider your abilities. In choosing a major, ability counts as much as interest. Einstein enjoyed playing the violin, but his love of music didn't override his choice of a career in science. In addition to considering what you enjoy, think about times and places when you excelled. List the courses that you aced, the work assignments that you mastered, and the hobbies that led to rewards or recognition. Let your choice of a major reflect a discovery of your passions *and* potentials.

Use formal techniques for self-discovery. Writing is a path to the kind of self-knowledge involved in choosing your major. Start with the exercises and Journal Entries in this book. Review what you've written, looking for statements about your interests and abilities.

Also consider questionnaires and inventories that are designed to correlate your interests with specific majors. Examples include the Strong Interest Inventory and the Self-Directed Search. Your academic advisor or someone in your school's job placement office can give you more details about these and related inventories. For some fun, take several of them and meet with an advisor to interpret the results.

Remember that there is no questionnaire, inventory, test, or formula for choosing a major or career. Likewise, there is no expert who can make these choices for you. Inventories can help you gain self-knowledge, and other people can offer valuable perspectives. However, what you *do* with all this input is entirely up to you.

Link to long-term goals. Your choice of a major can fall into place once you determine what you want in life. Before you choose a major, back up to a bigger picture. List your core values, such as contributing to society, achieving financial security and professional recognition, enjoying good health, or making time for fun. Also write down specific goals that you want to accomplish 5 years, 10 years, or even 50 years from today.

Many students find that the prospect of getting what they want in life justifies all of the time, money, and day-to-day effort invested in going to school. Having a major gives you a powerful incentive for attending classes, taking part in discussions, reading textbooks, writing papers, and completing other assignments. When you see a clear connection between finishing school and creating the life of your dreams, the daily tasks of higher education become charged with meaning.

Studies indicate that the biggest factor associated with completing a degree in higher education is commitment to personal goals.[8] A choice of major reflects those goals.

Ask other people. Key people in your life might have valuable suggestions about your choice of major. Ask for their ideas, and listen with an open mind. At the same time, distance yourself from any pressure to choose a major or career that fails to interest you. If you make a choice based solely on the expectations of other people, you could end up with a major or even a career you don't enjoy.

Gather information. Check your school's catalog or Web site for a list of available majors. Here is a gold mine of information. Take a quick glance, and highlight all the majors that interest you. Then talk to students who have declared them. Also read descriptions of courses required for these majors. Chat with instructors who teach courses in these areas, and ask for copies of their class syllabi. Go the bookstore and browse required texts.

Based on all this information, write a list of prospective majors. Discuss them with an academic advisor and someone at your school's career-planning center.

Invent a major. When choosing a major, you might not need to limit yourself to those listed in your school catalog. Many schools now have flexible programs that allow for independent study. Through such programs you might be able to combine two existing majors or invent an entirely new one of your own.

Consider a complementary minor. You can add flexibility to your academic program by choosing a minor to complement or contrast with your major. The student who wants to be a minister could opt for a minor in English; all of those courses in composition can help in writing sermons. Or the student with a major in psychology might choose a minor in business administration, with the idea of managing a counseling service some day. An effective choice of a minor can expand your skills and career options.

Think critically about the link between your major and your career. Your career goals might have a significant impact on your choice of major. For an overview of career planning and an immediate chance to put ideas down on paper, see Chapter 12: What's Next?

You might be able to pursue a rewarding career by choosing among *several* different majors. Even students planning to apply for law school or medical school have flexibility in their choice of majors. In addition, after graduation, many people are employed in jobs with little relationship to their major. And you might choose a career in the future that is unrelated to any currently available major.

Remember that many students who choose an "impractical" major go on to prosper in their careers. According to the National Committee for Latin and Greek, people who majored in classical civilizations and literature range from Ted Turner (founder of CNN) and James Baker (former U.S. secretary of state) to Toni Morrison (winner of the Noble Prize for Literature) and J. K. Rowling (author of the Harry Potter novels).[9]

Also remember that your required courses for general education can benefit you no matter what major or career you choose. For instance, English composition can help chemistry majors who will publish technical articles. Marketing courses will come in handy for editors who want to create a budget for promoting a new book.

2 Make a trial choice

At many schools, declaring a major offers some benefits. For example, you might get priority when registering for certain classes and qualify for special scholarships or grants.

Don't delay such benefits. Even if you feel undecided, you probably have a good idea about what major you will choose. One way to verify this is to conduct a simple experiment. Pretend that you have to choose a major today. Based on the options for a major that you've already discovered, write down the first three ideas that come to mind. Review the list for a few minutes, and then just choose one. This is one way to choose a trial major. Exercise #21, "Make a Trial Choice of Major" suggests another way to narrow down your choices.

Hold on to your list, however. It reflects your current intuition, or "gut feelings," and it may come in handy during the next step. Step 3 might confirm your trial choice of major—or return you to one of the other prospective majors in your original list.

3 Evaluate your trial choice

When you've made a trial choice of major, take on the role of a scientist. Treat your choice as a hypothesis, and then design a series of experiments to evaluate and test it. For example:

- Schedule office meetings with instructors who teach courses in the major. Ask about required course work and career options in the field.

- Discuss your trial choice with an academic advisor or career counselor.

- Enroll in a course related to your possible major. Remember that introductory courses might not give you a realistic picture of the workloads involved in advanced courses. Also, you might not be able to register for certain courses until you've actually declared a related major.

- Find a volunteer experience, internship, part-time job, or service learning experience related to the major.

- Interview students who have declared the same major. Ask them in detail about their experiences and suggestions for success.

- Interview someone who works in a field related to the major.

- Think about whether you can complete your major given the amount of time and money that you plan to invest in higher education.

- Consider whether declaring this major would require a transfer to another program or even another school.

If your "experiments" confirm your choice of major, celebrate that fact. If they result in choosing a new major, celebrate that outcome as well.

Also remember that higher education represents a safe place to test your choice of major—and to change your mind. As you sort through your options, help is always available from administrators, instructors, advisors, and peers.

4 Choose again

Keep your choice of a major in perspective. There is probably no single "correct" choice. Your unique collection of skills is likely to provide the basis for majoring in several fields.

exercise 22
Make a trial choice of major

This exercise presents another method for choosing a major. Look at your school's catalog for a list of majors, and cross out all of the majors that you already know are not right for you. You will probably eliminate well over half the list.

Now scan the remaining majors. Next to the ones that definitely interest you, write "yes." Next to majors that you're willing to consider and are still unsure about, write "maybe."

Focus on your "yes" choices. See if you can narrow them down to three majors. List those here.

_____

_____

_____

Finally, write an asterisk next to the major that interests you most right now. This is your trial choice of major.

Odds are that you'll change your major at least once—and that you'll change careers several times during your life. One benefit of higher education is mobility. You gain the general skills and knowledge that can help you move into a new major or career field at any time.

Viewing a major as a one-time choice that determines your entire future can raise your stress levels. Instead, look at choosing a major as the start of a continuing path that involves discovery, choice, and passionate action.

www Find more strategies for choosing a major online.

THINKING

7

Asking questions—learning through inquiry

Thinking is born of questions. Questions open up options that might otherwise remain unexplored. Questions wake up people and lead them to investigate more closely issues and assumptions that had previously gone unchallenged. Questions promote curiosity, create new distinctions, and multiply possibilities. Besides, teachers love them.

THERE'S A SAYING: "Tell me, and I forget; show me, and I remember; involve me, and I understand." Asking questions is a way to stay involved. One of the main reasons you are in school is to ask questions—a process called *inquiry-based learning*. This process takes you beyond memorizing facts and passing tests. Asking questions turns you into a lifelong learner.

Asking questions is also a way to improve relationships with friends and coworkers. When you ask a question, you offer a huge gift to people—an opportunity for them to speak their brilliance and for you to listen to their answers.

Students often say, "I don't know what to ask." If you have ever been at a loss for what to ask, here are some ways to construct powerful questions about any subject you study in school, or about any area of your life that you choose to examine.

Let your pen start moving. Sometimes you can access a deeper level of knowledge by taking out your pen, putting it on a piece of paper, and writing down questions—even before you know what to write. Don't think. Just watch the paper, and notice what appears. The results might be surprising.

Ask about what's missing. Another way to invent useful questions is to notice what's missing from your life and then ask how to supply it. For example, if you want to take better notes, you can write, "What's missing is skill in note taking. How can I gain more skill in taking notes?" If you always feel rushed, you can write, "What's missing is time. How do I create enough time in my day to actually do the things that I say I want to do?"

Pretend to be someone else. Another way to invent questions is first to think of someone you greatly respect. Then pretend you're that person, and ask the questions you think she would ask.

Begin a general question; then brainstorm endings. By starting with a general question and then brainstorming a long list of endings, you can invent a question that you've never asked before. For example:

What can I do when . . . ? What can I do when an instructor calls on me in class and I have no idea what to say? What can I do when a teacher doesn't show up for class on time? What can I do when I feel overwhelmed with assignments?

How can I . . . ? How can I get just the kind of courses that I want? How can I expand my career options? How can I become much more effective as a student, starting today?

When do I . . . ? When do I decide on a major? When do I transfer to another school? When do I meet with an instructor to discuss an upcoming term paper?

Ask questions to promote social change. If your friends are laughing at racist jokes, you have a right to ask why. If you're legally registered to vote and denied access to a voting booth, you have a right to ask for an explanation. Asking questions can advance justice.

Ask what else you want to know. Many times you can quickly generate questions by simply asking yourself, "What else do I want to know?" Ask this question immediately after you read a paragraph in a book or listen to someone speak.

Start from the assumption that you are brilliant, and begin asking questions that can help you unlock your brilliance. ✳

practicing critical thinking

The art of asking questions is just as important to critical thinking as answering them. One eye-opening way to create questions is to write something you're sure of and simply put a question mark after it. (You might need to rephrase the question for grammatical sense.) The question you create can lead to others.

For example, someone might say, "I would never take a philosophy course." This person can write, "I would never take a philosophy course?" That question suggests others: "In what ways would taking a philosophy course serve my success in school?" "Could taking a philosophy course help me become a better writer?"

In the space below, write three statements that you accept with certainty. Then rephrase each statement as a question.

Statement #1:

_____

_____

_____

_____

_____

Question #1:

_____

_____

_____

_____

_____

Statement #2:

_____

_____

_____

_____

Question #2:

_____

_____

_____

_____

Statement #3:

_____

_____

_____

_____

Question #3:

_____

_____

_____

_____

Think critically about information on the Internet

SOURCES OF INFORMATION on the Internet range from the reputable (such as the Library of Congress) to the flamboyant (such as the *National Enquirer*). This fact underscores the need for thinking critically about everything you see online. Taking a few simple precautions when you surf the Net can keep you from crashing onto the rocky shore of misinformation.

Look for overall quality. Examine the features of the Web site in general. Notice the effectiveness of the text and visuals as a whole. Also note how well the site is organized and whether you can navigate the site's features with ease. Look for the date that crucial information was posted, and determine how often the site is updated.

Next, take a more detailed look at the site's content. Examine several of the site's pages, and look for consistency of facts, quality of information, and competency with grammar and spelling. Are the links within the site easy to navigate?

Also evaluate the site's links to related Web pages. Look for links to pages of reputable organizations. Click on a few of those links. If they lead you to dead ends, it might indicate that the site you're evaluating is not updated often—a clue that it's not a reliable source for late-breaking information.

Look at the source. Think about the credibility of the person or organization that posts the Web site. Look for a list of author credentials and publications.

Notice evidence of bias or special interest. Perhaps the site's sponsoring organization wants you to buy a service, a product, or a point of view. This fact might suggest that the information on the site is not objective, and therefore questionable.

The domain in the uniform resource locator (URL) for a Web site can give you clues about sources of information and possible bias. For example, distinguish among information from a for-profit commercial enterprise (URL ending in .com); a nonprofit organization (.org); a government agency (.gov); and a school, college, or university (.edu).

Note: Wikis (peer-edited sites) such as Wikipedia do not employ editors to screen out errors or scrutinize questionable material before publication. Do not use these sites when researching a paper or presentation. Also, be cautious about citing blogs, which often are not reviewed for accuracy.

Look for documentation. When you encounter an assertion on a Web page or some other Internet resource, note the types and quality of the evidence offered. Look for credible examples, quotations from authorities in the field, documented statistics, or summaries of scientific studies. ✳

mastering technology

RETHINKING E-MAIL

When facing an inbox stuffed with hundreds of messages, some people choose to declare "e-mail bankruptcy." They send out a message to everyone on their contact list: "I'm going to delete all my e-mails. Please resend anything important. Sorry." That's one way to tame the e-mail tiger, but there are other options.

Change the Way You Use e-mail Spend a few minutes every day doing e-mail triage. If a message requires some kind of response from you, send it to a folder titled *action*. Check this folder often. If no response is required but you might refer to the message again, send it to a folder named *archives*. Trash all other messages.

In addition, be stingy. Send messages only when absolutely necessary, and keep them short. Reply to messages only when your response adds something essential to the conversation. Unsubscribe from mailing lists, and get the latest news with an online "feed reader" such as Google Reader or Bloglines.

Explore Alternatives To e-mail Use instant messaging, text messaging, and microblogging (for example, using Twitter) to send quick updates. Post more detailed messages via a page on Facebook, LinkedIn, or other social networking site. Consider a blog as a way to exchange comments with site visitors.

Use Your Voice, Feet, and Face Instead of sending an e-mail to a neighbor or coworker, pick up the phone. Or get away from the computer screen and make a personal visit. Your face can brighten someone's day more than impersonal lines on a computer screen.

THINKING

7

exercise 23

Translating goals into action

Goal setting is an exercise in decision making and problem solving. Choose one long-range goal, such as a personal project or a social change you'd like to help bring about. Examples include learning to scuba dive, eating a more healthful diet, studying to be an astronaut, improving health care for chronically ill children, inventing an energy-saving technology, increasing the effectiveness of American schools, and becoming a better parent. Write your long-range goal here.

_____

_____

_____

_____

_____

_____

Next, ask yourself, "What specific actions are needed in the short term to meet my long-range goal?" List those actions, focusing on those you could complete in less than 1 hour or could start in the next 24 hours.

_____

_____

_____

_____

_____

_____

_____

_____

_____

_____

journal entry 20

Discovery/Intention Statement

Reflect on Choosing a Major

Reflect for a moment on your experience with Exercise #22: "Make a Trial Choice of Major." If you had already chosen a major, did doing the exercise confirm that choice? Did you uncover any new or surprising possibilities for declaring a major?

I discovered that I . . .

_____

_____

_____

_____

_____

_____

_____

Now consider the major that is your current top choice. Think of publications you expect to find, resources you plan to investigate, and people you intend to consult in order to gather more information about this major.

I intend to . . .

_____

_____

_____

_____

_____

_____

Plan to repeat this Journal Entry and the preceding exercise several times. You might find yourself researching several majors and changing your mind. That's fine. The aim is to start thinking about your major now.

Find a Bigger Problem

It is impossible to live a life that's free of problems. Besides, problems serve a purpose. They provide opportunities to participate in life. Problems stimulate us and pull us forward.

Seen from this perspective, our goal becomes not to eliminate problems, but to find problems that are worthy of us. Worthy problems are those that draw on our talents, move us toward our purpose, and increase our skills. Solving these problems offers the greatest benefits for others and ourselves. Viewed in this way, bigger problems give more meaning to our lives.

Problems expand to fill whatever space is available. Suppose that your only problem for today is to write a follow-up letter to a job interview. You could spend the entire day thinking about what you're going to say, writing the letter, finding a stamp, going to the post office—and then thinking about all of the things you forgot to say.

Now suppose that you get a phone call with an urgent message: A close friend has been admitted to the hospital and wants you to come right away. It's amazing how quickly and easily that letter can get finished when there's a bigger problem on your plate.

True, the smaller problems still need to be solved. The goal is simply to solve them in less time and with less energy.

Bigger problems are easy to find—world hunger, child abuse, environmental pollution, terrorism, human rights violations, drug abuse, street crime, energy shortages, poverty, and wars. These problems await your attention and involvement.

Tackling a bigger problem does not have to be depressing. In fact, it can be energizing—a reason for getting up in the morning. A huge project can channel your passion and purpose.

When we take on a bigger problem, we play full out. We do justice to our potentials. We then love what we do and do what we love. We're awake, alert, and engaged. Playing full out means living our lives as if our lives depended on it.

Perhaps a little voice in your mind is saying, "That's crazy. I can't do anything about global problems." In the spirit of critical thinking, put that idea to the test. Get involved in solving a bigger problem. Then notice how you can, indeed, make a difference. And just as important, notice how your other problems dwindle—or even vanish.

 Learn more about finding bigger problems online.

Put it to Work

Applying thinking skills to practical decisions in the workplace such as ethical choices. Look for ways to apply the material in this chapter to work.

© Andresr/Shutterstock

Maria Sanchez graduated with an associate's degree in legal assistance and has been working for two years as a paralegal at a large law firm.

As a paralegal, Maria cannot set legal fees, give legal advice, or present cases in court. Despite these restrictions, she does many of the same things that lawyers do. Maria's current job centers on legal research—finding laws, judicial decisions, legal articles, and other materials that are relevant to her assigned cases.

Recently, Maria applied for a new job that opened up in the firm. In addition to legal research, this job involves drafting legal arguments and motions to be filed in court. It would mean a promotion and a raise for Maria.

When Maria applied for the job, she expressed strong interest in it. She believes that her chances are excellent. She also knows that Bill, the other paralegal in the firm, is not interested in the job and will soon announce that he's leaving the firm to pursue another career.

One day, Maria finds the first draft of an e-mail that her supervisor has printed out and accidentally placed in a stack of legal documents for Maria to read. The e-mail is a note of congratulations that offers the new paralegal job to Bill. Maria calls her parents and tells them that she faces an immediate decision: "Do I tell my supervisor that Bill plans to quit? Do I tell Bill about the e-mail? Do I keep quiet, or consider looking for a job in another firm? I'm confused about the ethical thing to do."

As a creative thinker, Maria has already begun brainstorming options. She also sees the importance of choosing her next step and taking action. List some strategies that she could use to make her decision:

_____

_____

_____

_____

If you face a decision at work that raises ethical issues, one option is to turn your personal moral standards into a set of practical questions. These questions can guide your thinking about possible actions to take. For example:

• Is this action legal?
• Is this action consistent with the mission, goals, and policies of my organization?
• Is this action consistent with my personal values?
• If I continue taking such actions, will I be happy with the kind of person I will become?
• Will I be able to defend this action tomorrow? Next month? Next year?
• In taking this action, will I set an example that I want other people to follow?
• Am I willing to make this action public—to talk about it openly with coworkers, family members, and friends?

Quiz

Name _____   Date ____/____/____

1. **List four questions described in this chapter that can guide you on your path to becoming a critical thinker.**
   a. Why am I considering this issue?   b. What are various points of view on this issue?   c. How well is each point of view supported?   d. What if I could combine various points of view or create a new one? (*Becoming a critical thinker,* p. 207)

2. **Briefly describe one strategy for answering each question you listed in your response to Question 1.**
   a. Seek a rationale for your learning, understand why a specific topic is important, arrive at a new conclusion, make a prediction, solve a problem, find a personal connection.   b. Define terms, look for assertions, look for at least three viewpoints, practice tolerance.   c. Look for logic and evidence, consider the source, understand before criticizing, watch for hot spots, be willing to be uncertain.   d. Create a critical thinking spreadsheet, write about it, accept your changing perspectives. (Answers will vary.)   (*Becoming a critical thinker,* p. 207)

3. **Briefly explain the difference between convergent and divergent thinking.**
   Convergent thinking is a narrowing-down process. Divergent thinking is a process of opening up to possibilities. (*Finding "aha!"—Creativity fuels creative thinking,* p. 211)

4. **Discuss what is meant in this chapter by *aha!***
   Aha! is the burst of creative energy that comes with the arrival of a new or original idea. (*Finding "aha!"—Creativity fuels creative thinking,* p. 211)

5. **Briefly describe three strategies for creative thinking.**
   List and describe three of the following: Conduct a brainstorm, focus and let go, cultivate creative serendipity, keep idea files, collect and play with data, create while you sleep, refine ideas and follow through, trust the process. (Answers will vary.) (*Ways to create ideas,* p. 212)

6. **Summarize the main steps in the process of choosing a major, as explained in this chapter.**
   1. Discover your options. You do this by brainstorming about the things you like to do. Taking your abilities into consideration, then use formal techniques for self-discovery.   2. Make a trial choice. Even if you are still undecided, you can narrow down your list and choose the one that most interests you now.   3. Evaluate your trial choice by meeting with instructors in your chosen field, discussing your choice with your advisor or counselor, enrolling in a course in that field, and/or finding a volunteer or part-time job in the related field.   4. Choose again. It's likely that you will change your major at least once during your college years. (*Choosing your major,* p. 222)

7. **List three types of logical fallacies, and give an example of each type.**
   a. Jumping to conclusions: Assuming that you failed the course and therefore dropping the class because you got a poor grade on one test.   b. Attacking the person: Diverting attention from political issues by making a personal attack on the opposing candidate or the candidate's family.   c. Appealing to authority: Thinking that a breakfast cereal is healthy for you because a professional athlete has endorsed it.   d. Pointing to a false cause: As children's vocabularies improve, they can get more cavities.   e. Thinking in all-or-nothing terms: Believing that all students these days are in school only to get high-paying jobs.   f. Basing arguments on emotions: Deciding that a politician who kisses babies and eats apple pie must be a nice person.   g. Faulty analogy: The people at the vitamin store are all very healthy, so if I take the vitamins they sell, I'll be healthy, too.   h. Creating a straw man: Saying that the quality of everyone's health care will go down if the United States adopts national health care.   i. Begging the question: Asserting that banning smoking in public places violates personal freedom.   j. Confusing fact and opinion: We must have tax cuts in order to create more jobs.   k. Creating a red herring: Emphasizing that Barack Obama's middle name is the same as Saddam Hussein's last name.   l. Appealing to tradition: We have to do it this way because historically we've always done it this way.   m. Appealing to "the people": Thinking that completing assignments in such a way as to please your instructor is the best way for you to learn.   n. Distracting from the real issue: Addressing a point that's only slightly related to the issue at hand because that's the only point you're knowledgeable enough to discuss.   o. Sliding a slippery slope: Concluding that because you failed one test, you are incapable of completing a college degree. (*Don't fool yourself,* p. 216)

8. **List an assumption that underlies the following statement: "Why save money? I want to enjoy life today."**
   Two assumptions that underlie the statement are that saving money is not enjoyable and that we can enjoy ourselves today only if we are spending money. (*Uncovering assumptions,* p. 219)

9. **Name at least one logical fallacy involved in this statement: "Everyone who's ever visited this school agrees that it's the best in the state."**
   Two logical fallacies in this statement are jumping to conclusions and all-or-nothing thinking. Depending on the context, the statement could also be an example of basing arguments on emotions. (*Don't fool yourself: Fifteen common mistakes in logic,* p. 216)

10. **According to the text, the words *choose* and *decide* are synonyms. True or False? Explain your answer.**
    False. Using the word *choose* frees up your thinking as it expresses a preference for one thing over another, rather than eliminating other options completely as happens when you "decide." (*Gaining skill at decision making,* p. 220)

Skills Snapshot

Now that you've experimented with some new strategies for thinking, take a few minutes to revisit your responses to the "Thinking" section of the Discovery Wheel exercise on page 27. Then complete the following sentences.

CREATIVE AND CRITICAL THINKING

When I'm asked to come up with a topic for a paper or speech, the first thing I do is . . .

When I'm asked for my opinion about a political candidate, the first thing I take into account about the candidate is . . .

APPLIED THINKING

In declaring my major, the steps I plan to take include . . .

One of the biggest problems I face right now is . . .

To come up with a solution for this problem, I will . . .

I'll know that I've reached a new level of mastery with critical and creative thinking skills when . . .

To reach that level of mastery, the most important thing I can do next is to . . .

Master Student PROFILE

Twyla Tharp

. . . is creative

© Petre Buzoianu/Corbis

Every creative person has to learn to deal with failure, because failure, like death and taxes, is inescapable. If Leonardo and Beethoven and Goethe failed on occasion, what makes you think you'll be the exception?

I don't mean to romanticize failure . . . . Believe me, success is preferable to failure. But there is a therapeutic power to failure. It cleanses. It helps you put aside who you aren't and reminds you of who you are. Failure humbles. . . .

When I tape a three-hour improvisational session with a dancer and find only thirty seconds of useful material in the tape, I am earning straight A's in failure. Do the math: I have rejected 99.7 percent of my work that day. It would be like a writer knocking out a two-thousand word chapter and upon re-reading deciding that only three words were worth keeping. Painful, yes, but for me absolutely necessary.

What's so wonderful about wasting that kind of time? It's simple: The more you fail in private, the less you will fail in public. In many ways, the creative act is editing. You're editing out all the lame ideas that won't resonate with the public. It's not pandering. It's exercising your judgment. It's setting the bar a little higher for yourself, and therefore for your audience. . . .

Some of my favorite dancers at New York City Ballet were the ones who fell the most. I always loved watching Mimi Paul; she took big risks onstage and went down often. Her falls reminded you that the dancers were doing superhuman things onstage, and when she fell, I would realize, "Damn, she's human." And hitting the ground seemed to transform Mimi: It was as though the stage absorbed the energy of her fall and injected it back into her with an extra dose of fearlessness. Mimi would bounce back up, ignore the fall, and right before my eyes would become superhuman again. I thought, "Go Mimi!" She became greater because she had fallen. Failure enlarged her dancing.

That should be your model for dealing with failure.

When you fail in public, you are forcing yourself to learn a whole new set of skills, skills that have nothing to do with creating and everything to do with surviving.

Jerome Robbins liked to say that you do your best work after your biggest disasters. For one thing, it's so painful that it almost guarantees that you won't make those mistakes again. Also, you have nothing to lose; you've hit bottom and the only place to go is up. A fiasco compels you to change dramatically. The golfer Bobby Jones said, "I never learned anything from a match I won." He respected defeat and profited from it. . . .

My heroes in *The Odyssey* are the older warriors who have been through many wars. They don't hide their scars, they wear them proudly as a kind of armor. When you fail— when your short film induces yawns or your photographs inspire people to say "That's nice" (ouch!) or your novel is trashed in a journal of opinion that matters to you—the best thing to do is acknowledge your battle scars and gird yourself for the next round. Tell yourself, "This is a deep wound. But it's going to heal and I will remember the wound. When I go back into the fray, it will serve me well."

Reprinted with the permission of Simon & Schuster, Inc., from *The Creative Habit: Learn It and Use It for Life* by Twyla Tharp with Mark Reiter. Copyright © 2003 W.A.T. Ltd. All rights reserved.

(1941–) A choreographer who has worked with her own company, the Joffrey Ballet, the Paris Opera Ballet, London's Royal Ballet, and the American Ballet Theatre. She also created dances for the films *Hair*, *Ragtime*, and *Amadeus*.

To learn more about the life and work of Twyla Tharp, visit the Master Student Hall of Fame online.

8 Communicating

Instructor Tools & Tips

> Listening means trying to see the problem the way the speaker sees it—which means not sympathy, which is feeling for him, but empathy, which is feeling with him.
>
> **—S. I. Hayakawa**
>
> You have two ears and one mouth. Remember to use them in more or less that proportion.
>
> **—Paula Bern**

Preview

Communicating effectively is discussed indirectly in many chapters of *Becoming a Master Student*. By taking a closer look at effective communication in this chapter, you can help your students in the related skills of speaking, listening, and writing now that they have the necessary foundations to work toward mastery. This chapter provides an opportunity to discuss conflict resolution, public speaking (including overcoming fear of public speaking), and plagiarism. Communication abilities are essential workplace skills that can be practiced and mastered in the college setting. Use this Annotated Instructor's Edition and other resources available to you to highlight and discuss key concepts in class and to devise assignments that allow students to practice communication skills outside the classroom. And consider this: Developing relationships through effective communication is essential for first-year student success and retention at your college.

Guest Speaker

A librarian or a colleague from the Speech/Communications department makes a timely guest speaker as a lead-in to the articles on plagiarism and public speaking. Share the related articles with the guest speaker ahead of time so that the speaker's presentation can be focused to complement the text. Let students know who is coming so that they can prepare questions to ask your guest speaker.

Lecture

Appropriate lecture topics for this chapter include active listening, effective writing, plagiarism, public speaking, and the Power Process: "Employ your word." Consider inviting a guest lecturer for one or more of these topics or using the PowerUP! DVD to lecture for you on the Power Process. For additional ideas, visit the Instructor Web site.

Exercises/Activities

1. **Five ways to say "I" (page 241)** Students who have not taken an interpersonal communications course often do not know how to create "I" statements. Dividing students into groups and having them practice writing and speaking "I" statements can help them understand how to do so and enable them to gauge their effectiveness in communicating.

2. **You deserve compliments (page 247)** This is one of Dave Ellis's favorite class activities. Ask students to pair up with a classmate they have gotten to know during the semester. One will be the speaker; the other, the listener. The speaker says, "What I like about you is…" and finishes the sentence with a quality he likes in that person. He continues to repeat this sentence for 45 seconds, each time stating a different quality. If your students get stuck and cannot think of a quality, encourage them to say, "What I like about you is *everything*" over and over again until they can think of another specific compliment. This keeps the barrage of compliments going. The listener receives the compliments and acknowledges them nonverbally. After 45 seconds, the students switch roles and repeat the exercise. Then have a class discussion about how it felt to *give* and to *receive* compliments.

3. **7 steps to effective complaints (page 248)** Students enjoy this short group activity. Ask your students to recall a recent consumer purchase that disappointed them. Then divide the students into small groups and have them share their experiences, including what happened and how they felt. Have them remain in the

groups and review the article for suggestions on how they might be more effective next time.

4. Mastering public speaking (page 260) In this activity, students prepare and present a 5-minute process speech about how to do or make something. This provides them with an opportunity to stand up and speak before the entire class. To lay the groundwork, review the criteria for an effective speech. Faculty Advisor Dean Mancina does a sample speech for the class to grade using his grading form. Students prepare and practice their speech at home and then sign up to present the speech during class. Students earn credit for essential points made during the introduction, body, and conclusion of their speech. This practice in a familiar and comfortable environment helps reduce speech anxiety for students who will likely make future presentations in other courses. For suggestions on grading student speeches, review information on the Instructor Web site.

5. Mastering public speaking (page 260) Participating in class is another excellent way for students to practice speaking in public. Many students experience communication apprehension when they are called on in class or when they must speak before a group. Ask your students to write a Discovery Statement about their memory of this type of situation. Have them describe their physical sensations, the effectiveness of their presentation, feedback from the audience, and so forth. Ask your students to write an Intention Statement concerning how they intend to participate in class in order to experience talking to a group of people. Ask them to be specific about which class they intend to speak in, how they will set up the opportunity to speak (e.g., having questions ready, sitting in front, asking to give a presentation, and so forth), and how they intend to record their observations of the experience. Connect this lesson with "Risk being a fool" and you have a practical application of the Power Process in Chapter 10.

6. Mastering public speaking (page 260) Students may be assigned to do many different types of oral reports for a course, but one form deserves particular attention: the classroom debate. Instructors use this assignment for many reasons. Debates:

- Teach students how to think critically about complex issues.

- Help students to understand, respect, and adapt to differences of opinion.
- Provide a way of comparing and contrasting different theories and viewpoints.
- Develop students' ability to create prompt, analytical responses to arguments.
- Teach students how to collect and analyze arguments and evidence.
- Teach audience members how to listen to and analyze arguments.
- Develop presentation skills and student confidence.[1]

Conversation/Sharing

This chapter is certainly one that your students will be energized to discuss. It will be especially easy for them to create schema using their prior knowledge of the subject before learning new information. Spend time focusing on the *What if?* in this chapter. Ask students *What if* they use the ideas presented in this chapter to help them succeed in the workplace. Ask your students to consider the importance of communication for the major they have chosen (connecting back to Chapter 7) or to their future career choice (looking ahead to Chapter 12).

Homework

Three phases of effective writing (page 253) Are you looking for an assignment that can help your students practice their writing *and* provide them with an opportunity to win a $1,000 scholarship? This is a perfect place to announce the Cengage Learning Scholarship Essay Contest. Host a contest in your classes, select the best essay (that answers the scholarship essay question, posted on the *Becoming a Master Student* Web site), and submit this winning essay to the national contest. Remind your students that they have the formula for writing a successful essay in their hands! Previous winning essays are available at the Student Web site for reflection.

Academic integrity: Avoid plagiarism (page 259) If students understand how to cite sources properly and feel confident about their ability to do so, many are less likely to "cheat," either intentionally or simply because they don't know how to cite. Consider asking students to go to your college library, find a current controversial topic, and use library reference material such as the *Opposing Viewpoints* series to choose a position on their controversial topic. Next, have them find three facts in periodicals or books that directly support their position. Finally, ask them to type their three facts and cite them properly using MLA or APA format. Many students don't know how to find topics in the library, locate reference books, and research a topic using the library's online catalog. Ask a librarian to explain how to do this to your students as a guest speaker or during a class visit to the library.

Power Process: Employ Your Word (page 265) To help illustrate the effectiveness of this Power Process, have students individually think about and then write two promises, one to themselves and one to a significant person in their lives. This helps demonstrate how to use the ideas in the article. Remind students that the promises they are making are, culturally, the highest level of commitment we make to each other.

Three phases of effective writing (page 253) Convincing your students that writing is as important in the workplace as it is in the classroom is an essential point to drive home. Stress that learning to write well pays many dividends and that writing effectively can help students express themselves. Writing will help them to organize information and adapt their ideas to different audiences. Finally, point out that good writing is a marketable skill. To verify this, have your students look at help wanted ads in the newspaper or online and determine how many job descriptions call for good writing skills. Have your students look for other transferable skills that they can master in the classroom and utilize in the workplace. Students can write Discovery and Intention Statements after reviewing the help wanted ads. Ask your students to highlight skills other than

writing that will be applicable to their intended career choice.

Master Student Profile: Mark Zuckerberg (page 269) Remind students that the Master Student Profiles can be a source of inspiration. You can also use the Master Student Profiles to discuss the topics covered in the article. Ask your students why they think that Mark Zuckerberg was selected for the communication chapter. You can assign additional reading or research (another opportunity for students to practice their writing) related to this article. Have your students begin with the biographical information and links that are provided on the *Becoming a Master Student* Web site.

Evaluation

Frequent quizzes ensure that students face attention during class and keep up with the text reading assignments. In addition, quizzes provide students with opportunities for written reflection regarding new discoveries and intentions. Evaluation instruments also help you identify topics and concept that students have not yet mastered. In addition to the questions listed here, find more test questions on the Instructor Web site.

Quiz ideas for Chapter 8:

- Ask students to describe ways to manage conflict.
- Present an example of a problem between a student and the Admissions/Records Office and ask students to share how they would effectively complain in order to get the situation resolved.
- Ask students for examples of how to stay safe during online social networking.
- Ask students to write Discovery and Intention Statements regarding the Power Process: "Employ your word."

Additional Digital Resources

Course Manual

The online *Course Manual* serves as an invaluable reference for those developing and teaching a College Success course with *Becoming a Master Student.* The *Course Manual* provides advice on general teaching issues such as preparing for classes, classroom management, grading, and communicating with students of various backgrounds as well as specific strategies on getting the most out of various features in *Becoming a Master Student* such as the Discovery Wheel, Learning Styles Inventory, and book-specific Web sites.

Instructor Web Site

The updated Instructor Web site provides resources to help you plan and customize your course. Content specific to Chapter 8 includes:

- ▶ Lecture Ideas
  - Communication Is Straightforward?
- ▶ In-Class Exercises
  - Assertiveness Inventory
  - Attendance Brainstorm
  - Turn a Complaint into a Request
  - Making Relationships Work While You're a Student
- ▶ In-Text Quiz Answers
- ▶ Learning Styles Application
- ▶ Discussion Topics
- ▶ PowerPoint Slides
- ▶ Reflection Questions
- ▶ Assessment Questions
- ▶ Experiment with chapter strategies

The Instructor Web site also contains the following book-specific content:

- ▶ ExamView Test Bank
- ▶ Online Course Manual
- ▶ Articles from previous editions
- ▶ Master Student Profiles from previous editions
- ▶ Sample Syllabi

Student Web Site

To help your students gain a better understanding of the topics discussed in *Becoming a Master Student,* encourage your students to visit the Student Web site, which provides the following resources specific to Chapter 8:

- ▶ Connect to Text content expands on specific topics marked with an icon within Chapter 8.

 www.cengage.com/success/bams13e

- ▶ Learning Style Applications invite students to cycle through the four styles of learning. In answering the four questions about conflict management posted in this chapter's Learning Styles Application, students explore the different modes and apply their new knowledge.

- ▶ Practice Tests allow students to see how well they understand the themes of *Becoming a Master Student.*

- ▶ Interactive Concept Maps promote critical thinking by highlighting related ideas to show relationships between concepts.

- ▶ Video Skillbuilders bring to life techniques that will help you to excel in college and beyond. The following videos should give your students more information regarding topics covered in Chapter 8:
  - Persuasive Communication: Effective Strategies
  - Persuasive Communication: Communicating in a Group

- ▶ Remembering Cultural Differences presents readers with brief articles that touch on aspects of diversity in our rapidly changing world. For Chapter 8, the following article will prompt your students to look at contemporary issues in a new way:
  - Ethnicity Issues in Communications

- ▶ Master Student Profiles provide additional information on the people covered in this book feature. For Chapter 8, students will find expanded coverage and links about:
  - Mark Zuckerberg

- ▶ Power Process Media contains video, PowerPoints, and audio files to take what your students have learned from the Power Processes in their book to the next level. For Chapter 8, students will find additional media on:
  - Employ your word

Along with the chapter-specific content, a General Resources folder is available that contains Toolboxes geared toward specific student types (Community College, Adult Learner, Student Athlete), the Plagiarism Prevention Zone, and the Career Resource Center.

[1]Isa Engleberg and Ann Raimes, *Pocket Keys for Speakers* (Boston: Cengage Learning, 2003), 210, 211.

8 Communicating

Master Student Map

as you read, ask yourself

what if . . . ?

I could consistently create the kind of relationships that I've always wanted?

why this chapter matters . . .

Your communication abilities are as important to your success as your technical skills.

how

you can use this chapter . . .

- Listen, speak, and write in ways that promote your success.
- Prevent and resolve conflict with other people.
- Use your capacity to make and keep agreements as a tool for creating your future.

what is included . . .

> **MASTER STUDENTS in *action***
>
> Dealing with conflict online is totally different than in person. I find that even if something is "resolved" online, it will probably come up in person anyway, so why not just talk face to face?
>
> **—CAT SALERNO**

Photo courtesy of Cat Salerno

Communicating creates our world

CERTAIN THINGS are real for us because we can see them, touch them, hear them, smell them, or taste them. Books, pencils, tables, chairs, and food all are real in this sense. They enter our world in a straightforward, uncomplicated way.

Many other aspects of our lives, however, do not have this kind of observable reality. None of us can point to a *purpose*, for example. Nor would a purpose step up and introduce itself or buy us lunch. The same is true about other abstract concepts, such as *quality, intelligence, trust, human rights,* or *student success.*

Concepts such as these shape our experience of life. Yet they don't really exist until we talk about them. These concepts come alive for us only to the degree that we have conversations about them. Communicating brings our world into being.

According to communication theorist Lee Thayer, there are two basic life processes. One is acquiring and processing energy. The other is acquiring and processing information, also known as *communication.*[1] From this point of view, communicating is just as fundamental to life as eating is.

Through communication, we take raw impressions and organize them into patterns. With our senses, we perceive sights, sounds, and other sensations. However, none of our sense organs is capable of perceiving *meaning.* We create meaning by finding patterns in our sensations and sharing them through conversation.

Communication can be defined as the process of creating shared meaning. When two people agree about the meaning of an event, they've communicated. However, communication is a constant challenge. Each of us creates meaning in a way that is unique.

When people speak or listen, they don't exchange meaning. They exchange symbols—words, images, gestures. And symbols are open to interpretation. This means that communication is always flawed to some extent. We can never be sure that the message we send is the message that others receive. This challenge will only grow as the technology of social networking connects us to people around the world.

Yet with practice we can overcome many of the difficulties inherent in human communication. That's what this chapter is about. As you enhance your skills at listening, speaking, and writing, you can create a new world. ✳

---

journal entry 21

Discovery/Intention Statement

Commit to Create Value from This Chapter

Think of a time when you experienced an emotionally charged conflict with another person. Were you able to resolve this dispute effectively? If so, list below the strategies you used.

I discovered that I . . .

_____

_____

_____

_____

Now scan this chapter for ideas that can help you get your feelings and ideas across more skillfully in similar situations. List at least four ideas here, along with the page numbers where you can read more about them.

Strategy   **Page number**

_____

_____

_____

Describe an upcoming situation in which you intend to apply these techniques. If possible, choose a situation that will occur within the next week.

I intend to . . .

_____

_____

_____

_____

Communication— keeping the channels open

In our daily contact with other people and the mass media, we are exposed to hundreds of messages. Yet the obstacles to receiving those messages accurately are numerous.

FOR ONE THING, only a small percentage of communication is verbal. We also send messages with our bodies and with the tone of our voices. Throw in a few other factors, such as a hot room or background noise, and it's a wonder we can communicate at all.

Written communication adds a whole other set of variables. When you speak, you supplement the meaning of your words with the power of body language and voice inflection. When you write, those nonverbal elements are absent. Instead, you depend on your skills at word choice, sentence construction, and punctuation to get your message across. The choices that you make in these areas can aid—or hinder—communication.

In communication theory, the term *noise* refers to any factor that distorts meaning. When noise is present, the channels of communication start to close. Noise can be external (a lawn mower outside a classroom) or internal (the emotions of the sender or receiver, such as speech anxiety). To a large extent, skillful communication means reducing noise and keeping channels open.

Mouth: © Moodboard/Corbis; *static:* © Paul Edmondson/Corbis; *ear:* © Masterfile Royalty Free; college by Walter Kopec

One powerful technique for doing these crucial things is to separate the roles of sending and receiving. Communication channels get blocked when we try to send and receive messages at the same time. Instead, be aware of when you are the receiver and when you are the sender. If you are receiving (listening or reading), just receive; avoid switching into the sending (speaking or writing) mode. When you are sending, stick with it until you are finished.

Communication works best when each of us has plenty of time to receive what others send *and* the opportunity

exercise 24
Practice sending or receiving

The purpose of this exercise is to help you slow down the pace of communication and clearly separate the roles of sending and receiving. Begin by applying the following steps to conversations on neutral topics. With some practice, you'll be ready to use this technique in situations that could escalate into an argument.

First, find a partner, and choose a topic for a conversation. Also set a time limit for doing this exercise. Then complete the following steps:

1. Get two 3x5 cards. Label one of them *sender*. Label the other *receiver*. Choose one card, and give the other one to your partner.

2. If you chose the *sender* card, then start speaking. If you chose the *receiver* card, then listen to your partner without saying a word.

3. When the sender is done speaking, exchange cards and switch roles. The person who listened in Step 2 now gets to speak. However, *do not exchange cards until the sender in Step 2 declares that she has expressed everything she wants to say*.

4. Keep switching cards and roles until your time is up.

After completing these steps, reflect on the experience. What has this exercise taught you about your current skills as a speaker and listener?

to send a complete message when it's our turn. Communication is a two-way street. When someone else talks, just listen. Then switch roles so that you can be the sender for a while. Keep this up until you do a reasonably complete job of creating shared meaning. ✳

Choosing to listen

Observe a person in a conversation who is not talking. Is he listening? Maybe. Maybe not. Is he focusing on the speaker? Preparing his response? Daydreaming?

EFFECTIVE LISTENING IS not easy. It calls for concentration and energy. But it's worth the trouble. People love a good listener. The best salespeople, managers, coworkers, teachers, parents, and friends are the best listeners.

Through skilled listening, you can gain insight into other people and yourself. You can also promote your success in school through more powerful notes, more productive study groups, and better relationships with students and instructors.

To listen well, begin from a clear intention. *Choose* to listen well. Once you've made this choice, you can use the following techniques to be even more effective at listening. Notice that these techniques start with nonverbal listening and continue with suggestions for verbal responses that can help you fully receive a speaker's message.

Nonverbal listening

Be quiet. Silence is more than staying quiet while someone is speaking. Allowing several seconds to pass before you begin to talk gives the speaker time to catch her breath and gather her thoughts. She might want to continue. Someone who talks nonstop might fear she will lose the floor if she pauses.

If the message being sent is complete, this short break gives you time to form your response and helps you avoid the biggest barrier to listening—listening with your answer running. If you make up a response before the person is finished, you might miss the end of the message, which is often the main point.

In some circumstances, pausing for several seconds might be inappropriate. Ignore this suggestion completely when someone asks in a panic where to find the nearest phone to call the fire department.

Maintain eye contact. Look at the other person while he speaks. Maintaining eye contact demonstrates your attentiveness and helps keep your mind from wandering. Your eyes also let you observe the speaker's body language and behavior. If you avoid eye contact, you can fail to see *and* fail to listen.

This idea is not an absolute. Maintaining eye contact is valued more in some cultures than others. Also, some people learn primarily by hearing; they can listen more effectively by turning off the visual input once in a while.

Display openness. You can display openness through your facial expression and body position. Uncross your arms and legs. Sit up straight. Face the other person, and remove any physical barriers between you, such as a pile of books.

Send acknowledgments. Let the speaker know periodically that you are still there. Words and nonverbal gestures of acknowledgment convey to the speaker that you are interested and that you are receiving his message. These words and gestures include "Umhum," "OK," "Yes," and head nods.

These acknowledgments do not imply your agreement. When people tell you what they don't like about you, your head nod doesn't mean that you agree. It just indicates that you are listening.

Release distractions. Even when your intention is to listen, you might find your mind wandering. Thoughts about what *you* want to say or something you want to do later might claim your attention. There's a simple solution: Notice your wandering mind without judgment. Then bring your attention back to the act of listening.

Another option is to ask for a quick break so that you can make a written note about what's on your mind. Tell the speaker that you're writing so that you can clear your mind and return to full listening.

Suspend judgments. Listening and agreeing are two different activities. As listeners, our goal is to fully receive another person's message. This does not mean that we're obligated to agree with the message. Once you're confident that you accurately understand a speaker's point of view, you are free to agree or disagree with it. The key to effective listening is understanding *before* evaluating.

Verbal listening

Choose when to speak. When we listen to another person, we often interrupt with our own stories, opinions, suggestions, and comments. Consider the following dialogue:

"Oh, I'm so excited! I just found out that I've been nominated to be in *Who's Who in American Musicians*."

"Yeah, that's neat. My Uncle Elmer got into *Who's Who in American Veterinarians*. He sure has an interesting job. One time I went along when he was treating a cow, and you'll never believe what happened next. . . ."

To avoid this kind of one-sided conversation, delay your verbal responses. This does not mean that you remain totally silent while listening. It means that you wait for an *appropriate* moment to respond.

Watch your nonverbal responses, too. A look of "Good grief!" from you can deter the other person from finishing his message.

Feed back meaning. Sometimes you can help a speaker clarify her message by paraphrasing it. This does not mean parroting what she says. Instead, briefly summarize. Psychotherapist Carl Rogers referred to this technique as *reflection.*[2]

Feed back what you see as the essence of the person's message: "Let me see if I understood what you said . . . ." or "What I'm hearing you say is . . . ." Often, the other person will say, "No, that's not what I meant. What I said was . . . ."

There will be no doubt when you get it right. The sender will say, "Yeah, that's it," and either continue with another message or stop sending when he knows you understand.

When you feed back meaning, be concise. This is not a time to stop the other person by talking on and on about what you think you heard.

Notice verbal and nonverbal messages. You might point out that the speaker's body language seems to convey the exact opposite of what her words do. For example: "I noticed you said you are excited, but you look bored."

Keep in mind that the same nonverbal behavior can have various meanings across cultures. Someone who looks bored might simply be listening in a different way.

Listen for requests and intentions. An effective way to listen to complaints is to look for the request hidden in them. "This class is a waste of my time" can be heard as "Please tell me what I'll gain if I participate actively in class." "The instructor talks too fast" might be asking "What strategies can I use to take notes when the instructor covers material rapidly?"

We can even transform complaints into intentions. Take this complaint: "The parking lot by the dorms is so dark at night that I'm afraid to go to my car." This complaint can result in having a light installed in the parking lot.

Viewing complaints as requests gives us more choices. Rather than responding with defensiveness ("What does he know anyway?"), resignation ("It's always been this way and always will be"), or indifference ("It's not my job"), we can decide whether to grant the request (do what will alleviate the other's

difficulty) or help the person translate his own complaint into an action plan.

Allow emotion. In the presence of full listening, some people will share things that they feel deeply about. They might shed a few tears, cry, shake, or sob. If you feel uncomfortable when this happens, see if you can accept the discomfort for a little while longer. Emotional release can bring relief and trigger unexpected insights.

Ask for more. Full listening with unconditional acceptance is a rare gift. Many people have never experienced it. They are used to being greeted with resistance, so they habitually stop short of saying what they truly think and feel. Help them shed this habit by routinely asking, "Is there anything more you want to say about that?" This question sends the speaker a message that you truly value what she has to say.

Be careful with questions and advice. Questions are directive. They can take conversations in a new direction, which may not be where the speaker wants to go. Ask questions only to clarify the speaker's message. Later, when it's your turn to speak, you can introduce any topic that you want.

Also be cautious about giving advice. Unsolicited advice can be taken as condescending or even insulting. Skilled listeners recognize that people are different, and they do not assume that they know what's best for someone else.

Take care of yourself. People seek good listeners, and there are times when you don't want to listen. You might be distracted with your own concerns. Be honest. Don't pretend to listen. You can say, "What you're telling me is important, and I'm pressed for time right now. Can we set aside another time to talk about this?" It's OK not to listen.

Stay open to the adventure of listening. Receiving what another person has to say is an act of courage. Listening fully—truly opening yourself to the way another person sees the world—means taking risks. Your opinions may be challenged. You may be less certain or less comfortable than you were before.

Along with the risks come rewards. Listening in an unguarded way can take your relationships to a new depth and level of honesty. This kind of listening can open up new possibilities for thinking, feeling, and behaving. And when you practice full listening, other people are more likely to receive when it's your turn to send. ✳

 Find more strategies for full listening online.

COMMUNICATING

8

Choosing to speak

You have been talking with people for most of your life, and you usually manage to get your messages across. There are times, though, when you don't. Often, these times are emotionally charged.

WE ALL HAVE this problem. Sometimes we feel wonderful or rotten or sad or scared, and we want to express it. Emotions, though, can get in the way of the message. And although you can send almost any message through tears, laughter, fist pounding, or hugging, sometimes words are better. Begin with a sincere intention to reach common ground with your listener. Then experiment with the suggestions that follow.

Replace "you" messages with "I" messages. It can be difficult to disagree with someone without his becoming angry or your becoming upset. When conflict occurs, we often make statements about the other person, or "you" messages:

"You are rude."

"You make me mad."

"You must be crazy."

"You don't love me anymore."

This kind of communication results in defensiveness. The responses might similar to these:

"I am not rude."

"I don't care."

"No, *you* are crazy."

"No, *you* don't love *me!*"

"You" messages are hard to listen to. They label, judge, blame, and assume things that might or might not be true. They demand rebuttal. Even praise can sometimes be an ineffective "you" message. "You" messages don't work.

Psychologist Thomas Gordon suggests that when communication is emotionally charged, consider limiting your statements to descriptions about yourself.[3] Replace "you" messages with "I" messages:

"You are rude" might become "I feel upset."

"You make me mad" could be "I feel angry."

"You must be crazy" can be "I don't understand."

"You don't love me anymore" could become "I'm afraid we're drifting apart."

Suppose a friend asks you to pick him up at the airport. You drive 20 miles and wait for the plane. No friend. You decide your friend missed her plane, so you wait 3 hours for the next flight. No friend. Perplexed and worried, you drive home. The next day, you see your friend downtown.

"What happened?" you ask.

"Oh, I caught an earlier flight."

"You are a rude person," you reply.

Look for and talk about the facts—the observable behavior. Everyone will agree that your friend asked you to pick her up, that she did take an earlier flight, and that you did not receive a call from her. But the idea that she is rude is not a fact—it's a judgment.

She might go on to say, "I called your home, and no one answered. My mom had a stroke and was rushed to Valley View. I caught the earliest flight I could get." Your judgment no longer fits.

When you saw your friend, you might have said, "I waited and waited at the airport. I was worried about you. I didn't get a call. I feel angry and hurt. I don't want to waste my time. Next time, you can call me when your flight arrives, and I'll be happy to pick you up."

"I" messages don't judge, blame, criticize, or insult. They don't invite the other person to counterattack with more of the same. "I" messages are also more accurate. They report our own thoughts and feelings.

At first, "I" messages might feel uncomfortable or seem forced. That's OK. Use the five ways to say "I" explained on page 241.

Remember that questions are not always questions. You've heard these "questions" before. A parent asks, "Don't you want to look nice?" Translation: "I wish you'd cut your hair, lose the blue jeans, and put on a tie." Or how about this question from a spouse: "Honey, wouldn't you love to go to an exciting hockey game tonight?" Translation: "I've already bought tickets."

We use questions that aren't questions to sneak our opinions and requests into conversations. "Doesn't it upset you?" means "It upsets me," and "Shouldn't we hang the picture over here?" means "I want to hang the picture over here."

Communication improves when we say, "I'm upset" and "Let's hang the picture over here."

Choose your nonverbal messages. How you say something can be more important than what you say. Your tone of voice and gestures add up to a silent message that you send. This message can support, modify, or contradict your words. Your posture, the way you dress, how often you shower, and even the poster hanging on your wall can negate your words before you say them.

Most nonverbal behavior is unconscious. We can learn to be aware of it and choose our nonverbal messages. The key is to be clear about our intention and purpose. When we know what we want to say and are committed to getting it across, our inflections, gestures, and words work together and send a unified message.

Notice barriers to sending messages. Sometimes fear stops us from sending messages. We are afraid of other people's reactions, sometimes justifiably. Being truthful doesn't mean being insensitive to the impact that our messages have on others. Tact is a virtue; letting fear prevent communication is not.

Assumptions can also be used as excuses for not sending messages. "He already knows this," we tell ourselves.

Predictions of failure can be barriers to sending, too. "He won't listen," we assure ourselves. That statement might be inaccurate. Perhaps the other person senses that we're angry and listens in a guarded way. Or perhaps he is listening and sending nonverbal messages we don't understand.

Or we might predict, "He'll never do anything about it, even if I tell him." Again, making assumptions can defeat our message before we send it.

It's easy to make excuses for not communicating. If you have fear or some other concern about sending a message, be aware of it. Don't expect the concern to go away. Realize that you can communicate even with your concerns. You can choose to make them part of the message: "I am going to tell you how I feel, and I'm afraid that you will think it's stupid."

Talking to someone when you don't want to could be a matter of educational survival. Sometimes a short talk with an advisor, a teacher, a friend, or a family member can solve a problem that otherwise could jeopardize your education.

Speak candidly. When we brood on negative thoughts and refuse to speak them out loud, we lose perspective. And when we keep joys to ourselves, we diminish our satisfaction. A solution is to share regularly what we think and feel. Psychotherapist Sidney Jourard referred to such openness and honesty as *transparency* and wrote eloquently about how it can heal and deepen relationships.[4]

Sometimes candid speaking can save a life. For example, if you think a friend is addicted to drugs, telling her so in a supportive, nonjudgmental way is a sign of friendship.

Imagine a community in which people freely and lovingly speak their minds—without fear or defensiveness. That can be your community.

This suggestion comes with a couple of caveats. First, there is a big difference between speaking candidly about your problems and griping about them. Gripers usually don't seek solutions. They just want everyone to know how unhappy they are. Instead, talk about problems as a way to start searching for solutions.

Second, avoid bragging. Other people are turned off by constant references to how much money you have, how great your partner is, how numerous your social successes are, or how much status your family enjoys. There is a difference between sharing excitement and being obnoxious.

Speak up! Look for opportunities to practice speaking strategies. Join class discussions. Start conversations about topics that excite you. Ask for information and clarification. Ask for feedback on your skills.

Also speak up when you want support. Consider creating a team of people who help one another succeed. Such a team can develop naturally from a study group that works well. Ask members if they would be willing to accept and receive support in achieving a wide range of academic and personal goals. Meet regularly to do goal-setting exercises from this book and brainstorm success strategies.

After you have a clear statement of your goals and a plan for achieving them, let family members and friends know. When appropriate, let them know how they can help. You may be surprised at how often people respond to a genuine request for support. ✳

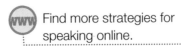 Find more strategies for speaking online.

Five ways to say "I"

An "I" message can include any or all of the following five elements. Be careful when including the last two element, though, because they can contain hidden judgments or threats.

Observations. Describe the facts—the indisputable, observable realities. Talk about what you—or anyone else—can see, hear, smell, taste, or touch. Avoid judgments, interpretations, or opinions. Instead of saying, "You're a slob," say, "Last night's lasagna pan was still on the stove this morning."

Feelings. Describe your own feelings. It is easier to listen to "I feel frustrated" than to "You never help me." Stating how you feel about another's actions can be valuable feedback for that person.

Wants. You are far more likely to get what you want if you say what you want. If someone doesn't know what you want, she doesn't have a chance to help you get it.

Ask clearly. Avoid demanding or using the word *need*. Most people like to feel helpful, not obligated. Instead of saying, "Do the dishes when it's your turn, or else!" say, "I want to divide the housework fairly."

Thoughts. Communicate your thoughts, and use caution. Beginning your statement with the word "I" doesn't automatically make it an "I" message. "I think you are a slob" is a "you" judgment in disguise. Instead, say, "I'd have more time to study if I didn't have to clean up so often."

Intentions. The last part of an "I" message is a statement about what you intend to do. Have a plan that doesn't depend on the other person. For example, instead of saying "From now on we're going to split the dishwashing evenly," you could say, "I intend to do my share of the housework and leave the rest."

25 exercise
Write an "I" message

First, pick something about school that irritates you. Then pretend that you are talking to a person who is associated with this irritation. In the space below, write down what you would say to this person as a "you" message.

Now write the same complaint as an "I" message. Include all of the elements suggested in "Five Ways to Say 'I.' "

8

Discovery/Intention Statement

Discover Communication Styles

The concept of *communication styles* can be useful when you want to discover sources of conflict with another person—or when you're in a conversation with someone from a different culture.

Consider the many ways in which people express themselves verbally. These characteristics can reflect an individual's preferred communication style:

- *Extroversion*—talking to others as a way to explore possibilities for taking action.
- *Introversion*—thinking through possibilities alone before talking to others.
- *Dialogue*—engaging in a discussion to hear many points of view before coming to a conclusion or decision.
- *Debate*—arguing for a particular point of view from the outset of a discussion.
- *Openness*—being ready to express personal thoughts and feelings early in a relationship.
- *Reserve*—holding back on self-expression until a deeper friendship develops.
- A *faster pace* of conversation—allowing people to speak quickly and forcefully while filling any gaps in conversation.
- A *slower pace* of conversation—allowing people to speak slowly and quietly while taking time to formulate their thoughts.

These are just a few examples of differences in communication styles. You might be able to think of others.

The point is that people with different communication styles can make negative assumptions about each other. For example, those who prefer fast-paced conversations might assume that people who talk slowly are indecisive. And people who prefer slower-paced conversations might assume that people who talk quickly are pushy and uninterested in anyone else's opinion.

Take this opportunity to think about your preferred communication styles and assumptions. Do they enhance or block your relationships with other people? Think back over the conversations you've had during the past week. Then complete the following sentences, using additional paper as needed.

1. I discovered that I prefer conversations that allow me to . . .

2. I discovered that I usually feel uncomfortable in conversations when other people . . .

3. When people do the things listed in Item 2, I tend to make certain assumptions, such as . . .

4. As an alternative to making the assumptions listed in Item 3, I intend to . . .

COMMUNICATING

8

Developing emotional intelligence

EMOTIONAL INTELLIGENCE MEANS recognizing feelings and responding to them in skillful ways. Daniel Goleman, author of *Emotional Intelligence: Why It Can Matter More Than IQ,* concludes that "IQ washes out when it comes to predicting who, among a talented pool of candidates *within* an intellectually demanding profession will become the strongest leader." At that point, emotional intelligence starts to become more important.[5]

If you're emotionally intelligent, you're probably described as someone with good "people skills." That's shorthand for being aware of your feelings, acting in thoughtful ways, showing concern for others, resolving conflict, and making responsible decisions. You can deepen these skills with the following strategies.

Recognize three elements of emotion

Even the strongest emotion consists of just three elements: physical sensations, thoughts, and action. Usually they happen so fast that you can barely distinguish them. Separating them out is a first step toward emotional intelligence.

Imagine that you suddenly perceive a threat—such as a supervisor who's screaming at you. Immediately your heart starts beating in double time and your stomach muscles clench (physical sensations). Then thoughts race through your head: *This is a disaster. She hates me. And everyone's watching.* Finally, you take action, which could mean staring at her, yelling back, or running away.

Name your emotions

Naming your emotions is a First Step to going beyond the "fight or flight" reaction to any emotion. Naming gives you power. The second that you attach a word to an emotion, you start to gain perspective. People with emotional intelligence have a rich vocabulary to describe a wide range of emotions. For examples, do an Internet search with the key words *feeling list.* Read through the lists you find for examples of ways that you can name your feelings in the future.

Accept your emotions

Another step toward emotional intelligence is accepting your emotions—*all* of them. This can be challenging if you've been taught that some emotions are "good" while others are "bad." Experiment with another viewpoint: Emotions are complicated. They have many causes that are beyond your control, including what *other* people do. Because you do not choose your emotional reactions from moment to moment, you cannot be held morally responsible for them. However, you can be held responsible for what you *do* in response to any emotion.

Express your emotions

One possible response to any emotion is expressing it. The key is to speak without blaming others for the way you feel. The basic tool for doing so is using "I" messages, as described on page 241.

Respond rather than react

The heart of emotional intelligence is moving from mindless reactions to mindful actions. See if you can introduce an intentional gap between sensations and thoughts on the one hand and your next action on the other hand. To do this more often:

- *Run a "mood meter."* Check in with your moods several times each day. On a 3x5 card, note the time of day and your emotional state at that point. Rate your mood on a scale of 1 (relaxed and positive) to 10 (very angry, very sad, or very afraid).

- *Write Discovery Statements.* In your journal, write about situations in daily life that trigger strong emotions. Describe these events—and your usual responses to them—in detail.

- *Write Intention Statements.* After seeing patterns in your emotions, you can consciously choose to behave in new ways. Instead of yelling back at the angry supervisor, for example, make it your intention to simply remain silent and breathe deeply until she finishes. Then say, "I'll wait to respond until we've both had a chance to cool down."

Make decisions with emotional intelligence

Emotional intelligence can help you make decisions. When considering a possible choice, ask yourself, "How am I likely to feel if I do this?" You can use "gut feelings" to tell when an action might violate your values or hurt someone.

Think of emotions as energy. Anger, sadness, and fear send currents of sensation through your whole body. Ask yourself how you can channel that energy into constructive action. ✳

 Learn more ways to develop emotional intelligence.

Managing conflict

Conflict management is one of the most practical skills you'll ever learn. Here are strategies that can help.

© Masterfile Royalty Free

THE FIRST FIVE strategies below are about dealing with the *content* of a conflict—defining the problem, exploring viewpoints, and discovering solutions. The remaining strategies are about finding a *process* for resolving any conflict, no matter what the content.

To bring these strategies to life, think of ways to use them in managing a conflict that you face right now.

Focus on content

Back up to common ground. Conflict heightens the differences between people. When this happens, it's easy to forget how much we still agree with each other.

As a first step in managing conflict, back up to common ground. List all of the points on which you are *not* in conflict: "I know that we disagree about how much to spend on a new car, but we do agree that the old one needs to be replaced." Often, such comments put the problem in perspective and pave the way for a solution.

State the problem. Using "I" messages, as explained earlier in this chapter, state the problem. Tell people what you observe, feel, think, want, and intend to do. Allow the other people in a particular conflict to do the same.

Each person might have a different perception of the problem. That's fine. Let the conflict come into clear focus. It's hard to fix something unless people agree on what's broken.

Remember that the way you state the problem largely determines the solution. Defining the problem in a new way can open up a world of possibilities. For example, "I need a new roommate" is a problem statement that dictates one solution. "We could use some agreements about who cleans the apartment" opens up more options, such as a resolving conflict about who will wash the dishes tonight.

State all points of view. If you want to defuse tension or defensiveness, set aside your opinions for a moment. Take the time to understand the other points of view. Sum up those viewpoints in words that the other parties can accept. When people feel that they've been heard, they're often more willing to listen.

Ask for complete communication. In times of conflict, we often say one thing and mean another. So before responding to what the other person says, use active listening. Check to see if you have correctly received that person's message by saying, "What I'm hearing you say is . . . . Did I get it correctly?"

Focus on solutions. After stating the problem, dream up as many solutions as you can. Be outrageous. Don't hold back. Quantity—not quality—is the key. If you get stuck, restate the problem and continue brainstorming.

Next, evaluate the solutions you brainstormed. Discard the unacceptable ones. Talk about which solutions will work and how difficult they will be to implement. You might hit upon a totally new solution.

Choose one solution that is most acceptable to everyone involved, and implement it. Agree on who is going to do what by when. Then keep your agreements.

Finally, evaluate the effectiveness of your solution. If it works, pat yourselves on the back. If not, make changes or implement a new solution.

Focus on the future. Instead of rehashing the past, talk about new possibilities. Think about what you can do to prevent problems in the future. State how you intend to change, and ask others for their contributions to the solution.

Focus on process

Commit to the relationship. The thorniest conflicts usually arise between people who genuinely care for each other. Begin by affirming your commitment to the other person: "I care about you, and I want this relationship to last. So I'm willing to do whatever it takes to resolve this problem." Also ask the other person for a similar commitment.

Allow strong feelings. Permitting conflict can also mean permitting emotion. Being upset is all right. Feeling angry is often appropriate. Crying is OK. Allowing other people to see the strength of our feelings can help resolve the conflict. This suggestion can be especially useful during times when differences are so extreme that reaching common ground seems possible.

Expressing the full range of your feelings can transform the conflict. Often what's on the far side of anger is love. When we express and release resentment, we might discover genuine compassion in its place.

Notice your need to be "right." Some people approach conflict as a situation where only one person wins. That person has the "right" point of view. Everyone else loses.

When this happens, step back. See if you can approach the situation in a neutral way. Define the conflict as a problem to be solved, not as a contest to be won. Explore the possibility that you might be mistaken. There might be more than one acceptable solution. The other person might simply have a different learning style than yours. Let go of being "right," and aim for being effective at resolving conflict instead.

© Masterfile Royalty Free

Sometimes this means apologizing. Conflict sometimes arises from our own errors. Others might move quickly to end the conflict when we acknowledge this fact and ask for forgiveness.

Slow down the communication. In times of great conflict, people often talk all at once. Words fly like speeding bullets, and no one listens. Chances for resolving the conflict take a nosedive.

When everyone is talking at once, choose either to listen or to talk—not both at the same time. Just send your message. Or just receive the other person's message. Usually, this technique slows down the pace and allows everyone to become more levelheaded.

To slow down the communication even more, take a break. Depending on the level of conflict, this might mean anything from a few minutes to a few days.

A related suggestion is to do something nonthreatening together. Share an activity with the others involved that's not a source of conflict.

Communicate in writing. What can be difficult to say to another person face to face might be effectively

journal entry 23

Discovery/Intention Statement

Re-create a Relationship

Think about one of your relationships for a few minutes. It can involve a parent, sibling, spouse, child, friend, hairdresser, or anyone else. In the space below, write down some things that are not working in the relationship. What bugs you? What do you find irritating or unsatisfying?

I discovered that . . .

_____

_____

_____

_____

_____

_____

_____

Now think for a moment about what you want from this relationship. More attention? Less nagging? More openness, trust, financial security, or freedom? Choose a suggestion from this chapter, and describe how you could use it to make the relationship work.

I intend to . . .

_____

_____

_____

_____

_____

_____

_____

communicated in writing. When people in conflict write letters or e-mails to each other, they automatically apply many of the suggestions in this article. Writing is a way to slow down the communication and ensure that only one person at a time is sending a message.

There is a drawback to this tactic, though: It's possible for people to misunderstand what you say in a letter or e-mail. To avoid further problems, make clear what you are *not* saying: "I am saying that I want to be alone for a few days. I am *not* saying that I want you to stay away forever." Saying what you are *not* saying is often useful in face-to-face communication as well.

Before you send your letter or e-mail, put yourself in the shoes of the person who will receive it. Imagine how your comments could be misinterpreted. Then rewrite your note, correcting any wording that might be open to misinterpretation.

There's another way to get the problem off your chest, especially when strong, negative feelings are involved: Write the nastiest, meanest e-mail response you can imagine, leaving off the address of the recipient so you don't accidentally send it. Let all of your frustration, anger, and venom flow onto the page. Be as mean and blaming as possible. When you have cooled off, see if there is anything else you want to add.

Then destroy the letter or delete the e-mail. Your writing has served its purpose. Chances are that you've calmed down and are ready to engage in skillful conflict management.

Get an objective viewpoint. With the agreement of everyone involved, set up a video camera, and record a conversation about the conflict. In the midst of a raging argument, when emotions run high, it's almost impossible to see ourselves objectively. Let the camera be your unbiased observer.

Another way to get an objective viewpoint is to use a mediator—an objective, unbiased third party. Even an untrained mediator—as long as it's someone who is not a party to the conflict—can do much to decrease tension. Mediators can help everyone get their point of view across. The mediator's role is not to give advice but to keep the discussion on track and moving toward a solution.

Allow for cultural differences. People respond to conflict in different ways, depending on their cultural background. Some stand close, speak loudly, and make direct eye contact. Other people avert their eyes, mute their voices, and increase physical distance.

When it seems to you that other people are sidestepping or escalating a conflict, consider whether your reaction is based on cultural bias.

Agree to disagree. Sometimes we say all we have to say on an issue. We do all of the problem solving we can

do. We get all points of view across. And the conflict still remains, staring us right in the face.

What's left is to recognize that honest disagreement is a fact of life. We can peacefully coexist with other people—and respect them—even though we don't agree on fundamental issues. Conflict can be accepted even when it is not resolved.

See the conflict within you. Sometimes the turmoil we see in the outside world has its source in our own inner world. A cofounder of Alcoholics Anonymous put it this way: "It is a spiritual axiom that every time we are disturbed, no matter what the cause, there is something awry with us."

When we're angry or upset, we can take a minute to look inside. Perhaps we are ready to take offense—waiting to pounce on something the other person said. Perhaps, without realizing it, we did something to create the conflict. Or maybe the other person is simply saying what we don't want to admit is true.

When these things happen, we can shine a light on our own thinking. A simple spot-check might help the conflict disappear right before our eyes. ✳

 Discover more ways to manage conflicts online.

Resolve conflicts with roommates

People who live together share a delicate bond. Relationships with even the best friends or closest relatives can quickly deteriorate over disagreements about who pays the bills or washes the dishes.

You can prevent conflicts with roommates by negotiating agreements now. For example, adopt a policy about borrowing. Loaning your roommate a book or a tennis racket might seem like a small thing. Yet these small loans can become a sore point in a relationship. Some people have difficulty saying no and resent lending things. If so, keep borrowing to a minimum.

Meet with your roommates to discuss the following:

- What you will do about sharing belongings such as computers, audio and video equipment, food, or clothing.

- How you will create a study environment at home.

- How you will split household costs and make sure that bills get paid on time.

- How you will resolve conflicts when either of you thinks the other is not keeping your agreements.

Expand this list to include other issues that matter to you. For maximum clarity, put your agreements in writing.

COMMUNICATING

8

Five ways to say no . . . gracefully

© Masterfile Royalty Free

ALL YOUR STUDY plans can go down the drain when a friend says, "Time to party!" Sometimes, succeeding in school means replying with a graceful and firm *no*.

Students in higher education tend to have many commitments. Saying no helps you to prevent an overloaded schedule that compromises your health and grade point average. You can use five strategies to say no in a respectful way—gracefully.

Think critically about your assumptions. An inability to say no can spring from the assumption that you'll lose friends if you state what you really want. But consider this: If you cannot say no, then you are not in charge of your time. You've given that right to whoever wants to interrupt you. This is not a friendship based on equality. True friends will respect your wishes.

Plan your refusal. You might find it easier to say no when you don't have to grasp for words. Choose some key words and phrases in advance—for example, "I'd love to, but not today"; "Thanks for asking, but I have a huge test tomorrow and want to study"; or "I'd prefer not do anything tonight; do you want to grab lunch tomorrow instead?"

When you refuse, align your verbal and nonverbal messages. Reinforce your words with a firm voice and a posture that communicates confidence.

Avoid apologies or qualifiers. People give away their power when they couch their no's in phrases such as "I'm sorry, but I just don't know if I want to" or "Would you get upset if I said no?"

You don't have to apologize for being in charge of your life. It's OK to say no.

Wait for the request. People who worry about saying no often give in to a request before it's actually been made. Wait until you hear a question. "Time to party!" is not a question. Nor is it a call to action. Save your response until you hear a specific request, such as "Would you go to a party with me?"

Remember that one no leads to another yes. *Yes* and *no* are complementary, not contradictory. Saying no to one activity allows you to say yes to something that's more important right now. Saying no to a movie allows you to say yes to outlining a paper or reading a textbook chapter. You can say an unqualified yes to the next social activity—and enjoy it more—after you've completed some key tasks on your to-do list. ✳

You deserve compliments

Some people find it more difficult to accept compliments than criticisms. Here are some hints for handling compliments.

Accept the compliment. People sometimes respond to praise with "Oh, it's really nothing" or "This old thing? I've had it for years." This type of response undermines both you and the person who sent the compliment.

Choose another time to deliver your own compliments. Automatically returning a compliment can appear suspiciously polite and insincere.

Let the compliment stand. Asking "Do you really think so?" questions the integrity of the message. It can also sound as if you're fishing for more compliments.

Accepting compliments is not the same as being conceited. If you're in doubt about how to respond, just smile and say, "Thank you!" This simple response affirms the compliment, along with the person who delivered it.

You are worthy and capable. Allow people to acknowledge that fact.

7 steps to effective complaints

Sometimes relationship building involves making a complaint. Whining, blaming, pouting, screaming, and yelling insults usually don't get results. Here are some guidelines for complaining effectively.

© Photodisc/Fotosearch

1 **Go to the source.** Start with the person who is most directly involved with the problem. This person will have the best understanding of the complaint, and talking directly with her can help to avoid any confusion.

2 **Present the facts without blaming anyone.** Consider how it might feel to receive complaints like these: "I put a lot of work into this project, but you gave me a C." "Your class is boring." "I just can't trust you." Your complaint will carry more weight if you document the facts. Keep track of names and dates. Note what actions were promised and what results actually occurred.

3 **Go up the ladder to people with more responsibility.** If you don't get satisfaction at the first level, go to that person's direct supervisor. Even requesting a supervisor's name will often get results. Write a letter to the company president if necessary.

4 **Ask for commitments.** When you find someone who is willing to solve your problem, get him to say exactly what he is going to do, and when.

5 **Use available support.** There are dozens of groups, as well as government agencies, willing to get involved in resolving complaints. Contact consumer groups of the Better Business Bureau. Trade associations can sometimes help. Ask city council members, county commissioners, state legislators, and senators and representatives. All of them want your vote, so they are usually eager to help.

6 **Take legal action, if necessary.** Small-claims court is relatively inexpensive, and they don't require you to hire a lawyer. These courts can handle cases involving small amounts of money (usually up to a few thousand dollars). Legal-aid offices can sometimes answer questions.

7 **Don't give up.** Assume that others are on your team. Many people are out there to help you. State what you intend to do, and ask for their partnership. ✳

Criticism really can be constructive

Although receiving criticism is rarely fun, it is often educational. Here are some ways to get the most value from it.

Avoid finding fault. When your mind is occupied with finding fault in others, you aren't open to hearing constructive comments about yourself.

Take criticism seriously. Some people laugh or joke to cover up their anger or embarrassment at being criticized. A humorous reaction on your part can be mistaken for a lack of concern.

React to criticism with acceptance. Most people don't enjoy pointing out another's faults. Your denial, argument, or joking makes it more difficult for them to give honest feedback. You can disagree with criticism and still accept it calmly.

Keep criticism in perspective. Avoid blowing the criticism out of proportion. The purpose of criticism is to generate positive change and self-improvement. There's no need to overreact to it.

Listen without defensiveness. You can't hear the criticism if you're busy framing your rebuttal.

exercise
26 V.I.P.s (very important persons)

Step 1. Under the column below titled "Name," write the names of at least seven people who have positively influenced your life. They might be relatives, friends, teachers, or perhaps persons you have never met. (Complete each step before moving on.)

Step 2. In the next column, rate your gratitude for this person's influence (from 1 to 5, with 1 being a little grateful and 5 being extremely grateful).

Step 3. In the third column, rate how fully you have communicated your appreciation to this person (again, 1 to 5, with 1 being not communicated and 5 being fully communicated).

Step 4. In the final column, put a U to indicate the persons with whom you have unfinished business (such as an important communication that you have not yet sent).

Name	Grateful (1–5)	Communicate Appreciation (1–5)	U

Step 5. Now select two persons with U's beside their names, and write each of them a letter. Express the love, tenderness, and joy you feel toward them. Tell them exactly how they have helped change your life and how glad you are that they did.

Step 6. You also have an impact on others. Write below the names of people whose lives you have influenced. Consider sharing with these people why you enjoy being a part of their lives.

COMMUNICATING

8

Collaborating for success

COLLABORATING SIMPLY MEANS working with others to achieve a common goal. In the workplace, things get done through collaboration. For example, the Boeing 747 airplane—among the world's largest aircraft—resulted from 75,000 blueprints that were created and implemented by a complex network of teams.[6]

To develop collaboration skills, take your cue from the Power Processes included throughout this book. Following are ways you can use four of the Power Processes to supercharge your next team project. Review the other Power Processes, and create more ideas of your own.

Discover what you want. To promote effective results, define your team's purpose, its expected results, and how it will be held accountable. Also ask for enough support—in terms of time, money, and other resources—to produce those results.

To define specific results, ask four questions based on the Master Student Map that begins each chapter of this book:

- Why is this project being done?
- What would a successful outcome for this project look like?
- How are we going to create a bridge from our current reality to that successful outcome?
- What if we truly made this outcome a high priority? What is the very next action that each of us would take to make it happen?

Ideas are tools. According to Frank LaFasto and Carl Larson, authors of *When Teams Work Best*, the most common barrier to effective teamwork is an atmosphere of defensiveness.[7] Teams tend to fizzle when they create new ideas that team members greet with immediate skepticism or outright rejection: *This suggestion will never work. . . . That's just not the way we do things around here. . . . We can't break with tradition. . . .* These responses are examples of "group think," which happens when a team automatically rules out new ideas simply because they're . . . well, new.

You can prevent this outcome by asking pointed questions before a team convenes its first meeting: *Are we truly interested in change? Are we willing to act on what the team recommends? Or are we just looking for a team to reinforce our current practices?*

Instead of automatically looking for what's wrong with a suggested idea, suggest that the team look for potential applications for that idea. Even a proposal that seems outlandish at first might become workable with a few modifications. In an empowered team, all ideas are welcome, problems are freely admitted, and any item is open for discussion.

Be here now. Concentration and focused attention are attributes of effective students—and effective teams. When a team tries to tackle too many problems or achieve too many goals, it gets distracted. Members can forget the team's purpose and lose their enthusiasm for the project. You can help restore focus by asking these questions: *What is the single most important goal that our team can meet?* and *What is the single most important thing we can do now to meet that goal?*

Notice your pictures and let them go. During much of the previous century, people worked in jobs with clearly defined tasks and limited responsibilities. Collaborations among employees in different departments were rare.

The concept of teamwork presents a different picture of how to operate a workplace. But old pictures die hard. Companies may give lip service to the idea of teams and yet fall back into traditional practices. Managers might set up teams but offer little training to help people function in this new working environment.

You can prepare for effective workplace practices now. While you are in school, seize opportunities to work collaboratively. Form study groups. Enroll in classes that include group projects. At the same time, keep in mind that not everyone will share your assumptions about the value of teams. By demonstrating your abilities, you can help them form new pictures. ✳

8

COMMUNICATING

Staying smart in cyberspace— safe social networking

SOCIAL NETWORKS ARE groups of people who connect with each other while they're online. These networks communities can create value. Web sites such as MySpace, Facebook, and LinkedIn are known as places to share news, photos, and personal profiles. You can also use such sites to form study groups, promote special events, and make job contacts. Microblogging services such as Twitter allow hour-by-hour and even minute-to-minute contact.

Activity in online communities can also have unexpected consequences. You might find examples of "cyberbullying"—hate speech or threats of violence. And some users find that embarrassing details from their online profiles come back to haunt them years later.

You can use simple strategies to stay in charge of your safety, reputation, and integrity any time you connect with people online.

Post only what you want made public and permanent. The Internet as a whole is a public medium. This is true of its online communities as well. Post only the kind of information about yourself that you *want* to be made public.

Friends, relatives, university administrators, potential employers, and police officers might be able to access your online profile. Don't post anything that could embarrass you later. Act today to protect the person that you want to be 4 or 5 years from now.

Remember that there is no delete key for the Internet. Web sites such as the Internet Archive and its "Wayback Machine" almost guarantee that anything you post online will stay online for a long time. Anyone with Internet access can take your words and images and post them on a Web site or distribute them via e-mail to

damage your reputation. In the virtual world, you never know who's following you.

To avoid unwanted encounters with members of online communities, also avoid posting the following:

- Your home address.
- Your school address.
- Your phone number.
- Your birth date.
- Your screen name for instant messaging.
- Your class schedule.
- Your financial information, such as bank account numbers, credit card numbers, your social security number, or information about an eBay or PayPal account.
- Information about places that you regularly go at certain times of the day.
- Information about places you plan to visit in the future.
- Provocative pictures or messages with sexual innuendos.
- Pictures of yourself at school or at work.

To further protect your safety, don't add strangers to your list of online friends.

Use similar caution and common sense when joining groups. Signing up for a group with a name like *Binge Drinking Forever* can have consequences for years to come.

Be honest. After you've chosen what information to post, make sure that it's accurate. False information can lead to expulsion from a community. For example,

mastering technology

MASTER STUDENTS—GET NETWORKED

Learning naturally occurs in social networks—that is, among groups of teachers and students. With technology, you can extend your network across the reach of the Internet. For example:

- Choose a topic that interests you, and search for related Web sites and podcasts.
- Use an RSS reader such as Google Reader, Bloglines, or NetNewsWire to get updated lists of articles on the Web sites you'd like to follow.

- Use e-mail and chat rooms to contact experts on your topic.
- Use videoconferencing Web sites to converse in real time with people across the world.
- Pay special attention to well-written blogs, and join the discussion by commenting on the postings.
- Create your own blog to document your learning, and welcome comments from others.

COMMUNICATING

8

MySpace administrators delete profiles of people who lie about their age.[8]

Also avoid flirting while you're online. People may not be who they say they are.

Use privacy features. Many online communities offer options for blocking messages from strangers, including instant messages and friendship invitations. Several social networking sites allow you to create both private and public profiles. (Look for a link on each site titled "Frequently Asked Questions," "Security Features," "Account Settings," or "Privacy Settings.") For further protection, review and update your list of contacts on a regular basis.

In addition, respect the privacy of other members. If you want to post something on their sites, send a message asking for permission first.

Be cautious about meeting community members in person. Because people can give misleading or false information about themselves online, avoid meeting them in person. If you do opt for a face-to-face meeting, choose a public place, and bring along a friend you trust.

Report malicious content. If you find online content that you consider offensive or dangerous, report it to site administrators. In many online communities, you can do this anonymously. You can help to prevent online forms of intolerance, prejudice, and discrimination. Set a positive counterexample by posting messages that demonstrate acceptance of diversity.

Remember netiquette. The word *etiquette* refers to common courtesy in interpersonal relationships. Its online equivalent is called *netiquette*—a set of guidelines for using computers, cell phones, or any other form of technology.

Certain kinds of exchanges can send the tone of online communications—including social networking, e-mail messages, and blog postings—into the gutter. To promote a cordial online community, abide by the following guidelines:

■ Respect others' time. People often turn to the Internet with the hope of saving time—not wasting it. You can accommodate their desires by typing concise messages. Adopt the habit of getting to your point, sticking to it, and getting to the end.

■ Fine-tune the mechanics. Proofread your message for spelling and grammar—just as you would a printed message. Some e-mail programs have built-in spelling checkers as an optional tool. Give your readers the gift of clarity and precision. Use electronic communications as a chance to hone your writing skills.

■ Avoid typing passages in ALL UPPERCASE LETTERS. This is the online equivalent of shouting.

■ Design your messages for fast retrieval. Avoid graphics and attachments that take a long time to download, tying up your recipient's computer.

■ Remember that the message is missing the emotion. When you communicate online, the people who receive your e-mail will miss out on voice inflection and nonverbal cues that are present in face-to-face communication. Without these cues, words can be easily misinterpreted. Reread your message before sending it to be sure you have clarified what you want to say and how you feel.

The cornerstone of netiquette is to remember that the recipient on the other end is a human being. Whenever you're at a keyboard or cell phone typing up messages, ask yourself one question: "Would I say this to the person's face?" ✳

 Learn more about smart social networking online.

Text message etiquette—Five key points

1. **Keep it short.** Limit text messages to about 150 characters. That's two to three sentences. If you go longer, your phone might split the message in two or even drop the last few words. In addition, long texts can be confusing. Send an e-mail or make a phone call instead.

2. **Double-check the outgoing number.** If a message intended for your boyfriend or girlfriend ends up going to your boss, the results can be alarming.

3. **At work and in other public places, set your phone on vibrate.** No one else wants to hear how many text messages you're getting.

4. **Keep the time in mind.** Save 2 a.m. text messages for special circumstances and your closest friends. A text can ring at the same volume as a phone call and wake people up.

5. **Reflect on the number of messages you send to each person.** Replacing in-person and phone contact with texting might send a message that the relationship is a low priority.

COMMUNICATING

8

Three phases of effective writing

Effective writing is essential to your success. Papers, presentations, essay tests, e-mail, social networking sites—and even the occasional text message—call for your ability to communicate ideas with force and clarity.

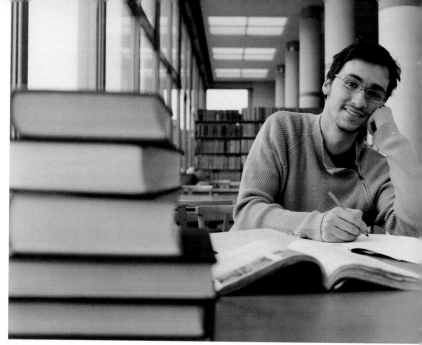
Digital Vision/Getty

THIS CHAPTER OUTLINES a three-phase process for writing anything:

1. Getting ready to write.
2. Writing a first draft.
3. Revising your draft.

PHASE 1: Getting ready to write

Schedule and list writing tasks

You can divide the ultimate goal—a finished paper—into smaller steps that you can tackle right away. Estimate how long it will take to complete each step. Start with the date your paper is due and work backward to the present. Say that the due date is December 1, and you have about 3 months to write the paper. To give yourself a cushion, schedule November 20 as your targeted completion date. Plan what you want to get done by November 1, and then list what you want to get done by October 1.

Generate ideas for a topic

Brainstorm with a group. There's no need to create in isolation. Forget the myth of the lonely, frustrated artist hashing out ideas alone in a dimly lit Paris café. You can harness the energy and the natural creative power of a group to assist you. For ideas about ways to brainstorm, see Chapter 7: Thinking.

Speak it. To get ideas flowing, start talking. Admit your confusion or lack of clear ideas. Then just speak.

By putting your thoughts into words, you'll start thinking more clearly. Novelist E. M. Forster said, "'Speak before you think' is creation's motto."[9]

Use free writing. Free writing, a technique championed by writing teacher Peter Elbow, sends a depth probe into your creative mind.[10] There's only one rule in free writing: Write without stopping. Set a time limit—say, 10 minutes—and keep your pencil in motion or your fingers dancing across the keyboard the whole time. Give yourself permission to keep writing. Ignore the urge to stop and rewrite, even if you think what you've written isn't very good. There's no need to worry about spelling, punctuation, or grammar. It's OK if you stray from the initial subject. Just keep writing, and let the ideas flow. Experiment with free writing as soon as your instructor assigns a paper.

Refine initial ideas

Select a topic and working title. It's easy to put off writing if you have a hard time choosing a topic. However, it is almost impossible to make a wrong choice of topic at this stage. You can choose a different topic later if you find the one you've chosen isn't working out.

Using your instructor's guidelines for the paper or speech, write down a list of topics that interest you. Write as many of these ideas as you can think of in 2 minutes. Then choose one topic. If you can't decide, use scissors to cut your list into single items, put them in a box, and pull one out. To avoid getting stuck on this step, set a precise time line: "I will choose a topic by 4 p.m. on Wednesday."

The most common pitfall is selecting a topic that's too broad. "Harriet Tubman" is not a useful topic for your American history paper. Instead, consider "Harriet Tubman's activities as a Union spy during the Civil

War." Your topic statement can function as a working title.

Write a thesis statement. Clarify what you want to say by summarizing it in one concise sentence. This sentence, called a *thesis statement*, refines your working title. It also helps in making a preliminary outline.

You might write a thesis statement such as "Harriet Tubman's activities with the Underground Railroad led to a relationship with the Union army during the Civil War." A thesis statement that's clear and to the point can make your paper easier to write. Remember, you can always rewrite your thesis statement as you learn more about your topic.

A thesis statement is different from a topic. Like newspaper headlines, a thesis statement makes an assertion or describes an action. It is expressed in a complete sentence, including a verb. "Diversity" is a topic. "Cultural diversity is valuable" is a thesis statement.

Consider your purpose

Effective writing flows from a purpose. Discuss the purpose of your assignment with your instructor. Also think about how you'd like your reader or listener to respond after considering your ideas. Do you want your audience to think differently, to feel differently, or to take a certain action?

How you answer these questions greatly affects your writing strategy. If you want someone to think differently, make your writing clear and logical. Support your assertions with evidence. If you want someone to feel differently, consider crafting a story. Write about a character your audience can empathize with, and tell how that character resolves a problem that the audience can relate to. And if your purpose is to move the reader into action, explain exactly what steps to take and offer solid benefits for doing so.

To clarify your purpose, state it in one sentence—for example, "The purpose of this paper is to define the term *success* in such a clear and convincing way that I win a scholarship from the publisher of this textbook."

Do initial research

At the initial stage, the objective of your research is not to uncover specific facts about your topic. That comes later. First, you want to gain an overview of the subject. Discover the structure of your topic—its major divisions and branches.

Say that you want to persuade the reader to vote for a certain candidate. You must first learn enough about this person to summarize his background and state his stands on key issues.

Outline

An outline is a kind of map. When you follow a map, you avoid getting lost. Likewise, an outline keeps you from wandering off the topic.

To start an outline, gather a stack of 3x5 cards. Brainstorm ideas you want to include in your paper. Write one phrase or sentence per card. Then experiment with the cards. Group them into separate stacks, each stack representing one major category. After that, arrange the stacks in order. Finally, arrange the cards within each stack in a logical order. Rearrange them until you discover an organization that you like. If you write on a computer, consider using the outlining feature of your word-processing software.

Do in-depth research

You can find information about research skills in Chapter 4: Reading and Chapter 5: Notes. The following are further suggestions.

Use 3x5 cards. If they haven't found their way into your life by now, joy awaits you. These cards work wonders when you conduct research. Just write down one idea per card. This makes it easy to organize—and reorganize—your ideas.

Organizing research cards as you create them saves time. Use rubber bands to keep source cards—cards that include the bibliographical information for a source—separate from information cards—cards that include nuggets of information from a source—and to maintain general categories.

You can also save time in two other ways. First, copy all of the information correctly. Always include the source code and page number on information cards. Second, be neat and organized. Write legibly, using the same format for all of your cards.

In addition to source cards and information cards, generate idea cards. If you have a thought while you are researching, write it down on a card. Label these cards clearly as containing your own ideas.

An alternative to 3x5 cards is a computer outlining or database program. Some word-processing packages also include features that can be used for outlining and note taking.

Discovery Statement

Take a First Step about Writing

This Journal Entry is for people who avoid writing. As with any anxiety, you can approach writing anxiety by accepting it fully. Realize that it's OK to feel anxious about writing. Others have shared this feeling, and many people have worked with it successfully.

Begin by telling the truth. Describe exactly what happens when you start to write. What thoughts or images run through your mind? Do you feel any tension or discomfort in your body? Where? Let the thoughts and images come to the surface without resistance. Complete the following statement.

When I begin to write, I discover that I . . .

PHASE 2: Writing a first draft

If you've planned your writing project and completed your research, you've already done much of the hard work. Now you can relax into writing your first draft.

TO CREATE YOUR draft, gather your notes and arrange them to follow your outline. Then write about the ideas in your notes. Write in paragraphs, with one idea per paragraph. If you have organized your notes logically, related facts will appear close to one another. As you complete this task, keep the following suggestions in mind.

Remember that the first draft is not for keeps

You can worry about quality later, when you revise. Your goal at this point is simply to generate lots of material.

Write freely

Many writers prefer to get their first draft down quickly. Their advice is just to keep writing, much as in free writing. Of course, you may pause occasionally to glance at your notes and outline. The idea is to avoid stopping to edit your work. You can save that for the next step.

Be yourself

Let go of the urge to sound "official" or "scholarly." Instead, write in a natural voice. Address your thoughts not to the teacher but to an intelligent student or someone you care about. Visualize this person, and choose the three or four most important things you'd say to her about the topic. This helps you avoid the temptation to write merely to impress.

Avoid ~~at all costs and at all times~~ the really, really terrible mistake of using ~~way too many~~ unnecessary words, ~~a mistake that some student writers often make when they sit down to write papers for the various courses in which they participate at the fine institutions of higher learning which they are fortunate to attend.~~

Ease into it

Some people find that it works well to forget the word *writing*. Instead, they ease into the task with activities that help generate ideas. You can free associate, cluster, meditate, daydream, doodle, draw diagrams, visualize the event you want to describe, talk into a voice recorder—anything that gets you started.

Make writing a habit

The word *inspiration* is not in the working vocabulary for many professional writers. Instead of waiting for inspiration to strike, they simply make a habit of writing at a certain time each day. You can use the same strategy. Schedule a block of time to write your first draft. The very act of writing can breed inspiration.

Respect your deep mind

Part of the process of writing takes place outside our awareness. There's nothing mysterious about this process. Many people report that ideas come to them while they're doing something totally unrelated to writing. Often this happens after they've been grappling with a question and have reached a point where they feel stuck. It's like the composer who said, "There I was, sitting and eating a sandwich, and all of a sudden this darn tune pops into my head." You can trust your deep mind. It's writing while you eat, sleep, and brush your teeth.

Get physical

Writing, like jogging or playing tennis, is a physical activity. You can move your body in ways that are in tune with the flow of your ideas. While working on the first draft, take breaks. Go for a walk. Speak or sing your ideas out loud. From time to time, practice relaxation techniques and breathe deeply.

Use affirmations and visualizations

Write with the idea that the finished paper or speech is inside you, waiting to be released. Affirmations and visualizations can help you with this. Imagine what your finished paper will look like. Construct a detailed mental picture of the title page and major sections of the paper. See a clean, typed copy, and speculate how it will feel to hold the paper and flip through the pages. Visualize the reaction of audience members after you've given your speech.

Then support your writing by sprinkling your self-talk with statements that affirm your abilities. For example: "I express myself clearly and persuasively." "I am using an effective process to write my paper." "I will be pleased with the results."

Hide it in your drawer for a while

Schedule time for rewrites before you begin, and schedule at least one day between revisions so that you can let the material sit. On Tuesday night, you might think your writing sings the song of beautiful language. On Wednesday, you will see that those same words, such as the phrase "sings the song of beautiful language," belong in the trash basket.

Ideally, a student will revise a paper two or three times, make a clean copy of those revisions, then let the last revised draft sit for at least 3 or 4 days. The brain needs that much time to disengage itself from the project. Obvious grammatical mistakes, awkward constructions, and lapses in logic are hidden from us when we are in the middle of the creative process. Give yourself time to step back, and then go over the paper one last time before starting the third phase of the writing process.

PHASE 3: Revising your draft

SCHEDULE TIME FOR rewrites before you begin, and schedule at least 1 day between revisions so that you can let the material sit. On Tuesday night, you might think your writing sings the song of beautiful language. On Wednesday, you will see that those same words, such as the phrase "sings the song of beautiful language," belong in the trash basket.

Plan to revise a paper two or three times, make a clean copy of those revisions, and then let the last revised draft sit for at least 3 or 4 days.

Keep in mind the saying "Write in haste; revise at leisure." When you edit and revise, slow down and take a microscope to your work. One guideline is to allow 50 percent of writing time for planning, researching, and writing the first draft. Then give the remaining 50 percent to revising.

An effective way to revise your paper is to read it out loud. The eyes tend to fill in the blanks in our own writing. The combination of voice and ears forces us to pay attention to the details.

Another technique is to have a friend look over your paper. This is never a substitute for your own review, but a friend can often see mistakes you miss. Remember, when other people criticize or review your work, they're not attacking you. They're just commenting on your paper. With a little practice, you can actually learn to welcome feedback.

Reading aloud and having a friend comment on your paper are techniques that can help you in each step of rewriting explained below.

Cut

Look for excess baggage. Avoid at all costs and at all times the really, really terrible mistake of using way too many unnecessary words, a mistake that some student writers often make when they sit down to write papers for the various courses in which they participate at the fine institutions of higher learning that they are fortunate enough to attend. (Example: The previous sentence could be edited to "Avoid unnecessary words.")

Approach your rough draft as if it were a chunk of granite from which you will chisel the final product. In the end, much of your first draft will be lying on the floor. What is left will be the clean, clear, polished product. Sometimes the revisions are painful. Sooner or later, every writer invents a phrase that is truly clever but makes no contribution to the purpose of the paper. Grit your teeth and let it go.

Note: For maximum efficiency, make the larger cuts first—sections, chapters, pages. Then go for the smaller cuts—paragraphs, sentences, phrases, words.

Paste

In deleting both larger and smaller passages in your first draft, you've probably removed some of the original transitions and connecting ideas. The next task is to rearrange what's left of your paper or speech so that it flows logically. Look for consistency within paragraphs and for transitions from paragraph to paragraph and section to section.

If all or part of your draft doesn't hang together, reorder your ideas. Imagine yourself with scissors and glue, cutting the paper into scraps—one scrap for each point. Then paste these points down in a new, more logical order.

Fix

Now it's time to look at individual words and phrases. Define any terms that the reader might not know, putting them in plain English whenever you can.

In general, rely on nouns and verbs. Using too many adjectives and adverbs weakens your message and adds unnecessary bulk to your writing. Write about the details, and be specific. Also, use the active rather than the passive voice.

Instead of writing in the passive voice:

A project was initiated.

You can use the active voice:

The research team began a project.

Instead of writing verbosely:

After making a timely arrival and perspicaciously observing the unfolding events, I emerged totally and gloriously victorious.

You can write to the point, as Julius Caesar did:

I came, I saw, I conquered.

Instead of writing vaguely:

The speaker made effective use of the television medium, asking in no uncertain terms that we change our belief systems.

You can write specifically:

The reformed criminal stared straight into the television camera and shouted, "Take a good look at what you're doing! Will it get you what you really want?"

Prepare

In a sense, any paper is a sales effort. If you hand in a paper that is wearing wrinkled jeans, its hair tangled and unwashed and its shoes untied, your instructor is less likely to buy it. To avoid this situation, format your paper following accepted standards for margin widths, endnotes, title pages, and other details.

Ask your instructor for specific instructions on how to cite the sources used in writing your paper. You can find useful guidelines in the *MLA Handbook for Writers of Research Papers,* a book from the Modern Language Association. Also visit the MLA Web site at *www.mla.org/style_faq.*

If you cut and paste material from a Web page directly into your paper, be sure to place that material in quotation marks and cite the source. And before referencing an e-mail message, verify the sender's identity. Remember that anyone sending e-mail can pretend to be someone else.

Use quality paper for your final version. For an even more professional appearance, bind your paper with a plastic or paper cover.

Proof

As you ease down the homestretch, read your revised paper one more time. This time, go for the big picture and look for the following:

- A clear thesis statement.

- Sentences that introduce your topic, guide the reader through the major sections of your paper, and summarize your conclusions.

- Details—such as quotations, examples, and statistics—that support your conclusions.

- Lean sentences that have been purged of needless words.

- Plenty of action verbs and concrete, specific nouns.

Finally, look over your paper with an eye for spelling and grammar mistakes.

When you're through proofreading, take a minute to savor the result. You've just witnessed something of a miracle—the mind attaining clarity and resolution. That's the aha! in writing. ✳

 Find more paths to effective writing online.

COMMUNICATING

8

Academic integrity:
Avoid plagiarism

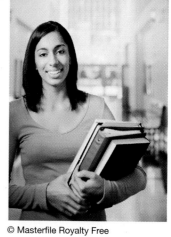

© Masterfile Royalty Free

USING ANOTHER PERSON'S words, images, or other original creations without giving proper credit is called *plagiarism*. Plagiarism amounts to taking someone else's work and presenting it as your own—the equivalent of cheating on a test. The consequences of plagiarism can range from a failing grade to expulsion from school.

Plagiarism can be unintentional. Some students don't understand the research process. Sometimes they leave writing until the last minute and don't take the time to organize their sources of information. Also, some people are raised in cultures where identity is based on group membership rather than individual achievement. These students may find it hard to understand how creative work can be owned by an individual.

To avoid plagiarism, ask an instructor where you can find your school's written policy on this issue. Read this document carefully, and ask questions about *anything* you don't understand.

The basic guidelines for preventing plagiarism are to cite a source for each phrase, sequence of ideas, or visual image created by another person. While ideas cannot be copyrighted, the way that any idea is *expressed* can be. You also need to list a source for any idea that is closely identified with a particular person.

The goal is to clearly distinguish your own work from the work of others. There are several ways to ensure that you do this consistently.

Identify direct quotes. If you use a direct quote from another writer or speaker, put that person's words in quotation marks. If you do research online, you might find yourself copying sentences or paragraphs from a Web page and pasting them directly into your notes. *This is the same as taking direct quotes from your source.* To avoid plagiarism, identify such passages in an obvious way.

Paraphrase carefully. Paraphrasing means restating the original passage in your own words, usually making it shorter and simpler. Students who copy a passage word for word and then just rearrange or delete a few phrases are running a serious risk of plagiarism. Consider this paragraph:

Higher education also offers you the chance to learn how to learn. In fact, that's the subject of this book. Employers value the person who is a "quick study" when it comes to learning a new job. That makes your ability to learn a marketable skill.

A proper paraphrase of this passage might be like this:

The author notes that when we learn how to learn, we gain a skill that is valued by employers.

Remember to cite a source for paraphrases, just as you do for direct quotes. When you use the same sequence of ideas as one of your sources—even if you have not paraphrased or directly quoted—cite that source.

Note details about each source. For books, details about each source include the author, title, publisher, publication date, location of publisher, and page number. For articles from print sources, record the article title and the name of the magazine or journal as well. If you found the article in an academic or technical journal, also record the volume and number of the publication. A librarian can help identify these details.

If your source is a Web page, record as many identifying details as you can find—author, title, sponsoring organization, URL, publication date, and revision date. In addition, list the date that you accessed the page.

Cite your sources as endnotes or footnotes to your paper. Ask your instructor for examples of the format to use.

Note: You do not need to credit wording that's wholly your own. Nor do you need to credit general ideas, such as the suggestion that people use a to-do list to plan their time. When you use your own words to describe such an idea, there's no need to credit a source. But if you borrow someone else's words or images to explain the idea, do give credit. ✳

 Find examples of the suggestions in this article online.

8

COMMUNICATING

© Masterfile Royalty Free

Mastering public speaking

Some people tune out during a speech. Just think of all the times you have listened to instructors, lecturers, and politicians. Remember all the wonderful daydreams you had during their speeches.

YOUR AUDIENCES are like you. The way you plan and present your speech can determine the number of audience members who will stay with you until the end. Polishing your speaking and presentation skills can also help you think on your feet and communicate clearly. You can use these skills in any course and in any career you choose.

Analyze your audience

Developing a speech is similar to writing a paper. Begin by writing out your topic, purpose, and thesis statement as described in "Phase 1: Getting Ready to Write" on page 253. Then carefully analyze your audience by using the strategies in the chart below.

Remember that audiences generally have one question in mind: *So what?* They want to know that your presentation relates to their needs and desires. To convince people that you have something worthwhile to say, think of your main topic or point. Then see if you can complete this sentence: *I'm telling you this because. . . .*

Organize your presentation

Consider the length of your presentation. Plan on delivering about a hundred words per minute. This is only a general guideline, however, so time yourself as you practice your presentation.

Aim for a lean presentation—enough words to make your point but not so many as to make your audience restless. Leave your listeners wanting more. When you speak, be brief and then be seated.

Speeches are usually organized in three main parts: the introduction, the main body, and the conclusion.

Write the introduction. Rambling speeches with no clear point or organization put audiences to sleep. Solve this problem with your introduction. The following introduction, for example, reveals the thesis and exactly what's coming. It

If your topic is new to listeners . . .	• Explain why your topic matters to them. • Relate the topic to something that listeners already know and care about. • Define any terms that listeners might not know.
If listeners already know about your topic . . .	• Acknowledge this fact at the beginning of your speech. • Find a narrow aspect of the topic that may be new to listeners. • Offer a new perspective on the topic, or connect it to an unfamiliar topic.
If listeners disagree with your thesis . . .	• Tactfully admit your differences of opinion. • Reinforce points on which you and your audience agree. • Build credibility by explaining your qualifications to speak on your topic. • Quote expert figures that agree with your thesis—people whom your audience is likely to admire. • Explain that their current viewpoint has costs for them, and that a slight adjustment in their thinking will bring significant benefits.
If listeners may be uninterested in your topic . . .	• Explain how listening to your speech can help them gain something that matters deeply to them. • Explain ways to apply your ideas in daily life.

reveals that the speech will have three distinct parts, each in logical order:

Dog fighting is a cruel sport. I intend to describe exactly what happens to the animals, tell you who is doing this, and show you how you can stop this inhumane practice.

Whenever possible, talk about things that hold your interest. Include your personal experiences and start with a bang. Consider this introduction to a speech on the subject of world hunger:

I'm very honored to be here with you today. I intend to talk about malnutrition and starvation. First, I want to outline the extent of these problems, then I will discuss some basic assumptions concerning world hunger, and finally I will propose some solutions.

You can almost hear the snores from the audience. Following is a rewrite:

More people have died from hunger in the past 5 years than have been killed in all of the wars, revolutions, and murders in the past 150 years. Yet there is enough food to go around. I'm honored to be here with you today to discuss solutions to this problem.

Some members of an audience will begin to drift during any speech, but most people pay attention for at least the first few seconds. Highlight your main points in the beginning sentences of your speech.

People might tell you to start your introduction with a joke. Humor is tricky. You run the risk of falling flat or offending somebody. Save jokes until you have plenty of experience with public speaking and know your audiences well.

Also avoid long, flowery introductions in which you tell people how much you like them, how thrilled you are to address them, and how humble you feel standing in front of them. If you lay it on too thick, your audience won't believe a word of it.

Draft your introduction, and then come back to it after you've written the rest of your speech. In the process of creating the main body and conclusion, your thoughts about the purpose and main points of your speech might change. You might even want to write the introduction last.

Write the main body. The main body of your speech is the content, which accounts for 70 to 90 percent of most speeches. In the main body, you develop your ideas in much the same way that you develop a written paper.

Transitions are especially important in speeches. Give your audience a signal when you change points. Do so by using meaningful pauses and verbal emphasis, as well as transitional phrases: "On the other hand, until the public realizes what is happening to

children in these countries . . ." or "The second reason hunger persists is . . . ."

In long speeches, recap from time to time. Also preview what's to come. Hold your audience's attention by using facts, descriptions, expert opinions, and statistics.

Write the conclusion. At the end of the speech, summarize your points and draw your conclusion. You started with a bang; now finish with drama. The first and last parts of a speech are the most important. Make it clear to your audience when you've reached the end. Avoid endings such as "This is the end of my speech." A simple standby is "So in conclusion, I want to reiterate three points: First, . . ." When you are finished, stop talking.

Create speaking notes. Some professional speakers recommend writing out your speech in full, and then putting key words or main points on a few 3x5 cards. Number the cards so that if you drop them, you can quickly put them in order again. As you finish the information on each card, move it to the back of the pile. Write information clearly and in letters large enough to be seen from a distance.

The disadvantage of the 3x5 card system is that it involves card shuffling. Some speakers prefer to use standard outlined notes. Another option is mind mapping. Even an hour-long speech can be mapped on one sheet of paper. You can also use memory techniques to memorize the outline of your speech.

Create supporting visuals. Presentations often include visuals such as overhead transparencies, flip charts, or slides created with presentation software. These visuals can reinforce your main points and help your audience understand how your presentation is organized.

Use visuals to *complement* rather than *replace* your speaking. If you use too many visuals—or visuals that are too complex—your audience might focus on them and forget about you. To avoid this fate,

- Use fewer visuals rather than more. Save them for illustrations, photos, charts, and concepts that are hard to express in words. For a 15-minute presentation, a total of five to ten slides is enough.

- Limit the amount of text on each visual. Stick to key words presented in short sentences or phrases, and in bulleted or numbered lists.

- Use a consistent set of plain fonts that are large enough for all audience members to see.

- Stick with a simple, coherent color scheme. Use light-colored text on a dark background, or dark text on a light background.

Overcome fear of public speaking

You may not be able to eliminate fear of public speaking entirely, but you can take steps to reduce and manage it.

Prepare thoroughly. Research your topic thoroughly. Knowing your topic inside and out can create a baseline of confidence. To make a strong start, memorize the first four sentences that you plan to deliver, and practice them many times. Delivering them flawlessly when you're in front of an audience can build your confidence for the rest of your speech.

Accept your physical sensations. You've probably experienced physical sensations that are commonly associated with stage fright: dry mouth, a pounding heart, sweaty hands, muscle jitters, shortness of breath, and a shaky voice. One immediate way to deal with such sensations is to simply notice them. Tell yourself, "Yes, my hands are clammy. Yes, my stomach is upset. Also, my face feels numb." Trying to deny or ignore such facts can increase your fear. When you fully accept sensations, however, they start to lose power.

Focus on content, not delivery. Michael Motley, a professor at the University of California–Davis, distinguishes between two orientations to speaking. People with a *performance orientation* believe that the speaker must captivate the audience by using formal techniques that differ from normal conversation. In contrast, speakers with a *communication orientation* see public speaking simply as an extension of one-to-one conversation. The goal is not to perform but to communicate your ideas to an audience in the same ways that you would explain them to a friend.[11]

Adopting a communication orientation can reduce your fear of public speaking. Instead of thinking about yourself, focus on your message. Your audiences are more interested in *what* you have to say than *how* you say it. Forget about giving a "speech." Just give people valuable ideas and information that they can use.

Practice your presentation

The key to successful public speaking is practice.

Use your "speaker's voice." When you practice, do so in a loud voice. Your voice sounds different when you talk loudly, and this fact can be unnerving. Get used to it early on.

Practice in the room in which you will deliver your speech. Hear what your voice sounds like over a sound system. If you can't practice your speech in the actual room, at least visit the site ahead of time. Also make sure that the materials you will need for your speech, including any audio-visual equipment, will be available when you want them.

Make a recording. Many schools have video recording equipment available for student use. Use it while you practice. Then view the finished recording to evaluate your presentation.

Listen for repeated words and phrases. Examples include *you know, kind of,* and *really,* plus any little *uh*'s, *umm*'s, and *ah*'s. To get rid of them, tell yourself that you intend to notice every time they pop up in your daily speech. When you hear them, remind yourself that you don't use those words anymore.

Keep practicing. Avoid speaking word for word, as if you were reading a script. When you know your material well, you can deliver it in a natural way. Practice your presentation until you could deliver it in your sleep. Then run through it a few more times.

Deliver your presentation

Before you begin, get the audience's attention. If people are still filing into the room or adjusting their seats, they're not ready to listen. When all eyes are on you, then begin.

Dress for the occasion. The clothing you choose to wear on the day of your speech delivers a message that's as loud as your words. Consider how your audience will be dressed, and then choose a wardrobe based on the impression you want to make.

Project your voice. When you speak, talk loudly enough to be heard. Avoid leaning over your notes or the podium.

Maintain eye contact. When you look at people, they become less frightening. Remember, too, that it is easier for the audience to listen to someone when that person is looking at them. Find a few friendly faces around the room, and imagine that you are talking to each of these people individually.

Notice your nonverbal communication. Be aware of what your body is telling your audience. Contrived or staged gestures will look dishonest. Be natural. If you don't know what to do with your

Making the grade in group presentations

When preparing group presentations, you can use three strategies for making a memorable impression.

Get organized. As soon as you get the assignment, select a group leader and exchange contact information. Schedule specific times and places for planning, researching, writing, and practicing your presentation.

At your first meeting, write a to-do list that includes all of the tasks involved in completing the assignment. Distribute tasks fairly, paying attention to the strengths of individuals in your group. For example, some people excel at brainstorming, while others prefer researching.

One powerful way to get started is to define clearly the topic and thesis, or main point, of your presentation. Then support your thesis by looking for the most powerful facts, quotations, and anecdotes you can find.

As you get organized, remember how your presentation will be evaluated. If the instructor doesn't give grading criteria, create your own.

Get coordinated. Coordinate your presentation so that you have transitions between individual speakers. Practice making those transitions smooth.

Also practice using visuals such as flip charts, posters, DVDs, videotapes, or slides. To give visuals their full impact, make them appropriate for the room where you will present. Make sure that text is large enough to be seen from the back of the room. For bigger rooms, consider using presentation software or making overhead transparencies.

Get cooperation. Presentations that get top scores take teamwork and planning—not egos. Communicate with group members in an open and sensitive way. Contribute your ideas, and be responsive to the viewpoints of other members. When you cooperate, your group is on the way to an effective presentation.

hands, notice that. Then don't do anything with them.

Notice the time. You can increase the impact of your words by keeping track of the time during your speech. It's better to end early than to run late.

Pause when appropriate. Beginners sometimes feel that they have to fill every moment with the sound of their voice. Release that expectation. Give your listeners a chance to make notes and absorb what you say.

Have fun. Chances are that if you lighten up and enjoy your presentation, so will your listeners.

Reflect on your presentation

Review and reflect on your performance. Did you finish on time? Did you cover all of the points you intended to cover? Was the audience attentive? Did you handle any nervousness effectively?

Welcome evaluation from others. Most of us find it difficult to hear criticism about our speaking. Be aware of resisting such criticism, and then let go of your resistance. Listening to feedback will increase your skill. ✳

practicing critical thinking

You might create a speech with the aim of changing the way your audience thinks or feels about a topic. Think critically about the complexity of this task. Consider your audience's *attitude system*, which has three key elements:

- *Attitudes* involve feelings of approval or disapproval.
- *Beliefs* reflect what people know—or think they know—about a topic.
- *Values* are broad, enduring principles that guide our behaviors.

Of these three elements, values are often the most resistant to change. In addition, people generally seek consistency in their attitudes, beliefs, and values.

This situation suggests a strategy for persuasion. Instead of trying to change your audience's values, see if you can persuade your audience members that one of their attitudes or beliefs *contradicts* their values. Then you can present a new attitude or belief that restores consistency to their attitude system.

Say that you are preparing to speak to a politically conservative audience about a single-payer health insurance system managed by the federal government. This proposal is not always popular with conservatives. However, many members of this political group also value organizational efficiency and cost savings. You could create a speech arguing that the American health insurance system contradicts this value because it is too expensive, and that shifting to a single-payer system would reduce costs.

To analyze the audience for your next speech, create a list of attitudes, beliefs, and values to consider. To organize your thinking, fill in the following chart.

Next, circle any attitudes or beliefs that contradict one of your audience's values. Then, in the space below, brainstorm and write down a new attitude or belief that you can propose, along with some key evidence for it.

_____

_____

_____

_____

_____

_____

_____

_____

_____

_____

_____

_____

_____

_____

_____

_____

_____

_____

_____

_____

Audience attitudes toward your topic	Audience beliefs about your topic	Audience values related to your topic

Employ Your Word

When you give your word, you are creating—literally. The person you are is, for the most part, a result of the agreements you make. Others know who you are by your words and your commitments. And you can learn who you are by observing which commitments you choose to keep and which ones you choose to avoid.

Relationships are built on agreements. When we break a promise to be faithful to a spouse, to help a friend move to a new apartment, or to pay a bill on time, relationships are strained.

The words we use to make agreements can be placed onto several different levels. We can think of each level as one rung on a ladder—the ladder of powerful speaking. As we move up the ladder, our speaking becomes more effective.

The lowest rung on the ladder is *obligation*. Words used at this level include *I should, he ought to, someone had better, they need to, I must,* and *I had to.* Speaking this way implies that something other than ourselves is in control of our lives. When we live at the level of obligation, we speak as if we are victims.

The next rung up is *possibility.* At this level, we examine new options. We play with new ideas, possible solutions, and alternative courses of action. As we do, we learn that we can make choices that dramatically affect the quality of our lives. We are not the victims of circumstance. Phrases that signal this level include *I might, I could, I'll consider, I hope to,* and *maybe.*

From possibility, we can move up to *preference.* Here we begin the process of choice. The words *I prefer* signal that we're moving toward one set of possibilities over another, perhaps setting the stage for eventual action.

Above preference is a rung called *passion.* Again, certain words signal this level: *I want to, I'm really excited to do that,* and *I can't wait.*

Action comes with the next rung—*planning.* When people use phrases such as *I intend to, my goal is to, I plan to,* and *I'll try like mad to,* they're at the level of planning. The Intention Statements you write in this book are examples of planning.

The highest rung on the ladder is *promising.* This is where the power of your word really comes into play. At this level, it's common to use phrases such as these: *I will, I promise to, I am committed,* and *you can count on it.* Promising is where we bridge from possibility and planning to action. Promising brings with it all of the rewards of employing your word.

 Find more ways online to employ your words.

Put it to Work

You can use strategies you learn in *Becoming a Master Student* to succeed at work. To discover ways in which your new communication skills can transfer to your career, reflect on the following case study.

Sanna Lindberg/PhotoAlto Agency RF Collections/Getty

Mark Hyland earned an associate's degree in dental hygiene and then completed a B.A. in business administration. Soon after graduating, he moved back to his hometown and went to work as an office manager for his family dentist.

Mark welcomed the chance to apply the skills he'd gained in school. He ordered supplies, managed the payroll, handled the day-to-day accounting chores, and filed tax returns for the business.

Everyone in the dental office admitted that Mark's skills in these areas were superb. His communication skills were another matter, though. Several long-term patients complained that Mark's manner was condescending—even harsh—during casual conversations at the office. One day, the dentist who hired Mark overheard him talking to a patient.

"I just happened to glance at your records and noticed that you've got a lot of plaque on your upper teeth," said Mark. "Do you ever floss?"

The patient tried to make light of the situation. "Oh well," she said, "we all have our vices, and . . . ."

"Yeah, but it's your teeth we're talking about here," Mark said, interrupting her. "They're really stained, too, from drinking too much coffee."

The dentist winced. He feared he was about to lose a valued patient. However, he'd known Mark for years and counted his parents as friends. He wanted to meet with Mark and give him feedback, yet the dentist knew that this conversation would be awkward for both of them. He found this meeting an easy thing to put off.

Review the suggestions given in this chapter for creating "I" messages. Then write an "I" message that the dentist could use to express his concerns with Mark.

_____

_____

List at least two other suggestions for managing conflict that the dentist could use.

_____

_____

_____

Finally, list two suggestions for Mark to keep in mind when talking to patients.

_____

_____

In addition, consider the following strategies for communicating effectively during your first crucial year as a new employee:

- Use memory techniques to learn coworkers' names quickly.
- Be honest when you don't understand directions—and willing to ask questions.
- Be open to feedback about your performance—and willing to change your behavior on the basis of that feedback.
- Be willing to complete the mundane tasks that are part of almost every job—understand what it means to "pay your dues" in a constructive way.
- To gain credibility in your organization, get involved in a high-profile project, and then perform well.
- Each day, look for a simple way to demonstrate a positive attitude and strong work ethic.

Quiz

chapter 8

- Put it to Work
◀ ◀ ◀ ◀ ◀
- Skills Snapshot
- Master Student Profile

Name _____   Date ____/____/____

1. According to the text, human communication is always flawed to some extent. True or False? Explain your answer.

   True. Because communication can be defined as the process of creating shared meaning, and meaning is based on our past experiences, thoughts, feelings, drives, and desires, human communication is always subject to our personal experience. This often results in miscommunication to some extent. (*Communicating creates our world,* p. 235)

2. During a conversation, if someone is trying to act as a sender when you want to be the sender, you can:

   (a) Stop sending and be the receiver.

   (b) Stop sending and leave the conversation.

   (c) Ask the other person to stop sending so that you can send.

   (d) Do any of the above.

   (d) Any of the above.   (*Communication—Keeping the channels open,* p. 236)

3. This chapter suggests techniques for nonverbal and verbal listening. Briefly explain the difference between these two approaches to listening, and give one example of each approach.

   During nonverbal listening, the listener does not speak and stays focused on what the sender is saying. Examples of nonverbal listening are (list one of the following) maintaining eye contact, displaying openness, sending acknowledgments, releasing distractions, and suspending judgments. During verbal listening, the listener responds to what the sender is saying to indicate that the listener understands what is being communicated. Examples of verbal listening are (list one of the following) feeding back meaning, noticing verbal and nonverbal messages, listening for requests and intentions, allowing emotion, asking for more, being careful with questions and advice, taking care of yourself, and staying open to the adventure of listening. (*Choosing to listen,* p. 237)

4. Reword the following complaint as a request: "You always interrupt when I talk!"

   Possible rewordings include "Before you begin to talk, please let me finish" and "I'd like to finish making my point; please allow me to do that." (*Choosing to listen,* p. 237)

5. List the five parts of an "I" message (the five ways to say "I").

   a. Observations. b. Feelings. c. Wants. d. Thoughts. e. Intentions. (*Five ways to say "I,"* p. 241)

6. You can listen skillfully to a speaker even when you disagree with that person's viewpoint. True or False? Explain your answer.

   True. Effective listening does not mean that we're obligated to agree with the message. It is essential to listen skillfully in order to understand and evaluate the message. (*Choosing to listen,* p. 237)

7. Which of the following is an effective thesis statement? Explain your answer.

   (a) Two types of thinking.

   (b) Critical thinking and creative thinking go hand in hand.

   (c) The relationship between critical thinking and creative thinking.

   (b) Critical thinking and creative thinking go hand in hand.   This is a complete sentence (including a verb) that makes an assertion.   (*Three phases of effective writing, Phase 1: Getting ready to write,* p. 253)

8. Define *plagiarism,* and explain ways to avoid it.

   Plagiarism is the use of another person's words, pictures, or other original creations without giving proper credit. While taking notes, clearly distinguish between your own ideas and those from others. Be sure to paraphrase and credit paraphrases in the same way you would credit direct quotes. (*Academic integrity: Avoid plagiarism,* p. 259)

9. Describe at least three techniques for practicing and delivering a speech.

   a. Practice using your "speaker's voice." b. Practice in the room in which you will deliver your speech. c. Make a recording of your speech. d. Listen for repeated phrases such as *you know, kind of,* and *really,* plus any *uh's, umm's,* and *ah's.* e. Practice until you can deliver your presentation in a natural way. f. Dress for the occasion. g. Project your voice. h. Maintain eye contact. i. Notice your nonverbal communication. j. Notice the time. k. Pause when appropriate. l. Have fun. (*Mastering public speaking,* p. 260)

10. Write one example of a statement on the lowest rung of the ladder of powerful speaking—and a statement on the highest rung.

   Lowest rung: I ought to study for my chemistry test this weekend. Highest rung: I am committed to studying for my chemistry test this weekend. (Answers will vary.) (*Power Process: Employ Your Word,* p. 259)

Skills Snapshot

By now you've had a chance to read this chapter and apply some of the suggestions it includes. Take a few minutes to revisit your responses to the "Communicating" section of the Discovery Wheel exercise on page 29. Then complete the following sentences.

The technique that has made the biggest difference in my skill at listening is . . .

When I hear an accomplished public speaker, the skill that I notice first and most admire is . . .

When I'm effective at managing conflict, I am remembering to . . .

I'll know that I've reached a new level of mastery with my communication skills when . . .

To reach that level of mastery, the most important thing I can do next is to . . .

Master Student PROFILE

Mark Zuckerberg

. . . is willing to change

© Kimberly White/Reuters/Corbis

The face of Facebook is Mark Zuckerberg, the mogul who's guiding its extraordinary growth. What everyone wants to know is: Is he old enough to be running a company some people say is the biggest thing since Google?

"I'm 23 right now," Zuckerberg tells Stahl when asked how old he is.

"And you're running this huge company," Stahl remarks.

"It's not that big," Zuckerberg says. . . .

"It used to be the case, like you'd switch jobs. And then maybe you wouldn't keep in touch with all the people that you knew from that old job. Just 'cause it was too hard," Zuckerberg explains. "But one of the things that Facebook does is it makes it really easy to just stay in touch with all these people.". . .

Facebook's headquarters in downtown Palo Alto look like a dorm room; the 400 employees, who get free food and laundry, show up late, stay late, and party really late.

Zuckerberg, who's made the cover of Newsweek and is reportedly worth $3 billion, sits at a desk like the other software engineers, writing computer code.

"Have you changed your lifestyle? You don't look like you're buyin' really expensive clothes," Stahl asks Zuckerberg, who showed up to the interview in a sweatshirt and sandals. . . .

"I have a little, like one bedroom apartment with a mattress on the floor. That's where I live," Zuckerberg says. . . .

Like the founders of Google, Larry Page and Sergey Brin, Mark Zuckerberg is looked up to in Silicon Valley as a visionary. . . .

He expanded access to Facebook from college students to high schoolers, then in 2006 to adults, his fastest growing demographic. Now he's inviting everyone on the site to create new software and pocket the profits themselves. It's a way to keep the next big thing on Facebook. New programs emerge daily, like Facebook Scrabble.

"I actually have a couple games going on now with my grandparents," Zuckerberg says, laughing. "So, they got on Facebook and we started playing Scrabble together."

So Facebook is changing the way we communicate with our friends, and with our grandparents. It's also changing politics. Every major candidate has a page. Zuckerberg says there seem to be more Republicans on the site than Democrats, and among them, Barack Obama —with his young persons following—is hugely popular. . .

"It used to be, first you went on 'Face The Nation' if you were a candidate. Then you went on Letterman. Now it seems the candidates have to be on Facebook. Are you changing the way candidates are running for president?" Stahl asks.

"Well, I think because politicians can communicate with tens of thousands of people at the same time, it's pretty effective for them in campaigning," Zuckerberg explains. . . .

Asked if he thinks his age is an asset or a liability, Zuckerberg says, "There's probably a little bit of both, right? I mean there are definitely elements of experience and stuff that someone who's my age wouldn't have. But there are also things that I can do that other people wouldn't necessarily be able to."

While 60 Minutes was working on this story, associate producer Ros Menon lost her wallet in a New York City cab. The good Samaritan who found it tracked her down by searching for her—you guessed it—on Facebook.

Adapted from "The Face Behind Face-book," January 13, 2008, http://www.cbsnews.com/stories/2008/01/10/60minutes/main3697442.shtml.

(1984–)
In a report for 60 Minutes, the CBS TV program, Lesley Stahl interviewed the founder and CEO of a company that began in a Harvard dorm room and is now estimated to be worth $15 billion.

To learn more about the life and work of Mark Zuckerberg, visit the Master Student Hall of Fame online.

9 Diversity

Instructor Tools & Tips

> Candor is a compliment; it implies equality. It's how true friends talk.
>
> **—Peggy Noonan**
>
> We don't see things as they are, we see things as we are.
>
> **—Anaïs Nin**

Preview

Becoming a Master Student values diversity as a key element to success at school, at work, and in our neighborhoods. This chapter focuses specifically on living with diversity and the benefits of learning to understand different customs and relate to different cultures. Communicating sets the stage for discussing diversity and the impact it has on your students' lives. The exercises and activities here and in the additional ancillaries encourage students to work together to build networks of peer support by exchanging ideas across cultures. In this way, students can learn to overcome stereotyping, respect differences, and embrace diversity.

Guest Speaker

Consider inviting a local employer to come to your class and discuss with your students antidiscrimination policies and diversity initiatives as they apply on a corporate level. Alternatively, a representative from your Human Resources department may be able to provide a similar presentation to your students. If Student Government coordinates a Diversity day, week, or month, seek out the student leaders of that effort and ask them to put together a student diversity panel to speak with your class. They can use this opportunity to recruit more volunteers to help with their event. A faculty member who teaches Cultural Anthropology could also present a relevant talk to your students. Or a representative from your Accessibility/Disabled Students Program could talk about the rights and issues of people with physical and/or mental challenges.

Lecture

The articles "Leadership in a diverse world," "Building relationships across cultures," and "Overcome stereotypes with critical thinking," as well as the Power Process: "Choose Your Conversations and Your Community," all can provide the basis for a lecture unit on Chapter 9. See additional lecture ideas on the Instructor Web site.

Exercises/Activities

Joanne Zitik, a diversity consultant for Center Focus, creates diversity exercises for workshops and courses for employees, managers, and executives in organizations. Some of her guidelines for the exercises also apply to the classroom. They include:

- Use adult learning approaches and techniques.
- Carefully consider the timing of when you introduce an exercise. For example, be sure to build trust among the students before tackling an exercise that encourages them to delve deeply into and/or reveal things about themselves.
- Make sure that students know that it is all right to "pass" and not participate in an exercise.
- Do not repeat derogatory words and phrases; try to move students away from stereotypes and derogatory language.
- Ask the students to observe confidentiality so that what is said during the exercise is not repeated outside the course.
- Make sure that the exercise is facilitated by a person who has had ample diversity and inclusion training.

Here are some other suggestions for activities:

1. Defining diversity Consider this chapter introduction idea:

> "When I start talking about diversity, students tend to focus on very obvious aspects of diversity, such as gender. To help them think more broadly about the many kinds of diversity, I put the students into groups of four or five. I ask them, in their groups, to list all the ways that people can be different from one another. I start them off with gender and ethnicity, and give them five minutes to brainstorm other differences. I have the students write these ideas on a flip chart. After they have brainstormed, I ask them to share the responses from their groups. They come up with many ideas and get additional ideas from the other groups—anything from political party preferences to shoe size. This exercise provides the students with a common starting point for the chapter and a much broader sense of what diversity can encompass.
>
> **—Michelle Martin, Faculty Advisor**

2. Diversity is real—and valuable (page 272) Here is a suggestion from an advisory board member:

> "I like to show my class a video, titled *Wealth, Innovation and Diversity,* that is narrated by futurist Joel Barker (published by Star Thrower Productions). Beginning with the Irish potato famine, the video illustrates the vital importance of diversity, casting it in a whole new light. It is diversity that makes human beings strong enough to survive. When we violate the principle of diversity, we pay a price in human suffering every time. When we celebrate diversity, we prosper as a people and as a nation.
>
> **—Eldon McMurray**

3. Using TV shows Many popular television series have included at least one episode with a theme of diversity. Watch programs with an eye and ear out for a segment or episode that you might be able to use in your classroom. Or challenge students to find such a program. For example, Faculty Advisor Dean Mancina uses an episode from the '90s television sitcom *3rd Rock from the Sun.* This show was about a family from another planet who came to earth to learn about humans. He uses the episode "Dick Like Me." When talking about a topic as sensitive as diversity, be cautious about using humor. Dean has shown his video to many diverse classes of students, and he has not received any negative feedback about it. For more details about how he uses this video in his classroom, go to the Instructor Web site.

4. Diversity circle Some diversity trainers use the diversity circle exercise to help workers appreciate diversity and overcome misperceptions. The exercise can be easily adapted for classroom use. Form a group of about ten students. Arrange your chairs into a circle, and put one additional chair in the center of the circle. A "diverse" group member volunteers to sit in the center chair and become the first "awareness subject." Because most people are diverse in some way, most people are eligible to occupy the center chair.

The person in the center tells the others how she has felt about being diverse or different and how people have reacted to her diversity. For example, an Inuit described how fellow workers were hesitant to ask him out for a beer because they worried about whether he could handle alcohol.

An equally effective alternative to the procedure just described is to ask each class member to come to the front of the class and describe a significant way in which he is different. After each class member has spoken, have the students discuss their observations and interpretations. Ask the students, "What lessons did you learn about interpersonal relations from this exercise that will help you be a more effective leader?"[1]

Conversation/Sharing

Appreciation for diversity often begins at home. You can increase your students' awareness of the role that family messages play in their own lives and in their perceptions of themselves. Start your class discussion by asking students to talk about the role of diversity in their lives, past and present.

What? What does embracing diversity mean to you?

How? How has diversity played a role in your life?

Why? Why does diversity matter to you?

To open a discussion on the impact of diversity, ask your students about discrimination. Have they ever been discriminated against for any reason?

What if? What if you were discriminated against? What if we could wipe out discrimination through education?

Overcome stereotypes with critical thinking (page 279) To begin a conversation with your students about generalizations and ways to decrease stereotyping, revisit the concepts presented in Chapter 7: Thinking. Then use this article to open up further discussion. The reinforcement will encourage your students to commit to using thinking strategies and to make connections between chapters. This answers the question, *What if* I use the strategies from the Thinking chapter and apply them to issues related to diversity?

Leadership in a diverse world (page 284) The topic of leadership provides another opportunity for in-class discussion. I ask my students who are leaders (on campus, in the workplace, at their church, at home, in their circle of friends) to share what it's like to be a leader. Then I divide the students into small groups and have them discuss the following questions: What are the advantages and disadvantages of being a leader? What are the challenges and perks?

Homework

Dealing with sexism and sexual harassment (page 282) Most colleges list sexual harassment policies in their student handbooks or post them online. Have your students obtain a copy of your college's policy, and encourage them to find out where to procure related materials provided by your campus and how to use them. After your students have reviewed the college's policy, engage them in a discussion—either in small groups or as a class—about this important issue.

Power Process: Choose Your Conversations and Your Community (page 289) Raise your students' "conversation consciousness" by asking them to reflect on the quality of the conversations they take part in daily. These conversations might occur during class meetings, course lectures, or social events, or even while reading or watching television. Students can describe a publication they read regularly (in print or online), pointing out the conversations they have when they read and the insights they gain from this material. Invite your

students to write Discovery and Intention Statements highlighting the amount of time they currently spend talking about the past, present, and future, and stating how they intend to change their conversations. A central thesis of *Becoming a Master Student* is that education works when it is value driven. We can choose to engage in value-driven conversations—those that move us toward our goals and affirm our intentions.

Strengthening diversity skills Here are four homework suggestions from an instructor:

> "I always prefer hands-on exercises and writing exercises to strengthen diversity skills. Examples can include the following:
>
> - Choose a situation where you encountered stereotypes or you were influenced by stereotypes you hold/held. Write a reaction paper explaining how you handled and ultimately resolved the situation. If it was unresolved, explain why.
>
> - Attend a meeting for an on-campus group that you normally would not attend. What did you learn? How did you feel?
>
> - Observe your campus cafeteria(s). Do members of racial, ethnic, or other groups sit together? Explain what you see.
>
> - What are some of the major groups on your campus? Describe each group. Describe your group. Do you think these groups could ever discover common ground? Why or why not?
>
> —**Letitia Thomas, State University of New York at Buffalo**

Evaluation

Ask students to write an essay about the value of diversity. Ask them to write about how to build relationships across cultures. Ask students to describe specific strategies for dealing with sexism and sexual harassment. Ask students to explain how choosing your conversations and community could promote student success. For more quiz and test questions, see the Instructor Web site.

Additional Digital Resources

Course Manual

The online *Course Manual* serves as an invaluable reference for those developing and teaching a College Success course with *Becoming a Master Student*. The *Course Manual* provides advice on general teaching issues such as preparing for classes, classroom management, grading, and communicating with students of various backgrounds, as well as specific strategies on getting the most out of various features in *Becoming a Master Student* such as the Discovery Wheel, Learning Styles Inventory, and book-specific Web sites.

Instructor Web Site

The updated Instructor Web site provides resources to help you plan and customize your course. Content specific to Chapter 9 includes:

- Lecture Ideas
  - Exploring the Common Ground
  - Culture Shock
- In-Class Exercises
  - Is There Only One Version of the American Dream?
  - Iceberg Concept and the Nature of Culture
  - Knocking Down Walls
- Writing Assignments
  - Proverbs We Grew Up With
  - Family Oral History
- In-Text Quiz Answers
- Learning Styles Application
- Discussion Topics
- PowerPoint Slides
- Reflection Questions
- Assessment Questions
- Experiment with chapter strategies

The Instructor Web site also contains the following book-specific content:

- ExamView Test Bank
- Online Course Manual
- Articles from previous editions
- Master Student Profiles from previous editions
- Sample Syllabi

Student Web Site

To help your students gain a better understanding of the topics discussed in *Becoming a Master Student,* encour-

www.cengage.com/success/bams13e

age your students to visit the Student Web site, which provides the following resources specific to Chapter 9:

- Connect to Text content expands on specific topics marked with an icon within Chapter 9.
- Learning Style Applications invite students to cycle through the four styles of learning. In answering the four questions about applying diversity skills posted in this chapter's Learning Styles Application, students explore the different modes and apply their new knowledge.
- Practice Tests allow students to see how well they understand the themes of *Becoming a Master Student.*
- Interactive Concept Maps promote critical thinking by highlighting related ideas to show relationships between concepts.
- Video Skillbuilders bring to life techniques that will help you to excel in college and beyond. The following video should give your students more information regarding topics covered in Chapter 9:
  - Diversity
- Remembering Cultural Differences presents readers with brief articles that touch on aspects of diversity in our rapidly changing world. For Chapter 9, the following article will prompt your students to look at contemporary issues in a new way:
  - Changing Families in the United States
- Master Student Profiles provide additional information on the people covered in this book feature. For Chapter 9, students will find expanded coverage and links about:
  - Sampson Davis
- Power Process Media contains video, PowerPoints, and audio files to take what your students have learned from the Power Processes in their book to the next level. For Chapter 9, students will find additional media on:
  - Choose your conversations and your community

Along with the chapter-specific content, a General Resources folder is available that contains Toolboxes geared toward specific student types (Community College, Adult Learner, Student Athlete), the Plagiarism Prevention Zone, and the Career Resource Center.

[1]Andrew J. Dubrin, *Leadership,* Fourth Edition. Copyright © 2004 by Houghton Mifflin Company. Reprinted by permission.

9 Diversity

Master Student Map

as you read, ask yourself

what if . . .

. . . I could create positive relationships with people from any culture?

why this chapter matters . . .

You're likely to learn and work with people from many different cultures.

what is included . . .

how you can use this chapter . . .

- Study effectively with people from many different cultures.
- Gain skills to succeed in a multicultural workforce.
- Choose conversations that promote your success.

MASTER STUDENTS in *action*

You have to fill in bubbles for your race and I remember raising my hand and asking the teacher what I should put because I wasn't sure (it said to only fill in one) . . . I just said, "My father is black and my mother is white; what should I put?" She leaned over, nodded knowingly, and just tapped the black option. . . . It was the first time I realized that despite how I might identify myself, that might not be how others perceive me.

—DANIELLA CICCONE

Photo courtesy of Daniella Ciccone

Waking up to diversity

LEARNING ABOUT DIVERSITY is an education in itself. This process can be frightening, frustrating, and even painful. It can also be exciting and enriching.

Consider that the people referred to as "minorities" in the United States are a numerical majority in other parts of the world. To make this idea more real, imagine the human race represented in a single village of just 100 people. If these villagers accurately reflected the Earth's total population, then only 18 would be white and just 31 would describe themselves as Christian. In addition, 80 would live in substandard housing, 67 would be illiterate, and only 7 would have Internet access.[1]

The diverse cultures of our planet are meeting daily through a growing world economy and a global network of computers. Discussions of diversity often focus on characteristics commonly linked to race—differences in skin tone, facial features, and hair texture. But grouping people according to such differences is arbitrary. We could just as easily classify them on the basis of height, weight, foot size, fingernail length, or a hundred other physical traits.

In this chapter, the word *diversity* refers to differences of any type. From this perspective, diversity can be compared to an iceberg. Only the top of an iceberg is visible; most of it is hidden under water. Likewise, only a few aspects of diversity are visible, such as obvious differences in physical appearance, language, social and economic background, and behavior. Much remains hidden from our awareness—different ideas about relationships, decision making, and problem solving; different assumptions about the meaning of love and duty, beauty and friendship, justice and injustice; and much more.

This chapter is titled "Diversity" because that term is widely accepted. You might gain more value from thinking about *cultural competence* instead. This term reminds us that even in the most culturally sensitive environment, people can fail at understanding each other and working toward shared goals. *Cultural competence* refers to gaining skills in these areas and actively using those skills in daily life.

You'll learn most by stepping outside your comfort zone and taking risks. Get involved in a study group or campus organization with people from different countries. Keep asking yourself, "What is the next action I could take to live and work more effectively in our global village?" The answers could change your life. ✳

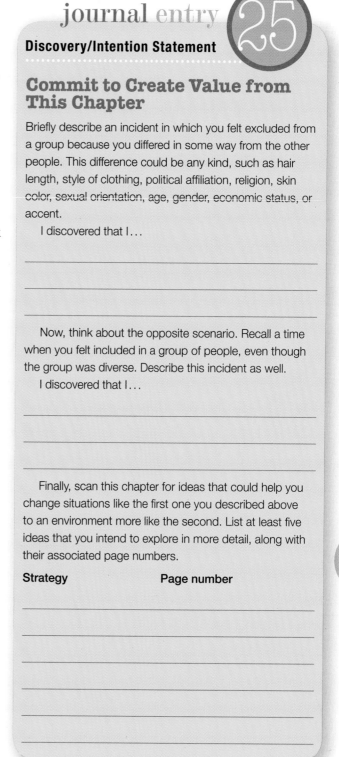

journal entry 25

Discovery/Intention Statement

Commit to Create Value from This Chapter

Briefly describe an incident in which you felt excluded from a group because you differed in some way from the other people. This difference could be any kind, such as hair length, style of clothing, political affiliation, religion, skin color, sexual orientation, age, gender, economic status, or accent.

I discovered that I…

_____

_____

_____

Now, think about the opposite scenario. Recall a time when you felt included in a group of people, even though the group was diverse. Describe this incident as well.

I discovered that I…

_____

_____

_____

Finally, scan this chapter for ideas that could help you change situations like the first one you described above to an environment more like the second. List at least five ideas that you intend to explore in more detail, along with their associated page numbers.

Strategy   **Page number**

_____

_____

_____

_____

_____

DIVERSITY

9

L-R: Ryan McVay/Getty; Hill Street Studios/Daniel Hebert/ Getty; LWA/Dann Tardif/Getty; Plush Studios/Getty; Martina Ebel / Shutterstock; 40260/Getty; Ragne Kabanova / Shutterstock; Jupiterimages/Getty; Ryan McVay/Getty; Indeed/Getty; collage by Walter Kopec

Diversity is real—and valuable

This country has a rich tradition of cultural diversity. Many of us come from families who immigrated to the United States or Canada within the last two or three generations. The things we eat, the tools we use, and the words we speak are a cultural tapestry woven by many different peoples.

THINK ABOUT A common daily routine. A typical American citizen awakens in a bed (an invention from the Near East). After dressing in clothes (possibly designed in Italy), she slices a banana (grown in Honduras) on her bowl (made in China) of cereal, and then brews coffee (shipped from Nicaragua). After breakfast, she reads the morning newspaper (printed by a process invented in Germany on paper, which was first made in China). Then she turns on her portable media player (made in Taiwan) and listens to music (possibly by a band from Cuba). This scenario presents just a few examples of how the cultures of the world meet in our daily lives.

The word *culture* embraces many kinds of differences. We can speak of the culture of large corporations or the culture of the fine arts. There are the cultures of men and women; heterosexual, homosexual, and bisexual people; and older and younger people. There are the cultures of urban and rural dwellers, the cultures of able-bodied people and people with disabilities, and the cultures of two-parent families and single-parent families. There are cultures defined by differences in standards of living and differences in religion.

Higher education might bring you into the most diverse environment that you will ever encounter. Your fellow students could come from many ethnic groups and countries. In addition, consider faculty members, staff members, alumni, donors, and their families. Think of all the possible differences in their family backgrounds, education, job experiences, religion, marital status, sexual orientation, and political viewpoints. Few institutions in our society can match the level of diversity found on many campuses.

A First Step to living effectively in a diverse world is to remember that many dimensions of culture are alive in you and in the people you meet every day. Once you recognize that such diversity is a fact, you can practice a new level of tolerance and respect for individual differences.

Discrimination is also real. The ability to live with diversity is now more critical than ever. Racism, homophobia, and other forms of discrimination exist in many settings, including higher education. According to the Federal Bureau of Investigation (FBI), nearly half of the hate crimes that took place in the United States during 2007 were motivated by racial bias.[2] Each year, thousands of bias-motivated threats and physical assaults occur on college campuses in the United States.[3]

Of course, discrimination can be far more subtle than hate crimes. Consider how you would respond to the following situations:

■ Members of a sociology class are debating the merits of reforming the state's welfare system. The instructor calls on a student who grew up on a reservation and says, "Tell us: What's the Native American perspective on this issue anyway?" Here the student is being typecast as a spokesperson for her entire ethnic group.

- Students in a mass media communications class are learning to think critically about television programs. They're talking about a situation comedy set in an urban high-rise apartment building with mostly African American residents. "Man, they really whitewashed that show," says one student. "It's mostly about inner-city black people, but they didn't show anybody on welfare, doing drugs, or joining gangs." The student's comment perpetuates common racial stereotypes.

- On the first day of the term, students taking English Composition enter a class taught by a professor from Puerto Rico. One of the students asks the professor, "Am I in the right class? Maybe there's been a mistake. I thought this was supposed to be an English class, not a Spanish class." The student assumed that only white people are qualified to teach English courses.

Forrest Toms, of Training Research and Development, defines racism as "prejudice plus power"—the power to define reality, to enshrine one culture as the "correct" set of lenses for viewing the world. The operating assumption is that differences mean deficits. When racism and other forms of intolerance live, we all lose—even if we belong to a group with social and political power. We lose the ability to make friends and to function effectively on teams. We crush human potential. And people without the skills to bridge cultures are already at a disadvantage.

Higher education offers a chance to change this situation. Campuses can become cultural laboratories—places where people of diverse cultures meet in an atmosphere of tolerance. Students who create alliances outside their familiar group memberships are preparing to succeed in both school and work.

Diversity is valuable. Synergy rests on the idea that the whole is more than the sum of its parts. A symphony orchestra consists of many different instruments; when played together, their effect is multiplied many times. A football team has members with different specialties; when their talents are combined, they can win a league championship.

Today we are waking up not only to the *fact* of diversity but also to the *value* of diversity. Biologists tell us that diversity of animal species benefits our ecology.

The same idea applies to the human species. Our goal in education can be to see that we are all part of a complex world—that our own culture is different from, not better than, other cultures. Knowing this, we can stop saying, "Ours is the way to work, learn, relate to others, and view the world." Instead, we can say, "Here is the way I have been doing it. I would also like to see your way."

The fact of diversity also presents opportunities in the workplace. Understanding cultural differences will help you to embrace others' viewpoints that lead to profitable solutions. Organizations that are attuned to diversity are more likely to prosper in the global marketplace.

It takes no more energy to believe that differences enrich us than it does to believe that differences endanger us. Embracing diversity adds value to any organization and can be far more exciting than just meeting the minimum requirements for affirmative action.

Accepting diversity does not mean ignoring the differences among cultures so that we all become part of an anonymous "melting pot." Instead, we can become more like a mosaic—a piece of art in which each element both maintains its individuality and blends with others to form a harmonious whole.

The more you can embrace diversity, the more friends you can make in school and the better prepared you'll be for the workforce of the twenty-first century. If you plan to pursue a career in health care, for example, you can prepare to work with patients from many ethnic groups. If you choose to start a business, you can prepare to sell to customers from many demographic groups. And if you plan to teach, you can prepare to assist every student who walks into your classroom.

Learning to thrive with diversity is a process of returning to "beginner's mind"—a place where we discover diversity as if for the first time. It is a magical place—a place of new beginnings and fresh options. It takes courage to dwell in beginner's mind—courage to go outside the confines of our own culture and worldview. It can feel uncomfortable at first. Yet there are lasting rewards to be gained.

Even if you've already attended diversity workshops in high school or at work, see if you can return to beginner's mind. Entering higher education can take your experience of diversity to a whole new level. ✳

Building relationships across cultures

Communicating with people of other cultures is a learned skill—a habit. According to Stephen R. Covey, author of *The Seven Habits of Highly Effective People*, a habit is the point at which desire, knowledge, and skill meet.[4] Desire is about wanting to do something. Knowledge is understanding what to do. And skill is the ability to do it.

Woman with glass: © Sven Hagolani/zefa/Corbis; *woman in hijab:* Peter Dazeley/Photographer's Choice/Getty

WHEN OUR ACTIONS are grounded in a sincere desire to understand others, we can be much more effective with our knowledge and skills. Once you are willing to embrace diversity and talk openly about it, you can make creative use of the following suggestions and invent more of your own.

Start with self-discovery

The first step to developing diversity skills is to learn about yourself and understand the lenses through which you see the world. One way to do this is to intentionally switch lenses—that is, to consciously perceive familiar events in a new way.

For example, think of a situation in your life that involved an emotionally charged conflict among several people. Now mentally put yourself inside the skin of another person in that conflict. Ask yourself, "How would I view this situation if I were that person?" You can also learn by asking, "What if I were a person of the opposite gender? Or if I were member of a different racial or ethnic group? Or if I were older or younger?" Do this exercise consistently, and you'll discover that we live in a world of multiple realities. There are many different ways to interpret any event—and just as many ways to respond, given our individual differences.

Also reflect on how people can have experiences of privilege *and* prejudice. For example, someone might tell you that he's more likely to be promoted at work because he's white and male—*and* that he's been called "white trash" because he lives in a trailer park.

See if you can recall incidents such as these from your own life. Think of times when you were favored because of your gender, race, or age—and times when you were excluded or ridiculed based on one of those same characteristics. In doing this, you'll discover ways to identify with a wider range of people.

Learn about other cultures

People from different cultures read differently, write differently, think differently, eat differently, and learn differently than you. If you know this from the beginning, you can be more effective with your classmates, coworkers, and neighbors.

One key to understanding styles is to look for several possible interpretations of any behavior. For example:

- Consider the hand signal that signifies *OK* to many Americans—thumb and index finger forming a circle. In France, that signal denotes the number zero. In Japan, it is a symbol for money. And in Brazil, it is considered an obscene gesture.

- When Americans see a speaker who puts her hands in her pockets, they seldom attribute any meaning to this behavior. But in many countries—such as Germany, Indonesia, and Austria—this gesture is considered rude.

- During a conversation, you might prefer having a little distance between yourself and another person. But in Iran, people may often get so close to you that you can feel their breath.[5]

These examples could be extended to cover many areas—posture, eye contact, physical contact, facial expressions, and more. And the various ways of interpreting these behaviors are neither right or wrong. They simply represent differing styles in making meaning out of what we see.

You might find yourself fascinated by the styles that make up a particular culture. Consider learning as much about that culture as possible. Immerse yourself in it. Read novels, see plays, go to concerts, listen to music, look at art, take courses, learn the language.

Look for differences between individualist and collectivist cultures

Individualist cultures flourish in the United States, Canada, and Western Europe. If your family has deep roots in one of these areas, you were probably raised to value personal fulfillment and personal success. You received recognition or rewards when you stood out from your peers by earning the highest grades in your class, scoring the most points during a basketball season, or demonstrating another form of individual achievement.

In contrast, collectivist cultures value cooperation over competition. Group progress is more important than individual success. Credit for an achievement is widely shared. If you were raised in such a culture, you probably place a high value on your family and were taught to respect your elders. Collectivist cultures dominate Asia, Africa, and Latin America.

In short, individualist cultures often emphasize "I." Collectivist cultures tend to emphasize "we." Forgetting about the differences between them can strain a friendship or wreck an international business deal.

If you were raised in an individualist culture:

- *Remember that someone from a collectivist culture may place a high value on "saving face."* This idea involves more than simply avoiding embarrassment. This person may *not* want to be singled out from other members of a group, even for a positive achievement. If you have a direct request for this person or want to share something that could be taken as a personal criticism, save it for a private conversation.

- *Respect titles and last names.* Although Americans often like to use first names immediately after meeting someone, in some cultures this practice is acceptable only among family members. Especially in work settings, use last names and job titles during your first meetings. Allow time for informal relationships to develop.

- *Put messages in context.* For members of collectivist cultures, words convey only part of an intended message. Notice gestures and other nonverbal communication as well.

If you were raised in a collectivist culture, you can creatively "reverse" the above list. Keep in mind that direct questions from an American student or coworker are meant not to offend but only to clarify an idea. Don't be surprised if you are called by a nickname, if no one asks about your family, or if you are rewarded for a personal achievement. In social situations, remember that indirect cues might not get another person's attention. Practice asking clearly and directly for what you want.

Reach out

If carrying out any of these suggestions feels awkward, just apply the Power Process: "Be here now." Then use the suggestions in this article. By intentionally expanding your comfort zone over time, you can break down social barriers and gain a new level of ease at being with people.

A more formal option is to arrange an intergroup dialogue—a "*facilitated*, face-to-face meeting between students from two or more social identity groups that have a history of conflict or potential conflict." Examples are Christians and Muslims, blacks and whites, and people with disabilities and those without disabilities. The goal is sustained and meaningful conversation about controversial issues.[6] Groups typically gather for 2-hour meetings over 6 to 12 weeks.

The format for intergroup dialogues was developed at the University of Michigan and is now being used at campuses across the country. Ask your academic advisor whether such a program is available at your school.

Look for common ground

Students in higher education often find that they worry about many of the same things—including tuition bills, the quality of dormitory food, and the shortage of on-campus parking spaces. More important, our fundamental goals as human beings—such as health, physical safety, and economic security—cross culture lines.

The key is to honor the differences among people while remembering what we have in common. Diversity is not just about our differences—it's also about our similarities. On a biological level, less than 1 percent of the human genome accounts for visible characteristics such as skin color. In terms of our genetic blueprint, we are more than 99 percent the same.[7]

Speak and listen with cultural sensitivity

After first speaking with someone from another culture, don't assume that you've been understood or that you fully understand the other person. The same action can have different meanings at different times, even for members of the same culture. Check it out. Verify what you think you have heard. Listen to see if what you spoke is what the other person received.

If you're speaking with someone who doesn't understand English well, keep the following ideas in mind:

- Speak slowly, distinctly, and patiently.
- To clarify your statement, don't repeat individual words over and over again. Restate your entire message with simple, direct language and short sentences.
- Avoid slang and figures of speech.
- Use gestures to accompany your words.
- English courses for non-native speakers often emphasize written English, so write down what you're saying. Print your message in capital letters.
- Stay calm, and avoid sending nonverbal messages that you're frustrated.

If you're unsure about how well you're communicating, ask questions: "I don't know how to make this idea clear for you. How might I communicate better?" "When you look away from me during our conversation, I feel uneasy. Is there something else we need to talk about?" "When you don't ask questions, I wonder if I am being clear. Do you want any more explanation?" Questions such as these can get cultural differences out in the open in a constructive way.

Look for individuals, not group representatives

Sometimes the way we speak glosses over differences among individuals and reinforces stereotypes. For example, a student worried about her grade in math expresses concern over "all those Asian students who are skewing the class curve." Or a white music major assumes that her black classmate knows a lot about jazz or hip-hop music. We can avoid such errors by seeing people as individuals—not spokespersons for an entire group.

Find a translator, mediator, or model

People who move with ease in two or more cultures can help us greatly. Diane de Anda, a professor at the University of California, Los Angeles, speaks of three kinds of people who can communicate across cultures. She calls them *translators, mediators,* and *models.*[8]

A *translator* is someone who is truly bicultural—a person who relates naturally to both people in a mainstream culture and people from a contrasting culture. This person can share her own experiences in overcoming discrimination, learning another language or dialect, and coping with stress.

Mediators are people who belong to the dominant or mainstream culture. Unlike translators, they might not be bicultural. However, mediators value diversity and are committed to cultural understanding. Often they are teachers, counselors, tutors, mentors, or social workers.

Models are members of a culture who are positive examples. Models include students from any racial or cultural group who participate in class and demonstrate effective study habits. Models can also include entertainers, athletes, and community leaders.

Your school might have people who serve these functions, even if they're not labeled translators, mediators, or models. Some schools have mentor or "bridge" programs that pair new students with teachers of the same race or culture. Ask your student counseling service about such programs.

Develop support systems

Many students find that their social adjustment affects their academic performance. Students with strong support systems—such as families, friends, churches, self-help groups, and mentors—are using a powerful strategy for success in school. As an exercise, list the support systems that you rely on right now. Also list new support systems you could develop.

Support systems can help you bridge culture gaps. With a strong base of support in your own group, you can feel more confident in meeting people outside that group.

Be willing to accept feedback

Members of another culture might let you know that some of your words or actions had a meaning other than what you intended. For example, perhaps a comment that seems harmless to you is offensive to them. And they may tell you directly about it.

Avoid responding to such feedback with comments such as "Don't get me wrong," "You're taking this way too seriously," or "You're too sensitive." Instead, listen without resistance. Open yourself to what others have to say. Remember to distinguish between the *intention* of your behavior and its actual *impact* on other people. Then take the feedback you receive, and ask yourself how you can use it to communicate more effectively in the future.

You can also interpret such feedback positively—a sign that others believe you can change and that they see the possibility of a better relationship with you.

If you are new at responding to diversity, expect to make some mistakes along the way. As long as you approach people in a spirit of tolerance, your words and actions can always be changed.

Speak up against discrimination

You might find yourself in the presence of someone who tells a racist joke, makes a homophobic comment, or utters an ethnic slur. When this happens, you have a right to state what you observe, share what you think, and communicate how you feel. Depending on the circumstance, you might say:

- "That's a stereotype, and we don't have to fall for it."

- "Other people are going to take offense at that. Let's tell jokes that don't put people down."

- "I realize that you don't mean to offend anybody, but I feel hurt and angry by what you just said."

- "I know that an African American person told you that story, but I still think it's racist and creates an atmosphere that I don't want to be in."

This kind of speaking may be the most difficult communicating you ever do. However, if you *don't* do it, you give the impression that you agree with biased speech.

In response to your candid comments, many people will apologize and express their willingness to change. Even if they don't, you can still know that you practiced integrity by aligning your words with your values.

Change the institution

None of us lives in isolation. We all live in systems, and these systems do not always tolerate diversity. As a student, you might see people of color ignored in class. You might see people of a certain ethnic group passed over in job hiring or underrepresented in school organizations. And you might see gay and lesbian students ridiculed or even threatened with violence. One way to stop these actions is to point them out.

You can speak more effectively about what you believe by making some key distinctions. Remember the following:

- *Stereotypes* are errors in thinking—inaccurate ideas about members of another culture.

- *Prejudice* refers to positive or negative feelings about others, which are often based on stereotypes.

- *Discrimination* takes places when stereotypes or prejudice gets expressed in policies and laws that undermine equal opportunities for all cultures.

Federal civil rights laws, as well as the written policies of most schools, ban racial and ethnic discrimination. If your school receives federal aid, it must set up procedures that protect students against such discrimination.

Throughout recent history, social change has been fueled by students. Student action helped to shift Americans' attitudes toward segregated universities, the Vietnam War, the military draft, and the invasion of Iraq. When it comes to ending discrimination, you are in an environment where you can make a difference. Run for student government. Write for school publications. Speak at rallies. Express your viewpoint. This is training for citizenship in a multicultural world. ✳

 Gain more strategies for building relationships across cultures.

9

DIVERSITY

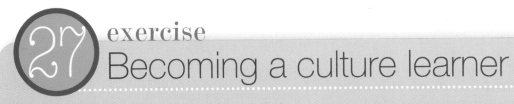

exercise 27
Becoming a culture learner

To learn about other cultures in depth, actively move through the cycle of learning described by psychologist David Kolb (and explained more fully in "Learning Styles—Discovering How You Learn" on page 32). This exercise, which has three parts, illustrates one way to apply the cycle of learning. Use additional paper as needed to complete each part.

Part 1: Concrete experience

Think of a specific way to interact with people from a culture different than your own. For example, attend a meeting for a campus group that you normally would not attend. Or sit in a campus cafeteria with a new group of people.

In the space below, describe what you will do to create your experience of a different culture.

_____

_____

_____

_____

_____

Part 2: Reflective observation

Describe the experience you had while doing Part 1 of this exercise. Be sure to separate your observations—what you saw, heard, or did—from your interpretations. In addition,

see if you can think of other ways to interpret each of your observations.

Use the table at the bottom of this page for this part of the exercise. An example is included to get you started.

Part 3: Abstract conceptualization

Next, see if you can refine your initial interpretations and develop them into some informed conclusions about your experience in Part 1. Do some research about other cultures, looking specifically for information that can help you understand the experience. (Your instructor and a librarian can suggest ways to find such information.) Whenever possible, speak directly to people of various cultures. Share your observations from Part 1, and ask for *their* interpretations.

Reflect on the information you gather. Does it reinforce any of the interpretations you listed in Part 2? Does it call for a change in your thinking? Summarize your conclusions in the space below.

_____

_____

_____

_____

_____

_____

_____

Observation	Your Initial Interpretation	Other Possible Interpretations
For 30 minutes starting at noon on Tuesday, I sat alone in the northeast section of the cafeteria in our student union. During this time, all of the conversations I overheard were conducted in Spanish.	I sat alone because the Spanish-speaking students did not want to talk to me. They are unfriendly.	The Spanish-speaking students are actually friendly. They were just not sure how to start a conversation with me. Perhaps they thought I wanted to eat alone or study. Also, I could have taken the initiative to start a conversation.

9
DIVERSITY

278 Chapter Nine   www.cengage.com/success/bams13e

Overcome stereotypes with critical thinking

CONSIDER ASSERTIONS such as these: "College students like to drink heavily," "People who speak English as a second language are hard to understand," and "Americans who criticize the president are unpatriotic."

These assertions are examples of stereotyping—generalizing about a group of people based on the behavior of isolated group members. When we stereotype, we gloss over individual differences and assume that every member of a group is the same.

Stereotypes infiltrate every dimension of human individuality. People are stereotyped on the basis of their race, ethnic group, religion, political affiliation, geographic location, birthplace, accent, job, age, gender, sexual orientation, IQ, height, hair color, or hobbies.

In themselves, generalizations are neither good nor bad. In fact, they are essential. Mentally sorting people, events, and objects into groups allows us to make sense of the world. But when we consciously or unconsciously make generalizations that rigidly divide the people of the world into "us" versus "them," we create stereotypes and put on the blinders of prejudice.

You can take several steps to free yourself from stereotypes.

Look for errors in thinking. Some of the most common errors in thinking are the following:

- *Selective perception.* Stereotypes can literally change the way we see the world. If we assume that homeless people are lazy, for instance, we tend to notice only the examples that support our opinion. Stories about homeless people who are too young or too ill to work will probably escape our attention.

- *Self-fulfilling prophecy.* When we interact with people based on stereotypes, we set them up in ways that confirm our thinking. For example, when people of color were denied access to higher education based on stereotypes about their intelligence, they were deprived of opportunities to demonstrate their intellectual gifts.

- *Self-justification.* Stereotypes can allow people to assume the role of victim and to avoid taking responsibility for their own lives. An unemployed white male might believe that affirmative action programs are making it impossible for him to get a job—even as he overlooks his own lack of experience or qualifications.

Create categories in a more flexible way. Stereotyping has been described as a case of "hardening of the categories." Avoid this problem by making your categories broader. Instead of seeing people based on their skin color, you could look at them on the basis of their heredity. (People of all races share most of the same genes.) Or you could make your categories narrower. Instead of talking about "religious extremists," look for subgroups among the people who adopt a certain religion. Distinguish between groups that advocate violence and those that shun it.

Test your generalizations about people through action. You can test your generalizations by actually meeting people of other cultures. It's easy to believe almost anything about certain groups of people as long as we never deal directly with individuals. Inaccurate pictures tend to die when people from different cultures study together, work together, and live together. Consider joining a school or community organization that will put you in contact with people of other cultures. Your rewards will include a more global perspective and an ability to thrive in a multicultural world.

Be willing to see your own stereotypes. The Power Process: "Notice your pictures and let them go" can help you see your own stereotypes. One belief about yourself that you can shed is *I have no pictures about people from other cultures.* Even people with the best of intentions can harbor subtle biases. Admitting this possibility allows you to look inward even more deeply for stereotypes.

Every time we notice an inaccurate picture buried in our mind and let it go, we take a personal step toward embracing diversity. ✳

 Find more examples of stereotypes and critical responses to them online.

9

DIVERSITY

Students with disabilities: Know your rights

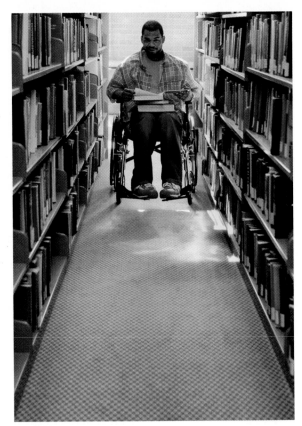
© Andersen Ross/Getty

IT USED TO be that students with disabilities faced a restricted set of choices in school. For instance, many had trouble majoring in subjects—engineering, science, or medicine—that call for using technical equipment. New technology, such as computers and calculators operated with voice commands, can change that. Students with disabilities can now choose from any course or major offered in higher education.

Even the most well-intentioned instructors, though, can forget about promoting learning for people with disabilities. To protect your rights, speak up. Ask for what you want. Begin with the suggestions in Chapter 8's "Five ways to say 'I'"; use "I" messages and listen actively. All these suggestions can help you succeed in school. So can the following ideas.

Learn about laws that apply to you

Equal opportunity for people with disabilities is the law. In the United States, both the Civil Rights Act of 1964 and the Rehabilitation Act of 1973 offer legal protection. The Americans with Disabilities Act of 1990 extends earlier legislation.

These laws give you the right to ask for academic adjustments based on your needs. The U.S. Department of Education gives these examples of adjustments:

- Arranging for priority registration.
- Reducing a course load.
- Substituting one course for another.
- Providing note takers, recording devices, and sign language interpreters.
- Equipping school computers with screen-reading, voice recognition, or other adaptive software or hardware.
- Installing a TTY in your dorm room if telephones are provided there.

In making an academic adjustment, your school is not obligated to change essential requirements for a course. For example, you can ask for extra testing time, but your instructor is not required to change the content of the test.

More details about legal protection for students with disabilities are available online at www.ed.gov/about/offices/list/ocr/transition.html.

Find out how to ask for an adjustment

If you want an academic adjustment, first identify yourself as having a disability. Then follow your school's procedures for getting the adjustment in place.

These procedures vary across campuses. Many schools have a person whose job it is to assist students with disabilities. If you cannot find this person, check with an admissions officer or counselor. And in any case, ask for your adjustment as early as possible.

Your school will probably ask you to document that you have a disability and need an adjustment. This documentation might include a written evaluation from a physician, psychologist, or other professional who has worked with you.

Use other available resources

Your school may offer services that go beyond the kinds of adjustments listed above. Libraries might furnish books in braille, on CD, or in another medium for the visually impaired. You might be able to get a permit that allows you to park closer to classrooms, or a shuttle bus for transportation between classes.

The student health center may offer certain services to people with disabilities, including learning disabilities. Some schools have disability resource centers with a full-time staff.

In addition, the Job Accommodation Network offers help in placing employees with learning or physical disabilities. For more information, call 1-800-526-7234 or go online to www.jan.wvu.edu.

Speak assertively

Tell instructors when it's appropriate to consider your disability. If you use a wheelchair, for example, ask for appropriate transportation on field trips. If you have a visual disability, request that instructors speak as they write on the chalkboard. Also ask them to use high-contrast colors and to write legibly.

Plan ahead

Meet with your counselor or advisor to design an educational plan—one that takes your disability into account. A key part of this plan is choosing instructors. Ask for recommendations before registering for classes. Interview prospective instructors, and sit in on their classes. Express an interest in the class, ask to see a course outline, and discuss any adjustments that could help you complete the course.

Use empowering words

Changing just a few words can make the difference between asking for what you want and apologizing for it. When people refer to disabilities, you might hear words such as *special treatment, accommodation,* and *adaptation.* Experiment with using the terms *adjustment* and *alternative* instead. The difference between these two groups of terms involves equality. Asking for an adjustment in an assignment or for an alternative assignment is asking for the right to produce equal work—not for special treatment that waters down the assignment.

Ask for appropriate treatment

Many instructors will be eager to help you. In fact, at times they might go overboard. For example, a student who has trouble writing by hand might ask to complete in-class writing assignments on a computer. "OK," the teacher might reply, "and take a little extra time. For you, there's no rush."

For some students this is a welcome response. Others, who have no need for an extended time line, can reply, "Thank you for thinking of me. I'd prefer to finish the assignment in the time frame allotted for the rest of the class."

Follow up when necessary

If the academic adjustment that you requested is not working, let your school know right away. Talk to the person who helped set up the adjustment. Remember that schools usually have grievance procedures for resolving conflicts about the services you're receiving.

Almost every school has a person who monitors compliance with disability laws. This person is often called the Section 504 coordinator, ADA coordinator, or disability services coordinator. If you think a school is discriminating against you because of your disability, this is the person to contact.

You can also file a complaint against the school in a court or with the Office of Civil Rights. Find out more online at www.ed.gov/ocr/docs/howto.html, or call 1-800-421-3481.

Take care of yourself

Many students with chronic illnesses or disabilities find that rest breaks are essential. If this is true for you, write such breaks into your daily or weekly plan.

A related suggestion is to treat yourself with respect. If your health changes in a way that you don't like, avoid berating yourself. Focus on finding an effective medical treatment or other solution.

It's important to accept compliments and periodically review your accomplishments in school. Fill yourself with affirmation. As you educate yourself, you are attaining mastery. ✳

Dealing with sexism and sexual harassment

Sexism and sexual harassment are real. Incidents that are illegal or violate organizational policies occur throughout the year at schools and in workplaces.

UNTIL THE EARLY nineteenth century, women in the United States were banned from attending colleges and universities. Today women make up the majority of first-year students in higher education, yet they still encounter bias based on gender. Although men also can be subjects of sexism and sexual harassment, women are more likely to experience this form of discrimination.

Bias based on gender can take many forms. For example, instructors might gloss over the contributions of women. Students in philosophy class might never hear of a woman named Hypatia, an ancient Greek philosopher and mathematician. Those majoring in computer science might never learn about Rear Admiral Grace Murray Hopper, who pioneered the development of a computer language named COBOL. And your art history textbook might not mention the Mexican painter Frida Kahlo or the American painter Georgia O'Keeffe.

Even the most well-intentioned people might behave in ways that hurt or discount women. Sexism is a factor in these situations:

- Instructors use only masculine pronouns—*he, his,* and *him*—to refer to both men and women.

- Career counselors hint that careers in mathematics and science are not appropriate for women.

- Students pay more attention to feedback from a male teacher than from a female teacher.

- Women are not called on in class, their comments are ignored, or they are overly praised for answering the simplest questions.

- People assume that middle-aged women who return to school have too many family commitments to study adequately or do well in their classes.

Many kinds of behavior—both verbal and physical—can be categorized as sexual harassment. This kind of discrimination involves unwelcome sexual conduct. Examples of such conduct in a school setting include the following:

- Sexual advances.

- Any other unwanted touch.

- Displaying or distributing sexually explicit materials.

- Sexual gestures or jokes.

- Pressure for sexual favors.

- Spreading rumors about someone's sexual activity or rating someone's sexual performance.

Sexual Harassment: It's Not Academic, a pamphlet from the U.S. Department of Education, quotes a woman who experienced sexual harassment in higher education: "The financial officer made it clear that I could get the money I needed if I slept with him."[9] That's an example of *quid pro quo harassment.* This legal term applies when students believe that an educational decision depends on submitting to unwelcome sexual conduct. *Hostile environment harassment* takes place when such incidents are severe, persistent, or pervasive.

The feminist movement has raised awareness about all forms of harassment. We can now respond to such incidents in the places we live, work, and go to school. Specific strategies follow.

Point out sexist language and behavior. When you see examples of sexism, point them out. Your message can be more effective if you use "I" messages instead of personal attacks, as explained in Chapter 8: Communicating.

Indicate the specific statements and behaviors that you consider sexist. To help others understand sexism, you might rephrase a sexist comment so that it targets another group, such as Jews or African Americans. People sometimes spot anti-Semitism or racism more readily than sexism.

Keep in mind that men can also be subjected to sexism, ranging from antagonistic humor to exclusion from jobs that have traditionally been done by women.

Observe your own language and behavior. Looking for sexist behavior in others is a good first step in dealing with it. Detecting it in yourself can be just as powerful. Write a Discovery Statement about specific comments that could be interpreted as sexist. Then notice if you say any of these things. Also ask people you know to point out occasions when you use similar

9

DIVERSITY

statements. Follow up with an Intention Statement that describes how you plan to change your speaking or behavior.

You can also write Discovery Statements about the current level of intimacy (physical and verbal) in any of your relationships at home, work, or school. Be sure that any increase in the level of intimacy is mutually agreed upon.

Encourage support for women. Through networks, women can work to overcome the effects of sexism. Strategies include study groups for women, women's job networks, and professional organizations, such as the Association for Women in Communications. Other examples are counseling services and health centers for women, family planning agencies, and rape prevention centers.

If your school does not have the women's networks you want, you can help form them. Help set up a 1-day or 1-week conference on women's issues. Create a discussion or reading group for the women in your class, department, residence hall, union, or neighborhood.

Take action. If you are sexually harassed, take action. Title IX of the Education Amendments of 1972 prohibits sexual harassment and other forms of sex discrimination. The law also requires schools to have grievance procedures in place for dealing with such discrimination. If you believe that you've been sexually harassed, report the incident to a school official. This person can be a teacher, administrator, or campus security officer. Check to see if your school has someone specially designated to handle your complaint, such as an affirmative action officer or Title IX coordinator.

You can also file a complaint with the Office for Civil Rights (OCR), a federal agency that makes sure schools and workplaces comply with Title IX. In your complaint, include your name, address, and daytime phone number, along with the date of the incident and a description of it. Do this within 180 days of the incident. You can contact the OCR at 1-800-421-3481. Or go online to wdcrobcolp01.ed.gov/CFAPPS/OCR/contactus.cfm.

Your community might offer more resources to protect against sexual discrimination. Examples are public interest law firms, legal aid societies, and unions that employ lawyers to represent students. ✳

Strategies for nonsexist communication

When speaking and writing, use language that includes both women and men. Following are some ways you can do this without twisting yourself into verbal knots.

1. **Use gender-neutral terms.** Instead of *policeman* or *chairman,* for example, use *police officer* or *chairperson.* In many cases, there's no need to identify the gender or marital status of a person. This fact allows us to dispose of expressions such as *female driver, male nurse,* and *lady doctor.*

2. **Use examples that include both men and women.** Effective writing and speaking thrives on examples and illustrations. As you search for details to support your main points, include the stories and accomplishments of women as well as men.

3. **Alternate pronoun gender.** In an attempt to be gender fair, some people make a point of mentioning both sexes whenever they refer to gender. Another method is to alternate male and female pronouns throughout a text or speech—the strategy used in this book.

4. **Switch to plural.** With this approach, a sentence such as *The writer has many tools at her disposal* becomes *Writers have many tools at their disposal.*

5. **Avoid words that imply sexist stereotypes.** Included here are terms such as *tomboy, sissy, office boy, advertising man, man-eater, mama's boy, old lady,* and *powder puff.*

Jeff Hunter/Getty

Leadership in a diverse world

MANY PEOPLE MISTAKENLY think that the only people who are leaders are those with formal titles such as *supervisor* or *manager*. In fact, though, some leaders have no such titles. Some have never supervised others. Like Mahatma Gandhi, some people change the face of the world without ever reaching a formal leadership position.

No one is born knowing how to lead. We acquire the skills over time. Begin now, while you are in higher education. Campuses offer continual opportunities to gain leadership skills. Volunteer for clubs, organizations, and student government. Look for opportunities to tutor, or to become a peer advisor or mentor. No matter what you do, take on big projects—those that are worthy of your time and talents.

The U.S. Census Bureau predicts that the groups once classified as minorities—Hispanics, African Americans, East Asians, and South Asians—will become the majority by the year 2042. For Americans under age 18, this shift will take place in 2023.[10] Translation: Your next boss or coworker could be a person whose life experiences and views of the world differ radically from yours.

We live in a world where Barack Obama, a man with ancestors from Kenya and Kansas, became president of the United States; where Bobby Jindal, the son of immigrants from India, became governor of Louisiana; and where Oprah Winfrey, an African American woman, can propel a book to the top of the best seller list simply by recommending it on her television show. These people set examples of diversity in leadership

that many others will follow. Prepare to apply your own leadership skills in a multicultural world.

To become a more effective leader, understand the many ways you can influence others. The following strategies can help you have a positive impact on your relationships with your friends, family members, and coworkers.

Own your leadership

Let go of the reluctance that many of us feel toward assuming leadership. It's impossible to escape leadership. Every time you speak, you lead others in some small or large way. Every time you take action, you lead others through your example. Every time you ask someone to do something, you are in essence leading that person. Leadership becomes more effective when it is consciously applied.

Be willing to be uncomfortable

Leadership is a courageous act. Leaders often are not appreciated or even liked. They can feel isolated—cut off from their colleagues. This isolation can sometimes lead to self-doubt and even fear. Before you take on a leadership role, be aware that you might experience such feelings. Also remember that none of them needs to stop you from leading.

Allow huge mistakes

The more important and influential you are, the more likely it is that your mistakes will have huge consequences. The chief financial officer for a large company can make a mistake that costs thousands or even millions of dollars. A physician's error could cost a life. As commander-in-chief of the armed forces, the president of a country can make a decision that costs thousands of lives. At the same time, these people are in a position to make huge changes for the better—to save thousands of dollars or lives through their power, skill, and influence.

People in leadership positions can become paralyzed and ineffective if they fear making a mistake. It's necessary for them to act even when information is incomplete or when they know a catastrophic mistake is a possible outcome.

Take on big projects

Leaders make promises. And effective leaders make big promises. These words—*I will do it* and *You can count on me*—distinguish a leader.

Look around your world to see what needs to be done, and then take it on. Consider taking on the biggest project you can think of—ending world hunger, eliminating nuclear weapons, wiping out poverty, promoting universal literacy. Think about how you'd spend your life if you knew that you could make a difference regarding these overwhelming problems. Then take the actions you considered. See what a difference they can make for you and for others.

Tackle projects that stretch you to your limits—projects that are worthy of your time and talents.

Provide feedback

An effective leader is a mirror to others. Share what you see. Talk with others about what they are doing effectively—and what they are doing ineffectively.

Keep in mind that people might not enjoy your feedback. Some would probably rather not hear it at all. Two things can help. One is to let people know up front that if they sign on to work with you, they can expect feedback. Also give your feedback with skill. Use "I" messages as explained in Chapter 8: Communicating. Back up any criticisms with specific observations and facts. And when people complete a task with exceptional skill, point that out, too.

Paint a vision

Help others see the big picture—the ultimate purpose of a project. Speak a lot about the end result and the potential value of what you're doing.

There's a biblical saying: "Without vision, the people perish." Long-term goals usually involve many intermediate steps. Unless we're reminded of the purpose for those day-to-day actions, our work can feel like a grind. Leadership is the art of helping others lift their eyes to the horizon—keeping them in touch with the ultimate value and purpose of a project. Keeping the vision alive helps spirits soar.

Model your values

"Be the change you want to see" is a useful motto for leaders. Perhaps you want to see integrity, focused attention, and productivity in the people around you. Begin by modeling these qualities yourself. It's easy to excite others about a goal when you are enthusiastic about it yourself. Having fun while being productive is contagious. If you bring these qualities to a project, others might follow suit.

Make requests—lots of them

An effective leader is a request machine. Making requests—both large and small—is an act of respect. When we ask a lot from others, we demonstrate our respect for them and our confidence in their abilities.

At first, some people might get angry when we make requests of them. Over time, however, many will see that requests are compliments and opportunities to expand their skills. Ask a lot from others, and they might appreciate you because of it.

Follow up

What we don't inspect, people don't respect. When other people agree to do a job for you, follow up to see how it is going. You can do so in a way that communicates your respect and interest—not your fear that the project might flounder. When you display a genuine interest in other people and their work, they are more likely to view you as a partner in achieving a shared goal.

Focus on problems, not people

Sometimes projects do not go as planned. Big mistakes occur. If this happens, focus on the project and the mistakes—not the personal faults of your colleagues. People do not make mistakes on purpose. If they did, we would call them "on-purposes," not mistakes. Most people will join you in solving a problem if your focus is on the problem, not on what they did wrong.

Acknowledge others

Express genuine appreciation for the energy and creativity that others have put into their work. Take the time to be interested in what others have done and to care about the results they have accomplished. Thank and acknowledge them with your eyes, your words, and the tone of your voice.

Share credit

As a leader, constantly give away the praise and acknowledgment that you receive. When you're congratulated for your performance, pass the praise on to others. Share the credit with the group.

When you're a leader, the results you achieve depend on the efforts of many others. Acknowledging that fact often is more than telling the truth—it's essential if you want to continue to count on the support of others in the future.

Delegate

Ask a coworker or classmate to take on a job that you'd like to see done. Ask the same of your family or friends. Delegate tasks to the mayor of your town, the governor of your state, and the leaders of your country.

Take on projects that are important to you. Then find people who can lead the effort. You can do this even when you have no formal role as a leader.

We often see delegation as a tool that's available only to those above us in the chain of command. Actually, delegating up or across an organization can be just as effective. Consider delegating a project to your boss. That is, ask him to take on a job that you'd like to see accomplished. It might be a job that you cannot do, given your position in the company.

Balance styles

Think for a moment about your own learning style. To lead effectively, assess your strengths, and look for people who can complement them. If you excel at gathering information and setting goals, for example, then recruit people who like to make decisions and take action. Also enlist people who think creatively and generate different points of view.

Look for different styles in the people who work with you. Remember that learning results from a balance between reflection, action, abstract thinking, and concrete experience. (For more information, see "Learning Styles: Discovering How You Learn" on page 32.) The people you lead will combine these characteristics in infinite variety. Welcome that variety, and accommodate it.

You can defuse and prevent many conflicts simply by acknowledging differences in style. Doing so opens up more options than blaming the differences on "politics" or "personality problems."

Listen

As a leader, be aware of what other people are thinking, feeling, and wanting. Listen fully to their concerns and joys. Before you criticize their views or make personal judgments, take the time to understand what's going on inside them. This is not merely a personal favor to the people you work with. The more you know about your coworkers or classmates, the more effectively you can lead them.

Practice

Leadership is an acquired skill. No one is born knowing how to make requests, give feedback, create budgets, do long-range planning, or delegate tasks. We learn these things over time, with practice, by seeing what works and what doesn't.

As a process of constant learning, leadership calls for all of the skills of master students. Look for areas in which you can make a difference, and experiment with these strategies. Right now there's something worth doing that calls for your leadership. Take action, and others will join you. ✳

 Gain more perspectives on leadership.

DIVERSITY

9

Discovery/Intention Statement

Removing Barriers to Communication

Effective leaders act as a mirror to others. They talk with others about what they are doing effectively—*and* what they are doing ineffectively.

People might not enjoy your feedback. Some would probably rather not hear it at all. Two things can help. One is to let people know up front that if they work with you, they can expect feedback. Also, give your feedback with skill.

Whenever you serve as a leader, examine your relationships. Then complete the following statements.

I discovered that I am not communicating about...

_____

_____

with...

_____

I discovered that I am not communicating about...

_____

_____

with...

_____

I discovered that I am not communicating about...

_____

_____

with...

_____

Now choose one idea from the article "Leadership in a diverse world" that can open communication with these people in these areas. Describe below how you will use this idea.

I intend to...

_____

_____

_____

_____

Discovery Statement

Reflect on the Quality of a Recent Conversation

Read the Power Process: "Choose your conversations and your community" on page 289. Then, in the space below, describe the circumstances of a conversation you had today and summarize its content.

_____

_____

_____

_____

_____

Now reflect on that conversation. Determine whether it aligned with your values and goals.

I discovered that...

_____

_____

_____

_____

9

DIVERSITY

practicing critical thinking

9

Write down the first words that come to mind when you hear the terms listed below. Do this now.

musicians

_____

_____

homeless people

_____

_____

football players

_____

_____

computer programmers

_____

_____

disabled persons

_____

_____

retired persons

_____

_____

adult learners

_____

_____

Next, exchange your responses to this exercise with a friend. Looking at both your responses and your friend's, did you discover stereotypes or other examples of bias? What counts as evidence of bias? Summarize your answers here.

_____

_____

_____

_____

_____

_____

(www) Complete this exercise online.

mastering technology

MAKING TECHNOLOGY ACCESSIBLE

Succeeding in school means doing research, writing papers, completing online assignments, and tackling other tasks that require hours at a keyboard and screen. If you have a disability, take special care to create a functional computer environment. For example, see if the operating system will allow you to do the following:

- Enlarge the cursor and adjust its blink rate.
- Enlarge all fonts and icons.
- Zoom in on all or a portion of the screen image.
- Adjust the screen display to remove all color and render images in black and white or gray scale.

- Use voice recognition rather than the keyboard for menu options.
- Turn on text-to-speech capabilities so that a computer-generated voice reads menu options, alerts, and web pages out loud.
- Choose a keyboard layout that's more convenient for typing with one hand or finger.

To access such features in Windows, select the Windows Control Panel or use the Accessibility Wizard. In Mac OS X, click on the Apple menu in the upper left corner of the screen and select "System Preferences." In the System Preferences pane, click on "Universal Access."

Choose Your Conversations and Your Community

Conversations can exist in many forms. One form involves people talking out loud to each other. At other times, the conversation takes place inside our own heads, and we call it *thinking*. Our observations about communications have three implications that wind their way through every aspect of our lives.

One implication is that conversations exercise incredible power over what we think, feel, and do. They shape our attitudes, our decisions, our opinions, our emotions, and our actions. If you want clues as to what a person will be like tomorrow, listen to what she's talking about today.

Second, given that conversations are so powerful, it's amazing that few people act on this fact. Most of us swim in a constant sea of conversations, almost none of which we carefully and thoughtfully choose.

The real power of this process lies in a third discovery: We can choose our conversations. Certain conversations create real value for us. They give us fuel for reaching our goals. Other conversations distract us from what we want. They might even create lasting unhappiness and frustration.

Suppose that you meet with an instructor to ask about some guidelines for writing a term paper. She launches into a tirade about your writing skills. This presents you with several options. One possibility is to talk about what a jerk the instructor is and give up on the idea of learning to write well. Another option is to refocus the conversation on what you can do to improve your writing skills, such as working with a writing tutor or taking a basic composition class. These two sets of conversations will have vastly different consequences for your success in school.

Another important fact about your conversations is that they are dramatically influenced by the people you associate with. If you want to change your attitudes about almost anything—prejudice, politics, religion, humor—choose your conversations by choosing your community. Spend time with people who speak about and live consistently with the attitudes you value. Use conversations to change habits and create new options in your life. It's as simple as choosing the next article you read or the next topic you discuss with a friend.

Begin applying this Power Process today. Start choosing your conversations, and watch what happens.

 Learn more about choosing your conversations.

Put it to Work

Strategies from *Becoming a Master Student* can help you succeed in your career, as well as in school. To start discovering how suggestions in this chapter apply to the workplace, reflect on the following case study.

Yuri Arcurs/Shutterstock

Linda Thompson graduated with a B.A. in marketing. Her major required her to take part in several internships. One of those experiences led to a full-time job with a Fortune 500 company based in Chicago that delivered training programs for clients across the world.

Linda quickly fell in love with her job. She worked in the part of the company that created incentive programs for employees. Her team's main task was to think of ways to reward divisions that met or exceeded their sales goals.

Within the company's home office, these incentive programs were widely viewed as successful. The plan was to extend them to employees in foreign offices.

Linda's team invited all of the company's employees to send a description of any group initiative that significantly increased sales. Linda's team would pick the twenty most successful initiatives and invite one representative from each of those groups to come to Chicago—an all-expenses-paid trip. These representatives would attend a rewards banquet and spend 3 days at a resort owned by the company. Linda's superiors thought that this program would be a great way to reward innovation and help employees start to build relationships across cultures.

More than a thousand responses flooded in. Linda worked overtime to review them in detail. After analyzing where the responses came from, however, Linda discovered a pattern: Most of the initiatives came from offices in northern Europe. Employees in Brazil, Argentina, and India had largely opted out.

Linda shared this information at a team meeting. "If you just looked at the number of submissions we got, you'd have to declare this program a success," she said. "But it fell flat with employees in some of the countries that we wanted to reach the most. I followed up with some of the division directors from these areas. Several of them said that their employees were offended by the program. I think we've got a clash of cultures here."

Linda's behavior demonstrated several techniques presented in this chapter. For example, she dealt with a potential source of conflict by citing facts about the program's results. She did not blame anyone on her team for the partial failure of the incentive program. Describe at least one other technique that might have been useful to Linda:

_____

_____

The next task for Linda's team is to discover why the program offended some employees. Describe a possible reason for this problem:

_____

_____

Finally, list a possible solution:

_____

_____

People of all races, ethnicities, and cultures can use several strategies to reach common ground in the workplace. Other techniques from this chapter that can be applied to the workplace are:

- **Expect differences.** To prevent misunderstandings, remember that culture touches every aspect of human behavior, ranging from the ways that people greet each other to the ways they resolve conflict.
- **Use language with care.** Also remember that nonverbal language differs across cultures. For example, people from India may shake their head from side to side to indicate agreement, not disagreement.
- **Put messages in context.** When speaking to people of another culture, you might find that words carry only part of an intended message. In many countries, strong networks of shared assumptions form a context for communication.

Quiz

Name _____   Date ____/____/____

1. **Explain the differences among *stereotypes*, *prejudice*, and *discrimination* as defined in the text.**
   Stereotypes are inaccurate ideas about members of another culture. *Prejudice* refers to positive or negative feelings about others, often based on stereotypes. *Discrimination* occurs when stereotypes or prejudice is expressed in policies and laws that undermine equal opportunities for all cultures. (*Building relationships across cultures,* p. 274)

2. **Give two examples of differences between individualist and collectivist cultures.**
   Individualist cultures value personal fulfillment and personal success and emphasize "I" over "we." Collectivist cultures value cooperation over competition and believe that group progress is more important than individual success. (*Building relationships across cultures,* p. 274)

3. **Briefly describe three strategies for communicating across cultures.**
   List and discuss three of the following (answers will vary):   a. Start with self-discovery.   b. Learn about other cultures.   c. Look for differences between individualist and collectivist cultures.   d. Reach out.   e. Look for common ground.   f. Speak and listen with cultural sensitivity.   g. Look for individuals, not group representatives.   h. Find a mediator, translator, or model.   i. Develop support systems.   j. Be willing to accept feedback.   k. Speak up against discrimination.   l. Change the institution.   (*Building relationships across cultures,* p. 274)

4. **Explain the difference between *self-fulfilling prophecy* and *self-justification* when it comes to detecting stereotypes.**
   Self-fulfilling prophecy, as it relates to stereotyping, involves interacting with people in ways that confirm our stereotyping of them. *Self-justification* occurs when the persons who are being stereotyped avoid taking responsibility for their own lives by assuming the role of victim and accepting the stereotypical portrayal of themselves and/or their culture. (*Overcome stereotypes with critical thinking,* p. 279)

5. **Define the terms *translator, mediator,* and *model* as explained in this chapter.**
   A *translator* is truly bicultural and relates skillfully to both people in a mainstream culture and people from a contrasting culture. *Mediators* belong to the dominant or mainstream culture. Though perhaps not bicultural, mediators value diversity and are committed to cultural understanding. *Models* are positive examples of members of a culture. Models may include entertainers, athletes, and community leaders. (*Building relationships across cultures,* p. 274)

6. **According to the text, skills in living with diversity help us focus on how people differ. True or False? Explain your answer.**
   False. By developing diversity skills, we focus on both similarities and differences in people. (*Building relationships across cultures,* p. 274)

7. **Explain a strategy for taking charge of the conversations in your life.**
   One strategy for taking charge of your conversations is to spend time with people who speak about and live consistently with the attitudes you value. See the page referenced for other strategies. (Answers will vary.) (*Power Process: Choose your conversations and your community,* p. 289)

8. **Briefly explain the difference between *quid pro quo harassment* and *hostile environment harassment.***
   Quid pro quo harassment occurs when students believe that an educational decision depends on their submitting to unwelcome sexual conduct, whereas *hostile environment harassment* takes place when such incidents are severe, persistent, or pervasive. (*Dealing with sexism and sexual harassment,* p. 282)

9. **Rewrite the following sentence so that it is gender neutral: "Any writer can benefit from honing his skill at observing people."**
   One possibility is switching to the plural: "Writers can benefit from honing their skills at observing people." (Answers will vary.) (*Strategies for nonsexist communication,* p. 283)

10. **Few of us get the chance to be leaders. True or False? Explain your answer.**
    False. We all have the capacity to make significant changes in the world around us. Almost all of us encounter situations in which we can function as leaders. (*Leadership in a diverse world,* p. 284)

Skills Snapshot

Now that you've reflected on the ideas in this chapter and experimented with some new strategies, revisit your responses to the "Diversity" section of the Discovery Wheel exercise on page 27. Then complete the following sentences.

QUESTIONING ASSUMPTIONS

The racial, ethnic, and gender stereotypes that I've heard include...

If I talk to people who express such stereotypes, I will respond by...

BRIDGING CULTURES

When I meet someone whose beliefs or customs differ in a major way from mine, my first reaction is...

Other ways I could respond to such differences include...

NEXT ACTION

I'll know that I've reached a new level of mastery with diversity when...

To reach that level of mastery, the most important thing I can do next is to...

Master Student PROFILE

Sampson Davis

. . . is determined

Medical school was one of the roughest periods of my life. Something unexpected was always threatening to knock me out of the game: family distractions, the results of my first state board exam, the outcome of my initial search for a residency. But through determination, discipline, and dedication, I was able to persevere.

I call them my three D's, and I believe that they are the perfect formula for survival, no matter what you are going through.

Determination is simply fixing your mind on a desired outcome, and I believe it is the first step to a successful end in practically any situation. When I made the pact with George and Rameck at the age of seventeen, I was desperate to change my life. Going to college and medical school with my friends seemed the best way to make that happen.

But, of course, I had no idea of the challenges awaiting me, and many times over the years I felt like giving up. Trust me, even if you're the most dedicated person, you can get weary when setbacks halt or interfere with your progress. But determination means nothing without the discipline to go through the steps necessary to reach your goal—whether you're trying to lose weight or finish college—and the dedication to stick with it.

When I failed the state board exam, the light in the tunnel disappeared. But I just kept crawling toward my goal. I sought counseling when I needed it, and I found at least one person with whom I could share the range of emotions I was experiencing. If you're going through a difficult time and can't see your way out alone, you should consider asking for help. I know how difficult that is for most guys....But reaching out to counselors I had come to trust over the years and talking to my roommate Camille helped me unload some of the weight I was carrying. Only then was I able to focus clearly on what I needed to do to change my circumstances.

I'm grateful that I took kung fu lessons as a kid, because the discipline I learned back then really helped me to stay consistent once I started meditating, working out, and studying every single day....

Another important ingredient of perseverance is surrounding yourself with friends who support your endeavor. I can't tell you how much it helped me to have George and Rameck in my life to help me reach my goal. Even though things were awkward between us for a while after I failed the state boards, just knowing they were there and that they expected me to succeed motivated me.

I found motivation wherever I could. One of my college professors once told me that I didn't have what it takes to be a doctor, and I even used that to motivate me. I love being the underdog. I love it when someone expects me to fail. That, like nothing else, can ignite my three D's.

And when success comes, I'm the one who's not surprised.

"Sam on Perseverance," from The Pact by Sampson Davis, George Jenkins, and Rameck Hunt, with Liza Frazier Page. Copyright © 2002 by Three Doctors LLC. Used by permission of Riverhead Books, an imprint of Penguin Group (USA), Inc.

© Michael Didyoung/
Retna Ltd./Corbis

(1973–) As a teenager growing up in Newark, New Jersey, made a pact with two of his friends to "beat the street," attend college, and become a physician.

For more biographical information about Sampson Davis, visit the Master Student Hall of Fame.

Instructor Tools & Tips

"There are people who have money and people who are rich.

—Coco Chanel

While we might vigorously maintain that we know that "money can't buy happiness" and "the best things in life are free," honesty requires that we look deeper. Our behavior tells a different story.

—Joe Dominguez and Vicki Robin

"My student success course is about students taking an honest look at themselves, learning new ways of being a student, and creating plans to achieve their created goals. While most of the class time is spent discussing strategies and sharing feelings in small groups and with the class as a whole, I always feel some concern when it comes to asking students to share about their finances. Maybe it is my personal bias that leads me to think money is too personal a topic to ask students to discuss with each other or with me. For example, the point that "most money problems result from spending more than is available" in the article "Three paths to financial freedom" seems important to discuss in class. And while a more personal discussion might be more powerful, I tend toward generalizations and let the students internalize these concepts and apply them privately to their individual financial circumstances.

—Dean Mancina

Preview

Money or rather the lack of money is the most common reason students give for withdrawing from college. This important issue has been covered in all editions of *Becoming a Master Student,* but with tuition increases on the rise in most states, the need for first-year college students to develop a mature financial literacy is crucial to their college survival. Understanding the economic aspects of completing a degree is more essential now than ever. New articles will help students explore ways to manage money during tough times and relate their learning style to how they spend their money. This chapter also challenges students to think about what money means to them and how they can use money to achieve their goals without letting money use them. The Money Monitor/Money Plan exercise has been redesigned to make it easier for students to complete this homework assignment.

Guest Speaker

Invite the Financial Aid Director from your campus to talk to students about financial aid opportunities, deadlines, and forms they need to fill out. You may discover that your students have more questions for this guest speaker than for any of the others!

Discussing money in class can raise student privacy concerns. Here's a guest speaker sharing his views on this issue:

Lecture

Here is a lecture idea from Faculty Advisor Eldon McMurray: There are three absolute financial disasters awaiting unsuspecting college students that can be avoided: Avoiding late fees, keeping a current account register, and protecting yourself from identity theft.

Avoid late fees. Prioritizing spending with a simple budget can help students avoid paying late fees. Discuss the importance of paying credit card bills on time. Point out that after just one late payment, some credit card companies boost interest rates beyond 31 percent and charge late fees of nearly $40. And some credit card companies raise rates if you miss a deadline on another card, even if you have a spotless record with them. Suggest that students pay scheduled bills automatically if possible. Setting up a separate account so that their set bills will be paid automatically from their bank account saves students the hassle of writing monthly checks and worrying about mail delays; it also protects them from costly missed deadlines.

Keep a current account register. Maintaining an up-to-date account register can be the difference between graduating and dropping out. Barry Oats, a former collegiate football player, suggests a trick he learned from legendary football coach Lavell Edwards that can help any student. Simply play your money like a weekly football game.

First, make a financial "game plan" for the week by predicting your income and expenses. On Thursday night do a "Half Time Check" to make sure your income tops your expenses. Finally, on Sunday afternoon reconcile your accounts by matching your receipts with your game plan. If you have cash leftover after accounting for all your spending, you win!

Protect yourself from identity theft. Protecting themselves from the ever-growing threat of identity theft can help students avoid financial nightmares. Purchase a simple paper shredder and destroy all ATM receipts as soon as the transactions appear on your monthly bank statement. *Never* give your credit or debit card or your PIN (personal identification number) to anyone. Always ask if you can swipe your own card in department stores. Watch your card from the moment it leaves your hand until the clerk returns it to you. Pay attention to what the clerk does with your card. Make sure that the clerk is not copying or imaging your card.

Exercises/Activities

1. Education by the Hour (page 308) Consider having your students complete this exercise during class. When all the students have computed their actual direct and indirect costs of attending one class meeting, have them write the figure anonymously on a 3x5 card and put the cards on the chalk/whiteboard tray in order from lowest to highest. Then point out that the amount on the card is also the amount that students throw away each time they miss a class meeting during the term. I bring $100 in $1 bills and select a card with an amount that is close to $100 without going over it. I dramatically pull the hundred bills out of my pocket and count out the total on the 3x5 card,

tossing the $1 bills onto a table one by one. Then I pick up the wad of cash and throw it into the classroom trash can as a graphic illustration of how money is lost every time a class meeting is skipped. Without fail, you'll likely hear students gasp! Of course, the money loss is just one aspect of missing class, but students will get the point. Ask them each to retrieve their card and put it where they will see it frequently and be reminded of the cost of missing classes.

Preparation note: While students are doing their calculations and filling out their cards, sneak over to the trash can and line it with another trash bag to protect the dollar bills you'll throw in it later! Don't worry about forgetting to retrieve your cash—the students' eyes won't leave the trash can until you pull out the liner with the cash! (Note: I adapted this activity from a similar presentation by Dave Ellis when he was teaching me and other instructors how to illustrate the articles in *Becoming a Master Student.*)

P.S.: Perhaps you should worry just a little about forgetting to retrieve your money. Here's a story from an instructor, after he did a similar activity using thirty-five $1 bills:

> Some time after doing this exercise in front of a large class in the library, my office phone rang. The caller wanted to know if anyone from the morning's assembly in the library auditorium was missing any money—$35 to be exact! Thanks to an honest maintenance worker, who had emptied the basket and saw the bills fall out, I got my money back—less the reward that he richly deserved.
>
> Yes, I did tell the class the next day. And, no, I don't use real cash anymore.
>
> **—Jeff Swanberg, Rockford Business Center**

2. Take charge of your credit (page 307) A month before you get to Chapter 10, tell students to keep all credit card offers they receive in the mail. Have them bring the offers to class on a specific day. Divide the class into groups and ask them to analyze the offers in terms of the promotional interest rate, regular interest rate, credit limits, annual fees, and penalties for late payments. Students who did not receive any offers can borrow some from students who received several daily! Then ask the students if any of the offers in their group provides a better deal than the rate, limit, fees, and penalties on the credit card(s) they currently use. Most students won't know these facts about their current credit card(s). This is a good lead-in to a homework assignment to investigate their credit cards.

3. Master Student Profile: Lisa Price (page 319) After students have read this inspirational story, divide them into groups and ask them to brainstorm a money-making product or service idea. Then brainstorm five steps that would be necessary to bring this idea to fruition and five marketing ideas that would help promote the product or service. Ask each group to make a 2-minute summary report to the rest of the class.

Conversation/Sharing

Power Process: Risk Being a Fool (page 315) Begin the discussion of this Power Process by asking students, "What percentage of the shots you never take in a basketball game will you miss?" (Zero percent is the answer.) Then follow up with this question: "Will you ever win a game?" The answer, of course, is no. This example helps students connect to this Power Process by thinking about the risks they are taking—or not taking. Then we cycle through the learning styles reasoning model.

Why? Why is "Risk being a fool" a Power Process that applies to you?

What? What do you have to understand in order to practice "Risk being a fool"?

How? How can you transfer the power out of this process and into your life as a student?

What if? What if you apply "Risk being a fool" in your other classes? Or what if you don't?

Homework

The ultimate question This is a good time to use an "ultimate question" activity to encourage students to read this chapter and engage in a critical thinking approach to exploring the ideas and learning how they can manage money. Many students waste their second

most valuable resource—money (the most valuable is study time)—by not keeping track of their spending. For some students, this is simply due to a lack of skills. In contrast, knowing what financial resources they have at any given moment is characteristic of master students. Begin this chapter by having your students ask themselves the "ultimate question": "*What* do I not know about money that I need to know?" Then encourage your students to learn *how* they can acquire this knowledge. Ask them to predict *what if* they were to apply these new skills to their course work—and in the workplace. Use the Master Student Map in the textbook to take this exercise a step further. Have your students review the list of articles under "What is included…" and put an X by the topics they do know and a check mark by the items they don't know or are unsure of. As they go through the list, they can also rate their knowledge of the topic or their confidence in their skills using a scale of 1 to 10 (with 10 being very knowledgeable or confident). Then they can do a chapter reconnaissance by touching each page of the chapter. When this approach is finished, your students will have created an active framework in their mind for the financial literacy information in this chapter.

The Money Monitor/Money Plan (page 296) Note that this exercise has been revised for the thirteenth edition of *Becoming a Master Student.* Tell your students that this is similar to the Time Monitor/Time Plan in Chapter 2. The first step in managing their money is to see objectively how much money they have and how they spend it. If they think back to the invaluable knowledge they obtained from the Time Monitor/Time Plan, they will be willing to spend the time to complete this admittedly lengthy task for the awareness it will provide them.

Evaluation

Ask students to describe ways of making more money while in college. Ask students to write specific Intention Statements about protecting their money online. Ask students how they intend to spend less money. Ask them to discuss one or more money management strategies that are especially useful during tough economic times. Ask students how they can take charge of their credit cards.

Additional Digital Resources

Course Manual

The online *Course Manual* serves as an invaluable reference for those developing and teaching a College Success course with *Becoming a Master Student.* The *Course Manual* provides advice on general teaching issues such as preparing for classes, classroom management, grading, and communicating with students of various backgrounds, as well as specific strategies on getting the most out of various features in *Becoming a Master Student* such as the Discovery Wheel, Learning Styles Inventory, and book-specific Web sites.

Instructor Web Site

The updated Instructor Web site provides resources to help you plan and customize your course. Content specific to Chapter 10 includes:

- ▶ Lecture Ideas
  - • Money Makes the World Go Around
- ▶ In-Class Exercises
  - • Education by the Hour
  - • The Long-Term Budget
  - • Where Does All the Money Go?
- ▶ In-Text Quiz Answers
- ▶ Learning Styles Application
- ▶ Discussion Topics
- ▶ PowerPoint Slides
- ▶ Reflection Questions
- ▶ Assessment Questions
- ▶ Experiment with chapter strategies

The Instructor Web site also contains the following book-specific content:

- ▶ ExamView Test Bank
- ▶ Online Course Manual
- ▶ Articles from previous editions
- ▶ Master Student Profiles from previous editions
- ▶ Sample Syllabi
- ▶ Detailed Transition Guide

Student Web Site

To help your students gain a better understanding of the topics discussed in *Becoming a Master Student,* encourage your students to visit the Student Web site, which provides the following resources specific to Chapter 10:

 www.cengage.com/success/bams13e

- ▶ Connect to Text content expands on specific topics marked with an icon within Chapter 10.
- ▶ Learning Style Applications invite students to cycle through the four styles of learning. In answering the four questions about increasing your income or decreasing your expenses posted in this chapter's Learning Styles Application, students explore the different modes and apply their new knowledge.
- ▶ Practice Tests allow students to see how well they understand the themes of *Becoming a Master Student.*
- ▶ Interactive Concept Maps promote critical thinking by highlighting related ideas to show relationships between concepts.
- ▶ Video Skillbuilders bring to life techniques that will help you to excel in college and beyond. The following video should give your students more information regarding topics covered in Chapter 10:
  - • Managing Your Finances
- ▶ Remembering Cultural Differences presents readers with brief articles that touch on aspects of diversity in our rapidly changing world. For Chapter 10, the following article will prompt your students to look at contemporary issues in a new way:
  - • Aging in the Future
- ▶ Master Student Profiles provide additional information on the people covered in this book feature. For Chapter 10, students will find expanded coverage and links about:
  - • Lisa Price
- ▶ Power Process Media contains video, PowerPoints, and audio files to take what your students have learned from the Power Processes in their book to the next level. For Chapter 10, students will find additional media on:
  - • Risk being a fool

Along with the chapter-specific content, a General Resources folder is available that contains Toolboxes geared toward specific student types (Community College, Adult Learner, Student Athlete), the Plagiarism Prevention Zone, and the Career Resource Center.

10 Money

Master Student Map

as you read, ask yourself

what if . . .

I could adopt habits that would free me from money worries for the rest of my life?

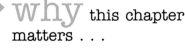

why this chapter matters . . .

Money no longer has to be a barrier to getting what you want from school—and from your life.

how you can use this chapter . . .

- Discover the details about how money flows in and out of your life.
- Experiment with ways to increase your income and decrease expenses.
- Gain strategies for saving, investing, and reducing debt.
- Find ways to pay for your education.

what is included . . .

MASTER STUDENTS in *action*

My money management strategies include waiting until I have the money to buy something and searching for the best deal. I'm a fiend when it comes to searching for coupons online. I could spend less money on food if I went out to eat less. I figured out I could save $100-to-$150 a month by packing a lunch.—**JAKE ZUCKER**

Courtesy of Jake Zucker

Three paths to financial freedom

"I CAN'T AFFORD IT" is a common reason that students give for dropping out of school. "I don't know how to pay for it" or "I don't think it's worth it" are probably more accurate ways to state the problem.

Money produces more unnecessary conflict and worry than almost anything else. And it doesn't seem to matter how much money a person has. People who earn $10,000 a year never have enough. People who earn $100,000 a year also say that they never have enough.

Let's say they earned $1 million a year. Then they'd have enough, right? Not necessarily.

Most money problems result from spending more than is available. It's that simple, even though we often do everything we can to complicate the problem.

The solution also is simple: *Don't spend more than you have.* If you are spending more than you have, then increase your income, decrease your spending, or do both. This idea has never won a Nobel Prize in Economics, but you won't go broke applying it.

Money management may be based on a simple idea, but there is a big incentive for us to make it seem more complicated than it really is. If we don't understand money, then we don't have to be responsible for it. After all, if you don't know how to change a flat tire, then you don't have to be the one responsible for fixing it.

Choosing to remain ignorant of money matters will almost surely lead to severe problems. Using the strategies in this chapter could free you from money worries. That's a bold statement—perhaps even an outrageous one. But what if it's true? Approach this idea with an open mind. Then experiment with it, using your own life as the laboratory.

The strategies you're about to learn are not complicated. In fact, they're not even new. The strategies are all based on the cycle of discovery, intention, and action that you've already practiced with the Journal Entries in this book. With these strategies and the abilities to add and subtract, you have everything you need to manage your money.

There are three main steps in money management:

- First, tell the truth about how much money you have and how much you spend (discovery).

- Second, commit to spend less than you have (intention).

- Finally, apply the suggestions for earning more money, spending less money, or both (action).

If you do these three things consistently, you can eventually say goodbye to most money worries.

This chapter about money does not tell you how to become a millionaire, though you can certainly adopt that as a goal if you choose. Instead, the following pages reveal what many millionaires know—ways to control money instead of letting money control you.

 Find more perspectives on the nature of financial freedom online.

journal entry 28

Discovery/Intention Statement

Commit to a New Experience of Money

Reflect on your overall experience of money. List any statements you've made about your money during the last month—anything from "I never have enough" to "I have some extra money to invest, and I'm wondering where to put it." Write your statements here.

When speaking about my money, I discovered that I . . .

_____

_____

_____

Scan this chapter with an eye for strategies that could help you increase your income, decrease your expenses, or both. List three money strategies that you'd like to use right away.

I intend to . . .

_____

_____

_____

10

MONEY

The Money Monitor/Money Plan

Many of us find it easy to lose track of money. It likes to escape when no one is looking. And usually, no one *is* looking. That's why the simple act of noticing the details about money can be so useful—even if this is the only idea from the chapter that you ever apply.

Use this exercise as a chance to discover how money flows into and out of your life. The goal is to record all the money you receive and spend over the course of 1 month. This sounds like a big task, but it's simpler than you might think. Besides, there's a big payoff for this action. With increased awareness of income and expenses, you can make choices about money that will change your life. Here's how to begin.

1. Tear out the Money Monitor/Money Plan form on page 299

Make photocopies of this form to use each month. The form helps you do two things. One is to get a big picture of the money that flows in and out of your life. The other is to plan specific and immediate changes in how you earn and spend money.

2. Keep track of your income and expenses

Use your creativity to figure out how you want to carry out this step. The goal is to create a record of exactly how much you earn and spend each month. Use any method that works for you. And keep it simple. Following are some options:

Carry 3x5 cards in your pocket, purse, backpack, or briefcase. Every time you buy something or get paid, record a few details on a card. List the date. Add a description of what you bought or what you got paid. Note whether the item is a source of income (money coming in) or an expense (money going out). Be sure to use a separate card for each item. This makes it easier to sort your cards into categories at the end of the month and fill out your Money Monitor/Money Plan.

Save all receipts and file them. This method does not require you to carry any 3x5 cards. But it does require that you faithfully hang on to every receipt and record of payment. Every time you buy something, ask for a receipt. Then stick it in your wallet, purse, or pocket. When you get home, make notes about the purchase on the receipt. Then file the receipts in a folder labeled with the current month and year (for example, *January 2011*). Every time you get a paycheck during that month, save the stub and add it to the folder. If you do not get a receipt or record of payment, whip out a 3x5 card and create one of your own. Detailed receipts will help you later on when you file taxes, categorize expenses (such as food and entertainment), and check your purchases against credit card statements.

Use personal finance software. Learn to use Quicken or a similar product that allows you to record income and expenses on your computer and to sort them into categories.

Use online banking services. If you have a checking account that offers online services, take advantage of the records that the bank is already keeping for you. Every time you write a check, use a debit card, or make a deposit, the transaction will show up online. You can use a computer to log in to your account and view these transactions at any time. If you're unclear about how to use online banking, go in to your bank and ask for help.

Experiment with several of the above options. Settle into one that feels most comfortable to you. Or create a method of your own. Anything will work, as long as you end each month with an *exact and accurate* record of your income and expenses.

3. On the last day of the month, fill out your Money Monitor/Money Plan

Pull out a blank Money Monitor/Money Plan. Label it with the current month and year. Fill out this form using the records of your income and expenses for the month.

Notice that the far left column of the Money Monitor/Money Plan includes categories of income and expenses. (You can use the blank rows for categories of income and expenses that are not already included.) Write your total for each category in the middle column.

For example, if you spent $300 at the grocery store this month, write that amount in the middle column next to *Groceries*. If you work a part-time job and received two paychecks for the month, write the total in the middle column next to *Employment*. See the sample Money Monitor/Money Plan on the next page for more examples.

Remember to split expenses when necessary. For example, you might write one check each month to pay the balance due on your credit card. The purchases listed on your credit card bill might fall into several categories. Total up your expenses in each category, and list them separately.

Suppose that you used your credit card to buy music online, purchase a sweater, pay for three restaurant meals, and buy two tanks of gas for your car. Write the online music expense next to *Entertainment*. Write the amount you paid for the sweater next to *Clothes*. Write the total you spent at the restaurants next to *Eating Out*. Finally, write the total for your gas stops next to *Gas*.

Now look at the column on the far right of the Money Monitor/Money Plan. This column is where the magic happens. Review each category of income and expense. If you plan to reduce your spending in a certain category during the next month, write a minus sign (–) in the far right column. If you plan a spending increase in any category next month, write a plus sign (+) in the far right column. If you think that a category of income or expense will remain the same next month, leave the column blank.

Look again at the sample Money Monitor/Money Plan. This student plans to reduce her spending for clothes, eating out, and entertainment (which for her includes movies and DVD rentals). She plans to increase the total she spends on groceries. She figures that even so, she'll save money by cooking more food at home and eating out less.

4. After you've filled out your first Money Monitor/Money Plan, take a moment to congratulate yourself

You have actively collected and analyzed the data needed to take charge of your financial life. No matter how the numbers add up, you are now in conscious control of your money. Repeat this exercise every month. It will keep you on a steady path to financial freedom.

 Do this exercise online.

No budgeting required

Notice one more thing about the Money Monitor/Money Plan: It does not require you to create a budget. Budgets—like diets—often fail. Many people cringe at the mere mention of the word *budget*. To them it is associated with scarcity, drudgery, and guilt. The idea of creating a budget conjures up images of a penny-pinching Ebenezer Scrooge shaking a bony, wrinkled finger at them and screaming, "You spent too much, you loser!"

That's not the idea behind the Money Monitor/Money Plan. In fact, there is no budget worksheet for you to complete each month. And no one is pointing a finger at you. Instead of budgeting, you simply write a plus sign or a minus sign next to each expense or income category that you *freely choose* to increase or decrease next month. There's no extra paperwork, no shame, and no blame.

Sample Money Monitor/Money Plan
Month_____ Year_____

Income	This Month	Next Month		Expenses	This Month	Next Month
Employment	500			Books and Supplies		
Grants	100			Car Maintenance		
Interest from Savings				Car Payment		
Loans	300			Clothes		–
Scholarships	100			Deposits into Savings Account		
				Eating Out	50	–
				Entertainment	50	–
				Gas	100	
				Groceries	300	+
				Insurance (Car, Life, Health, Home)		
				Laundry	20	
				Phone	55	
				Rent/Mortgage Payment	400	
				Tuition and Fees		
				Utilities	50	
Total Income	1000			Total Expenses	1025	–

10

MONEY

Money Monitor/Money Plan
Month_____ Year_____

Income	This Month	Next Month	Expenses	This Month	Next Month
Employment			Books and Supplies		
Grants			Car Maintenance		
Interest from Savings			Car Payment		
Loans			Clothes		
Scholarships			Deposits into Savings Account		
			Eating Out		
			Entertainment		
			Gas		
			Groceries		
			Insurance (Car, Life, Health, Home)		
			Laundry		
			Phone		
			Rent/Mortgage Payment		
			Tuition and Fees		
			Utilities		
Total Income			Total Expenses		

Money Monitor/Money Plan
Month_____ Year_____

Income	This Month	Next Month
Employment		
Grants		
Interest from Savings		
Loans		
Scholarships		
Total Income		

Expenses	This Month	Next Month
Books and Supplies		
Car Maintenance		
Car Payment		
Clothes		
Deposits into Savings Account		
Eating Out		
Entertainment		
Gas		
Groceries		
Insurance (Car, Life, Health, Home)		
Laundry		
Phone		
Rent/Mortgage Payment		
Tuition and Fees		
Utilities		
Total Expenses		

10

MONEY

Discovery/Intention Statement

Reflect on your Money Monitor/Money Plan

Now that you've experimented with the Money Monitor/ Money Plan process, reflect on what you're learning. To start creating a new future with money, complete the following statements.

After monitoring my income and expenses for 1 month, I was surprised to discover that . . .

_____

_____

_____

_____

_____

_____

When it comes to money, I am skilled at . . .

_____

_____

_____

_____

_____

_____

_____

When it comes to money, I am *not* so skilled at . . .

_____

_____

_____

_____

_____

_____

I could increase my income by . . .

_____

_____

_____

_____

_____

_____

I could spend less money on . . .

_____

_____

_____

_____

_____

_____

After thinking about the most powerful step I can take right now to improve my finances, I intend to . . .

_____

_____

_____

_____

_____

_____

_____

10

MONEY

Make more money

FOR MANY PEOPLE, finding a way to increase income is the most appealing way to fix a money problem. This approach is reasonable, but it has a potential problem: When their income increases, many people continue to spend more than they make. This means that money problems persist, even at higher incomes.

To avoid this problem, manage your expenses no matter how much money you make.

If you do succeed at controlling your expenses over the long term, then increasing your income is definitely a way to build wealth. Among the ways to make more money are to focus on your education, consider financial aid, work while you're in school, and do your best at every job.

Focus on your education. Your most important assets are not your bank accounts, your car, or your house—they are your skills. As Henry Ford said, "The only real security that a person can have in this world is a reserve of knowledge, experience, and ability. Without these qualities, money is practically useless."[1]

That's why your education is so important. Right now, you're developing knowledge, experience, and abilities that you can use to create income for the rest of your life.

Once you graduate and land a job in your chosen field, continue your education. Look for ways to gain additional skills or certifications that lead to higher earnings and more fulfilling work assignments.

Consider financial aid. Student grants and loans can play a major role in your college success by freeing you up from having to work full-time or even part-time. Many students erroneously assume they don't qualify for educational grants or low-interest student loans.

Remember, though, that loans—even student loans at reduced interest rates—can burden students after they complete their degrees. So consider loans with caution.

Work while you're in school. If you work while you're in school, you earn more than money. You gain experience, establish references, interact with a variety of people, and make contact with people who might hire you in the future. And regular income in any amount can make a difference in your monthly cash flow.

Many students work full-time or part-time jobs. Work and school don't have to conflict, especially if you plan carefully (see Chapter 2: Time) and ask for your employer's support.

On most campuses, the financial aid office employs a person whose job it is to help students find work while they're in school. See that person. In addition, check into career planning and job placement services at your school. Using these resources can greatly multiply your job options.

Most jobs are never advertised. In fact, a key source of information about new jobs is people—friends, relatives, coworkers, and fellow students. Tell all of them that you're looking for a job.

In addition, make a list of several places where you would like to work. Then go to each place on your list, and tell someone that you would like a job. He might say that he doesn't have a job available. No problem. Ask to be considered for future job openings. Then check back periodically.

Some part-time jobs are just made for students. Serving or delivering food may not be glamorous, but the tips can make a real difference in your monthly income. Other jobs, such as working the reference desk at the campus library or monitoring the front desk in a dorm, can offer quiet times that are ideal for doing some extra studying.

Another option is to start your own business. Consider a service you could offer—anything from lawn mowing to computer consulting. Students can boost their income in many other ways, such as running errands, giving guitar lessons, walking pets, and house sitting. Charge reasonable rates, provide impeccable service, and ask your clients for referrals.

See if you can find a job related to your chosen career. Even an entry-level job in your field can provide valuable experience. Once you've been in such a job for a while, explore the possibilities for getting a promotion—or a higher-paying job with another employer.

Self-employment during higher education can blossom into amazing careers. For example, David Filo and Jerry Yang started making lists of their favorite Web sites while they were graduate students. They went on to create Yahoo!, which became the world's most popular site.[2]

Do your best at every job. Once you get a job, make it your intention to excel as an employee. A positive work experience can pay off for years by leading to other jobs, recommendations, and contacts.

No matter what job you have, be as productive as possible. Look for ways to boost sales, increase quality, or accomplish tasks in less time. Every day, ask yourself how you can create value for your employer by solving a problem, reducing costs, improving service, or attracting new clients or customers.

To maximize your earning power, keep honing your job-hunting and career-planning skills. You can find a wealth of ideas on these topics in Chapter 12: What's Next?

Finally, keep things in perspective. If your job is lucrative and rewarding, great. If not, remember that almost any job can support you in becoming a master student and reaching your educational goals. ✳

 Discover more ways to increase your income.

mastering technology

PROTECT YOUR MONEY ONLINE

Avoid scams. Con artists have been around ever since money was invented. Today, they're active online, looking for high-tech ways to peddle their schemes. Don't fall for them. One strategy is called *phishing*. It works like this: You receive an e-mail that looks as if it came from a bank or credit card company. The e-mail asks you to verify your account number, PIN, password, social security number, or other private information by clicking on a link.

If you get such a message, trash it. No reputable business asks for this kind of information via e-mail. People who forget this fact set themselves up for identity theft.

Guard your money data. To prevent other security breaches when managing money, regularly monitor your online bank accounts:

* Keep account information—including your social security number—private.
* For money transactions, use Web sites with an address (URL) that begins with *https://* rather than *http://*. The extra *s* stands for *secure,* meaning that any data you send will be encrypted and virtually impossible to steal.
* Check the lower right-hand corner of your browser for an icon that looks like a closed lock. This also indicates a secure site.
* Don't manage your money on public computers. Other users could see your information displayed on the screen and watch the keyboard as you type in passwords.

* Don't let your Web browser store passwords and other log-in information for sites that you use to manage money. People who know how to access this information could hack in to your accounts.
* Take any financial documents you print out or receive in the mail and shred them before throwing them away.

Prevent identity theft. If someone learns your social security number, credit card numbers, or bank account numbers, she could get access to your money. To prevent this problem, shred all your financial documents, and keep your social security card in a secret place. If any of your confidential information is stolen, file a police report right away. Also contact your bank and credit card companies. Afterward, keep checking your bank statements and credit card bills to make sure that problem has stopped. For more help, go online to the Federal Trade Commission's identity theft site at www.ftc.gov/bcp/edu/microsites/idtheft.

In addition, use a strong password whenever you pay bills or buy something online. Such a password will look like a string of random characters to anyone but you. To create a strong password, make it at least eight characters long, and include a combination of letters, numbers, and symbols. Choose characters from across the entire keyboard rather than characters that are located close together.

Also consider using a *pass phrase*—several words with a space between each word. Choose a phrase that's easy for you to remember but difficult for anyone else to guess.

10

MONEY

Spend less money

CONTROLLING YOUR EXPENSES is something you can do right away, and it's usually easier than increasing your income. Use ideas from the following list, and invent more of your own.

Look to big-ticket items. When you look for places to cut expenses, start with the items that cost the most. Choices about where to live, for example, can save you thousands of dollars. Sometimes a place a little farther from campus, or a smaller house or apartment, will be much less expensive. You can also keep your housing costs down by finding a roommate. Offer to do repairs or maintenance in exchange for reduced rent. Pay your rent on time, and treat property with respect.

Another high-ticket item is a car. Take the cost of buying or leasing and then add expenses for parking, insurance, repairs, gas, maintenance, and tires. You might find that it makes more sense to walk, bike, use public transportation, ride a campus shuttle, and call for an occasional taxi ride. Or, carpool. Find friends with a car, and chip in for gas.

Use Exercise #28: "The Money Monitor/Money Plan" on page 296 to discover the main drains on your finances. Then focus on one or two areas where you can reduce spending while continuing to pay your fixed monthly bills, such as rent and tuition.

Look to small-ticket items. Reducing or eliminating the money you spend on low-cost purchases can make the difference between saving money or going into debt. For example, $3 spent at the coffee shop every day adds up to $1,095 over a year. That kind of spending can give anyone the jitters.

Ask for student discounts. Movie theaters, restaurants, bars, shopping centers, and other businesses sometimes discount prices for students. Also go to your bank, and ask whether you can open a student checking and savings account with online banking. The fees and minimum required amounts could be lower. Go online to check your balances weekly so that you avoid overdraft fees.

Do comparison shopping. Prices vary dramatically. Shop around, wait for off-season sales, and use coupons. Check out secondhand stores, thrift stores, and garage sales. Before plunking down the full retail price for a new item, consider whether you could buy it used. You can find "preowned" clothes, CDs, furniture, sports equipment, audio equipment, and computer hardware in retail stores and on the Internet.

Be aware of quality. The cheapest product is not always the least expensive over the long run. Sometimes, a slightly more expensive item is the best buy because it will last longer. Remember, there is no correlation between the value of something and the amount of money spent to advertise it. Carefully inspect things you are considering to buy, and see if they are well made.

Save money on eating and drinking. This single suggestion could significantly lower your expenses. Instead of hitting a restaurant or bar, head to the grocery store. Fresh fruits, fresh vegetables, and whole grains are not only better for you than processed food—they also cost less. In addition, clip food coupons. Sign up for a shopper's discount card.

Cooking for yourself doesn't need to take much time if you do a little menu planning. Create a list of your five favorite home-cooked meals. Learn how to prepare them. Then keep ingredients for these meals always on hand. To reduce grocery bills, buy these ingredients in bulk.

If you live in a dorm, review the different meal plans you can buy. Some schools offer meal plans for students who live off campus. These plans might be cheaper than eating in restaurants while you're on campus.

Lower your phone bills. If you use a cell phone, pull out a copy of your latest bill. Review how many minutes you used last month. Perhaps you could get by with a less expensive phone, fewer minutes, fewer text messages, and a cheaper plan.

Do an Internet search on *cell phone plan comparison*, and see if you could save money by switching providers. Also consider a family calling plan, which might cost less than a separate plan for each person. In addition, consider whether you need a home phone (a land line) *and* a cell phone. Dropping the home phone could save you money right away.

Go "green." To conserve energy and save money on utility bills, turn out the lights when you leave a room. Keep windows and doors closed in winter. In summer, keep windows open early in the day to invite lots of cool air into your living space. Then close up the apartment or house to keep it cool during the hotter hours of the day. Leave air-conditioning set at 72 degrees or above. In cool weather, dress warmly and keep the house at 68 degrees or less. In hot weather, take shorter, cooler showers.

Unplug any electric appliances that are not in use. Appliances like microwaves, audio systems, and cell phone chargers use energy when plugged in even when they're not in use. Also, plug computer equipment into power strips that you can turn off while you sleep.

Explore budget plans for monthly payments that fluctuate, such as those for heating your home. These plans average your yearly expenses so you pay the same amount each month.

Pay cash. To avoid interest charges, deal in cash. If you don't have the cash, don't buy. Buying on credit makes it more difficult to monitor spending. You can easily bust next month's money plan with this month's credit card purchases.

Postpone purchases. If you plan to buy something, leave your checkbook or credit card at home when you first go shopping. Look at all the possibilities. Then go home and make your decision when you don't feel pressured. When you are ready to buy, wait a week, even if the salesperson pressures you. What seems like a necessity today may not even cross your mind the day after tomorrow.

Notice what you spend on "fun." Blowing your money on fun is fun. It is also a fast way to blow your savings. When you spend money on entertainment, ask yourself what the benefits will be and whether you could get the same benefits for less money. You can read magazines for free at the library, for example. Most libraries also loan CDs and DVDs for free.

Use the envelope system. After reviewing your monthly income and expenses, put a certain amount of cash each week in an envelope labeled *Entertainment/Eating Out.* When the envelope is empty, stop spending money on these items for the rest of the week. If you use online banking, see if you can create separate accounts for various spending categories. Then deposit a fixed amount of money into each of those accounts. This is an electronic version of the envelope system.

Don't compete with big spenders. When you watch other people spend their money, remember that you don't know the whole story. Some students have parents with deep pockets. Others head to Mexico every year for spring break but finance the trips with high-interest credit cards. If you find yourself feeling pressured to spend money so that you can keep up with other people, stop to think about how much it will cost over the long run. Maybe it's time to shop around for some new friends.

Use the money you save to prepare for emergencies and reduce debt. If you apply strategies such as those listed above, you might see your savings account swell nicely. Congratulate yourself. Then choose what to do with the extra money. To protect yourself during tough times, create an emergency fund (see "Money for the Future" on page 310). Then reduce your debt by paying more than the minimum on credit card bills and loan payments (see "Take Charge of Your Credit" on page 307).

Spend less, and feel the power. Cutting your spending might be challenging at first. Give it time. Spending less is not about sacrificing pleasure. It's about something that money can't buy—the satisfaction of choosing exactly where your money goes and building a secure financial future. Every dollar that you save on a frivolous expense is a dollar you can invest in something that truly matters to you.

 Discover more cost-cutting strategies online.

29 exercise
Show me the money

See if you can use *Becoming a Master Student* to create a financial gain that is many times more than the cost of the book. Scan the entire text, and look for suggestions that could help you save money or increase income in significant ways; for example:

- Use suggestions for career planning and job hunting in Chapter 12: What's Next? to find your next job more quickly—and start earning money sooner.

- Negotiate a higher salary for your next job using strategies from the article "Use Interviews and Résumés to Hire an Employer" on page 364.

- Use suggestions for goal setting from Chapter 2: Time to create a detailed plan to acquire a skill that will make it easier for you to get a higher-paying job.

In the space below, write your ideas for creating more money from your experience of this book. Use additional paper as needed.

10

MONEY

Managing money during tough times

The biggest factor in your long-term financial well-being is your own behavior. Taking informed action is a way to cut through financial confusion and move beyond fear. An added benefit: The habits that help you survive tough times will also help you manage money when the economy rebounds.

zimmytws/Shutterstock

START BY DOING Exercise #28: The "Money Monitor/Money Plan" on page 296. This exercise will give you the details about what you're spending and earning right now. With that knowledge, you can choose your next strategy from among the following.

Spend less and save more. The less you spend, the more money you'll have on hand. Use that money to pay your monthly bills, pay off your credit cards, and create an emergency fund to use in case you lose your job or a source of financial aid. See "Spend less money" on page 304 for ideas.

Author Suze Orman recommends three actions to show that you can reduce spending at any time: (1) do not spend money for 1 day, (2) do not use your credit card for 1 week, and (3) do not eat out for 1 month. Success with any of these strategies can open up your mind to other possibilities for spending less and saving.[3]

Make sure that your savings are protected. The Federal Deposit Insurance Corporation (FDIC) backs individual saving accounts. The National Credit Union Administration (NCUA) offers similar protection for credit union members. If your savings are protected by these programs, every penny you deposit is safe. Check your statements to find out, or go online to www.myfdicinsurance.gov.

Invest only after saving. The stock market is only for money that you can afford to lose. Before you speculate, first save enough money to live on for at least 6 months in case you're unemployed. Then consider what you'll need over the next 5 years to finish your schooling and handle other major expenses. Save for these expenses before taking any risks with your money.

Think about your next job. During an economic crisis, you can get laid off even if you're a star employee. Prepare for this situation now. Create a career plan that describes the next job you want, the skills that

you'll develop to get it, and the next steps you'll take to gain those skills. Stay informed about the latest developments in your field. Find people who are already working in this area, and contact them for information interviews.

Research unemployment benefits. Unemployment benefits have limits and may not replace your lost wages. However, they can cushion the blow of losing a job while you put other strategies in place. To learn about the benefits offered in your state, go online to www.servicelocator.org.

Get health insurance. A sudden illness or lengthy hospital stay can drain your savings. Health insurance can pick up all or most the costs instead. If possible, get health insurance through your school or employer. Another option is private health insurance. To find coverage, go to the National Association of Health Underwriters (www.nahu.org) and www.ehealthinsurance.com.

Get help that you can trust. Avoid debt consolidators that offer schemes to wipe out your debt. What they don't tell you is that their fees are high, and that using them can lower your credit rating. Turn instead to the National Foundation for Credit Counseling (www.nfcc.org).

Choose your money conversations. To manage stress, talk about what you'll do to take charge of your money. Talk about what gives your life meaning beyond spending money. Use this chance to embrace the truth about your money life rather than resist it. ✳

 Find more ways online to thrive during tough times.

Take charge of your credit

© Michele Constantini, PhotoAlto/Getty

A GOOD CREDIT rating will serve you for a lifetime. With this asset, you'll be able to borrow money any time you need it. A poor credit rating, however, can keep you from getting a car or a house in the future. You might also have to pay higher insurance rates, and you could even be turned down for a job.

To take charge of your credit, borrow money only when truly necessary. If you do borrow, make all of your payments, and make them on time. This is especially important for managing credit cards and student loans.

Use credit cards with caution

A credit card is compact and convenient. That piece of plastic seems to promise peace of mind. Low on cash this month? Just whip out your credit card, slide it across the counter, and relax. Your worries are over—that is, until you get the bill. Credit cards often come with a hefty interest rate—sometimes as high as 30 percent.

A 2009 report by Sallie Mae, a student loan corporation, reveals that the average credit card debt among undergraduate students is $3,173.[4] However, many students are carrying higher amounts of debt, with costs that can soar over time. Suppose that a student owes $7,000 on a credit card with an annual percentage rate of 18.9 percent. Also suppose that he pays only the minimum balance due each month and charges nothing else to the account. He'll need to make payments for 16 years and pay $7,173 in interest.[5]

Credit cards do offer potential benefits, of course. Having one means that you don't have to carry around a checkbook or large amounts of cash, and they're pretty handy in emergencies. Getting a card is one way to establish a credit record. Some cards offer rewards, such as frequent flier miles and car rental discounts.

Used unwisely, however, credit cards can create a debt that takes decades to repay. This debt can seriously delay other goals—paying off student loans, financing a new car, buying a home, or saving for retirement.

Use the following strategies to take control of your credit cards. Write these ideas on a 3x5 card, and don't leave home without it.

Pay off the balance each month. An unpaid credit card balance is a sure sign that you are spending more money than you have. To avoid this outcome, keep track of how much you spend with credit cards each month. Pay off the card balance each month, on time, and avoid finance or late charges.

If you do accumulate a large credit card balance, go to your bank and ask about ways to get a loan with a lower interest rate. Use this loan to pay off your credit cards. Then promise yourself never to accumulate credit card debt again.

Scrutinize credit card offers. Beware of cards offering low interest rates. These rates are often only temporary. After a few months, they could double or even triple. Also look for annual fees, late fees, and other charges buried in the fine print.

Be especially wary of credit card offers made to students. Remember that the companies who willingly dispense cards on campus are not there to offer an educational service. They are in business to make money by charging you interest.

Avoid cash advances. Due to their high interest rates and fees, credit cards are not a great source of spare cash. Even when you get cash advances on these cards from an ATM, it's still borrowed money. As an alternative, get a debit card tied to a checking account, and use that card when you need cash on the go.

Check statements against your records. File your credit card receipts each month. When you get the bill for each card, check it against your receipts for accuracy. Mistakes in billing are rare, but they can happen. In addition, checking your statement reveals the interest rate and fees that are being applied to your account.

Use just one credit card. To simplify your financial life and take charge of your credit, consider using only one card. Choose one with no annual fee and the lowest interest rate. Don't be swayed by offers of free T-shirts or coffee mugs. Consider the bottom line, and be selective.

Get a copy of your credit report. A credit report is a record of your payment history and other credit-related items. You are entitled to get a free copy each year. Go to your bank and ask someone there how to do this. You can also request a copy of your credit report online at https://www.annualcreditreport.com. This site was created by three nationwide consumer credit–reporting companies—Equifax, Experian, and TransUnion. Check your report carefully for errors or accounts that you did not open. Do this now, before you're in financial trouble.

Protect your credit score. Whenever you apply for a loan, the first thing a lender will do is check your credit score. The higher your score, the more money you can borrow at lower interest rates. To protect your credit score, pay all your bills on time, hold on to credit cards that you've had for a while, and avoid applying for new credit cards. Pay off your credit card balance every month. Pay your bills on time. Never charge more than your limit.

Manage student loans

A college degree is one of the best investments you can make. But you don't have to go broke to get that education. You can make that investment with the lowest debt possible.

Choose schools with costs in mind. If you decide to transfer to another school, you can save thousands of dollars the moment you sign your application for admission. In addition to choosing schools on the basis of reputation, consider how much they cost and the financial aid packages that they offer.

Avoid debt when possible. The surest way to manage debt is to avoid it altogether. If you do take out loans, borrow only the amount that you cannot get from other sources—scholarships, grants, employment, gifts from relatives, and personal savings.

Also set a target date for graduation, and stick to it. The fewer years you go to school, the lower your debt.

Shop carefully for loans. Go the financial aid office and ask if you can get a Stafford loan. These are fixed-rate, low-interest loans from the federal government. If you qualify for a subsidized Stafford loan, the government pays the interest due while you're in school. Unsubsidized Stafford loans do not offer this benefit, but they are still one of the cheapest student loans you can get. Remember that *anyone* can apply for a Stafford loan. Take full advantage of this program before you look into other loans. For more information on the loans that are available to you, visit www.studentaid.ed.gov.

If your parents are helping to pay for your education, they can apply for a PLUS loan. There is no income limit, and parents can borrow up to the total cost

exercise 30
Education by the hour

Determine exactly what it costs you to go to school. Fill in the blanks below using totals for a semester, quarter, or whatever term system your school uses.

Note: Include only the costs that relate directly to going to school. For example, under "Transportation," list only the amount that you pay for gas to drive back and forth to school—not the total amount you spend on gas for a semester.

Tuition	$_____
Books	$_____
Fees	$_____
Transportation	$_____
Clothing	$_____
Food	$_____
Housing	$_____
Entertainment	$_____
Other expenses (such as insurance, medical costs, and child care)	$_____
Subtotal	$_____
Salary you could earn per term if you weren't in school	$_____
Total (A)	$_____

Now figure out how many classes you attend in one term. This is the number of your scheduled class periods per week multiplied by the number of weeks in your school term. Put that figure below:

Total (B) _____

Divide the **Total (B)** into the **Total (A),** and put that amount here:

$_____

This is what it costs you to go to one class one time.

On a separate sheet of paper, describe your responses to discovering this figure. Also list anything you will do differently as a result of knowing the hourly cost of your education.

 Do this exercise online. _____

10

MONEY

of their children's education. With these loans, your parents—not you—are the borrowers. A new option allows borrowers to defer repayment until after you graduate. PLUS loans cost more than Staffords but are still less expensive than private loans. If at all possible, avoid private loans.

Some lenders will forgive part of a student loan if you agree to take a certain job for a few years, such as teaching in a public school in a low-income neighborhood or working as a nurse in a rural community. This arrangement is called an *income-based repayment plan*. Ask someone in the financial aid office if it is an option for you.

If you take out student loans, find out exactly when the first payment is due on each of them. Don't assume that you can wait to start repayment until you find a job. Any bill payments that you miss will hammer your credit score.

Also ask your financial aid office about whether you can consolidate your loans. This means that you lump them all together and owe just one payment every month. Loan consolidation makes it easier to stay on top of your payments and protect your credit score. ✳

If you're in trouble . . .

Financial problems are common. Solve them in ways that protect you for the future.

Get specific data. Complete Exercise #28: "The Money Monitor/Money Plan" included earlier in this chapter.

Be honest with creditors. Determine the amount that you are sure you can repay each month, and ask the creditor if that would work for your case.

Go for credit counseling. Most cities have agencies with professional advisors who can help straighten out your financial problems.

Change your spending patterns. If you have a history of overspending (or underearning), change *is* possible. This chapter is full of suggestions.

 Find more strategies online for credit mastery.

Common credit terms

Annual fee—a yearly charge for using a credit card, sometimes called a *membership fee* or *participation fee*.

Annual percentage rate (APR)—the interest that you owe on unpaid balances in your account. The APR equals the periodic rate times the number of billing periods in a year.

Balance due—the remaining amount of money that you owe a credit card company or other lender.

Balance transfer—the process of moving an unpaid debt from one lender to another lender.

Bankruptcy—a legal process that allows borrowers to declare their inability to pay their debts. People who declare bankruptcy transfer all their assets to a court-appointed trustee and create a plan to repay some or all of their borrowed money. Bankruptcy protects people from harassment by their creditors and lowers their credit scores.

Credit score—a three-digit number that reflects your history of repaying borrowed money and paying other bills on time (also called a *FICO score*—an acronym for the Fair Isaac Corporation, which was the first company to create credit ratings). This number ranges from 300 to 850. The higher the number, the better your credit rating.

Default—state of a loan when the borrower fails to make required payments or otherwise violates the terms of the agreement. Default may prompt the creditor to turn the loan over to a collection agency, which can severely harm the borrower's credit score.

Finance charge—the total fee for using a credit card, which includes the interest rate, periodic rate, and other fees. Finance charges for cash advances and balance transfers can be different than finance charges for unpaid balances.

Grace period—for a credit card user who pays off the entire balance due, a period of time when no interest is charged on a purchase. When there is no grace period, finance charges apply immediately to a purchase.

Interest rate—an annual fee that borrowers pay to use someone else's money, normally a percentage of the balance due.

Minimum payment—the amount you must pay to keep from defaulting on an account; usually 2 percent of the unpaid balance due.

Payment due date—the day that a lender must receive your payment—*not* the postmarked date or the date you make a payment online. Check your statements carefully, as credit card companies sometimes change the due dates.

Periodic rate—an interest rate based on a certain period of time, such as a day or a month.

Money for the future

Start saving now

You can begin saving now even if you are in debt and living in a dorm on a diet of macaroni. Saving now helps you establish a habit that will pay off in the future.

Create an emergency fund. Take some percentage of every paycheck you receive, and immediately deposit that amount in a savings account. Start by saving 10 percent of your income. Then see if you can increase that amount over time.

The first purpose of this savings account is to have money on hand for surprises and emergencies—anything from a big repair bill to a sudden job loss. For peace of mind, have an emergency fund equal to at least 6 months of living expenses. Once you have that amount in place, save for longer-term goals. Examples are a new car, a child's education, and your own retirement.

Keep your savings in liquid investments such as an FDIC-insured savings account at a bank. The word *liquid* means that you can withdraw the money immediately. Other options for saving include certificates of deposit and Treasury securities (bills, notes, and bonds backed by the federal government). These are not as liquid as a savings account. However, they are low-risk ways to save for longer-term goals.

Save for retirement. It's never too early to start thinking about your retirement. Many employers offer 401(k) plans and other retirement plans. Some companies will match employee contributions to these accounts. Ask your employer if this benefit is offered to you. If it is, take full advantage of it.

Invest carefully

Investing in stocks, corporate bonds, and mutual funds can be risky. Do so only if you regularly save money and pay off the full balance on your credit cards each month. Even then, only invest money that you can afford to lose.

Successful investing requires extensive homework. Educate yourself by taking a class about personal finance and getting coaching from an independent, certified financial planner. No matter how you choose to invest, put time on your side. Invest as much as you can—keeping in mind the tips above—and invest as early as you can.

Be a wise car shopper

A car is a lousy investment. The minute you drive it off the dealer's lot, it loses value. And the trade-in value will never be enough to pay off a car loan.

If you borrow money to buy a car, keep the costs as low as possible. Reduce interest charges by sticking to a 3-year loan rather than extending it to 4 or 5 years. Check out certified, preowned cars. These are used cars that come with a warranty from the manufacturer, not the car dealer.

Stick to regular loans rather than leasing. Once you pay off a 3-year loan, you can keep on driving the car with no monthly payments. If you lease a car for 3 years, you won't own the car when the lease is up, and you might find it tempting to lease another car.

Save on insurance

Protect your assets by getting insurance for your home, car, life, and health. If you live in an apartment, get renters' insurance.

Find an independent insurance agent who can help you with all these policies. Ask about discounts for buying more than one policy from the same insurance company. Also ask if you can lower your premiums by raising your deductibles.

There are basically two kinds of life insurance: term and whole life. Term insurance is the least expensive. It pays if you die, and that's it. Whole life is more expensive. It pays if you die, and it also accumulates money like a savings plan does. However, you'll often get a higher return on your money if you buy the lower-priced term insurance and invest your extra dollars in something other than insurance.

Many schools offer competitive health insurance for students. Find out what's available on your campus. ✳

 Find more ways online to create a secure financial future.

You can pay for school

MILLIONS OF DOLLARS are waiting for people who take part in higher education. But the funds flow only to students who know how to find them.

There are many ways to pay for school. The kind of help you get depends on your financial need. In general, financial need equals the cost of your schooling minus what you can reasonably be expected to pay.

Financial aid includes money you don't pay back (grants and scholarships), money you do pay back (loans), and work-study programs. Most students who get financial aid receive a package that includes several examples of each type.

To find out more, visit your school's financial aid office on a regular basis. Also go online. Start with FinAid, at www.finaid.org.

Once you've lined up financial aid, keep it flowing. Find out the requirements for renewing loans, grants, and scholarships. Remember that many financial aid packages depend on your making "satisfactory academic progress." Also, programs change constantly. Money may be limited, and application deadlines are critical.

Scholarships, grants, and loans backed by the federal government are key sources of money for students. State governments often provide grants and scholarships as well. So do credit unions, service organizations such as Kiwanis International, and local chambers of commerce. Sometimes relatives will provide financial help. For more information on loans, refer back to the article "Take Charge of Your Credit" earlier in this chapter.

Determine how much money you need to complete your education and where you will get it. Having a plan for paying for your entire education makes it easier to finish your degree. ✳

 Discover more ways online to pay for school.

Education is worth it

Education is one of the few things you can buy that will last a lifetime. It can't rust, corrode, break down, or wear out. It can't be stolen, burned, repossessed, or destroyed. Once you have a degree, no one can take it away. That makes your education a safer investment than real estate, gold, oil, diamonds, or stocks.

Think about all the services and resources that your tuition money buys: academic advising to help you choose classes and select a major; access to the student health center and counseling services; career planning and job placement offices that you can visit even after you graduate; athletic, arts, and entertainment events at a central location; and a student center where you can meet people and socialize.

If you live on campus, you also get a place to stay with meals provided, all for less than the cost of an average hotel room. And by the way, you get to attend classes. Consider how much nonstudents would have to pay for such an array of services. You can see that higher education is a bargain.

The benefits go even further. A 2007 study released by the College Board reports that higher levels of education are associated with the following:

- Higher incomes for both men and women in all racial and ethnic groups.
- Higher levels of volunteer work and voting.
- Higher tax revenues for governments, which fund libraries, schools, parks, and other public goods.
- Lower levels of unemployment and dependence on social services, as well as lower smoking rates.[6]

In short, education is a good deal for you and for society. It's worth investing in it periodically to update your skills, reach your goals, and get more of what you want in life.

Why   What   How   What if

Car: Michael Shake/Shutterstock; *money:* Tomislav Forgo/Shutterstock; *bank:* Sebastian Kaulitzki/Shutterstock; *bike:* Marina Krasnorutskaya/Shutterstock; *woman:* PhotoAlto/Michele Constantini/Getty; collage by Walter Kopec

Your learning styles and your money

"LEARNING STYLES: Discovering how you learn" on page 32 explains four learning styles—unique ways of perceiving and processing our experiences. You can see these different styles at work in the ways that people spend and earn money.

For example, some people buy quickly once they find a product or service that connects to something they care about deeply (*active experimentation*). Others take the time to shop around and compare prices before they spend much (*reflective observation*). Some people are curious about how the stock and bond markets work and will take the time to analyze the field (*abstract conceptualization*). Others want to jump right in and experiment with ways to make more money (*concrete experience*).

When you face a financial decision, ask the following four questions. They will help you gain the benefits of using each learning style and make a more balanced choice.

Ask: *Why* **am I considering spending this money?** We buy when we see something to be gained. This could involve a small benefit, such as spending a couple of dollars on a soft drink to satisfy your thirst. Or it could be a larger benefit, like spending thousands of dollars on a car to satisfy your desire for convenience and mobility. Before you hand over your cash or credit card, be clear about what you want to gain.

Ask: *What* **are the facts I need to know?** The answer to this question is useful even with small purchases. In the case of the soft drink, for example, check out the ingredients on the label. Then think about whether you want to put that stuff in your body. If you're buying a car, find out exactly how much it will cost beyond the sticker price. If you plan to borrow money, research the available options. Your bank or credit union may offer a better interest rate than the car dealer. Or maybe a relative would consider giving you a no-interest loan.

Ask: *How* **would this purchase affect my life?** Many purchases come with a cost that goes beyond money. That soft drink might come with hidden costs—excess sugar and calories. Buying or renting a bigger home could tie you into higher payments. And that might require you to work more hours or see less of your family. When you spend your time, energy, and money for one purpose, those resources are not available for other purposes.

Ask: *What if* **I could get the same benefit without spending money?** You could save a couple dollars, reduce calories, *and* quench your thirst by using a drinking fountain instead of buying an overpriced drink. You could get around town *and* save thousands of dollars by getting a used car, or by using public transportation and paying for an occasional taxi ride. And you could gain more living space by building a small addition to your current home, or by simply cleaning out some cluttered rooms. Before you spend a dime, ask whether you can get the same benefit for no money down—or no money at all. ✳

We live like royalty

STEP BACK IN time just a few centuries, and imagine how a king, queen, or other wealthy person might have lived.

These people had enough to eat. Sometimes they even had feasts. They would serve food seasoned with spices from the four corners of the Earth. Guests would eat until they were stuffed. After the meal, they summoned entertainment with the snap of a finger.

Transportation was no problem. Horses were always ready, and a driver would chauffeur the king or queen from kingdom to kingdom.

Dress was lavish. Monarchs wore the latest fashions. The king and queen got new clothes at least once a year and never had to wear anything that was full of holes.

Royal families often lived in castles. Sometimes they were drafty and chilly, yet the inhabitants were safe from nature and usually safe from intruders.

True, infectious disease was common in those days, and life spans were shorter than they are now. Yet the richest people lived out their years in relative ease.

In short, these people lived a royal existence.

And they lacked central heating, air conditioners, refrigerators, stoves, public transportation, public parks, libraries, television, CDs, DVDs, computers, and many other comforts and conveniences that most of us enjoy today.

Most people don't say to themselves, "We live like royalty." They don't see the riches they possess right now. Through their selective perceptions, they create lives based on scarcity rather than abundance. They might roll their eyes if you told them that real wealth is all about loving relationships, fulfilling work, and continuous opportunities to learn. Tell them that money worries are unnecessary, and they might even get upset.

This article is not meant to upset anyone. The point is to consider a new way of thinking. Ideas such as "Wealth means more than having money" and "I am already rich" can change how you feel about money. They can open you up to new possibilities for making and saving money. And that can affect how much money you actually have.

Test this idea for yourself. For example, see if you can apply each of the Power Processes to your relationship with money. You can ease frustration by being here now, detaching, surrendering, letting go of your pictures of how much money you ought to have, loving your frustration to death, or looking at how you create your money problems. ✳

Jose Marines/Shutterstock

Free fun

Sometimes it seems that the only way to have fun is to spend money. Not true. Search out free entertainment on campus and in your community. Beyond this, your imagination is the only limit. Some suggestions are listed below. If you think they're silly or boring, create better ideas of your own.

- Browse a bookstore.
- Volunteer at a child care center.
- Draw.
- Exercise.
- Find other people who share your hobby, and start a club.
- Give a massage.
- Do yoga with a friend.
- Play Frisbee golf.
- Make dinner for your date.
- Picnic in the park.
- Take a long walk.
- Ride your bike.
- Listen to music that you already own but haven't heard for a while.

 Find more options for free fun.

practicing critical thinking

The money management articles in this chapter are based on three core ideas:

- Money problems have a simple source: You spend more than you have.
- The solution to money problems is also simple: Spend less than you have.
- You can implement this solution with three broad strategies: Increase your income, decrease your expenses, or both.

In this exercise, you will think critically about these statements by completing the following four steps:

1. First, test the logic of these assertions. Are they clear? Are they consistent with one another? And are they based on sound assumptions?

   For example, the first assertion is based on the assumption that problems can have a single cause. You might argue that this is simplistic and that most problems have more than one cause.

   Summarize your thinking about the logic of the three assertions in the space below:

   _____
   _____
   _____
   _____
   _____
   _____
   _____
   _____
   _____
   _____
   _____
   _____

2. Next, consider the evidence for these assertions. See if you can think of examples to support them. Also see if you can think of any counterexamples. For instance, you might be able to list money problems that are not due to spending more than you have.

Summarize your evidence for and against the three assertions here:

_____
_____
_____
_____

3. The third assertion states three broad financial goals that you could adopt: Increase your income, decrease your expenses, or both. Think about whether these goals imply actions that you could reasonably take. For example, could you actually decrease your expenses by finding a cheaper place to live or by spending less on entertainment?

   In the space below, summarize your ideas about whether you can truly apply the main strategies in this chapter:

   _____
   _____
   _____
   _____
   _____

4. Finally, if you agree to act on the strategies in this chapter, write a specific intention and take action. Also make a note on your calendar to return to this exercise in 1 month and assess the results. Did you carry through on your planned action? If so, do the results support or contradict the assertions listed above?

   Summarize your ideas in the space below:

   _____
   _____
   _____
   _____
   _____
   _____
   _____
   _____

Risk Being a Fool

A master student has the courage to take risks. And taking risks means being willing to fail sometimes—even being willing to be a fool. This idea can work for you because you already are a fool.

Don't be upset. All of us are fools at one time or another. There are no exceptions. If you doubt it, think back to that stupid thing you did just a few days ago. You know the one. Yes . . . *that* one. It was embarrassing, and you tried to hide it. You pretended you weren't a fool. This happens to everyone.

We are all fallible human beings. Most of us, however, spend too much time and energy trying to hide our foolhood. No one is really tricked by this—not even ourselves. It's OK to

look ridiculous while dancing. It's all right to sound silly when singing to your kids. Sometimes it's OK to be absurd. It comes with taking risks.

This Power Process comes with a warning label: Taking risks does *not* mean escaping responsibility for our actions. "Risk being a fool" is not a suggestion to get drunk at a party and make a fool of yourself. It is not a suggestion to fool around or do things badly. Mediocrity is not the goal.

The point is that mastery in most activities calls for the willingness to do something new, to fail, to make corrections, to fail again, and so on.

"Risk being a fool" means that foolishness—along with courage, cowardice, grace, and clumsiness—is a human characteristic. We all share

it. You might as well risk being a fool because you already are one, and nothing in the world can change that. Why not enjoy it once in a while?

There's one sure-fire way to avoid any risk of being a fool, and that's to avoid life. The writer who never finishes a book will never have to worry about getting negative reviews. The center fielder who sits out every game is safe from making any errors. And the comedian who never performs in front of an audience is certain to avoid telling jokes that fall flat. The possibility of succeeding at any venture increases when we're comfortable with making mistakes—that is, with the risk of being a fool.

 Learn more about taking risks online.

Ted Humble-Smith/RF/Getty

Put it to Work

Strategies from *Becoming a Master Student* can help you succeed in your career, as well as in school. To start discovering how suggestions in this chapter apply to the workplace, reflect on the following case study.

PhotosIndia.com/Getty

Vijit Ramcha graduated from college during a recession and felt lucky to land a job within a month after leaving school. He'd done an internship at a small nonprofit organization and was inspired by the sense of mission that its employees showed. He then began working full-time for the same organization as an accountant.

On Vijit's first day, his supervisor laid out the hard news about the organization's finances. Its primary source of income was a single funder—a foundation created by a local family. The economic downturn had delivered a hard blow to just about everyone's investment portfolio, and the foundation had decided to reduce its upcoming grant to Vijit's organization by 40 percent. To make ends meet, Vijit's supervisor now wanted to reduce their organization's expenses by 10 percent each month during the first quarter of the new fiscal year.

Vijit rose to the challenge. He was full of suggestions: Ask vendors for discounts. Rent out a rarely used conference room in the organization's office. Ask employees to take a temporary wage cut rather than lay off anyone. Put off doing a major upgrade of the organization's computer system.

"Those are all useful ideas," said Vijit's supervisor. "And, they're all focused on the short term. Let's back up a minute and get a bigger picture. We've been through hard times in the past, and we'll make it through the current recession. The question is, How can we start planning for the next recession *before* it arrives?"

Both Vijit and his supervisor demonstrated money strategies that are presented in this chapter: Reduce expenses. Postpone purchases. List some other short-term strategies that might be useful to Vijit's organization:

_____

_____

_____

_____

What would you say in response to the following question from Vijit's supervisor: "How can we start planning for the next recession *before* it arrives?"

_____

_____

_____

_____

_____

Like Vijit, you might get a job that requires preparing budgets, making financial forecasts, and adjusting income and expenses to meet an organization's financial goals. The ability to handle such tasks successfully is called *workplace financial literacy.* To get the most from your education, plan to develop this form of literacy. Following are some strategies to consider:

- Think about the ways you'll be handling money in your chosen career.
- Find out more by interviewing people who work in your field and asking them about how they handle money on the job.
- After listing the financial skills you need, consider which courses you'll take to develop them.
- Look for work-study assignments and internships that can help you to develop financial skills.
- Throughout your career, keep track of the positive outcomes you produce at work, including financial successes. Summarize these results in a sentence or two. Add them to your résumé.

Quiz

chapter 10

■ Put it to Work
◀ ◀ ◀ ◀ ◀
■ Skills Snapshot
■ Master Student Profile

Name _____   Date ____/____/____

1. List five sources of money to help students pay for their education.

   Student loans, grants, scholarships, and work-study programs, all of which may be included in financial aid packages; financial help may also be available from relatives. (*You can pay for school*, p. 311)

2. Describe at least three ways to decrease your expenses while you are in school.

   List any three of the following (answers will vary):   a. Look to big-ticket items.   b. Look to small-ticket items.   c. Ask for student discounts.   d. Do comparison shopping.   e. Be aware of quality.   f. Save money on eating and drinking.   g. Lower your phone bills.   h. Go "green."   i. Pay cash.   j. Postpone purchases.   k. Notice what you spend on "fun."   l. Use the envelope system.   m. Don't compete with big spenders.   n. Use the money you save to prepare for emergencies and reduce debt.   o. Spend less and feel the power.   (*Spend less money*, p. 304)

3. How can you avoid getting into financial trouble when you use credit cards?

   Some ways to control credit cards and use them with caution are the following (answers will vary):   a. Pay off the balance each month.   b. Scrutinize credit card offers.   c. Avoid cash advances.   d. Check statements against your records.   e. Use just one credit card.   f. Get a copy of your credit report.   g. Protect your credit score.   (*Take charge of your credit*, p. 307)

4. If you are in financial trouble, which of the following strategies is *least* likely to help?

   (a) Monitor your income and expenses.

   (b) Borrow additional money.

   (c) Be honest with creditors.

   (d) Go for credit counseling.

   (e) Change your spending patterns.

   (b) Borrow additional money.   (*If you're in trouble . . .*, p. 308)

5. The text asserts that investing in your education is safer than investing in real estate, gold, oil, or stocks. List the reasons given for this assertion.

   Education is safer because it will last a lifetime. It can't rust, corrode, break down, or wear out; it can't be stolen, burned, repossessed, or destroyed. (*Education is worth it*, p. 311)

6. A First Step approach to managing money is to:

   (a) Admit that you probably don't have enough money.

   (b) Admit that money management is complicated.

   (c) Tell the truth about how much money you have and how much you spend.

   (d) All of the above.

   (e) None of the above.

   (c) Tell the truth about how much money you have and how much you spend.   (*Three paths to financial freedom*, p. 295)

7. Privately owned companies generally offer better student loans than the federal government. True or False? Explain your answer.

   False. Most privately owned companies offer variable-interest loans, which could cost much more than the federal government's fixed-interest loans. (*Take charge of your credit*, p. 307)

8. Power Process: "Risk being a fool" suggests that sometimes you should take action without considering the consequences. True or False? Explain the answer.

   False. Taking risks does not mean escaping responsibility for our actions. (*Power Process: Risk Being a Fool*, p. 315)

9. Describe three strategies for increasing your income.

   List any three of the following: focus on your education, consider financial aid, work while you're in school, and do your best at every job. (Answers will vary.) (*Make more money*, p. 302)

10. List three ways to make online transactions more secure.

    List any three of the following (answers will vary):   a. Keep account information private.   b. Use https:// Web sites.   c. Check the lower right-hand corner of the browser window for the secure "lock" symbol.   d. Don't manage your money on public computers.   e. Don't let your Web browser store passwords.   f. Shred financial documents you print out before throwing them away. (*Mastering Technology: Protect your money online*, p. 303)

Skills Snapshot

Now that you've reflected on the ideas in this chapter and experimented with some new strategies, revisit your responses to the "Money" section of the Discovery Wheel exercise on page 27. Think about the most powerful action you could take in the near future toward financial mastery. Complete the following sentences.

MANAGING INCOME AND EXPENSES

Right now my main sources of income are . . .

My three biggest expenses each month are . . .

One monthly expense that I could reduce right away is . . .

To begin reducing this expense, I could . . .

PAYING FOR SCHOOL

I plan to graduate by (month and year) . . .

I plan to pay for my education next year by . . .

TAKING THE NEXT ACTION

I'll know that I've reached a new level of mastery with money when . . .

To reach that level of mastery, the most important thing I can do next is to . . .

Master Student PROFILE

Lisa Price
. . . is willing to take risks

© Bennett Raglin/WireImage/
Getty Images

(1962–) Transformed Carol's Daughter, a line of all-natural body care products, from a hobby into a multimillion-dollar business.

I have loved fragrance since I was a small child. I used my allowance to buy perfume, not clothes. I was a huge Prince fan, and I read that he had a fragrance bar on his dresser so he could mix scents. So I found a way to make my own fragrances blending perfume oils.

Over the years, it became something I did to relax. My mother was the one who suggested I start selling my body cream at a church flea market in the summer of 1993.

By the end of that first day, I was pretty much sold out. I made another batch and spent most of that summer at street fairs and flea markets, paying close attention to my customers. I noticed that they were looking for hair products. So I started making things for hair to keep them from walking away from my table.

My day job was in television and film production, but customers started to call me for refills. The weather was too cold for flea markets, so I had them come to my apartment. I continued selling out of my home until 1996, when I was expecting my first child. I quit TV because I knew I couldn't do that, be a mom, be a wife and do this business.

I came up with the name at the very beginning. I made a list of things that I was and a list of things I wanted to become. There were other things on the list, like Robert's daughter and Gordon's girlfriend. But when I said Carol's daughter, I got goose bumps. It sounded right.

My mother and I used to joke about it over the years. She would say, "Have you made enough money for me to sue you for using my name?" When she died, someone at her wake said to me, "It's so wonderful that you honored your mother while she was still here." My mother spent most of her adult life sick. When she was in her early 20s, she was diagnosed with polymyositis. It's a collagen vascular disease, and it attacks the muscles and the nervous system. She never complained, but I can remember times when I would hear her scream because her legs had cramped up. We would have to massage her legs and help her breathe through it.

As I was growing the business, I would sometimes feel overwhelmed. But my mother taught me to smile through adversity, to know that I wouldn't be given the job if I couldn't do it. It's appropriate that the company is named after her. . . .

Carol's Daughter has made other people in the beauty business look at African American consumers in a different way. When I first started to do this, the black products were always at the back of the drugstore on the lower shelves. They were always dusty, dirty and sticky; they looked like nobody ever touched them. That's changing. . . . It's great to be part of that shift.

Adapted with permission from "The Sweet Smell of Success: What Mom Taught Lisa Price, Founder of Carol's Daughter," *Newsweek,* October 13, 2008, www.newsweek.com/id/162352 (accessed April 2, 2009).

For more biographical information about Lisa Price, visit the Master Student Hall of Fame.

Instructor Tools & Tips

> To be somebody you must last.
> —**Ruth Gordon**
>
> Emotion, which is suffering, ceases to be suffering as soon as we have a clear picture of it.
> —**Baruch Spinoza**

Preview

Staying healthy while pursuing higher education is an important skill all students need to master. Juggling work, college courses, and family responsibilities can be quite stressful. It is essential that first-year students start their education on the right foot with strategies for maintaining their "machine." The revised "Health" chapter in the thirteenth edition of *Becoming a Master Student* provides resources for beginning conversations about such topics as eating well, exercising, personal safety, self-esteem, alcohol abuse, and addiction. Don't hesitate to seek an opinion—from your campus health center or a community outreach program—when you need an expert's voice to support the text.

Some of you may feel uncertain *how* to begin discussing serious health issues in your classroom. One way to do this is to have students revisit the answers they filled in on their Discovery Wheel. Using the Discovery and Intention Journal Entry system, a discussion about stress can begin with *what* factors are causing your students to feel stress, and this can lead to asking *why* these issues might be considered stressful. As a class, you can brainstorm possible *what if* scenarios to reduce students' stress. Then have your students write Intention Statements about steps they can take the next time they are experiencing high levels of stress.

Guest Speaker

Invite a guest speaker from the student wellness or health center for this portion of the class. You could even contact your county health department as a resource. Often, students will pay more attention to a visiting professional. Ask your presenter to discuss the importance of health and the relationship of health to learning. Be sure to allow time for a question-and-answer period.

Another idea is to ask if a local chapter of Alcoholics Anonymous or Narcotics Anonymous can provide a guest speaker or, better yet, a panel of speakers. Although these programs emphasize anonymity, some participants, as part of their program of recovery, choose to share their story as a way of educating others. These individuals can have a powerful impact on your students.

Or, use the Video Skillbuilders that were designed to go along with this chapter. **Keeping your mind and body and shape:** Students often overlook the role their health plays in their success in college. Many college students are living on their own for the first time, and may not know how to cook and prepare healthy meals. Many students don't have time to prepare meals, and fall into the fast food habit. In this video, students talk about being overwhelmed by school and work, and not efficiently managing their days in order to provide time for meal preparation and eating, exercise, and a good night's sleep.

Healthy Living: Making the right choices: Difficulties encountered by college students don't always originate during freshman year. Problems may begin during high school. They may occur at home. But college is a different environment and students may be distracted. Whether it's about living arrangements, time management, or new friends, students have many choices to make. Drinking, sexually transmitted diseases, and psychological problems may create unsafe and unhealthy conditions. The students on the video relate examples of the results of extreme behavior.

Lecture

Here is a lecture idea from an instructor:

" I've been involved in AIDS education since the 1980s. The best weapon we have to fight HIV/AIDS is education, so we spend about 30 to 45 minutes on this topic in my College Success classes. The college years are the time for many students to experiment with sexual behaviors. Many know that they need to practice abstinence to be totally safe or, if sexually active, to practice safer sex. However, many students do not know what behaviors are considered risky or what skills are involved in practicing safer sex. So I teach not only the fact that condoms may prevent the transmission of HIV but also specific skills in condom usage. My primary objectives are for students to learn effective communication skills in negotiating the use of a condom with their partners as well as learning the skills needed to stay safe during sexual activities. I use explicit language; I incorporate humor and frank discussion, as well as a demonstration on how to use a condom. This is one topic where you will find the entire class will "Be here now."

—Deborah Warfield, Seminole Community College

Exercises/Activities

1. **Avoiding negative thinking** Here is a suggestion from an instructor:

" When change is requested of students, they often unconsciously say, "I can't. . . ." I ask my students to take a closer look at times when they say these statements and begin to replace the "I can't" with "I won't."

Have your students make a list of those "I can't" statements. From this list, have them select one and restate the sentence with "won't" instead of "can't." Then, ask students to describe any distinction between these two statements. Generally students will say that the "I won't" statement implies some choice in the matter, and the experience changes from being one of victimization to taking some responsibility.

The last step is to have students replace the "I won't" with "I don't know how." Again I ask students to describe any distinction between this statement and the "I won't" statement. Students often experience a weight off their shoulders or realize they were operating under a false expectation such as, "I should know this." Students at this point can write a Discovery and Intention Statement about their experience.

Chapter 11 provides students with an opportunity to practice taking more responsibility for their thoughts (intrapersonal communications) and to use the steps in critical thinking.

I have students list some of their negative thinking. They often say things like "I'll never get as much sleep as suggested," or "I'll never reduce my anxiety before test taking."

I ask student to rewrite their sentences to look like this: "I thought I would never get enough sleep," or "I thought I would never reduce my anxiety before test taking."

I have students rewrite these statements over and over again, emphasizing the word *thought*. At some point, students will smile and say, "Oh I get it, I just 'thought' I would never get enough sleep," or "I see it now, I 'thought' I would never reduce my anxiety before test taking."

We often turn our thoughts into reality or a belief without going through the steps in critical thinking. This is related to a self-fulfilling prophecy, or self-efficacy, described in the article "Developing self-efficacy" in Chapter 11 and the Power Process: "I create it all" in Chapter 5.

—Fred Kester, Yavapai College

2. Master Student Profile: Randy Pausch (page 351)
After students read the inspirational story about Randy Pausch, ask them to think about how their childhood dreams can be connected to their career goals.

Conversation/Sharing

Power Process: Surrender (page 347) Use the following example to open a discussion about this Power Process with your students:

> Sally and Jane leave work on Friday at the same time. Both are caught in rush-hour traffic. Sally frets, honks her horn, and changes lanes as frequently as possible with the hope of saving time. She curses the light when it changes to red, gets aggravated at cars that don't start moving fast enough when the light changes to green, frantically listens to the traffic reports on the radio, agonizes about all the things she's missing at home, worries because she is getting very low on gas, and arrives home at 6:09 p.m. with a headache. Jane surrenders. Rather than fighting and resisting the traffic, she accepts it and flows with it. She listens to her favorite radio station, plans her activities for the weekend, thinks of a better way for taking purchase orders at work, sees a new Chinese restaurant she wants to try, notices the trees and plants telling her that spring is here, repeats her affirmations about self-improvement, anticipates the warm greeting she will receive from her family, and arrives home at 6:09 with a smile.

More examples like this one are available on the Instructor Web site.

Homework

Choose to rest (page 326) College students frequently complain that they have trouble getting a good night's sleep. For a homework assignment, have them research solutions to sleep disorders online and bring an interesting article to class. Have them share these articles in small groups and then discuss the body's need for rest and how sleep deprivation can affect their schoolwork.

Alcohol, tobacco, and drugs: The truth (page 339)
Some college students are trying to enhance their focus, memory, and brain performance by taking controlled medications that are prescribed for other purposes. These drugs include Ritalin, Adderall, and Provigil. Assign students to research the intended medical purposes of these drugs as well as the precautions and side effects associated with them.

Evaluation

Frequent quizzes ensure that students face attention during class and keep up with the text reading assignments. In addition, quizzes provide students with opportunities for written reflection regarding new discoveries and intentions. Evaluation instruments also help you identify topics and concept that students have not yet mastered. In addition to the questions listed here, find more test questions on the Instructor Web site.

Quiz ideas for Chapter 11:

- Ask students to describe strategies to find more time to exercise.
- Ask students to write Discovery and Intention Statements about ways to develop self-esteem.
- Ask students to describe tools for dealing with emotional pain.
- Ask students to identify several strategies that can be used to quit smoking.

Additional Digital Resources

CHAPTER 11

Course Manual

The online *Course Manual* serves as an invaluable reference for those developing and teaching a College Success course with *Becoming a Master Student.* The *Course Manual* provides advice on general teaching issues such as preparing for classes, classroom management, grading, and communicating with students of various backgrounds, as well as specific strategies on getting the most out of various features in *Becoming a Master Student* such as the Discovery Wheel, Learning Styles Inventory, and book-specific Web sites.

Instructor Web Site

The updated Instructor Web site provides resources to help you plan and customize your course. Content specific to Chapter 11 includes:

- ▶ Lecture Ideas
  - Addiction—Some Facts to Consider
  - Getting Trapped and Getting Out
  - Recognizing and Beating "Burnout"
- ▶ In-Class Exercises
  - Speeches Promote Learning
  - What I Like About Myself
  - A Nutrition Journal
- ▶ In-Text Quiz Answers
- ▶ Learning Styles Application
- ▶ Discussion Topics
- ▶ PowerPoint Slides
- ▶ Reflection Questions
- ▶ Assessment Questions
- ▶ Experiment with chapter strategies

The Instructor Web site also contains the following book-specific content:

- ▶ ExamView Test Bank
- ▶ Online Course Manual
- ▶ Articles from previous editions
- ▶ Master Student Profiles from previous editions
- ▶ Sample Syllabi

Student Web Site

To help your students gain a better understanding of the topics discussed in *Becoming a Master Student,* encourage your students to visit the Student Web site, which provides the following resources specific to Chapter 11:

www.cengage.com/success/bams13e

- ▶ Connect to Text content expands on specific topics marked with an icon within Chapter 11.
- ▶ Learning Style Applications invite students to cycle through the four styles of learning. In answering the four questions about setting health goals posted in this chapter's Learning Styles Application, students explore the different modes and apply their new knowledge.
- ▶ Practice Tests allow students to see how well they understand the themes of *Becoming a Master Student.*
- ▶ Interactive Concept Maps promote critical thinking by highlighting related ideas to show relationships between concepts.
- ▶ Video Skillbuilders bring to life techniques that will help you to excel in college and beyond. The following videos should give your students more information regarding topics covered in Chapter 11:
  - Healthy Living: Making the Right Choices
  - Keeping Your Mind and Body in Shape
- ▶ Remembering Cultural Differences presents readers with brief articles that touch on aspects of diversity in our rapidly changing world. For Chapter 11, the following article will prompt your students to look at contemporary issues in a new way:
  - A Holistic Approach to Health
- ▶ Master Student Profiles provide additional information on the people covered in this book feature. For Chapter 11, students will find expanded coverage and links about:
  - Randy Pausch
- ▶ Power Process Media contains video, PowerPoints, and audio files to take what your students have learned from the Power Processes in their book to the next level. For Chapter 11, students will find additional media on:
  - Surrender

Along with the chapter-specific content, a General Resources folder is available that contains Toolboxes geared toward specific student types (Community College, Adult Learner, Student Athlete), the Plagiarism Prevention Zone, and the Career Resource Center.

ANNOTATED INSTRUCTOR'S EDITION

BECOMING A MASTER STUDENT AIE

11 Health

Master Student Map

as you read, ask yourself

what if . . .

I could meet the demands of daily life with energy and optimism to spare?

why this chapter matters . . .

Success calls for physical and emotional well-being.

what is included . . .

how you can use this chapter . . .

- Maintain your physical and mental energy.
- Enhance your self-esteem.
- Make decisions about alcohol and other drugs in a way that supports your success.

MASTER STUDENTS in *action*

I start every week with my Success Triangle: (1) Prioritize what needs to be done now and what can be done by others; (2) make a schedule, and check it daily (or more often as needed); and (3) reward myself—eat right, exercise, and get more rest. When I stick to my plan there's less stress in my life. **—KAREN GRAJEDA**

Courtesy of Karen Grajeda

Wake up to health

SOME PEOPLE SEE health as just a matter of common sense. These people might see little value in reading a health chapter. After all, they already know how to take care of themselves. Yet *knowing* and *doing* are two different things. Health information does not always translate into healthy habits.

We expect to experience health challenges as we age. Even youth, though, is no guarantee of good health. Over the last 3 decades, obesity among young adults has tripled. Twenty-nine percent of young men smoke. And 70 percent of deaths among adults age 18 to 29 result from unintentional injuries, accidents, homicide, and suicide.[1]

As a student, your success in school is directly tied to your health. Lack of sleep and exercise have been associated with lower grade point averages among undergraduate students. So have alcohol use, tobacco use, gambling, and chronic health conditions.[2] And any health habit that undermines your success in school can also undermine your success in later life.

People often misunderstand what the word *health* means. Remember that this word is similar in origin to *whole, hale, hardy,* and even *holy*. Implied in these words are qualities that most of us associate with healthy people: alertness, vitality, vigor. Healthy people meet the demands of daily life with energy to spare. Illness or stress might slow them down for a while, but then they bounce back. They know how to relax, create loving relationships, and find satisfaction in their work.

Perhaps *health* is one of those rich, multilayered concepts that we can never define completely. That's okay. We can still adopt habits that sustain our well-being. One study found that people lengthened their lives an average of 14 years by adopting just four habits: staying tobacco-free, eating more fruits and vegetables, exercising regularly, and drinking alcohol in moderation if at all.[3]

In the end, your definition of *health* comes from your own experience. The proof lies not on these pages but in your life—in the level of health that you create, starting now. You have two choices. You can remain unaware of habits that have major consequences for your health. Or you can become aware of current habits (discovery), choose new habits (intention), and take appropriate action.

Health is a choice you make every moment, with each action that you take. Wake up to this possibility by experimenting with the suggestions in this chapter. ✳

---

journal entry 30

Discovery Statement

Take a First Step about Your Health

This structured Discovery Statement allows you to look closely at your health. If you look and feel healthy, understanding your body better can help you be aware of what you're doing right. If you are not content with your present physical or emotional health, you might discover some ways to adjust your personal habits and increase your sense of well-being.

Complete the following statements in the space provided. As with the Discovery Wheel exercise in Chapter 1, the usefulness of this Journal Entry will be determined by your honesty and courage.

Eating

1. What I know about the way I eat is . . .

2. What I would most like to change about my diet is . . .

3. My eating habits lead me to be . . .

_____

_____

_____

_____

HEALTH

11

Exercise

1. The way I usually exercise is . . .
2. The last time I did 20 minutes or more of heart/lung (aerobic) exercise was . . .
3. As a result of my physical conditioning, I feel . . .
4. And I look . . .
5. It would be easier for me to work out regularly if I . . .
6. The most important benefit for me in exercising more is . . .

_____

_____

_____

_____

_____

_____

_____

Substances

1. My history of cigarette smoking is . . .
2. An objective observer would say that my use of alcohol is . . .
3. In the last 10 days, the number of alcoholic drinks I have had is . . .
4. I would describe my use of coffee, colas, and other caffeinated drinks as . . .
5. I have used the following illegal drugs in the past week:
6. When it comes to drugs, what I am sometimes concerned about is . . .
7. I take the following prescription drugs:

_____

_____

_____

_____

_____

_____

Relationships

1. Someone who knows me fairly well would say I am emotionally . . .
2. The way I look and feel has affected my relationships by . . .
3. My use of drugs or alcohol has been an issue with the following people . . .
4. The best thing I could do for myself and my relationships would be to . . .

_____

_____

_____

_____

_____

_____

Sleep

1. The number of hours I sleep each night is . . .
2. On weekends I normally sleep . . .
3. I have trouble sleeping when . . .
4. Last night I . . .
5. The quality of my sleep is usually . . .

_____

_____

_____

_____

_____

In general

What concerns me more than anything else about my health is . . .

Looking back at my responses to this exercise, I feel . . .

_____

_____

_____

_____

Choose your fuel

FOOD IS YOUR primary fuel for body and mind. And even though you've been eating all your life, entering higher education is bound to change the way that you fuel yourself.

There have been hundreds of books written about nutrition. One says don't drink milk. Another says the calcium provided by milk is an essential nutrient we need daily. Although such debate seems confusing, take comfort. There is actually wide agreement about how to fuel yourself for health.

Today, federal nutrition guidelines are summarized visually as a *food pyramid*. The idea is to eat more of the foods shown in the bigger sections of the pyramid and less of those in the smaller sections. To see an example and build your personal food pyramid, go online to www.mypyramid.gov.

The various food pyramids agree on several core guidelines:[4]

- Emphasize fruits, vegetables, whole grains, and fat-free or low-fat milk and milk products.

- Include lean meats, poultry, fish, beans, eggs, and nuts.

- Choose foods that are low in saturated fats, trans fats, cholesterol, salt (sodium), and added sugars.

Michael Pollan, a writer for the *New York Times Magazine,* spent several years sorting out the scientific literature on nutrition.[5] He boiled the key guidelines down to seven words in three sentences:

© Iconotec/
Wonderfile

- *Eat food.* In other words, choose whole, fresh foods over processed products with a lot of ingredients.

- *Not too much.* If you want to manage your weight, then control how much you eat. Notice portion sizes. Pass on snacks, seconds, and desserts—or indulge just occasionally.

- *Mostly plants.* Fruits, vegetables, and grains are loaded with chemicals that help to prevent disease. Plant-based foods, on the whole, are also lower in calories than foods from animals (meat and dairy products).

Finally, forget diets. *How* you eat can matter more than *what* you eat. If you want to eat less, then eat slowly. Savor each bite. Stop when you're satisfied instead of when you feel full. Use meal times as a chance to relax, reduce stress, and connect with people. ✳

 Discover more strategies online for fueling your body.

Prevent and treat eating disorders

Eating disorders affect many students. These disorders involve serious disturbances in eating behavior. Examples are overeating or extreme reduction of food intake, as well as irrational concern about body shape or weight. Women are much more likely to develop these disorders than are men, though cases are on the rise among males.

Bulimia involves cycles of excessive eating and forced purges. A person with this disorder might gorge on a pizza, doughnuts, and ice cream and then force herself to vomit. Or she might compensate for overeating with excessive use of laxatives, enemas, or diuretics.

Anorexia nervosa is a potentially fatal illness marked by self-starvation. People with anorexia may practice extended fasting or eat only one kind of food for weeks at a time.

These disorders are not due to a failure of willpower. They are real illnesses in which harmful patterns of eating take on a life of their own.

Eating disorders can lead to many complications, including life-threatening heart conditions and kidney failure. Many people with eating disorders also struggle with depression, substance abuse, and anxiety. They need immediate treatment to stabilize their health. This is usually followed by continuing medical care, counseling, and medication to promote a full recovery.

If you're worried you might have an eating disorder, visit a doctor, campus health service, or local public health clinic. If you see signs of an eating disorder in someone else, express your concern with "I" messages, as explained in Chapter 8: Communicating.

For more information, contact the National Eating Disorders Association at 1-800-931-2237 or online at www.nationaleatingdisorders.org.

© Brand X (X Collection)/Wonderfile

Choose to exercise

OUR BODIES NEED to be exercised. The world ran on muscle power back in the era when we had to hunt down a woolly mammoth every few weeks and drag it back to the cave. Now we can grab a burger at a drive-up window. Today we need to make a special effort to exercise.

Exercise promotes weight control and reduces the symptoms of depression. It also helps to prevent heart attack, diabetes, and several forms of cancer.[6] Exercise also refreshes your body and your mind. If you're stuck on a math problem or blocked on writing a paper, take an exercise break. Chances are that you'll come back with a fresh perspective and some new ideas.

If you get moving, you'll create lean muscles, a strong heart, and an alert brain. You don't have to train for the Boston Marathon, however. And if the word *exercise* turns you off, think *physical activity* instead. Here are some things you can do:

Stay active throughout the day. Park a little farther from work or school. Do your heart a favor by walking some extra blocks. Take the stairs instead of riding elevators. For an extra workout, climb two stairs at a time.

An hour of daily activity is ideal, but do whatever you can. Some activity is better than none.

No matter what you do, ease into it. For example, start by walking briskly for at least 15 minutes every day. Increase that time gradually, and add a little jogging.

Adapt to your campus environment. Look for exercise facilities on campus. Search for classes in aerobics, swimming, volleyball, basketball, golf, tennis, and other sports. Intramural sports are another option. School can be a great place to get in shape.

Do what you enjoy. Stay active over the long term with aerobic activities that you enjoy. You might enjoy martial arts, kickboxing, yoga, ballroom dance classes, stage combat classes, or mountain climbing. Check your school catalog for such courses.

Vary your routine. Find several activities that you enjoy, and rotate them throughout the year. Your main form of activity during winter might be ballroom dancing, riding an exercise bike, or skiing. In summer, you could switch to outdoor sports. Whenever possible, choose weight-bearing activities such as walking, running, or stair climbing.

Get active early. Work out first thing in the morning. Then it's done for the day. Make it part of your daily routine, just like brushing your teeth.

Exercise with other people. Making exercise a social affair can add a fun factor and raise your level of commitment.

Join a gym without fear. Many health clubs welcome people who are just starting to get in shape.

Look for gradual results. If your goal is to lose weight, be patient. Since 1 pound equals 3,500 calories, you might feel tempted to reduce weight loss to a simple formula: *Let's see . . . if I burn away just 100 calories each day through exercise, I should lose 1 pound every 35 days.*

Actually, the relationship between exercise and weight loss is complex. Many factors—including individual differences in metabolism and the type of exercise you do—affect the amount of weight you actually lose.[7]

When you step on the bathroom scale, look for small changes over time rather than sudden, dramatic losses. Gradual weight loss is more healthy, anyway—and easier to sustain over the long term.

Weight loss is just one potential benefit of exercise. Choosing to exercise can also lift your mood, increase your stamina, strengthen your bones, stabilize your joints, and help prevent heart disease. It can also reduce your risk of high blood pressure, diabetes, and several forms of cancer. If you do resistance training—such as weight machines or elastic-band workouts—you'll strengthen your muscles as well. For a complete fitness program, add stretching exercises to enjoy increased flexibility.[8]

Before beginning any vigorous exercise program, consult a health care professional. This is critical if you are overweight, over age 60, in poor condition, or a heavy smoker, or if you have a history of health problems. ✳

 Discover more ways online to follow through on your exercise goals.

Choose mental health

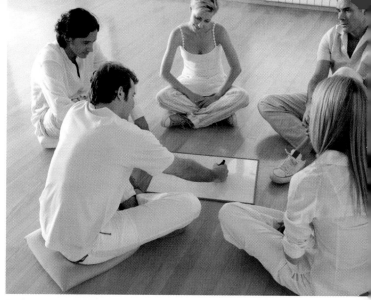

ZenShui/Alix Minde/Getty

THE NUMBER OF students in higher education who have mental health problems is steadily increasing.[9] According to the American College Health Association, 31 percent of college students report that they have felt so depressed that it was difficult to function. Almost half of students say that they've felt overwhelming anxiety, and 60 percent report that they've felt very lonely.[10]

Mental health includes many factors: your skill at managing stress, your ability to build loving relationships, your capacity to meet the demands of school and work, and your beliefs about your ability to succeed. People with mental illness have thoughts, emotions, or behaviors that consistently interfere with these areas of life.

You can take simple and immediate steps to prevent mental health problems or cope with them if they do occur. Remember that strategies for managing test-related stress can help you manage *any* form of stress. (See "Let go of test anxiety" on page 188.) Here are some other suggestions to promote your mental health.

Take care of your body. Your thoughts and emotions can get scrambled if you go too long feeling hungry or tired. Follow the suggestions in this chapter for eating, exercise, and sleep.

Solve problems. Although you can't "fix" a bad feeling in the same way that you can fix a machine, you can choose to change a situation associated with that feeling. There might be a problem that needs a solution. You can use feeling bad as your motivation to solve that problem.

Sometimes an intense feeling of sadness, anger, or fear is related to a specific situation in your life. Describe the problem. Then brainstorm solutions, and choose one to implement. Reducing your course load, cutting back on hours at work, getting more financial aid, delegating a task, or taking some other concrete action might solve the problem and help you feel better.

Stay active. A related strategy is to do something—*anything* that's constructive, even if it's not a solution to a specific problem. For example, mop the kitchen floor. Clean out your dresser drawers. Iron your shirts. This sounds silly, but it works.

The basic principle is that you can separate emotions from actions. It is appropriate to feel miserable when you do. It's normal to cry and express your feelings.

It is also possible to go to class, study, work, eat, and feel miserable at the same time. Unless you have a diagnosable problem with anxiety or depression, you can continue your normal activities until the misery passes.

Japanese psychiatrist Morita Masatake, a contemporary of Sigmund Freud, based his whole approach to treatment on this insight: We can face our emotional pain directly and still take constructive action. One of Masatake's favorite suggestions for people who felt depressed was that they tend a garden.[11]

Share what you're thinking and feeling. There are times when negative thoughts and emotions persist even after you take appropriate action. Tell a family member or friend about them. This is a powerful way to gain perspective. The simple act of describing a problem can sometimes reveal a solution or give you a fresh perspective.

Focus on one task at a time. It's easy to feel stressed if you dwell on how much you have to accomplish this year, this term, this month, or even this week. One solution is to plan using the suggestions in Chapter 2: Time.

Remember that an effective plan for the day does two things. First, it clarifies what you're choosing *not* to do today. (Tasks that you plan to do in the future are listed on your calendar or to-do list.) Second, an effective plan reduces your day to a series of concrete tasks—such as making phone calls, going to classes, running errands, or reading chapters—that you can do one at a time.

If you feel overwhelmed, just find the highest-priority task on your to-do list. Do it with total attention until it's done. Then go back to your list for the next high-priority task. Do *it* with total attention. Savor the feeling of mastery and control that comes with crossing each task off your list.

11

HEALTH

Don't believe everything you think. According to Albert Ellis and other cognitive psychologists, stress results not from events in our lives but from the way we *think* about those events.[12] If we believe that people should always behave in exactly the way we expect them to, for instance, we set ourselves up for misery. The same happens if we believe that events should always turn out exactly as we want. A more sane option is to dispute such irrational beliefs and replace them with more rational ones: *I can control my own behavior but not the behavior of others.* And: *Some events are beyond my control.* Changing our beliefs can reduce our stress significantly.

Another way to deal with stressful thoughts is to release them altogether. Meditation is a way to do this. While meditating, you simply notice your thoughts as they arise and pass. Instead of reacting to them, you observe them. Eventually, your stream of thinking slows down. You might enter a state of deep relaxation that also yields life-changing insights.

Many religious organizations offer meditation classes. You can also find meditation instruction through health maintenance organizations, YMCAs or YWCAs, and community education programs.

Find resources on or off campus. Student health centers are not just for treating colds, allergies, and flu symptoms. Counselors expect to help students deal with adjustment to campus, changes in mood, academic problems, and drug abuse and dependence. Students with anxiety disorders, clinical depression, bipolar disorder, and other diagnoses might get referred to a psychiatrist or psychologist who works off campus. The referral process can take time, so seek help right away. Your tuition helps to pay for these services. It's smart to use them now.

You can find resources to promote mental health even if your campus doesn't offer counseling services. First, find a personal physician—one person who can coordinate all of your health care. (For suggestions, go to your school's health center.) A personal physician can refer you to a mental health professional if it seems appropriate. Second, remember a basic guideline about *when* to seek help: whenever problems with your thinking, moods, or behaviors consistently interfere with your ability to sleep, eat, go to class, work, or create positive relationships. These two suggestions can also work after you graduate. Promoting mental health is a skill to use for the rest of your life. ✳

 Find more pathways to robust mental health online.

Choose to rest

A lack of rest can decrease your immunity to illness and impair your performance in school. You still might be tempted to cut back drastically on your sleep once in a while for an all-night study session. Instead, read Chapter 2: Time for some time management ideas. Depriving yourself of sleep is a choice you can avoid.

If you have trouble falling asleep, experiment with the following suggestions:

- Exercise daily. For many people, regular exercise promotes sounder sleep. However, finish exercising several hours before you want to go to sleep.

- Avoid naps during the daytime.

- Monitor your caffeine intake, especially in the afternoon and evening.

- Avoid using alcohol to feel sleepy. Drinking alcohol late in the evening can disrupt your sleep during the night.

- Develop a sleep ritual—a regular sequence of calming activities that end your day. You might take a warm bath and do some light reading. Turn off the TV and computer at least 1 hour before you go to bed.

- Keep your sleeping room cool.

- Keep a regular schedule for going to sleep and waking up.

- Sleep in the same place each night. When you're there, your body gets the message: "It's time to go to sleep."

- Practice relaxation techniques while lying in bed. A simple one is to count your breaths and release distracting thoughts as they arise.

- Make tomorrow's to-do list before you go to sleep so you won't lie there worrying that tomorrow you'll forget about something you need to do.

- Get up and study or do something else until you're tired.

- See a doctor if sleeplessness persists.

11

HEALTH

Choose to stay safe

MOST SCHOOLS ARE relatively safe. While on campus, you might feel insulated from the outside world and believe that you have special protection. Yet there are people who know how to take advantage of this belief. Some criminals target students who are alone. Others monitor dorm activity. They know that rooms are often unlocked and stashed with computers and other valuables.

Take general precautions

Three simple actions can significantly increase your personal safety. One is to always lock doors when you're away from home. If you live in a dorm, follow the policies for keeping the front doors secure. Don't let an unauthorized person walk in behind you. If you commute to school or have a car on campus, keep your car doors locked.

The second action is to avoid walking alone, especially at night. Many schools offer shuttle buses to central campus locations. Use them. As a backup, carry enough spare cash for a taxi ride.

Third, plan for emergencies. Look for emergency phones along the campus routes that you normally walk. If you have a cell phone, you can always call 911 for help.

Also, be willing to make that call when you see other people in unsafe situations. For example, you might be at a party with a friend who drinks too much and collapses. In this situation, some underage students might hesitate to call for help. They fear getting charged with illegal alcohol possession. Don't make this mistake. Every minute that you delay calling 911 puts your friend at further risk.

Prevent sexual assault

You need to know how to prevent sexual assault while you're on campus. This problem could be more common at your school than you think. People often hesitate to report rape for many reasons, such as fear, embarrassment, and concerns that others won't believe them.

Both women and men can take steps to prevent rape from occurring in the first place:

- Get together with a group of people for a tour of the campus. Make a special note of danger spots, such as unlighted paths and unguarded buildings. Keep in mind that rape can occur during daylight and in well-lit places.

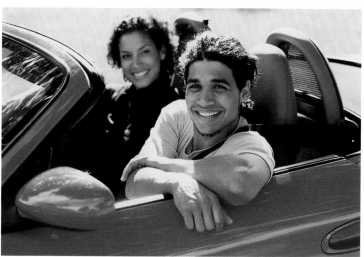

© George Shelley/Masterfile

- Ask if your school has escort services for people taking evening classes. These might include personal escorts, car escorts, or both. If you do take an evening class, ask if there are security officers on duty before and after the class.

- Take a course or seminar on self-defense and rape prevention. To find these courses, check with your student counseling service, community education center, or local library.

If you are raped, get medical care right away. Go to the nearest rape crisis center, hospital, student health service, or police station. Also arrange for follow-up counseling. It's your decision whether to report the crime. Filing a report does not mean that you have to press charges. And if you do choose to press charges later, having a report on file can help your case.

Date rape—the act of forcing sex on a date—is a common form of rape among college students. Date rape is rape. It is a crime.

Drugs such as Rohypnol (flunitrazepam) and GHB (gamma-hydroxybutyrate) have been used in date rape. These drugs, which can be secretly slipped into a drink, reduce resistance to sexual advances and produce an effect similar to amnesia. People who take these drugs might not remember the circumstances that led to their being raped. To protect yourself, don't leave your drinks unattended, and don't let someone else get drinks for you.

Take further steps to protect yourself from sexual assault. Decide what kind of sexual relationships you want. Then set firm limits, and communicate them clearly and assertively. Make sure that your nonverbal

11

HEALTH

messages match your verbal message. If someone refuses to respect your limits, stay away from that person.

Also make careful decisions about using alcohol or drugs. Be wary of dates who get drunk or high. Consider providing your own transportation on dates. Avoid going to secluded places with people you don't know well. Forcing someone to have sex is *never* acceptable. You have the right to refuse to have sex with anyone—dates, your partner, your fiancée or fiancé, or your spouse.

Prevent accidents

Accidents due to unsafe conditions and behaviors can lead to disability and even death. Following are ways you can greatly reduce the odds of accidents:

- Don't drive after drinking alcohol or using psychoactive drugs.
- Drive with the realization that other drivers may be preoccupied, intoxicated, or careless.
- Put poisons out of reach of children, and label poisons clearly.

- Keep stairs, halls, doorways, and other pathways clear of shoes, toys, newspapers, and other clutter.
- Don't smoke in bed.
- Don't let candles burn unattended.
- Keep children away from hot stoves. Turn pot handles inward.
- Check electrical cords for fraying, loose connections, or breaks in insulation. Don't overload extension cords.
- Keep a fire extinguisher handy.
- Install smoke detectors where you live and work. Most run on batteries that need occasional replacement. Follow the manufacturer's guidelines.
- Watch for ways that an infant or toddler could suffocate. Put away or discard small objects that can be swallowed, old refrigerators or freezers that can act as air-tight prisons, unattended or unfenced swimming pools, kerosene heaters in tightly closed rooms, and plastic kitchen or clothing bags. ✳

Observe thyself

You are an expert on your body. You are more likely to notice changes before anyone else does. Pay attention to these changes. They are often your first clue about the need for medical treatment or intervention.

Watch for the following signs:

- Weight loss of more than 10 pounds in 10 weeks with no apparent cause.
- A sore, scab, or ulcer that does not heal in 3 weeks.
- A skin blemish or mole that bleeds; itches; or changes size, shape, or color.
- Persistent or severe headaches.
- Sudden vomiting that is not preceded by nausea.
- Fainting spells.
- Double vision.
- Difficulty swallowing.
- Persistent hoarseness or a nagging cough.
- Blood that is coughed up or vomited.

- Shortness of breath for no apparent reason.
- Persistent indigestion or abdominal pain.
- A big change in normal bowel habits, such as alternating diarrhea and constipation.
- Black and tarry bowel movements.
- Rectal bleeding.
- Pink, red, or unusually cloudy urine.
- Discomfort or difficulty when urinating or during sexual intercourse.
- Lumps or thickening in a breast.
- Vaginal bleeding between menstrual periods or after menopause.

If you are experiencing any of these symptoms, get help. Even if you think it might not be serious, check it out. Without timely and proper treatment, a minor illness or injury can lead to serious problems. Begin with your doctor or school health service.

HEALTH

11

Choose sexual health:
Prevent infection

PEOPLE WITH A sexually transmitted infection (STI) might feel no symptoms for years and not even discover that they are infected. Know how to protect yourself.

STIs can result from vaginal sex, oral sex, anal sex, or any other way that people contact semen, vaginal secretions, and blood. Without treatment, some of these infections can lead to blindness, infertility, cancer, heart disease, or even death.[13]

There are at least twenty-five kinds of STIs. Common examples are chlamydia, gonorrhea, and syphilis. Sexual contact can also spread the human papillomavirus (HPV, the most common cause of cervical cancer) and the human immunodeficiency virus (HIV, the virus that causes AIDS).

Most STIs can be cured if treated early. (Herpes and AIDS are important exceptions.) Prevention is better. Some guidelines for prevention follow.

Abstain from sex. Abstain from sex, or have sex exclusively with one person who is free of infection and has no other sex partners. These are the only ways to be absolutely safe from STIs.

Talk to your partner. Before you have sex with someone, talk about the risk of STIs. If you are infected, tell your partner.

Use condoms. Male condoms are thin membranes stretched over the penis prior to intercourse. Condoms prevent semen from entering the vagina. For the most protection, use latex condoms—not ones made of lambskin or polyurethane. Use a condom every time you have sex, and for any type of sex.

Condoms are not guaranteed to work all of the time. They can break, leak, or slip off. In addition, condoms cannot protect you from STIs that are spread by contact with herpes sores or warts.

Talk to your doctor before using condoms, lubricants, spermicides, and other products that contain nonoxynol-9. This chemical can irritate a woman's vagina and cervix and actually increase the risk of STIs.

Stay sober. People are more likely to have unsafe sex when drunk or high.

Do not share needles. Sharing needles or other paraphernalia with other drug users can spread STIs.

Take action soon after you have sex. Urinate soon after you have sex. Wash your genitals with soap and water.

Get vaccinated. Vaccines are available to prevent hepatitis B and HPV infection. See your doctor.

Get screened for STIs. The only way to find out whether you're infected is to be tested by a health care professional. If you have sex with more than one person, get screened for STIs at least once each year. Do this even if you have no symptoms. Remember that many schools offer free STI screening.

The more people you have sex with, the greater your risk of STIs. You are at risk even if you have sex only once with one person who is infected.

The U.S. Centers for Disease Control and Prevention recommends chlamydia screening for all sexually active women under age 26. Women age 25 and older should be screened if they have a new sex partner or multiple sex partners.[14]

Recognize the symptoms of STIs. Symptoms include swollen glands with fever and aching; itching around the vagina; vaginal discharge; pain during sex or when urinating; sore throat following oral sex; anal pain after anal sex; sores, blisters, scabs, or warts on the genitals, anus, tongue, or throat; rashes on the palms of your hands or soles of your feet; dark urine; loose and light-colored stools; and unexplained fatigue, weight loss, and night sweats.

Get treated right away. If you think you have an STI, go to your doctor, campus health service, or local public health clinic. Early treatment might prevent serious health problems. To avoid infecting other people, abstain from sex until you are treated and cured. ✳

 Go online to learn more about preventing sexually transmitted infections.

11

HEALTH

Choose sexual health:
Prevent unwanted pregnancy

YOU AND YOUR partner can avoid unwanted pregnancy. There are many options. But choosing among them can be a challenge. Think about whether you want to have children someday, the number of sexual partners you have, your comfort with using a birth control method, possible side effects, and your overall health.

Even birth control methods that are usually effective can fail when used incorrectly. To prevent pregnancy, make sure you understand your chosen method. Then use it *every* time you have sex. Start with the ideas listed below. Also talk to your doctor.

Abstinence

Abstinence is choosing *not* to have sex—vaginal, oral, or anal. You might feel pressured to change your mind about this choice. However, many people exist happily without having sex. Abstinence, when practiced without exception, is the only sure way to prevent pregnancy and sexually transmitted infections (STIs).

Natural family planning

Natural family planning is based on abstaining from sex when a woman is most fertile (likely to become pregnant). It is sometimes called the "rhythm method." For women with a regular menstrual cycle, this fertile time is about 9 days each month. It includes the days right before and after ovulation. There are no side effects with natural family planning. However, it is difficult to know for sure when a woman is ovulating. Before you consider natural family planning, talk to a qualified instructor.

Barrier methods

Several methods of birth control create barriers that prevent sperm from reaching a woman's egg. One is the sponge. This is a soft disk made of polyurethane that contains nonoxynol-9—a spermicide (chemical that kills sperm). To use a sponge, a woman runs it under water and then places it inside her vagina to cover the cervix (the opening to the womb). If you choose to use the sponge, ask your doctor for instructions on when to remove it after you have intercourse. Keep in mind that nonoxynol-9 can irritate tissue in the vagina and anus with frequent use. This makes it easier for STIs to enter the body. Remember also that some women are sensitive to nonoxynol-9 so the sponge is not an option for them.

Other barrier methods include the diaphragm, cervical cap (FemCap), and cervical shield (Lea's Shield). These are cups made out of silicone or latex. The woman fills them with a spermicide and then places them inside her vagina to cover the cervix before having sex. The diaphragm and cervical cap come in various sizes, meaning that a woman has to see her doctor to get fitted for one. The cervical shield comes in only one size. Again, ask a doctor about when to remove these devices.

Male condoms, another type of barrier, are wrapped over an erect penis before sex. For better protection, use them with a spermicide. Also, use a new condom every time you have sex. The male latex condom is the only form of birth control known to protect against STIs.

If you use male condoms, keep some precautions in mind. Do not use them with oil-based lubricants such as petroleum jelly, lotions, baby oil, or massage oils. All of these can cause condoms to break. Instead, use lubricated condoms or add a water-based lubricant, such as K-Y Jelly. Remember that "natural" condoms—condoms made from lambskin—do not prevent STIs. Also, storing condoms in a warm place—such as a car or wallet—can weaken them and lead to breakage.

Female condoms are made of polyurethane. They are lubricated and placed inside the woman's vagina. Carefully follow the instructions about when to insert the female condom. Use a new condom each time you have sex. Do not use a female condom and a male condom at the same time.

Spermicides come in several forms: tablets, suppositories, cream, film, gel, and foam. They work best with a barrier method, such as a condom, cervical cap, or diaphragm. Note that some spermicides include nonoxynol-9, which can irritate tissue in the vagina and anus and make it easier for STIs to enter the body. Also, vaginal yeast infections can make spermicides less effective.

Hormonal methods

There are several hormonal methods for preventing pregnancy. These methods work by preventing ovulation, fertilization, or implantation of a fertilized egg.

An oral contraceptive—the *Pill*—is a synthetic hormone that "tells" a woman's body not to produce eggs. Many kinds are available. Talk to your doctor to make an informed choice. You might be advised to avoid the Pill if you are older then 35 and smoke, if you've had blood clots, or if you've had cancer. Antibiotics can interfere with the Pill, so ask your doctor about other methods of birth control when you're taking this medication.

Women can choose from several methods that release hormones to stop ovulation. These include a skin patch (Ortho Evra), an injection (Depo-Provera), and a vaginal ring (NuvaRing). Again, ask your doctor about possible side effects. Also get specific instructions on how to use these methods.

Implants

Some devices for preventing pregnancy are placed inside a woman's body and left there for several years. These devices release a hormone that prevents sperm from reaching an egg. They can also prevent a fertilized egg from implanting in the lining of the uterus. The rod (Implanon) goes under the skin of the upper arm. Intrauterine devices (IUDs) go inside a woman's uterus. They include the copper IUD (ParaGard) and the hormonal IUD (Mirena).

Talk to your doctor about how implants are inserted, how long they stay inside you, and which option would be most effective for you.

Emergency contraceptives

When women have vaginal sex without using birth control, or when they use birth control that fails, they can take "morning-after" pills. These pills are taken in two doses, 12 hours apart. The pills release hormones that stop ovulation or stop sperm from fertilizing an egg. This method works best when the pills are taken within 72 hours after sex.

Permanent methods

Some birth control methods are only for people who do not want to have children, or want to stop having children. One method is surgical sterilization. For women this means cutting, tying, or sealing the fallopian tubes (where eggs travel to get implanted in the uterus). Men get a vasectomy, which prevents sperm from going to the penis. Remember that sperm can stay in a man's body for about 3 months after surgery. Use another form of birth control during this time.

Women can also be sterilized without surgery. The doctor inserts an implant (Essure) that causes scar tissue to form in the fallopian tubes. Until the scarring appears—usually in about 3 months—another form of birth control is needed.

Where to get birth control

You can buy condoms, sponges, and spermicides over the counter at a store. Other birth control devices—including morning-after pills for women under age 18—require a prescription.

Note: Withdrawal does not work

Withdrawal happens when a man takes his penis out of the woman's vagina before he has an orgasm. Don't rely on this method for birth control. It requires extraordinary self-control. In addition, men can release some sperm before they have an orgasm. This can lead to pregnancy. The withdrawal method also does not prevent the spread of infection from an STI.

Evaluate birth control methods

Be sure you know how to use your chosen method of birth control. A doctor might assume that you already have this knowledge. If you don't, ask questions freely. Remember that some methods require practice and special techniques. For example, male condoms have an inside and outside surface, and they work best when there's a little space left at the tip for fluid.

The chart on the following page summarizes the effectiveness of various birth control methods and possible side effects. However, effectiveness rates can only be estimated. The estimates depend on many factors—for example, the health of the people using them, their number of sex partners, and how often they have sex. *Remember that a method can work only if used consistently and correctly.* ✱

 Learn more online about preventing pregnancy.

11

HEALTH

Method	Failure rate (the number of pregnancies expected per 100 women)	Some side effects and risks
Sterilization surgery for women	Less than 1	• Pain • Bleeding • Complications from surgery • Ectopic (tubal) pregnancy
Sterilization implant for women (Essure)	Less than 1	• Pain • Ectopic (tubal) pregnancy
Sterilization surgery for men	Less than 1	• Pain • Bleeding • Complications from surgery
Implantable rod (Implanon)	Less than 1 Might not work as well for women who are overweight or obese.	• Acne • Weight gain • Ovarian cysts • Mood changes • Depression • Hair loss • Headache • Upset stomach • Dizziness • Sore breasts • Changes in period • Lower interest in sex
Intrauterine device (ParaGard, Mirena)	Less than 1	• Cramps • Bleeding between periods • Pelvic inflammatory disease • Infertility • Tear or hole in the uterus
Shot/injection (Depo-Provera)	Less than 1	• Bleeding between periods • Weight gain • Sore breasts • Headache • Bone loss with long-term use
Oral contraceptives (combination pill, or "the Pill")	5 Being overweight may increase the chance of getting pregnant while using this pill.	• Dizziness • Upset stomach • Changes in period • Changes in mood • Weight gain • High blood pressure • Blood clots • Heart attack • Stroke • New vision problems
Oral contraceptives (continuous/extended use, or "no-period pill")	5 Being overweight may increase the chance of getting pregnant while using this pill.	• Same as the combination pill • Spotting or bleeding between periods • Hard to know if pregnant

11

HEALTH

Method	Failure rate (the number of pregnancies expected per 100 women)	Some side effects and risks
Oral contraceptives (progestin-only pill, or "minipill")	5 Being overweight may increase the chance of getting pregnant while using this pill.	• Spotting or bleeding between periods • Weight gain • Sore breasts
Skin patch (Ortho Evra)	5 May not work as well in women weighing more than 198 pounds.	• Similar to the combination pill • Greater exposure to estrogen than with other methods
Vaginal ring (NuvaRing)	5	• Similar to side effects of the combination pill • Swelling of the vagina • Irritation • Vaginal discharge
Male condom	11–16	• Allergic reactions
Diaphragm with spermicide	15	• Irritation • Allergic reactions • Urinary tract infection • Toxic shock if left in too long
Sponge with spermicide (Today sponge)	16–32	• Irritation • Allergic reactions • Hard time taking it out • Toxic shock if left in too long
Cervical cap with spermicide	17–23	• Irritation • Allergic reactions • Abnormal Pap smear • Toxic shock if left in too long
Female condom (Reality condom)	20	• Irritation • Allergic reactions
Natural family planning (rhythm method)	25	None
Spermicide alone	30 It works best if used along with a barrier method, such as a condom.	• Irritation • Allergic reactions • Urinary tract infection
Emergency contraception ("morning-after pill," "Plan B")	15 It must be used within 72 hours of having unprotected sex. It should not be used as regular birth control; only in emergencies.	• Upset stomach • Vomiting • Stomach pain • Fatigue • Headache

Source: womenshealth.gov, "Birth Control Methods: Frequently Asked Questions," www.4women.gov/faq/birth-control-methods.cfm#b, March 19, 2009 (accessed April 8, 2009).

11

HEALTH

Men, consider your health

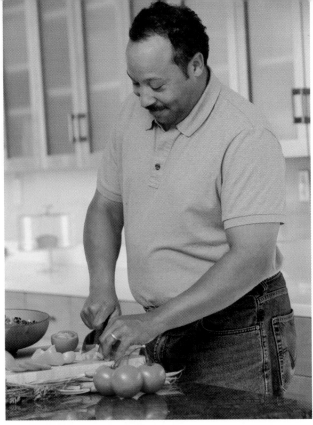

Ariel Skelley/Getty

IN A POLL conducted by Louis Harris and Associates, researchers found that one in three men did not have a doctor they saw regularly for medical advice. This might be one reason why life expectancy for men averages 6 years less than that for women.[15] The U.S. Preventive Services Task Force suggests that men do the following:

- Have your body mass index (BMI) calculated to screen for obesity.

- Have your cholesterol checked regularly starting when you turn 35. If you smoke or have diabetes, or if heart disease runs in your family, start having your cholesterol checked at age 20.

- Have your blood pressure checked at least every 2 years.

- Begin regular screening for colorectal cancer starting at age 50. Ask your doctor about which test is best for you.

- Have a test to screen for diabetes if you have high blood pressure or high cholesterol.

- Talk to your doctor about a screening for depression if you've felt despondent and have had little interest or pleasure in your regular activities for 2 weeks straight.

- Talk to your doctor to see whether you should be screened for STIs, such as HIV infection.

Daily steps that you can take are to stay tobacco-free, be physically active, eat a healthy diet, stay at a healthy weight, and take preventive medicines if you need them.[16] ✳

mastering technology

SETTING LIMITS ON SCREEN TIME

Access to wireless communication offers easy ways to procrastinate. We call it "surfing," "texting," "IMing,"—and sometimes "researching" or "working." Author Edward Hallowell coined a word to describe these activities when done compulsively—*screensucking*.[17]

Digital devices create value. With a computer you can stream music, watch videos, listen to podcasts, scan newspapers, read books, check e-mail, and send instant messages. With a cell phone you can be available to key people when it counts. And any of these activities can become addicting distractions.

Discover how much time you spend online. To get an accurate picture of your involvement in social networking and other online activity, use the Time Monitor/Time Plan exercise included in Chapter 2. Then make conscious choices about how much time you want to spend online and on the phone. Don't let social networking distract you from meeting personal and academic goals.

Go offline to send the message that other people matter. It's hard to pay attention to the person who is right in front of you when you're hammering out text messages or updating your Twitter stream. You can also tell when someone else is doing these things and only half-listening to you.

An alternative is to close up your devices and "be here now." When you're eating, stop answering the phone. Notice how the food tastes. When you're with a friend, close up your laptop. Hear every word he says. Instead of using a computer or cell phone to rehash the past or plan the future, rediscover where life actually takes place—in the present moment.

Developing interpersonal intelligence requires being with people and away from a computer or cell phone. People who break up with a partner through text messaging are not developing that intelligence. True friends know when to go offline to resolve a conflict. They know when to go back home and support a family member in crisis.

Developing self-efficacy

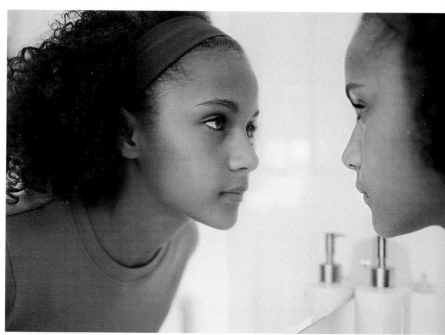

The challenge of higher education often puts self-esteem at risk. The rigors of class work, financial pressures, and new social settings can test our ability to adapt and change.

© Masterfile Royalty Free

OUR SELF-ESTEEM can erode in ways that are imperceptible to us. Over time, we can gradually buy into a reduced sense of our own possibilities in life. This orientation makes it less likely that we'll take risks, create a vision for the future, and accomplish our goals.

During the past 30 years, psychologists have produced several key studies about *self-efficacy*. The word *efficacy* refers to the ability to produce a desired effect. *Self-efficacy* refers to your belief in your ability to determine the outcomes of events—especially outcomes that are strongly influenced by your own behavior. A strong sense of self-efficacy allows you to tackle problems with confidence, set long-term goals, and see difficult tasks as creative challenges rather than potential disasters. With a strong sense of self-efficacy, you believe that your action counts. You have the capacity to make a difference in the world.

The field of self-efficacy research is closely associated with psychologist Albert Bandura of Stanford University.[18] While the word *self-esteem* refers to an overall impression of your abilities, *self-efficacy* is more exact. It points to specific factors that influence the ways you think, feel, and act. According to Bandura, self-efficacy has several sources. You can use specific strategies to strengthen these resources.

Set up situations in which you can win

Start by planning scenarios in which you can succeed. Bandura calls these "mastery situations." For example, set yourself up for success by breaking a big project down into small, doable tasks. Then tackle and complete the first task. This accomplishment can help you move on to the next task with higher self-efficacy. Success breeds more success.

Set goals with care

If you want to boost self-efficacy, be picky about your goals. According to the research, goals that you find easy to meet will not boost your self-efficacy. Instead, set goals that call on you to overcome obstacles, make persistent effort, and even fail occasionally.

At the same time, it's important to avoid situations in which you are *often* likely to fail. Setting goals that you have little chance of meeting can undermine your self-efficacy. Ideal goals are both challenging *and* achievable.

Adopt a model

In self-efficacy research, the word *model* has a special definition. This term refers to someone who is similar to you in key ways and who succeeds in the kinds of situations in which you want to succeed.

To find a model, gather with people who share your interests. Look for people with whom you have a lot in common—and who have mastered the skills that you want to acquire. Besides demonstrating strategies and techniques for you to use, these people hold out a real possibility of success for you.

Change the conversation about yourself

Monitor what you say and think about yourself. Remember that your self-talk might be so habitual that you don't even notice it. Whether or not you are fully aware of these thoughts, they can make or break your sense of self-efficacy.

Pay close attention. Notice when you speak or think negatively about yourself. Telling the truth about your weaknesses is one thing. Consistently underrating yourself is another. In the conversation about yourself, go for balance. Tell the truth about the times you set a goal and missed it. Also take the time to write and speak about the goals you meet and what works well in your life.

People with a strong sense of self-efficacy attribute their failures to skills that they currently lack—and that they can acquire in the future. This approach chooses not to look on failures as permanent, personal defects. Rather than saying "I just don't have what it takes to become a skilled test taker," say "I can adopt techniques to help me remember key facts even when I feel stressed."

Interpret stress in a new way

Achieving your goals might place you right in the middle of situations in which you feel stress. You might find yourself meeting new people, leading a meeting, speaking in public, or doing something else that you've never done before. That can feel scary.

Remember that stress comes in two forms—thoughts and physical sensations. Thoughts can include mental pictures of yourself making mistakes or being publicly humiliated. They also can be statements such as "This is the worst possible thing that could happen to me." Sensations can include shortness of breath, dry mouth, knots in the stomach, tingling feelings, headaches, and other forms of discomfort.

The way you interpret stress as you become aware of it can make a big difference in your sense of self-efficacy. During moments when you want to do well, you might rely on a stream of personal impressions to judge your performance. In those moments, see if you can focus your attention. Rather than attaching negative interpretations to your experience of stress, simply notice your thoughts and sensations. Release them instead of dwelling on them or trying to resist them. As you observe yourself over time, you might find that the physical sensations associated with your sense of stress and your sense of excitement are largely the same. Instead of viewing these sensations as signs of impending doom when they are caused by stress, see them as a boost of energy and enthusiasm that you can channel into performing well.

Compare yourself to yourself

Our own failures are often more dramatic to us than the failures of others. Our own successes are often more invisible to us. When we're unsure of ourselves, we can look in any direction and see people who seem more competent and more confident than we do. When we start the comparison game, we open the door to self-doubt.

There is a way to play the comparison game and win: Instead of comparing yourself with others, compare yourself to yourself. Measure success in terms of self-improvement rather than in terms of triumphs over others. Take time to note any progress you've made toward your goals over time. Write Discovery Statements about that progress. Celebrate your success in any area of life, no matter how small that success might seem.

Soak in the acknowledgments of others

Instead of deflecting compliments ("It was nothing"), fully receive the positive things that others say about you ("Thank you"). Also, take public credit for your successes. "Well, I was just lucky" can change to "I worked hard to achieve that goal." ✳

Emotional pain is not a sickness

Emotional pain has gotten a bad name. This reputation is undeserved. There is nothing wrong with feeling bad. It's OK to feel miserable, depressed, sad, upset, angry, dejected, gloomy, or unhappy.

IT MIGHT NOT be pleasant to feel bad, but it can be good for you. Often, bad is an appropriate way to feel. When you leave a place you love, sadness is natural. When you lose a friend or lover, misery might be in order. When someone treats you badly, it is probably appropriate to feel angry.

When a loved one dies, for example, it is necessary to grieve. The grief might appear in the form of depression, sadness, or anger. There is nothing wrong with extreme emotional pain. It is natural, and it doesn't have to be fixed.

If depression, sadness, or anger persists, get help. Otherwise, allow yourself to experience these emotions. They're usually appropriate and necessary for personal growth.

Sometimes students think that this whole idea of allowing yourself to feel bad is a joke, reverse psychology, or something else. It isn't. This suggestion is based on the notion that mental health means allowing yourself to feel the full range of your emotions.

The following suggestion—when applied with care—can sometimes help: If you feel absolutely useless, ugly, and unlovable, look in the mirror. Tell yourself over and over again how useless, ugly, and unlovable you are. It might be hard to berate yourself for very long and keep a straight face. Another option is to throw a pity party for yourself and talk about how rotten things have been going for you. Be prepared for your depressed mood to change quickly.

If you are determined to feel sorry for yourself, go all the way. Increase your misery by studying a few extra hours. It might go like this: You get some extra studying done and start feeling like a good student. Maybe you are more worthwhile than you thought. You fight it, but you can't help feeling pleased with yourself. The misery subsides. Feeling good about yourself has an interesting side effect—usually, others start feeling good about you, too.

Following are other good ways to feel bad.

Don't worry about reasons. Sometimes we allow ourselves to feel bad only if we have a good reason. For example: "Well, I feel very sad, but that is because I just found out my best friend is moving to Europe." It's all right to know the reason why you are sad. It's also fine not to know. You can feel bad for no apparent reason. The reason doesn't matter. Since you cannot directly control any feeling, simply accept it.

Connect with people. Talking to people is a way of healing. Do things with other people. Include old friends. Make new friends. If friends and family members can't help, see a counselor at your campus health center.

Reassure others. Sometimes other people—friends or family members, for example—have a hard time letting you feel bad. They might be worried that they did something wrong and want to make it better. They want you to quit feeling bad. Tell them you will. Assure them that you will feel good again, but that for right now, you just want to feel bad.

Remember that pain passes. Emotional pain does not last forever. Often it ends in a matter of weeks. One case disappeared in 4 hours and 12 minutes. There's no need to let a broken heart stop your life. Although you can find abundant advice on the subject, just remember a simple and powerful idea: This, too, shall pass. ✳

11

HEALTH

Suicide is no solution

WHILE PREPARING for and entering higher education, people typically face major changes. The stress they feel can lead to depression and anxiety. Both are risk factors for suicide—the second leading cause of death on college campuses.[19]

Recognize danger signals

Suicide rarely comes out of the blue. Most people who attempt suicide drop definite hints before they act. Here are some common signals:

- *Talking about suicide.* People who attempt suicide often talk about it first. They might say, "I just don't want to live anymore." Or "I want you to know that no matter what happens, I've always loved you." Or "Tomorrow night at 7:30 I'm going to end it all with a gun."

- *Planning for it.* People planning suicide will sometimes put their affairs in order. They might close bank accounts, give away or sell precious possessions, or make or update a will. They might even develop specific plans on how to kill themselves.

- *Having a history of previous attempts.* The American Foundation for Suicide Prevention estimates that up to 50 percent of the people who kill themselves have attempted suicide at least once before.[20]

- *Dwelling on problems.* Expressing extreme helplessness or hopelessness about solving problems can indicate that someone might be considering suicide.

- *Feeling depressed.* Although not everyone who is depressed attempts suicide, almost everyone who attempts suicide feels depressed.

Take prompt action

Most often, suicide can be prevented. If you suspect that someone you know is considering suicide, do whatever it takes to ensure the person's safety. Let this person know that you will persist until you are certain that she's safe. Any of the following actions can help.

- *Take it seriously.* Taking suicidal comments seriously is especially important when you hear them from young adults. Suicide threats are more common in this age group and might be dismissed as normal. Err on the side of being too careful rather than negligent.

- *Listen fully.* Encourage the person at risk to express thoughts and feelings appropriately. If he claims that he doesn't want to talk, be inviting, be assertive, and be persistent. Be totally committed to listening.

- *Speak powerfully.* Let the person at risk know that you care. Trying to talk someone out of suicide or minimizing problems is generally useless. Acknowledge that problems are serious and that they can be solved. Point out that suicide is a permanent solution to a temporary problem—and that help is available.

- *Get professional help.* Suggest that the person see a mental health professional. If she resists help, offer to schedule the appointment for her and to take her to it. If this fails, get others involved, including the depressed person's family or school personnel.

- *Remove access to firearms.* Most suicides are attempted with guns. Get rid of any guns that might be around. Also remove all drugs and razors.

- *Ask the person to sign a "no-suicide contract."* Get a promise, in writing, that the person will not hurt himself before speaking to you. A written promise can provide the "excuse" he needs not to take action.

- *Handle as an emergency.* If a situation becomes a crisis, do not leave the person alone. Call a crisis hotline, 911, or a social service agency. If necessary, take the person to the nearest hospital emergency room, clinic, or police station.

- *Follow up.* Someone in danger of attempting suicide might resist further help even if your first intervention succeeds. Ask the person if she's keeping counseling appointments and taking prescribed medication. Help this person apply strategies for solving problems. Stay in touch.

Take care of yourself

If you ever begin to think about committing suicide, remember that you can apply any of the above suggestions to yourself. For example, look for warning signs, and take them seriously. Seek out someone you trust. Tell this person how you feel. If necessary, make an appointment to see a counselor, and ask someone to accompany you. When you're at risk, you deserve the same compassion that you'd willingly extend to another person.

Find out more on this topic from the American Foundation for Suicide Prevention at 1-800-273-8255 or www.afsp.org. ✳

Alcohol, tobacco, and drugs:
THE TRUTH

THE TRUTH is that getting high can be fun. In our culture, and especially in our media, getting high has become synonymous with having a good time. Even if you don't smoke, drink, or use other drugs, you are certain to come in contact with people who do.

Patrick Strattner/Getty

In addition to the payoffs, there are costs. For some people, the cost is much greater than the payoff. Even if drug use doesn't make you broke, it can make you crazy. This is not necessarily the kind of crazy where you dress up like Napoleon. Rather, it is the kind where you care about little else except finding more drugs—friends, school, work, and family be damned.

For centuries, human beings have devised ways to change their feelings and thoughts by altering their body chemistry. The Chinese were using marijuana 5,000 years ago. Herodotus, the ancient Greek historian, wrote about a group of people in eastern Europe who threw marijuana on hot stones and inhaled the vapors. More recently, during the American Civil War, customers could buy opium and morphine at neighborhood stores.[21]

Today we are still a drug-using society. Of course, some of those uses are therapeutic and lawful, including taking drugs as prescribed by a doctor or psychiatrist. The problem comes when we turn to drugs as *the* solution to any problem. Are you uncomfortable? Often the first response is "Take something."

We live in times when reaching for instant comfort via chemicals is not only condoned but encouraged. If you're bored, tense, or anxious, you can drink a can of beer, down a glass of wine, or light up a cigarette. If you want to enhance your memory, take a "smart drug," which includes prescription stimulants and caffeine. And these are only the legal options. If you're willing to take risks, you can pick from a large selection of illegal drugs on the street. And if that seems too risky, you can abuse prescription drugs.

There is a big payoff in using alcohol, tobacco, caffeine, cocaine, heroin, or other drugs—or people wouldn't do it. The payoff can be direct, such as relaxation, self-confidence, comfort, excitement, or the ability to pull an all-nighter. At times, the payoff is avoiding rejection or defying authority.

Substance abuse is only part of the picture. People can also relate to food, gambling, money, sex, and even work in compulsive ways.

Some people will stop abusing a substance or activity when the consequences get serious enough. Other people don't stop. They continue their self-defeating behaviors, no matter the consequences for themselves, their friends, or their families. At that point, the problem goes beyond abuse. It's addiction.

With addiction, the costs can include overdose, infection, and lowered immunity to disease. These can be fatal. Long-term heavy drinking, for example, damages every organ system in the human body. And about 440,000 Americans die annually from the effects of cigarette smoking.[22]

Lectures about the reasons for avoiding alcohol and drug abuse and addiction can be pointless. We don't take care of our bodies because someone says we should. We might take care of ourselves when we see that the costs of using a substance outweigh the benefits.

Acknowledging that alcohol, tobacco, and other drugs can be fun infuriates a lot of people. Remember that this acknowledgment is *not* the same as condoning drug use. The point is this: People are more likely to abstain when they're convinced that using these substances leads to more pain than pleasure over the long run. You choose. It's your body. ✳

(31) exercise
Addiction: How do I know?

People who have problems with drugs and alcohol can hide this fact from themselves and from others. It is also hard to admit that a friend or loved one might have a problem. The purpose of this exercise is to give you an objective way to look at your relationship with drugs or alcohol. There are signals that indicate when drug or alcohol use has become abusive or even addictive. This exercise can also help you determine if a friend might be addicted.

Answer the following questions quickly and honestly with yes, no, or n/a (not applicable). If you are concerned about someone else, rephrase each question using that person's name.

_____ Are you uncomfortable discussing drug abuse or addiction?

_____ Are you worried about your own drug or alcohol use?

_____ Are any of your friends worried about your drug or alcohol use?

_____ Have you ever hidden from a friend, spouse, employer, or coworker the fact that you were drinking? (Pretended you were sober? Covered up alcohol breath?)

_____ Do you sometimes use alcohol or drugs to escape lows rather than to produce highs?

_____ Have you ever gotten angry when confronted about your use?

_____ Do you brag about how much you consume? ("I drank her under the table.")

_____ Do you think about or do drugs when you are alone?

_____ Do you store up alcohol, drugs, cigarettes, or caffeine (in coffee or soft drinks) to be sure you won't run out?

_____ Does having a party almost always include alcohol or drugs?

_____ Do you try to control your drinking so that it won't be a problem? ("I drink only on weekends now." "I never drink before 5 p.m." "I drink only beer.")

_____ Do you often explain to other people why you are drinking? ("It's my birthday." "It's my friend's birthday." "It's Veterans Day." "It sure is a hot day.")

_____ Have you changed friends to accommodate your drinking or drug use? ("She's OK, but she isn't excited about getting high.")

_____ Has your behavior changed in the last several months? (Grades down? Lack of interest in a hobby? Change of values or of what you think is moral?)

_____ Do you drink or use drugs to relieve tension? ("What a day! I need a drink.")

_____ Do you have medical problems (stomach trouble, malnutrition, liver problems, anemia) that could be related to drinking or drugs?

_____ Have you ever decided to quit drugs or alcohol and then changed your mind?

_____ Have you had any fights, accidents, or similar incidents related to drinking or drugs in the last year?

_____ Has your drinking or drug use ever caused a problem at home?

_____ Do you envy people who go overboard with alcohol or drugs?

_____ Have you ever told yourself you can quit at any time?

_____ Have you ever been in trouble with the police after or while you were drinking?

_____ Have you ever missed school or work because you had a hangover?

_____ Have you ever had a blackout (a period you can't remember) during or after drinking?

_____ Do you wish that people would mind their own business when it comes to your use of alcohol or drugs?

_____ Is the cost of alcohol or other drugs taxing your budget or resulting in financial stress?

_____ Do you need increasing amounts of the drug to produce the desired effect?

_____ When you stop taking the drug, do you experience withdrawal?

_____ Do you spend a great deal of time obtaining and using alcohol or other drugs?

_____ Have you used alcohol or another drug when it was physically dangerous to do so (such as when driving a car or working with machines)?

_____ Have you been arrested or had other legal problems resulting from the use of a substance?

Now count the number of questions you answered yes. If you answered yes more than once, then talk with a professional. This does not necessarily mean that you are addicted. It does point out that alcohol or other drugs are adversely affecting your life. Talk to someone with training in recovery from chemical dependency. Do not rely on the opinion of anyone who lacks such training.

If you filled out this questionnaire about another person and you answered yes two or more times, then your friend might need help. You probably can't provide that help alone. Seek out a counselor or a support group such as Al-Anon. Call the local Alcoholics Anonymous chapter to find out about an Al-Anon meeting near you.

Some facts . . .

The National Institute on Alcohol Abuse and Alcoholism reports the following consequences of excessive and underage drinking by college students.[23] For more information, go online to www.collegedrinkingprevention .gov.

Alcohol abuse and dependence	In a recent survey, 31 percent of college students met criteria for a diagnosis of alcohol abuse. Six percent met criteria for alcohol dependence.	Academic problems	About 25 percent of college students report missing class, falling behind, doing poorly on exams or papers, or receiving lower grades due to drinking.
Unsafe sex	In another survey, 400,000 students between ages 18 and 24 reported having unprotected sex. About 100,000 said that they had been too intoxicated to know if they had consented to sex.	Vandalism	About 11 percent of college student drinkers report that they have damaged property while under the influence of alcohol.
		Injury	599,000 students between the ages of 18 and 24 are unintentionally injured under the influence of alcohol.
Sexual abuse	Nearly 97,000 students between the ages of 18 and 24 are victims of alcohol-related sexual assault or date rape.	Death	About 1,700 college students between the ages of 18 and 24 die each year from alcohol-related injuries, including traffic accidents.

© Photodisc/Fotosearch

From dependence to recovery

THE TECHNICAL TERM for drug addiction is *drug dependence*. This disease is defined by the following:

- *Loss of control*—continued substance use or activity in spite of adverse consequences.
- *Pattern of relapse*—vowing to quit or limit the activity or substance use and continually failing to do so.
- *Tolerance*—the need to take increasing amounts of a substance to produce the desired effect.
- *Withdrawal*—signs and symptoms of physical and mental discomfort or illness when the substance is taken away.[24]

This list can help you determine if dependence is a barrier for you right now. The items above can apply to anything from cocaine use to compulsive gambling.

If you have a problem with dependence in any form, get help. Consider the following suggestions.

Use responsibly. Show people that you can have a good time without alcohol or other drugs. If you do choose to drink, consume alcohol with food. Pace yourself. Take time between drinks.

Avoid promotions that encourage excess drinking. "Ladies Drink Free" nights are especially dangerous. Women are affected more quickly by alcohol, making them targets for rape. Also stay out of games that encourage people to guzzle. And avoid people who make fun of you for choosing not to drink.

Pay attention. Whenever you use alcohol or another drug, do so with awareness. Then pay attention to the consequences. Act with deliberate decision rather than out of habit or under pressure from others.

Look at the costs. There is always a tradeoff to dependence. Drinking six beers might result in a temporary high, and you will probably remember that feeling. You might feel terrible the morning after consuming six beers, but some people find it easier to forget *that* pain. Stay aware of how dependence makes you feel.

Before going out to a restaurant or bar, set a limit for the number of drinks you will consume. If you consistently break this promise to yourself and experience negative consequences afterward, then you have a problem.

Admit the problem. People with active dependencies are a varied group—rich and poor, young and old, successful and unsuccessful. Often these people do have one thing in common: They are masters of denial. They deny that they are unhappy. They deny that they have hurt anyone. They are convinced that they can quit any time they want. They sometimes become so adept at hiding the problem from themselves that they die.

Take responsibility for recovery. Nobody plans to become an addict. If you have pneumonia, you seek treatment and recover without guilt or shame. Approach drug dependence in the same way. You can take responsibility for your recovery without blame, shame, or guilt.

Get help. People cannot treat dependence on their own. Behaviors tied to dependence are often symptoms of an illness that needs treatment.

Two broad options exist for getting help. One is the growing self-help movement. The other is formal treatment. People recovering from addiction often combine the two.

Many self-help groups are modeled after Alcoholics Anonymous (AA). AA is made up of recovering alcoholics and addicts. These people understand the problems of abuse firsthand, and they follow a systematic, twelve-step approach to living without it. AA is one of the oldest and most successful self-help programs in the world. Chapters of AA welcome people from all walks of life, and you don't have to be an alcoholic to attend most meetings. Programs based on AA principles exist for many other forms of dependence as well.

Some people feel uncomfortable with the AA approach. Other resources exist for them, including private therapy and group therapy. Also investigate organizations such as Women for Sobriety, the Secular Organizations for Sobriety, and Rational Recovery. Use whatever works for you.

Treatment programs are available in almost every community. They might be residential (you live there for weeks or months at a time) or outpatient (you visit several hours a day). Find out where these treatment centers are located by calling a doctor, a mental health professional, or a local hospital. If you don't have insurance, it is usually possible to arrange some other payment program. Cost is no reason to avoid treatment.

Get help for a friend or family member. You might know someone whose behavior meets the criteria for dependence. If so, you have every right to express your concern to that person. Wait until the person is clearheaded. Then mention specific incidents. For example: "Last night you drank five beers when we were at my apartment, and then you wanted to drive home. When I offered to call a cab for you instead, you refused." Also be prepared to offer a source of help, such as the phone number of a local treatment center. ✳

 Learn more online about recovery from dependence.

Succeed in quitting smoking

There is no magic formula for becoming tobacco-free. However, you can take steps to succeed sooner rather than later. The American Cancer Society suggests the following.[25]

Make a firm choice to quit. All plans for quitting depend on this step. If you're not ready to quit yet, then admit it. Take another look at how smoking affects your health, finances, and relationships.

Set a date. Choose a "quit day" within the next month. That's close enough for a sense of urgency—and time to prepare. Consider a date with special meaning, such as a birthday or anniversary. Let friends and family members know about the big day.

Get personal support. Involve other people. Sign up for a quit smoking class. Attend Nicotine Anonymous or a similar group.

Consider medication. Medication can double your chances of quitting successfully.[26] Options include bupropion hydrochloride (Zyban) and varenicline (Chantix), as well as the nicotine patch, gum, nasal spray, inhaler, and lozenge.

Prepare the environment. Right before your quit day, get rid of all cigarettes and ashtrays at home and at work. Stock up on oral substitutes such as sugarless gum, candy, and low-fat snacks.

Deal with cravings for cigarettes. Distract yourself with exercise or another physical activity. Breathe deeply. Tell yourself that you can wait just a little while longer until the craving passes. Even the strongest urges to smoke will pass. Avoid alcohol use, which can increase cravings.

Learn from relapses. If you break down and light up a cigarette, don't judge yourself. Quitting often requires several attempts. Think back over your past plans for quitting and how to improve on them. Every relapse contains a lesson about how to succeed next time.

11

HEALTH

practicing critical thinking

11

This exercise is about clarifying the differences between behaviors and interpretations. A behavior is factual and observable. An interpretation is subjective and often based on observed behaviors. Understanding this distinction can help you think clearly about your behaviors—including those that affect your emotional health by influencing your key relationships.

For instance, arriving 10 minutes after a lecture starts or pulling a dog's tail are both observable behaviors. In contrast, an interpretation is a conclusion we draw on the basis of the observed behavior: "She's either too rude or too irresponsible to get to a lecture on time." "He hates animals. Just look at how he pulled that dog's tail!" Keep in mind that other interpretations are possible. Perhaps the person's car broke down on the way to the lecture. And maybe the owner of the dog is playing a game that his pet enjoys.

Consider another example. "She shouted at me, left the room, and slammed the door" is a statement that describes behaviors. "She was angry" is one interpretation of the social significance or meaning of the observed behavior.

With this distinction in mind, brainstorm a list of behaviors you have seen in others when they were in conflict with you. Use the space here to record your brainstorm. Afterward, review your list to see if some of the behaviors you noted are actually interpretations.

_____

_____

_____

_____

_____

_____

_____

_____

_____

_____

_____

_____

_____

journal entry 31

Discovery/Intention Statement

Choose a New Level of Health

Review your responses to Journal Entry 30: "Take a First Step about Your Health" on page 321. This Discovery Statement asked you to reflect on your current state of health. Review what you wrote. Then summarize your top three health concerns on a separate sheet of paper.

I discovered that . . .

If you've read the preceding articles, you've learned about ways to choose good health in a variety of areas—by eating, exercising, sleeping, protecting your mental health, and staying safe. In the space below, list some suggestions that could help you respond positively to your top health concerns:

I discovered that . . .

Next, choose one of the above suggestions that you would like to use immediately. Write an Intention Statement about turning this behavior into a daily habit:

I intend to . . .

Finally, introduce some accountability. Share your Intention Statement with someone else. Consider asking this person to check in with you during the next month and ask how your plan to adopt a new habit is going. Alternatively, review the "Ways to Change a Habit" article in the Introduction to this book to help you make your intention into a new habit.

Note: You can use above process to change your behavior—discovery, intention, and action with accountability—and adopt *any* new habit.

Warning: Advertising can be dangerous to your health

> The average American is exposed to hundreds of advertising messages per day. Unless you are stranded on a desert island, you are affected by commercial influences.

ADVERTISING SERVES a useful function. It helps us make choices about how we spend our money. We can choose among cars, kitchen appliances, health clubs, books, plants, groceries, home builders, dog groomers, piano tuners, vacation spots, locksmiths, movies, amusement parks—the list is endless. Advertising makes us aware of the options.

Advertising space is expensive. Advertisers craft their messages carefully to get the most value for the cost. Advertisements can play on our emotions and be dangerously manipulative. For example, consider the messages that relate to your health. Advertising alcohol, tobacco, and pain relievers is a big business. Much of the revenue earned by newspapers, magazines, radio, television, and Web sites comes from advertisements for these products.

Advertising affects what we eat. The least nutritious foods often bring in the most advertising money. So multimedia advertisers portray the primary staples of our diet as sugary breakfast cereals, candy bars, and soft drinks.

Ads for alcohol glorify drinking. Advertisers imply that daily drinking is the norm. Pleasant experiences are enhanced by drinking. Holidays naturally include alcohol. Parties are a flop without it. Relationships are more romantic over cocktails. Everybody drinks.

Advertising can affect our self-image. A typical advertising message is "You are not OK unless you buy our product." These messages are painstakingly programmed to get us to buy clothes, makeup, and hair products to make us look OK; drugs, alcohol, and food to make us feel OK; perfumes, toothpaste, and deodorants to make us smell OK. Advertising also promotes the idea that buying the right product is essential to having valuable relationships in our lives.

A related problem concerns images of women. The basic message in many ads is that women love to spend hours discussing floor wax, deodorants, tampons, and laundry detergent—and that they think constantly about losing weight and looking sexy. In some ads, women handle everything from kitchen to bedroom to boardroom—true superwomen.

Images such as these are demeaning to women and damaging to men. Women lose when they allow their self-image to be influenced by ads. Men lose when they expect real-life women to look and act like the women on television. Advertising photography creates illusions. The next time you're in a crowd, notice how few people look like those in the media.

Advertising is making progress in representing diversity. However, it often excludes realistic presentations of people of color. If our perceptions were based solely on advertising, we would be hard-pressed to know that our society is racially and ethnically diverse. See how many examples of cultural stereotypes you can find in the ads you encounter this week.

Use advertising as a continual opportunity to develop the qualities of a critical thinker. Be aware of how a multibillion-dollar industry affects your health. ✳

journal entry 32

Discovery/Intention Statement

Advertisements and Your Health

Think of a time when—after seeing an advertisement or a commercial—you craved a certain food or drink, or you really wanted to buy something. Describe a specific ad and exactly how it affected you.

I discovered that I . . .

_____

_____

_____

Now describe anything you'd like to do differently in the future when you notice that advertising affects you in the way you just described.

I intend to . . .

_____

_____

_____

Crazed glazed donut runs amok

Editor's note: For those of you who think this article might be a bit cutesy, please understand that it is included here to lighten up a subject that is often approached with the guilt and solemnity of a final exam.

By Bill Harlan

PANCREAS CITY, IOWA— A glazed donut, apparently out of control, caused a multisugar pileup here early yesterday.

The entire state is reeling in lethargy, and the governor has called in extra fatty tissue.

Kelpfish/ Shutterstock

The pileup occurred shortly after 9 a.m., when assistant brain cells in Hypothalamusville noticed an energy shortage. They telephoned the state procurement office in Right Hand with a request for a glazed donut.

Procurement officers delivered the donut to Mouth, two miles north of Throat, at 9:04 a.m. "We were only following orders," one said.

When the donut reached Stomach, the town was nearly deserted. "No one had been here since dinner the night before," a witness said. The donut raced straight through Duodenum Gap and into Intestine County.

Records indicate that the energy level throughout the state did rise for more than a half-hour. However, about 45 minutes after the donut was delivered, residents in Eyelid noticed what one witness described as "a sort of drooping effect." Within 90 minutes the whole state was in a frenzy. Energy levels dropped. Tremors were reported in Hand. A suspicious "growl" was heard near Stomach.

By that time, confusion reigned in Pancreas. Officials there later claimed the donut was pure glucose, the kind of sugar that causes an immediate but short-lived energy boost. The glazed perpetrator apparently burned itself out in a metabolic rampage. Soon, only the smoking traces of burned glucose remained.

Minutes later, terror-stricken cells near Stomach began screaming, "Send down a candy bar." The cry was taken up throughout the state, as cells everywhere begged for more sugar.

For the rest of the day, the state reeled under an assault of caffeine and sugar. Three candy bars. Four soft drinks. Pie and coffee.

By evening, the governor's office had called up the Alcohol Reserves. "We've been recommending complex carbohydrates and small amounts of protein since Tuesday," said a highly placed source, who was reached on vacation at the Isle of Langerhans in Lake Pancreas. "Carbohydrates and proteins burn energy gradually, all day. An egg, some cereal, a piece of fruit, and this tragedy could have been avoided. Heck, a burger would have been better. This donut thing has got to stop."

This morning, a saddened state lies under a layer of fat. "I'm guessing it will take a hard 10-mile run to get this mess cleaned up," an administrative assistant in Cerebellum said.

Officials in Legs could not be reached. ✻

Surrender

Life can be magnificent and satisfying. It can also be devastating.

Sometimes there is too much pain or confusion. Problems can be too big and too numerous. Life can bring us to our knees in a pitiful, helpless, and hopeless state. A broken relationship with a loved one, a sudden diagnosis of cancer, total frustration with a child's behavior problem, or even the prospect of several long years of school are situations that can leave us feeling overwhelmed—powerless.

In these troubling situations, the first thing we can do is to admit that we don't have the resources to handle the problem. No matter how hard we try and no matter what skills we bring to bear, some problems remain out of our control. When this is the case, we can tell the truth: "It's too big and too mean. I can't handle it."

Desperately struggling to control a problem can easily result in the problem's controlling us. Surrender is letting go of being the master in order to avoid becoming the slave.

Many traditions make note of this idea. Western religions speak of surrendering to God. Hindus say surrender to the Self. Members of Alcoholics Anonymous talk about turning their lives over to a Higher Power. Agnostics might suggest surrendering to the ultimate source of power. Others might speak of following their intuition, their inner guide, or their conscience.

In any case, surrender means being receptive to help. Once we admit that we're at the end of our rope, we open ourselves up to receiving help. We learn that we don't have to go it alone. We find out that other people have faced similar problems and survived. We give up our old habits of thinking and behaving as if we have to be in control of everything. We stop acting as general manager of the universe. We surrender. And that creates a space for something new in our lives.

Surrender is not "giving up." It is not a suggestion to quit and do nothing about your problems. Giving up is fatalistic and accomplishes nothing. You have many skills and resources. Use them. You can apply all of your energy to handling a situation and still surrender at the same time. Surrender includes doing whatever you can in a positive, trusting spirit. So let go, keep going, and recognize when the true source of control lies beyond you.

 Learn more about the power of this Power Process online.

Yasuhide Fumoto/Getty

Put it to Work

Strategies from Becoming a Master Student can help you succeed in your career, as well as in school. To discover how suggestions in this chapter can apply to the workplace, reflect on the following case study.[27]

For weeks David had been bothered by aching muscles, loss of appetite, restless sleep, and fatigue. Eventually he became so short-tempered and irritable that his wife insisted he get a checkup.

Now, sitting in the doctor's office, David barely noticed when Theresa took the seat beside him. They had been good friends when she worked in the front office at the plant. He hadn't seen her since she left 3 years ago to take a job as a customer service representative. Her gentle poke in the ribs brought him around. Within minutes they were talking freely.

"You got out just in time," he told her. "Since the reorganization, nobody feels safe. It used to be that as long as you did your work, you had a job. Now they expect the same production rates even though two guys are now doing the work of three. We're so backed up that I'm working 12-hour shifts 6 days a week. Guys are calling in sick just to get a break."

"Well, I really miss you guys," she said. "In my new job, the computer routes the calls, and they never stop. I even have to schedule my bathroom breaks. All I hear the whole day are complaints from unhappy customers. I try to be helpful and sympathetic, but I can't promise anything until I get my boss's approval. Most of the time I'm caught between what the customer wants and company policy. The other reps are so uptight and tense they don't even talk to one another. We all go to our own little cubicles and stay there until quitting time. No wonder I'm in here with migraine headaches and high blood pressure."

David and Theresa are using a powerful strategy to promote health—talking about how they feel with a person they trust. List three other strategies that might be useful to them:

_____

_____

_____

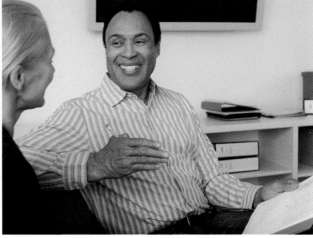

Image Source/Getty

Imagine that you suggested those three strategies to David and Theresa. They responded, "Those are good ideas, but we can't get relief from stress until our working conditions change. And that's up to our supervisors, not us." How would you respond to them?

_____

_____

_____

Consider these other strategies for staying healthy under pressure.

Ask for change. Use your skill with "I" messages (see Chapter 8: Communicating) to make suggestions and ask for specific changes in working conditions. If your employer conducts a survey of workers' satisfaction with their jobs, answer honestly and completely—especially if responses are kept anonymous.

Deal with depression. Untreated depression costs the American economy as much as heart disease or AIDS.[28] However, many employees don't report symptoms of depression. They worry about confidentiality in the workplace and about paying for treatment. Yet confidential and free or low-cost help is often available through employee assistance plans. Find out whether your employer offers such a plan.

Check the full range of your health benefits. In addition to screening and treatment for depression, your employee health benefits might include screenings for other conditions, paid time off for medical appointments, and discounts for health club memberships. Set up a meeting with someone at work who can explain all the options available to you.

Quiz

Name _____   Date ____/____/____

1. Explain three ways you can respond effectively if someone you know threatens to commit suicide.
   List and explain three of the following (answers will vary):   a. Take it seriously.   b. Listen fully.   c. Speak powerfully.
   d. Get professional help.   e. Remove access to firearms.   f. Ask the person to sign a "no-suicide contract."
   g. Handle as an emergency.   h Follow up.   (*Suicide is no answer*, p. 338)

2. Key signs of dependence include
   (a) Loss of control.
   (b) A pattern of relapse.
   (c) Tolerance.
   (d) Withdrawal.
   (e) All of the above.
   (e) All of the above.   (*From dependence to recovery*, p. 342)

3. How is the Power Process: "Surrender" different from giving up?
   Surrender is not a suggestion to quit and do nothing about your problems. Surrender includes doing whatever you can in a
   positive, trusting spirit. Surrender is the ability to let go and keep going, knowing the true source of control lies just ahead.
   (*Power Process: Surrender*, p. 347)

4. A person with a sexually transmitted infection might have no symptoms for months—or sometimes years. True or
   False? Explain your answer.
   True. Many times, those who have a sexually transmitted infection don't even know that they are infected. (*Choose sexual
   health: Prevent infection*, p. 329)

5. Define *date rape*, and describe at least two ways to protect yourself against it.
   Date rape is the act of forcing sex on a date. It is the most common form of rape among college students. List any two of
   the following ways to protect yourself (answers will vary):   a. Don't leave your drinks unattended.   b. Don't let someone
   get drinks for you.   c. Set firm limits about the kind of sexual relationships you want.   d. Communicate your limits clearly
   and assertively.   e. Make sure your nonverbal messages match your verbal ones.   f. Stay away from people who do
   not respect your limits.   g. Be wary of dates who get drunk or high.   h. Consider providing your own transportation on
   dates.   i. Avoid going to secluded places with people you don't know well.   (*Choose to stay safe*, p. 327)

6. Define the term *self-efficacy*, and list a strategy to develop it.
   Self-efficacy is the belief in your ability to determine the outcomes of events, especially those that are influenced by your
   behavior. List one of the following strategies to develop it (answers will vary):   a. Set up situations in which you can
   win.   b. Set goals with care.   c. Adopt a model.   d. Change the conversation about yourself.   e. Interpret stress in a
   new way.   f. Compare yourself to yourself.   g. Soak in the acknowledgments of others.   (*Developing self-efficacy*, p. 335)

7. One of the suggestions for dealing with addiction is "Pay attention." This implies that it's OK to use drugs, as long as you
   do so with full awareness. True or False? Explain your answer.
   False. The suggestion to "Pay attention" refers to being aware of the consequences of behavior under the influence of
   drugs. Respond to that awareness with deliberate decision rather than out of habit or under pressure from others. (*From
   dependence to recovery*, p. 342)

8. Name at least three methods for preventing unwanted pregnancy.
   List at least three of the following (answers will vary):   a. Abstinence.   b. Natural family planning.   c. Barrier methods.
   d. Hormonal methods.   e. Implants.   f. Emergency contraceptives.   g. Permanent methods.   (*Choose sexual health:
   Prevent unwanted pregnancy*, p. 330)

9. Briefly describe one of the ways to improve mental health.
   Describe one of the following (answers will vary):   a. Take care of your body.   b. Solve problems.   c. Stay active.
   d. Share what you're thinking and feeling.   e. Focus on one task at a time.   f. Don't believe everything you think.
   g. Find resources on or off campus.   (*Choose mental health*, p. 325)

10. The only option for long-term recovery from dependence is treatment based on the steps of Alcoholics Anonymous.
    True or False? Explain your answer.
    False. Many recovery groups are based on the AA system, but there are many other systems, such as private therapy. People should explore different systems and pursue the one that works best for them. (*From dependence to recovery*, p. 342)

Skills Snapshot

Now that you've reflected on the ideas in this chapter and experimented with some new strategies, revisit your responses to the "Health" section of the Discovery Wheel exercise on page 27. Think about the most powerful action you could take in the near future toward mastery in this area of your life. Complete the following sentences.

DISCOVERY

To monitor my current level of health, I look for specific changes in . . .

After reading and doing this chapter, my top three health concerns are . . .

INTENTION

My top three intentions for responding to these concerns are . . .

NEXT ACTION

I'll know that I've reached a new level of mastery with health when . . .

To reach that level of mastery, the most important intention for me to act on next is . . .

Master Student PROFILE

Randy Pausch
. . . was energetic

© ABCNews.com

I t's a thrill to fulfill your own childhood dreams, but as you get older, you may find that enabling the dreams of others is even more fun.

When I was teaching at the University of Virginia in 1993, a twenty-two-year-old artist-turned-computer-graphics-wiz named Tommy Burnett wanted a job on my research team. After we talked about his life and goals, he suddenly said, "Oh, and I have always had this childhood dream."

Anyone who uses "childhood" and "dream" in the same sentence usually gets my attention.

"And what is your dream, Tommy?" I asked.

"I want to work on the next *Star Wars* film," he said.

Remember, this was in 1993. The last *Star Wars* movie had been made in 1983, and there were no concrete plans to make any more. I explained this. "That's a tough dream to have because it'll be hard to see it through," I told him. "Word is that they're finished making *Star Wars* films."

"No," he said, "they're going to make more, and when they do, I'm going to work on them. That's my plan."

Tommy was six years old when the first *Star Wars* film came out in 1977. "Other kids wanted to be Hans Solo," he told me. "Not me. I wanted to be the guy who made the special effects—the space ships, the planets, the robots."

He told me that, as a boy, he read the most technical *Star Wars* articles he could find. He had all the books that explained how the models were built, and how the special effects were achieved. . . . I figured Tommy's big dream would never happen,

but it might serve him well somehow. I could use a dreamer like that. I knew from my NFL desires that even if he didn't achieve his, they could serve him well, so I asked him to join our research team. . . .

When I moved to Carnegie Mellon, every member of my team from the University of Virginia came with me—everyone except Tommy. He couldn't make the move. Why? Because he had been hired by producer/director George Lucas' company, Industrial Light & Magic. And it's worth noting that they didn't hire him for his dream; they hired him for his skills. In his time with our research group, he had become an outstanding programmer in the Python language, which as luck would have it, was the language of choice in their shop. Luck is indeed where preparation meets opportunity.

It's not hard to guess where this story is going. Three new *Star Wars* films would be made—in 1999, 2002, and 2005—and Tommy ended up working on all of them.

On *Star Wars Episode II: Attack of the Clones,* Tommy was a lead technical director. There was an incredible fifteen-minute battle scene on a rocky red planet, pitting clones against droids, and Tommy was the guy who planned it all out. He and his team used photos of the Utah desert to create a virtual landscape for the battle. Talk about cool jobs. Tommy had one that let him spend each day on another planet.

From the book *The Last Lecture* by Randy Pausch with Jeffrey Zaslow, pp. 117-119. Copyright © 2008 Randy Pausch. Reprinted by permission of Hyperion. All rights reserved.

(1960–2008) A professor at Carnegie Mellon University, who, shortly after being diagnosed with pancreatic cancer, gave a "last lecture"—a reflection on his personal and professional journey—that became a hit on YouTube (this lecture was later adapted into a book of the same title). He devoted the remaining 9 months of his life to creating a legacy.

Learn more about Randy Pausch online at the Master Student Hall of Fame.

Instructor Tools & Tips

> Live as if you were to die tomorrow. Learn as if you were to live forever.
>
> **—Gandhi**

> Learning is not a task or a problem—it is a way to be in the world. Man learns as he pursues goals and projects that have meaning for him.
>
> **—Sidney Jourard**

Preview

As this student success course comes to an end, it's time to celebrate accomplishments and prepare to take the next step. Use your class sessions at the end of the semester to help students understand that time spent in school is a stepping-stone to the future. Revisit goals set earlier in the term to help guide students from "school is something I have to do for now" to "school is the First Step toward achieving the goals I have set for my life." When students choose life missions that direct and energize their efforts both in and out of class, you and your students can celebrate this true sign of success—yours and theirs.

Faculty Advisor Dean Mancina shares his thoughts on the semester's end:

> I know from my own experience that as each semester draws to a close, we are madly rushing to get through all the material that has to be completed before final exams. For some instructors, that means skipping the last one or two chapters of a textbook. However, Chapter 12 of *Becoming a Master Student* provides so much reflection and closure that it's essential to plan your course carefully so students will have time to read and complete the writing activities in this final chapter. You and your students will especially want to see the results of Exercise #35: "The Discovery Wheel—Coming Full Circle" (page 375).

Guest Speaker

A local employer who looks to your institution to find workers is an appropriate choice for a guest speaker for this chapter. Another possibility is to invite a career counselor who specializes in helping students prepare to apply for jobs, interview, and enter the workplace.

Now is also the time to ask your current students to consider coming back next term to be your guest speakers on the first day of class. Your new students will be very interested in meeting your former students. They can be an inspiration to new students who are not fully committed to continuing in your class.

Lecture

Appropriate lecture topics for this chapter include:

- What students can do next term to keep the tools learned in this course fresh in their minds.
- The connection between the skills learned in this course and the skills employers are looking for.
- Putting together an effective résumé.
- Interviewing successfully for a job.
- Skills for starting a new job.
- Service-learning and other types of contributing.

Exercises/Activities

1. The Discovery Wheel—Coming Full Circle (page 375) Begin this in-class assignment by having your students complete the Discovery Wheel in this final chapter. Ask them to compare the scores they have just given themselves with the scores from the Discovery Wheel they completed in Chapter 1. Then have students subtract their first Discovery Wheel scores from their second Discovery Wheel scores. This difference can be very insightful. It represents the change in the students' self-confidence. Many students see dramatic improvements. This comparison is a powerful tool—the Discovery Wheel reveals the truth about students to themselves.

Some students also like to divide the first Discovery Wheel scores by the second Discovery Wheel scores and note the percentage change. They describe the result as a percentage increase in their academic awareness.

Note: Occasionally, you will have a student whose scores go down. This is an important example of the power of telling the truth and how the truth can change.

2. **Power Process: Be It (page 381)** As this class nears its completion, it's exciting for students to reflect on their educational and career goals one last time before exiting the course. Once they learn to use the tools and strategies presented in *Becoming a Master Student,* many students raise their level of expectation to include additional educational and career achievements. They now know how easy it can be for them to pursue goals they would never have considered before. In class, ask them to brainstorm individually a list of their hopes, dreams, and goals. Have them answer the following questions on a sheet of paper: What do you want to be? What do you want to do? What do you want to have? For example, a student might write:

I want to be a poet.

I want to go to Stanford University.

I want to have a career that enables me to travel throughout the world.

Then ask the students to sit in a large circle. Ask them to change the *want*'s to *be*'s. In the example above, the changes might look like this:

I am a poet.

I am a Stanford University student.

I am in a career that enables me to travel throughout the world.

Ask them to look at their revised statements and read them silently to themselves. Seeing this change on paper will make students feel as if the future is happening in the present! Ask the students to read their affirmation statements out loud to their classmates. This is an opportunity to proclaim their goals. It's a First Step of the Power Process: "Be it."

3. **Create your next semester** Here's a suggestion from an instructor:

> I try to make sure all my students know what a degree plan is, how to file one, and how to follow one. Remind students that college is a long progression of acquiring knowledge and learning how to use that knowledge, but it is also a chance to explore life and take risks. Learning from the mistakes of others shows real maturity. Invite students to remember another time in life when they began a project, followed the appropriate sequence, and completed the project successfully. Examples can be anything from baking a cake to teaching swimming lessons.
>
> The chapter might also remind students that a successful semester in college isn't necessarily a 4.0 grade point average. In college, being successful means growing, learning, and evolving into a better person. Invite students to challenge themselves in nontraditional ways.
>
> **—Joseph Fly, South Plains College**

Conversation/Sharing

The culminating chapter of *Becoming a Master Student* focuses on the transfer of knowledge that is best displayed by Mode 4 learners who ask *what if?* Your students will have practiced using the metacognitive map for a whole semester. Now you can challenge them to think of questions related to Chapter 12 and Mode 4. *What if* they apply the skills they learned in this course to all of their future courses? *What if* they apply these skills in the workplace? *What if* they select one major and then want to change majors because they have changed career goals? This is a great way to introduce a discussion about transferable skills.

Encourage your students to look ahead to the following semester and make a commitment to review the chapters of this textbook, one per week, to keep the concepts and strategies fresh in their mind. As part of the final week's assignment, have students reread the textbook's Introduction: Making Transitions, which will make even more sense to them now that they have read the entire book. This assignment demonstrates the benefits of a later, second reading of the text. Ask students to engage in a group conversation about what they discovered on rereading the Introduction.

Homework

Exercise #32: Create Your Career Plan—Now (page 359) This exercise will help students focus and commit to considering a specific career, and to identifying in writing the steps to get there.

Exercise #34: Do Something You Can't (page 365) In this powerful exercise, students face their fears and take a risk. Then they write about what they discovered.

Practicing Critical Thinking 12 (page 373) This unique activity will challenge students to create their own student success course and identify what they see as the key elements of such a class. This is not only a powerful, creative homework assignment for them, but it can also provide the instructor with valuable feedback about what to keep in the course next term, and what to change.

Creating portfolios Your first-year student success course is a perfect place for students to begin collecting their work in a way that reflects their academic development and accomplishments. Encourage students to use the following portfolio exercise suggestions to personalize their portfolios and help them reflect on their growth over time. A portfolio is a work in progress. Each student's portfolio will be unique and different from all others at the conclusion of the course. Consider having a sharing day and end-of-semester celebration at the end of your course so that students can review and reflect on one another's portfolios.

- **Create a personal profile.** Personal profiles help to catalog your students' background, education, employment, activities, hobbies, and college skills. The profile can be used as a resource for learning more about your students. A sample personal profile form is available for downloading and distributing to your students from the Instructor Web site. Consider customizing the profile to your liking and to your campus. Consider allowing students to omit sensitive items if they prefer not to answer them (especially if you are requiring that they submit the profile for a grade).

- **Review goal-setting exercises.** *Becoming a Master Student* provides students with many opportunities for setting goals. Beginning with Exercise #10:

"Get Real with Your Goals" (page 70), students can begin to plan long-term goals, mid-term goals and short-term goals. Periodically, they are encouraged to revisit these goals and make updates. Filing this material in a portfolio enables them to easily measure their growth and note their changes throughout their semester and college experience.

The CL Assessment and Portfolio Builder provides students with another opportunity for self-reflection and future planning. The CL Assessment and Portfolio Builder is an online tool that you can use in your classroom to reinforce goal setting, accomplishments, attitudes, and values to your students. Have your students assess the skills that they come to college with, and work with your students to plan for accomplishments throughout their college experience and their future in the workplace.

- **Prepare for the future.** As students assess their majors and career interests, they can use their portfolios to keep track of their education plans, lists of courses they need to complete in order to graduate, and other program requirements. Suggest that students also consider what types of materials may be relevant to share with prospective employers. For example, if a student writes for a publication on your campus, he can add his published articles to his portfolio and share them during an interview. If a student participates in campus organizations or service-learning projects, she can add photographs and materials documenting her activities to her portfolio.[1]

Evaluation

Here are some ideas for final exam questions for your course:

1. Which Master Student Profile in the text inspired you the most, and why?

2. What were the three most valuable textbook articles that you read in this course? How did they change the way you are as a student?

3. If you were to write a top ten list of reasons why students entering college should take this course their first semester, what would be your top five reasons?

4. Name the five most important skills you learned in this course, and explain how you will ensure that you use, and do not lose, these skills as you continue your college experience after this course ends.

Additional Digital Resources

Course Manual

The online *Course Manual* serves as an invaluable reference for those developing and teaching a College Success course with *Becoming a Master Student.* The *Course Manual* provides advice on general teaching issues such as preparing for classes, classroom management, grading, and communicating with students of various backgrounds, as well as specific strategies on getting the most out of various features in *Becoming a Master Student* such as the Discovery Wheel, Learning Styles Inventory, and book-specific Web sites.

Instructor Web Site

The updated Instructor Web site provides resources to help you plan and customize your course. Content specific to Chapter 12 includes:

► Lecture Ideas
  • How School Fits into the Rest of Students' Lives
  • Rehearsing Success
  • Use the SCANS Reports to Create Value for Your Students
► In-Class Exercises
  • From Paper to Action
  • Career Planning
  • Creating Your Diploma: A Goal-Setting Exercise
► In-Text Quiz Answers
► Learning Styles Application
► Discussion Topics
► PowerPoint Slides
► Reflection Questions
► Assessment Questions
► Experiment with chapter strategies

The Instructor Web site also contains the following book-specific content:

► ExamView Test Bank
► Online Course Manual
► Articles from previous editions
► Master Student Profiles from previous editions
► Sample Syllabi

Student Web Site

To help your students gain a better understanding of the topics discussed in *Becoming a Master Student,* encour-

 www.cengage.com/success/bams13e

age your students to visit the Student Web site, which provides the following resources specific to Chapter 12:

► Connect to Text content expands on specific topics marked with an icon within Chapter 12.
► Learning Style Applications invite students to cycle through the four styles of learning. In answering the four questions posted about applying what you've learned in this book in this chapter's Learning Styles Application, students explore the different modes and apply their new knowledge.
► Practice Tests allow students to see how well they understand the themes of *Becoming a Master Student.*
► Interactive Concept Maps promote critical thinking by highlighting related ideas to show relationships between concepts.
► Video Skillbuilders bring to life techniques that will help you to excel in college and beyond. The following videos should give your students more information regarding topics covered in Chapter 12:
  • Career Planning: In College
  • Career Planning: After College
► Remembering Cultural Differences presents readers with brief articles that touch on aspects of diversity in our rapidly changing world. For Chapter 12, the following article will prompt your students to look at contemporary issues in a new way:
  • Align Yourself with Tomorrow's Employment Trends
► Master Student Profiles provide additional information on the people covered in this book feature. For Chapter 12, students will find expanded coverage and links about:
  • Lisa Ling
► Power Process Media contains video, PowerPoints, and audio files to take what your students have learned from the Power Processes in their book to the next level. For Chapter 12, students will find additional media on:
  • Be it

[1]Some ideas for this homework assignment were collected from the work of Eve Evans Walden, *Portfolio to Accompany Becoming a Master Student,* Ninth Edition. Copyright © 2001 by Houghton Mifflin Company. Reprinted by permission.

12 What's Next?

Master Student Map

as you read, ask yourself

what if . . .

I could begin creating the life of my dreams—starting today?

why this chapter matters . . .

You can use the techniques introduced in this book to set and achieve goals for the rest of your life.

how

you can use this chapter . . .

- Choose the next steps in your education and career.
- Highlight your continuing success on résumés and in interviews.
- Experience the joys of contributing.
- Use a Power Process that enhances every technique in this book.

what is included . . .

MASTER STUDENTS in *action*

The feeling of accomplishment is a feeling like no other. To know what it is like to finish what you started and what it took to get there. . . . I believe that success is not about what you have gained, but what you have gone through.

—ALEX DENIZARD

Photo courtesy of Alex Denizard

Now that you're done—begin

IF YOU USED this book fully—if you actively participated in reading the contents, writing the Journal Entries, doing the exercises, practicing critical thinking, and applying the suggestions—you have had quite a journey.

Recall some high points of that journey. The first half of this book is about the nuts and bolts of education—the business of acquiring knowledge. It helps prepare you for making the transition to higher education and suggests that you take a First Step by telling the truth about your skills and setting goals to expand them. Also included are guidelines for planning your time, training your memory, improving your reading skills, taking useful notes, and succeeding at tests.

All of this activity prepares you for another aim of education—generating new knowledge and creating a unique place for yourself in the world. Meeting this aim leads you to the topics in the second half of this book: thinking for yourself, enhancing your communication skills, embracing diversity, learning to manage money, and living with vibrant health. All are steps on the path of becoming a master student.

Now what? What's the next step?

As you answer this question, remember that the process of experimenting with your life never ends. At any moment, you can begin again.

Consider the possibility that you can create the life of your dreams. Your responses to any of the ideas, exercises, and Journal Entries in this book can lead you to think new thoughts, say new things, and do what you never believed you could do. If you're willing to master new ways to learn, the possibilities are endless. This message is more fundamental than any individual tool or technique you'll ever read about.

There are people who scoff at the suggestion that they can create the life of their dreams. These people have a perspective that is widely shared. Please set it aside.

You are on the edge of a universe so miraculous and full of wonder that your imagination, even at its most creative moment, cannot encompass it. Paths are open to lead you to worlds beyond your wildest dreams.

If this sounds like a pitch for the latest recreational drug, it might be. That drug is adrenaline, and it is automatically generated by your body when you are

learning, planning, taking risks, achieving goals, and discovering new worlds inside and outside your skin.

One of the first articles in this book is about transitions. You are about to make another transition—not just to another chapter of this book, but to the next chapter of your life. Each article in this chapter is about creating your future through the skills you've gained in this course. Use the following pages to choose what's next for you. ✳

journal entry 33

Discovery/Intention Statement

Revisiting What You Want and How You Intend to Get It

Review the Power Process: "Discover what you want" on page 23. Then complete the following sentences with the first thoughts that come to mind.

I discovered that what I want most from life is . . .

_____

_____

_____

_____

_____

_____

_____

To get what I want from my life, I intend to . . .

_____

_____

_____

_____

_____

WHAT'S NEXT?

12

"...use the following suggestions to continue..."

Keep a journal. Psychotherapist Ira Progoff based his Intensive Journal System on the idea that regular journaling can be a path to life-changing insights.[1] To begin journaling, consider buying a bound notebook in which to record your private reflections and dreams for the future. Get a notebook that will be worthy of your personal discoveries and intentions. Write in this journal daily. Record what you are learning about yourself and the world.

Write about your hopes, wishes, and goals. Keep a record of significant events. Consider using the format of Discovery Statements and Intention Statements that you learned in this book.

Take a workshop. Schooling doesn't have to stop at graduation, and it doesn't have to take place on a campus. In most cities, a variety of organizations sponsor ongoing workshops covering topics from cosmetology to cosmology. Take workshops to learn skills, understand the world, and discover yourself. You can be trained in cardiopulmonary resuscitation (CPR), attend a lecture on developing nations, or take a course on assertiveness training.

Read, watch, and listen. Publications related to the topic of becoming a master student are recommended in the Additional Reading at the end of this book. Also, ask friends and instructors what they are reading. Sample a variety of newspapers and magazines. None of them has all of the truth. Most of them have a piece of it. In addition to books, many bookstores and publishing houses offer CDs and DVDs on personal growth topics. Record your most exciting discoveries in an idea file.

Take an unrelated class. Sign up for a class that is totally unrelated to your major. If you are studying economics, take a physics course. If you are planning to be a doctor, take an accounting course. Take a course that will help you develop new computer skills and expand your possibilities for online learning.

© Photodisc

You can discover a lot about yourself and your intended future when you step out of old patterns. In addition to formal courses offered at your school, check into local community education courses. They offer a low-cost alternative that poses no threat to your grade point average.

Travel. See the world. Visit new neighborhoods. Travel to other countries. Explore. Find out what it looks like inside buildings that you normally have no reason to enter, museums that you never found interesting before, cities that are out of the way, forests and mountains that lie beyond your old boundaries, and far-off places that require planning and saving to reach.

Get counseling. Solving emotional problems is not the only reason to visit a counselor, therapist, or psychologist. These people are excellent resources for personal growth. You can use counseling to look at and talk about yourself in ways that might be uncomfortable for anyone except a trained professional. Counseling offers a chance to focus exclusively on yourself—something that is usually not possible in normal social settings.

Form a support group. Just as a well-organized study group can promote your success in school, an organized support group can help you reach goals in other areas of your life.

Today, people in support groups help one another lose weight, stay sober, cope with chronic illness, recover from emotional trauma, and overcome drug addiction.

Groups can also brainstorm possibilities for job hunting, career planning, parenting, solving problems in relationships, promoting spiritual growth—strategies for reaching almost any goal you choose.

Find a mentor—or become one. Seek the counsel of experienced people you respect and admire. Use them as role models. If they are willing, ask them to be sounding boards for your plans and ideas. Many people are flattered to be asked.

You can also become a mentor. If you want to perfect your skills as a master student, teach them to someone else. Offer to coach another student in study skills in exchange for child care, free lunches, or something else you value. A mentor relationship can bridge the boundaries of age, race, and culture.

Redo this book. Start by redoing one chapter, or maybe just one exercise, in this book. If you didn't get everything you wanted from this book, it's not too late.

You can also reread and redo portions of the book that you found valuable. As you plan your career and hunt for jobs, you might find that the Put It to Work articles in each chapter acquire new meaning. Redo the quizzes to test your ability to recall certain information. Redo the exercises that were particularly effective for you. They can work again. Many of the exercises in this book can produce a different result after a few months. You are changing, and your responses change, too.

The Discovery Wheel can be useful in revealing techniques you have actually put into practice. This exercise is available online. You can redo it as many times as you like. You can also redo the Journal Entries. If you keep your own journal, refer to it as you rewrite the Journal Entries in this book.

As you redo this book or any part of it, reconsider techniques that you skimmed over or skipped before. They might work for you now. Modify the suggestions, or add new ones. Redoing this book can refresh and fine-tune your study habits.

Another way to redo this book is to retake your student success course. People who do this often say that the second time is much different from the first. They pick up ideas and techniques that they missed the first time around and gain deeper insight into things they already know. ✳

 Find more suggestions online for continuing the path toward mastery.

mastering technology

CONTINUE YOUR EDUCATION AT INTERNET UNIVERSITY

You can use online resources as tools for lifelong learning. Begin by doing an Internet search on any topic that interests you. In addition, try the following suggestions.

Access Web sites devoted to learning. Examples are eduFire (www.edufire.com), eHow (www.ehow.com), MindTools.com (www.mindtools.com), and About.com (www.about.com).

Use a newsreader to stay informed. Applications such as Google Reader, FeedDemon, and NewsGator (also called *RSS feeders*) will check your favorite Web sites for hourly or daily updates. This new content is displayed as a list of headlines with summaries.

Subscribe to audio and video podcasts. Podcasts are essentially radio and television programs delivered on demand. You can subscribe to podcasts through iTunes and Web sites such as Odeo (odeo.com). For a comprehensive directory of free podcasts, go online to www.LearnOutLoud.com, and click on the "Free Stuff" link.

Access university classes. Through iTunes U, colleges and universities across the world offer courses as podcasts for anyone to download. Also check your own school's Web site for podcasts.

Go to library Web sites. If you're interested in continuing education, then library Web sites are pure gold. Check your local library's online calendar for upcoming events and classes.

Find more. For additional ways to learn online, do an Internet search using key words such as *online education, virtual education, instructional Web sites,* and *distance learning.* Make the world your classroom.

Create your career *now*

There's an old saying: "If you enjoy what you do, you'll never work another day in your life." If you clearly define your career goals and your strategy for reaching them, you can plan your education effectively and create a seamless transition from school to the workplace.

Terry Vine/Blend Images/RF/Getty

CAREER PLANNING INVOLVES continuous exploration. There are dozens of effective paths to take. Begin now with the following ideas.

You already know a lot about your career plan

When people learn study skills and life skills, they usually start with finding out things they don't know. That means discovering new strategies for taking notes, reading, writing, managing time, and the other subjects covered in this book.

Career planning is different. You can begin your career planning education by realizing how much you know right now. You've already made many decisions about your career. This is true for young people who say, "I don't have any idea what I want to be when I grow up." It's also true for midlife career changers.

Consider the student who can't decide if she wants to be a cost accountant or a tax accountant and then jumps to the conclusion that she is totally lost when it comes to career planning. It's the same with the student who doesn't know if he wants to be a veterinary assistant or a nurse.

These people forget that they already know a lot about their career choices. The person who couldn't decide between veterinary assistance and nursing had already ruled out becoming a lawyer, computer programmer, or teacher. He just didn't know yet whether he had the right bedside manner for horses or

for people. The person who was debating tax accounting versus cost accounting already knew she didn't want to be a doctor, playwright, or taxicab driver. She did know she liked working with numbers and balancing books.

In each case, these people have already narrowed their list of career choices to a number of jobs in the same field—jobs that draw on the same core skills. In general, they already know what they want to be when they grow up.

Demonstrate this for yourself. Find a long list of occupations. (One source is *The Dictionary of Occupational Titles,* a government publication available at many libraries.) Using a stack of 3x5 cards, write down about a hundred randomly selected job titles, one title per card. Sort through the cards, and divide them into two piles. Label one pile "Careers I've Definitely Ruled Out for Now." Label the other pile "Possibilities I'm Willing to Consider."

You might go through a stack of a hundred such cards and end up with ninety-five in the "definitely ruled out" pile and five in the "possibilities" pile. This demonstrates that you already have a career in mind.

Your career is a choice, not a discovery

Many people approach career planning as if they were panning for gold. They keep sifting through the dirt, clearing the dust, and throwing out the rocks. They are hoping to strike it rich and discover the perfect career.

Other people believe that they'll wake up one morning, see the heavens part, and suddenly know what they're supposed to do. Many of them are still waiting for that magical day to dawn.

You can approach career planning in a different way. Instead of seeing a career as something you discover, you can see it as something you choose. You don't find the right career. You create it.

There's a big difference between these two approaches. Thinking that there's only one "correct" choice for your career can lead to a lot of anxiety: "Did I choose the right one?" "What if I made a mistake?"

Viewing your career as your creation helps you relax. Instead of anguishing over finding the right career, you can stay open to possibilities. You can choose one career today, knowing that you can choose again later.

Suppose that you've narrowed your list of possible careers to five, and you still can't decide. Then just choose one. Any one. Many people will have five careers in a lifetime anyway. You might be able to pursue all five of your careers, and you can do any one of them first. The important thing is to choose.

One caution is in order. Choosing your career is not something to do in an information vacuum. Rather, choose after you've done a lot of research. That includes research into yourself—your skills and interests—and a thorough knowledge of what careers are available.

After you've gathered all of the data, there's only one person who can choose your career: you. This choice does not have to be a weighty one. In fact, it can be like going into your favorite restaurant and choosing from a menu that includes only your favorite dishes. At that point, it's difficult to make a mistake. Whatever your choice, you know you'll enjoy it.

You have a world of choices

Our society offers a limitless array of careers. You no longer have to confine yourself to a handful of traditional categories, such as business, education, government, or manufacturing. People are constantly creating new products and services to meet emerging demands. The number of job titles is expanding so rapidly that we can barely keep track of them.

In addition, people are constantly creating new goods and services to meet emerging needs. For instance, there are people who work as *ritual consultants,* helping people plan weddings, anniversaries, graduations, and other ceremonies. *Space planners* help individuals and organizations arrange furniture and equipment efficiently. *Auto brokers* visit dealers, shop around, and buy a car for you. *Professional organizers* will walk into your home or office and advise you on managing time and paperwork. *Pet psychologists* will help you raise a happy and healthy animal. And *life coaches* will assist

you in setting and achieving goals relating to your career or anything else.

The global marketplace creates even more options for you. Through Internet connections and communication satellites that bounce phone calls across the planet, you can exchange messages with almost anyone, anywhere. Your customers or clients could be located in Colorado or China, Pennsylvania or Panama. Your skills in thinking globally and communicating with a diverse world could help you create a new product or service for a new market—and perhaps a career that does not even exist today.

Plan by naming names

One key to making your career plan real and to ensuring that you can act on it is naming. Go back over your plan to see if you can include specific names whenever they're called for:

■ *Name your job.* List the skills you enjoy using, and find out which jobs use them (the *Occupational Outlook Handbook* is a good resource for this activity). What are those jobs called? List them. Note that one job might have a number of different names.

■ *Name your company—the agency or organization you want to work for.* If you want to be self-employed or start your own business, name the product or service you'd sell. Also list some possible names for your business. If you plan to work for others, name the organizations or agencies that are high on your list.

■ *Name your contacts.* Take the list of organizations you just compiled. Find out which people in these organizations are responsible for hiring. List those people, and contact them directly. If you choose self-employment, list the names of possible customers or clients. All of these people are job contacts.

■ *Name your location.* Ask if your career choices are consistent with your preferences about where to live and work. For example, someone who wants to make a living as a studio musician might consider living in a large city such as New York or Toronto. This contrasts with the freelance graphic artist who conducts his business mainly by phone, fax, and e-mail. He might be able to live anywhere and still pursue his career.

Now expand your list of contacts by brainstorming with your family and friends. Come up with a list of names—anyone who can help you with career planning and job hunting. Write each of these names on a 3x5 card or Rolodex card. You can also use a spiral-bound notebook, computer, or personal digital assistant.

Next, call the key people on your list. Ask them about their career experiences, tell them about the career path you're considering, and probe their knowledge

WHAT'S NEXT?

12

BECOMING A MASTER STUDENT 357

of the industry you're interested in. After you speak with them, make brief notes about what you discussed. Also jot down any actions you agreed to take, such as a follow-up call.

Consider everyone you meet as a potential member of your job network. Be prepared to talk about what you do. Develop a "pitch"—a short statement of your career goal that you can easily share with your contacts. For example: "After I graduate, I plan to work in the travel business. I'm looking for an internship in a travel agency for next summer. Do you know of any agencies that take interns?"

Describe your ideal lifestyle

In addition to choosing the content of your career, you have many options for integrating work into the context of your life. You can work full-time. You can work part-time. You can commute to a cubicle at a major corporate office. Or you can work at home and take the 30-second commute from your bedroom to your desk.

Close your eyes. Visualize an ideal day in your life after graduation. Vividly imagine the following:

- Your work setting.
- Your coworkers.
- Your calendar and to-do list for that day.
- Other sights and sounds in your work environment.

This visualization emphasizes the importance of finding a match between your career and your lifestyle preferences—the amount of flexibility in your schedule, the number of people you see each day, the variety in your tasks, and the ways that you balance work with other activities.

Consider self-employment

Instead of joining a thriving business, you could create one of your own. If the idea of self-employment seems far-fetched, consider that as a student, you already *are* self-employed. You are setting your own goals, structuring your time, making your own financial decisions, and monitoring your performance. These are all transferable skills that you could use to become your own boss. Remember that many successful businesses—including Facebook and Yahoo!—were started by college students.[2]

Test your choice—and be willing to change

Career-planning materials and counselors can help you test your choice and change it if you decide to do so. Read books about careers. Search for career-planning Web sites. Ask career counselors about skills assessments that can help you discover more about your skills and identify jobs that call for those skills. Take career-planning courses and workshops sponsored by your school. Visit the career-planning and job placement offices on campus.

Once you have a career choice, translate it into workplace experience. For example:

- Contact people who are actually doing the job you're researching, and ask them a lot of questions about what it's like (an *information interview*).
- Choose an internship or volunteer position in a field that interests you.
- Get a part-time or summer job in your career field.

If you find that you enjoy such experiences, you've probably made a wise career choice. And the people you meet are possible sources of recommendations, referrals, and employment in the future. If you did *not* enjoy your experiences, celebrate what you learned about yourself. Now you're free to refine your initial career choice or go in a new direction.

Career planning is not a once-and-for-all proposition. Rather, career plans are made to be changed and refined as you gain new information about yourself and the world.

Career planning never ends. If your present career no longer feels right, you can choose again—no matter what stage of life you're in. The process is the same, whether you're choosing your first career or your fifth.

Remember your purpose

While digging deep into the details of career planning, take some time to back up to the big picture. Listing skills, researching jobs, writing résumés—all these activities are necessary and useful. At the same time, though, attending to these tasks can obscure your broadest goals. To get perspective, you need to go back to the basics—a life purpose.

Your deepest desire might be to see that hungry children are fed, to make sure that beautiful music keeps getting heard, or to help alcoholics become sober. When such a large purpose is clear, smaller decisions about what to do are often easier.

A life purpose makes a career plan simpler and more powerful. It cuts through the stacks of job data and employment figures. Your life purpose is like the guidance system for a rocket. It keeps the plan on target while revealing a path for soaring to the heights.[3] ✳

 Find more strategies online for career planning.

32 exercise
Create Your Career Plan—Now

Write your career plan. Now. Start the process of career planning, even if you're not sure where to begin. Your response to this exercise can be just a rough draft of your plan, which you can revise and rewrite many times. The point is to get your ideas in writing.

The final format of your plan is up to you. You might include many details, such as the next job title you'd like to have, the courses required for your major, and other training that you want to complete. You might list companies to research and people that could hire you. You might also include target dates to complete each of these tasks.

Another option is to represent your plan visually through flowcharts, time lines, mind maps, or drawings. You can generate these by hand or use computer software.

For now, experiment with career planning by completing the following sentences. Use the space provided, and continue on additional paper as needed. When answering the first question below, write down what first comes to your

mind. The goal is to begin the process of discovery. You can always change direction after some investigation.

1. The career I choose for now is . . .

_____

_____

2. The major steps that will guide me to this career are . . .

_____

_____

3. The immediate steps I will take to pursue this career are . . .

_____

_____

33 exercise
Recognize Your Skills

This exercise about discovering your skills includes three steps. Before you begin, gather at least a hundred 3x5 cards and a pen or pencil. Allow about 1 hour to complete the exercise.

Step 1
Recall your activities during the past week or month. To refresh your memory, review your responses to Exercise #7: "The Time Monitor/Time Plan Process" in Chapter 2. (You might even benefit from doing that exercise again.)

Write down as many activities as you can, listing each one on a separate 3x5 card. Include work-related activities, school activities, and hobbies. Next, recall and write down any rewards you've received or recognition of your achievements during the past year. Examples include scholarship awards, athletic awards, or recognitions for volunteer work. Spend 20 minutes on this step.

Step 2
Next, take another 20 minutes to list any specialized knowledge or procedures needed to complete the activities

or merit those awards and recognitions you've listed. These are your *work-content skills*. For example, tutoring a French class requires a working knowledge of that language. Write each skill on a separate card, and label it "work-content skills."

Step 3
Go over your activity cards one more time. Look for examples of *transferable skills*—those skills that can be applied to a variety of situations. For instance, working as a salesperson in a computer store requires the ability to persuade people. Tuning a car means that you can attend to details and troubleshoot. These are all transferable skills. Write each of your transferable skills on a separate card labeled "transferable skills."

Congratulations—you now have a detailed picture of your skills. Keep your lists of skills on hand when writing your résumé, preparing for job interviews, and doing other career-planning tasks. As you think of new skills, add them to the lists.

Sample career plans

FOLLOWING ARE SOME examples of mind maps, pie charts, and lists that you can use to visually represent your career plan.

Skill: Speaking candidly

Skill: Observing physical and mental states

Skill: Listening

Love

Health

Skill: Changing habits

Skill: Resolving conflict

CORE VALUES

Skill: Creating budgets

Learning

Wealth

Skill: Teaching

Skill: Counseling

Skill: Monitoring expenses

Skill: Raising funds

Sample 1

A mind map that links personal values to desired skills that could be used in a variety of careers.

Sample 2

A pie chart summarizing the amounts of time devoted to career-related activities.

Time spent supervising others

Time for planning and gaining new skills

Time for developing new products

Cushion (unplanned time)

Sample 3

A list of career goals sorted by priority. In this case, each goal is assigned a number from 1 to 100. Higher numbers denote higher priority.

- Consult college career services department on law school options (100)
- Prepare rigorously for LSAT and do well (100)
- Get into top-10 law school (95)
- Get position as editor on *Law Review* (90)
- Graduate in top of class at law school (85)
- Work for state district attorney's office (80)
- Use my position and influence to gain political and judicial contacts (75)
- Found private law firm focused on protection of workers' rights (70)
- Win major lawsuits in defense of individual liberties in the workplace (60)
- Leave law practice to travel to developing countries in aid of poor for two years (60)
- Found international agency for protection of human rights (50)
- Win Nobel Prize (30)

 Find more sample career plans online.

Jumpstart your education with transferable skills

FEW WORDS ARE as widely misunderstood as *skill*. Defining it carefully can have an immediate and positive impact on your career planning.

Identify two kinds of skills

One dictionary defines *skill* as "the ability to do something well, usually gained by training or experience." Some skills—such as the ability to repair fiber-optic cables or do brain surgery—are acquired through formal schooling, on-the-job training, or both. These abilities are called *work-content skills*. People with such skills have mastered a specialized body of knowledge needed to do a specific kind of work.

However, there is another category of skills that we develop through experiences both inside and outside the classroom. We may never receive formal training to develop these abilities, yet they are key to success in the workplace. These are *transferable skills*. Transferable skills indicate the kind of abilities that help people thrive in any job—no matter what work-content skills they have.

Perhaps you've heard someone described this way: "She's really smart and knows what she's doing, but she's got lousy people skills." People skills—such as *listening* and *negotiating*—are prime examples of transferable skills. Other examples are listed on this page.

Succeed in many situations

Transferable skills are often invisible to us. The problem begins when we assume that a given skill can be used in only one context, such as being in school or working at a particular job. Thinking in this way places an artificial limit on our possibilities.

As an alternative, think about the things you routinely do to succeed in school. Analyze your activities to isolate specific skills. Then brainstorm a list of jobs where you could use the same skills.

Consider the task of writing a research paper. This calls for the following skills:

- *Planning,* including setting goals for completing your outline, first draft, second draft, and final draft.
- *Managing time* to meet your writing goals.
- *Interviewing* people who know a lot about the topic of your paper.
- *Researching* using the Internet and campus library to discover key facts and ideas to include in your paper.

> **When meeting with an academic advisor, you may be tempted to say, "I've just been taking general education and liberal arts courses. I don't have any marketable skills." Think again.**

- *Writing* to present those facts and ideas in an original way.
- *Editing* your drafts for clarity and correctness.

Now consider the kinds of jobs that draw on these skills.

For example, you could transfer your skill at writing papers to a possible career in journalism, technical writing, or advertising copywriting.

You could use your editing skills to work in the field of publishing as a magazine or book editor.

Interviewing and research skills could help you enter the field of market research. And the abilities to plan, manage time, and meet deadlines will help you succeed in all the jobs mentioned so far.

Use the same kind of analysis to think about transferring skills from one job to another. Say that you work part-time as an administrative assistant at a computer dealer that sells a variety of hardware and software. You take phone calls from potential customers, help current customers solve problems using their computers, and attend meetings where your coworkers plan ways to market new products. You are developing skills at *selling, serving customers,* and *working on teams.* These skills could help you land a job as a sales representative for a computer manufacturer or software developer.

The basic idea is to take a cue from the word *transferable.* Almost any skill you use to succeed in one situation can *transfer* to success in another situation.

The concept of transferable skills creates a powerful link between higher education and the work world. Skills are the core elements of any job. While taking any course, list the specific skills you are developing and how you can transfer them to the work world. Almost everything you do in school can be applied to your career—if you consistently pursue this line of thought.

WHAT'S NEXT?

12

Ask four questions

To experiment further with this concept of transferable skills, ask and answer four questions derived from the Master Student Map.

Why identify my transferable skills? Getting past the "I-don't-have-any-skills" syndrome means that you can approach job hunting with more confidence. As you uncover these hidden assets, your list of qualifications will grow as if by magic. You won't be padding your résumé. You'll simply be using action words to tell the full truth about what you can do.

Identifying your transferable skills takes a little time, but the payoffs are numerous. A complete and accurate list of transferable skills can help you land jobs that involve more responsibility, more variety, more freedom to structure your time, and more money. Careers can be made—or broken—by the skills that allow you to define your job, manage your workload, and get along with people.

Transferable skills help you thrive in the midst of constant change. Technology will continue to develop. Ongoing discoveries in many fields could render current knowledge obsolete.

In the economy of the twenty-first century, you might not be able to count on job security. What you *can* count on is "skills security"—abilities that you can carry from one career to another or acquire as needed. Even though he only completed 8 years of formal schooling,[4] Henry Ford said, "The only real security that a person can have in this world is a reserve of knowledge, experience, and ability. Without these qualities, money is practically useless."[5]

What are my transferable skills? Discover your transferable skills by reflecting on key experiences.

Recall a time when you performed at the peak of your ability, overcame obstacles, won an award, gained a high grade, or met a significant goal.

For a more complete picture of your transferable skills, describe the object of your action. Say that one of the skills on your list is *organizing*. This could refer to organizing ideas, organizing people, or organizing objects in a room. Specify the kind of organizing that you like to do.

How do I perform these skills? You can bring your transferable skills into even sharper focus by adding adverbs—words that describe *how* you take action. You might say that you edit *accurately* or learn *quickly*. Use a three-column chart to list your transferable skills. For example:

Verb	Object	Adverb
Organizing	Records	Effectively
Serving	Customers	Courteously
Coordinating	Special events	Efficiently

Add a specific example of each transferable skill to your skills list, and you're well on the way to an engaging résumé and a winning job interview.

What if I could expand my transferable skills? In addition to thinking about the skills you already have, consider the skills you'd like to acquire. Describe them in detail. List experiences that can help you develop them. Let your list of transferable skills grow and develop as you do. ✳

 Learn more about transferable skills online.

65 transferable skills

WHAT'S NEXT?

There are literally hundreds of transferable skills. To learn more, check out O*Net OnLine, a Web site from the federal government at online.onetcenter.org. There you'll find tools for discovering your skills and matching them to specific occupations. Additional information on careers and job hunting is available through CareerOneStop at www.careeronestop.org.

Self-discovery and self-management skills

1. Assessing your current knowledge and skills.
2. Seeking out opportunities to acquire new knowledge and skills.
3. Choosing and applying learning strategies.
4. Showing flexibility by adopting new attitudes and behaviors.

For more information about self-discovery skills, review the Introduction to this book and Chapter 1.

Time management skills

5. Scheduling due dates for project outcomes.
6. Scheduling time for goal-related tasks.
7. Choosing technology and applying it to goal-related tasks.
8. Choosing materials and facilities needed to meet goals.
9. Designing other processes, procedures, or systems to meet goals.
10. Working independently to meet goals.
11. Planning projects for teams.

12. Managing multiple projects at the same time.

13. Monitoring progress toward goals.

14. Persisting in order to meet goals.

15. Delivering projects and outcomes on schedule.

For more information about time management skills, review Chapter 2.

Reading skills

16. Reading for key ideas and major themes.

17. Reading for detail.

18. Reading to synthesize ideas and information from several sources.

19. Reading to discover strategies for solving problems or meeting goals.

20. Reading to understand and follow instructions.

For more information about reading skills, review Chapter 4.

Note-taking skills

21. Taking notes on material presented verbally, in print, or online.

22. Creating pictures, graphs, and other visuals to summarize and clarify information.

23. Organizing information and ideas in digital and paper-based forms.

24. Researching by finding information online or in the library.

25. Gathering data through field research or working with primary sources.

For more information about note-taking skills, review Chapter 5.

Test-taking and related skills

26. Assessing personal performance at school or at work.

27. Using test results and other assessments to improve performance.

28. Working cooperatively in study groups and project teams.

29. Managing stress.

30. Applying scientific findings and methods to solve problems.

31. Using mathematics to do basic computations and solve problems.

For more information about this group of skills, review Chapters 3, 6, and 11.

Thinking skills

32. Thinking to create new ideas, products, or services.

33. Thinking to evaluate ideas, products, or services.

34. Evaluating material presented verbally, in print, or online.

35. Thinking of ways to improve products, services, or programs.

36. Choosing appropriate strategies for making decisions.

37. Choosing ethical behaviors.

38. Stating problems accurately.

39. Diagnosing the sources of problems.

40. Generating possible solutions to problems.

41. Weighing benefits and costs of potential solutions.

42. Choosing and implementing solutions.

43. Interpreting information needed for problem solving or decision making.

For more information about thinking skills, review Chapter 7.

Communication skills

44. Assigning and delegating tasks.

45. Coaching.

46. Consulting.

47. Counseling.

48. Editing publications.

49. Giving people feedback about the quality of their performance.

50. Interpreting and responding to nonverbal messages.

51. Interviewing people.

52. Leading meetings.

53. Leading project teams.

54. Listening fully (without judgment or distraction).

55. Preventing conflicts (defusing a tense situation).

56. Resolving conflicts.

57. Responding to complaints.

58. Speaking to diverse audiences.

59. Writing.

60. Editing.

For more information about communication skills, review Chapters 8 and 9.

Money skills

61. Monitoring income and expenses.

62. Raising funds.

63. Decreasing expenses.

64. Estimating costs.

65. Preparing budgets.

For more information about money skills, review Chapter 10.

 Find an expanded list of transferable skills online.

Use résumés and interviews to "hire" an employer

The logical outcome of your career plan is a focused job hunt.

© Thinkstock/Alamy

MENTION THE PHRASE *job hunting,* and many people envision someone poring through the help-wanted sections in newspapers or on Web sites, sending out hundreds of résumés, or enlisting the services of employment agencies to find job openings and set up interviews.

There's a big problem with these job-hunting strategies: *Most job openings are not advertised.* Many employers turn to help-wanted listings, résumés, and employment agencies only as a last resort. When they have positions to fill, they prefer instead to hire people they know—friends and colleagues—or people who walk through the door and prove that they're excellent candidates for available jobs.

Remembering this can help you overcome frustration, tap the hidden job market, and succeed more often at getting the position you want. One powerful source of information about new jobs is people. Ask around. Tell everyone—friends, relatives, coworkers, and fellow students—that you want a job. In particular, tell people who have the power to hire you. Some jobs are created on the spot when a person with potential simply shows up and asks.

Richard Bolles, author of *What Color Is Your Parachute? A Practical Manual for Job-Hunters and Career-Changers,* recommends the following steps in job hunting:

- Discover which skills you want to use in your career, and which jobs draw on the skills you want to use.
- Interview people who are doing the kind of jobs you'd want to do.
- Research companies you'd like to work for, and find out what kinds of problems they face on a daily basis.
- Identify your contacts—a person at each one of these companies who has the power to hire you.
- Arrange an interview with that person, even if the company has no job openings at the moment.
- Stay in contact with the people who interviewed you, knowing that a job opening can occur at any time.[6]

Use résumés to get interviews. A résumé is a piece of persuasive writing, not a dry recitation of facts or a laundry list of previous jobs. It has a basic purpose—to get you to the next step in the hiring process, usually an interview.

Begin your résumé with your name, address, phone number, and e-mail address. Then name your desired job, often called an "objective" or "goal." Follow with the body of your résumé—your skills, work experience, and education.

Write your résumé so that the facts leap off the page. Describe your work experiences in short phrases that start with active verbs: "*Supervised* three people." "*Wrote* two annual reports." "*Set up* sales calls." Also leave reasonable margins and space between paragraphs.

As you draft your résumé, remember that every organization has problems to solve. Show in your résumé that you know about those problems and can offer your skills as solutions. Give evidence that you've used those skills to get measurable results. Show a potential employer how you can contribute value and help create profits.

Use interviews to screen employers. You might think of job interviews as times when potential employers size you up and possibly screen you out. Consider another viewpoint—that interviews offer you a chance to size up potential employers and possibly screen *them* out.

To get the most from your interviews, learn everything you can about each organization that interests you. Get a feel for its strong points. Learn about its successes in the marketplace. Also find out what challenges the organization faces. As in a résumé, use interviews to present your skills as unique solutions for those challenges.

Job interviewers have many standard questions. Most of them boil down to a few major concerns:

■ How did you find out about us?

■ Would we be comfortable working with you?

■ How can you help us?

■ Will you learn this job quickly?

■ What makes you different from other applicants?

Before your interview, prepare some answers to these questions.

If you get turned down for the job after your interview, don't take it personally. Every interview is a source of feedback about what works—and what doesn't work—in contacting employers. Use that feedback to interview more effectively next time.

Counter bias and discrimination. During your job hunt, you might worry about discrimination based on your race, ethnic background, gender, or sexual orientation. Protect yourself by keeping records, including copies of all correspondence from prospective employers. Remember that Title VII of the Civil Rights Act bans discrimination in almost all aspects of the workplace, from hiring to firing. Congress set up the Equal Employment Opportunity Commission (EEOC) to enforce this act. You can contact this agency at 1-800-669-4000 and get more information through its Web site at www.eeoc.gov.

Give yourself a raise before you start work. Preparing for salary negotiation can immediately increase your income by hundreds or thousands of dollars. To get the money you deserve:

■ Use Exercise #28: "The Money Monitor/Money Plan" in Chapter 10 to determine how much you'll need each month to meet your expenses—and still have some money left over to save.

■ Maintain flexibility by settling on a salary *range* that you want rather than a specific figure.

■ Through informational interviews, library research, and Internet searches, discover typical salary ranges for jobs in your field.

■ Based on your research, estimate how much the employer is likely to offer you.

■ Postpone salary discussions until the end of the interview process—when you're confident an employer wants to hire you.

■ Let the employer be the first to mention a salary range.

■ Ask for a figure near the top of that range.

■ Ask if there's room to negotiate benefit packages and vacation time as well.

Use what you have learned in becoming a master student to constantly update your skills, manage job transitions, and stay in charge of your career path. ✳

 Go online to discover more job-hunting strategies.

34 exercise
Do Something You Can't

Few significant accomplishments result from people sticking to the familiar. You can accomplish much more than you think you can. Doing something you can't involves taking risks. This exercise has three parts. Complete this exercise on a separate piece of paper.

Part 1
Select something that you have never done before, that you don't know how to do, that you are fearful of doing, or that you think you probably can't do.

Perhaps you've never learned to play an instrument, or you've never run a marathon. Be smart. Don't pick something that will hurt you physically, such as flying from a third-floor window.

Part 2
Do it. Of course, this is easier to say than to do. This exercise is not about easy. It is about discovering capabilities that stretch your self-image.

To accomplish something that is bigger than your self-perceived abilities, use any of the tools you have gained from this book. Develop a plan. Divide and conquer. Stay focused. Use outside resources. Let go of self-destructive thoughts.

Summarize the tools you will use.

Part 3
Write about the results of this exercise.

12

Creating and using *portfolios*

PHOTOGRAPHERS, CONTRACTORS, and designers regularly show portfolios filled with samples of their work. Today, employers and educators increasingly see the portfolio as a tool that's useful for everyone. Some schools require students to create them, and some employers expect to see a portfolio before they hire.

When you create a portfolio, experiment with a four-step process.

1. Collect and catalog artifacts. An artifact is any object that's important to you and that reveals something about yourself. Examples include photographs, awards, recommendation letters, job descriptions for positions you've held, newspaper articles about projects you've done, lists of grants or scholarships you've received, programs from performances you've given, transcripts of your grades, audio or video recordings you've created, or models you've constructed.

To save hours when you create your next portfolio, start documenting your artifacts. On a 3x5 card, record the "five W's" about each artifact: who was involved with it, what you did with it, when it was created, where it was created, and why the artifact is important to you. File these cards and update them as you collect new artifacts. Another option is to manage this information with a computer, using word processing or database software.

2. Plan your portfolio. When you're ready to create a portfolio for a specific audience, write your purpose—for example, to demonstrate your learning or to document your work experience as you prepare for a job interview.

Also list some specifics about your audience. Write a description of anyone who will see your portfolio. List what each person already knows about you and predict what else these people will want to know. Answer their questions in your portfolio.

Screen artifacts with your purpose and audience in mind. If a beautiful artifact fails to meet your purpose or fit your audience, leave it out for now.

When you plan your portfolio, also think about how to order and arrange your artifacts. One basic option is a chronological organization. For example, start with work samples from your earliest jobs and work up to the present.

Another option is to structure your portfolio around key themes, such as your values or work skills. When preparing this type of portfolio, you can define work to include any time you used a job-related skill, whether or not you got paid.

3. Assemble your portfolio. With a collection of artifacts and a written plan, you're ready to assemble your portfolio. Arranging artifacts according to your design is a big part of this process. Also include elements to orient your audience members and guide them through your portfolio. These elements can include:

- A table of contents.
- An overview or summary of the portfolio.
- Titles and captions for each artifact.
- An index to your artifacts.

Although many portfolios take their final form as a collection of papers, remember that this is just one possibility. You can also create a bulletin board, a display, or a case that contains your artifacts. You could even create a recording or a digital portfolio in the form of a personal Website.

4. Present your portfolio. Your audience might ask you to present your portfolio as part of an interview or oral exam. If that's the case, rehearse your portfolio presentation the way you would rehearse a speech. Write down questions that people might ask about your portfolio. Prepare some answers, then do a dry run. Present your portfolio to friends and people in your career field, and request their feedback.

That feedback will give you plenty of ideas about ways to revise your portfolio. A portfolio is a living document. Update it as you acquire new perspectives and skills. ✳

Surviving your first day on a new job

Woman with papers: Phil Boorman/Getty; *man at copier:* Christopher Robbins/Getty; *woman with boxes:* Somos/Veer/Getty; *woman on stairs:* Anthony Marsland/Getty; *man watering plant:* John Lund/Sam Diephuis/Getty; collage by Walter Kopec

YOU'VE LANDED a new job. Congratulations! Now prepare to walk into the office and make a place for yourself. Well-meaning people may advise you to "just be yourself" when you show up for your first day of work. The following checklist offers more specifics.

Dress the part. To make a positive impression, put special effort into looking your best on your first day. Some students cultivate an eclectic wardrobe, and that won't pass the test for a new job. Even employers with "casual days" prefer to meet new employees in standard business attire. Think back to what people in the office were wearing when you showed up for your job interview. Then dress at that level or slightly above it.

Arrive early. Don't underestimate the power of this simple suggestion. Arriving late for your first day of work sends mixed messages. To you, it may be a simple mistake. Your supervisor might interpret it as being careless or having an "attitude." Remove all possibility of misunderstanding by showing up with at least 15 minutes to spare.

Notice your "nonverbals." Remember to shake hands firmly and say hello in a friendly voice. Make eye contact and smile. Also be aware of your other nonverbal messages. In meetings, for example, check to see if your posture says, "I'm here now, and I am paying attention to what you say."

Start decoding the culture. Even if you graduated from school with a straight-A average—a real accomplishment—your new coworkers are not likely to know or care. Unless you're working in education, prepare for a business rather than an academic environment. Your job on your first day is to start adapting to this environment rather than remaking it. (Remaking might come later—*after* you pay some dues.)

Keep your eyes open. Notice when people arrive for work, how they greet each other, when they leave for lunch, how often they take breaks, how they make requests, and when they go home. Look for clues to the workplace culture: the unwritten rules that seem to shape peoples' behavior.

Take notes. During your first day, you'll cover lots of details. First, there's the obvious stuff—where to sit, where to park, where to eat, where to make photocopies, where to take breaks, where to go to the bathroom. Then there's higher-level stuff, such as phone numbers, and user IDs and passwords for Internet access. Be prepared with paper and a pen so you can write this information down. Besides aiding your memory, taking notes gives you something to do with your hands if you feel nervous.

Pack a briefcase. Companies just love to push paper at new employees—brochures, forms, maps, manuals, and more. When you receive these things, look at them for a few seconds. This communicates in a small and significant way that you pay attention to details. Then place the papers in a professional-looking folder or briefcase.

Do not say these words. Avoid saying, "Wow, that's not how we did things at my last job!" This invites an inevitable response: "Well, then why did you leave that job?" Expect procedures to differ from job to job. Look for chances to suggest improvements in the future—but not right away.

Go easy on yourself. Notice whether there's a self-critical voice in your head that's saying something like this: "You're not fooling anyone—you really have no idea what you're doing here." No one else hears that voice. And no one expects you to perform to perfection on your first day.

Remember that your boss has already scoped out your qualifications. Since she hired you, she's probably confident that you can handle job tasks now, or learn to do them within a reasonable period. To really shine as a new employee, focus on your people skills. If you demonstrate that you're willing to listen and learn, you'll have done good work on your first day. ✳

WHAT'S NEXT?

12

Choosing schools . . . *again*

© PhotoAlto/Alamy

If you ever choose to change schools, you won't be alone. The *New York Times* reports that about 60 percent of students graduating from college attend more than one school.[7]

THE WAY THAT you choose a new school will have a major impact on your education. This is true if you're transferring from a community or technical college to a 4-year school or if you're choosing a graduate school.

Even if you don't plan to go through the process of choosing schools again, you can use the following ideas to evaluate your current school.

Know key terms

As you begin researching schools, take a few minutes to review some key terms.

Articulation agreements are official documents that spell out the course equivalents that a school accepts.

An *associate of arts (A.A.)* or *associate of science (A.S.)* is the degree title conferred by many 2-year colleges. Having a degree from a 2-year college can make it easier to change schools than transferring without a degree.

Course equivalents are courses you've already taken that another school will accept as meeting its requirements for graduation.

Prerequisites are courses or skills that a school requires students to complete or have before they enter or graduate.

Gather information

To research schools, start with publications. These include print sources, such as school catalogs, and school Web sites. Next, contact people—academic advisors, counselors, other school staff members, and current or former students from the schools you're considering. Contact the advisor at the new school to find out what the acceptance and graduation requirements will be. Finally, take trips to the two or three schools that interest you most.

Use your research to dig up key facts about each school you're considering, such as the following:

- Location.
- Number of students.
- Class sizes.
- Possibilities for contact with instructors outside class.
- Percentage of full-time faculty members.
- Admissions criteria.
- Availability of degrees that interest you.
- Tuition and fees.
- Housing plans.
- Financial aid programs.
- Religious affiliation.
- Diversity of students and staff.
- Course requirements.
- Retention rates (how many students come back to school after their freshman year).

To learn the most about a school, go beyond the first statistics you see. For example, a statement that "30 percent of our students are persons of color" doesn't tell you much about the numbers of people from specific ethnic or racial groups.

Also, you could transfer to a school that advertises student-instructor ratios of 15 to 1 and then find yourself in classes with 100 people. Remember that any statement about average class size is just that—an average. To gain more details, ask how often you can expect to enroll in smaller classes, especially during your final terms.

12

In addition, gather facts about your current academic profile. Include your grades, courses completed, degrees attained, and grade point average (GPA). Standardized test scores are important. They include your scores on the SAT, ACT, Graduate Record Examinations (GRE), and any advanced placement tests you've taken.

Choose your new school

If you follow the above suggestions, you'll end up with stacks of publications and pages of notes. As you sort through all this information, remember that your impressions of a school will go beyond a dry list of facts. Also pay attention to your instincts and intuitions—your "gut feelings" of attraction to one school or hesitation about another. These impressions can be important to your choice. Allow time for such feelings to emerge.

You can also benefit from putting your choice of schools in a bigger context. Consider the purposes, values, and long-term goals you've generated by doing the exercises and Journal Entries in this book. Consider which school is most likely to support the body of discoveries and intentions that you've created.

As you choose your new school, consider the needs and wishes of your family members and friends. Ask for their guidance and support. If you involve them in the decision, they'll have more stake in your success.

At some point, you'll just choose a school. Remember that there is no one "right" choice. You could probably thrive at many schools—perhaps even at your current one. Use the suggestions in this book to practice self-responsibility. Take charge of your education no matter which school you attend.

Succeed at your new school

Be willing to begin again. Some students approach a transfer with a "been there, done that" attitude.

Having enrolled in higher education before, they assume that they don't need the orientation, advising, or other student services available at their new school.

Consider an alternative. Since your tuition and fees cover all these services, you might as well take advantage of them. By doing so, you could uncover opportunities that you missed while researching schools. At the very least, you'll meet people who will support your transition.

Your prior experience in higher education gives you strengths. Acknowledge them, even as you begin again at your new school. While celebrating your past accomplishments, you can explore new paths to student success.

Connect to people. At your new school, you'll be in classes with people who have already developed social networks. To avoid feeling left out, seek out chances to meet people. Join study groups, check out extracurricular activities, and consider volunteering for student organizations. Making social connections can ease your transition to a new academic environment.

Check credits. Make sure that credits and grade point averages from your previous school transferred as you planned. No two schools offer the same curriculum, so determining course equivalents is often a matter of interpretation. In some cases, you might be able to persuade a registrar or the admissions office to accept some of your previous courses. Keep a folder of syllabuses from your courses for this purpose. Ask your academic advisor for help. Taking care of these details can help you graduate from your new school on time, with the education that you want. ✳

Contributing:
The art of selfishness

This book is about contributing to yourself—about taking care of yourself, being selfish, and filling yourself up by fulfilling your own needs. The techniques and suggestions in these pages focus on ways to get what you want out of school and out of life.

Leland Bobbe/Getty

ONE OF THE results of all this successful selfishness is the capacity for contributing—for giving to others. Contributing is what's left to do when you're satisfied—when your needs are fulfilled. It completes the process.

People who are satisfied with life can share that satisfaction with others. It is not easy to contribute to another person's joy until you experience joy yourself. The same is true for love. When people are filled with love, they can more easily contribute love to others.

Our interdependence calls for contributing. Every day we depend on contributing. We stake our lives on the compassion of other people. When we drive, we depend on others for our lives. If a driver in an oncoming lane should cross into our own lane, we might die. We also depend on the sensibilities of world leaders for our safety.

People everywhere are growing more interdependent. A plunge in the U.S. stock market reverberates in markets across the planet. A decrease in oil prices gives businesses everywhere a shot in the arm. A nuclear war would ignore national boundaries and devastate life on the planet. Successful arms negotiations allow all people to sleep a little easier.

In this interdependent world, there is no such thing as win/lose. If others lose, their loss directly affects us. If we lose, it is more difficult to contribute to others. The only way to win and to get what we want in life is for others to win, also. When we contribute, the whole human family benefits.

Besides, contributing means getting involved with other people. This is one way to break the ice in a new community and meet people with interests similar to your own. If you want to build community, then contribute.

You can start to experience the advantages of contributing right now. Don't wait for disasters such as a terrorist attack, flood, or hurricane to motivate your volunteerism. The world will welcome your gifts of time, money, and talent.

A caution. The idea of contributing is not the same as knowing what is best for other people. We can't know that.

There are people who go around "fixing" others: *I know what you need. Here's some free advice.* That is not contribution, and it can lead to harm. The person we are "helping" might become dependent on us.

True contribution occurs only after you find out what another person wants or needs. Then you can lovingly support that person as he seeks to achieve his goals, helping him in a way that supports his learning and personal effectiveness.

How you can begin contributing. When you've made the decision to contribute, the next step is knowing how. There are ways to contribute in your immediate surroundings. Visit a neighbor, take a family member to a movie, or offer to tutor a roommate.

Another option is volunteering. In addition to the joy of contribution, volunteering offers a way to explore possible career choices.

You can choose from hundreds of organizations. For example, Big Brothers Big Sisters offers a chance for kids to gain mentors. Boys & Girls Clubs of America, Girl Scouts of the USA, and Boy Scouts of America all need volunteers. So do the Sierra Club, Greenpeace, the National Audubon Society, the World Wildlife Fund, and similar organizations that are dedicated to protecting the environment and endangered species.

Amnesty International investigates human rights violations. It assists people who are imprisoned or tortured for peacefully expressing their points of view.

Hospitals and hospice programs often depend on volunteers to supplement patient care provided by the professional staff. Nursing homes welcome visitors who are willing to spend time listening to and talking with residents. Most communities have volunteer-based programs for people living with HIV infection or AIDS. These programs provide daily hot meals to men, women, and children too ill to cook for themselves.

The American Red Cross provides disaster relief. Local community care centers use volunteers to help feed homeless people.

Political parties, candidates, and special interest groups need volunteers to stuff envelopes, gather petition signatures, distribute literature, and knock on doors.

Service organizations such as Lions Club International, Rotary International, and Kiwanis International create projects to benefit communities across the world.

Other organizations promote the success of women and people of color. Examples are Business and Professional Women/USA, the National Association of Professional Women, and the National Association for the Advancement of Colored People.

Volunteering for some organizations allows you to tackle global problems. For example, there are groups devoted to ending world hunger, such as Oxfam America, CARE, and The Hunger Project. The Environmental Defense Fund and the Natural Resources Defense Council want you to help stop global warming. And the World Bank, UNICEF, the Grameen Bank, and the United Nations are devoted to reducing poverty. This problem kills 26,000 children under the age of 5 each day.[8]

Daily life as contribution. We often see contribution as one task among the many others in our lives. From another perspective, however, we can see our daily life as an act of contribution. For instance, you can live green—and sometimes save money—by recycling waste, reducing your electricity consumption, reusing paper, and driving less. Your efforts will be joined by companies that are building more energy-efficient offices, reducing their greenhouse gas emissions, and changing other daily operations to protect the environment.

The strategies in this book can help you learn efficiently, think critically, communicate clearly, and collaborate effectively. These skills promote your personal success—and the success of any effort you make to contribute. Use this book to load yourself up with skills. Then, make a difference. ✱

Becoming a Master Student goes green

Cengage Learning, publisher of *Becoming a Master Student,* aims to do business in a way that protects the environment. For example, a division of the company called iChapters (www.ichapters.com) offers full books and individual chapters that you can purchase online and read on your computer. You can use this Web site to get discounted prices on some required texts and experience a green alternative to printed books.

Along with the International Code Council, Cengage also hosts www.TheGreenDestination.com. This is a Web site for businesses and homeowners who are interested in sustainable building construction.

In addition, a Cengage office building in Boston, Massachusetts, was remodeled with LEED (Leadership in Energy and Environmental Design) standards in mind. For example:

- Much of the previously existing interior was preserved, but older windows and mechanical systems were replaced with energy-efficient products.
- The carpet tile was made from recycled goods, and the carpet itself can be recycled.
- The linoleum in the lunchroom and copy area is a renewable and reusable product.
- The creation of the work surfaces in cubicles and much of the office furniture involved a water-based adhesive.
- Many of the chairs are made from recycled material and can be recycled again.
- Doors from the old office building have been reused in several areas of the remodeled building, including the lobby and lunch areas.

WHAT'S NEXT?

12

Service-learning: The art of learning by contributing

AS PART OF a service-learning project for a sociology course, students volunteer at a community center for older adults. For another service-learning project, history students interview people in veterans' hospitals about their war experiences. These students plan to share their interview results with a psychiatrist on the hospital staff.

Meanwhile, business students provide free tax-preparation help at a center for low-income people. Students in graphic arts classes create free promotional materials for charities. Other students staff a food cooperative and a community credit union.

These examples of actual projects from the National Service-Learning Clearinghouse demonstrate the working premise of service-learning—that volunteer work and other forms of contributing can become a vehicle for higher education.

Service-learning generally includes three elements: meaningful community service, a formal academic curriculum, and time for students to reflect on what they learn from service. That reflection can include speeches, journal writing, and research papers.

Service-learning creates a win/win scenario. For one thing, students gain the satisfaction of contributing. They also gain experiences that can guide their career choices and help them develop job skills.

At the same time, service-learning adds to the community a resource with a handsome return on investment. For example, participants in the Learn and Serve America program (administered by the Corporation for National and Community Service) provided community services valued at four times the program cost.[9]

When you design a service-learning project, consider these suggestions:

- **Choose partners carefully.** Work with a community agency that has experience with students. Make sure that the agency has liability insurance to cover volunteers.

- **Handle logistics.** Integrating service-learning into your schedule can call for detailed planning. If your volunteer work takes place off campus, arrange for transportation, and allow for travel time.

- **Reflect on your service-learning project.** Turn to a tool you've used throughout this book—the Discovery and Intention Journal Entry system. Write Discovery Statements about what you want to gain from service-learning and how you feel about what you're doing. Follow up with Intention Statements about what you'll do differently for your next volunteer experience.

- **Include ways to evaluate your project.** From your Intention Statements, create action goals and outcome goals. *Action goals* state what you plan to do and how many people you intend to serve; for instance, "We plan to provide 100 hours of literacy tutoring to ten people in the community." *Outcome goals* describe the actual impact that your project will have: "At the end of our project, 60 percent of the people we tutor will be able to write a résumé and fill out a job application." Build numbers into your goals whenever possible. That makes it easier to evaluate the success of your project.

- **Build long-term impact into your project.** One potential pitfall of service-learning is that the programs are often short-lived. After students pack up and return to campus, programs can die. To avoid this outcome, make sure that other students or community members are willing to step in and take over for you when the semester ends.

- **Build transferable skills.** Review the list of sixty-five transferable skills on page 362. Use this list as a way to stimulate your thinking. List the specific skills that you're developing through service-learning. Keep this list. It will come in handy when you write a résumé and fill out job applications. And before you plan to do another service-learning project, think about the skills you'd like to develop from that experience.

- **Celebrate mistakes.** If your project fails to meet its goals, have a party. State—in writing—the obstacles you encountered and ways to overcome them. The solutions you offer will be worth gold to the people who follow in your footsteps. Sharing the lessons learned from your mistakes is an act of service in itself. ✳

practicing critical thinking

Imagine that you are about to teach a student success course. Analyze the topic of student success. Then create a brief outline or syllabus for the course. Choose the main subtopics you will cover, any texts or other materials you will use, and any guest speakers you will invite. Write down your ideas in the space below.

_____
_____
_____
_____
_____
_____
_____
_____
_____
_____
_____
_____
_____
_____
_____
_____
_____
_____
_____
_____
_____
_____
_____
_____

Now reflect on what you just wrote. What results do you want students to achieve in this course? For each result you list, include ways that you, as a teacher, can help students achieve these results.

_____
_____
_____
_____
_____
_____
_____
_____
_____
_____
_____
_____
_____
_____
_____
_____
_____
_____
_____
_____

Finally, look over the lists you just wrote. Circle any ideas that you can use right now to enhance the value that you take away from this student success course.

WHAT'S NEXT?

12

Define your values; align your actions

SOME PEOPLE ARE guided by values that they automatically adopt from others or by values that remain largely unconscious. Other people focus on short-term gain and forget about how their behavior violates their values over the long term (a perspective that helped to create the recent economic recession). All these people could be missing the opportunity to live a life that's truly of their own choosing.

Becoming a Master Student is based on a particular set of values:

- Focused attention
- Self-responsibility
- Integrity
- Risk taking
- Contributing

You'll find these values and related ones directly stated in the Power Processes throughout the text. For instance:

"Discover What You Want" is about the importance of living a purpose-based life.

"Ideas Are Tools" points to the benefits of being willing to experiment with new ideas.

"Be Here Now" expresses the value of focused attention.

"Love Your Problems (and Experience Your Barriers)" is about seeing difficulties as opportunities to develop new skills.

"Notice Your Pictures and Let Them Go" is about adopting an attitude of open-mindedness.

"I Create It All" is about taking responsibility for our beliefs and behaviors.

"Detach" reminds us that our core identity and value as a person does not depend on our possessions, our circumstances, or even our accomplishments.

"Find a Bigger Problem" is about offering our lives by contributing to others.

"Employ Your Word" expresses the value of making and keeping agreements.

"Choose Your Conversations and Your Community" reminds us of the power of language, and that we can reshape our lives by taking charge of our thoughts.

One key way to choose what's next in your life is to define your values. Values are the things in life that you want for their own sake. Values influence and guide your choices, including your moment-by-moment choices of what to do and what to have. Your values define who you are and who you want to be.

"Risk Being a Fool" is about courage—the willingness to take risks for the sake of learning something new.

"Surrender" points to the value of human community and the power of asking for help.

"Be It" is specifically about the power of attitudes—the idea that change proceeds from the inside out as we learn to see ourselves in new ways.

In addition, most of the skills you read about in these pages have their source in values. The Time Monitor/Time Plan process, for example, calls for focused attention. Even the simple act of sharing your notes with a student who missed a class is an example of contributing.

Gaining a liberal education is all about adopting and acting on values. As you begin to define your values, consider the people who have gone before you. In creeds, scriptures, philosophies, myths, and sacred stories, the human race has left a vast and varied record of values. Be willing to look everywhere, including sources that are close to home. The creed of your local church or temple might eloquently describe some of your values. So might the mission statement of your school, company, or club. Another way to define your values is to describe the qualities of people you admire.

Also translate your values into behavior. Although defining your values is powerful, it doesn't guarantee any results. To achieve your goals, take actions that align with your values. ✳

35

The Discovery Wheel—
Coming Full Circle

This book doesn't work. It is worthless. Only you can work. Only you can make a difference and use this book to become a more effective student.

The purpose of this book is to give you the opportunity to change your behavior. The fact that something seems like a good idea doesn't necessarily mean that you will put it into practice. This exercise gives you a chance to see what behaviors you have changed on your journey toward becoming a master student.

Answer each question quickly and honestly. Record your results on the Discovery Wheel on page 377. Then compare it with the one you completed in Chapter 1.

The scores on this Discovery Wheel indicate your current strengths and weaknesses on your path toward becoming a master student. The last Journal Entry in this chapter provides an opportunity to write about how you intend to change. As you complete this self-evaluation, keep in mind that your commitment to change allows you to become a master student. *Your scores might be lower here than on your earlier Discovery Wheel.* That's OK. Lower scores might result from increased self-awareness and honesty, as well as other valuable assets.

Note: The online version of this exercise does not include number ratings, so the results will be formatted differently than described here. If you did your previous Discovery Wheel online, do it online again. This will help you compare your two sets of responses more accurately.

5 points: This statement is always or almost always true of me.

4 points: This statement is often true of me.

3 points: This statement is true of me about half the time.

2 points: This statement is seldom true of me.

1 point: This statement is never or almost never true of me.

1. _____ I enjoy learning.

2. _____ I understand and apply the concept of multiple intelligences.

3. _____ I connect my courses to my purpose for being in school.

4. _____ I make a habit of assessing my personal strengths and areas for improvement.

5. _____ I am satisfied with how I am progressing toward achieving my goals.

6. _____ I use my knowledge of learning styles to support my success in school.

7. _____ I am willing to consider any idea that can help me succeed in school—even if I initially disagree with that idea.

8. _____ I regularly remind myself of the benefits I intend to get from my education.

_____ **Total score (1) Attitude**

1. _____ I set long-term goals and periodically review them.

2. _____ I set short-term goals to support my long-term goals.

3. _____ I write a plan for each day and each week.

4. _____ I assign priorities to what I choose to do each day.

5. _____ I plan review time so I don't have to cram before tests.

6. _____ I plan regular recreation time.

7. _____ I adjust my study time to meet the demands of individual courses.

8. _____ I have adequate time each day to accomplish what I plan.

_____ **Total score (2) Time**

1. _____ I am confident of my ability to remember.

2. _____ I can remember people's names.

3. _____ At the end of a lecture, I can summarize what was presented.

4. _____ I apply techniques that enhance my memory skills.

5. _____ I can recall information when I'm under pressure.

6. _____ I remember important information clearly and easily.

7. _____ I can jog my memory when I have difficulty recalling.

8. _____ I can relate new information to what I've already learned.

> _____ **Total score (3) Memory**

1. _____ I preview and review reading assignments.

2. _____ When reading, I ask myself questions about the material.

3. _____ I underline or highlight important passages when reading.

4. _____ When I read textbooks, I am alert and awake.

5. _____ I relate what I read to my life.

6. _____ I select a reading strategy to fit the type of material I'm reading.

7. _____ I take effective notes when I read.

8. _____ When I don't understand what I'm reading, I note my questions and find answers.

> _____ **Total score (4) Reading**

1. _____ When I am in class, I focus my attention.

2. _____ I take notes in class.

3. _____ I am aware of various methods for taking notes and choose those that work best for me.

4. _____ I distinguish important material and note key phrases in a lecture.

5. _____ I copy down material that the instructor writes on the chalkboard or overhead display.

6. _____ I can put important concepts into my own words.

7. _____ My notes are valuable for review.

8. _____ I review class notes within 24 hours.

> _____ **Total score (5) Notes**

1. _____ I use techniques to manage stress related to exams.

2. _____ I manage my time during exams and am able to complete them.

3. _____ I am able to predict test questions.

4. _____ I adapt my test-taking strategy to the kind of test I'm taking.

5. _____ I understand what essay questions ask and can answer them completely and accurately.

6. _____ I start reviewing for tests at the beginning of the term.

7. _____ I continue reviewing for tests throughout the term.

8. _____ My sense of personal worth is independent of my test scores.

> _____ **Total score (6) Tests**

1. _____ I have flashes of insight and think of solutions to problems at unusual times.

2. _____ I use brainstorming to generate solutions to a variety of problems.

3. _____ When I get stuck on a creative project, I use specific methods to get unstuck.

4. _____ I see problems and tough choices as opportunities for learning and personal growth.

5. _____ I am willing to consider different points of view and alternative solutions.

6. _____ I can detect common errors in logic.

7. _____ I construct viewpoints by drawing on information and ideas from many sources.

8. _____ As I share my viewpoints with others, I am open to their feedback.

> _____ **Total score (7) Thinking**

12

1. _____ I am candid with others about who I am, what I feel, and what I want.

2. _____ Other people tell me that I am a good listener.

3. _____ I can communicate my upset and anger without blaming others.

4. _____ I can make friends and create valuable relationships in a new setting.

5. _____ I am open to being with people I don't especially like in order to learn from them.

6. _____ I can effectively plan and research a large writing assignment.

7. _____ I create first drafts without criticizing my writing, then edit later for clarity, accuracy, and coherence.

8. _____ I know ways to prepare and deliver effective speeches.

_____ **Total score (8) Communicating**

1. _____ I build rewarding relationships with people from backgrounds different from my own.

2. _____ I use critical thinking to overcome stereotypes.

3. _____ I point out examples of discrimination and sexual harassment and effectively respond to them.

4. _____ I am constantly learning ways to thrive with diversity in school and/or the workplace—attitudes and behaviors that will support my success.

5. _____ I can effectively resolve conflict with people from other cultures.

6. _____ My writing and speaking are free of sexist expressions.

7. _____ I take diversity into account when assuming a leadership role.

8. _____ I respond effectively to changing demographics in my country and community.

_____ **Total score (9) Diversity**

1. _____ I am in control of my personal finances.

2. _____ I can access a variety of resources to finance my education.

3. _____ I am confident that I will have enough money to complete my education.

4. _____ I take on debts carefully and repay them on time.

5. _____ I have long-range financial goals and a plan to meet them.

6. _____ I make regular deposits to a savings account.

7. _____ I pay off the balance on credit card accounts each month.

8. _____ I can have fun without spending money.

_____ **Total score (10) Money**

1. _____ I have enough energy to study and work—and still enjoy other areas of my life.

2. _____ If the situation calls for it, I have enough reserve energy to put in a long day.

3. _____ The way I eat supports my long-term health.

4. _____ The way I eat is independent of my feelings of self-worth.

5. _____ I exercise regularly to maintain a healthy weight.

6. _____ My emotional health supports my ability to learn.

7. _____ I notice changes in my physical condition and respond effectively.

8. _____ I am in control of any alcohol or other drugs I put into my body.

_____ **Total score (11) Health**

1. _____ I see learning as a lifelong process.

2. _____ I relate school to what I plan to do for the rest of my life.

3. _____ I learn by contributing to others in need.

4. _____ I have a written career plan and update it regularly.

5. _____ I am gaining skills to support my success in the workplace.

6. _____ I take responsibility for the quality of my education—and my life.

7. _____ I live by a set of values that translates into daily actions.

8. _____ I am willing to accept challenges even when I'm not sure how to meet them.

_____ **Total score (12) Purpose**

Filling in your Discovery Wheel

Using the total score from each category, shade in each section of the Discovery Wheel on this page. Use different colors, if you want. For example, you could use green to denote areas you want to work on. When you have finished, complete the Journal Entry on page 378.

 Complete this exercise online.

Discovery/Intention Statement

Revisiting Your Discovery Wheels

The purpose of this Journal Entry is to (1) review both of the Discovery Wheels you completed in this book, (2) summarize your insights from doing them, and (3) declare how you will use these insights to promote your continued success in school.

Again, a lower score on the second Discovery Wheel does not necessarily indicate decreased personal effectiveness. Instead, the lower score could result from increased honesty and greater self-awareness.

Enter your Discovery Wheel scores from both chapters in the space below.

	Chapter 1	Chapter 12
Attitude		
Time		
Memory		
Reading		
Notes		
Tests		
Thinking		
Communicating		
Diversity		
Money		
Health		
Purpose		

Comparing the Discovery Wheel in this chapter with the Discovery Wheel in Chapter 1, I discovered that I . . .

_____

_____

_____

_____

_____

_____

In the next 6 months, I intend to review the following articles from this book for additional suggestions I could use:

_____

_____

_____

_____

_____

_____

_____

_____

---

36 exercise
This Book Shouts, "Use me!"

Becoming a Master Student is designed to be used for years. The success strategies presented here are not likely to become habits overnight. There are more suggestions than can be put into action immediately. Some of what is discussed might not apply to your life right now, but it might be just what you need in a few months.

Plan to keep this book and use it again. Imagine that your book has a mouth. (Visualize the mouth.) Also imagine that it has arms and legs. (Visualize them.)

Now picture your book sitting on a shelf or table that you see every day. Imagine a time when you are having trouble in school and struggling to be successful as a student. Visualize your book jumping up and down, shouting, "Use me! Read me! I might have the solution to your problem, and I know I can help you solve it."

This is a memory technique to remind you to use a resource. Sometimes when you are stuck, all you need is a small push or a list of possible actions. At those times, hear your book shout, "Use me!"

WHAT'S NEXT?

12

Create Your Next Semester or Term

This exercise offers a chance to celebrate your successes during the past term—and to think in specific ways about what you want to create next term.

Part 1: Update your First Step

Looking back on this past semester or term, you might be surprised at how quickly it went by. You might also be surprised at how much you learned, both inside and outside the classroom.

In the space below, list three things that you did well during the current term. Perhaps you took the initiative to meet a new person or created an effective way to take notes in class. Write down any success that you find personally significant, no matter how small it might seem to others. Use additional paper as needed.

1. _____

2. _____

3. _____

Now take a moment to write about three things that did not go as well as you wanted during the past term. Give yourself permission to explore whatever comes to mind—anything from a simple embarrassment to a major mistake. If you missed a class because you set your alarm for 7 p.m. instead of 7 a.m., you can write about that. If you failed a test, you might describe that experience as well.

As you practice truth telling, remember to keep it light. It's fine to acknowledge breakdowns and to laugh at yourself as you do.

1. _____

2. _____

3. _____

Part 2: Determine what you want next

You've come a long way since first setting foot on campus. Now consider where you want to go next term. Brainstorm some intentions in several areas of your life. Then channel them into some new behaviors.

Do this activity by building on the writing you did in Part 1 of this exercise. Reflect on ways to maintain or expand on the successes you listed. Also consider ways to change or prevent some of the experiences you didn't like.

Determine what you want from academics. For instance, you could set a goal to raise your grade point average to a specific number, or to declare your major by a certain date. Complete the following sentence.

In my academic life, I want to . . .

_____

_____

_____

Now consider your social life. Perhaps you want to resolve a conflict with an instructor or roommate. Or you might want to deepen a connection with someone you already know and make this person a friend for life. Put such goals in writing by completing the following sentence.

In my social life, I want to . . .

_____

_____

_____

Finally, brainstorm a list of specific actions you can take to meet the goals you just described. Write these actions below. Reflect on which ones might work best for you and record them in your calendar or to-do list. For more suggestions on goal setting, see Chapter 2.

_____

_____

_____

_____

_____

_____

_____

_____

Be It

Use this Power Process to enhance all of the techniques in this book.

Consider that most of our choices in life fall into three categories. We can do the following:

- Increase our material wealth (what we have).
- Improve our skills (what we do).
- Develop our "being" (who we are).

Many people devote their entire lifetime to the first two categories. They act as if they are "human havings" instead of human beings. For them, the quality of life hinges on what they have. They devote most of their waking hours to getting more—more clothes, more cars, more relationships, more degrees, more trophies. "Human havings" define themselves by looking at the circumstances in their lives—what they have.

Some people escape this materialist trap by adding another dimension to their identities. In addition to living as "human havings," they also live as "human doings." They thrive on working hard and doing everything well. They define themselves by how efficiently they do their jobs, how effectively they raise their children, and how actively they participate in clubs and organizations. Their thoughts are constantly about methods, techniques, and skills.

In addition to focusing on what we have and what we do, we can also focus on our being. That last word describes how we *see* ourselves.

All of the techniques in this book can be worthless if you operate with the idea that you are an ineffective student. You might do almost everything this book suggests and still never achieve the success in school that you desire.

Instead, picture yourself as a master student right now. Through higher education, you are simply gaining knowledge and skills that reflect and reinforce this view of yourself. Change the way you see yourself. Then watch your actions and results shift as if by magic.

Remember that "Be it" is not positive thinking or mental cheerleading. This Power Process works well when you take a First Step—when you tell the truth about your current abilities. The very act of accepting who you are and what you can do right now unleashes a powerful force for personal change.

If you can first visualize where you want to be, if you can go there in your imagination, if you can *be* it today, then you set yourself up to succeed.

If you want it, be it.

 Learn more about this Power Process online.

Put it to Work

Strategies from *Becoming a Master Student* can help you succeed in your career, as well as in school. To discover how suggestions in this chapter can apply to the workplace, reflect on the following case study.

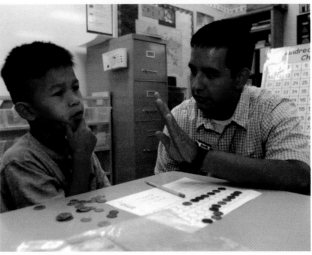

© Ed Kashi/CORBIS

Duane Bigeagle earned his B.A. in elementary education and found a job teaching kindergarten in an urban public school.

To his surprise, the hardest thing about the job was not interacting with students—whom he enjoyed greatly—but interacting with his coworkers. Although Duane had heard of office politics, he did not expect to encounter them much in an educational setting.

Duane's greatest concern was a colleague named Reneé, a teacher with 25 years of experience. During weekly staff meetings, the school's principal asked teachers to share any problems they were experiencing with students and to collectively brainstorm solutions. Reneé smiled a lot, offered suggestions, and freely offered praise for anyone who was willing to share a problem. During informal conversations with Duane before or after school, however, Reneé complained bitterly about other teachers on staff—including those she'd just praised during staff meetings.

Being new to the school and a first-year teacher, Duane decided that he wanted to avoid making enemies. His goal in relating to staff members was simply to learn everything he could from them. With that goal in mind, Duane adopted the habits of carefully observing the classroom strategies used by other teachers and listening without judgment to any coaching they offered him.

Reneé talked with Duane every day and, after gossiping about other teachers, freely offered advice for managing his classroom. By the end of the school year, Duane had had enough of this. He worried that Reneé was taking on the role of a self-appointed mentor to him, and he disagreed with many of her ideas about teaching. He also worried that other teachers would perceive that he and Reneé were a "team," and that her mixed reputation in the workplace would reflect negatively on him as well.

During his first year on a new job, Duane is using several transferable skills, including listening without judgment. Describe some other transferable skills that he demonstrates:

_____

_____

_____

Also describe some strategies that Duane could use to resolve his conflict with Reneé:

_____

_____

_____

You can use other techniques from this chapter in the workplace. Think about a larger issue—your life beyond this student success course. To get continuing benefits from this course, continue the conversation about creating success in the workplace and every other area of your life:

Put your vision in front of you. Write your goals on 3x5 cards or sticky notes. Place these reminders of your vision in places where you can't miss them—your desk, your bathroom mirror, your car.

Start a book group focused on success. There are plenty of books about success that complement this one. (See Additional Reading on page 391.) Gather with friends to digest and discuss some of them.

Quiz

Name _____   Date ____/____/____

1. According to the text, you can create a career plan through the process of "naming names." True or False? Explain your answer.

   True. Naming names means being very specific: Name your specific job, name the company you want to work for, name your contacts in securing that job, and name where you want to live and work. (*Create your career now,* p. 356)

2. Explain how *work-content skills* and *transferable skills* differ. Give one example of each kind of skill.

   A work-content skill is an ability gained by training or experience. It involves a specialized body of knowledge needed to do a specific kind of work. An example is the ability to repair fiber-optic cable. A transferable skill is an ability developed without formal training that helps people thrive in any job. Examples include listening and negotiating. (Answers will vary.) (*Jumpstart your education with transferable skills,* p. 361)

3. Explain how career planning can become a process of choosing instead of a process of discovery.

   While we may discover skills through career planning, we don't find the right career. We create it. We choose our careers because we are the only ones who can do research into ourselves and truly know our own skills and interests. Knowing that we make the choice can be relaxing. There is not just one "correct" choice for a career. (*Create your career now,* p. 356)

4. List three suggestions for designing an effective service-learning project.

   List at least three of the following (answers will vary):   a. Choose partners carefully.   b. Handle logistics.   c. Reflect on your project using the Discovery and Intention Journal Entry system.   d. Include ways to evaluate your project.   e. Build long-term impact into your project.   f. Celebrate mistakes.   (*Service-learning: The art of learning by contributing,* p. 371)

5. Describe the three main types of life choices explained in the Power Process: "Be It."

   List and describe the following: a. What we have.   b. What we do.   c. Who we are.   (*Power Process: Be It,* p. 380)

6. List at least three strategies for negotiating a starting salary during the interview process.

   List any three of the following (answers will vary):   a. Use the Money Monitor/Money Plan to determine how much money you'll need.   b. Maintain flexibility by settling on a salary range rather than a specific figure.   c. Discover typical salary ranges for jobs in your field.   d. Estimate how much the employer is likely to offer you.   e. Postpone salary discussions until the end of the interview process (when you're confident the employer wants to hire you).   f. Let the employer be the first to mention a salary range.   g. Ask for a figure near the top of the employer-proposed salary range.   h. Ask if there's room to negotiate benefit packages and vacation time.   (*Use résumés and interviews to "hire" an employer,* p. 364)

7. If your scores are lower on the Discovery Wheel the second time you complete it, this means your skills have not improved. True or False? Explain your answer.

   False. Lower scores the second time you complete the Discovery Wheel might result from increased self-awareness and honesty, among other valuable assets. (*Exercise #35: The Discovery Wheel—Coming Full Circle,* p. 374)

8. Give three examples of ways to test your career choice.

   Three ways to test a career choice are to interview people who are actually doing the job, obtain an internship or volunteer position in that field, and get a part-time or summer job in that field. For example, a person considering a career as a veterinarian might interview and ask questions of a working veterinarian, seek out a volunteer or internship position at a local animal care shelter, and get a part-time job at a veterinarian's office for the summer. (Answers will vary.) (*Create your career now,* p. 356)

9. Describe a flaw associated with the typical job-hunting strategy of looking through help-wanted advertisements. Then briefly describe an alternative approach to job hunting.

   A major flaw is that most job openings are never advertised. Many employers use help-wanted listings, along with résumés and employment agencies, only as a last resort. An example of a strategy that might be used instead is to research a company you would like to work for, identify a contact there, and arrange an interview with that person. Employers often prefer to hire people they know. (*Use résumés and interviews to "hire" an employer,* p. 364)

10. List at least four ways in which you can continue on your path of becoming a master student after completing this book.

    List at least four (answers will vary):   a. Keep a journal.   b. Take a workshop.   c. Read, watch, and listen.   d. Take an unrelated class.   e. Travel.   f. Get counseling.   g. Form a support group.   h. Find a mentor—or become one.   i. Redo this book.   (". . . use the following suggestions to continue . . . ," p. 354)

Skills Snapshot

Jerry Seinfeld told one aspiring comedian that "the way to be a better comic was to create better jokes and the way to create better jokes was to write every day."[10] Seinfeld also revealed his own system for creating a writing habit: He bought a big wall calendar that displayed the whole year on one page. On each day that he wrote jokes, Seinfeld marked a big red "X" on the appropriate day on the wall calendar. He knew that he'd established a new habit when he looked at the calendar and saw an unbroken chain of "X's."

So much of success boils down to changing habits. Take a snapshot of your habits as they exist today, after reading and doing this book. Then take the next step toward mastery by committing to a specific action in the near future.

DISCOVERY

During this course, it has been my intention to change the following habits . . .

I would describe my skill at changing those habits as . . .

INTENTION

Three habits that I am committed to changing in the future are . . .

NEXT ACTION

Of the three habits listed above, the one I would like to focus on next is . . .

To experience a new level of mastery at making this habit change, I will . . .

Master Student PROFILE

Lisa Ling

. . . is inquisitive

© Michael Quan/ZUMA/Corbis

I had heard about auditions for a teen magazine show called *Scratch*. They were holding auditions in a mall, and one Saturday in Sacramento I showed up along with hundreds of other students. They chose four of us to host this show—a fun teen magazine where I interviewed celebrities and did makeovers and silly things like that. But what was cool was that it was produced by a local news affiliate, and I used that entrée into the station to get an internship in the newsroom. I hung out with the writers and learned to run the teleprompter. I was sort of an eager and aggressive young kid who wanted to learn about the business, and I would show up at the TV station at 4:30 or 5:00 in the morning before classes.

After doing three years on a teen magazine show, I was ready to go to college. Then the director of Channel One called me and said, "We'd like you to come audition." I did and got the job. It was based in Los Angeles, so I ended up going to the University of Southern California while doing Channel One at the same time.

Channel One has been plagued by . . . controversy because it airs commercials within the broadcast. But for me as a reporter it was the most incredible opportunity, and the editorial content of Channel One I would put up against any network news show. I was a 19- and 20-year old kid covering the civil war in Afghanistan, the Russian referendum elections, the civil war in Algeria, the drug war in Colombia, overpopulation in China, globalization in India. I would work on a series about the democracy movement in Iran in 1995 that would run about twenty-five minutes throughout the course of a week. And at that time what news outlet would cover Iran for twenty-five minutes?

I actually think that was some of my best journalism. While I did do research on the various stories and countries, I kind of went in to them not knowing so much—just being open and not having a lot of preconceived ideas or notions. You know, these days we are almost brainwashed. When our leadership characterizes entire countries as evil, how do you *not* go into stories with preconceived ideas? What we did as young people was pick these places in the world that no one was covering and went there. We didn't tell our viewers what to think. We just gave them an opportunity to experience what *we* were experiencing.

I majored in history because I wanted to have as broad-based an education as I could possibly get. My history background and my political science background and my travels have been my biggest assets as a journalist.

People are always asking me: How did you get your job? And my answer is, I just got it. I just kind of willed it into existence. I just kind of created this situation.

My advice to young people is: Before you get hampered by a job and family and financial obligations, try to get out of your comfort zone. If you can, live in another country for a year or so. You won't regret it.

Excerpted from "Journalist and Correspondent Lisa Ling," broadcast on *Profiles,* a radio program from WFIU, Indiana University, and hosted by Owen Johnson, November 11, 2007, http://wfiu.org/profiles/lisa-ling.

(1973–)
Host of National Geographic Channel's *Explorer*, special correspondent for *The Oprah Winfrey Show*, and a former cohost of ABC's *The View*, was one of the youngest reporters for Channel One News, whose programming is aimed at middle and high schools.

Learn more about Lisa Ling at the Master Student Hall of Fame.

Endnotes

Introduction

1. U.S. Department of Labor, Bureau of Labor Statistics, "Education Pays…," April 15, 2008, http://www.bls.gov/emp/emptab7.htm (accessed January 30, 2009); National Center for Education Statistics, "Annual Earnings of Young Adults," http://nces.ed.gov/programs/coe/2008/section2/indicator20.asp, 2008 (accessed January 30, 2009).

2. Robert Mager, *Preparing Instructional Objectives* (Belmont, CA: Fearon, 1975).

3. Randy Moore, "The Importance of Admissions Scores and Attendance to First-Year Performance," *Journal of the First-Year Experience & Students in Transition* 18, no. 1 (2006): 105–125.

4. Albert Bandura, *Social Foundations of Thought and Action* (Englewood Cliffs, NJ.: Prentice-Hall, 1986).

5. U.S. Census Bureau, "Facts for Feature: Back to School 2007–2008," http://www.prnewswire.com/cgi-bin/stories.pl?ACCT=104&STORY=/www/story/06-14-2007/0004608454&EDATE=, June 14, 2008 (accessed February 2, 2009).

6. Robert Reich, *The Work of Nations: Preparing Ourselves for 21st Century Capitalism* (New York: Vintage, 1991).

7. National Commission on Writing, *Writing: A Ticket to Work…Or a Ticket Out* (New York: College Board, 2004), http://www.writingcommission.org/prod_downloads/writingcom/writing-ticket-to-work.pdf (accessed February 2, 2009).

8. Secretary's Commission on Achieving Necessary Skills, *Skills and Tasks for Jobs: A SCANS Report for America 2000* (Washington, DC: U.S. Department of Labor, 1991), http://wdr.doleta.gov/SCANS/whatwork/whatwork.pdf (accessed February 2, 2009).

9. James O. Prochaska, John C. Norcross, and Carlo C. DiClemente, *Changing for Good* (New York: Avon, 1994).

10. Richard Malott, "Self Management Checklist," Counselling Services, University of Victoria, 2003, http://www.coun.uvic.ca/learn/program/hndouts/slfman.html (accessed October 13, 2006).

11. B. F. Skinner, *Science and Human Behavior* (Boston: Free Press, 1965).

12. Excerpts from *Creating Your Future*. Copyright © 1998 by David B. Ellis. Adapted by permission of Houghton Mifflin Company. All rights reserved.

Chapter 1

1. David A. Kolb, *Experiential Learning: Experience as the Source of Learning and Development* (Englewood Cliffs, NJ: Prentice-Hall, 1984).

2. Douglas A. Bernstein, Louis A. Penner, Alison Clarke-Stewart, and Edward J. Roy, *Psychology* (Boston: Houghton Mifflin, 2006), 368–369.

3. Howard Gardner, *Frames of Mind: The Theory of Multiple Intelligences* (New York: Basic Books, 1993).

4. Neil Fleming, "VARK: A Guide to Learning Styles," 2006, www.vark-learn.com (accessed February 13, 2009).

5. Carl Rogers, *Freedom to Learn* (Columbus, OH: Merrill, 1969).

6. Ezra Pound, *The ABC of Reading* (New York: New Directions, 1934).

7. Robert Hutchins, *The Great Books of the Western World,* vol. 1, *The Tradition of the West* (Chicago: Encyclopaedia Britannica, 1952).

Chapter 2

1. Alan Lakein, *How to Get Control of Your Time and Your Life* (New York: New American Library, 1973; reissue 1996).

2. Linda Sapadin, with Jack Maguire, *It's About Time! The Six Styles of Procrastination and How to Overcome Them* (New York: Penguin, 1997).

3. Stephen R. Covey, *The Seven Habits of Highly Effective People: Restoring the Character Ethic* (New York: Simon & Schuster, 1990).

4. David Allen, *Getting Things Done: The Art of Stress-free Productivity* (New York: Penguin, 2001).

Chapter 3

1. Donald Hebb, quoted in D. J. Siegel, "Memory: An Overview," *Journal of the American Academy of Child and Adolescent Psychiatry* 40, no. 9 (2001): 997–1011.

2. Donald Hebb, *Essay on Mind* (Hillsdale, NJ: Erlbaum, 1980).

3. Daniel L. Schacter, *The Seven Sins of Memory: How the Mind Forgets and Remembers* (Boston: Houghton Mifflin, 2001), 14.

4. From *Information Anxiety* by Richard Saul Wurman. Copyright © 1989 by Richard Saul Wurman. Used by permission of Doubleday, a division of Bantam Doubleday Dell Publishing Group, Inc.

5. D. J. Siegel, "Memory: An Overview," *Journal of the American Academy of Child and Adolescent Psychiatry* 40, no. 9 (2001): 997–1011.

6. Schacter, *The Seven Sins of Memory*, 14.

7. Alzheimer's Association, "Brain Health," 2009, http://www.alz.org/brainhealth/overview.asp (accessed February 19, 2009).

Chapter 4

1. From *Master Student Guide to Academic Success* (Boston: Houghton Mifflin, 2005), 111.

2. G. S. Gates, "Recitation as a Factor in Memorizing," *Archives of Psychology* 40 (1917).

3. R. Rosnow and E. Robinson, eds., *Experiments in Persuasion* (New York: Academic Press, 1967).

4. From *Master Student Guide to Academic Success*, 115.

5. Adapted from Ann Raimes, *Universal Keys for Writers* (Boston: Houghton Mifflin, 2004), 709–712.

6. Jakob Nielsen, "How Users Read on the Web," October 1, 1997, www.useit.com/alertbox/9710a.html (accessed February 26, 2009).

7. National Endowment for the Arts, To Read or Not to Read: A Question of National Consequence, November 2007, arts.endow.gov/research/ToRead.pdf (accessed February 26, 2009).

Chapter 5

1. Walter Pauk and Ross J. Q. Owens, *How to Study in College*, 8th ed. (Boston: Houghton Mifflin, 2005).
2. Tony Buzan, *Use Both Sides of Your Brain* (New York: Dutton, 1991).
3. Gabrielle Rico, *Writing the Natural Way* (Los Angeles: J. P. Tarcher, 1983).
4. Joseph Novak and D. Bob Gowin, *Learning How to Learn* (New York: Cambridge University Press, 1984).

Chapter 6

1. Linda Wong, *Essential Study Skills*, Fourth Edition. Copyright © 2003 by Houghton Mifflin Company. Reprinted with permission.
2. Joe Cuseo, "Academic-Support Strategies for Promoting Student Retention and Achievement during the First Year of College," University of Ulster Office of Student Transition and Retention, http://www.ulst.ac.uk/star/data/cuseoretention.htm#peestud (accessed September 4, 2003).
3. Ibid.
4. Jonathan D. Glater, "Colleges Chase as Cheats Shift to Higher Tech," *New York Times*, May 18, 2006, http://www.nytimes.com/2006/05/18/education/18cheating.html (accessed March 1, 2009).
5. MayoClinic.com, "Generalized Anxiety Disorder," www.mayoclinic.com/health/generalized-anxiety-disorder/DS00502/DSECTION=symptoms, September 11, 2007 (accessed March 1, 2009).
6. Jon Kabat-Zin, *Full Catastrophe Living: How to Cope with Stress, Pain and Illness Using Mindfulness Meditation* (London: Piatkus Books, 2001).
7. Steven C. Hayes, *Get Out of Your Mind and Into Your Life: The New Acceptance and Commitment Therapy* (Oakland, CA: New Harbinger, 2004).
8. This article incorporates detailed suggestions from reviewer Frank Baker.
9. Jena McGregor, William C. Symonds, Dean Foust, Diane Brady, and Moira Herbst, "How Failure Breeds Success," *Business Week*, July 10, 2006, http://www.businessweek.com/magazine/content/06_28/b3992001.htm (accessed March 1, 2009).

Chapter 7

1. Quoted in Theodore A. Rees Cheney, *Getting the Words Right: How to Rewrite, Edit and Revise* reprint (Cincinnati, OH: Writer's Digest Books, 1990).
2. Mortimer Adler and Charles Van Doren, *How to Read a Book: The Classic Guide to Intelligent Reading* (New York: Simon and Schuster, 1972).
3. William G. Perry, Jr., *Forms of Intellectual and Ethical Development in the College Years: A Scheme* (New York: Holt, Rinehart, and Winston, 1970).

4. Peter A. Facione, *Critical Thinking: A Statement of Expert Consensus for Purposes of Educational Assessment and Instruction* (Millbrae, CA.: California Academic Press, 1990).
5. Arthur Koestler, *The Act of Creation* (New York: Dell, 1964).
6. Martin E. P. Seligman, *Authentic Happiness: Using the New Positive Psychology to Realize Your Potential for Lasting Fulfillment* (New York: Simon and Schuster, 2002).
7. Quoted in Alice Calaprice, ed., *The Expanded Quotable Einstein* (Princeton, NJ: Princeton University Press, 2000).
8. Joe Cuseo, "Academic-Support Strategies for Promoting Student Retention and Achievement during the First Year of College," University of Ulster Office of Student Transition and Retention, www.ulst.ac.uk/star/data/cuseoretention.htm#peestud (accessed September 4, 2003).
9. National Committee for Latin and Greek, www.promotelatin.org/Default.htm#famous, March 5, 2006 (accessed March 12, 2009).

Chapter 8

1. Lee Thayer, "Communication—Sine Qua Non of the Behavioral Sciences," in *Vistas in Science*, ed. David L. Arm (Albuquerque: University of New Mexico, 1968).
2. Carl Rogers, *On Becoming a Person* (Boston: Houghton Mifflin, 1961).
3. Thomas Gordon, *Parent Effectiveness Training: The Tested New Way to Raise Responsible Children* (New York: New American Library, 1975).
4. Sidney Jourard, *The Transparent Self* (New York: Van Nostrand, 1971).
5. Daniel Goleman, *Emotional Intelligence: Why It Can Matter More Than IQ* (New York: Bantam, 1995), xiv–xv.
6. Frank LaFasto, "The Zen of Brilliant Teams," Center for Association Leadership, July 2002, www.asaecenter.org/PublicationsResources/articledetail.cfm?ItemNumber=13295 (accessed March 17, 2009).
7. LaFasto, "The Zen of Brilliant Teams."
8. MySpace, "Safety Tips," www1.myspace.com/misc/safetyTips.html (accessed March 20, 2009).
9. Quoted in Richard Saul Wurman, Loring Leifer, and David Sume, *Information Anxiety #2* (Indianapolis: QUE, 2001), 116.
10. Peter Elbow, *Writing with Power: Techniques for Mastering the Writing Process* (New York: Oxford University Press, 1981).
11. M. T. Motley, *Overcoming Your Fear of Public Speaking: A Proven Method* (New York: Houghton Mifflin, 1998).

Chapter 9

1. Family Care Foundation, "If the World Were a Village of 100 People," www.familycare.org/news/if_the_world.htm (accessed March 25, 2009).
2. Federal Bureau of Investigation, "Uniform Crime Reports," www.fbi.gov/ucr/ucr.htm#hate (accessed March 26, 2009).
3. Anti-Defamation League, "Members of Congress Urged: Retain Campus Hate Crime Data Collection Improvements," 2009, www.adl.org/combating_hate/letter_campus_hcd.asp (accessed March 26, 2009).

4. Stephen R. Covey, *The Seven Habits of Highly Effective People: Restoring the Character Ethic* (New York: Simon & Schuster, 1989).

5. Vincent A. Miller, *Guidebook for International Trainers in Business and Industry* (New York: Van Nostrand Reinhold, 1979), 46–55.

6. Ximena Zúñiga, "Fostering Intergroup Dialogue on Campus: Essential Ingredients," *Diversity Digest,* www.diversityweb.org/Digest/W98/fostering.html (accessed March 27, 2009).

7. Maia Szalavitz, "Race and the Genome," Howard University Human Genome Center, March 2, 2001, www.genomecenter.howard.edu/article.htm (accessed March 27, 2009).

8. Diane de Anda, *Bicultural Socialization: Factors Affecting the Minority Experience* (Washington, DC: National Association of Social Workers, 1984).

9. Office for Civil Rights, *Sexual Harassment: It's Not Academic,* U.S. Department of Education, www.ed.gov/about/offices/list/ocr/docs/ocrshpam.html (accessed October 5, 2006).

10. U.S. Census Bureau, "An Older and More Diverse Nation by Midcentury," August 14, 2008, www.census.gov/Press-Release/www/releases/archives/population/012496.html (accessed March 27, 2009).

Chapter 10

1. Fordcarz.com, "Quotations from Henry Ford," www.fordcarz.com/henry_ford_quotes.htm (accessed April 3, 2009).

2. Saul Hansell, "Yahoo Feels Breath on Neck; These Days, No. 1 Portal Seems to Be a Step Behind," *New York Times,* October 11, 2006.

3. Suze Orman, *Suze Orman's 2009 Action Plan* (New York: Spiegel & Grau, 2009).

4. "How Undergraduate Students Use Credit Cards: Sallie Mae's National Study of Usage Rates and Trends 2009," www.salliemae.com/NR/rdonlyres/0BD600F1-9377-46EA-AB1F-6061FC763246/10739/SLMCreditCardUsageStudy41309FINAL1.pdf (accessed April 17, 2009).

5. Marie O'Malley, "Educating Undergraduates on Using Credit Cards," Nellie Mae, 2008, www.nelliemae.com/library/cc_use.html (accessed April 2, 2009).

6. Sandy Baum and Jennifer Ma, "Education Pays 2007: The Benefits of Higher Education for Individuals and Society," College Board, 2007, http://professionals.collegeboard.com/data-reports-research/trends/education-pays-2006 (accessed July 10, 2009).

Chapter 11

1. Centers for Disease Control and Prevention, "Health Habits of Adults Aged 18-29 Highlighted in Report on Nation's Health," February 18, 2009, www.cdc.gov/media/pressrel/2009/r090218.htm (accessed April 10, 2009).

2. University of Minnesota, "Health and Academic Performance: Minnesota Undergraduate Students," www.bhs.umn.edu/reports/HealthAcademicPerformanceReport_2007.pdf, 2007 (accessed April 10, 2009).

3. Kay-Tee Khaw, Nicholas Wareham, Sheila Bingham, Ailsa Welch, Robert Luben, and Nicholas Day, "Combined Impact of Health Behaviours and Mortality in Men and Women: The EPIC-Norfolk Prospective Population Study," *PLoS Medicine* 5, no. 1 (2008), www.plosmedicine.org/article/info:doi/10.1371/journal.pmed.0050012 (accessed April 10, 2009).

4. U.S. Department of Agriculture, "MyPyramid.gov," mypyramid.gov/guidelines/index.html, 2009 (accessed April 10, 2009).

5. Michael Pollan, "Unhappy Meals," *New York Times,* January 28, 2007, www.nytimes.com/2007/01/28/magazine/28nutritionism.t.html (accessed April 10, 2009).

6. Harvard Medical School, *HEALTHbeat: 20 No-Sweat Ways to Get More Exercise* (Boston: Harvard Health Publications, October 14, 2008).

7. Jane Brody, "Exercise = Weight Loss, Except When It Doesn't," *New York Times,* September 12, 2006, www.nytimes.com/2006/09/12/health/nutrition/12brody.html (accessed April 9, 2009).

8. Harvard Medical School, *HEALTHbeat Extra: The Secret to Better Health—Exercise* (Boston: Harvard Health Publications, January 27, 2009).

9. Mary Duenwald, "The Dorms May Be Great, but How's the Counseling?" *New York Times,* October 26, 2004, www.nytimes.com/2004/10/26/health/psychology/26cons.html?_r=1 (accessed April 9, 2009).

10. American College Health Association, *American College Health Association–National College Health Assessment II: Reference Group, Executive Summary Fall 2008,* www.acha-ncha.org/docs/ACHA-NCHA_Reference_Group_ExecutiveSummary_Fall2008.pdf, 2009 (accessed April 9, 2009).

11. Morita Masatake's ideas are discussed in David Reynolds, *A Handbook for Constructive Living* (New York: Morrow, 1995), 98.

12. Albert Ellis, *Overcoming Destructive Beliefs, Feelings, and Behaviors: New Directions for Rational Emotive Behavior Therapy* (Amherst, NY: Prometheus, 2001).

13. Centers for Disease Control and Prevention, "Trends in Reportable Sexually Transmitted Diseases in the United States, 2007," www.cdc.gov/nchhstp/newsroom/docs/STDTrendsFactSheet.pdf, 2009 (accessed April 9, 2009).

14. Centers for Disease Control and Prevention, "CDC Fact Sheet: Most Widely Reported, Curable STDs Remain Significant Health Threat," www.cdc.gov/nchhstp/newsroom/docs/STDFastFacts-3.27.09-508%20Compliant.pdf, 2009 (accessed April 9, 2009).

15. David Sandman, Elisabeth Simantov, and Christina An, "Out of Touch: American Men and the Health Care System," www.commonwealthfund.org/Content/Publications/Fund-Reports/2000/Mar/Out-of-Touch--American-Men-and-the-Health-Care-System.aspx, The Commonwealth Fund, 2000 (accessed April 10, 2009).

16. Agency for Healthcare Research and Quality, "Men: Stay Healthy at Any Age," February 2007, www.ahrq.gov/ppip/healthymen.htm (accessed April 10, 2009).

17. Edward Hallowell, *CrazyBusy: Overstretched, Overbooked, and About to Snap!* (New York: Ballantine, 2006), 71–85.

18. Albert Bandura, "Self-Efficacy," in *Encyclopedia of Human Behavior,* vol. 4, ed. V. S. Ramachaudran (New York: Academic Press, 1994), 71–81.

19. M. Schaffer, E.L. Jeglic, and B. Stanley, "The Relationship between Suicidal Behavior, Ideation, and Binge Drinking among College Students," *Archives of Suicide Research* 12, no. 2 (2008): 124–132.

20. American Foundation for Suicide Prevention, "Risk Factors for Suicide," www.afsp.org/index.cfm?page_id=05147440-E24E-E376-BDF4BF8BA6444E76, 2009 (accessed April 10, 2009).

21. Andrew Weil and Winifred Rosen, *From Chocolate to Morphine: Everything You Need to Know About Mind-Altering Drugs* (Boston: Houghton Mifflin, 1993), 45.

22. U.S. Centers for Disease Control and Prevention, "The Health Consequences of Smoking: A Report of the Surgeon General," www.cdc.gov/tobacco/sgr/sgr_2004/index.htm, 2004 (accessed April 10, 2009).

23. National Institutes of Health, National Institute on Alcohol Abuse and Alcoholism, "A Snapshot of Annual High-Risk College Drinking Consequences," July 11, 2007, www.collegedrinking prevention.gov/StatsSummaries/snapshot.aspx (accessed April 10, 2009).

24. American Psychological Association, *Diagnostic and Statistical Manual of Psychoactive Substance Abuse Disorders* (Washington, DC: American Psychological Association, 1994).

25. American Cancer Society, "Guide to Quitting Smoking," www.cancer.org/docroot/PED/content/PED_10_13X_Guide_for_Quitting_Smoking.asp, 2008 (accessed April 10, 2009).

26. American Cancer Society, "Double Your Chances of Quitting Smoking," www.cancer.org/docroot/PED/content/PED_10_3x_Double_Your_Chances.asp, 2008 (accessed April 10, 2009).

27. Adapted from National Institute of Occupational Safety and Health, *Stress...at Work,* http://www.cdc.gov/niosh/docs/99-101/.

28. Mental Health America, "Depression in the Workplace," www.mentalhealthamerica.net/go/information/get-info/depression/depression-in-the-workplace, 2009 (accessed April 10, 2009).

Chapter 12

1. Ira Progoff, *At a Journal Workshop* (New York: Dialogue House, 1975).

2. Adapted from *From Master Student to Master Employee* (Boston: Houghton Mifflin, 2006), 279.

3. Adapted from Dave Ellis, Stan Lankowitz, Ed Stupka, and Doug Toft, *Career Planning,* Third Edition. Copyright © 2003 by Houghton Mifflin Company. Reprinted by permission.

4. Encyclopaedia Britannica Online Reference Center, "Ford, Henry," www.library.eb.com/eb/article-22461 (accessed April 15, 2009).

5. FordCarz, "Henry Ford Quotations," 2003, www.fordcarz.com/henry_ford_quotes.htm (accessed April 15, 2009).

6. Richard N. Bolles, *What Color Is Your Parachute? A Practical Manual for Job-Hunters and Career-Changers* (Berkeley, CA: 2005), 38.

7. Kate Zernike, "College, My Way," *New York Times*, April 23, 2006, www.nytimes.com/2006/04/23/education/edlife/zernike.html (accessed April 15, 2009).

8. United Nations Children's Fund, *The State of the World's Children 2008: Child Survival,* (New York: UNICEF, 2007), www.unicef.org/sowc08/docs/sowc08.pdf (accessed April 15, 2009).

9. Center for Human Resources, *National Evaluation of Learn and Serve America,* www.cpn.org/topics/youth/k12/pdfs/Learn_and_Serve1999.pdf, July 1999 (accessed April 15, 2009).

10. Brad Isaac, "Jerry Seinfeld's Productivity Secret," *Lifehacker,* July 24, 2007, lifehacker.com/software/motivation/jerry-seinfelds-productivity-secret-281626.php (accessed April 15, 2009).

Adler, Mortimer, and Charles Van Doren. *How to Read a Book: The Classic Guide to Intelligent Reading.* New York: Touchstone, 1972.

Allen, David. *Getting Things Done: The Art of Stress-Free Productivity.* New York: Penguin, 2001.

Allen, David. *Ready for Anything: 52 Productivity Principles for Work and Life.* New York: Viking, 2003.

Bandler, Richard, and John Grinder. *Frogs into Princes: Neuro-Linguistic Programming.* Moab, UT: Real People, 1979.

Becoming a Master Student Athlete. Florence, KY: Cengage, 2006.

Bolles, Richard N. *What Color Is Your Parachute? A Practical Manual for Job-Hunters and Career-Changers.* Berkeley, CA: Ten Speed, updated annually.

Boston Women's Health Book Collective. *The New Our Bodies, Ourselves.* New York: Simon & Schuster, 1996.

Brown, Alan C. *Maximizing Memory Power.* New York: Wiley, 1986.

Buzan, Tony. *Make the Most of Your Mind.* New York: Simon & Schuster, 1977.

Chaffee, John. *Thinking Critically.* Florence, KY: Cengage, 2009.

Coplin, Bill. *10 Things Employers Want You to Learn in College.* Berkeley, CA: Ten Speed, 2003.

Covey, Stephen R. *The Seven Habits of Highly Effective People: Powerful Lessons in Personal Change.* New York: Simon & Schuster, 1989.

Davis, Deborah. *The Adult Learner's Companion.* Florence, KY: Cengage, 2007.

Downing, Skip. *On Course: Strategies for Creating Success in College and in Life,* 4th ed. Florence, KY: Cengage, 2008.

Dumond, Val. *The Elements of Nonsexist Usage.* New York: Prentice Hall, 1990.

Elgin, Duane. *Voluntary Simplicity.* New York: Morrow, 1993.

Ellis, Dave. *Falling Awake: Creating the Life of Your Dreams.* Rapid City, SD: Breakthrough Enterprises, 2000.

Facione, Peter. *Critical Thinking: What It Is and Why It Counts.* Millbrae, CA: California Academic Press, 1996.

Fletcher, Anne. *Sober for Good.* Boston: Houghton Mifflin, 2001.

From Master Student to Master Employee. Florence, KY: Cengage, 2009.

Gawain, Shakti. *Creative Visualization.* New York: New World Library, 1998.

Gibaldi, Joseph. *MLA Handbook for Writers of Research Papers.* New York: Modern Language Association, 1999.

Glasser, William. *Take Effective Control of Your Life.* New York: HarperCollins, 1984.

Golas, Thaddeus. *The Lazy Man's Guide to Enlightenment.* New York: Bantam, 1993.

Greene, Susan D., and Melanie C. L. Martel. *The Ultimate Job Hunter's Guidebook.* Florence, KY, 2008.

Hallowell, Edward M. *CrazyBusy: Overstretched, Overbooked, and About to Snap!* New York: Ballantine, 2006.

Higbee, Kenneth L. *Your Memory: How It Works and How to Improve It.* Englewood Cliffs, NJ: Prentice Hall, 1996.

Hill, Napolean. *Think and Grow Rich.* New York: Fawcett, 1996.

James, William. *Talks to Teachers on Psychology and to Students on Some of Life's Ideals.* New York: Norton, 1983.

Keyes, Ken, Jr. *Handbook to Higher Consciousness.* Berkeley, CA: Living Love, 1974.

Keyes, Ralph. *Timelock: How Life Got So Hectic and What You Can Do about It.* New York: HarperCollins, 1991.

Kolb, David A. *Experiential Learning: Experience as the Source of Learning and Development.* Englewood Cliffs, NJ: Prentice Hall, 1984.

Lathrop, Richard. *Who's Hiring Who?* Berkeley, CA: Ten Speed, 1989.

LeBoeuf, Michael. *Imagineering: How to Profit from Your Creative Powers.* New York: Berkley, 1990.

Levy, Frank, and Richard J. Murname. *The New Division of Labor: How Computers Are Creating the Next Job Market.* Princeton, NJ: Princeton University Press, 2004.

Lucas, Jerry, and Harry Lorayne. *The Memory Book.* New York: Ballantine Books, 1975.

Mallow, Jeffry V. *Science Anxiety: Fear of Science and How to Overcome It.* New York: Thomond, 1986.

Manning, Robert. *Credit Card Nation: The Consequences of America's Addiction to Credit.* New York: Basic Books, 2000.

Newport, Cal. *How to Win at College.* New York: Random House, 2005.

Nolting, Paul D. *Math Study Skills Workbook,* 3rd ed. Florence, KY: Cengage, 2008.

Pauk, Walter, and Ross J. Q. Owens. *How to Study in College.* Florence, KY: Cengage, 2008.

Pennebaker, James W. *Opening Up: The Healing Power of Confiding in Others.* New York: Morrow, 1990.

Pirsig, Robert. *Zen and the Art of Motorcycle Maintenance.* New York: Perennial Classics, 2000.

Raimes, Anne, and Maria Jerskey. *Universal Keys for Writers.* Florence, KY: Cengage, 2008.

Robinson, Adam. *What Smart Students Know: Maximum Grades, Optimum Learning, Minimum Time.* New York: Crown, 1993.

Ruggiero, Vincent Ryan. *Becoming a Critical Thinker.* Florence, KY: Cengage, 2009.

Schacter, Daniel L. *Searching for Memory: The Brain, the Mind, and the Past.* New York: HarperCollins, 1997.

Scharf-Hunt, Diana, and Pam Hait. *Studying Smart: Time Management for College Students.* New York: HarperPerennial, 1990.

Schlosser, Eric. *Fast Food Nation.* Boston: Houghton Mifflin, 2001.

Strunk, William, Jr., and E. B. White. *The Elements of Style.* New York: Macmillan, 1979.

Tobias, Sheila. *Succeed with Math: Every Student's Guide to Conquering Math Anxiety.* New York: College Board, 1995.

Toft, Doug, ed. *Master Student Guide to Academic Success.* Florence, KY: Cengage, 2005.

Trapani, Gina. *Lifehacker: 88 Tech Tricks to Turbocharge Your Day.* Indianapolis, IN: Wiley, 2007.

Ueland, Brenda. *If You Want to Write: A Book about Art, Independence and Spirit.* St. Paul, MN: Graywolf, 1987.

U.S. Department of Education. *Funding Education Beyond High School: The Guide to Federal Student Aid.* Published yearly. http://studentaid.ed.gov/students/publications/student_guide/index.html

Watkins, Ryan, and Michael Corry. *E-learning Companion: A Student's Guide to Online Success.* Florence, KY: Cengage, 2008.

Weil, Andrew. *Health and Healing.* Boston: Houghton Mifflin, 1998.

Welch, David. *Decisions, Decisions: The Art of Effective Decision Making.* Amherst, NY: Prometheus, 2002.

Wurman, Saul Richard. *Information Anxiety 2.* Indianapolis, IN: QUE, 2001.

Master Instructor Notes

Master Instructor Notes

Master Instructor Notes

ANNOTATED INSTRUCTOR'S EDITION

Master Instructor Notes